A HISTORY OF
CHINA

THE BLACKWELL HISTORY OF THE WORLD

General Editor: **R. I. Moore**

★ Denotes title published

A HISTORY OF
CHINA

MORRIS ROSSABI

WILEY Blackwell

Blackwell Publishing was acquired by John Wiley & Sons in February 2007. Blackwell's publishing program has been merged with Wiley's global Scientific, Technical, and Medical business to form Wiley-Blackwell.

Registered Office
John Wiley & Sons Ltd, The Atrium, Southern Gate, Chichester, West Sussex, PO19 8SQ, UK

Editorial Offices
350 Main Street, Malden, MA 02148-5020, USA
9600 Garsington Road, Oxford, OX4 2DQ, UK
The Atrium, Southern Gate, Chichester, West Sussex, PO19 8SQ, UK

For details of our global editorial offices, for customer services, and for information about how to apply for permission to reuse the copyright material in this book please see our website at www.wiley.com/wiley-blackwell.

Library of Congress Cataloging-in-Publication Data

Rossabi, Morris.
  A history of China / Morris Rossabi.
    pages   cm. – (The Blackwell history of the world)
  Includes bibliographical references and index.
  ISBN 978-1-55786-078-1 (hardback : alk. paper) – ISBN 978-1-57718-113-2 (pbk. : alk. paper)
  1. China–History.   I. Title.
  DS735.R68 2014
  951–dc23

                                   2013006410

A catalogue record for this book is available from the British Library.

Cover image: Wang Ruihui, Grandparents and Grandchildren before a portrait of Mao, Gouache on paper, 57 × 43.2 cm, 20th century. Princeton University Art Museum, NJ. Photo: Bruce M. White. © 2013. Princeton University Art Museum/Art Resource NY/ Scala, Florence
Cover design by Nicki Averill

Set in 10/12pt Plantin by SPi Publisher Services, Pondicherry, India
Printed in Malaysia by Ho Printing (M) Sdn Bhd

1 2014

CONTENTS

SERIES EDITOR'S PREFACE

There is nothing new in the attempt to understand history as a whole. To know how humanity began and how it has come to its present condition is one of the oldest and most universal of human needs, expressed in the religious and philosophical systems of every civilization. But only in the past few decades has it begun to appear both necessary and possible to meet that need by means of a rational and systematic appraisal of current knowledge. Until the middle of the nineteenth century, history itself was generally treated as a subordinate branch of other fields of learning, of literature, rhetoric, law, philosophy, or religion.

When historians began to establish history's independence as a field of scholarship in its own right, with its own subject matter and its own rules and methods, they made it in practice not the attempt to achieve a comprehensive account of the human past but the history of western Europe and of the societies created by European expansion and colonization. In laying the scholarly foundations of their discipline, they also reinforced the Enlightenment's belief in the advance of "civilization" (and, more recently, of "western civilization"), and made it, with relatively minor regional variation, the basis of the teaching of history almost everywhere for most of the twentieth century. Research and teaching of the histories of other parts of the world developed mainly in the context of area studies like those of ancient Greece and Rome, dominated by philology, and conducted through the exposition of the canonical texts of their respective languages. World history as such remained the province of thinkers and writers principally interested in constructing theoretical or metaphysical systems. Only toward the very end of the century did the community of academic historians begin to recognize world history as a proper and even urgent field for the application of their knowledge and skills.

The inadequacy of the traditional parameters of the discipline is now widely – though not universally – acknowledged, and the sense is growing that a world facing a common future of headlong and potentially catastrophic transformation needs its common history. Its emergence has been delayed, however, by simple ignorance on the one hand – for the history of enormous stretches of space and time was known not at all, or so patchily and superficially as not to be worth revisiting – and on the other by the lack of a widely acceptable basis upon which to organize and discuss what is nevertheless the enormous and enormously diverse knowledge that we have.

The first of those obstacles is now being rapidly overcome. There is almost no part of the world or period of its history that is not the subject of vigorous and sophisticated investigation by archaeologists and historians. The expansion of the horizons of academic history since the 1980s has been dramatic. The quality and quantity of historical research and writing has risen exponentially in each decade, and the advances have been most spectacular in the areas previously most neglected. Nor have the academics failed to share the results of their labors. Reliable and accessible accounts are now readily available of regions, periods, and topics that even twenty years ago were obscure to everyone but a handful of specialists. In particular, collaborative publication, in the form of volumes or sets of volumes in which teams of authors set forth, in more or less detail, their expert and up-to-date conclusions in the field of their research, has been a natural and necessary response to the growth of knowledge. Only in that way can non specialists, at any level, be kept even approximately in touch with the constantly accelerating accumulation of information about the past.

Yet the amelioration of one problem exacerbates the other. It is truer than it has ever been that knowledge is growing and perspectives are multiplying more quickly than they can be assimilated and recorded in synthetic form. We can now describe a great many more trees in a great deal more detail than we could before, but it does not always follow that we have a better view of the wood. Collaboration has many strengths, but clarity, still less originality, of vision is rarely among them. History acquires shape, structure, relevance – becomes, in the fashionable catch-phrase, something for think-ing with – by advancing and debating new propositions about what past societies were like; how they worked and why they changed over long periods of time; and how they resembled and why they differed from contemporane-ous societies in other parts of the world. Such insights, like the sympathetic understanding without which the past is dead, are almost always born of individual creativity and imagination.

There is a wealth of ways in which world history can be written. The oldest and simplest view, that it is best understood as the history of contacts between peoples previously isolated from one another, from which (as some think) all change arises, is now seen to be capable of application since the earliest times. An influential alternative focuses upon the tendency of economic exchange to create self-sufficient but ever expanding "worlds" that sustain successive systems of power and culture. Another seeks to understand the differences between societies and cultures, and therefore the particular character of each, by comparing the ways in which their values, social relationships, and struc-tures of power have developed. The rapidly emerging field of ecological history returns to a very ancient tradition of seeing interaction with the physical environment, and with other animals, at the centre of the human predicament, while insisting that its understanding demands an approach that is culturally, chronologically, and geographically comprehensive. More recently still, "Big History" (one of the leaders of which is among the contributors to this series) has begun to show how human history can be integrated with that not only of the natural but also of the cosmic environment, and better understood in consequence.

Each volume of the *Blackwell History of the World* offers a substantial account of a portion of the history of the world large enough to permit, and indeed demand, the reappraisal of customary boundaries of regions, periods, and topics, and in doing so reflects the idiosyncrasies of its sources and its subjects, as well as the vision and judgment of its author. The series as a whole seeks not to embody any single approach but to support them all, as it will use them all, by providing a modern, comprehensive, and accessible account of the entire human past. Its plan combines the indispensable narratives of very-long-term regional development with global surveys of developments across the world at particular times, of interaction between regions and what they have experienced in common, or visited upon one another. In combination these volumes will provide a framework in which the history of every part of the world can be viewed, and a basis upon which most aspects of human activity can be compared across both time and space. A frame offers perspective. Comparison implies respect for difference. That is the beginning of what the past has to offer the future.

R. I. Moore

SERIES EDITOR'S ACKNOWLEDGMENTS

The editor is grateful to all of the contributors to the *Blackwell History of the World* for advice and assistance on the design and contents of the series as a whole as well as on individual volumes. Both editor and contributors wish to place on record their immense debt, individually and collectively, to John Davey, formerly of Blackwell Publishers. The series would not have been initiated without his vision and enthusiasm, and could not have been realized without his energy, skill, and diplomacy.

PREFACE

I have deliberately titled this book *A History of China*. It is not *The History of China*. In fact, such an all-encompassing book has not been and probably will never be written. Chinese history is beyond the scope of a single volume. In this work, much in the history of China has been omitted, partly due to size restrictions. I have tried to replicate the course on Chinese history I have taught at a variety of universities. However, I have left out some anecdotes and have eschewed documentary overkill. I have had to select from a vast array of political, economic, social, and cultural developments.

Yet this work offers a survey of Chinese history, with one innovation. The basic events and trends are described, but I have emphasized China as part of a larger world, starting with its contacts with its neighbors in early times and stretching to west, south, and southeast Asia, Korea, and Japan in later eras. From the Mongol age in the thirteenth century onward, I portray China in the context of global developments and history. Specific Chinese policies and practices can be understood as, in part, responses to foreign influences. Indeed, non-Chinese peoples have ruled China for almost half of its history since 1279, the date the Mongols crushed the Southern Song dynasty. In the past, some histories depicted the Mongol and Manchu rulers who governed China during that time as typical Chinese potentates and their people as highly sinicized. This history and many recent scholarly studies have challenged that interpretation, and I devote more space than most texts to describing Mongol and Manchu societies and analyzing their impact on China. In addition, since 1279, China has had a significant non-Chinese population, mostly along strategic frontier areas. Again, I have emphasized these peoples' histories in this book, often devoting more space to the subject than almost all other histories of China.

Such emphases on China in global history and on the non-Chinese population living in the country have not been my sole perspective. To be sure, many developments in China generally reflected internal events and were not responses to foreign pressures or stimuli. Chinese officials, military commanders, artists, scientists, and philosophers most often reacted to indigenous political or cultural challenges. Yet China and the Chinese were not isolated; they had contacts with foreigners adjacent to their lands, and the Mongol Empire linked them with Eurasia (a connection that was never truly severed). Events and trends in other parts of Eurasia – and indeed in other parts of the world – have influenced China. Similarly, developments in China occasionally reverberated in Europe, west Asia, the Americas, and, to an extent, Africa. Such external impacts did not necessarily determine the course of events or the development of discoveries or ideas. Yet a conception of China from a global perspective provides unique insights. Consideration of domestic causes of events in Chinese history will be of primary concern, but, unlike many other appraisals of Chinese society, a new global perspective, capitalizing on recent research, will also be presented and will, I trust, add to the understanding of Chinese history.

On another note, even within the country, there have been many different Chinas. China's population has long been sizable and the territory under its control substantial. In traditional times, various regions faced numerous obstacles in transport and communications. Thus, different parts of the country and different peoples had differing values and differing histories. A peasant in Sichuan, an official in the city of Changan (modern Xian), a merchant in the city of Quanzhou, and a woman in a remote village in Gansu all had different histories.

Until the late nineteenth century, the elite produced nearly all the written sources, which described the lives, activities, concerns, and values of a single group of people who derived from the same social background. They hardly portrayed other groups of Chinese. Peasants, the vast majority of the population, barely appeared in these texts. Women also received short shrift, and only through painstaking perusals of numerous texts have scholars begun to piece together aspects of their roles in Chinese history. Confucian officials, who wrote most of the histories, relegated merchants and artisans to a lowly social status and scarcely mentioned them in historical accounts; thus, information about these two groups is limited. The available sources are not as multidimensional and diverse as historians would like. Scholars have used the briefest of mentions in texts and material remains to offer a glimpse of the lives and roles of merchants and artisans. Nonetheless, until changes in nineteenth-century Chinese history, most sources, both written and visual, center on the careers and roles of the imperial families and officials. The reader needs to bear this in mind in reading this book.

A historian would find that traditional Chinese historical texts portrayed Confucianism as the system of values governing personal relations and the philosophical view that shaped people's lives. Yet he or she could wonder whether popular religions played as important or greater roles for the ordinary Chinese. However, little is known about popular religions in certain eras of Chinese history because of the nature of the sources. Such religions were generally the province of ordinary Chinese, nearly all of whom were illiterate. Written texts that described these religions have, by and large, not survived (if they existed in the first place). Because the elite embraced Confucianism, wrote extensively about it, and appear to have led lives shaped by it, historians may assume that it was pervasive because the surviving texts portray it as such. This may not have been the case for ordinary people.

I have chosen to organize this history based on the various dynasties of China. I realize, of course, that changes in dynasties do not necessarily coincide with or reflect transformations in society and economy, cultural and ideological patterns, technological and scientific knowledge, or other equally significant developments. I am aware that a Japanese scholar has divided Chinese history in two, arguing that dramatic changes in the eleventh and twelfth centuries CE changed the course of Chinese society. Other historians have adopted a variety of schemes for the periodization of Chinese history, including a disputed one centering on China's response to the West. I have referred to some of these interpretations, describing them while also alluding to crucial assessments and critiques of these theories. However, in many years of teaching, I have found that students are better able to grasp the fundamentals of Chinese history through the lens of dynasties. Because this book is aimed at students and the nonspecialist reader, the dynastic approach appears to be less confusing and more optimal for a work of this kind.

Despite this choice, I do not subscribe to the concept of the dynastic cycle, a traditional and stereotypical paradigm of Chinese history. Advocates of this theory assert that a dynasty's first rulers were honest, courageous, and powerful and cared for their people, creating conditions of prosperity and longevity, but that the later rulers were oppressive and corrupt and were unconcerned about their people, leading to decline and increasing chaos. This approach does not jibe with actual events and overemphasizes the roles of the emperors and the courts in shaping the history of China. Another misconception that arose from the dynastic-cycle paradigm was an idea of the insignificance of eras that lacked either strong dynasties or dynasties that ruled over all of China. Periods of decentralization were equated with chaos and no important cultural innovations. Yet Confucianism, Daoism, and other philosophies of a golden age of classical thought developed in precisely such an era – known as the Warring States period – and Buddhism flourished after the collapse of the great Han dynasty and before the Sui and Tang dynasties restored centralized government in China. Suffice it to say that I use "dynasties" as the organizational scheme for the reader's convenience and ease.

FURTHER READING

The Further Reading sections, which can be found at the end of each chapter, consist principally of works that are accessible both to undergraduate students and the general educated reader. The selections are weighted toward books that offer summaries of highly scholarly studies. The major exceptions to this principle are the general reference works cited below, which provide guidance on more specialized studies. Journal articles are excluded because they are less accessible to nonspecialists. Another reason for some of the selections is that I enjoyed reading them.

An important general work is *The Cambridge History of China*, a multivolume and chronological political and economic history of China, with essays written by leading specialists in the various fields covered. Each volume provides an extensive bibliography, in a variety of languages, for those intending further serious study.

Eugene Anderson, *The Food of China* (New Haven: Yale University Press, 1990).
Kathryn Bernhardt, *Women and Property in China, 960–1949* (Stanford: Stanford University Press, 1999).

Caroline Blunden and Mark Elvin, *Cultural Atlas of China* (New York: Checkmark Books, 1998).

Howard Boorman and Richard Howard, eds., *A Biographical Dictionary of Republican China* (New York: Columbia University Press, 4 vols., 1967–1979).

K. C. Chang, ed., *Food in Chinese Culture* (New Haven: Yale University Press, 1977).

Craig Clunas, *Art in China* (Oxford: Oxford University Press, 1997).

Patricia Ebrey, *The Cambridge Illustrated History of China* (Cambridge: Cambridge University, rev. ed., 2010).

Mark Elvin, *The Pattern of the Chinese Past* (Stanford: Stanford University Press, 1973).

Mark Elvin, *The Retreat of the Elephants: An Environmental History of China* (New Haven: Yale University Press, 2006).

John Fairbank and Merle Goldman, *China: A New History* (Cambridge, MA: Harvard University Press, 2006).

Herbert Franke, ed., *Song Biographies* (Wiesbaden: Steiner, 4 vols., 1976).

L. Carrington Goodrich and Chao-ying Fang, eds., *A Dictionary of Ming Biography* (New York: Columbia University Press, 2 vols., 1976).

Arthur Hummel, ed., *Eminent Chinese of the Ch'ing Period* (Washington: US Government Printing Office, 1943–1944).

Donald Klein and Anne Clark, eds., *Biographic Dictionary of Chinese Communism, 1921–1965* (Cambridge, MA: Harvard University Press, 1971).

James Liu, *The Art of Chinese Poetry* (Chicago: University of Chicago Press, 1966).

Victor Mair, *The Columbia History of Chinese Literature* (New York: Columbia University Press, 2001).

F. W. Mote, *Imperial China, 900–1800* (Cambridge, MA: Harvard University Press, 2003).

Igor de Rachewiltz, ed., *In the Service of the Khans: Eminent Personalities of the Mongol-Yüan Period* (Wiesbaden: Harrassowitz, 1993).

Jonathan Spence, *The Search for Modern China* (New York: W. W. Norton, 1999).

John Wills, *Mountain of Fame* (Princeton: Princeton University Press, 1996).

ACKNOWLEDGMENTS

This book has evolved from courses I have taught since 1965 on Chinese history. Through their positive and negative reactions, my students have led me to incorporate changes in this survey course – additions and deletions that have, I believe, benefited this volume. I am grateful to these students for their questions and insights because they have had a substantial influence on my thinking. They are now occupational therapists, teachers, lawyers, policemen, doctors, soldiers, and workers, among other occupations, and are perhaps far removed from the study of Chinese history, but their contributions to this work ought to be mentioned. Similarly, I want to acknowledge the numerous secondary-school teachers and instructors in colleges who took part in outreach programs designed to assist them in introducing units on Chinese history in their curricula. In my presentations to them, I had to compress a whole semester's worth of lectures into a week or two of intensive talks. Such condensation prompted me to focus on what I perceived to be the most important developments and themes in the history of China, and this process was an invaluable contribution to this book.

I learned a great deal in discussions with Hans Bielenstein, the late L. C. Goodrich, and the late Morton Fried, all of Columbia University; Roderick Ptak and the late Herbert Franke of the University of Munich; the late John Langlois of Bowdoin College; John Meskill of Barnard College; the late Hok-lam Chan of the University of Washington; the late Frederick Wakeman of the University of California at Berkeley; the late Michael Gasster of Rutgers University; the late Frederick Mote of Princeton University; the late Joseph Fletcher of Harvard University; John Wills and Bettine Birge of the University of Southern California; David Robinson of Colgate University; Edward Farmer of the University of Minnesota; Ralph Kauz and Veronika Veit of Bonn University; Liu Yingsheng of Nanjing University; Leonard Blusse of Leiden University; Angela Schottenhammer of Salzburg University; Joanna Waley-Cohen of New York University; Pamela Crossley of Dartmouth College; Nancy S. Steinhardt of the University of Pennsylvania; John Chaffee of the University of Binghamton; Caroline Humphrey of Cambridge University; and the late Father Henry Serruys, Dr. Paula Harrell, Dr. Stan Czuma, and the late Dr. Sherman Lee of the Cleveland Museum of Art. Professor Robert Moore, the editor of this series of volumes on world history, has offered invaluable suggestions for revisions, and Tessa Harvey of Wiley Blackwell has been extremely patient and supportive. Two anonymous reviewers provided extraordinarily helpful comments. I am certain that I have omitted the names of other colleagues and friends who have influenced my conception of Chinese history and hope that they will forgive me for my failing memory.

My own family has been extremely supportive over the years. My older brother Mayer, whose life was cut short by a virulent form of brain cancer in 1998, taught me so much – from a concern for social justice to skills such as swimming – that it is difficult to imagine what I would have become without his influence. I think of him daily and hope he realized how important he was in my life and career. Like their father Mayer, Joseph and Amiel Rossabi are decent and honorable, and they have been helpful to me and my immediate family over the years. My daughter Amy and my son Tony and their respective families – Howard, Sarah, and Nathan Sterinbach and Anna and Julia Rossabi – have been a source of joy, stimulation, and assistance throughout the writing of this book, although Julia, now two years old, is probably not aware of her contribution.

My wife Mary is always mentioned last but should be first, and I don't say so merely because she will be the first person to read these acknowledgments. Indeed, she has read every book and article (even my doctoral dissertation!) that I've ever written and has improved all of them through her suggestions for change. We have also collaborated on five books over the years, pleasurable experiences for both of us. Her intelligence, energy, and sense of humor have enriched both of our lives.

LIST OF ILLUSTRATIONS

LIST OF MAPS

A NOTE ON ROMANIZATION

I studied the Chinese language when the Wade-Giles system of Romanization was standard. Around 1980, books and articles about China started to use the *pinyin* system, although a few stayed with Wade-Giles. I am not entirely satisfied with the *pinyin* scheme, but I have used it for the convenience of the reader because nearly all publications he or she will encounter will employ it.

I have eschewed diacritical marks, with the exception of the umlaut, for all Arabic, Iranian, and Turkic terms and names.

I have adopted Antoine Mostaert's scheme for the transliteration of Mongolian, as modified by Francis W. Cleaves, except for these deviations:

- *č* is ch
- *γ* is gh
- ĵ is j
- q is kh
- š is sh

PART I

China among "Barbarians"

[1] EARLY HISTORY, TO 1027 BCE

Land and Settlement
Early Mankind
Agricultural Revolution in the Neolithic Era
Xia: The First Dynasty?
The Shang and the Origins of Chinese
    Civilization
Oracle Bones
Ritual Objects as Historical Sources
Shang Society

LAND AND SETTLEMENT

Along with Russia and the USA, China is one of the world's largest countries, stretching about three thousand miles from the east coast to its boundaries to the west in central Asia, the Himalayan states, and Vietnam. This vast domain embraces the tropical island of Hainan and the subarctic areas of Manchuria. Its landscape of plains, deserts, and lofty mountains has created various kinds of economies, based upon the environment. There are multiple Chinas, depending on the topography and the inhabitants' differing responses to the lands in which they reside. Two-thirds of the land consists of mountains or other demanding terrain, with limited or almost no opportunities for transport, precluding the development of agriculture. However, the melting snows from the mountains provide water and, in modern times, hydroelectric power. The Tibetan plateau (Tibet and Qinghai province) has the most daunting mountains. The lands east of the mountains are China's agricultural heartland.

A History of China, First Edition. Morris Rossabi.
© 2014 Morris Rossabi. Published 2014 by Blackwell Publishing Ltd.

Within the traditional boundaries of China, the north and south regions differ. The Qinling Mountains and the Yangzi River divide the country. Flowing from Tibet to north China and then to the original core of Chinese civilization in Shanxi and Shaanxi provinces, the Yellow River (or Huang He) is vital to the northern economy. Loess soil blowing from Inner Mongolia into these provinces and Gansu province permits sedentary agriculture. The yellowish soil builds up with silt and mud in the Yellow River and necessitates the construction of embankments to protect against floods. The river is, in many sections, fifty meters or more above the plains, and proper maintenance of embankments is essential to prevent flooding and changes in the course of the river, which could ravage the land. When a government, in traditional times, did not undertake such flood-control projects, the dynasty declined and peasants suffered, leading to frequent disorder and rebellions. At the same time, the north suffered from a lack of precipitation and endured severe droughts. Deficiencies in water and a short growing season due to an early onset of low temperatures limited staple crops to wheat, oats, and millet. Rice required considerable water and could be grown only in the south.

At this time, the Yangzi River dominated south China. The largest waterway in the country, it was navigable and readily linked the southeast coast to its hinterland to the southwest. Abundant precipitation and good soil offered optimal conditions for a rice-based intensive agriculture in the southeast. The Sichuan Basin, in the southwest, with its mild and humid climate, was also a rich agricultural region. Even farther to the south, below the Nanling mountain range, a tropical climate permitted the planting of two crops a year. West of the Nanling, Guizhou and Yunnan provinces also had a bountiful agricultural base. The southeast coast has excellent ports, and ships from southeast, south, and west Asia reached these harbors, but traditional China generally, with some exceptions, oriented itself inland throughout its history. Like the north, the south has not always been blessed by nature. The southeast coast has been prone to typhoons and monsoons and the attendant flooding and loss of life.

Both natural and man-made disasters have afflicted China. Floods have threatened the Yellow River basin as well as the southeast coast; earthquakes have proved to be devastating throughout the country (in recent years, they have caused damage and much loss of life in an area not far from Beijing and in Sichuan); and dust storms emanating from Inner Mongolia have created hazardous conditions in the north. Such a listing of catastrophes does not include locusts and predatory birds and animals and their effects on crops. Human error or lack of concern for the environment has had similarly devastating consequences. Felling of trees and erosion, especially in the north, has resulted in growing desertification, leading, for example, to the increased size of the Gobi desert. In modern times, the use of coal for heating and unregulated emissions from automobiles have contributed to poor air quality in many cities, including Beijing, while chemical effluents from factories and untreated wastes have fouled numerous lakes, rivers, and streams, further jeopardizing the relatively paltry supplies of potable water in the north.

China's territorial parameters have changed throughout its history. Modern China controls much more land than the Han or Tang, the great traditional dynasties, did. The Han did not totally dominate south China, and the Tang did not control parts of the contemporary southwest. Yunnan province did not become part of China until the thirteenth century, and the region of Xinjiang (comprising one-sixth of modern China's land) was not ruled by a dynasty from China until the eighteenth century. Like the histories of Russia and the USA, China's lengthy past is a narrative of colonization. China in the second century CE did not encompass many areas that are now considered to be part of its lands. It was a much lesser domain – at least in territorial extent – than contemporary China.

As a result, there have been many Chinas. Starting with a base around the Yellow River, China expanded to the south and the west. As the Chinese added territory and peoples, they also incorporated new cultural patterns and values that they adopted from the native inhabitants. When they advanced along the current northern borderlands, they gained control over non-Chinese peoples, which contributed to the cultural mix. Localism prevailed, as many areas retained their own identities. Although these regions fell under central control, they often persisted in their own lifestyles. Yet historians cannot readily identify these deviations and regional variations because the written records, most of which derived from the central authorities, ignored both local patterns and opposition to the dynasties' institutions and policies. Nonetheless, readers should be aware that the trends and policies described in this book may not apply to all regions at all times in Chinese history. There was considerable variation in this large land mass.

Before China expanded into the regions of the non-Chinese peoples, geography determined the divisions between it and its neighbors. Chinese peasants spread to lands suited for farming. They planted in terraces on mountains, constructed canals, built banks to tame rivers, and created ditches to preserve water for irrigation and to avert floods. The available land imposed limits on such sedentary agriculture. Mountainous and desert terrain, especially in the north and west, prevented farming in those regions. The areas north of China proper had short growing seasons, low temperatures, and soil unsuited for intensive agriculture, precluding Chinese settlements. This territory was principally the nomads' land. Hunting and fishing prevailed in the northeast area in northern Manchuria, which resembled the Siberian territories. Directly north was the Gobi desert, which prevented Chinese colonization, and, farther north in modern Inner Mongolia and Mongolia, nomadic herders dominated. Only late in history (the seventeenth and eighteenth centuries) did Qing China, governed by the Manchus, attempt to encroach on the northern lands of Mongolia and Xinjiang. Because the Tarim Basin and the Tian Shan in Xinjiang have proved to possess oil, coal, and precious ores, Chinese expansion in that region has been important. However, it has resulted in considerable turbulence because the Turkic (principally Muslim) population in the area has repeatedly chafed under Chinese domination.

EARLY MANKIND

The study of China in its preliterate stage has undergone dramatic changes since the establishment of the People's Republic of China in 1949. New construction, the opening up of more arable land, and systematic surveys of ancient sites all have contributed to discoveries of a treasure trove of fossils and artifacts. Major finds were also made before the founding of the People's Republic, but the pace of discovery has accelerated since then. For example, a leading text on the archeology of ancient China, first published in 1963, was revised and enlarged on four separate occasions before 2000 because of the rapid increase in knowledge during that time. Thus, generalizations about preliterate China are quickly dated and often require emendation. The specific portrait drawn in this text will no doubt be superseded, although the general outline may remain valid for some time to come.

The most spectacular and significant site of the Middle Pleistocene (about 400,000 years ago) is Zhoukoudian, a complex of caves about forty kilometers west of Beijing. Found by the Swedish paleontologist J. G. Andersson around 1921, these limestone hills proved to have a wealth of materials for the reconstruction of early hominid life in China. Scholars have identified about fifteen geological strata in the caves and various different levels of culture. The most renowned fossil in the cave was the so-called Beijing Man or, to paleontologists, *Sinanthropus pekinensis* or *Pithecanthropus pekinensis*. Isolated skulls, bones, and teeth of forty individuals were found in this site; forty percent of those individuals had died before the age of fourteen. Their diet consisted of the meat of other animals, including the ancestors of deer, leopards, elephants, water buffaloes, and horses. They also gathered and ate nuts and berries. They had discovered how to make fire and how to produce stone tools and implements. However, having been found after half a million years, the fossils were lost only twenty years after their discovery. In 1941, the Chinese and the Americans responsible for the remains feared the growing turbulence in China and decided to send the fossils to the USA for safekeeping. However, the USA's entry into the Second World War in December of 1941 upset these plans, and the fossils were either lost in a ship bound for the USA when it was sunk by the Japanese navy or were simply stolen while awaiting shipment to the USA or later.

These fossils found in the Zhoukoudian caves are among the most significant evidence of Paleolithic culture in China, but sites throughout the country have yielded other Paleolithic remains. In recent years, excavations (which have uncovered Paleolithic sites in southwest China, Manchuria, and Inner Mongolia, among other locales) have proven that the earliest evidence of hominid life is not limited, as previously believed, to the areas around the Yellow River. Many scholarly controversies have developed about the interpretation of these hominids, including so-called Beijing Man. Additional discoveries may help to resolve some of these issues.

AGRICULTURAL REVOLUTION IN THE NEOLITHIC ERA

Those finds that can be definitively linked with modern Chinese people date from the Neolithic era. Evidence about the Neolithic age is plentiful and historians have sifted through it to provide a clear image of cultural and technological innovations. The most significant changes from the Paleolithic to the Neolithic were the development of agriculture and a growing dependence on farming for survival. A fragile hunting and fishing economy became a more stable, agrarian-based society. Archeological excavations since 1949 have challenged the earlier view that China had two, and only two, demarcated Neolithic cultures. At least four such cultures have been identified, and the sites are scattered throughout the country. The new discoveries have considerably altered the previously accepted dates for the Neolithic. J. G. Andersson, who excavated one of the Neolithic sites in the early 1920s, had given 2500 BCE as the approximate onset of the Neolithic, but more-accurate dating techniques have shown that his village was founded as early as the fifth millennium BCE and that other Neolithic sites existed around 6500 BCE, if not earlier.

The earliest known sites can be found as far apart as southern Hebei province and eastern Gansu province, and several have been found in south China. The residences and cemeteries excavated in the northern areas share specific characteristics – round or square houses, underground storage pits, use of specialized stone tools including knives, axes, hammers, and mortars and pestles, and simple handmade red or brown pots. Pigs and dogs had been domesticated, and this may serve to explain why (in an indication of the vital role of the pig in early China) the Chinese character for "pig" placed under the character for "roof" came to form a new character meaning "family" or "household." The dead were buried singly in individual graves and provided with pottery or stone tools. Many of the sites in south China are located in caves, again scattered across a wide variety of regions in the provinces of Jiangxi, Guangxi, and Guangdong. Judging from the tools found in these sites, the cave dwellers worked the land but also hunted and fished. Bones of deer, sheep, rabbits, and birds indicate the range of animals they hunted. Like their contemporaries in the north, they had domesticated the pig, and the large number of pig bones indicates the animal's value to the inhabitants.

The Yangshao sites are doubtless the most renowned of the early Neolithic cultures. Discovered in 1921 by J. G. Andersson, they provide a wealth of data on the peoples and economies located in the area. Banpo village in the modern city of Xian is a typical example of these sites. Excavated by archeologists starting in 1953, the site has been turned into a well-arranged museum with helpful descriptions of the original layout of the village. Because it has been left in pristine condition, it provides a glimpse of Neolithic life. The discovery of the bones of various animals, including deer, raccoons, and foxes, confirms that that the Banpo villagers, like their counterparts in Paleolithic cultures, hunted for part of their sustenance. The uncovering of seeds from trees verifies that the inhabitants also gathered food. Yet their generally sedentary existence and their larger populations necessitated a steadier source of supply than hunting and gathering. Since agriculture offered greater control of their environment, the villagers turned to farming for most of their needs. Millet was their principal food crop, and rudimentary farm implements, such as hoes and spades, exemplify some of their technological sophistication. Fishing provided variety to their diet and appears to have been a significant economic activity, as evidenced by the numerous representations of fish on their pottery.

Banpo was a well-laid-out village. Its inhabitants placed their sturdy houses, which were either at or below ground level, at the center of the village complex. Plastered floors and walls, as well as roofs supported by wooden posts, gave an appearance of permanence to the dwellings. Adjacent to the houses were storage pits, with pottery containers often used as granaries, and enclosed areas for domesticated animals. A cemetery (in which more than a hundred skeletons of adults were discovered) and a kiln were located on the fringes of the village. A communal dwelling was found at the center of the village, and the doors of the individual dwellings opened out onto the center. The large number of infants and children buried in the cemetery and in burial urns near the houses attests to the fragility of life in this era.

Like most of the other Neolithic sites in the north, Banpo was situated near a tributary of the Yellow River. The nearby waters provided the foundations for agriculture. The river conveyed the fine grains of sand that had, probably for millennia, been transported from the Mongolian deserts. After the sand was deposited and weathered, it eventually formed the loess soil that made the land productive. Layers of loess soil deposited over thousands of years facilitated farming, partly due to the ability of the loess to absorb water, and the river provided the water to nourish the soil. However, the river could cause havoc to neighboring villages. Accumulation of substantial amounts of loess in the river could, on occasion, result in water

Figure 1.1 Ceramic urn, Gansu province, Neolithic period. Freer Gallery of Art, Smithsonian Institution, USA / The Bridgeman Art Library

spilling over the banks and flooding. Villages downstream felt the full energy of the river. The reaction to such flooding was simply to move to higher grounds to avoid the onrushing water. Later, substantial irrigation projects would be devised to control the river.

Banpo's inhabitants had made great strides in the production of pottery, which varied considerably in color, decoration, and shape. They used a red pigment to paint a large number of the pottery vessels, but not all were painted; some were gray or black. The shapes of the vessels, which were remarkably diverse, were often dictated by their use, from tripods for cooking to thin-topped but large-bodied jars for storage to both small and large bowls for food and for ritual observances. The decorative motifs were also varied, with geometric designs, realistic depictions of fish and deer, and abstract representations of fish and animals. These depictions of fish and animals reflected the continued significance of hunting and, particularly, fishing in the economy of the village. Symbols on some of the pottery may have indicated ownership or the sign of the potter and may have signaled the beginnings of a written language.

The village's tools and ornaments were more numerous and diversified than similar artifacts of the Paleolithic era. Stone chisels, polishing tools, hoes, and spades supplemented the stone axes, knives, and arrowheads of earlier times. Antler needles, fishhooks, spearheads, and polishers showed significant improvements in technology. The fashioning of decorative items such as rings and beads made of jade and other semiprecious and precious stones indicated the development of an economy producing more than subsistence products.

The Banpo village and the original Yangshao villages were not the only north China sites of Neolithic culture. Since the 1920s, other such sites have been excavated in the provinces of Gansu (the so-called Painted Pottery Culture), southern Hebei, central Henan, and Shaanxi. They shared some of the same cultural and economic traits of Banpo, but there were nonetheless variations in the sizes of the villages, the types of pottery and stone implements, and the methods of burial. Such differences presaged a characteristic of much of Chinese history and a persistent theme in this book – the local deviations from central patterns or, later, from central government's demands and laws.

South China also witnessed the development of early Neolithic cultures, but the early and late Neolithic sites found in the province of Shandong (in the northeast) were most closely related to the earliest true Chinese civilization. Like the Yangshao, the Dawenkou culture of Shandong, which originated later than the Yangshao culture, was based upon millet production, but its tools, pottery, weaponry, and crafts were more complex in design and in performance. In addition, excavation of the graves revealed growing complexity in social organization. A few were extremely elaborate, with exquisite pottery and stone implements, while most were bare or had relatively few furnishings. Such evidence points to a more hierarchical social structure. In addition, it is apparent that Dawenkou had been

Figure 1.2 Ting tripod bowl, Longshan culture (third or early second millennium BCE) from Shandong province. The Art Archive/Genius of China Exhibition

influenced by other Neolithic cultures. The borrowing of practices confirmed that the various Neolithic communities were in touch with and affected each other.

The Longshan culture of Shandong, which succeeded the Dawenkou, was the culmination of the interrelationship of the earlier Neolithic sites. Relatively few Longshan villages have been totally excavated, but the ones that have reveal significant changes from Yangshao villages. The pottery, for example, was principally black and gray, differing from the painted pottery of the Yangshao. Most vessels were relatively unadorned, although some were decorated with incisions and appliqués. The tripods, jars, and other shapes characteristic of Yangshao were also found in the Longshan assemblages, but new forms, such as steamers and cups with handles, were introduced in the Shandong cultural complex. Stone and bone implements and weapons in both cultures were similar, but the preponderance of arrowheads and spearheads in Longshan indicated a greater concern for defense from troublesome outsiders.

The very concept of "outsiders" was a new formulation; it shaped some unique features of the Longshan and provided even sharper distinctions from the Yangshao. Defense against perceived or actual enemies heightened the Longshan villagers' sense of identity and unity. They began to recognize that they shared certain beliefs, customs, practices, and institutions that clearly distinguished them from others. The most tangible manifestation of distinctiveness was the construction of walls around their villages, a practice that most Chinese cities would later follow. The Longshan village of Chengziya built the earliest known such wall, to an average height of about six meters. Defense was the paramount consideration for the villagers; yet the walls reflect an affinity of interests – familial, clan, and political – that required protection. The inhabitants of these walled villages sensed that they belonged together and were distinct from other groups.

In addition to stamped-earth walls, Longshan culture exhibited other features that would be found in the earliest Chinese dynasty. Longshan appears thus to be a direct link between the Neolithic era and the origins of Chinese civilization. Not only did Longshan and the earliest Chinese civilization build walls around their villages but they also both used the practice of scapulimancy. Diviners or community leaders burned animal scapulae to generate cracks that they would then interpret to foretell the future. These so-called oracle bones, pervasive throughout the Longshan sites, constituted a step in the development of the Chinese written language and yield invaluable information about the Shang, the first attested dynasty. They also reveal an increasing concern for rituals, which is also shown in the unusual animal-mask decorations on the distinctive black pottery, tools, and other objects and in the markedly different burials from those found in Yangshao sites. The Longshan devoted considerable resources to burials, which is an indication of increasing attention to ceremonies concerning an afterlife and of a more stratified social structure. A few burials in the cemeteries consisted of sizable graves with wooden caskets and numerous furnishings; a slightly larger number had a few caskets and some scattered goods; and the largest number had no caskets and no furnishings. It appears that the more elaborate the burial, the higher the socials status of the deceased.

Attention to rituals and ceremonies, together with walled villages and oracle bones, link Longshan to the earliest Chinese civilization; in addition, new materials for tools and weapons and clearer political and social distinctions relate this Neolithic culture to the first recognizable entity that can legitimately be called China. Objects made of copper and several bronze vessels, which were discovered in a number of Longshan sites, mark the transition from a stone-age to a metal-age culture. The Bronze Age dynasties were still at some remove, but the appearance of metal tools indicates technological advances on the path to the full-blown metallurgical centers of early Chinese civilization. Warfare and burial practices and other ceremonies point to demarcated territories and political groups and to a stratified society, still another step toward the first Chinese dynasty. Political power within the Longshan groups became more concentrated, and wealth varied considerably. Such differentiations presaged the social distinctions found at the early stages of Chinese culture.

Although Longshan was associated principally with the province of Shandong, other sites sharing the same characteristics were widely dispersed in the third millennium BCE. Farther to the south, around the modern cities of Hangzhou and Shanghai and other centers along the Yangzi River, archeologists have excavated villages exhibiting the same cultural features as the prototypical sites in Shandong. To the west, some villages inthe provinces of Shaanxi, Gansu, and Henan, associated with the Yangshao culture, gradually manifested traits of the Longshan, and their material culture and social differentiation resembled those of the Longshan. Even farther away, archeologists have uncovered Longshan-like sites as distant as Fujian and Guangdong in the south and the Liaodong peninsula in the north.

These discoveries challenge the earlier view that Chinese civilization originated only along the bend of the Yellow River in north China. Archeological evidence now points to the existence of many regional cultures, which shared basic traits but differed sufficiently to be distinctive. This pattern of regional traits, which on occasion translated into regional autonomy, characterized China even after the creation of a so-called common culture and the establishment of a centralized government that, in theory, ruled the entire country. Historians have begun to question the concept of a monolithic China and to acknowledge the significance of regional variations, both culturally and politically. Evidence of there being many Chinas can be found for any given time in Chinese history, even this early stage of culture. Paucity of information, however, often limits knowledge and consideration to the central authorities and the reputed dominant culture.

XIA: THE FIRST DYNASTY?

Throughout the third millennium BCE, regional cultures were in touch with each other. Groups living along the bend of the Yellow River, in Shandong, and in the middle Yangzi River valley were the most significant. Some relations within and between these three groups were peaceful and resulted in rudimentary commerce, while others involved violent struggles for power. Absence of written records impedes precise knowledge of the causes of these conflicts, but control of land and water and clashes between ambitious leaders no doubt provoked some of this warfare. More powerful villages swallowed up weaker ones, although in the process they were influenced by the traits and practices of the vanquished. Indeed, interaction, whether peaceful or adversarial, among these regions inevitably affected the customs and beliefs of the various regions and brought them closer together into a peaceful Sinitic culture. By around 2000 BCE, the stage had been set for cohesion and the establishment of a state.

Early Chinese legends traditionally attributed the founding of a state to a much earlier period and to a heroic man or god named Yu who, according to long-held beliefs, reputedly founded the Xia, the first dynasty. Yu was one of the last semidivine, semihuman figures who, mythical accounts claim, were responsible for vital technological and cultural advances, the origins of the state, and even the beginnings of the Earth. A divinity named Pangu is credited with the creation of the Earth. He divided Heaven and Earth and, after his demise, his body was transformed into the various features of the Earth's environment. His blood flowed to create the lakes, rivers, and oceans; his eyes turned into the sun and moon, the brightest phenomena seen by mankind; his hair grew into the trees and plants; and even his body lice were changed – they formed human beings and animals.

Pangu, who appeared only in later texts, established the foundations of the reputed innovations and discoveries of the mythical Three Sovereigns (*Sanhuang*) and Five Emperors (*Wudi*). Paradoxically, some of the figures who supposedly trod the Earth after Pangu are noted in earlier sources. In fact, the later they are said to have lived, the earlier their appearance in Chinese historical texts.

In addition, in these texts, the figures who reputedly inhabited the Earth in late times resemble humans and have been stripped of their characteristics as divinities. Naturally, the earlier figures retain their godlike attributes.

The Three Sovereigns, for example, assumed strange, nonhuman shapes and made extraordinary contributions to Chinese civilization. Fuxi and his consort Nuwa, who is variously described as his wife or his sister, are portrayed with human heads but serpents' bodies. The sources laud Fuxi for introducing animal husbandry and marriage and creating musical instruments and the calendar. Shennong, the second of the Three Sovereigns, was China's great economic benefactor because he reputedly initiated agriculture and commerce, and Zhurong, the last of the Three Sovereigns, allegedly instructed the Chinese in the use of fire.

The Five Emperors generally contributed to human relations rather than to techniques and inventions and were depicted in human form. Huangdi (the Yellow Emperor) reputedly devised the governmental structure and expelled the non-Chinese "barbarians" from China's core territories, permitting the development of Chinese civilization. His wife served as a model for women, originating sericulture and undertaking domestic chores, and his principal minister created the first written symbols. Yao and Shun, the last two emperors, exemplified the Chinese values of wisdom and competence for rulers and embodied the highest virtues, as was later articulated by Confucius and his followers. Early accounts credit them with devising the characteristic Chinese governmental institutions and with setting political precedents. For example, Yao emphasized the principle of merit in the selection of officials and leaders, although his own family lost out as a result. He chose the commoner Shun rather than his own son as his successor. He judged Shun to be the most competent person to rule the territory of China under his control and forsook heredity as the main criterion for succession. Yao was particularly impressed with Shun's unswerving devotion to filial piety, despite the cruel and inhumane treatment he received at the hands of his stepmother and father. Yao eventually gave the throne and two of his daughters in marriage to Shun, who supposedly came to be an exceptional ruler, proving that Yao's confidence in him was not misplaced.

When Shun, in turn, needed to choose his own successor, he followed Yao's example, overriding the hereditary or flesh-and-blood imperative in order to select the most competent person. In this case, he tapped Yu, who became a great cultural hero and is repeatedly mentioned and praised for his accomplishments in the Chinese histories. Yu tamed the Great Flood, which had caused havoc and devastation and threatened the survival of the sedentary agricultural civilization created near the Yellow River and its tributaries in north China. In effect, the sources depict him as the originator of the irrigation projects that permitted the continuance of Chinese civilization. Without flood control and simultaneous conservation of the occasionally scarce water resources of north China, agriculture could not have been sustained.

Having saved civilization through strenuous, life-long efforts, Yu was poised to follow his predecessors in selecting a successor. However, his people rejected his choice and selected his son as the heir, thereby legitimizing the principle of hereditary succession and originating the concept of a dynasty or a family-ruled state. His son's succession to the throne resulted in the founding of the first reputed dynasty in the Chinese tradition, the Xia. The dynasty, which in theory flourished around 2000 BCE, survived until the reign of the cruel and tyrannical Jie, who so alienated his own people that they rebelled, enabling a virtuous leader named Tang to overthrow the Xia and found the Shang (ca. 1600–1027 BCE) dynasty. This portrait of a virtuous and wise founder and a depraved and evil last ruler of a dynasty became still another precedent in Chinese historical writings. The sources depict nearly every succeeding dynasty with just such a pattern – clearly attempts by usurpers to justify the overthrow of the previous rulers.

Because the history of the Xia appears to be intermingled with legendary accounts and mythical heroes and because no specific site has been definitively ascribed to the dynasty, some scholars have speculated that later rulers, probably in the Zhou (1027–256 BCE) dynasty, fabricated its existence to legitimize their own destruction of the previous dynasty. These rulers would have argued that, just as the Shang was justified in deposing the Xia, whose rulers had lost the people's support because of misrule, they too were right in overthrowing the corrupt and declining previous dynasty. In this view, invention of the "Xia" was merely a convenient means of sanctioning rebellion against an existing dynasty.

On the other hand, some scholars have attempted to substantiate the historicity of the Xia, and finds at Erlitou in the province of Henan in 1957 have provided support for this interpretation. The site appears to be a cultural midpoint between the Longshan Neolithic era and the Shang dynasty. Scholars who reject the existence of the Xia label Erlitou as Early Shang, while others who are impressed by the Chinese historical sources assert that it represents a distinct phase differing from the Shang. The most obvious difference between the Erlitou and the Longshan sites is two sizable residences of "palatial foundations" (in the words of the distinguished archeologist K. C. Chang).[1] Reconstruction by the on-site archeologists indicates that one of the residences had a gabled roof and a timber framework. Tombs adjacent to the residences show the sharp social distinctions that had developed. A few – the graves of the elite – had lacquered coffins and other valuables, but the depredations of grave robbers make it impossible to assess the exact nature of the ritual and practical objects placed in these tombs. Others were bare and appear to contain the remains of ordinary people of nonelite background. A few individual residences were sizable, reflecting the rise of a newly prosperous elite. In sum, the scale of the palaces and a few of the tombs reveal a much more highly developed culture than that of the Longshan.

Although stone tools and objects made of bone and shell similar to those found at Longshan predominated, artifacts composed of other materials less frequently found (if at all) at Longshan occurred at Erlitou. Stone tools comprised the vast majority of agricultural implements excavated at the site, and a few farm tools were shaped from bone and shell. Yet the inhabitants of Erlitou also used bronze knives and chisels. Gray, black, and red pottery provided most of the food and storage containers, but bronze wine vessels also appeared in larger numbers. Bronze weapons and musical instruments supplemented the stone varieties and were found even more frequently than in the Longshan sites. Objects made of new and more valuable materials and probably used for rituals and ceremonies surfaced more often from this era. Jade ceremonial knives and axes, lacquer drums and cups, and turquoise plates constituted new objects not represented in Longshan sites. On the other hand, like the Longshan peoples, the inhabitants used oracle bones, but, unlike the Shang, they did not produce inscriptions, thus revealing the absence of a written language.

In short, Erlitou represents a mixture of Longshan and Shang, but can it be identified as a distinct phase that coincided with the Xia dynasty? This question continues to be controversial and, like much else in the prehistory of China, the archeological evidence is, as yet, insufficient to provide incontrovertible proof. Also, like much else in the study of Chinese archeology, it has become entangled with feelings of nationalism and attitudes about traditional Chinese historical sources. For a few scholars (certainly not the majority), ethnic pride has become bound up with proving the veracity of the Chinese historical accounts, which are among the most prized and revered writings in China, and with verifying traditional beliefs in and descriptions of the Xia. No doubt they, as well as scholars who have no particular national pride invested in this controversy but who nonetheless subscribe to their views, have developed a strong case to confirm the existence of a Xia dynasty. Longshan, Erlitou, and Shang lie along a continuum, but there are marked differences between the three. The bronzes, burials, and palaces of Erlitou are larger in scale and more diverse in decoration than the similar objects and buildings of the Longshan, whose inhabitants certainly did not erect palaces of any size. The congruence of the dates of Erlitou and the Xia (2100–1800 BCE) also buttresses the claims for an independent dynasty distinct from the Shang. Yet the most striking evidence is that Erlitou sites have been found in precisely the places mentioned in later texts as the locations of the Xia capitals. According to some scholars, this geographic congruence corroborates the information on the Xia in the Chinese historical texts. However, unless written evidence confirming the identification of Erlitou with the Xia is uncovered, the controversy will continue to rage.

Some of the most critical questions swirling around the study of early Chinese civilization center on the origins of its most characteristic cultural and technological elements. To put it simply, did the Chinese develop these institutions and practices independently or did many derive from neighboring cultures from which the Chinese borrowed? The evidence generally bears out the view that the unique features of Chinese civilization developed in China, although useful contributions were introduced from other lands, and careful archeological and linguistic studies may indicate closer links and diffusion between China and other cultures. Analysis of bronzes produced in central Asia may, for example, testify to their predating and influencing the so-called unique bronzes of ancient China; similarly, study of eastern Siberia may show that scapulimancy developed earlier there than in Longshan; finally, the Chinese numerals and writing may have antecedents elsewhere. In short, as more information becomes available, closer links and interchanges between China and the surrounding cultures may be revealed.

THE SHANG AND THE ORIGINS OF CHINESE CIVILIZATION

The Shang is not only the first attested dynasty of China but also the first era to provide an array of rich source materials. More abundant information translates into more precise reconstruction of its history than at any previous time in China's history. Excavations in the last Shang capital of Anyang have uncovered artifacts, such as bronzes, pottery, jades, and oracle bones, offering vivid glimpses of society. The names of about thirty kings have been identified in the oracle-bone inscriptions, and archeologists have located the sites of eight different capitals of the dynasty. Later written accounts yield stereotypical portraits of the kings, providing insights into the later dynasties but primarily offering anecdotes with a specific moral message about the Shang. For example, these sources depict Cheng Tang, the first ruler, as a great unifier who represented, in Chinese eyes, the highest moral standards. According to these accounts, many regions voluntarily accepted his rule because they recognized that he embodied the virtues prized in Chinese culture. The same sources depict his adversaries, in particular King Jie, the last ruler of the so-called Xia dynasty, as despicable exploiters and oppressors of their subjects. Victory for Cheng Tang was almost predictable, for, in these later accounts, the moral superiority of the new ruler would naturally attract others to join him in defeating the evil and dissolute tyrant.

The other leading Shang figures are also portrayed in dubious stereotypes that served to support the orthodox political morality. The written sources laud rulers of probity but vilify licentious and corrupt kings in order to justify rebellion and usurpation. Pan Geng, for example, is portrayed as a hero because he reputedly moved the capital city to Yin at a propitious time. On the other hand, King Zhou, the last ruler of the dynasty, is presented as a grotesque monster. According to these later sources, he ignored the government, sponsored outrageous orgies, and exacted higher taxes to pay for the lavishness at court. Critics of his policies and activities took their lives in their hands. He had recalcitrant ministers sliced open so that he could examine their hearts; he used the so-called "grilled roast" technique to incinerate, in a most painful way, any dissenters; and he killed a female bedmate who was apparently not enchanted with his sexual proclivities. This horrifying portrait of a brutal tyrant naturally served to justify the Zhou dynasty's overthrow of the Shang in the eleventh century BCE. The political motives underlying this depiction arouse suspicions about its accuracy. Nor can the Shang's fall be attributed to a depraved and blood-thirsty monster. Economic, social, and political factors, some of which will never be known because of the limitations of the written sources and the material artifacts, contributed much more to its decline than the alleged brutality of a loathsome, almost inhuman king.

Despite these lacunae, archeological data and written inscriptions reveal considerable development in almost every area of endeavor. The Shang, the dates of which are still in dispute, though it certainly ended in 1028 BCE, witnessed remarkable changes from Neolithic cultures. Cities rather than towns were built. Rituals and ceremonies were more elaborate, and a recognizable system of writing was created. The populations of the cities were larger, necessitating a more complicated social system. Nearly every site and institution was on a larger scale than in the Neolithic.

The modern city of Anyang (in modern Henan province), in which the Shang capital of Yin was located, has turned out to be a treasure house of Shang civilization. The site stretches beyond the old city walls of Anyang to include small villages and tomb complexes. The village of Xiaotun, the principal site thus far excavated, consisted of rectangular houses with stamped-earth bases, large tombs adjacent to smaller burial pits, and ritual areas also with burial pits. The excavations indicate that Xiaotun was inhabited prior to the shifting of the capital. Even in this early period, the several hundred or so residences uncovered had drainage ditches, and graves of seemingly important individuals contained bronze ritual vessels, as well as the remains of human sacrifices.

With the establishment of the capital near Xiaotun, the buildings assumed larger proportions – evidence of a more sophisticated society. The inhabitants erected several large above-ground structures, some with thirty layers of stamped earth, which have been identified as palaces and temples. The sizable quantity of below-ground pit dwellings, which contained animal bones, pottery, and tools, attest to the large number of ordinary residents who farmed the fields or acted as service personnel for the palace inhabitants. Enormous underground storage pits, which preserved the goods of the royal family and the elite, and numerous bronze, jade, and stone workshops were built near the palaces. Also adjacent were colossal tombs, with human and dog sacrifices; sixteen people (men, women, and children) were sacrificed in one such tomb. Precious objects overflowed within the pit, the coffin, and other parts of the grave. Hundreds of jades, bronzes, and pottery vessels, among other goods, were scattered throughout the tombs. Other objects placed in the tombs included weapons, musical instruments, and cowry shells (which were used as money).

ORACLE BONES

Knowledge of the Shang has emerged not only from the era's physical remains but also from oracle-bone inscriptions, of which about 100,000 pieces have survived. The Shang advanced beyond the Neolithic forms of scapulimancy in using turtle shells (generally female) along with cattle bones in divination and incising responses on the scapula, thus producing the first conscious Chinese writing. Workmen chiseled or bored holes in the bone or shell, and diviners applied heat and produced cracks, which were then interpreted. A craftsman, perhaps the same workman, recorded the circumstances surrounding the actual divination – the date and the name of the diviner (who, as the Shang progressed, was almost always the king) as well as its actual content. Divinations concerned potential military ventures and hunting expeditions, the harvests, sacrifices to the ancestors, and the weather and other natural phenomena.

Figure 1.3 Tortoise shell with divinatory text of the reign of Geng Ding, Shang dynasty, fourteenth/thirteenth century BCE. The Art Archive / Musée Guimet Paris / Gianni Dagli Orti

The diviners sought responses from the ancestors and from Di (who was particularly identified with the Shang royal family), a deity who, along with the river, mountain, and wind gods, controlled the natural world as well as warfare, illness, and other human crises. The king's interpretation of the cracks foretold the future. On occasion, the bones recorded the actual outcome, which most often confirmed the prognostication. The whole operation – the chiseling of holes, the proper creation of systematic cracks, and the recording of the divination – required enormous effort, time, and expertise, indicating divination's value to Shang society.

The oracle bones afford glimpses of Shang society. Nearly every aspect of Shang culture, from agriculture to sickness to the interpretation of dreams, was addressed in these records of divination. Since the king himself, reflecting a theocratic system, was the principal diviner, the bones often convey the objectives and aspirations of the elite, as well as their spiritual views. However, Shang religions consisted of more than oracle bones. The bones themselves allude only to rituals, dances, music, and ceremonies, without providing additional details. Thus, they convey only a partial – though invaluable – view of Shang religion and society. Though the bones that have survived constitute less than ten percent of the total actually produced for divination, most specialists believe that they are representative in theme and subject matter of the rest. Some historians believe that the divination inscriptions provide a general picture of the elite's worldviews; they also recognize that knowledge of Shang China will not, unless new remarkable sources are uncovered, achieve the same level of detail about rulers, the military, and the economy as exists regarding later dynasties.

RITUAL OBJECTS AS HISTORICAL SOURCES

Other sources that provide information about the Shang include signs and actual writings on bones, pottery, and jade, but no doubt the most important are ritual bronze vessels. The bronzes reflect sophistication and advances in arts and crafts but also yield information on religion, social relations, and government. Some of these data derive from fragmentary and sometimes cryptic inscriptions on the bronzes. Unlike the bronze inscriptions of the next dynasty, the Zhou, the Shang artifacts are brief, none amounting to more than fifty Chinese characters. Nonetheless, they occasionally narrate the circumstances under which the bronzes were cast, for several were produced to commemorate military expeditions, gifts, or special rituals. Many were designed for ritual purposes and served as drinking vessels, food containers, or cooking implements on ceremonial occasions. Bronze craftsmen also fashioned musical instruments, chariots, weapons, and farm tools.

Figure 1.4 Bronze vessel bearing the *taotie* design, Shang dynasty. Ashmolean Museum, University of Oxford, UK / The Bridgeman Art Library

In addition, the decorations on the bronzes may yield insights about the Shang ethos and religion. Descriptions of fantastic animals, which sometimes combined features of different animals, were characteristic of the motifs found on the bronzes. The so-called *taotie* mask is the most distinctive of these mythical figures. Readily recognized by its prominent and large eyes, which gaze directly at the observer, the *taotie* has puzzled scholars who have tried to understand its possible ritual or religious importance. Speculation on its meaning ranges from its use to protect humans to its identification as a grotesque, malevolent monster. What appear to be its jaws, as well as its horns and snout, give it a ferocious appearance, but its symbolic significance remains elusive. There are also variations in the depictions of the *taotie* in the Shang bronzes, and the eyes often are the only means to identify the creature. A number of other animals, including dragons, are represented, although once again their precise meaning is unclear.

The diverse shapes of the vessels, some of which derive from shapes of Neolithic pottery, and their decorations reveal the skill of the bronze craftsmen. Art historians have identified at least five stages of decoration, with each evincing a more elaborate style and more detailed decoration of the objects. The origins of the decorations and indeed of the high level of bronze casting are unknown, but the quality and the large number of bronzes indicate the presence of a sizable industry and skilled artisans. The artisans were favored in this social structure; for example, they lived in houses with floors of stamped earth rather than in the virtually underground residences of ordinary folk.

Along with a sophisticated bronze industry, the Shang also produced jade, ceramic, and lacquer objects. Jade carving developed in the Neolithic, but

Figure 1.5 *Cong* (jade tube), Neolithic culture, 3300–2250 BCE. Freer Gallery of Art, Smithsonian Institution, USA / Gift of Charles Lang Freer / The Bridgeman Art Library

more jade artifacts have survived from the Shang. Jade knives, weapons, and jewelry, often with incised decorations of animals or simple geometric designs, have been found in many burial sites. Their appearance at burial sites may indicate that they had a ritual or religious significance. They may, for example, have served as offerings to the spirits or the ancestors. The *bi* ring, a disc in the shape of a circle, probably had such ceremonial associations and may have been used in divining the future. Some of the jade probably came from outside the core area of Shang culture, testifying to the development of commerce during this era. Lacquerware has also been discovered in some Shang tombs. Like the motifs on jade and ceramics, the designs on lacquer reveal an interest in the depiction of animals.

SHANG SOCIETY

The Shang's more populous settlements, larger towns, elaborate and grander tombs, bronze industry, and ceramics and jade production, as well as the greater emphasis accorded to divination, presume a more organized society, an efficient mobilization of resources, and a highly developed division of labor. However, details about the structure of government and the social system are difficult to tease out of the sources. Careful study of the fragmentary writings and artifacts has offered glimpses of the Shang elite, but information about commoners is scanty, and knowledge of their lives and values will probably remain limited.

The key figures in the elite were the king and the royal family. As the oracle bones attest, the king was clearly the main diviner, a ritual and religious function that at some early stage translated into secular political power. As he expanded his authority in the capital at Anyang, he instructed specific clans to settle in new towns and provided their leaders with tangible symbols of power, helping to legitimize their rule in these sites. The kings and their consorts derived from a small group of clans, among whom the royal succession rotated. Because primogeniture was not the norm, officials who were part of the elite advised the king on the choice of a suitable successor who could assume the religious, political, and military responsibilities. The king's ritual tasks evolved throughout the dynasty but always involved offerings to the ancestors and earlier kings, as well as divinations concerning war, hunts, and other matters of importance. Depending on the era, kings also made offerings to deities associated with nature or performed rituals to produce more bountiful harvests.

Elite status conferred privileges and responsibilities on both men and women. Royal consorts played an active role in the public sphere. They could conduct sacrifices and act in the name of the king, and at least one took part in a military campaign. In short, they played active social roles rather than spending their lives in the shadowy private spheres of household and harem. Other members of the elite included princes, diviners, ministers, officials, and landlords who were granted land or walled towns by the king. Members of the elite had the right to accompany the king on hunts, often used to train the military, and to assume the responsibility of supporting him on military expeditions. By participating in the hunts, they had access to the animals bagged – a valuable resource for their own domains. In theory, the land accorded them was still owned by the king, and they were obligated to offer tribute to him. In practice, however, distance and time influenced the king's ability to control them and to demand and receive tribute. The farther away their domains from the capital, the less leverage the king could have over them. Similarly, at times when weak monarchs were on the throne, they fulfilled their obligations with neither alacrity nor regularity. Yet their power derived from the titles that the king conferred upon them as lords over walled towns within the Shang state.

The princes and lords commanded the armies, but the social status of the military is not discernible from the sources. Naturally the king was the commander in chief of the state's army, and the princes and lords led the military within their own domains – the military forces that could be mobilized were apparently sizable. Descriptions of the battles, of the captives, and of the human sacrifices of prisoners of war in the tombs of the elite attest to the participation of substantial numbers of soldiers in particular campaigns. The military achieved a degree of specialization, with specific units of archers, foot soldiers, and charioteers who used bows and arrows, halberds, and chariots.

Knowledge of the nonelite is even sketchier. The divination inscriptions describe what appear to be collectives of peasants who worked under the strict supervision of the king and lords. They worked together to farm the fields, served as soldiers, offered tribute, and were compelled to perform corvée labor. Although most were servile, labeling them "slaves" is an overstatement. Unlike slaves, most could not be bought or sold. To be sure, slavery existed in the Shang; prisoners of war were often enslaved and forced to work in the fields or were sacrificed at tombs of kings or lords. Yet the vast majority of the nonelite were not slaves, although they undoubtedly were accorded little status, were economically exploited, and were dominated by the kings and lords. As suggested earlier, artisans had a higher position in the social hierarchy, lived more comfortably, and had access to more goods than ordinary commoners. Specific clans dominated particular trades such as woodcarving, bronze casting, and jade carving, and craft production was often a monopoly transmitted from one generation to another.

Although records on finances are absent, it appears that the king collected taxes from all his subjects. He received tribute of grain, principally millet, from the peasants, who also sent cattle (for his divinations), sheep, and horses to the capital. During his hunts (and possibly tours of inspection), he also requisitioned supplies from the peasants for his entourage. The quantity of taxes levied by the king is not recorded, but it must have been sufficient to pay for military campaigns and the elaborate tombs and other material possessions of the royal household. Simultaneously, the king received goods that the artisans had fashioned. The furnishings at the royal tombs, as well as those of the elite, attest to the considerable number of bronzes, jades, and pottery items commandeered from craftsmen. Merchants surely played a role in transmitting grain and craft articles from the various towns to the capital and vice versa, but they are scarcely mentioned on the oracle bones. Cowry shells were used as currency, and the modern Chinese word for "merchant" (*shangren*) uses the same Chinese characters as "man of Shang." Yet the paucity of data precludes efforts to assay the role of trade and the status of merchants during this era.

The available information, however, permits us to conclude that the population was divided into defined groups and classes. The king and the royal family were at the apex, with the monarch performing ritual functions (including divination), commanding military forces, and amassing considerable quantities of grain, craft articles, and other valuables. The lords to whom the king entrusted land for the construction of new settlements held sway over these territories, as well as over the inhabitants. They too received substantial amounts of the goods produced within their domains. Less privileged were the peasants, slaves, craftsmen, and merchants. Peasants did not own the land they farmed and turned over much of the produce to the king and the lords. Known as *zhongren* (multitude), they could be conscripted into the military or for labor service. Often captives of war, slaves could count themselves fortunate if they were employed to farm the land or to act as servants and unfortunate if they were selected to be sacrificial victims. Although craftsmen had a higher status and lived better than the *zhongren* and the slaves, the articles they fashioned were most often designed for the king and the nobility.

This generally stable social structure contributed to a popularly accepted conception of the uniqueness of Shang culture. Some archeologists asserted that its culture and artifacts were primarily indigenous. Even more significant was that the inhabitants of the Shang perceived themselves as a different people. They had, after all, developed a sophisticated culture, with a worked-out political system, a highly organized bronze industry, a unique burial system, and a written language. Their pictorially based written language, found mostly on the oracle bones and perhaps in some signs and symbols on ceramics, contributed, in large measure, to the Shang people's feelings of identity. The language, with its initial associations with divination and religion, proved a powerful vehicle for the fostering of their sense of affinity.

With the growth of such feelings of identity, the Shang distinguished itself from other neighboring regions, which were sometimes adversaries. Most attacks against Shang territory originated from its north and northwest, and the final onslaught, which overwhelmed the dynasty and permitted the rival Zhou dynasty to take power, derived from the northwest. Competition for land and for control of mineral deposits and other natural resources provoked crises and conflicts between the Shang and nearby territories. Such hostilities bedeviled relations between these various states. Ironically, conflict may have resulted in interaction and borrowing among a few, which enlarged the territory in which cultural homogeneity prevailed.

NOTES

1 K. C. Chang, *The Archaeology of Ancient China* (New Haven: Yale University Press, 4th ed., 1986), p. 310.

FURTHER READING

E. J. W. Barber, *The Mummies of Ürümchi* (New York: W. W. Norton, 1999).

K. C. Chang, *Shang Civilization* (New Haven: Yale University Press, 1980).

K. C. Chang, *The Archaeology of Ancient China* (New Haven: Yale University Press, 4th ed., 1986).

David Keightley, *Sources of Shang China: The Oracle Bone Inscriptions of Bronze Age China* (Berkeley: University of California Press, 1985).

Harry Shapiro, *Peking Man* (London: Allen & Unwin, 1974).

[2] CLASSICAL CHINA, 1027–256 BCE

"Feudalism"?
Changes in Social Structure
Political Instability in the Eastern Zhou
Transformations in the Economy
Hundred Schools of Thought
Daoism
Popular Religions
Confucianism
Mohism
Legalism
Book of Odes and *Book of Documents*
Secularization of Arts

"FEUDALISM"?

Although the Zhou lasted longer than any other dynasty in Chinese history, its longevity may be deceptive. There was a sharp break in the dynasty, for in 771 BCE it was compelled to move its capital. During the first phase, known as the Western Zhou, its administrative center was located in the Wei river valley, west of the modern city of Xian; in the succeeding phase, known as the Eastern Zhou, the capital was transferred to Chengzhou (near the present-day location of Luoyang), which the Western Zhou had used as a secondary capital. The remaining five centuries of Eastern Zhou rule witnessed a rapid deterioration in its ability to govern, leading to a chaotic struggle for power between areas reputedly under its jurisdiction during the so-called Warring States period (403–221 BCE).

A History of China, First Edition. Morris Rossabi.
© 2014 Morris Rossabi. Published 2014 by Blackwell Publishing Ltd.

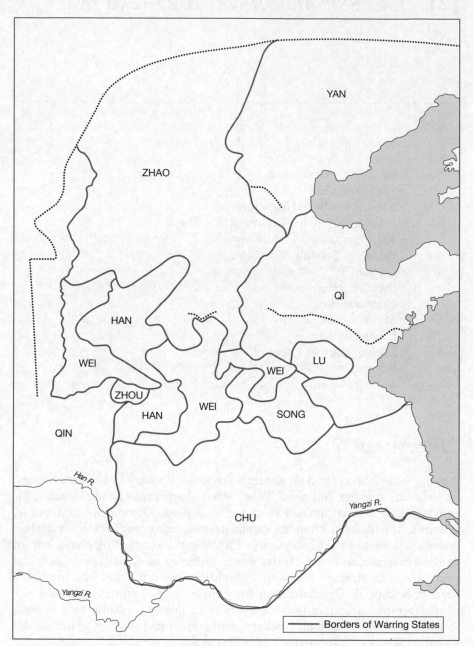

Map 2.1 Warring States-era divisions

The Zhou had from its inception set up a decentralized government, which some scholars identify as similar to the European system of feudalism. However, the concept of feudalism is also murky. In its simplest form, it consisted of a legal and military system based on a relationship between a lord and a vassal. A lord who owned land turned over possession of a portion of that land (known as a fief) to a vassal in return, principally, for military services. Their mutual obligations and rights entailed a pledge of loyalty to the lord by the vassal and a pledge of protection of the vassal by the lord. Peasants who worked the land on manors for the lords and vassals or in Church estates were also part of this feudal society. Yet there were so many variations of "feudalism" in Europe that some scholars have stopped using the term in relation to China. Thus, the Western Zhou may be best described as a society in which the local nobility often supplanted the kings as true wielders of power. The rudimentary levels of transport, communications, and technology clearly reduced the opportunities for centralization. Even so, the Zhou political system, particularly the Eastern Zhou, tilted further toward localism than such limitations would have mandated.

Decentralization stemmed from the initial Zhou conquests, though it should be noted that disentangling myth from reality concerning its early years is difficult. Part of the problem is that texts allegedly written in the Zhou actually derive from later periods. Many Chinese accepted the earlier dates. The sources all concur that the Zhou peoples traced their ancestry to Hou Ji, whose second name translates as "millet." This semidivine figure reputedly instructed his descendants in the basics of farming. Inhabiting as it did the areas west of the Shang kingdom in the Wei river valley, the Zhou had often bellicose relations with its neighbor for several generations before their final confrontation in the eleventh century BCE. Despite these conflicts, the Zhou was influenced by the Shang. Designs and techniques of early Zhou bronzes and ceramics resembled Shang prototypes, and their rituals were often similar.

Culmination of the strained relationship occurred during the reigns of the stereotyped, almost legendary father-and-son monarchs, Wen and Wu of Zhou. The sources endow Wen (his name signifying "accomplished" or "learned") with the attributes of a sage-ruler. Intelligent and benevolent, Wen believed in negotiations and compromise in relations with others and in governing his own people. His remarkable character paved the way for his son Wu (his name meaning "martial') to battle with and overwhelm the Shang. The sources praise Wu for his military successes, but Wen represented the ideal. Even at this early stage in Chinese culture, civil virtues were more highly prized than military skills. The sources, for example, extol the Zhou for their magnanimity toward their defeated enemies. Instead of adopting a military solution and extirpating the Shang royal family, the leaders of Zhou gave them land in order to permit them to continue their ancestral rituals.

Early Chinese attitudes can be discerned even more clearly in the descriptions of the Duke of Zhou, the leading cultural hero of the period. The Duke of Zhou, Wu's brother, was first a regent and later a minister for King Cheng, his young nephew. In later accounts, he is credited with stabilizing the Zhou by enfeoffing collateral members of the royal family and other nobles who had been instrumental in the overwhelming victory over the Shang. Recognizing that the Zhou needed to reward these loyal retainers, the Duke of Zhou initiated the practice of granting them land and allowing them to govern their domains, relieving the Zhou court of a task it did not have the administrative or military capability to undertake. He is also revered for his patronage of scholars, a quintessential Chinese value in later times. He is most celebrated, however, for his promotion of the concept of the Mandate of Heaven. This view justified the Zhou usurpation of the throne because the mandate to rule offered by Heaven (Tian, who became the most important deity and superseded the Di and the wind, mountain, and other Shang deities) was not granted in perpetuity. Future rulers could lose the mandate, which would be revealed by their lack of concern for their subjects' welfare. When rulers lost such support, their subjects had the right, if not the obligation, to depose them. The Duke of Zhou and other exponents sought to use the theory to exonerate themselves from accusations of sedition and to legitimize the new dynasty. According to the Duke of Zhou, the Shang kings had not performed the divinely ordained rituals, had scarcely concerned themselves with government, and had selected ministers with hardly any interest in public welfare. Thus, the Zhou was absolutely justified in overthrowing the discredited and disreputable Shang kings. In this view, the king's role was essential. It is all the more ironic, then, that the Duke of Zhou took the initiative in developing a decentralized political system that eventually circumscribed the king's authority and turned over much of the responsibility for the public welfare to the nobility. The question is: did the Zhou kings and the Duke of Zhou have any other choice in light of the technological limitations of centralized government at that time?

The early Zhou rulers devised a set of offices for the central government, but the operation of these agencies and their division of functions were vague. It is perhaps too much to expect a precise table of organization at this early stage of culture, and it is true that the Zhou distinguished between household personnel, or the inner court, and the various ministries. However, the confusion concerning these offices probably reflected the lack of true Western Zhou centralization. The scanty evidence confirms the informality of the political structure, as those close to the king (who were not an officially designated bureaucracy) often wielded power and increasingly dominated the court aristocrats. The Zhou's financial administration was as vague as its political system. Though the land, in theory, belonged to the king, the peasants generally did not pay taxes to the court. Whatever revenue reached the court derived from the vassals whom the king enfeoffed and from taxes on commerce. This imprecise financial system initially fulfilled the Western Zhou's revenue needs. Yet, as the court continued to decline, its reliance on so-called tribute from its vassals revealed its vulnerability because these very same retainers sought to supplant the king and were not willing to meet his revenue demands.

This decentralized system eventually offered vassals the opportunity to dominate on the local level, to garner taxes from their subjects, to administer justice, and to raise and command their own military forces. Nonetheless, some scholars have argued, on the basis of inscriptions and early texts, that the kings still maintained power during the Western Zhou and that they mandated a feudal system. Such a system was essential because the Zhou adopted a process of incorporating many non-Zhou peoples and needed help from their relatives and retainers, the feudal lords, to do so. Since definitions of "feudal" vary in the histories of "feudal" China and Europe, it may seem pointless to characterize the Zhou as "feudal" rather than as a decentralized political system with its own unique characteristics. The sparse materials on the early Zhou, in contrast to the relatively more abundant extant sources on medieval Europe, compound the difficulties of using the term "feudal." Yet, since comparative history, on occasion, proves illuminating, a few distinctions as well as several similarities between the two ought to be mentioned.

Like the lords in medieval Europe, the kings in Zhou China played pivotal roles. The kings enfeoffed their vassals (who were relatives, retainers, or allies and numbered about a hundred or so), giving them various ritual objects of authority and entrusting them with lands over which they had considerable control. As in Europe, the ceremonies for such enfeoffment became increasingly more elaborate as the dynasty developed, but at first the kings generally did not demand an oath of allegiance. This may indicate that the kings were so confident of their retainers' loyalty that they could not have conceived of demanding such a pledge. In the Western Zhou, these enfeoffments did not take place at the altar of the god of the soil (as in the Eastern Zhou), another indication of the lack of ceremonies or perhaps of the appointment of trustworthy retainers to positions of local authority. On the other hand, this may imply that these enfeoffments were only a formality and did not entail subservience and loyalty. The contractual obligations of European feudalism did not appear as clearly in the Zhou system. Nonetheless, once the vassal was invested, he was, in theory, obligated to provide tribute and to supply laborers and soldiers when requested to do so. Again, in theory, he served as the king's representative to ensure peace and stability on the local level.

Some of the practices of enfeoffed vassals resembled practices in the European system but others diverged. Like their European counterparts, vassals perceived themselves to be distinctive, tended to marry among themselves, and had a code of conduct (*li*), which could include and did resemble chivalry. Eventually they coalesced into a real hierarchy composed of dukes (*gong*), marquises (*hou*), earls (*bo*), barons (*zi*), and vice-barons (*nan*). However, these vassals did not receive their titles in perpetuity. Unlike in the European feudal system, their sons did not automatically inherit their positions. Each successive inheritor of a fief needed the court's sanction and required the king's blessing and enfeoffment. Such investitures entailed a personal visit to the king's court for the enfeoffment ceremonies. In other areas, family and kinship played a much more significant role in the Zhou than in medieval Europe. Kinship ties frequently superseded contractual obligations in the enfeoffment of vassals and in the lord–vassal relationship. Since family considerations were vital in Chinese culture, it seems natural that kinship would, on occasion, supplant merit in the court's selection of officials – still another deviation from the European model of feudalism.

Despite such kinship ties, vassals often went their own ways within their local domains, partly because they controlled their own military forces. Warfare was, in theory, a gentleman's activity throughout the Western Zhou and until the Warring States period and thus had well-defined rules of conduct. The chariot, though unwieldy and often a liability in uneven or rutted terrain, was characteristic of gentlemanly or aristocratic warfare. It did not provide a haven for combatants, judging from the numerous aristocrats killed while riding in such a vehicle. Scholars have repeatedly challenged its efficiency in battle, but it offered mobility for the commander, who could use it to survey the entire battlefield; it also enabled him to transport his troops from one location to another rapidly. Though its role in warfare was limited, it had symbolic value as a means to impress allies and enemies. It had prestige but was infrequently decisive in battles. As the dynasty wore on, the infantry became increasingly significant, and wars were fought on a grander scale. Archery, as well as hand-to-hand combat, became important, and the larger scope of war necessitated more sophisticated analyses of strategy.

A military handbook could be useful in fulfilling this need. Other hand-books probably preceded it, but the *Ping fa* (*Art of War*), probably written in the fourth century BCE by Sunzi, offered such guidance. The Zhou vassals used this handbook as a guidebook for fending off enemies and ensuring authority in their domains. Although it dealt with battle tactics and strategy, it also emphasized supposed auxiliary aspects of warfare such as espionage and intelligence information, support from the populace, and cleverness in deploying troops rather than simply focusing on manpower and weaponry. The writer asserted that the best commanders would gain their objectives without a battle, an example of so-called soft power. Military historians often refer to it as one of the first descriptions of guerilla warfare.

The *Zhanguoce* (*Intrigues of the Warring States*), another contemporary text, also reflected the difficult times. The work offered a guide to proper diplomacy for the often hostile states in this period and provided means of avoiding conflict. Pointing to reportedly real historical events, the work inculcated a set of diplomatic principles that could be used in averting catastrophic wars against other states.

Meanwhile, raids by non-Chinese peoples along the country's frontiers, together with the increasing disaffection of its vassals, contributed to the grow-ing decentralization of the Western Zhou. Natural catastrophes, including a serious earthquake in the reign of the last king, added to its troubles. The dynasty was increasingly vulnerable, and it should come as no surprise that foreign forces – so-called barbarians – raided the capital in 771 BCE, killing the king and compelling the dynasty to transfer its capital eastward to the Luo River valley, near modern Luoyang. Abandonment of the capital and the onset of the Eastern Zhou signaled a significant diminution of the central govern-ment's authority. For the remaining five centuries of the dynasty, vassals often acted on their own. The court did not have a military force and did not have the power to command its vassals to provide troops for any campaigns. It also could not count on regular tribute or tax payments, precluding the develop-ment of essential large-scale public-works projects and the creation of a loyal bureaucracy. In short, the court had scarcely any political or military power, and the king was principally a figurehead who undertook ceremonial and ritual functions and, on occasion, adjudicated disputes or questions of legitimacy concerning specific lords. The Eastern Zhou thus consisted of a number of independent states that over the last three centuries of the dynasty were intermittently at war in order to determine who would succeed the ineffective Zhou rulers.

CHANGES IN SOCIAL STRUCTURE

Peasants constituted by far the largest segment of the population, although written sources about them are scarce. They grew millet, wheat, rice, hemp seeds, and beans and divided their produce with the lord, who also demanded corvée labor from them. Later writers, notably the philosopher Mencius (the Latinized version of his personal name, Meng Ko), also called Meng Zi (Master Meng), asserted that the land had been divided according to a so-called "well-field system." Eight families tilled a plot of land each, and they also farmed a ninth plot, which belonged to the lord. The pattern of fields, which looked like a tic-tac-toe board, also resembled the Chinese character for "water well," lending the system its name. It is unclear whether the well-field system ever actually existed. The sources indicate that the peasants provided tribute and corvée service while the lord offered land and protection – a typical "feudal" arrangement – though it may be stretching the comparison with Europe to refer to the peasants as "serfs."

Differences in style of life, based on position in the hierarchy, were also apparent. Lords ate far more meat while farmers subsisted on vegetables and soups at best and on stale grain and leaves at worst. Clothing for aristocrats was more elaborate and included more luxurious materials, such as jade and silk, than the dress worn by peasants. The lords led the peasants on hunts in the winter to train them as a military force. The ceremonies practiced by the elite and the peasants did not differ considerably, though the elite's rituals were more lavish. Even at this early stage, marital ceremonies emphasized the submissiveness of women – though, as will be explained later, women may in fact have been more assertive than this stereotyped portrait. In any event, parents urged the prospective bride to be obedient, and she herself moved into her husband's home having been advised to serve and to submit to her new family. Despite similarities in marital and ancestral ceremonies, the differences in the lifestyles of the lords and the peasants were striking.

POLITICAL INSTABILITY IN THE EASTERN ZHOU

The shift of the capital and the establishment of the Eastern Zhou in 770 BCE ushered in political and military turmoil, but paradoxically it also witnessed extraordinary economic and technological developments and the onset of great intellectual ferment. On several occasions in their history, the Chinese reacted to chaotic conditions with economic and institutional changes and either new or refurbished ideologies designed to create unity or at least foster a more stable environment. Major philosophies and religions frequently made their first appearances during unsettled times in China. Daoism, Confucianism, and Buddhism, the three dominant religions or cults in the history of the Middle Kingdom, all emerged during troubled eras in Chinese society.

The Eastern Zhou was certainly a troubled, unsettled time. This era is often divided into two discrete segments, the Spring and Autumn period (722–481 BCE) and the Warring States period (403–221 BCE). The appellation "Spring and Autumn" derives from the *Spring and Autumn Annals (Chun qiu)*, a text perhaps written by the great philosopher Confucius that offered a factual, if somewhat tedious, account of interstate relations at that time. This work lacks interpretation and the fullness of a true history, leading to speculation about Confucius's motives in compiling the text. Some students have suggested that Confucius may have valued the *Annals* because it was the first attempt to set down events in Chinese history in chronological order without embroidering the facts with invented dialogues and fabricated evidence meant to underscore a moral. Later scholars wrote commentaries designed to flesh out the spare details offered in the text and to provide it with a moral and didactic framework. It eventually became associated with the *Zuo Commentary (Zuo zhuan)*, a source dealing with many of the same events (through 468 BCE) but with more elaborate and more colorful and lengthier descriptions. Both texts described turbulent times.

The founding of the Eastern Zhou coincided with the virtual disintegration of the king's power. The nobility was autonomous and no longer felt obliged to provide military service and tribute to the Zhou ruler. Nor did nobles appear in person at the Zhou court to be invested with authority. Some formed their own states that were not controlled by the king. The proliferation of such states engendered fears of strife. Thus, in the seventh century BCE an overlord or hegemon (*ba*), supported by lesser leaders, sought to impose order with the blessing, for whatever it was worth, of the king. Five rulers in succession assumed the role of hegemon and are credited with stemming disorder for a time, but interstate hostility intensified throughout this era.

The principal states were in the Central Plain, which was surrounded by so-called barbarian groups. These states comprised Jin, Lu, Qi, Wei, Song, and Cheng while the states on the fringes of what was perceived to be Chinese civilization consisted of Qin (the westernmost of the states), Yan (which included the area around modern Beijing), Wu (along the eastern coast, near modern Shanghai), Yue (directly south of Wu), and Chu (in the southwest). In general, the states on the periphery were in more advantageous positions because they had room in which to expand and could avoid conflict until they themselves were prepared to do battle. However, until the third century BCE, these states waxed and waned depending on their conditions at particular times, for each had unique strengths and weaknesses. Qi, for example, had reserves of iron and salt, perhaps facilitating its construction of weapons and enriching itself through sale of its precious salt. It also had the advantage of the administrative reforms introduced by Guan Zhong (ca. 720–645 BCE), the influential counselor to its lords and the author of an important work of political philosophy, the *Guanzi*. Jin, on the other hand, controlled much of the territory around the bend of the Yellow River.

A precarious balance prevailed among these states throughout the seventh and sixth centuries but it eventually collapsed late in the fifth century. Hegemons, marital alliances, and conferences between potential belligerents all averted chaos and warfare during what became known as the Spring and Autumn period. The states of the Central Plain often joined together in fear of the "barbaric" Chu in the southwest, and the state of Jin, in particular, checked the power of that state. However, in 453 BCE, internal conflicts within Jin led to its breakup into three smaller and more vulnerable states. Earlier in the century, Yue had conquered Wu and had initiated the deterioration into the Warring States period. Peace conferences and interstate alliances could no longer maintain the peace. For the next two and a half centuries, intermittent warfare plagued the central core of Chinese civilization. An authoritarian state with policies that conformed to the Legalist philosophy (to be considered later), Qin began a seemingly inexorable drive toward conquest and unification of China in the third century BCE. In 256 it overthrew the last remnants of the Zhou kingdom and over the next three decades destroyed one state after another, so that in 221 BCE it was the uncontested unifier of China.

Though violence and brute force characterized the politics of the Warring States period, momentous technological and cultural developments occurred. The implications for China's history of this volatile period cannot be over-stated. Wars themselves resulted in undeniable changes. The scale of warfare increased throughout this era so that, by the time of the Warring States, battles involved much larger numbers of troops, entailed attacks on populous towns and cities, and were fought over a much broader expanse of territory. The resulting casualties were substantial, and the number of prisoners who were executed, enslaved, or, on occasion, incorporated into the victorious army was equally sizable. With the advent of larger confrontations and battles, warfare changed from struggles between a limited number of aristocrats to encounters between masses of people. Infantry began to supplant the chariot as the most important component on the battlefield. Chariots were, in any case, ineffective in mountainous, uneven, or rutted terrain. Moreover, learning to drive a chariot and to shoot a bow and arrow from a moving chariot required considerable time, expense, and effort. Thus, hand-to-hand combat, which inflicted heavy losses on both sides in battle, tended to replace the more "gentlemanly" fighting associated with chariots. Despite the decline of the chariot, the value of the horse actually grew. There is no doubt that the use of cavalry was introduced by the nomads on China's northern frontiers, and this offered them the tactical advantage of mobility. They could engage in hit–and–run raids, with impunity, on China's borders, fleeing on their steeds to the steppe lands in order to elude pursuing Chinese forces. Archers who could shoot accurately while riding at full speed gave a decided advantage over armies that did not have a cavalry.

The Chinese themselves began to make use of the horse in warfare, which, together with the development of the crossbow, strengthened the military. The threats posed by the nomads, who were more adept on horseback than the Zhou, also prompted some of the northern Chinese states to build walls to deter attacks from the pastoral peoples. Nonetheless, the need for horses continued to increase, as did their uses. They could facilitate communications within China, contributing eventually to unification. Horses also hastened travel between various parts of Asia, leading to the introduction of innovations from west Asia in China and vice versa. Speedier travel would pave the way for commercial and cultural relations throughout Asia, and technological innovations and ideas would flow into China from the Indian subcontinent, central Asia, Persia, and west Asia. Finally, horseback riding influenced Chinese dress. It necessitated the use of functional outfits rather than the long and more cumbersome traditional robes. Trousers, boots, and belt buckles were developed to enable the cavalry to ride with ease. The horse thus had a pervasive influence on Zhou culture and would continue to affect China until recent times.

The scale of warfare and the resulting value of able military tacticians and strategists altered the Chinese social structure. Rulers and ministers who lacked military skills or were incapable of adjusting to the new types of military conflict lost influence. Because the much larger engagements meant more loss of life, opportunities for social mobility increased. Nobles and military commanders died, paving the way for men of lower-class origins to rise quickly up the social ladder. Even without the deaths of the old aristocrats and rulers, the new warrior groups attained higher status because the various states, desperate for any means to bolster their power, recruited them with ever more lavish inducements. Competent military men of uncertain or varying social backgrounds became dominant figures, as the aristocrats no longer monopolized power and sons of rulers did not automatically succeed their fathers. The group that profited the most from the turbulence and changes of the Warring States period was the *shi*, a class that might tentatively be described as part of the lower nobility. Literate and conversant with the sacrifices and ceremonies of the time, the *shi* were trained in the military arts, giving them the opportunity to step into power if the aristocrats faltered, died, or simply needed their expertise.

The states that emerged victorious in these struggles grew large and acquired new characteristics. Control over a much larger area required greater concentration of power in the hands of the ruler rather than the old "feudal" structure, which had resulted in a dispersal of authority. In turn, the ruler needed to recruit a corps of competent experts (rather than aristocrats who could perform the proper rituals) to help him with the more complicated governmental apparatus for his new state. These new officials, many of whom derived from the *shi* class, had to have training, mostly from master tutors, that would qualify them for positions guaranteeing wealth, power, and rank. Tutors would offer them practical exercises but would also use the essays and treatises written during this great period in Chinese philosophy to instruct their charges. The Warring States period thus benefited and offered mobility to this new group. Competence rather than birth often determined the staffing of positions.

TRANSFORMATIONS IN THE ECONOMY

The economic transformations derived, in part, from the more fluid social system. With the decline of the old aristocracy, new patterns of land ownership evolved. The earlier manorial system in which peasants tilled the land granted by the ruler to the nobility gradually shifted to a system of private ownership. Peasants could now own land previously in the hands of the hereditary aristocratic families who had suffered as a result of the conflicts. The peasants' lot did not necessarily improve because the various state governments now imposed stiff taxes on them, and many of them eventually had to sell or give up their land to local landlords or usurers. Tenancy increased, and land became increasingly concentrated in estates owned by the new elite. Paradoxically, ownership of land and the relative ease with which it could be purchased and sold did not generally lead to better conditions for the peasantry. Large landholders benefited most from the transition to private ownership of land. Many peasants continued to till the land but now as tenants. A few who were deprived of their land became floating vagabonds, at times cooperating with bandits or potential rebels, which naturally exacerbated the turmoil afflicting China during this era.

The scenario described above characterized many periods in Chinese history. Stiff taxes, heavy corvée demands, encroachments by landlords, and high, burdensome rates of interest charged by moneylenders harmed many peasants, compelling some to sell or entrust their land to landlords, who had managed to achieve a tax-free status. The recurrence of such patterns has given rise to the concept of dynastic cycles – that is, each dynasty went through a regular ebb and flow, with the same factors as in preceding dynasties leading to its rise and eventual collapse. However, though certain patterns seem to be similar, scholars now question the idea of a "dynastic cycle" because there were just as many, if not more, differences contributing to the growth and decline of individual dynasties.

Another paradox was that agronomy and trade actually developed during this period of warfare. Better irrigation systems and new farming techniques led to greater food production. The conflicts prompted the construction and repair of roads, which naturally facilitated trade. The individual states gained control of more territory, with the result that, when peace prevailed, merchants could travel unhindered in a larger expanse. As contacts with other states increased, demands for new or previously unknown products developed, and merchants sought to fill these demands. Bronze money appeared to facilitate commerce. Money in the shapes of knives and spades came into wider circulation, particularly in the cities, which proliferated and now became more populated and more market oriented. Merchants could aspire to higher social positions because social status was not as fixed as it had been in the Western Zhou dynasty. Using their newly won gains, they could buy land or a government office, easing their way into the elite.

Commerce fostered exchanges of all sorts and led to the introduction of new products and new technologies, not to mention new ideas. Even before the Eastern Zhou, developments in areas to the west influenced China. For example, the chariot probably entered into China from modern Kazakhstan, where it likely originated as early as 2000 BCE. The ox-drawn plow, which was invented in west Asia, appeared during the Eastern Zhou. Central Asia, where many animals had been domesticated, was in touch with China, judging from the introduction of camels and donkeys toward the end of the Zhou. Along with the horse, the arrival of these two beasts of burden marked an important economic advance because they facilitated transport and commerce.

Economic vibrancy also culminated in domestic innovations and inventions. Iron started to be substituted for bronze (but did not entirely supplant it). Agricultural implements such as shovels, plowshares, sickles, hoes, and rakes were the most common tools, and the use of iron plows permitted greater efficiency in farming, enabling peasants to work previously uncultivable land. The use of oxen as draft animals allowed peasants to farm larger plots of land. Hammers, chisels, axes, knives, and other iron tools were also plentiful, as were items of daily usage such as cups, nails, and belt buckles. Unlike bronze, iron was not generally used for the production of ritual and ceremonial vessels. Bronzes continued to be produced in large quantities and with some new features. More elaborate designs, including new motifs of intertwined dragons or snakes, characterized some of the bronzes. The Eastern Zhou rulers also lavished more attention on bronze weapons because of the unstable and strife-torn conditions, and bronze mirrors appeared in larger numbers than in the past, particularly in the state of Chu. Distinctive lacquered objects, including drums, cups, and boxes, have been found in Chu tombs. Musical instruments, utilitarian vessels for food and drink, and mortuary objects, all made of lacquer, have been excavated and were highly valued, as evidenced by their positions in tombs. Gold and silver bowls and jade ornaments revealed a high level of craftsmanship, and their placement in graves indicates the great value accorded to these objects. All of these luxury goods, in addition, attest to the existence of a prosperous elite that could afford them.

HUNDRED SCHOOLS OF THOUGHT

Perhaps even more significant for Chinese civilization was a profusion of new ideas and philosophies that generated the so-called Hundred Schools of Thought, an outburst that coincided with a philosophical flowering in many of the great civilizations of the era. The development of new and vastly influential philosophies in Eurasia during this time is astonishing. In the sixth century BCE, Zoroastrianism developed in Iran, Shakyamuni described the path to Buddhist Nirvana, and (at approximately the same time) Isaiah and Jeremiah prophesied mostly manifold disasters; in the fifth century, Socrates took part in the dialogues that gradually but inexorably revealed his metaphysical and epistemological views; and, from the sixth to the fourth centuries, Chinese philosophy flourished. Pervasive theories about direct links between these intellectual developments have proliferated, resulting in unverifiable and occasionally absurd speculations. According to such often-ill-informed hypotheses,

Daoism was an east Asian version of Buddhism, and the Buddha was actually Lao Zi, the alleged founder of Daoism, who moved to India after completing his mission in China. A chance overlapping in chronology led to such unsubstantiated and incredible assertions. It is true that comparisons between the various philosophies and religions that originated at this time may prove instructive, but direct links and influences are more difficult to establish.

To be sure, the philosophers and religious thinkers of this era shared some of the same concerns. Both Socrates and Confucius sought to identify the nature of a just society in which each individual recognized his or her position in the social hierarchy and performed the tasks required of that status. The two thinkers also offered visions of the ideal man – an individual of high moral probity for Confucius and a philosopher of superior intellectual abilities and ethical astuteness for Socrates; each emphasized education. They resembled each other even in the style they used to present their views, as each shunned a direct, explicit account of his beliefs. Instead they tantalized their listeners with dialogues or anecdotes from which their philosophies could be gleaned. Similarly, Lao Zi and Siddhartha Gautama, the historical Buddha, both described roads to spiritual enlightenment, an objective they shared, though they differed on the paths they advocated. Each disparaged the rewards of this world as ephemeral, and Buddhism, in particular, perceived human life as engulfed in suffering.

The convergence of some themes in the philosophies and religions of that time does not imply a direct relationship between them. It would have been highly unlikely for Chinese philosophers of this era, for example, to have had knowledge of Buddhism. Comforting and satisfying as it may be to conceive of and actually attest to a link and to mutual influences between these philosophies and religions from different Asian civilizations, there is absolutely no evidence for such inferences.

In addition, the Chinese philosophers of this era were responding to the specific social circumstances of Eastern Zhou China. The turmoil of the Warring States period had overturned not only the social system but also societal values. Turbulence had also caused destruction and death. Under these circumstances, the populace needed solace as well as a new moral code and social system. Thus, philosophies that provided comfort or that offered the prospect of social stability and harmony were likely to find a receptive audience. Two philosophical strains emerged to fill China's needs. One (i.e. Daoism) sought to comfort a population beset by warfare, roving bands of brigands, and generally chaotic conditions while the other (i.e. Confucianism) presented plans for an orderly society.

The economic and political changes of the Warring States period reverberated in the new philosophies of the time. The seemingly greater opportunities for social mobility were mirrored in opposition to the use of social position as the means of selecting officials. Most of the philosophies emphasized merit rather than birth as the main criterion for recruitment as well as for social advancement. Confucianism, Mohism, and Legalism, three of the principal philosophies that developed in the Warring States period, paid the greatest attention to the individual's qualifications in assessing his suitability for office.

They also judged his moral worth on the basis of his own actions and values, not the circumstances of his birth. According to their thinking, because family status and personal relations would be insufficient to guarantee a prominent position at court, the ruler and his ministers would have a more contractual compact rather than a hereditary, personalized arrangement. Similarly, a number of the leading philosophers, perhaps reacting to some of the inhumane, even malevolent heads of state in the Warring States period, wrote that the ruler himself ought to be subject to the same kind of scrutiny.

The Warring States period thus witnessed the development of the conditions necessary for a unified China and the rise of a new governing class based, in theory, on merit. The hereditary principle for ministers and officials was overturned, and new men rose to positions of authority because of their capabilities. Opportunities increased for them because of the warfare that punctuated the era and that resulted in the deaths of many in the nobility. Since the new men had military, diplomatic, and administrative skills essential for the states seeking to survive these tumultuous times, the various rulers courted them. Simultaneously, ambitious men, who were not part of the nobility, began to supersede the "feudal" lords as landowners, and merchants capitalized on the demand for products that was precipitated by increased contact between the states; these merchants reaped sizable fortunes, creating still another wealthy, non-noble class. The philosophies espoused during this time undermined the rigid hierarchical structure that favored the old elite and instead supported the aspirations of the newly risen commoners and prized competence above birth in the recruitment of officials and rulers.

DAOISM

Daoism, the first of the major Eastern Zhou schools of thought to develop, poses a paradox to potential interpreters. Like other mystical philosophies, it disdains easy transmission of its principles. For Daoists, the spoken or written word often distorts the fundamental message. Even the most sympathetic of interpreters who seek to describe or define the *dao* inevitably alter it. Explaining its basic features is thus no easy task. A straightforward starting point is the *dao*, which simply meant the "road" or the "path." Yet *dao* eventually assumed the connotation of a manner of conduct entailing an affinity for nature. Chaotic conditions may have prompted Daoists to turn away from society. They took refuge in nature and perceived society, government, and civilization as artificial and hazardous. Advocating withdrawal from active involvement with society, they proposed detachment as an important value. Unlike Confucianism, with its emphasis on the family, the group, and society at large, Daoists appealed to Chinese individualism. If the individual followed a course that blended with the natural order, he or she would be at peace and would move in the direction of the *dao*. Yet, for the Daoists, the *dao* could not be truly defined because such attempts entailed the delineation of distinctions, which would distort the *dao*, symbolized by wholeness rather than artificial separation.

The *Daodejing* offered the first statement of Daoist beliefs. Lao Zi, its reputed author, remains a shadowy figure. Although some scholars have credited him with writing the text, others over the centuries have questioned his very existence. Some have asserted that the text is a compilation of the works of several authors that was finally completed in the fourth or third centuries BCE. Some have accepted the traditional sixth–fifth centuries BCE dating of the work but have denied the ascription of authorship to the mysterious Lao Zi. The numerous myths that have gathered around the life and career of Lao Zi have compounded these difficulties. One that was the focus of later disputes between Buddhists and Daoists concerned his alleged departure to the so-called Western Regions. Having transmitted the Daoist message as clearly as he could to his own people, he is said to have traveled to India, where he expounded the doctrine to the historical Buddha, whose ideas were simply an adaptation and ultimately a degradation of Daoism.

The *Daodejing* itself is an elliptical, cryptic text composed of eighty-one short poetical passages. As befits a system of thought that questions the ability of words to convey Daoist reality, these terse observations are often murky and difficult to translate and interpret. Having proposed that the *dao* (Way) is the vast primary force in the universe, the text then defines the *de* in a variety of ways, including as the power derived from the *dao*. It identifies the *dao* with nature and relates it to the development and deterioration of material phenomena. The constant changes in the world simply reflect the manifestations of the *dao*. Study of texts or use of the senses will not necessarily lead to greater understanding of the *dao*. Only by looking inward will an individual be in touch with and understand the *dao*. Neither science nor reason will result in true knowledge. Like other mystical texts, the *Daodejing* envisioned a sudden illumination as a means of gaining insight into one's kinship with the universe.

The *dao* did not necessarily translate into tangible benefits, nor could morality or good behavior guarantee rewards. The later Confucian emphasis on virtue and on proper, occasionally deferential conduct toward others struck Daoists as irrelevant. The *dao* would not intervene in human affairs on behalf of those who had received illumination. It bore no relation to human standards of morality. Daoism offered solace to the individual in an era of chaos and social fragmentation. Liberated from obligations to society and from expectations of specific ethical behavior, the individual was free to cultivate himself and to achieve a union with the *dao*. When he became enlightened, he would rise above the tribulations of his times and would experience inner peace and harmony.

Daoism, as described in the *Daodejing*, also proffered what it believed to be beneficial advice to rulers, which included a response to the turbulence of the Warring States period. It asserted that the best rulers practiced a policy of nonaction (*wu-wei*). If they wanted to cope with banditry, plundering, and rebellion, the terrible plagues of this unsettled time, they would simply avoid doing anything. The more laws or restrictions that the ruler imposed, the greater the deterioration he would face. Inaction and initially yielding to others would eventually lead to success. Through inaction, compassion, and avoidance of distinctions between good and evil, the ruler often reflected the people's views and at other times persuaded others by his example. Compulsion and harsh laws would not be effective in achieving order and stability.

Though Lao Zi perceived nonaction as a sound political philosophy for the rulers and for the entire population, his impact on politics was negligible. Centralization and unification were essential during the Warring States period, and the rulers of the various "feudal" states were not persuaded that Daoism provided a proper vehicle for their political needs. Instead Daoism, with its affinity for nature and its espousal of a harmonious and contemplative life, appealed principally to those artists and intellectuals who sought refuge from difficult and dangerous times.

Zhuang Zi (or Zhuang Zhou), a Daoist who lived in the fourth and third centuries BCE, amplified the ideas found in the *Daodejing*. Instead of cryptic verses, Zhuang Zi used anecdotes and paradoxes to illustrate the principles of Daoism. His amusing yet pointed stories provided revealing introductions to the basic Daoist precepts and also poked fun at and satirized contemporary and earlier thinkers.

Like the *Daodejing*, Zhuang Zi sought unison with the Way (*dao*), identified with nature or Heaven. Such an effort required liberation from social standards. Conventional morality and behavior would lead the individual astray, and only actions divorced from a desire for material gain or any other kinds of advantage deserved praise. Spontaneous and intuitive actions reflected the Way. Zhuang Zi repeatedly praised artisans who produced beautiful and useful artifacts instinctively without the burden of ponderous intellectualizing about their craft. He valued imagination and freedom from convention more than incessant intellectual discourse. His views on morality and on overreliance on intellect and reason thus clashed with the philosophy of Confucius, who appears in several of Zhuang Zi's anecdotes. In Zhuang Zi's accounts, he deflated Confucius with ridicule rather than with scathing denunciations of the earlier philosopher's ideas. He valued those who forgot about morality, about the untenable distinctions between good and evil, and about constant use of reason.

As a mystic, Zhuang Zi tended to distrust knowledge derived from the senses or so-called experience. He wrote that the true sage looked inward rather than to external reality in order to become enlightened. Dependence on the senses would mislead and would be deadening. One of Zhuang Zi's anecdotes, in the translation by Burton Watson, aptly demonstrates his views of the senses. Two emperors frequently met "in the territory of [emperor] Hundun, and Hundun treated them very generously." They "discussed how they could repay his kindness. 'All men,' they said, 'have seven openings so they can see, hear, eat, and breathe. But Hundun alone doesn't have any. Let's try boring him some.' Every day they bored another hole, and on the seventh day Hundun died."[1]

Zhuang Zi's connections with Lao Zi, the reputed founder of Daoism, are uncertain. Since Lao Zi is not an attested figure and the exact dating of the *Daodejing* is contested, the possible links between the philosophers will probably remain unknown. Zhuang Zi mentions Lao Zi in several of his anecdotes but does not cite the *Daodejing*. Yet this does not prove that Lao Zi was a real figure because Zhuang Zi mentions numerous legendary and mythical personages. In any event, both the *Daodejing* and Zhuang Zi have attracted the attention of numerous translators in the West. Their mysticism, their occasional playfulness, and their elusiveness have appealed to Western interpreters of east Asian thought, making them among the most translated texts in world literature.

In their own times, neither Lao Zi nor Zhuang Zi appealed to the political elite. Their ideas did not appear to provide useful guides to decision making or to bolstering the power of individual rulers. Unlike the other pragmatic moral and political philosophies of the era, Daoism offered scant practical aid to rulers seeking to expand their territories and to promote unity within their domains. Its murkiness and its espousal of nonaction were deemed too unrealistic by political leaders. By emphasizing social order and by prescribing proper conduct between the governors and the governed, Confucianism, Legalism, and the other philosophies of the time seemed more attuned to the rulers' needs; Daoism did not appear as useful politically. Yet the eventual success of Confucianism did not lead to the extirpation of Daoism. Indeed, Confucianism and Daoism were not mutually exclusive. Because each dealt with different needs and facets of mankind – Confucianism with the political and the social and Daoism with the individual, the aesthetic, and emotions – they could and did coexist.

POPULAR RELIGIONS

Popular religions offered another means of solace in unstable times, although written sources for such expressions are limited. However, glimpses may be garnered through inference. Some texts cite belief in spirits and in deities associated with nature, but details about specific rituals are scarce. A work of poetry, known as the *Chu ci* (*Songs of the South* or *Songs of Chu*), mentions shamanism, which was an easily accessible religion because it did not depend on written sources. With the help of musical instruments and a whirling dance, a shaman could allegedly reach the sky and speak in the names of the spirits. Judging from modern shamanism in Japan and Korea, shamans also provided rudimentary medical care. To be sure, shamanism developed different forms and practices in northeast Asia, including Manchuria and Mongolia. In any event, the *Chu ci* includes a poem called "Li Sao" (Departing in Sorrow), which had profound reverberations on Chinese history and yielded set themes about a badly treated official who commits suicide in response and, in that manner, clears his name. Qu Yuan (343–278 BCE), the writer of the poem, himself had been dismissed from government service for warning about taking precautions against the state of Qin. His warnings fell on deaf ears and the Qin conquered his region. In despair, Qu committed suicide. The annual Dragon Boat Festival, on the fifth day of the fifth lunar month, commemorates this heroic figure.

Popular religions may have had as great an influence on the ordinary person as Daoism and other clearly defined philosophies. They had few specific texts and no clergy except for practitioners. The lack of a canon made these views accessible to the largest segment of the population, most of whom could not read or write. Worshippers did not limit themselves to set beliefs and instead borrowed, combined, and adapted them from local traditions and other religions and cults. They believed in such supernatural beings as gods, ancestors, and ghosts and prayed to them to provide rain, to avert natural catastrophes, and to prevent illnesses. They incorporated veneration of the ancestors and a belief in an afterlife. Gods and ancestors became central, but worshippers showed the same reverence to ghosts because they feared them. A cult of the dead developed, with ancestral tablets playing important roles in prayer.

The gods might respond to prayers if provided with temples and shrines, which were situated according to the principles of geomancy. Statues honoring them, festivals, and offerings of food, drink, and incense would also prompt responses. Practitioners would perform divinations and would interpret the gods' and ancestors' responses. The Jade Emperor, a towering figure, was in many cases the leading deity, but he remained aloof and somewhat inapproachable. Indeed, before the twelfth century CE, many gods were remote and were associated with mountains, the earth, natural phenomena, and heroes of a distant age. Local deities, such as a city god who was responsible for public safety and justice and a kitchen god whose image adorned many households, were more approachable, but even the kitchen god offered an annual report on household members to the Jade Emperor, an indication of the greater power of the more remote deities. Naturally, there were many regional and local variations in such worship and performance.

CONFUCIANISM

Confucianism has cast such a large shadow over Chinese history that Chinese society cannot be understood without knowledge of Confucius's life and ideas. His theories of human nature, proper conduct, and interpersonal relations dominated much of Chinese history from the Han dynasty (206 BCE–220 CE) on. Since then, Confucius has been so inextricably linked with Chinese civilization that the term "Confucian China" seems commonplace. Students, recognizing the significance of Confucianism, often ask whether it is a philosophy or a religion. They implicitly assume that Confucianism was so vital to the legitimacy and functioning of Chinese society that it needed to be more than a philosophy. However, Confucianism's emphasis on this life differentiates it from most religions.

Confucius (551–479 BCE) or Kong Fuzi (Master Kong) or Kong Qiu lived and died believing that he had failed in his objectives. Born in the state of Lu (in the modern province of Shandong), he was descended from a noble family that had suffered setbacks as a result of the turbulence in the Warring States period. Confucius was determined to influence the politics of his times and believed that an appeal to rulers provided the optimal opportunity to do so. He attempted to persuade the nobles in various states to adopt his teachings in order to restore stability in China, which for most of these rulers meant unification and centralization of the country. Although he succeeded in gathering around him a group of students and disciples, he failed in his efforts to secure an official position in the states through which he traveled. Nor did the rulers subscribe to or implement his philosophy. His disciples also traveled throughout China to spread his teachings but they too were often rebuffed. Facing such disappointments and encountering such resistance, Confucius returned to Lu in his sixties and died there in 479 BCE. Despite the tenacity of his students and disciples, he came to the end of his life without having had much of an impact on Chinese society.

Because Confucius directed his efforts at gaining support from rulers, his philosophy tended to be conservative, focusing on a return to a golden age of the past. In general, he did not call for dramatic social change because he did not wish to be perceived as challenging or undermining the authority of his potential patrons. An image as a disrupter of the social system would not serve his interests. Yet his teachings would actually subvert the power of the hereditary aristocracy and would enable a less entrenched, mobile class, if not a meritocracy, to supplant it as the ruling authority. To a limited extent, his philosophy generated social change.

Confucius sought social stability. Believing that social order resulted from proper moral conduct, he identified five basic relationships in society: ruler–ruled, father–son, elder brother–younger brother, friend–friend, and husband–wife. Women played an explicit role in only one of these relationships – an indication of their lesser position in Confucian society. In any event, Confucius believed that if the ethical principles he espoused characterized these five relationships, a good society would emerge. There is no doubt that Confucius's principal objective was the establishment of a harmonious and ethical society. Although he referred to spirits, sacrifices, and Heaven, he simply mentioned them in passing and devoted barely any attention to metaphysical and cosmological speculation. He probably accepted the major beliefs embodied in the ancient Shang and Zhou religions (though certainly not the practice of human sacrifice), but these views scarcely intruded on his teachings because they dealt with the realm beyond mankind's control. Thus, other than a concern for harmony in the cosmos, Confucius did not generally address theological questions. One exception was his rejection of the concepts of destiny and fate. Instead he affirmed his belief that a man's abilities, efforts, and ethical code determined his own fate and his own potential to become a *junzi* or gentleman – for Confucius, the person most suited to govern and the embodiment of the highest ideals. According to Confucius, a man succeeded because of his self-cultivation, merit, and virtue, not because of heredity or fate. Yet this view appeared to clash with his repeated attempts to appeal to the ruling classes and his emphasis on acceptance of a social hierarchy.

It is difficult to reconcile these contradictory elements in Confucius's thought because of the nature of the sources available to us. The *Analects* (*Lunyu*), which is attributed to Confucius and contains the most lucid explanation of his teachings, was compiled at least a century after his death. The schools founded by his disciples probably organized the work and prepared it for wider distribution. The quotes attributed to Confucius cannot be authenticated. Some may have been emendations from his disciples. Because Confucius perceived or at least portrayed himself as a transmitter of the ancients' teachings, other quotes may have been the words of earlier thinkers whose views he was reiterating. Even more complicated, the *Lunyu* consists of anecdotes and sayings rather than a straightforward, logical exposition of Confucius's teachings. It is not a systematic, coherent rendering of his philosophy; instead it contains his most esteemed and remembered sayings. This kind of presentation accounts for the vagueness enveloping some elements of his philosophy.

Nonetheless, the most significant features of Confucianism readily emerge from the text. The clearest characteristic of the school is its practicality. In its view, the adoption and implementation of a moral code would inevitably lead to a harmonious family and from there to a well-ordered society. A good government presumed and was based upon stable families, which in turn centered upon the adoption of specific values. Filial piety (*xiao*) was essential for the ideal Confucian family, and such submissiveness was similarly vital for the state. The *Xiaojing* (*Classic of Filial Piety*), a text written about a hundred years after Confucius's death and frequently found in many households in later years, illustrated the principles of filial piety toward the family, the ruler, and officials. As numerous students of Confucianism have noted, the Confucians perceived the state as an extension of the family. The individual aspiring to become a *junzi* and the body politic, however, both required other virtues to achieve stability and harmony. *Ren* was, for Confucius, a supreme virtue, but curiously the term remains vague and ill defined. "Goodness" and "humaneness" provide the closest approximations, but those definitions too are nebulous. Examination of the specific uses of *ren* in the *Analects* reveals characteristics such as generosity and loyalty to others, attention to rituals, and actions that bespeak the highest morality. Humane treatment of and humane behavior toward others offer concise descriptions of the qualities associated with goodness.

The other virtues flowed from goodness. Wisdom or knowledge (*zhi*), another trait vital of the "good man," entailed more than knowledge and academic pursuits. It was linked to morality, for wisdom meant knowledge of proper conduct and acting in accordance with its dictates. Again, Confucius repeatedly stressed the practical value of these virtues. *Xin* or faithfulness or truth also had practical ramifications. For Confucians, it signified carrying out commitments to others. Like all the other virtues, its greatest significance lay in its application in relations with others. Confucius emphasized the importance of a network of stable relationships. *Yong*, or courage or loyalty, still another trait valued by Confucius, entailed acting pursuant to the dictates of right conduct. *Yi*, or righteousness and *li*, or ritual correspondence, were also critical virtues. They did not refer to manners but to proper moral principles. Morals rather than etiquette were Confucius's main concern. Yet, along with moral conduct, *li* presupposed proper performance of ceremonies. It prescribed specific rites for burial and mourning of the dead, including formulas for eulogies and designated diet and clothing for mourners. It also entailed continuation of music and dance ceremonies of the ancients. Confucians valued music for its promotion of morality. Musical performances during court rituals and among the population in general contributed to harmony and higher moral standards. Confucians asserted that music helped to transmit and inculcate the most significant personal and social values. The *Yili* (or *Record of Rituals*) confirmed the importance of music and the other arts in fostering a good society. Poetry, calligraphy, and the casting of bronze ritual vessels, among other arts, were also invested with these same objectives. The ruler himself had a special responsibility to perform rituals associated with the agricultural cycle. *Li*, however, could not simply be formalistic; it had to be carried out with singleness of purpose and good faith. Perfunctory performance of the rituals would be ineffective.

Confucius perceived that the separation of content and name, as exemplified in such formalism, resulted in social disarray. Because his teachings were designed to avert such instability, he placed great faith in *zheng ming* or "to rectify the names." Lack of congruence between reality and form signified an inability to fulfill the Confucian moral code and to establish an orderly social system. Thus, the first step in achieving a stable network of relationships was a proper correlation between name and reality. *Zheng ming* also implied that each individual could more easily identify and understand the expectations of his own position and tasks in these relationships and would more readily accept his status in the social hierarchy.

However, Confucius did not advocate a stagnant society in which the individual had no opportunities for advancement. The value he placed on education, merit, and moral worth would clash with systems that lacked or prevented social mobility. He conceived of himself as a teacher and obviously valued education as a means of promoting a high standard of morality. Thus, he suggested that study of the classic texts and ritual works and participation in music and dance would improve the individual's character and could lead to the development of a *junzi*. To Confucius, this nonspecialized education would enable the *junzi* to assume positions of leadership. From his perspective, the *junzi* did not need any specialized training to govern a region, devise a budget, or plan and build irrigation projects. His ideal officials and rulers were rational and moral gentlemen who had a sense of social responsibility and who derived from any social background, not necessarily from the entrenched aristocracy. In Confucius's view, morality could not be separated from education, particularly in the chaotic times in which he lived. He wanted gentlemen to receive the moral training that would enable them to serve as a striking contrast to the often duplicitous and amoral officials of the Warring States period. He looked to a golden age of the past in which such men dominated society.

Thus, Confucius's teachings offered a flexible, rational, and moral alternative to the chaos prevailing in China. They were conservative in confirming a defined, hierarchical social structure. Yet they were liberal in challenging the hereditary aristocracy, in supporting a system that encouraged the recruitment of talented and moral men of any social background into high officialdom, and in legitimizing social mobility. They had the additional advantage of making educated and socially responsible men available to rulers who required counsel and assistance in administration. Although the leaders of the Zhou era did not recognize the value of Confucianism, the Han dynasty, which ruled China within several decades after their fall, would promote Confucianism, and later dynasties would adopt it as a state cult.

Mencius followed in Confucius's footsteps but supplemented his predecessor's teachings. Born around 372 BCE, he was active about a century and a half after the death of the revered philosopher. Like Confucius, he became a teacher and traveled widely to disseminate Confucian values and ideas. Until his death in 289 BCE, he continued to expand upon Confucius's philosophy. Also like Confucius, he encountered frustrations in his efforts to secure support from the rulers of the various states for his own version of Confucian philosophy.

Mencius was doubtless more optimistic than Confucius about the individual. He started with the premise that mankind was basically good. Yet he diverged sharply from those who advocated a concept of universal goodness. He suggested instead that the extent of a person's goodness toward others depended on the closeness and social status of the other. Behavior and attitude toward others was based, in part, on one's position in the social hierarchy. Righteousness (yi) mandated specific treatment of others, and the individual had defined obligations toward those of higher or lower social status. Like Confucius, Mencius accepted a hierarchical social structure.

However, on closer examination it turns out that Mencius also demanded proper conduct and benevolence from rulers. In one of his conversations, he admonished a king for focusing on profit rather than on humaneness and righteousness. He said that, if the king would emphasize a humane administration, the rest of the population, modeling its behavior on his, would act humanely toward one another. A humane administration would, in turn, guarantee the people's livelihood, ensuring that ordinary folk would not suffer deprivation or want. Proper land distribution was vital because most Chinese eked out their livelihoods from their farms. Mencius's humane government would mandate a more equitable arrangement, which was the well-field system that had reputedly been the foundation of a golden age in the past. Under this scheme, each so-called well field would be divided into nine equal sections, with eight households working eight plots while one was a community-farmed public field. This utopian, egalitarian system never truly operated in Mencius's own time or in some great earlier era in Chinese civilization. Nonetheless, Mencius proposed it as the ideal way to avert instability in the countryside. He did not, however, advocate absolute equality because he believed that society required rulers. Equality also would not prevail within the family because sons needed to obey their fathers and younger brothers their elder brothers, in accordance with the principle of filial piety. Rulers had a responsibility toward the ruled. Mencius reiterated the Mandate of Heaven theory that had dominated political thinking for centuries. Heaven entrusted power to the ruler who, in turn, upheld his mandate by benefiting the people.

Xun Zi (?312–230 BCE), the third of the most prominent Confucian thinkers, diverged somewhat from his predecessors. However, the oft-depicted idea of Mencius and Xun Zi as representing antithetical poles of the Confucian school of thought is too simplistic. Both emphasized the value of government and civilization; both emphasized morality above profitability; both had an abiding faith in the educability and perfectability of mankind; and, unlike the Daoists, both regarded mankind as the center of the universe. Yet, having endured a longer period of chaos, strife, and brutality during the Warring States period, Xun Zi disputed Mencius's overly rosy assessment of mankind.

Indeed, in his principal work, known as the *Xun Zi*, Xun Zi baldly stated that "Man's nature is evil" and that "goodness is the result of conscious activity." Corrupt governments, unprincipled rulers, and use of magic and prayers attested, in his view, to the chaos generated in an unregulated and disorderly society. Study of the classical texts and practice of the Confucian rituals, which served to curb mankind's evil yearnings, offered the basic prescription for a peaceful land. Xun Zi had faith in education, stating that once a man was shown the proper path he would follow it. Sages who had studied the classics and become morally purified through proper conduct of rituals would lead the people to pursue the same course. Although humans were intrinsically evil, they could be trained to strive for the good. According to Xun Zi, sages should exhort the people to perform music, dance, funeral, and wedding ceremonies properly and not to be distracted by criticisms of these elaborate and expensive rituals. He attributed vital functions to *li*; it helped people to cope with, regulate, and express emotions of happiness, loss, and failure and to develop proper respect for others in the social hierarchy. However, he rejected belief in prayers for rain and in the intrusion by ghosts and demons into human affairs, treating belief in such figures as superstitions, not rituals.

Unlike the earlier Confucian thinkers, Xun Zi presented his arguments in a logical narrative rather than in anecdotes. Relying on a rational exposition of his views and shunning the elliptical and illustrative stories used by his predecessors, he summarized the main tenets of Confucianism in a direct and forceful style. His work consisted of straightforward exposition instead of the imaginary dialogues concocted by earlier philosophers. He also differed from his Confucian predecessors in offering a trenchant critique of the thinking of non-Confucian philosophers instead of merely satirizing or lampooning them. He disparaged Daoism, for example, for its seeming otherworldliness and its lack of concern for human affairs.

Like Confucius, Xun Zi supported a carefully graded social hierarchy, with every individual recognizing his or her position. Social order necessitated class distinctions, and equality would be disastrous. Similarly, he insisted on proper naming of things and concepts on the grounds that they defined distinctions between groups in society – distinctions that facilitated governance and social order.

Despite Xun Zi's faith in education, he still believed in the need for coercion. Mankind, on occasion, had to be forced to pursue the right path. Unlike Mencius, Xun Zi was hardheaded and not totally confident in mankind's self-control and drive toward the good. Lacking some of Mencius's idealism, he proposed a harsher means of curbing mankind's evil impulses. The rulers to whom both sought to appeal found Xun Zi's ideas more realistic, and it is thus no accident that he was the only one of these three major Confucians to become a government official. He served in the states of Qi and then the Chu for about three decades.

However, Xun Zi's realism and pragmatism eventually undermined his standing with Confucians. Late in life he traveled to the state of Qin, where he attracted two disciples – Han Fei Zi, later a principal spokesperson for Legalism, and Li Si, a state minister – who ultimately castigated Confucianism. Yet he himself condemned the authoritarianism of Qin.

In addition to the writings of Confucius, Mencius, and Xun Zi, a number of other texts were associated with Confucianism and were incorporated into the Confucian canon. Two of the most significant derived from a specific work, the *Book of Rites* (*Liji*). Written by members of the Confucian school possibly as late as 200 BCE, it nonetheless reflects some of Confucius's views. Like the *Analects*, the "Great Learning" (*Daxue*) section seems often to be directed to rulers, though its teachings apply to the rest of the population as well. It links ruling well with good relations within the family, which, in turn, entailed abiding by the proper moral code. The individual needed to cultivate himself if he were to succeed as the ruler of a good government. In effect, proper conduct by the individual and the ruler would inevitably result in a proper government. If the individual and the family embodied humaneness, the country as a whole would be properly regulated.

The "Mean" (*Zhongyong*), the other passage, was addressed to rulers as well as to ordinary subjects. As its title implies, this section proposed moderation, the Aristotelian mean, as the proper mode of behavior and governance. If the ruler genuinely adopted the moral code that emphasized goodness, he would attract the men he required to establish a stable and benevolent government. *Li* (rituals) mandated a set of reciprocal obligations between the ruler and those he ruled. As a person with a superior status, he still needed to treat those with inferior status according to the proper ritual principles. In essence, his actions ought to reflect his station in life, a view that surely confirmed the existing social hierarchy.

MOHISM

Mo Zi (ca. 470–391 BCE) also responded to the chaos of the times, but his diagnosis and prescriptions diverged markedly from those of the Confucians and Daoists. Little is known of Mo Zi's own life or his writings, which his immediate disciples and later Mohists supplemented, edited, and revised. For almost three centuries, his ideas competed, with some success, with Confucianism, but Mohism's own limitations, as well as the appeal of the Confucian ethical code, led to its decline after the second century BCE, save for in small and dedicated bands who owed absolute obedience to the supreme leaders of their respective groups.

Mo Zi's failure to attract a wide following may have resulted from his principal concerns. Looking at a strife-torn China, he emphasized profit and universal love as a means of restoring stability and peace. He offered a simple utilitarian test for evaluation of behavior: he lauded conduct that provided material benefit or that resulted in the greatest profit for the greatest number. Productive use of resources was equated with moral value. Thus, Mo Zi denounced waste, urging the elimination of costly expenditures. The Confucian advocacy of elaborate and expensive funeral and marital ceremonies scandalized him and exacerbated his antipathy for what he perceived to be Confucianism's corrupting influences on men. The emphasis on music and on the finest food and drink in rituals struck him as overly lavish and extravagant. For Mo Zi, the most wasteful human activity was warfare because of the harm it inflicted on people and the destruction it wrought on the land. He reviled aggressors because expansionist aims would divert leaders' attention from internal affairs and farmers' attention from work on the land, not to mention the damage such aims would cause to horses, weapons, chariots, and supplies. His condemnation of offensive war was based primarily upon its destruction and waste, and less so upon ethical concerns. Because aggressive wars were unprofitable, good rulers ought to shun them.

These pragmatic considerations entailed indirect criticism of contemporary rulers and aristocrats. Mo Zi objected to their abuses – wastefulness in useless and costly rituals and in destructive military conflicts. He appeared on the surface to reflect the aspirations and values of the lower and middle classes, for they suffered disproportionately from the excesses of the aristocracy and from warfare. Moreover, his obsession with waste, his denunciation of needless consumption, and his opposition to elegant and expensive refinements coincided with the interests of the common people. He also represented their needs in asserting that rulers should appoint capable and virtuous men to positions in government, which implied that merit, not birth, should be the principal criterion. Like the Confucians, he argued that aristocratic background ought not to be a prerequisite for prominence in government; worthiness and ability were more crucial.

Yet his identification with the common people clashed with the means he used to promote his views. Like Confucius, Mencius, and many other philosophers of this era, he traveled from one state to another to persuade rulers and aristocrats to adopt and implement his philosophy. Thus, he could not afford to alienate his prospective patrons by calling for radical changes in the social system. Because such an effort would be self-defeating, he moderated his diatribes against the aristocracy and the elite, instead urging subordinates to avoid engaging in class warfare. In short, he accepted the idea of a hierarchy and undermined his own views on esteeming the worthy and recruiting them in government, believing that the vast majority of those at the bottom would simply accept their lot because the head of the local community and the lord of the region knew what was best. Mo Zi left it to the existing leadership to curb the excesses of the aristocracy and to select good men from whatever class to help the rulers govern. This injunction of obedience to superiors naturally made his views less threatening to the elite.

Mo Zi's advocacy of universal love also would not challenge the existing social hierarchy: it was simply a vehicle for ameliorating conflicts between the strata. He criticized the Confucian particularistic doctrine of different levels of devotion, which emphasized love for the family above all else, with less emphasis on affection for the clan and other Chinese who were unrelated. His more generous vision encouraged loving Chinese men and women of other families and even non-Chinese as heartily as one loved one's parents or family. Such unselfishness countered the particularism of mere love of family and of filial piety. However, Mo Zi undercut some of the credit he might have secured for this remarkable and benevolent concept by justifying it on simplistic grounds. He stressed that universal love would result in material benefits and could readily be mandated by forceful rulers. The idealism and innovation of this grand conception did not emerge in Mo Zi's practical description. He failed to portray a vision that could galvanize and inspire his followers.

He and his disciples linked their championing of universal love to their condemnation of offensive warfare. They encouraged fellow Mohists to support and to come to the defense of weaker states threatened by bellicose states. Manifesting their love for the less powerful and the endangered, they sided with the weak and ultimately became skilled in warfare, earning a reputation as adept military strategists. Yet Mo Zi surely did not have this in mind when he first expounded his views about universal love and the destructiveness and wastefulness of warfare.

Another questionable ramification of his views related to his attempted justification of his moral order. He repeatedly appealed to the supernatural as a force that sanctioned his vision. Believing that spirits and ghosts could intervene in human affairs, he asserted that they could punish or reward behavior. The Supreme Spirit was the dominant deity, the progenitor of all creatures, which worked its will through its earthly representative, the Son of Heaven. Mo Zi, seeking to induce fear, depicted the Supreme Spirit as awesome. This turn to the supernatural did not jibe with the developing rationalism of this era and may have alienated potential adherents.

Mohism's appeal was also undermined by other flaws, one of which was confusion concerning the audience for Mo Zi's views. He was critical of the lifestyles and morals of the aristocracy and many of the ideas he expounded, including his abhorrence of waste and his utilitarianism, reflected lower-class or middle-class attitudes. Yet he devoted much of his career to appeals to the aristocracy, which contributed to a blurring of his message and confusion and contradictions in his philosophy. Moreover, Mohism was too simplistic for many aristocrats. Mo Zi's repeated injunctions against waste and luxury did not endear him to the elite, nor did his references to ghosts and spirits mesh with the growing rationalism and secularism of the age. Similarly, his emphasis on universal love clashed with the Chinese esteem of family. Finally, his utilitarianism did not offer a systematic, cohesive morality. The repetitiousness of his style also diminished its wider appeal. In short, Mo Zi did not identify sufficiently with any specific group or class in China, nor did he take into account Chinese sensitivities and sensibilities.

LEGALISM

The Legalist thinkers, who have been given credit for the Qin dynasty's success in unifying the country (see Chapter 3), have been termed un-Chinese because of the harshness of their philosophy and the severity of the sanctions they proposed to enforce their views. Reacting to the crises of fragmentation and disorder, the Legalists prescribed policies aimed at unity and centralization. These objectives were not in themselves objectionable; however, the methods of implementing them eventually provoked unrest. The Legalists' doctrines had become so discredited that, once the Qin dynasty fell, no statesman in Chinese history who wished to be successful could propound the philosophy, though it continued to influence Chinese governmental practices.

Most students associate Legalism with the Qin, but the development of its principles predated the rise of that absolutist dynasty. According to earlier sources, Guan Zhong (d. 645 BCE), a minister of the state of Qi, had attempted to persuade his ruler, Duke Huan, to initiate policies that would strengthen the state. In a work entitled *Guan zi* (*Master Guan*), which actually appears to have been compiled several centuries later, Guan Zhong's later disciples described the institution of the *ba* (hegemon), a powerful figure who imposed peace and stability on the fractious states of his era in the name of the Zhou king, whose survival he perceived to be essential. He proposed the granting of authority to a ruler who had a mandate to strengthen the military, to enact laws governing an extraordinary range of behavior, to promote a growth in population (since a large population was said to be an indication of state power), and to enrich the state through government monopolies on salt, iron, and wine and other fiscal practices. Guan Zhong's realistic statecraft, as well as his emphasis on law and a powerful state with great influence over its subjects' lives, presaged and perhaps influenced the Legalist thinkers of later centuries.

Like Guan Zhong, Wei Yang (d. 338 BCE) or Gongsun Yang (more commonly known as Lord Shang) was a political actor as well as a principal exponent of Legalism. Born in the state of Wei, he subsequently shifted his allegiance to the state of Qin, served Duke Xiao, and helped to subjugate his own native land. Later sources credit Lord Shang with unifying and centralizing the "feudal" lands of Qin and with curbing the nobility's authority. The centralized state of Qin appointed officials to enforce its will on the population. He argued that peasants should own their land and should be obligated to pay taxes directly to the state rather than turning over a share of their produce to "feudal" nobles. A state with full granaries would be both prosperous and powerful. Lord Shang also proposed that the population be organized into groups of five or ten men who would be encouraged to denounce subversives or those among them who challenged the state.

Lord Shang relied on law (*fa*) to regulate society. In this turbulent time, he believed in a strong state that would conquer the rest of China and ensure stability and peace. The state needed to be prosperous and seemingly invincible to achieve this goal, a task that entailed control of its people. A system of rewards and punishments had to be instituted in order to enforce state power. The state's interest would prevail over the individual's rights and concerns, and obedience to the law was the single most important value to be impressed upon the people. The values associated with Confucianism (righteousness, benevolence, and wisdom), as well as the rituals of music, dance, and filial piety, were irrelevant, if not harmful. Lord Shang was unabashedly amoral, for he believed that the Confucian virtues would create a weaker state.

He proposed a system that would enable governments to be the absolute masters, and argued that laws were essential in restraining the evil and depraved nature of mankind. Though the rare gifted man could overcome the general depravity, laws and administrative methods could not be abandoned if the state wished to avert chaos. Most men could not control their evil ways without the sanction of harsh punishments to keep them in line. Thus, the ruler needed to enforce the laws evenhandedly and punish transgressors from any and all classes. For the first time, the nobility would be treated in the same way as the rest of the population and would be liable to the same sanctions as ordinary people.

Lord Shang's views reputedly influenced Duke Xiao, who adopted many of his adviser's suggestions to strengthen Qin. However, Lord Shang did not benefit from the Qin state's success. When his patron died, the new ruler turned out to be one of his earlier antagonists, which compelled him to flee in order to survive. The army he quickly organized was routed, and he was captured and torn apart by chariots, a grisly end for a man who, ironically, advocated harsh punishments.

In the following century, Han Fei Zi (?280–233 BCE) emerged as the leading Legalist philosopher. Born to a noble family in the small state of Han, as a young adult he studied with the renowned Confucian Xun Zi in Chu. Returning to his own state, he continually offered advice to the rulers, but they repeatedly rejected his suggestions. Thus, he disseminated his ideas by writing a work that attracted the attention of the Qin king, who eventually subjugated and united China and became the first emperor in the Chinese tradition. Qin attacked Han Fei Zi's native land in 234 BCE, and the panicked rulers called upon the philosopher whom they had earlier rebuffed to serve as an envoy to their attackers. The Qin king was, at first, hospitable to Han Fei Zi, but his chief minister, Li Si, who had also studied with the Confucian Xun Zi, persuaded the king that Han Fei Zi was duplicitous and treacherous. Han Fei Zi was imprisoned and subsequently committed suicide with poison provided by Li Si.

Han Fei Zi's death serves an ironic counterpoint to his realistic, tough-minded political philosophy. He appealed to the rulers of the "feudal" states, counseling them to tighten control over the economy and government and to crush dissenting and troublesome individuals. Like the Lord of Shang, he emphasized law and governing policies rather than morality and family as the principal means of social control. Harsh laws were required in turbulent times, such as the late Zhou period, and proper administrative regulations were essential in controlling the aristocracy as well as the bureaucracy that the ruler recruited to govern the state. The ruler had to be all-powerful yet he ought to refrain from day-to-day decision making, turning that responsibility over to his administrators. Han Fei Zi had an extremely harsh view of human motivations, advising the ruler to be wary of his closest associates. The ruler also ought not to show much compassion because mercy would undermine state stability. Only by severe laws would the ruler manage to dominate the five vermin – the scholars who question the laws, the speechmakers who champion deceitful policies, the wealthy who seek to evade military service, the soldiers who transgress upon the laws, and the merchants and craftsmen who produce wasteful, luxury goods. Han Fei Zi argued that the ruler should encourage agriculture, develop a powerful military, and enforce harsh laws. Only then would China achieve stability and order.

Legalism thus offered a severe though initially effective philosophy. The emphasis on harsh punishments, centralized government, promotion of agriculture, growth of the military, and authoritarianism and curbs on the aristocracy enabled Qin to expand its power and to enlarge the territory under its control. Initially situated in the Wei river valley in the modern province of Shaanxi, Qin had a splendid base from which to annex neighboring lands. The "feudal" states on the eastern coast of China were hemmed in whereas Qin was not surrounded. It faced no states to the west since non-Chinese nomadic peoples roamed the region. Encounters with these foreigners exposed the Qin to cavalry warfare and refined their military skills. The Qin thus had definite advantages when it began to move eastward, seeking to centralize and unify China.

Although this golden age of Chinese philosophy played a vital role in the definition of Chinese civilization, social changes (including the eventual centralization of the country and the rise of the *shi*, or merit-based class) and also military and technological developments (such as the use of cavalry, more sophisticated irrigation works, and bronze and jade ornaments, weapons, and coinage) were also significant in the rise of a great empire.

BOOK OF ODES *AND* BOOK OF DOCUMENTS

The Chinese literary tradition, especially poetry, also developed during the Zhou. The Chinese have traditionally excelled in the writing of poetry, yet very few pre-Han dynasty works are extant. Many more poems were written, but most have not survived. The most renowned early anthology of poetry was the *Book of Odes* (*Shijing*), which consists of about three hundred poems. The poems were designed to be sung and were edited to incorporate rhymes within a specific dialect. Over the centuries, Chinese commentators interpreted these poems to fit the specific social and political values their society wished to inculcate. The poems assumed a didactic and moralistic tone. In the commentators' hands, love poems were transformed into paeans advocating filial piety and proper performance of rituals. Similarly, songs lamenting the absence of a loved one became critiques of student truants. Such far-fetched and moralistic interpretations persisted for a long time. Because the *Book of Odes* was accepted as one of the Five Confucian Classics, these interpretations, even if outlandish, need to be considered because of their pervasive influence.

The poems derive from diverse origins. The largest number, the so-called "airs" section, is composed of folk songs that were probably revised and refined at court. These short poems yield insights into the daily lives, aspirations, and activities of ordinary people. They deal with love and marriage, festivals, work, and rituals. The songs give voice to soldiers lamenting separation from their loved ones and to wives or husbands betrayed or ignored by their spouses. Some clearly express discontent with the inequities in Chinese society. They criticize oppressive officials, avaricious kings, and constant turbulence and warfare. Commentators naturally read political judgments and criticism into other seemingly bland poems. They did so often by reinterpreting the nature symbolism found in the songs. Because the contemporary meaning of various animals, birds, and natural phenomena was unknown, later commentators could assert that they represented criticisms of political and social conditions of the time. Despite the numerous over-interpretations, however, this section of the *Odes* reveals the common people's dissatisfactions with the chaos, misrule, and exploitation that enveloped them.

Other sections in the *Book of Odes* have distinctly different themes, reflecting, in particular, the interests and activities of the nobility. The *xiaoya* and *daya* ("lesser odes" and "greater odes") describe festivals, hunts, music and dancing, and sacrifices and provide details about clothing, meals, and transport. Surprisingly, a few poems offer social critiques, consisting of denunciations of officials who do not perform their assigned tasks, of oppressive governments, and of scandalously opulent lifestyles for some in the nobility in the face of poverty and starvation for many commoners.

These complaints attest to the unsettled times and to exploitation and misgovernment. The hymns (*song*), the final section of the *Odes*, differ from the rest because they do not include a litany of complaints, laments, and accusations. Instead they offer praise for the kings' military victories and proper performance of rituals and for the dynasty's accomplishments. They glow with optimism about the deeds of the nobility, and few rumblings of discontent emerge.

Although some of the poems offer trenchant or, on occasion, covert critiques of Zhou society, many appear to be straightforward evocations of hopes, wishes, and reality. Some are exactly what they purport to be, with no symbolic or hidden messages. They include courtship poems, songs of lovesick or neglected young men or women, and verses reflecting the woes of disillusioned and abused wives. These poems are direct and unencumbered with larger political or social meanings.

However, because the compilation of the *Book of Odes* was often attributed to Confucius, individual poems have been accorded a moral or didactic interpretation. One traditional view was that Confucius selected the three hundred poems from a larger anthology while another was that he simply gave his imprimatur to an existing collection. Whatever the true origin of the poems, Confucius emphasized their significance in the education of a gentleman. According to the *Analects*, he urged his disciples to study the *Odes* in order to broaden their sensibilities, refine their language, and enlarge their knowledge of nature. He insisted that officials needed to be conversant with the *Odes* because others made repeated references to them when discussing and negotiating state affairs. Because many officials had memorized the poems, could allude to them, and accepted the rather labored and exaggerated interpretations of individual songs, Confucius advised his disciples to ponder and seek to understand the *Odes* for the very practical reason of fulfilling their public roles and responsibilities. Additional evidence that Confucius played a role in the compilation or editing of the work is the large number of hymns deriving from the state of Lu, his native land.

Confucius is also credited with amassing the various passages that constituted another of the Five Classics, the *Book of Documents* (*Shujing*). However, some sections of the work date from after Confucius's death. A text written in archaic language, the *Book of Documents* consists of legendary, semihistorical, and historical passages with no underlying unity or at least little effort to produce a coherent narrative. Much of the text is composed of speeches. Since the writers or historians could not have been present during most of these discourses, the speeches cannot be considered authentic, although they may, on occasion, convey the general sense of what transpired. The parts of the work that deal with the Zhou dynasty are more reliable than descriptions of much earlier, semilegendary figures. Although many of the speeches and incidents cannot be attested, they nonetheless reveal the general themes and values that the compiler(s) wished to inculcate.

The most important of these themes was the Mandate of Heaven theory, which, according to the *Documents*, the early Zhou rulers expounded to Shang citizens whom they had just conquered. In seeking to justify the overthrow of the Shang kings, the Zhou leaders, in particular the Duke of Zhou, explained that Heaven, an amorphous force that controlled the Earth, bestowed a specific leader or group with a mandate to rule. As long as these designated rulers and their descendants continued to govern virtuously, they would retain Heaven's support. Should they, however, abandon virtue and encourage corruption and exploitation, Heaven would retract its mandate, offering it instead to a new leader or group. How would one discover Heaven's displeasure? If the new leaders emerged victorious, Heaven had surely bestowed its favor on them; here pragmatism merged with morality. In sum, each successive leader needed to prove himself morally fit to maintain the mandate, for Heaven did not grant the throne to descendants in perpetuity. The Zhou rulers asserted that their own overthrow of the Shang, which had lost the mandate, was thus justified. The *Documents*, in this way, contributed to a historical tradition of portraying the first rulers of a dynasty as honest, benevolent, and courageous and the last rulers as evil and immoral. New dynasties could therefore justify their usurpation of the throne. The implication was that no dynasty lasted forever.

In addition to the Mandate of Heaven theory, the *Documents* offers a specific and unusual view of the transfer of power. The text lauds legendary figures who selected the most meritorious candidate to succeed them instead of turning authority over to their sons. The mythical ruler Yao, for example, did not tap his son as his successor but rather chose a commoner named Shun. In turn, Shun handed over power to his minister Yu, not to any of his own progeny. Eventually, the principle of family succession, usually father to son, took hold, and the *Documents* ultimately confirm this mode of transfer of authority. Yet, considering the prestige accorded to the *Documents*, it is puzzling that the value of family seems to be superseded in these early examples. One explanation is that the work reflects the views and aspirations of the traveling group of philosophers during Confucius's time. Deriving from nonelite backgrounds, they attempted to secure positions in government. Using the *Documents*, they could show that the legendary revered heroes of the past had selected successors on the basis of merit, not heredity. The lesson would presumably not have been lost on the contemporary rulers from whom they requested employment.

SECULARIZATION OF ARTS

Despite the political decentralization and weakness of the Western Zhou, its cultural achievements were not negligible and indeed paved the way for the efflorescence of the Eastern Zhou. Although Zhou bronzes initially resembled Shang models in technique and decoration, the weapons and ritual vessels now had inscriptions. As the number of bronze workshops increased, the vessels fashioned at these centers were no longer exclusively used for rituals. Output grew rapidly, and the more bronzes that were produced, the less well decorated and more secular they became. As a result, they were not a monopoly of the aristocracy. The Zhou decorations began to differ from those of the Shang. The shapes became less complex, and different animal forms were rarely combined to depict the legendary animals of the Shang. The vessels no longer portrayed the grotesque *taotie* mask, and some represented animals and particularly birds (which were now frequently depicted) in a much more naturalistic style than during the Shang.

Basic changes in decoration reveal even more clearly the transformation from Shang to Zhou thought and attitudes. These changes mirror the development in Yangshao pottery decorations from realistic portraits of animals and fish to more geometric conceptions. The animal forms in Zhou bronzes similarly turned away from realism to abstraction. At the same time, the Zhou bronzes show a greater emphasis on decorative designs. This focus on decoration may reflect a changing societal conception of the bronzes, which now had a wider and more secular audience. Instead of bronzes being produced for court rituals and awe-inspiring purposes as in the Shang, the Western Zhou bronzes were often used for ordinary occasions, eroding their evocation of majesty and their religious functions. The inscribed bronzes also indicated that the Zhou elite had them cast to commemorate significant events (victory in battle, marriage, etc.) or to communicate with the ancestors. They thus offer valuable data that supplement knowledge of the dynasty. Most inscriptions start with precise indications of the date and location, contributing to their historical value. They then describe a particular activity – a military campaign, a sacrifice, the investiture of an official, or an alliance. However, the number of divinations mentioned diminished, implying a change in attitude about direct spiritual or ancestral involvement in human affairs. Decorative objects that had little ritual significance (such as bronze mirrors and belt buckles) were often produced, and some imitated the "animal-style art" of the nomadic pastoral peoples who dealt with the Chinese.

The religious attitudes of the Western and later Eastern Zhou elite diverged from those of the Shang. Earlier beliefs centered on a variety of coequal divinities associated with nature, with Di represented as the dominant figure. The Western Zhou supplanted Di with Tian (Heaven), vital for the concept of the Mandate of Heaven, and tended to deemphasize animal and nature deities.

Proper performance of ancestral rituals became at least as significant as obeisance to deities. Another indication of increasing secularism entailed transformations in the tombs. Human and animal sacrifices at burial sites diminished considerably. At these same tombs, various jade objects were buried with prominent individuals. *Bi* discs, symbolizing Heaven, as well as jade artifacts representing Earth and jade plugs for the openings of the deceased's body to protect it from harm, served as important mortuary pieces. Later, in the Han dynasty, the custom of using jade to protect the body of the dead reached its height with the creation of elaborate jade suits for members of the elite. However, not all jades were designed as mortuary objects; many were fashioned as ornaments.

Despite its glorious philosophical, literary, and artistic masterpieces, the Zhou dynasty encountered difficulties in its last years. The Warring States era, with no centralized government, needed economic and political changes. Standardized currency and writing systems, regular taxes on agriculture and commerce, a local and regional administration that ensured safety and security and basic restraints on the seemingly all-powerful nobility, and a policy for dealing with occasionally obstreperous foreigners on China's northern frontiers were required for greater stability and peace. The victory of one of the Warring States and the resulting unification and centralization of China brought about such a transformation.

NOTES

1 Burton Watson, trans., *Chuang Tzu: Basic Writings* (New York: Columbia University Press, 1996), p. 95.

FURTHER READING

Roger Ames, trans., *Sun-tzu: The Art of Warfare* (New York: Ballantine Books, 1993).

Roger Ames, *Analects of Confucius: A Philosophical Translation* (New York: Ballantine Books, 1998).

Hsu Cho-yun, *Ancient China in Transition* (Stanford: Stanford University Press, 1965).

Victor Mair, trans., *Tao-te-ching* (New York: Bantam Books, 1990).

Benjamin Schwartz, *The World of Thought in Ancient China* (Cambridge, MA: Harvard University Press, 1980).

Burton Watson, *The Tso Chuan* (New York: Columbia University Press, 1989). Burton Watson's translations of classic philosophic and literary texts are invaluable for the general reader. See his *Han Feizi: Basic Writings, Zhuangzi: Basic Writings, Xunzi: Basic Writings*, and *Mozi: Basic Writings* (New York: Columbia University Press, 2003).

[3] THE FIRST CHINESE EMPIRES, 221 BCE–220 CE

Development of the Qin State
Qin Achievements
Failures of the Qin
Han and New Institutions
Han Foreign Relations
Emperor Wu's Domestic Policies and Their
    Ramifications
Wang Mang: Reformer or Usurper?
Restoration of a Weaker Han Dynasty
Spiritual and Philosophical Developments
    in the Han
Han Literature and Art

IT is perhaps trite to observe that certain short-lived periods represent vital watersheds in civilizations and provide essential structures for later glorious eras. The Qin dynasty (221–207 BCE), with its brevity, exemplifies this assertion. It marked the transition from a China of small kingdoms and petty states to a China of great empires. The first Qin ruler was the first emperor of China. He and his principal ministers developed institutions that laid the foundations for centralization and were adapted and adopted by later dynasties. Traditional accounts have castigated the dynasty for its cruelty and its authoritarianism. However, any rulers would surely have had to use force to impose one government on the fractious political entities of the Warring States period. The Qin was doubtless more ruthless in its policies, but domination over the "feudal" lords, the aristocratic families, and the *shi* could not have been accomplished without violence. The Legalist rulers of the Qin were

A History of China, First Edition. Morris Rossabi.
© 2014 Morris Rossabi. Published 2014 by Blackwell Publishing Ltd.

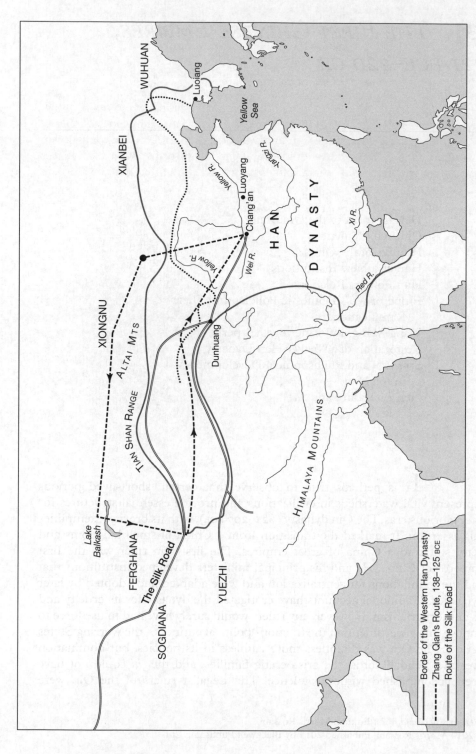

Map 3.1 Western (or Former) Han Dynasty

Border of the Western Han Dynasty
Zhang Qian's Route, 138–125 BCE
Route of the Silk Road

WUHUAN

XIANBEI

XIONGNU

ALTAI MTS

TIAN SHAN RANGE

Lake
Balkash

FERGHANA

The Silk Road

SOGDIANA

YUEZHI

Luolang

Yellow
Sea

Luoyang

Chang'an

HAN

DYNASTY

Yellow R.

Yellow R.

Yangzi R.

Wei R.

Xi R.

Red R.

Dunhuang

HIMALAYA MOUNTAINS

enthusiastic advocates of force in attaining their objectives and thus aroused the hostility of the previously powerful families, who eventually allied with military commanders to overthrow them.

Having governed China for less than two decades, the Qin rulers scarcely had the time or resources to record the history of their own achievements. Instead, their successors in the Han dynasty shaped later Chinese perceptions of the Qin. Sima Qian (ca. 145–ca. 86 BCE), the author of the *Shiji* (*Records of the Grand Historian of China*), offered the principal written account of Qin history. Though he was one of China's greatest historians, he lived less than a century after the defeat of the Qin and was bound to reflect Han antagonism toward its rival. The reader should thus bear in mind that Chinese sources tend to magnify the Qin's nefariousness though they often acknowledge, if somewhat half-heartedly, its considerable achievements.

DEVELOPMENT OF THE QIN STATE

The Qin capitalized on the changes in the late Zhou to become sufficiently dominant for its fame to spread as far away as the Hellenistic and Roman worlds. The warfare of the late Zhou era resulted in the displacement of "feudal" nobles by professional military men, the rise of infantry rather than the cumbersome and clumsy war chariots, and the development of the crossbow, which led to the use of mounted archers and the integration of cavalry into the military. It also fostered the centralization of states, the decline of the "feudal" nobility, the emergence of the *shi* and a new landlord class (which was not part of the old nobility) to positions of power, the rise of professional administrators (the ancestors of the scholar-officials of later eras), and the growth of local administrative units controlled by the central state authorities.

A different pattern of land distribution emerged, with peasant owners and landlords having obligations to the state rather than to "feudal" lords. Agricultural production increased, as did population; and, with somewhat more prosperous conditions, commerce (particularly in luxury products) grew and some merchants accumulated considerable fortunes. The new schools of thought that developed during this time complemented these political, economic, and social developments by asserting that (1) rulers and officials ought to be chosen because of their own qualifications, not because of the accident of birth, (2) individuals needed to perform the tasks incumbent on their social status, and (3) political unity and a shared cultural identity were essential for social stability. Qin was probably the first Chinese state to promote these changes and proved to be the initial beneficiary of these successful transformations.

First based in the modern province of Gansu, Qin arose on the fringes of the Zhou dynasty. It confronted hostile non-Chinese groups, which compelled its rulers to maintain a large military force. Frequent battles with a group known as the Rong offered the Qin military experience and resulted, by the mid fourth century BCE, in the creation of the best army among the Chinese states.

The reforms advocated by the Lord of Shang, the Legalist thinker, bolstered the strength of the state. Seeking to undermine the power of the local lords, the Lord of Shang organized the state into thirty-one counties, each governed by a centrally appointed official who was, in turn, under the administrators in the capital at Xianyang, on the outskirts of the modern city of Xian. Simultaneously, he encouraged the dispersal of land ownership to the peasants, reducing further the authority and property of the "feudal" lords. Conceiving of agriculture and warfare as basic pursuits, he promoted the interests of the peasantry and the military while imposing restrictions on merchants and artisans who, he perceived, played a lesser role in the economy and the state. Partly to regularize and facilitate economic transactions and partly to protect gullible peasants and consumers, he standardized weights and measures within the state. As befits his allegiance to Legalism, he stressed well-publicized laws by which everyone, even the most prominent and powerful, would be judged. Punishments for infractions were severe, but rewards (e.g. for meritorious military service and production of more than the quota of tax in kind) included lavish inducements such as exemption from labor service and the granting of honorary titles. Bestowals of these honorary ranks naturally diminished the value of the old "feudal" titles – still another means of subverting the position of the "feudal" nobles.

The Lord of Shang's reforms paved the way for Qin success, although the state's final victory was due to the mobility of its forces and its ability to impose strict discipline on them. The Lord of Shang's influence initiated Qin's drive toward centralizing China, but the pace of expansion quickened about one hundred years after his death in 338 BCE. Qin destroyed the Zhou dynasty only in 256 BCE, and then from 230 to 221 overwhelmed, in rapid succession, the states of Han, Zhao, Yan, Wei, Chu, and Qi. Within a decade, Qin conquered and then annexed the lands of its principal rivals. By 221, its leader had become the uncontested ruler of a mostly centralized China. Scholars have attributed Qin's victory first to geographical happenstance. Its base in western China was protected by three mountains, which were well guarded, enabling its leaders to have few concerns about external attacks. Geographic isolation also permitted Qin to avert the traditionalism of the central states and to be more receptive to new and more effective practices and institutions. Its struggles with so-called barbarians strengthened its military and gave primacy to martial virtues and discipline. Its emphasis on agriculture resulted in more technological innovations and ingenious irrigation works that increased output. These irrigation complexes, a few of which have survived to the present day, enriched the state. The highly centralized government, the tightly controlled administrative machinery, the uniform laws, and the influence of Legalist principles concerning a powerful state (enriched by promotion of agriculture) offer the likeliest explanations for its triumph.

Probably just as critical was Qin's willingness to accept the assistance of people from beyond its borders, which set a precedent for future dynasties. For example, the non-Chinese who would from time to time subjugate and then rule China throughout Chinese history could not have succeeded without recruiting talented Chinese counselors. Such foreign rulers generally constituted a small population compared to the Chinese and required the assistance of the Chinese in administration and governing. Like the later non-Chinese dynasties, the Qin, which originally lay outside the Chinese cultural sphere (although its people were ethnically Chinese), needed and obtained assistance from outsiders. Lü Buwei (291?–235 BCE), an extremely wealthy merchant, arrived in Qin just at the beginning of its final phase of expansion. Serving as a court adviser for several decades, he also turned over his concubine, who may already have been pregnant, as a wife to the Qin ruler, who believed the child was his and accepted him as his successor. This child grew up to become the first emperor of China. Li Si (ca. 280–208 BCE), another Chinese, proved to be the this emperor's most trusted adviser and engineered many of the most important policies promulgated by the Qin.

Centralization and standardization were the keynotes of these policies. Adopting Li Si's suggestions, the Qin rulers abolished the old "feudal" states and instead adapted their own administrative machinery to the newly subjugated territories. Dividing the country into thirty-six commanderies, with each composed of a number of counties, they placed centrally appointed and paid officials in charge of local government. To avert the meddling of the formerly powerful elites, the court moved many of them to Xianyang, providing them with suitable accommodation and stipends. Centralization of local regions was accompanied by concentration of power in the hands of the Qin ruler, who now sought a title that differed from and appeared superior to the Zhou designation of "king." The eventual choice of the title "Huangdi" (Yellow Emperor) was inspired because *di* designated the Shang dynasty's deity and had religious and political associations with the Zhou as well. The title, with its reverberations of a glorious heritage, provided the new dynasty with the majesty and legitimacy it sought. The Qin ruler who united China, a charismatic and dominant figure, assumed the title of Shi Huangdi ("First Emperor," r. 246–210 BCE) and established the first empire in the Chinese tradition. To encourage even greater centralization, he imposed the Qin state's legal code, with its emphasis on group responsibility for individual crimes and on harsh punishments (though not markedly more severe than those the Zhou states imposed), on the entire country.

Such policies subverted the authority and sometimes resulted in the dispossession of the old local aristocracy. Seeking to prevent a resurgence of localism, the Qin thus alienated and, in a sense, created potential enemies. Its bias against commerce, in addition, fostered opposition from merchants. The Qin's perhaps overly radical program and its enthusiastic implementation of these policies drew the hostility of influential groups who no doubt awaited an opportunity to reassert their lost claims to power.

QIN ACHIEVEMENTS

Partly to bolster his legitimacy in the face of such opposition but also to foster centralization and standardization, the First Emperor organized mammoth building projects. The most important such enterprise was the construction of the so-called Great Wall (which ought not to be confused with the present Great Wall, most of which dates from the sixteenth century), designed to protect against incursions by the non-Chinese steppe peoples residing north of China. Chinese sources may have exaggerated the expanse and length of the Wall and may have omitted the fact that part of the construction merely entailed merging and repairing walls already built by the individual states during the seemingly incessant warfare that afflicted the late Zhou period. Nonetheless, whatever the overstatements, considerable effort and resources were devoted to this enterprise. Although scholars have questioned the Wall's value as a deterrent, it was surely an expensive project. The sources indicate that 300,000 workers labored on the construction, and the number of fatalities was high. Forced labor was required on still another of the First Emperor's projects, the construction of roads. He ordered Meng Tian (d. 210 BCE), a leading general who also supervised the Great Wall project, to build a five-hundred-mile highway stretching from Xianyang to an area in modern Inner Mongolia within the confines of the Wall. He also promoted the construction of other roads radiating from Xianyang, which naturally facilitated centralized control and the movement of Qin armies while simultaneously fostering commerce. Large numbers of laborers were assigned to these road-building efforts. Similarly, many peasants were forced to migrate to the capital to construct elaborate palaces for the old aristocratic families and for the emperors. Seeking a more grandiose palace than the one from which his predecessors ruled, the First Emperor recruited even more laborers to build a new residence and a hall for court affairs south of the Wei river.

Figure 3.1 Terracotta Warriors, Xian, Shaanxi, China. © Jon Arnold Images Ltd / Alamy

Figure 3.2 Horse, terracotta figure from tomb of Qin Shi Huangdi, 221–210 BCE, emperor of China, Qin dynasty, 221–207 BCE, from Lintong, Shaanxi province, China. Discovered 1974. © The Art Archive / Alamy

Like the Egyptian pharaohs, the First Emperor began almost as soon as he acceded to the throne to prepare for his death and to create a suitable burial place. He was probably eager to fashion an awe-inspiring and majestic structure as a means of bolstering his own and his descendants' legitimacy. The tumulus that began to be built in the last years of his reign was indeed imposing. Although it still has not been excavated, literary sources reveal that its interior was stocked with precious valuables from all parts of the empire and was encircled by pools of mercury and ceilings. The walls and floors were lined with depictions of the sky and Heaven and of the lands the Qin ruled. Eventually, when the emperor died, several of his concubines joined him in death. Some of the unfortunate laborers were also entombed in order to prevent them from telling potential grave robbers about safe passageways into the tumulus (in addition, these passageways were guarded by elaborate death traps to deter such tampering). The 1974 discovery of an adjacent site confirmed the painstaking, expensive, and monumental plans for this burial location. In the vault was discovered an "army" of more than seven thousand life-size terracotta statues built to defend the tumulus, accompanied by statues of horses, bronze chariots, and weapons. Such a massive project necessitated the use of large numbers of corvée laborers, most of whom had to leave their homelands for long periods of time and many of whom perished as a result of their arduous labor and the unsanitary conditions.

The First Emperor's ambitious projects also imposed additional burdens on the peasantry. Under the leadership of the ubiquitous Meng Tian, Qin forces swept into Inner Mongolia, and other commanders occupied regions in the modern provinces of Guangxi, Guangdong, and Fujian. Not only were peasants recruited into the army but they were also, together with convicts and other malefactors, forcibly moved to become colonists in the newly conquered lands. Wrenched from their families and environments, many of these colonists could hardly have been pleased with the treatment the government accorded them. Thus, the dynasty created still another unhappy and potentially disloyal group.

The Qin's efforts at standardization, however, did not generate animosity and indeed generally received enthusiastic responses. It mandated the use of the same weights and measures developed during the Lord of Shang's era, which facilitated economic dealings. Despite its bias against merchants, it encouraged trade by instituting a standard metal currency, consisting principally of a circular coin with a square hole in the center, which eliminated the diverse and confusing knife and spade coins used previously. It abetted transport and, by extension, commerce by prescribing a standard gauge for vehicles, which made travel less cumbersome. Perhaps the most important standardization entailed the written script. The written language had developed somewhat helter-skelter during the Zhou dynasty, with quite a few regional variations. In a policy instigated by Li Si, Qin scholars simplified the script, converted it from so-called Large Seal to Small Seal characters, and promoted this uniform writing system throughout the domain, contributing immeasurably to cultural homogeneity and to feelings of shared identity.

FAILURES OF THE QIN

The Qin's other cultural ventures earned fewer plaudits and, in fact, alienated still another group of its subjects. Li Si's policies and their apparent deviation from tradition, as well as the First Emperor's edicts and laws, had stimulated objections from many intellectuals who often (and effectively) cited past events to criticize present developments. In 213 BCE, Li Si responded by calling for the burning of such texts as the *Book of Odes* and the *Book of Documents* and the writings of Confucian and other non-Legalist philosophers. All copies of these works had to be turned over to the government within thirty days. Only copies in the state's own library would be preserved; the rest would be destroyed. Li Si warned that obstreperous intellectuals who continued to cite these texts to vilify Qin rule would be severely punished. Contemporary sources hostile to the Qin accused the First Emperor of executing quite a number of scholars. Later historians perhaps exaggerated the number of texts destroyed and probably overstated the number of executions of intellectuals. However, Qin hostility toward the literati and its deliberate and systematic extirpation of books in a culture that reputedly valued the written word enraged scholars and bequeathed to history an image of the Qin as an authoritarian state opposed to learning and to the educated. However fair or unfair this essentially negative perception of the

Qin may be, many scholars turned against the dynasty, which led to a critical loss of support for the First Emperor and his Legalist adherents.

The alienation of the literati is ironic in light of the flexibility with which the Qin approached the three leading philosophies of the time (Legalism, Confucianism, and Daoism). Although the Qin ministers, from the Lord of Shang to Lü Buwei to Li Si, adhered to Legalism, they applied its principles less dogmatically than implied in traditional Confucian sources. They believed in severe sanctions and in group responsibility, yet other contemporary states had similarly harsh punishments for those perceived to be deviants or lawbreakers. Qin's aggressive efforts at centralization and its grandiose public-works projects may have alienated just as many of its newly subjugated subjects as its reputedly harsh laws. Qin leaders also did not dismiss Confucianism and on occasion cloaked themselves in Confucian garb and morality. Portraying himself at times as a wise Confucian ruler, the First Emperor proclaimed his devotion to right-eousness, unity, and humaneness – virtues also associated with Confucianism.

In addition, the First Emperor was attracted to a vulgarized form of Daoism, which had been influenced by folk and popular religion. This type of Daoism, which Lao Zi and Zhuang Zi might not have recognized and would probably have repudiated, comprised an amalgamation of superstitions and a smatter-ing of the original form of the philosophy. It appealed to Chinese rulers, par-ticularly because it sought formulas for longevity. Popular Daoism would eventually, in part, transform the spiritual path (*dao*) of the philosophical Daoists in their search for physical immortality. As he reached middle age, the First Emperor expressed great interest in efforts to discover formulas for pro-longing life. A number of mysterious masters, magicians, and adepts per-suaded the emperor to dispatch a mission composed of several hundred boys and girls to find an island populated by immortals. This party never returned, giving rise to the curious legend that the children reached the shores of Japan, where they chose to remain. Despite repeated failures, the emperor persisted in his support for men who pledged to produce an elixir of immortality.

In short, the Qin, its ministers, and its emperor did not simplistically apply Legalist doctrine in their political, social, and cultural policies. Their deliberate destruction of Confucian texts notwithstanding, they portrayed themselves as embodiments of some of the Confucian virtues. Despite their authoritarianism and elitism, they were often patrons of popular religions, and the First Emperor was captivated by the claims of a variety of popular religions. Yet the image of the Qin as an inflexible regime and of the First Emperor as a tyrannical despot has lingered, with the later Confucian dynasties contributing to that percep-tion. To be sure, the Qin had created many enemies via its aggressive, even ruthless, implementation of its policies and vision. However, it should be noted that other Chinese rulers have been brutal. They have recruited, exploited, and mistreated corvée laborers at public-works projects; they have censored and, on occasion, destroyed texts; and, every so often, they have severely punished elites and peasants alike. However, perhaps such practices were not carried out on as comprehensive a scale as during the Qin. Moreover, because Confucian rulers implemented these policies, the sources did not excoriate them as much as they did the Qin.

Nonetheless, the Qin generated hostility among its contemporary subjects. Its abolition of "feudal" titles and states stimulated considerable animosity toward the First Emperor. The Qin's numerous enemies were given a golden opportunity to challenge the dynasty because of the irregularities in its last years. The First Emperor, one of whose favorite activities was making tours of inspection throughout his domains, partly for his own pleasure and partly for ceremonial and military purposes, died in 210 BCE during one of these processions. His aging chief minister, Li Si, and a certain Zhao Gao (d. 207 BCE), the first in a long line of powerful eunuchs at the Chinese courts, concealed news of his death until his caravan had returned to the capital while they hatched a (successful) plot to derail the succession of the First Emperor's eldest son in favor of a younger son whom Zhao Gao had tutored and had influence over. Despite their success in hiding the emperor's death until their return to the capital, they could not avert uprisings against the tottering dynasty. The usurpation of the throne made the second emperor appear to be lacking in legitimacy, which gave rise to opposition and then to outright rebellion. Having to face an increasingly more volatile situation shattered the fragile unity at the Qin court. These rifts led, in rapid succession, to the execution of Li Si, the suicide of the second emperor, and the murder of Zhao Gao. Disaffection was so pronounced that the dynasty collapsed without much resistance. In 206, one of the rebel armies marched into and devastated the capital at Xianyang, burning numerous buildings and destroying palaces, artifacts, and texts. The Qin had ruled for barely fifteen years – a striking contrast to the eight centuries of the Zhou, its predecessor, and the four centuries of its successor, the Han. Yet it cannot be sufficiently emphasized that it laid the foundations for the Han, considered by the Chinese to be one of their greatest dynasties.

The disparity in length of the Qin and the other dynasties was often attributed to the oppressiveness of the Legalist-inspired government, but that explanation is simplistic. A sounder interpretation is that the Qin displaced the Zhou nobility, creating a ready-made opposition that would pounce on any of its missteps. Another valid explanation is the Qin's audaciousness and ambition. It undertook too many projects in too short a time, resulting in a straining of China's capacities. Forced labor and forced exactions of taxes in order to perform these manifold endeavors fostered the real opposition to the court. These public-works projects were valuable and turned out to be essential for China's political and economic development, but the Qin embarked upon them without considering the impact of such rapid and dramatic construction projects on the already stretched resources of the country. The burdens, both financial and labor related, fell inordinately on the most vulnerable segments of the population, principally the peasantry, creating a sizable reservoir of discontented and angry people. However, the Qin's disastrous miscalculations and its authoritarian rule should not obscure its considerable achievements in unifying China. Its efforts led to the creation of a bureaucracy, standardization of important functions and agencies, and centralization of the country.

The Qin also attempted to develop a system of imperial succession. However, the Han, the successor dynasty, truly implemented it. An emperor's transfer of power to a son became entrenched during the Han. Nonetheless, the Qin had conceived of such a transfer, but its brevity prevented it from carrying out a proper succession. The Han adopted the system, which lent stability to the dynasty. To be sure, the new system did not always prevail. After the death of Emperor Wu, the most renowned of the Han rulers, the succession was messy, partly due to the length of the emperor's reign and partly due to the death of his alleged chosen successor. Also, toward the end of the first century BCE, infants and young boys were enthroned, necessitating the appointment of regents. Yet the conception of a regular and orderly system of succession was frequently accepted and implemented.

The Qin and Han were the first imperial dynasties. Yet "dynasty" has to be understood in its Chinese context. Like the Western conception of the term, "dynasty" mandated governance by a specific family and hereditary succession, with the ruler perceived as part of a collective entity and not merely as an individual. The reigning emperor would choose his own successor, usually a son. To be sure, figures other than the emperor may have, in some eras, wielded power with the reigning emperor serving as a figurehead. A significant number of emperors were either uninterested in governance or dominated by others – for example, an official, a mother, a wife, or a eunuch. Yet the idea of dynasty persisted, with the most significant of them lasting for three centuries or more. Symbolism and rituals contributed to their survival. A dynasty constructed temples for its ancestors; its rulers conducted rituals associated with assurance of a bountiful harvest; its founder selected earth, fire, wood, metal, or water as its primary element, allegedly giving it strength for its future; and its family name could no longer be used as a surname by anyone in the country. Performance of the rituals lent considerable legitimacy, strength, and stability to the dynasty, even if a specific emperor was inadequate or had scant authority. The power of this model prompted usurpers to seek to found their own dynasties. Wang Mang (ca. 45 BCE–23 CE), who overthrew the Former Han dynasty in 9 CE, and the Empress Wu (624–705 CE), empress of the Tang dynasty in the seventh century CE and the only woman to seek to govern on her own, were perhaps the two most prominent examples of powerful but ignominious failures in those who sought to establish their own dynasties. Their efforts reveal the attractiveness and significance of the concept of "dynasty."

The stability of the Chinese dynastic model contrasted sharply with the problems of succession of many of the nomadic pastoral peoples on China's borders and with the foreign and often originally nomadic peoples who conquered and imposed their own dynasties on China. These foreigners devised a variety of different forms of succession to the throne, although a few adopted the Chinese pattern. Those who retained their own systems were often unstable. For example, the Mongol nobility traditionally convened to choose one of the descendants of Chinggis Khan (or Genghis Khan) as their new khan (or emperor). Conflicts often arose, and on occasion they resulted in chaos. This system was inherently unstable, and, after the Mongol conquest of China, successions to the throne led, at times, to assassinations and even battles between contending forces. The Chinese generally had a more regular and orderly system of succession.

HAN AND NEW INSTITUTIONS

The Han (206 BCE–220 CE), the next dynasty, which was split into the Former Han (206 BCE–9 CE) and the Later Han (25–220 CE), proved to be not only enduring but also pivotal for Chinese history. Chinese prize the dynasty so highly that they often refer to themselves even today as "men of Han." The dynasty devised institutions and policies that remained in place for much of Chinese history, and it witnessed the triumph of Confucianism as the dominant philosophy, the underlying ethical system, and the means of legitimizing the dynasty through rituals and the reputed blessing of Heaven. The Han pursued the Qin aim of unifying China and was determined to avert a reversion to the Zhou-era profusion of bitterly hostile states, whose conflicts had resulted in a descent into chaos. To ensure such unification, the Han needed to establish a government and to persuade the populace that it was sanctioned by Heaven.

The Han came to power partly due to the turbulence at the end of the Qin but also partly as a result of the ability, canniness, and vision of its founder, Liu Bang (256 or 247–195 BCE), or Emperor Gaozu. Of peasant background, he had originally thrown in his lot with Xiang Yu (232–202 BCE), previously a leading figure in the Qin army but by 207 BCE the primary commander of the rebel forces. Xiang attempted to restore a decentralized system of government reminiscent of Zhou times, a system composed of nineteen states with himself as the principal ruler. Such a scheme contrasted sharply with the Qin mania for control and a unified government. Xiang and Liu initially cooperated, but their alliance barely survived the immediate fall of the Qin. Twice Xiang let victory slip out of his hands in the ensuing struggle, and ultimately the more unscrupulous and rough-and-tumble Liu overwhelmed his rival, causing the former commander to commit suicide.

Naming his dynasty "Han" from the name of the territory he had controlled under Xiang's system of nineteen states, Liu set about establishing a government. He first selected the Qin capital around the modern city of Xian as its approximate site because it was easily defended and was closer to provisions for the burgeoning population at the center of government. Then, imitating the Qin governmental structure, he set up a policy-making group (*sangong*) composed of a chancellor (*chengxiang*), an imperial counselor (*yushi dafu*), and a supreme commander (*taiwei*), the last of whom, in theory, commanded the army. In practice, the chancellor was the most powerful figure, partly because he sifted through the reports and memorials from officials throughout the empire to determine which merited the emperor's attention. The imperial counselor had the specific responsibility of supervising the bureaucracy while the supreme commander, who was reputedly in charge of military affairs, was in fact often superseded by the chancellor – an example of the professed Chinese tradition of civilian supremacy over the military. Nine ministers, with carefully delineated responsibilities, carried out the policies devised principally by the emperor and the chancellor. Several agencies, such as the superintendents of the palace, the guards, transport, and the imperial clan, provided services almost exclusively for the imperial family and the court. Others concerned themselves with state functions. The superintendent of ceremonials managed the empire's rituals, cults, and religions while the superintendent of state took charge of foreign envoys and leaders who came to China. Legal matters fell into the jurisdiction of the superintendent of trials, and the superintendent of agriculture received land taxes that were used to pay officials and to support the military. Finally, the superintendent of the lesser treasury gathered the revenues derived from nonagricultural, generally minor taxes.

As the Han progressed, however, fear of granting too much power to any single official or agency resulted in a rudimentary checks–and-balances system. The emperors' concerns about potential threats to their authority led to limits on the responsibility of any minister or chancellor over any government function. In various areas, two or more agencies were frequently granted authority over single aspects of rule. This system of overlapping functions prevented specific administrators or agencies from dominating any aspect of government. For example, the superintendents of agriculture and the lesser treasury shared jurisdiction over finances; similarly, the superintendent of the lesser treasury, by his power to shape the amount of revenue provided to the military, restricted the supreme commander's authority. Such a system reduced the institutional opportunities for challenges to imperial authority but simultaneously set the stage for possible irreconcilable disputes among top officials and agencies. These disputes impeded or, in some cases, totally undercut timely decision making and thus occasionally led to stagnation or to a lack of resolution of serious problems. This system of checks and balances shaped government operations throughout much of Chinese history, leading to similar problems for many dynasties.

Having devised the institutions required for a central government, the Han then faced the perennial question of how to gain and maintain control over local regions, an issue that plagued many dynasties from this time on. Because Liu Bang had relied on various powerful regional commanders to vanquish Xiang Yu, he could not simply renounce them, nor could he demand that they give up their arms and abide by the dictates of the central government. The Han system of local administration would thus need to consider these powerful regional figures. Indeed, the early emperors worked out a compromise, permitting the creation of kingdoms and commanderies in local regions. The kings enjoyed considerable leeway in governing their domains until 145 BCE, though Han rulers attempted to have their own relatives or retainers succeed as kings. In 145, the Han court, by now more self-confident than in its first years, seized the power to appoint the officials who directly served the kings, thus starting to undermine the kingdoms' independence. As the Han wore on, it gained greater authority over the kings. From its earliest days, the Han had exerted quite a bit of influence over the commanderies, dispatching governors to enforce central-government financial and military policies. It sought also to control the lower-level administrative units that composed the kingdoms and commanderies – the counties (*xian*) and the marquisates (*hou*). The court selected magistrates to collect taxes, to administer justice, to maintain peace and order, and often to supervise public-works projects. The counties and marquisates, in turn, appointed officials to head lower administrative units such as districts, and these officials dealt more frequently with ordinary people.

This carefully and elaborately constructed system of provincial and local administration did not necessarily ensure the dominance of the central government, either in the Han or later dynasties. Decentralization was in the best interests of many local elite families in the provinces, and throughout the dynasty they would be opposed to and would, in fact, contest central-government attempts to enforce its policies and to control them. Chinese history had vacillated and would continue to alternate between periods of centralized control and successful regional challenges to centralization. This tension would rage for centuries, on occasion leading to the same kind of collapse as in the Warring States period. Even during strong dynasties, local elites and local governments frequently wielded considerable power. In addition, rudimentary transport and communications impeded the central government's efforts to enforce its will on local elites and to implement its policies and edicts.

The military offered one means of dominating local areas, but its early failure against China's most vaunted enemy, the non-Chinese peoples north of China, was not comforting. In theory, universal military service for a two-year term was mandated for all males aged between twenty-three and fifty-six. Most received assignments among the troops guarding the capital or protecting the borders. Those stationed along the frontiers went on reconnaissance missions to ascertain the intentions of foreign forces that might attack China, warned the court of potential threats, and attempted to rebuff incursions. The court appointed commanders when the need arose, and officers conducted training exercises to ensure that the soldiers were ready for battle. The early Han mandated that accurate records of the delivery of supplies and mail and of the actual military training be kept so as to avert corruption and to guarantee the preparedness of the troops. However, despite their meticulous efforts, their initial campaigns against the Xiongnu (a new confederation of tribes based in modern Inner Mongolia and Mongolia) resulted in a resounding defeat. In 201 BCE, the Xiongnu routed a Han army and almost captured the emperor, best known by his temple name, Gaozu. The military alone would not resolve China's frontier problems.

To meet its military and other needs, the new dynasty required revenue, much of which would ultimately derive from agriculture. As early as 205 BCE, a tax on land had been imposed that amounted to a rate of one-fifteenth of total yield, later reduced to one-thirtieth of total yield. This tax was not, by itself, burdensome, but a poll tax, together with a property tax, added to the levies demanded from the peasantry. Some measures were introduced in an attempt to assist peasants – for example, irrigation and flood-control projects. However, labor service of one month a year for all males of working age and the military requirements described earlier meant even more heavy responsibilities. Peasants who barely eked out their subsistence could not afford to meet their tax obligations. The onset of disastrous locusts, floods, and droughts exacerbated their difficulties. Many fell into debt, and the high rates of interest charged by usurers forced them into bankruptcy. They eventually had to sell their holdings to large landowners who often permitted them to rent the land. Increasingly, many peasants were compelled to give up their lands, and large (frequently tax-exempt) estates proliferated, resulting in a further diminution of court revenues as well as fiscal dilemmas for the dynasty.

Income from other taxes did not compensate for the reduced revenue derived from land. The court, through the superintendent of the lesser treasury, imposed taxes on the products of hills and seas, including fishing and iron and salt production, and on merchants and their profits. A poll tax on merchants was still another means of raising government funds. Within sixty years of the founding of the dynasty, these fiscal devices and the revenues they raised were insufficient for the court's needs, compelling the Han emperors to resort to other measures to finance the government.

Yet initially Gaozu and his immediate successors did not encounter financial difficulties and concentrated instead on developing and bolstering Han institutions of governance. Gaozu's closest associates had been military men, but he quickly recognized that he needed civilian administrators. Faced first with the need to recruit officials, he and his successors experimented with various means to select capable men. In 192 BCE, he conducted the first civil-service examinations to choose the most competent men. Centuries later, examinations would be the most important method of staffing the bureaucracy, but at this earlier time appointments and family relationships to prominent figures were as significant. Then, with the counsel of advisers such as Jia Yi (201–169 BCE), the emperors gradually reduced the power and territories controlled by the kingdoms, and they overcame efforts by relatives of Gaozu's wife, the Empress née Lü, to dominate the court (though she remained powerful after her husband's death until her own demise in 180 BCE). She was the first in a line of empresses who sought power and were thus vilified in the traditional Chinese histories. Since these sources were written by allies of the bureaucracy, their portrait of the empress, as well as of other indomitable women, ought perhaps to be somewhat discounted. The empress's career challenges the stereotyped portrait of women as submissive and having scant involvement in public life. She was the first but not the last woman in the history of the Chinese court to wield power and, in fact, to dominate Chinese policy making.

Emperor Gaozu, Empress née Lü, and the court accomplished much in the first thirty years or so of the Han, including the design and construction of a capital at Changan, northwest of the present city of Xian. Surrounded by four walls, each about twenty-six feet high, with twelve gates permitting entry into the city, Changan was built on a grid pattern, with the Weiyang district as the principal palace complex. At least two sizable markets were established to cater to the growing population. A period of stability set in, during which the court attempted to solidify its institutions but scarcely embarked upon new initiatives or efforts to expand the territory under its control.

HAN FOREIGN RELATIONS

Instead the court sought peace, at least until the accession of Emperor Wu (r. 140–87 BCE). Officials and emperors warned against adventurism and urged caution in foreign relations. They were concerned about the economic and political repercussions that could result from the unstable border and from raids and incursions.

The greatest threat was from the peoples living north of China in the area now known as inner Asia. Because their land was unsuited to agriculture, many of these peoples practiced a pastoral economy that necessitated seasonal migrations to find the water and grass essential for the survival of their animals. Their own survival depended upon the sheep, goats, yaks, camels, or horses that they transported (or that transported them). Such reliance made them peculiarly vulnerable to any difficulties that afflicted their herds. Drought, overgrazing, disease among their animals, or a bad winter (during which an ice cover over the land denied the animals access to life-preserving grass) threatened their existence. Their mobility, which limited their ability to carry a surplus in case of emergency, exacerbated the difficulties inherent in their fragile economy and compelled them to seek grain, manufactured goods, and metals from neighboring civilizations, particularly China. Simultaneously, their migrations imposed limits on the number of people in any group, the optimal size amounting to several thousand individuals. Thus, if they were denied trade by China, their only recourse was hit-and-run raids, which surely troubled but did not imperil their neighbor. However, if they were to unite and form a larger confederation of groups under centralized leadership, they would offer a more serious threat to China, and some confederations did begin to arise. One way in which the rulers of the confederations ensured the loyalty of their people was to secure booty from neighboring civilizations. They sought either to extort wealth or to obtain trade, not necessarily to conquer. According to some recent studies, the rise of such confederations was actually, in part, a response to the growth of a strong Chinese dynasty. To secure the goods they required either through trade or raids, the pastoral peoples organized themselves into larger units to counteract China's increased power.

The Xiongnu, one of the first of these steppe nomadic confederations, arose in Mongolia at precisely the same time that the Han unified and consolidated China. Under the leadership of their leader, who was known by his Chinese name Maodun, the Xiongnu united many of the pastoral nomads of Mongolia and central Asia into one powerful unit. Maodun himself defeated the Donghu and Yuezhi confederations on his road to power. He then took a major step for a nomadic ruler by establishing a fixed site for an annual meeting of all his people, a site that could potentially become the capital for an empire. He also initiated religious ceremonies, as well as such basic elements in creating a government as conducting a census. Maodun's new policy raised the possibility of the establishment of a sedentary government. With experience in operating a regular administration, the Xiongnu would clearly be a more serious threat because they could not only occupy but also rule Chinese territory.

Responding to this potential threat, Gaozu initially mounted a punitive expedition and led his army in person against the Xiongnu. Maodun employed the tactic of a feigned retreat to entice the Chinese army into a trap in the modern province of Shanxi. He besieged the Han forces for a week and withdrew his troops only because of turbulence caused by the disaffection and disloyalty of two of his allies. The lifting of the siege did not conclude the hostilities, for the Xiongnu invaded again in 200 and 196 BCE. Smarting over his precarious position, Gaozu sought a peaceful accommodation. He did so through a so-called marital alliance. In 192, a young Chinese woman who was supposed to be a princess became one of Maodun's consorts, and the Han dynasty also promised to provide annual gifts of silk, grain, and wine in return for a pledge of nonaggression. Later the court permitted the Xiongnu to trade for Chinese products in specially designated markets on the Chinese border. Marital alliances and trade led to peace for about fifty years.

The accession of Emperor Wu altered this period of stability. Wu was determined to pursue a less conciliatory and more aggressive policy toward the Xiongnu. In 138, he dispatched a palace official named Zhang Qian (d. 114 BCE) to travel toward central Asia to seek allies among the Xiongnu's vaunted enemies. The underlying assumption was that such an alliance would translate into a concerted military campaign on two fronts against the Xiongnu. A Chinese army could launch an expedition from the south while their allies could move from the west to pacify the Xiongnu. Knowing of the enmity between the Xiongnu and the Yuezhi, who had been forced to move westward by Maodun's attacks, Zhang traveled to the so-called Western Regions to sign a pact with the Xiongnu's enemies. After a harrowing voyage during which he was captured and detained in the Xiongnu encampment for about a decade, he finally reached the Yuezhi territories only to find that the Xiongnu's adversaries were reluctant to imperil themselves with an attack against their former enemies. They rebuffed Zhang's overtures. The dejected Chinese envoy headed back to China, but the Xiongnu captured him once again. After a year, Zhang managed to escape and returned to China. His mission appeared, on the surface, to be a fiasco. However, he offered an invaluable report on the states and regions through which he had traveled. He implied that some could be lured into accepting Chinese sovereignty while others offered products appealing to China. The Ferghana region in modern Uzbekistan had fine horses, which intrigued Wu and the court because China simply did not breed sufficient steeds for its military needs. Similarly, the region around Ferghana produced grape wine, and Zhang ought to be credited with making the Chinese aware of grapes and alfalfa. However, he failed to achieve the diplomatic objectives of his mission. Nonetheless, the emperor sent him with gold and silk and a Chinese princess to lure still another group in the Western Regions, the Wusun, into an alliance. Though commerce developed between China and the Wusun, they did not reach an agreement on a joint expedition against the Xiongnu. Thus, Zhang's contribution lay in fostering trade, leading eventually to the renowned Silk Roads commerce, rather than in developing a solution for China's problems with the Xiongnu.

Wu adopted a forceful policy even before learning of the results of Zhang's first mission. He abandoned the policy of marital alliances and instead ordered several surprise attacks on Xiongnu positions. In 127, 121, and 119 BCE, Han forces routed the "barbarians" of the north, compelling them to move ever farther north, but these reputed successes were costly. Moreover, the Han dynasty histories, which were often based on reports by commanders who sought to inflate their achievements, exaggerated the Xiongnu losses. Had the

Xiongnu suffered as many casualties as described in the Chinese accounts, they would have needed decades to recover from the devastation. In fact, the Xiongnu repeatedly attempted to avoid direct confrontations with large Chinese forces, preferring to flee farther into the steppelands. A pursuing Chinese army would encounter serious logistical difficulties because it would have to carry, by oxen, its own supplies for men and animals for an extended period of time, while the Xiongnu would simply butcher a few of their animals and continue to flee. Such campaigns in the rugged terrain in the north led to great losses among the troops and animals, particularly the oxen, which had fragile constitutions and suffered under the heavy loads they had to transport in desolate areas where they could not adequately graze.

Thus, although Wu's campaigns played a role, the real weakening of the Xiongnu confederation resulted from internal turbulence. Unity within this newly established confederation was always fragile, and each supreme leader's authority over his various underlings had to be earned – a demanding task. About two decades after Wu's accession, conflicts erupted in the Xiongnu leadership, weakening the confederation. One supreme leader after another succeeded to power over the next sixty years, culminating in greater regional power and a diminution of central authority. Facing such internal disunity and unrest, the supreme leaders were more willing to abide by the system of foreign relations devised by the Chinese. Assuming their civilization was the most advanced in the world, the Chinese created a system that demanded acknowledgment of their superiority. They pointed out that they had a sophisticated culture, a written language, a well-worked-out ethical code, and magnificent cities and palaces, all of which their nomadic neighbors to the north lacked. Thus they portrayed their neighbors as uncivilized, crude, intractable, and occasionally treacherous. The Chinese claimed that they had the responsibility, through their own example of creating an orderly society, of encouraging foreigners to "come and be transformed" – that is, to become increasingly sinicized. The Chinese emperor, who had a mandate from Heaven to rule his own people, was allegedly vital because his conduct inspired the foreigners to seek the benefits of Chinese culture. His benevolence, compassion, and generosity served as a model for foreign rulers and drew them and their people closer to China. Though the Xiongnu and other foreign peoples to the north and west of China did not necessarily subscribe to this ideological viewpoint, they recognized that China was the most important country in east Asia at that time and often abided by Chinese regulations in order to obtain diplomatic and commercial gains.

The tribute system governed foreigners' relations with the Chinese. In order to deal with China, foreign rulers were required to send tribute embassies periodically to the Chinese emperor. When an embassy reached the Chinese border, Chinese officials immediately took charge and accompanied the envoys to the capital. The Chinese government bore all the expenses of the embassy during its stay in China. Its officials taught the envoys the proper etiquette for their appearance at court. After the envoys had been prepared, they had an audience with the emperor. They performed the rituals, including the kowtow, a symbolic recognition of their inferiority and, more important, of their acknowledgment of their status as envoys of a "vassal" state or group. Their conduct at court implied that their ruler was subordinate to the emperor. They then offered their tribute of rare and precious goods to him, and he, in turn, bestowed valuable gifts upon them and their ruler. The audience ended, and the envoys then had three to five days to trade with Chinese merchants. The Chinese court could, in theory, control this relationship. It determined the frequency with which embassies could be admitted into China, the number of men in each embassy, and the length of the embassy's stay in the country. Court officials supervised the foreigners' trade with Chinese merchants, regulating the prices and profits and ensuring that neither side exploited the other. The court asserted that it did not gain from such tribute and trade relations. China, it contended, was economically self-sufficient, and the gifts that the foreigners brought to the court were superfluous. On the other hand, the Chinese products granted to the foreigners were vital and valuable. Although the court appeared to be bribing the foreigners in order to secure peace, Chinese officials hesitated to describe the relationship in those terms. They could use the threat of a suspension of tribute and trade to pacify the foreigners, since they gained little from the relationship while the foreigners gained much.

Why would the Xiongnu, who were often China's military equals, accept, even in theory, an inferior status in dealings with the Chinese court? One likely explanation is that they profited enormously from tribute and trade with China. The lavish goods they received from the emperors (e.g. silk) and the essential products they obtained in trade with Chinese merchants compensated for the less than exalted position they occupied in their relations with China. They would acquiesce to the Chinese system as long as they secured the products they needed. Only when China sought to limit or eliminate tribute and trade did they renounce the system and use their forces to challenge Chinese hegemony. Another explanation for the acquiescence of foreign rulers is that investiture by the Chinese emperor enhanced the prestige of the foreign ruler among his own and neighboring groups. Such Chinese support could be extremely useful to a new ruler, particularly one who faced rivals or opposition within his own land.

Thus the tribute system enabled China to devise its own world order. The Chinese court dealt with foreigners on its own terms. Equality with China was ruled out, and the court could not conceive of equitable international relations. It could not accept other states or tribes as equals. The court would not tolerate rulers who did not abide by this world order and would not permit entry to those who rejected this system of foreign relations. The Chinese emperor was the Son of Heaven, the undisputed leader of the east Asian peoples, if not the world.

Because Emperor Wu's reign came at the apogee of the Han dynasty's power, he could enforce the regulations of the tribute system, particularly when he faced a Xiongnu leadership that was in disarray. Nonetheless, his earlier military campaigns had been expensive. In addition, his expansionist policies in other regions were similarly costly, although some merchants profited. Following up on Zhang Qian's mission, in 108 BCE, Wu's troops attacked and then occupied Turfan, a vital gateway to central Asia. From there, they made forays farther to the west to ensure passage for travel. The resulting development of the so-called Silk Roads trade enriched some merchants and brought China in touch with a wider world, offering opportunities for cultural and commercial exchanges. Naturally, many regions in central Asia, India, Persia, and west Asia (and, eventually, the Roman Empire) benefited from this trade because it gave them ready access to the silk they coveted. China became increasingly attractive to many foreign merchants. Nonetheless, the maintenance of troops in Turfan and other oases and towns along the Silk Roads contributed to the court's financial burdens.

Wu's adventurist foreign policies stretched from the southwest to the northeast and included the southern coast as well. Some of his expeditions were prompted by reports of the great wealth accruing to some areas due to trade; others resulted from turbulence that he feared might spill over into China; and still others entailed attempts to establish buffer zones for China's territories. In III BCE, his troops set up garrisons and commanderies in the kingdom of Dian in the modern province of Yunnan and in the kingdom of Yelang in modern Guizhou. A few years later, other military expeditions affirmed Chinese control and established commanderies in the provinces of Guangdong and Guangxi and in northern Vietnam, as well as on the island of Hainan. Simultaneously, Han forces occupied the kingdoms of Dongyue and Minyue (in the modern province of Fujian) in reprisal for the killing of Chinese officials. In the northeast, the various inhabitants of Korea had been in touch with China for several centuries, and Chinese settlers had probably introduced features of Chinese civilization into the Korean peninsula. However, Wu was now determined to gain control. In 109, claiming that Koreans harbored Chinese defectors, he dispatched an army that created several commanderies, the most important of which were Lelang (near modern P'yongyang), Lintun, Zhenfan, and Xuantu. Archeological evidence, including numerous Chinese goods found at tomb sites and tombs of prominent Chinese, confirms the Chinese presence in Korea over the next century.

Despite the impetus to commercial and cultural contacts, Wu's expansionism did not necessarily result in permanent territorial gains. Many commanderies were eventually abandoned. The extent of their control beyond the immediate region occupied by Chinese troops is unclear. These forays, nonetheless, fostered trade. In sum, Wu's expansion had immediate benefits, but some of the long-term consequences may not have been salubrious, and the expenditures for the campaigns were staggering.

EMPEROR WU'S DOMESTIC POLICIES AND THEIR RAMIFICATIONS

The same mixed results characterized Wu's domestic fiscal policies, which were shaped, in large part, by the court's pressing need for revenue to finance the mounting costs of foreign expansionism. The court increased taxes on property and vehicles, but – even more critical – the government imposed monopolies on salt and iron and took over the copper mines in order to gain control over the production and minting of copper coins. These monopolies would turn out to be important sources of revenue but would simultaneously raise the prices of these vital commodities. Wu also permitted the growth of large estates, which would, in theory, provide additional taxes but which would also lead to further impoverishment of the peasantry. Dong Zhongshu (179–104 BCE), the leading Confucian of this era, warned of the instability generated by the growing disparity between poor peasants and the landlords, but his warnings did not translate into new policies. Instead the owners of large estates would become increasingly powerful and would successfully seek to exclude their lands from the tax rolls. Thus, the court's fiscal problems remained and weighed down even harder on later reigns. Wu went on to sell military honors and government offices in order to meet the court's growing expenditures – a particularly dangerous precedent. Sale of positions in the bureaucracy offered opportunities for unscrupulous men to gain political power.

A similarly unorthodox bureaucratic change Wu initiated fostered still other opportunities for profiteering and power-hungry individuals to move into positions of authority. The Secretariat, which had been a relatively innocuous and lesser office, began to be entrusted with greater responsibilities. Wu and later emperors used the Secretariat in this way to circumvent the regular bureaucracy, avoid opposition, and evade the formalities that might cause delays or obstructions in implementation of their desires and policies. With such strong emperors as Wu, decisions and authority remained in the ruler's hands. However, when the weaker and less competent of his descendants came to the throne, the Secretariat often gained tremendous power. Eunuchs, who comprised a large number of the Secretariat's employees, became more prominent at these times.

An additional trait of Wu's reign that contributed to problems later in the dynasty was the superstition that prevailed among the elite and the emperor himself. A witchcraft episode in 91 BCE, to which Wu gave credence, resulted in the suicide of Wu's heir apparent. Accusations of witchcraft, perhaps inspired by Wu, were leveled at the emperor's in-laws and maternal relatives. Such fractiousness at court weakened the dynasty and caused growing disarray, which led to several irregular successions to the throne over the next few decades. On Wu's death in 87 BCE, a nine-year-old was enthroned and a powerful regent governed in his name. Purges of influential officials and imperial relatives, as well as various cliques striving for power, characterized the remaining century of the Former Han dynasty.

Disputes among the different factions in the government added to the confusion. One faction focused on strengthening and enriching the state, while another emphasized limiting court demands on the individual. The first supported government monopolies on vital commodities as a means of raising revenues, advocated the seemingly Legalist principle of harsh laws to achieve order, and sought controls on the population to empower the state so as to confront and dominate its bellicose neighbors to the north, mostly the

Xiongnu. The opposition believed that monopolies would provide insufficient revenues and would, in any case, harm the population. It argued that agriculture was more vital than the proposed monopolies and that promoting peasant interests ought to be the fundamental government objective. This faction concluded by asserting that morality rather than severe laws would assure stability and that a conciliatory policy toward the Xiongnu would be less expensive and less harmful than an expansionist strategy. The government alternated between these two policies throughout the rest of the Former Han dynasty. Emperor Xuan (74–49 BCE), a decisive and incorruptible ruler, briefly halted the dynasty's slide by curbing court expenditures, peasant exploitation, and aristocrats' avoidance of taxes.

After Xuan's reign, however, the dynasty persisted in its downward spiral. The kingdoms, which had earlier been abolished, were restored, and aristocrats who had previously held power in certain regions regained some of their authority, weakening the central government.

To its credit, the court repeatedly attempted to reduce costly excesses, including lavish rituals, ceremonies, and religious services. However, such austerity simply could not compensate for the limited revenues flowing to the government (which were principally due to the fact that many in the aristocracy had secured tax-free status for their estates). With fewer resources at its command, the court did not adequately maintain the dikes along the Yellow River, leading to frequent floods and fatalities.

The Xiongnu, who had been China's principal foreign antagonist, could not capitalize on the Han's difficulties. Unity proved elusive for this tribal confederation, and constant struggles for succession weakened it. Finally, in 53 BCE, the Xiongnu leader Huhanye, faced with such divisiveness, made his peace with China in order to receive the handsome rewards that the Han court pledged. Traveling in person to the court, he accepted Chinese demands, including payment of tribute and leaving behind a son as a hostage. Delighted with his acquiescence, the Han court and its merchants provided him with silk, gold, and grain, which he could then use to win over previously recalcitrant underlings. Several of his successors continued to arrive in person at the Han court to obtain lavish gifts, and they recognized that they did not need to organize massive and costly raids across the border to secure the Chinese goods they needed. For more than half a century, China thus established peace with its most hostile neighbor.

Similarly, the Former Han's last years witnessed other successes in foreign policy that somewhat mitigated its slide into domestic turbulence. It set up military colonies (*tuntian*) in the northwest, which consisted of soldiers who worked the land and thus did not require government supplies. These colonies protected, at a minimal cost, the caravan trails along the Silk Roads. Because of the colonies' effective system of watchtowers and garrisons, they preserved trade with central and west Asia. The court also dealt adroitly with the Qiang, who probably formed one of the constituent groups of the modern Tibetan peoples. It sent troops to establish military colonies in the Qiang's territories in the modern provinces of Qinghai, Gansu, and Sichuan (a policy similar to the one it devised for the Silk Roads). Simultaneously, it encouraged the settlement of some of the more sedentary Qiang well within China.

WANG MANG: REFORMER OR USURPER?

After Emperor Xuan's reign, the Former Han's achievements in foreign relations were not matched at the court. The imperial family was torn asunder by assassinations, plots, and coups. Lack of stability at the court, which reputedly resulted from the ambitions and schemes of concubines and empresses and their relatives, simply aggravated the wider society's unrest. During the last three unsettled decades of the Former Han, the Wang family, who often acted as regents for child emperors, assumed control of the Secretariat. Wang Mang, the last important family member, became regent for a child emperor and then in 9 CE capitalized on several so-called omens to overthrow his charge and proclaim the founding of his own dynasty, which he called the Xin (New) dynasty, a dynasty that Chinese historians do not consider legitimate.

Wang Mang's ultimate failure stigmatized him and shaped the Chinese historians' depiction of him and his policies. A failed usurper does not get much sympathy from traditional historians. From their viewpoint, Wang Mang had not received a mandate from Heaven to rule and, as such, was clearly a fraud and a rebel, if not worse. Historians offered scant empathy for the last emperors of a dynasty or for pretenders to the throne. Losers, like Wang Mang, were generally not accorded fair treatment. Historians judged his very appearance to be wanting, in contrast to successful emperors who looked the part and whose features were described in grandiose, exaggerated, and even false terms. The historians portray Wang Mang as having a huge mouth and a loud voice, bad omens in the Chinese view of physiognomy.

A more balanced appraisal of Wang Mang's policies offers a more complex portrait. Wang's edicts hardly seem radical. Some were merely continuations of previous policies. For example, Wang reaffirmed state monopolies on salt, liquor, iron implements, revenues from mountains and marshes, and minting of coins – a slight addition to the list of goods monopolized during Emperor Wu's reign. He also banned the purchase and sale of slaves, who admittedly comprised only a small segment of the population. His other policies, including a tax on merchants and artisans and a lowering of the value of coinage, did not diverge significantly from Han practices. Indeed, Wu had pursued the same policies. Even the "ever-normal granary," Wu's principal innovation, could not be deemed harmful. Officials would buy grain in times of surplus to avert a decline in prices paid to producers and would sell it from government storehouses in times of shortage to ward off high prices and gouging of consumers. By stabilizing prices, the "ever-normal granary" ensured greater regularity, surely a policy that could hardly have antagonized any significant segment of the population. Indeed Henry Wallace, the US Secretary of Agriculture during the Depression, adopted just such policies to ameliorate the problems faced by farmers and consumers.

Similarly, Wang Mang's foreign policies did not deviate dramatically from Han precedents. The dynastic histories charge that he unnecessarily provoked the Xiongnu, causing them to abandon the tribute system that the Han had so patiently fostered and to initiate aggressive forays into China. A more likely scenario is that the Xiongnu recognized the disturbances within China and deliberately capitalized on the turbulence to challenge the Han's territorial and commercial interests. In any case, the Xiongnu had certainly not been passive in the last decades of the Former Han. With the accession of their leader Huduershi in 18 CE, Xiongnu pressure on the Chinese borders intensified. Wang Mang's troops held their own within China itself, but the Xiongnu disrupted Chinese control over the central Asian oases along the Silk Roads. Caravans faced a more perilous journey because the towns en route were not entirely secured. Isolated uprisings erupted in Korea (where Wu had established commanderies) and in the southwest (where the Han had attempted to maintain trade routes to Burma and India), but these outbreaks did not result from dramatic changes in policy. They reflected, in part, the ongoing jockeying for position in these regions, as well as awareness of China's vulnerability during what turned out to be a turbulent era.

Because Wang Mang's policies did not deviate sharply from Han precedents, his downfall cannot truly be attributed to disastrous programs or, as the dynastic histories would have us believe, a pugnacious personality that repelled many Chinese. To be sure, he had opponents among the old aristocracy who had supported Han rule. They certainly would have sought any pretext to challenge his authority. However, the most important factor in his downfall may have been a catastrophic shift in the course of the Yellow River, where maintenance and repair of dikes and embankments had not received sufficient attention over a long period of time. The river changed its course southward, particularly in Shandong, leading to devastating floods, shortage of food, and disease and death. Many succumbed to starvation and disease in the aftermath of the floods, and the ensuing famine, with which the government could not cope, caused many to move south. These refugees scavenged for and stole food, and as larger crowds developed they began to rampage over an increasingly wider territory. They became more organized and sought to establish their own identity by painting their foreheads red. Soon known as the Red Eyebrows, they became a threat to Wang Mang. However, they did not have the skills – literacy, experience, and leadership – required to form a government. The old aristocracy saw its chance to capitalize on these disturbances, and a descendant of the Han dynasty, known by his posthumous name of Guangwu (r. 25–57 CE), emerged as the leader of these rebel groups and defeated Wang Mang by 23 CE.

RESTORATION OF A WEAKER HAN DYNASTY

After suppressing challenges to his rule and compelling the somewhat anarchic Red Eyebrows to submit, Emperor Guangwu began to chart policies that would vastly influence the new Later Han dynasty (25–220 CE). He first moved the capital to Luoyang, a site where the court could not as easily be trapped as in Changan. A well-planned city with an adequate water supply and with altars for ceremonial and ritual purposes, Luoyang became such a magnet for the Chinese that within a few decades the population reached more than half a million. Because Guangwu had had substantial support in coming to power, he needed to make concessions to his allies. Thus he restored some of the marquisates and kingdoms that had been abandoned in the earlier Han dynasty. Although the kings would from this time on often be the emperors' sons, the fact that the emperors reverted to kingdoms and marquisates revealed a weakening of central authorities. Most of the Later Han's administrative institutions resembled those of the Former Han, save that the Secretariat became more prominent and the government itself became increasingly decentralized. In addition, court rivalries and struggles bedeviled Guangwu's reign and would continue to plague the Later Han. The incessant irregularities and infighting at court lowered its prestige and undermined efforts to deal seriously with domestic and foreign problems. Empress dowagers, on several occasions, wielded power in the name of their young and inexperienced sons, which added to the instability at court.

Power struggles at court brought still another group, the eunuchs, into prominence. The eunuchs' original responsibility was supervision of the imperial harem. However, their connections with the emperors led to close relations and eventually to greater imperial trust of and reliance on these castrated males, whose lack of issue meant that they posed no threat to the dynasty. Emperors began to entrust eunuchs with additional duties and responsibilities. Recognizing that whatever power accrued to the eunuchs was based on their patronage, the emperors had more faith in them than they did in the regular bureaucracy. In addition, the eunuchs were more malleable and responsive to the emperors' wishes than their counterparts among the officials. Their increasing involvement in politics added still another cast of characters to the volatile mixture of interests and groups at court. They often served to counter the growing power of the relatives of the empresses. Thus, by around 100, empresses' relatives, influential families, the bureaucracy, and eunuchs all competed for authority. Groups that had not specifically been granted decision-making authority began to supersede the designated officials, a trend that could and did lead to abuses.

Court politics in the first and second centuries yield a portrait of conflict, confusion, and corruption. No wonder that instability wracked the Later Han. Some officials exacted inordinately heavy taxes from the peasantry and then pocketed the proceeds. They meted out harsh punishments to even minor offenders or innocents who somehow alienated them. Avaricious eunuchs and relatives of the empresses misappropriated funds meant for state projects and instead used them for their own pursuits and pleasures. Although several officials attempted reforms to curb such excesses and corruption, they were unable to overcome the resistance of those who dominated the government. Repeated protests by officials about the indecisiveness of the emperors, the growth in power of the Secretariat, the insolence and cupidity of the consort families, the purchase of government offices and titles, and the rapaciousness of eunuchs did not lead to change. It was no accident that disorders and rebellions erupted before the middle of the second century. Earthquakes and other natural disasters offered critics opportunities to remonstrate with the later emperors about their lack of will in governing properly and eliminating corruption. Such criticisms had scant discernible effects, as the emperors generally were either manipulated by others or remained above court politics. In 168, the eunuchs consolidated their power by quelling a coup by a leading family. They were so entrenched that they even became military commanders in charge of dealing with domestic insurrections and foreign attacks.

In response to the court corruption and the impoverishment of the peasantry, a "Five Pecks of Rice" movement (consisting of Daoists who annually donated that amount of rice to their religious leaders) arose in Sichuan in opposition to the dynasty. Subsequently, a religious figure named Zhang Jue (d. 184) led uprisings against the dynasty in 184. Within a year, a rebel group known as the Yellow Turbans, whose leader proclaimed himself to be the Son of Heaven, had organized itself. Government forces, with the assistance of mercenaries from north of China, defeated them and the Five Pecks of Rice movement, but other rebel forces arose to challenge the Han. Simultaneously, the Qiang took advantage of the tumult to attack Han positions in northwest China. The Xiongnu and the Xianbei (a new nomadic confederation) joined against the Han to contest territory and towns along the northern frontiers. As the power of the military grew, the eunuchs were undercut. In 189, a coalition of military commanders and influential families surprised the eunuch leaders and killed many at court, a massacre that ended eunuch preeminence and even political involvement at court. Military commanders dominated the remainder of the dynasty. Cao Cao (155–220), the most important of these commanders, gained control over the court and assumed the appellation "King of Wei," challenging the Han practice of granting the title "king" only to those of imperial blood. For the ensuing two decades he increased the territory under his control, but the empire itself continued to fragment. A weak emperor and court proved to be tantalizing to power-hungry leaders. Thus, shortly after Cao Cao's death, his son Cao Pi (187–226) compelled the last Han emperor to abdicate and then, like his father, proclaimed himself to be the King of Wei, no doubt with the intention of establishing his own dynasty. Four centuries of Han rule came to an end, and in the next three hundred or so years China splintered into different regions, with no single dynasty able to unify the country. China appeared to revert to circumstances similar to the Warring States period, when numerous rulers struggled to bring the country under one sword.

Traditional interpretations of the Han have attributed its collapse to the eunuchs, the consort families, callow emperors, and manipulative regents. To be sure, each of these groups played a role in the dynasty's decline. However, larger forces should not be discounted. The power of a few aristocratic families, who often successfully evaded taxation, on occasion undermined the court's ability to rule and to perform the public works and security tasks required of government. The court's resulting need for revenue prompted it to impose extraordinary levies on the less potent and more vulnerable segments of the population and to persist in the sale of offices and the ransoming of prisoners – practices initiated during Emperor Wu's reign. Such policies fueled unrest and led to rebellions such as those organized by the Yellow Turbans, which further enfeebled the dynasty.

Despite its failings, the Later Han experienced some notable successes. In the first century, it had triumphs in foreign relations, particularly in central Asia. The Xiongnu were twice expelled from Silk Roads oases – which they had occupied during the turbulence accompanying Wang Mang's reign – first in 73 (by Commander Dou Gu, d. 88) and second in 91 (by Commander Ban Chao, 32–102, a member of an illustrious family whose siblings included the historian Ban Gu, 32–92, and the reputed foremost woman scholar of ancient China, Ban Zhao, 45–ca. 116). Han troops then set up colonies in Turfan, Hami, and other gateways to central Asia. With Chinese control or at least influence over these neighboring towns, commerce flourished, and the Silk Roads became ever more traveled. By the middle of the second century, however, the costs of Chinese domination, which included expenses for the formation of military colonies near the frontiers, had mounted up. As the century came to an end and as the Han's fiscal resources continued to plummet, the dynasty began to abandon its bases. Trade with central Asia and Persia diminished.

In addition to the Xiongnu, the Later Han had to contend with the Xianbei, groups who had resided in Manchuria and eastern Inner Mongolia but had started to expel the Xiongnu from Mongolia. By the middle of the second century, a strong and charismatic Xianbei leader had defeated Han troops in several battles. The Xianbei refused to accept a tributary status, partly because their ruler did not wish to be treated as a vassal and partly because he resented limitations on commerce. He wanted direct access to Chinese grain, textiles, pottery, and luxury products. The resulting impasses about diplomatic status and about commerce repeatedly erupted into conflicts. Even after the death of the hostile Xianbei leader, battles between the Xianbei and the Han persisted.

Despite the weak government and the turbulence of the last century of Later Han rule, a few aspects of the economy flourished and social and cultural innovations were not necessarily curtailed. Some merchants and landlords who engaged in trade prospered from commerce, and agriculture too created wealth for the landowning elite, as sizable estates, which employed numerous laborers, were established. Farm workers and landowners fashioned a variety of arrangements, from tenancy to sharecropping. Many landowners attempted, through bribery or other tactics, to prevent their land from being registered on the tax rolls. The landowners also benefited because the court did not impose heavy land taxes. Similarly, peasants profited from the generally light land taxes but were harmed by the poll tax and the demand for corvée labor, both regressive burdens that fell disproportionately on the peasantry. Suffering from such burdens, many peasants required relief from the court in order to survive. For the first century of the Later Han, the court provided grain or waived taxes, but in the last half of the dynasty the government did not have the resources to assist the peasants. Many peasants either starved or were compelled to abandon their lands.

SPIRITUAL AND PHILOSOPHICAL DEVELOPMENTS IN THE HAN

The major philosophical development in the Han was the elite's adoption of Confucianism as the state cult. As early as the first reign in the Former Han, emperors began to practice Confucian rituals and ceremonies. Some of these rituals predated Confucianism, deriving from the Shang and early Zhou dynasties, but their incorporation into court ceremonies bolstered Confucianism. The Han emperors worshipped Heaven (which was associated with previous dynasties), continued their ancestral cults, and performed sacrifices at such revered sites as Mount Tai. The court also persisted in the divination practices of earlier eras, including scapulimancy and the interpretation of omens. However, it supplemented these rituals with the underlying rational philosophy of Confucianism. The Confucian texts were standardized, and the Confucian virtues were restated. The court prepared a new calendar, an important Confucian responsibility, and a water clock was developed to demarcate the day's divisions. The emperors mandated, in accordance with Confucian rituals, the use of music and dance at court.

They also emphasized proper funerary practices and continued, like earlier dynasties, to construct elaborate tombs laden with precious bronzes, jades, and textiles, with walls emblazoned with portraits of attendants of the dead, whom they might need in the next life. Perhaps as critical, funerary officials and coffin makers tried to preserve bodies or at least to arrest their disintegration. In several instances, they showed great faith in the restorative powers of jade by encasing corpses in jade suits to prevent natural deterioration. Such efforts did not live up to expectations, but the use of several coffins and additional precautions to ward off environmental influences, notably in the Mawangdui tombs discovered in Changsha in the modern province of Hunan, turned out to be effective. These bodies had not decomposed when they were found two thousand years later.

Naturally, the court's and the elite's rituals did not encompass the spiritual activities of ordinary Chinese. Popular cults that sought union with and assistance from ghosts and spirits flourished, as did others that worshipped the Queen Mother of the West. However, without much evidence, knowledge of their practices and beliefs remains limited. Divination and searches for techniques leading to immortality were no doubt features of the practices of ordinary Chinese. Despite repeated criticism of the costs of these rituals, the court, as well as Chinese of relatively modest means, persisted in conducting these ceremonies. Rational critiques of the value of such rituals fared little better. Wang Chong (27–ca. 100), a materialist philosopher, sought, in his *Lunheng* (*Discourses Weighed in the Balance*), to deflate what he perceived to be the superstitious or fallacious beliefs that informed the rituals. He scorned the efficacy of shamans and diviners and rejected the possibilities of an afterlife and of Heaven's intrusion into human affairs. Arguing that only tangible, material phenomena could affect human beings, he challenged such activities as funeral ceremonies and consultation of oracles. His views contrasted sharply with those of the Former Han Confucian thinker Dong Zhongshu, a principal exponent of the hypothesis that natural catastrophes were Heaven-sent indicators of displeasure with the emperor. Dong Zhongshu championed the Mandate of Heaven theory, emphasizing an emperor's moral failings and his unethical conduct of government as causes of natural disasters afflicting China and as indications of Heaven's growing dissatisfaction with an emperor's rule. This view bolstered official attempts to use untoward events to criticize a particular emperor and to promote new and different policies and interpretations. As a Son of Heaven, the emperor, in theory, had a direct connection with Heaven, and dislocations in the natural sphere attested to imperial misrule.

Yin-yang and the Five Phases (or Elements) theory also contributed to the proliferation of rituals at court and in Chinese society. In the third century BCE, Zou Yan (305–240 BCE) had laid out an explanation of the operation of the universe based on these conceptions, an explanation many Confucians adopted during the Han dynasty. He maintained that the interaction of *yin*, identified with inertness, passivity, and feminine traits, and *yang*, identified with dynamism, activity, and masculine traits, resulted in the cycles of change and development with which mankind is familiar. In line with the Five Phases theory, he asserted that the cycles consisted of five stages. Indeed, that number characterized most classifications. For example, the principal colors in the Five Phases theory were green, red, yellow, white, and black, and the principal animals were sheep, fowl, ox, dog, and pig. The seasons, emotions, and tastes were intertwined and integrated with the Five Phases. According to this interpretation, the most important constituents were wood, earth, fire, metal, and water. Proponents of the scheme engaged in pseudoscientific speculation and tried to derive political significance from the Five Phases. The theoretical frameworks of *yin-yang* and the Five Phases, which posited that the forces of the Phases influenced each other without any direct physical links, encouraged the development of explanations that went beyond the immediately visible. A number of thinkers, who were swayed by these theories, began to formulate explanations based upon nonobservable phenomena about objects not directly in touch with each other. Zhang Heng (78–139), the most prominent of these thinkers, determined the numerical value of *pi*, a nonobservable phenomenon, and developed the seismograph, a device that measured the severity of earthquakes, even those occurring a considerable distance away. Others used the Five Phases scheme to devise reputed cures for a variety of ailments, because illness often became defined as an excess of either *yin* or *yang*. A concoction that contained the exact opposite of the abundant element, either *yin* or *yang*, supposedly served as an ideal antidote. Medicine thus often became a by-product of *yin-yang* in attempting to achieve a balance in the human body.

This orderly conception of the universe also proved to be a potent political symbol. Successive founders of dynasties selected an element and the associated color to represent the new rulers. The choice was largely determined by their predecessors' symbols, which appeared in a continuum of fire, water, earth, wood, and metal, with each transcending and overwhelming its predecessor. Han rulers chose at least two distinct representations, the earth with the matching color of yellow and fire with its attendant color of red. They also abided by the other elements – taste, animals, etc. – in the rituals and ceremonies carried out at court. The linking of *yin-yang* and the Five Phases, which apparently enjoyed widespread popular support during the dynasty, no doubt bolstered Han rule.

However, Confucianism provided the repository for the major ideas, beliefs, and rituals of the dynasty. The Han became associated with Confucianism. Dong Zhongshu probably had as much as anyone to do with the emergence of Confucianism, for his views influenced Emperor Wu, who became a patron, initiated Confucian rituals at court, established the Imperial Academy (Taixue) where potential officials could be trained, and promoted scholarship, including the selection of the Five Classics as the main orthodox texts. Commentaries were written to provide official interpretations of these somewhat cryptic texts. For example, the Guliang and Gongyang commentaries attempted to supply greater moral significance to the dry accounts preserved in the *Spring and Autumn Annals.* The appointment of Confucian tutors to the emperors early in the Former Han solidified links between Confucian scholars and the government. The court appeared to value education, and, although scholars did not dominate government, learning slowly became a criterion in the selection of officials. With growing acceptance at court, Confucianism and its attendant practices of ancestor worship and filial piety took hold among the populace.

Confucianism also sought to define the role of women during this time. Ban Zhao, an extraordinarily accomplished woman who completed the first dynastic history of China, wrote *Lessons for Women* (*Nüjie*), on proper behavior. She counseled women to be submissive to their husbands and to respect their male relatives, including brothers, fathers-in-law, and brothers-in-law. She also advised women to remain faithful and to allow their husbands to bring concubines into their households. On the other hand, her text states that women ought to become well educated, mostly in order to assist their husbands. Ban Zhao herself was prodigiously talented. In addition to editing the final version of the Former Han dynastic history and writing the *Lessons for Women*, she composed poems and expressed considerable interest in mathematics and astronomy. Yet obedience to males was her principal message for women. From this time on, educated women throughout traditional Chinese history read and memorized the text, and even women who could not read or write were taught to memorize the work.

Although Ban Zhao's prescriptions for women may have been well known, it is unclear whether they reflected reality. Were gender roles and statuses as clear cut as Ban Zhao specified them? In practice, did women have more rights than Ban Zhao's text has us believe? In a few of the later dynasties, women could own property, and some in the upper classes took an active role in society. Were they submissive within the family or did they have leverage, especially after giving birth to a male heir? Similarly, kinship relations, as described in Confucian texts, may not have always fit the stereotypes of filial piety and of younger generations owing respect, if not obeisance, to the older generation. Even at court, there were examples of sons not on good terms with and, on occasion, challenging their fathers. Such unfilial behavior was replicated among ordinary folk in other dynasties. Evidence about women and kinship relations in the

Han is limited. Gender and family relations in later dynasties, for which more information is available, will be covered later in the book.

The shocking events at the Later Han court and the accompanying turbulence in society at large were disturbing. Like other court institutions, the Imperial Academy lost its vigor, and its scholars and students became less attentive and increasingly corrupt. Confucian scholars who advocated reform scarcely had much influence. In these trying times, some Confucians sought remedies by proposing harsher laws and better means of recruiting moral officials. Invocations to abide by Confucian morality and veiled warnings about the loss of the Mandate of Heaven did not forestall the decay, corruption, and disarray at court. Disputes among the Confucian scholars about their doctrines and about Confucius himself also undercut the status of Confucianism. The fall of the Later Han therefore dealt a damaging blow to the philosophy that provided its ideological underpinning.

HAN LITERATURE AND ART

Han literature is often closely identified with the works of the historians Sima Qian and Ban Gu. According to tradition, Sima Qian's *Shiji* (or *Records of the Grand Historian*) owes its origins, in part, to filial piety. Sima Tan (ca. 165–110 BCE), Sima Qian's father and the grand historian and astrologer during Emperor Wu's reign, had conceived a plan to record events of the past and to write accounts of the great historical figures. He collected source materials but died before actually beginning to produce this historical record. Traditional sources portray a touching deathbed scene in which the grand historian elicited a pledge from his son, his successor in the post at court, to finish the grandiose project he had embarked upon. Sima Qian (145 or 135–86 BCE) fulfilled his promise, despite numerous obstacles and personal losses. One such setback resulted from his support for Li Ling (d. 74 BCE), a general who had been defeated and then captured by the Xiongnu. In defending Li Ling and arguing that his troops had been ill-supplied and had been hastily dispatched to meet the enemy, Sima Qian alienated the emperor, who in his anger had the grand historian castrated. Customarily, people so punished committed suicide. Instead Sima Qian persisted in his work, believing that the future would absolve him for not bowing to the customary dictates of his time. He had a filial obligation to complete the history, but he also believed that his work would clear his reputation from the aspersions cast upon it because he had not followed societal norms.

His work, particularly its organization, would provide a model for future histories. He divided his book into four sections, a pattern that would be followed by the twenty-five subsequent official dynastic histories. The first section, known as the "Basic Annals," consisted of a year-by-year account of dynasties and rulers of the past, focusing primarily on events at court. The second section was composed of chronological tables citing the significant dates and events in the country's various regions and "feudal" states, while the third part contained treatises or essays concerning taxation, the calendar, rituals, the military, and religions. The last section provided biographies of leading officials, princes, consorts, philosophers, merchants, assassins, and poets and descriptions of foreign lands and states.

Sima Qian was the first Chinese historian to devote much of his work to accounts of the merits and defects of individuals. History, in his hands, became the study of great men, their attributes, and their actions. The biographical format served as a splendid vehicle for the didacticism implicit in the work, and the actions of both the virtuous and the treacherous offered models of proper and improper behavior. The emphasis on anecdotes in the biographies conveyed the values that Sima Qian and his society perceived as the most conducive to the development of good moral individuals and a harmonious society. He focused on the eminent, but, unlike earlier Chinese histories, did not ignore commoners or individuals with nonelite occupations. Such a widening of the scope of biographies was useful, for ordinary people could more readily identify with this work than with an account that dealt exclusively with the upper classes. Sima Qian often added a personal touch to the biographies, making his own value judgments and criticizing the actions of some of his subjects while praising others. He did not pretend to be totally objective.

The "Basic Annals" and the accounts of the Zhou and early Han were relatively straightforward, but Sima Qian occasionally appended his own comments. Despite his critical and didactic analyses, much of the work, particularly about the distant past, consists of paraphrases and summaries and, in some cases, verbatim copies from earlier texts. As the history approached his own times, however, his own original writing surfaced. In these sections, he no longer simply followed the accounts and interpretations of other texts but offered original conceptions of events closer to his times. Much of the section on the Han was new, reflecting Sima Qian's own views. In these sections, his didacticism surfaced. He presented these accounts so that readers would be exposed to proper role models. This didactic emphasis in the *Shiji* would have a remarkable impact on future historical writing. The dynastic histories would use the same or similar organizational schemes as the *Shiji*, as well as using history for didactic purposes.

While the next major history shared the *Shiji*'s didactic motivations and organization, it diverged somewhat and became the closest model for later dynastic histories. Like the *Shiji*, it originated with the father of those historians who received credit for it. Ban Biao (3–54), who lived through and witnessed the career of Wang Mang, had decided to continue the *Shiji* through the Former Han dynasty. He died before he got very far, but his son Ban Gu, like Sima Tan's son Sima Qian, assumed the task that his father had just begun. Yet Ban Gu charted a different course, for he was determined to produce a work that could stand on its own. He elected to write an independent study of the Former Han, ending with Wang Mang's usurpation. The work he compiled was the *Han shu* (or *History of the [Former] Han*), the first of the dynastic histories. He too did not live to complete the work, dying in prison while awaiting the results of an investigation into totally trumped-up charges against him. The court recruited his remarkable sister, Ban Zhao, to finish the history, but Ban Gu has traditionally been credited as the compiler.

The *Han shu* borrowed from the *Shiji*, but eventually included new material concerning the period after Sima Qian's death. Unlike the *Shiji*, it confined itself to a single dynasty, and its relative closeness to the events described made it less prone to accepting legendary and dubious accounts. Ban Gu was generally more reliable than Sima Qian but could, on occasion, be as credulous. Yet his work is more precise than the *Shiji*, and, unlike Sima Qian, he rarely intruded his personal judgments. He adopted a more formal and more balanced tone and excluded the revealing asides that Sima Qian incorporated in his work. Ban Gu's more impersonal style served as a more fitting model because the later dynastic histories, which were produced under court sponsorship, were collaborative efforts and precluded personal touches. Despite its significance as a model, the *Han shu* has been overshadowed by Sima Qian's work, with its more idiosyncratic and colorful style and anecdotes.

It should come as no surprise that the first political unification of China engendered valuable developments in both poetry and prose. The court itself contributed to such developments. Emperor Wu founded a Music Bureau in 120 BCE to devise music and verse for official ceremonies. He and later emperors commissioned Bureau officials to compose songs for court occasions. These commissions led to the creation of new poetic forms to evoke some of the traditional themes of Chinese poetry – sorrow at separation, love, and capture by the enemy in warfare. The *fu* (or prose poem), which supplemented the telegraphic and concise language and images of other kinds of poetry with descriptions beyond the constraints of the poetic lines of the times, became an important form and occasionally received court patronage. Descriptions in some *fu* of the capital cities and palaces and of court entertainments yield evidence of Han splendor. The greater length and expansiveness of the *fu* coincidentally dovetailed with the Han expansionist foreign policy, particularly during Emperor Wu's reign.

Figure 3.3 Belt buckle, Han dynasty (206 BCE–220 CE), China, third–second century BCE, gilt bronze, H. 2¼″ (5.7 cm), W. 1½″ (3.8 cm). New York, Metropolitan Museum of Art, Rogers Fund, 1918. Acc.no. 18.33.1. © 2013. Image copyright The Metropolitan Museum of Art / Art Resource / Scala, Florence

Figure 3.4 Flying or galloping horse, western or "celestial" breed, standing on a swallow, bronze, Eastern Han dynasty, second century CE, from Wuwei, Gansu province, China, 34.5 cm. © The Art Archive / Alamy

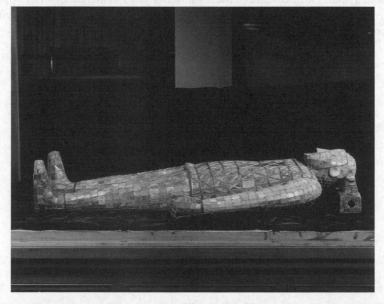

Figure 3.5 Funeral suit of Princess Tou Wan, wife of prince Liu Sheng, jade, Western Han dynasty, late second century BCE, from her tomb at Mancheng, Hebei province, China, 172 cm, seen from side. © The Art Archive / Alamy

Figure 3.6 Han-dynasty animal pen. New York, Metropolitan Museum of Art, Charlotte C. and John C. Weber Collection, Gift of Charlotte C. and John C. Weber, 1994. Inv. no. 1994.605.21. © 2013. Image copyright The Metropolitan Museum of Art / Art Resource / Scala, Florence

Artistic developments also often reflected the grandeur of Han aspirations. Elaborate tombs with numerous burial objects confirm the desire for majesty and ornateness. The varieties of shapes (rectangular, square), materials (stone, brick), and motifs (bedrooms and a kitchen for the comfort of the deceased in the afterlife) reflect the differing regions in which the tombs have been uncovered. The tombs of Liu Sheng (d. 113 BCE; Emperor Wu's elder brother) and his wife, Dou Wan, which were discovered in 1968, offer evidence of attempts to show off the court's majesty. The corpses were clothed in suits composed of about two thousand pieces of jade, linked with gold thread. This elaborate, costly, and painstaking work, which was designed to preserve the bodies but also meant to show the dynasty's majesty, indicates the grandiose ambitions of the Han elite. Both life-size and miniature sculptures reveal similar objectives: the desire for grandiosity and the intricacy of exquisite detail. Large statues in front of the tombs honored Han generals and officials, and relatively small clay figurines of servants, animals, and entertainers were buried with the deceased. Because members of the elite planned to recreate their lavish lifestyle in the afterlife, they required the services of these clay representations of men and animals who had served them during their sojourn on Earth. The era of sacrifices, particularly human victims, had passed long ago. The Han elite thus substituted models (*mingqi*), which included watchtowers, musicians, acrobats, and domestic animals, to accompany the corpses on their presumed journeys after death. These exquisitely detailed figurines and objects, which required vast amounts of labor, confirm the grandness of the elite's vision of themselves and their society. Like the tombs of earlier dynasties, Han graves contained numerous bronze artifacts, including harnesses, swords, drums, belt buckles, and mirrors, which were often embellished with elaborate decorations of real and mythical animals, humans, and symbols representing the prevalent *yin-yang* and Five Phases cosmogony. Jade objects (e.g. the burial suits for Liu Sheng and Dou Wan), and lacquer bowls, baskets, and boxes, with depictions of humans, animals, and landscapes, also testify to the Han's majestic and ostentatious aspirations.

Han art, in addition, attests to China's increasing contacts with the outside world. Chinese silks, which were transported via the numerous silk roads that led to the west, were highly valued. To the south, the silks reached India, but the Indian practice of cremation of the dead in full dress, as well as the hot and humid climate, meant that few such textiles survived in the neighboring subcontinent. India also exported Chinese textiles to the Roman Empire, another reason few remain in India. A further outlet for the textiles was the Xiongnu elite, whose demand for Chinese silks was met by the development of a new silk road that wound its way to Mongolia. Chinese silk panels and fabrics have been uncovered at the tombs of Xiongnu leaders at Noyan Ula, an indication of the value accorded them by the nomadic rulers. Designs with animals, as well as cloud motifs, appealed to the nomadic pastoral elite. Such designs apparently attracted the peoples of central Asia, west Asia, and the Roman Empire.

Silk Roads caravans wound their way from various centers in China to its northwestern frontiers, where they encountered the inhospitable Taklamakan Desert, which they skirted via such northern towns and oases as Turfan and Hami or via the south through such towns as Khotan. They then intersected at Kashgar and headed west through Persia to west Asia. A number of silks and silk fragments have been found at Turfan and other Silk Roads oases; some were clearly designed for an export market. As will be apparent later, China's growing contacts with the outside world influenced its culture, challenging the view that China was self-sufficient and isolated.

Painting, the other great art form identified with the Chinese, has left barely a trace in this era. Wall paintings enlivened many Han palaces and homes, but these have not survived. Paintings on silk generally met the same fate. Paper had been developed, but painters scarcely understood the possibilities of this new medium. Some paintings in tombs have survived. They range from depictions of daily life (including farming, hunting, and fishing tableaux) to representations of human figures and divinities illustrating Confucian morality and Daoist ideals. It seems likely that the paintings that have not survived dealt with similar motifs – human figures symbolizing Confucian tenets described and analyzed in the Five Classics, clouds and other natural scenes, and palaces, houses, and other buildings. Depictions on lacquerware, the finest examples of which were produced in Sichuan, focus on the same subjects: animals and natural scenes and humans representing Confucian or Daoist precepts. Like silk, lacquer appears to have been highly prized abroad because boxes and other lacquer vessels have been found in a wide area, ranging from Korea to central Asia. The names of two painters have been found inscribed on lacquer objects unearthed in Lelang, Korea; by a remarkable coincidence, these same names were also found on a lacquer artifact unearthed in Noyan Ula.

A variety of foreign discoveries filtered into Han China. Glass and pearls reached China by sea via the Indian Ocean; alfalfa, a feed for horses, and grapes were central Asian and Persian contributions that Zhang Qian probably introduced; and oranges and lichee nuts became familiar as the Han colonized south China. Pomegranates, walnuts, and other products from Persia and central Asia that were attributed to Zhang Qian's mission actually arrived later, when China had even more extended contacts with the outside world. Cultural imports were as significant. The Chinese lute, known as the *pipa*, had central Asian ancestry, and its prototype is reflected on earlier sculptures found in central Asia. In the south, the Chinese were exposed to the zither.

In addition to music, other entertainments owed much to foreign influence. Persian and central Asian jugglers and acrobats brought their skills to the court. A few foreign dancers may have reached Han China, but the real vogue for foreign dancing developed in later dynasties. Falconry, a practice associated with the pastoral peoples on the northern frontier, also began to reach the sedentary agricultural Chinese.

Figure 3.7 Female dancer, Western Han dynasty (206 BCE–9 CE), second century BCE, earthenware with slip and pigments, H. 21″ (53.3 cm). New York, Metropolitan Museum of Art, Charlotte C. and John C. Weber Collection, Gift of Charlotte C. and John C. Weber, 1992. Acc.no.: 1992.165.19. Photo: Seth Joel. © 2013. Image copyright The Metropolitan Museum of Art / Art Resource / Scala, Florence

This vibrant culture also manifested itself in technical and scientific discoveries. Paper was invented in the Later Han, but at that time the Chinese scarcely made use of it. They were more aware of and made use of bricks, another discovery, in tomb construction. As was to be expected of an agricultural society so concerned with Heaven and with possible natural threats to its livelihood, astronomy made great strides. Han astronomers discovered sunspots, calculated with precision the number of days in a year, and ascertained the moon's exact orbit. Zhang Heng's invention of a seismograph – evidence of the pragmatic nature of China's scientific efforts and of its focus on natural disasters – has already been mentioned. Pragmatism and a scientific attitude were also evident in the writings of Zhang Heng and Wang Chong, who both emphasized a critical attitude as a guideline for inquiry about and analysis of natural phenomena.

In sum, despite its failures and eventual collapse, the Han played a central role in the development of Chinese civilization. It created the first effective governmental institutions to rule the entire country and adopted Confucianism as the state cult. Confucianism defined proper relationships between the generations and designated gender roles, and Ban Zhao, the foremost woman scholar of ancient China, described proper behavior for women. The Han delineated a new system of foreign relations, and, by creating ritualized, economic, and political methods of dealing with foreigners, it simultaneously affirmed the identities of those within its borders as different from the outsiders. It established institutions for local government and performed vital societal tasks, including conducting a census – perhaps the first such undertaking in world history. The census registered a total of over fifty-five million people, making China the world's most populous country. The greater population was mostly in the rural areas, but the capital city and a few other cities attested to the first significant urbanization in Chinese history. Economic growth and greater agricultural production in the countryside permitted the development of such urban centers.

FURTHER READING

Bret Hinsch, *Women in Early Imperial China* (Lanham, MD.: Rowman & Littlefield, 2002).

Mark Lewis, *Early Chinese Empires: Qin and Han History* (Cambridge, MA: Harvard University Press, 2007).

Michael Loewe, *Everyday Life in Early Imperial China During the Han Period, 202 B.C.–A.D. 220* (New York: Putnam, 1968).

Yu Ying-shih, *Trade and Expansion in Han China* (Berkeley: University of California Press, 1967).

[4] CHAOS AND RELIGIOUS AND POLITICAL RESPONSES, 220–581

Three Kingdoms
Rise of South China
Foreigners and North China
Northern Wei
Spiritual Developments, Post-Han
Buddhism Enters China
Literature, Science, and the Arts
   in a Period of Division

THREE KINGDOMS

The immediate aftermath of the Han's collapse saw the fragmentation of China into the Three Kingdoms (*Sanguo*). In 220, Cao Pi (187–226) overthrew the Later Han and established his own Wei dynasty in China's traditional heartland. He gambled that his control over Luoyang and Changan, the two preeminent capital cities, would offer him legitimacy and would quell political challenges to his rule. His gamble did not pay off, for shortly thereafter Liu Bei (161–223), a descendant of the Han imperial family, created his own dynasty in Sichuan, Guizhou, and Hunan. Chinese later dubbed Liu's dynasty the Shu Han, the Shu deriving from the name of the state in Sichuan during the Zhou dynasty. In 222, a certain Sun Chuan (182–252) also broke away, founding the Wu dynasty in the region to the south, adjacent to the Yangzi River. The Three Kingdoms clashed repeatedly as each jockeyed for position and sought to dominate as the principal unifier of China.

A History of China, First Edition. Morris Rossabi.
© 2014 Morris Rossabi. Published 2014 by Blackwell Publishing Ltd.

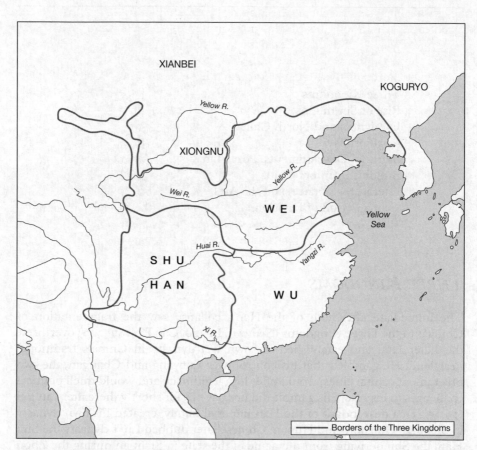

Map 4.1 The Three Kingdoms

Chinese accounts later romanticized this era's warfare. Contemporaries, however, confronted chaotic conditions. Nonetheless, the romantic versions were eventually gathered together and compiled into an episodic, lengthy, and popular fourteenth-century novel, the *Sanguozhi yanyi* (*The Romance of the Three Kingdoms*), by Luo Guanzhong (ca. 1330–1400). Because these later accounts embroidered upon the stories of this era's commanders and strategists, the military leaders became legendary heroes. The Shu Han kingdom perhaps provided the most important heroes. Liu Bei became portrayed as a benevolent sage in the Confucian tradition and was worshipped, specifically in the city of Chengdu in Sichuan. His leading general, Guan Yu (d. 219), depicted as red-faced with a long beard, was transformed in folk religion to Guan Di, the God of War, a subduer of demons in the Daoist pantheon and an important figure in Buddhism. Similarly, the brilliant tactician Zhuge Liang (181–234) was idealized as the military genius par excellence. They have continued their hold on the Chinese through portrayals in temples, operas, films, television, and restaurants, and even in card and video games.

Each kingdom initially expanded its territory but then faltered. Shu Han overwhelmed the groups along the Sichuan frontiers; Wu moved into modern Vietnam; and Wei steadily gained influence over Korea and southern Manchuria. Yet the real conflict remained in China, since Wei, which controlled the area historically known as the Middle Kingdom and had access to its resources, had a decided advantage. By 263, it had defeated and expanded into Shu Han, and in 280 the Western Jin (265–316), its successor, once again brought China under one rule by subjugating Wu, thus ending the Three Kingdoms period. Unity, however, proved to be elusive. Within Wei itself, internal rivalries and turmoil undermined efforts at consolidation. Internecine struggles among military commanders plagued Wei, as the Cao family lost control. Finally, in 265, Sima Yan (236–290), one of the military leaders, defeated the other generals, overthrew Wei, and established himself as Emperor Wu of a new Western Jin dynasty.

The Western Jin's victory in 280 hardly created the stability needed for a strong dynasty. Sima Yan could not galvanize support from the great aristocratic families, who did not wish to knuckle under to a powerful central government. The tensions between centralization and the authority of local families had not subsided and would not abate for the rest of Chinese history. Such internal struggles weakened China and compelled it to make concessions that prevented it from exercising the power required to govern. Sima Yan tried to bring the elite families under his control and to reduce their independent authority. He sought to place the peasantry and the estate owners on the tax rolls but was unable to enforce his will on the elite families. The large estates often evaded taxes, and the aristocratic families frequently prevented census takers from including the peasants who worked estate lands on the tax rolls. Without such revenue, Sima Yan could not perform the tasks expected of an emperor, and the dynasty increasingly lost support. His death in 290 ended whatever stability had existed. Within a short time, the steppe nomads north of China attempted to fill the vacuum caused by the lack of an effective government.

RISE OF SOUTH CHINA

Non-Chinese peoples, recognizing the disarray in China, capitalized to form Chinese-style dynasties in north China, causing many Chinese to flee to the south. Fearing the threat posed to their culture by so-called northern barbarians, they migrated to a region where they could retain control. The less organized non-Chinese and Chinese of the south were no match for the immigrants, who took charge and whose efforts led to the growing assimilation of the native populations. The south was gradually integrated into Chinese civilization. Over at least three centuries if not longer, the Chinese spread throughout the south, which offered the bonus of more-fertile territory. In time, the Chinese in the south began to perceive of themselves as the standard bearers of Chinese culture and started to portray their compatriots in the north as less suited to inherit the mantle of Confucian civilization because they had fallen under foreign domination, had been influenced by foreign customs and institutions, and had strayed from Confucian orthodoxy. As a result, the south and the north were divided, and each section had separate dynasties – a development that lent its name to the era, the *Nanbeichao* (Period of Southern and Northern Dynasties, 220–581).

Yet, despite their brave invocations of traditional Chinese history and culture, the Chinese of the south could not unify the country. Six dynasties chose capitals at Nanjing (then known as Jiankang), but none could galvanize sufficient support within their own regions to overwhelm the north. In 317, the first of these dynasties selected Jin, the same dynastic name that Sima Yan had chosen several decades earlier. Scholars refer to the dynasty as the Eastern Jin (317–420) to distinguish it from its predecessor, which had been based in the north. None of the six dynasties could control the aristocratic landowning elite that often dominated the military. Struggles among commanders were common, and the ensuing wars and revolts led to the decline and fall of some previously prominent families, which resulted in increased social mobility as new families came to the fore. Thus, the great families of the Han faced challenges from newly powerful families who had made better adjustments to the new environment they encountered in the south. When one dynasty finally restored unity in the sixth century, great aristocratic families would still play significant political roles, but their composition would differ somewhat from that of the families of the Han. This so-called oligarchy did not remain monolithic, as the fortunes of individual families varied considerably.

Each succeeding southern dynasty was wracked with the same frustrating impediments. All wanted to reoccupy the traditional northern heartland of China. Although the Eastern Jin succeeded in conquering the southwest, including Sichuan, it could never consistently challenge and gain additional territory from the northern foreign dynasties. In 420, its failures and internal weaknesses permitted Liu Yu (363–422), one of the dynasty's leading commanders, to overthrow its last ruler and to establish his own short-lived dynasty, the Song (often referred to as the Liu Song, 420–479, to distinguish it from the later and more renowned Song dynasty), and to assume the title of

Emperor Wu. Although the new ruling group was initially promising because of Liu Yu's own abilities, it barely lasted for two generations before falling to rival leaders, who established the Southern Qi (479–502) dynasty. Yet again the Southern Qi could not suppress internal dissidents, and indeed divisions arose in the ruling family, culminating when one family member overthrew the last emperor and founded the Liang (502–579) dynasty.

Emperor Wu, the Liang founder, differed from most other rulers of this era in the longevity of his reign. His almost five decades on the throne witnessed a period of domestic peace, offering opportunities to strengthen the state and to emerge as a potential unifier of China. Wu also had the advantage of state sponsorship of Buddhism, which ensured the support of its monks. An ardent convert to Buddhism, he issued regulations banning the use of animals or parts of them for sacrifices or medicines. He also built temples, encouraged wealthy and pious patrons to donate funds to the monasteries, and lectured and wrote explanations and interpretations of Buddhist texts. His attempts to limit the practice of Daoism and the activities of Daoists were the first indications of tensions between the two religions. However, Wu's devotion to Buddhism and particularly his attacks on Daoism alienated many in his domains and undermined efforts at unity. In addition, some Confucian scholars deplored the gains made by the Buddhists and criticized them and their ideas as "barbarian." Wu's patronage, nonetheless, bore fruit, as later sources reveal that the total number of monks increased from 32,500 to 82,700 during his reign.

Yet hostility based on his favoritism toward Buddhism and, even more important, his inability to control his own commanders and the elite led to the same disunity that prevailed among the earlier dynasties. The ensuing weakness permitted a non-Chinese commander from the north to seize most of the dynasty's lands and to briefly occupy the Liang capital. After this loss, the Liang made a feeble attempt at restoration in its southern domains, with a different city as the capital, but its vulnerability had been revealed. Within a decade, Chen Baxian (503–559), still another military commander, led a successful coup d'état and founded the Chen (557–589), the last of these southern dynasties. The Chen controlled less territory and was thus weaker than the Liang, which reduced its chances of survival. Like its predecessors, the Chen was plagued by internal rifts and weak government, which rendered it vulnerable when the Sui, a northern dynasty, challenged it in the 580s.

The southern Chinese dynasties could not resolve the problems that the northern immigrants had brought with them to the south. Leading families, who supplied the most important military commanders, continued to challenge and thus enfeeble the central government. Large landowners evaded taxes and had their own military forces, which undermined the dynasties' efforts to dominate their domains. Conversion to a new religion such as Buddhism, which often served to unify people in a state or region, did not translate into an effective and cohesive government. Turbulence in the form of coup d'états and struggles for succession confronted each dynasty. Assertions of China's indigenous traditions and affirmations of Buddhism were insufficient for restoration of the Chinese empire.

FOREIGNERS AND NORTH CHINA

North China was the region influenced by non-Chinese peoples during this era. The turbulence of the Three Kingdoms period left China vulnerable, permitting foreigners living north of China to make incursions on or conquests of Chinese soil. China was no doubt influenced by these foreigners, who established dynasties to govern north China. They introduced powerful military forces and martial values into the north. One of the foreign dynasties fostered Buddhism and played a vital role in its transmission. None of the dynasties initiated an attack on Confucianism or on Chinese tradition. Indeed they frequently portrayed themselves as accommodating to Chinese culture in order to gain the allegiance of the subjugated Chinese population. Nonetheless, with ever-greater influence from the so-called barbarians, the north became, to the Chinese who migrated to the south, less and less regarded as Chinese. Yet a strong core of Chinese traditions and institutions survived in the north.

For almost a century after the fall of the Han, Chinese dynasties managed to rule much of the north. The Wei and then after 265 the Western Jin ruled much of the north, but their internal squabbles undermined them and disrupted relations with the northern frontier peoples. Trade with China, which was a vital source of income for the northern steppe peoples, gradually diminished, prompting frustration and then foreigners' efforts to obtain, by force, products denied them by chaotic conditions within China. In these difficult times, the perpetual agreement whereby a descendant of the Xiongnu leaders (or *shanyu*s) was a hostage at the Chinese court ended. With China fragmenting, the successors of the original Xiongnu groups had little to gain from such cooperation or submissiveness to the Chinese court. In 304, the *shanyu* hostage fled from the Western Jin capital and declared his independence. Having been exposed to Chinese culture, he adopted a Chinese name for his dynasty. Han, or Later Han, the name he initially selected, naturally resonated in China and revealed an effort to win over the Chinese by appearing to have become sinicized. The Later Han dynasty (later renamed the Zhao) moved so briskly to capitalize on China's internal conflicts that it occupied Luoyang in 311 and Changan in 316, in the process imprisoning two emperors of the tottering Western Jin dynasty.

Having gained control of much of the north, the Later Han/Zhao rulers sought to win the allegiance of the people by establishing a Chinese-style dynasty. However, this attempt created fissures among the conquerors. Many wished to retain their traditional nomadic society, with occasional forays into China to expropriate its resources, and opposed the creation of a Chinese-like sedentary society. Unlike the founders of the Later Han/Zhao, they sought to avert Chinese influence for fear of "spiritual pollution" of their traditional way of life. Also unlike their more sinicized brothers, they did not wish to recruit and cooperate with the Chinese to set up an administration capable of ruling the vast Chinese empire. Raids and conquests, not governance, were their goals. Attacks, pillaging, and retreat into the northern steppe lands had customarily been their tactics, and they did not relish abandoning their freer and more mobile existence. These attitudes clashed with those of the Later Han/ Zhao rulers, who employed Chinese bureaucrats to assist them in ruling China. The growing accommodation to Chinese culture of the Later Han/ Zhao elite provoked hostility among the nomads, which rapidly resulted in a violent rift and the undermining of the dynasty's attempts to establish a stable rule over China.

The Later Han/Zhao's efforts to fuse a nomadic military society with a Chinese-style administration thus foundered. Shortly after the proclamation of the dynasty, Shi Le (274–333), one of the commanders who opposed the dynasty's acculturation to China, began covertly to undermine his increasingly sinicized confreres by organizing leaders against them. Moving cautiously and gradually, he finally rebelled, crushed the Later Han/Zhao, and established his own Later Zhao dynasty. The Later Han/Zhao rulers had recognized the importance of creating a bureaucracy to administer their domains, but they did not succeed in attracting the support of nomadic pastoral leaders for this effort. Their inability to persuade these leaders of the need for a Chinese-style administration spelled disaster. Relying principally on Chinese officials to help them proved to be insufficient to maintain their fragile confederation. They could not retain the loyalty of nomadic leaders who were unaccustomed to a regular stable governmental organization.

Yet, ironically, Shi Le and other more traditionally minded leaders who persisted in raids and conquests also could not maintain the allegiance of their own people beyond one generation because such loyalty was granted to a specific person and could not readily be bequeathed or transferred to successors or descendants. Thus Shi Le's nephew Shi Hu (295–349) was faced with the disaffection of most of his father's previously staunch allies, and their hostility eventually led to a complete rift, culminating within a few years in the collapse of the Later Zhao dynasty. The first attempt of a steppe people to create a Chinese-style administration thus failed.

The peoples and tribes northeast of China, along the Manchurian frontier, proved to be more effective in establishing more-enduring Chinese-style dynasties. The regions they inhabited had a mixed economy of pastoral nomadism, subsistence agriculture, and hunting and fishing. The sedentary agricultural domain gave rise to a Chinese-style administration, providing experience and exposure to a more tightly centralized bureaucratic system. Success in establishing control over north China entailed both military power and a bureaucracy, which the peoples of the northeast frontier developed more readily than had the steppe nomads directly north of China. A leader who aspired to govern China needed to satisfy and yet tame his own people's military force and its leaders, organize an administration capable of ruling the Chinese, and also gradually limit the authority of their own chiefs. The governor or eventually emperor had to dominate both the tribes and the bureaucracy. He would rely mostly on Chinese to staff the bureaucracy but would retain military power for his own people.

The Yan (337–370) dynasties, composed principally of the Xianbei peoples, witnessed the first attempt to handle this delicate balancing act. Founded in the middle of the fourth century, the Former Yan made great strides toward administration of an empire. Its rulers recruited Chinese advisers to help them govern; the Chinese were willing to serve the Yan because, unlike the Chinese dynasties, it had maintained order and stability. Thus the Yan began to expand from its base in Liaodong and shortly incorporated much of the modern provinces of Anhui, Hunan, and Shaanxi, subjugating or sometimes merely assimilating both Chinese and non-Chinese peoples in their new domains. By 342, it had resisted an incursion from the marauder Shi Hu and had planned and constructed a splendid capital in Longcheng, west of the Longshan mountains in the modern province of Liaoning, partly to celebrate this success. Ironically, as the Yan rulers accommodated to Chinese culture, they eventually confronted the same problems as the Chinese dynasties in the south. To attract the support of Chinese advisers, as well as the Chinese landowning elite, they made financial concessions, which weakened them considerably and exposed their vulnerabilities. Similarly, like other groups from the region north of China, they encountered difficulties in developing a regular and orderly system of succession to the throne, which was still more debilitating to the dynasty. In short, they could not balance the traditional military and the Chinese bureaucratic traditions without major disruptions and without giving in to one or the other.

The Yan rulers' fiscally damaging accommodation to the Chinese elite and their internal squabbles and divisions finally proved to be their undoing. In 370, Fu Jian (337–385), a leader of the Di peoples of southwestern China and Tibet and emperor of a Chinese-style dynasty known as the Former Qin (perhaps to conjure up images of the Qin dynasty, which had reunified China after the Warring States period), conquered and destroyed the Yan dynasty en route to his own attempt to unify China. However, Fu subsequently failed because of his inability to control his underlings. Like non-Chinese rulers from across the northern Chinese borders, he could retain his people's loyalty only through fear and through military successes. When he extended his conquests to much of north China, they remained with him. However, in 383, when he apparently suffered a defeat at the battle of the Fei River in an effort to expand into south China, his associates began to sever their links with him, and within a couple of years he had been murdered.

NORTHERN WEI

The Tavghach, a people known in Chinese transcription as the Tuoba, turned out to be the most sophisticated, successful, and influential of the northern peoples whom the Chinese had encountered. The Chinese sources record that the Tavghach, part of the Xianbei peoples, had devised their own written script, which would give them the signal honor of having developed the first written language of any of the Altaic groups, but no evidence of this script has survived. Nonetheless, creation of a written language indicated a significant advance and provided the potential for a true administrative structure. Yet the Tuoba did not dispense with reliance on the military. Their leaders were simply more successful at the balancing act of maintaining strong links with both their own armies and the sedentary bureaucracy. They did this by establishing two parallel lines of organization – one for the military directed by the commanders who proclaimed their loyalty to the Tuoba emperor, and the other for the bureaucracy with Chinese advisers and administrators under the emperor's supervision. On the one hand, this system offered enormous power to the emperor; on the other, it averted conflicts between the Chinese and Tuoba leadership because they had overlapping but different responsibilities. Each group was cohesive and performed its functions separately but remained under the direction of one man, the emperor.

Such unity enabled the Tuoba to annex additional lands and increase their power. As they incorporated new territories, they assumed the Chinese dynastic name of Northern Wei (386–534). They first attacked (and in 410 overwhelmed) the remnants of the declining Yan dynasty, thus adding much of northwest China to their lands. Having succeeded in this campaign, they then built a capital in Pingcheng, east of the modern city of Datong, along the frontiers between the steppes and the Chinese cultural areas. Steppe peoples would doubtless construe this choice of a site for the capital, so close to China, as an indication of growing acculturation to Chinese civilization. The Rouran, an amalgamation of nomadic groups north of the Wei in modern Mongolia, became dominant in the steppes. Not bound by the limitations of traditional Chinese dynasties, the Wei could compete with the Rouran not only within China but also in the steppes. In 425, their troops launched an attack all the way to northern Mongolia and defeated the Rouran. From that time on, the Rouran were on the defensive, and in 458 the Wei dealt them a devastating blow, compelling them to migrate west toward central Asia, where they occupied several towns and oases along the Silk Roads. The Northern Wei eventually forced the Rouran to move even farther west, where they probably merged with other groups to become known to Europeans as the Avars.

While the Wei gained victories over various groups, they were increasingly involved with China and its culture. Yet the Tuoba elite had to avoid an overly close identification with China if they were to maintain their identity, and for the first decades of their rule they managed to maintain their distance. However, they needed a system of thought or philosophy to justify their rule and to gain the acquiescence, if not support, of the Chinese majority whom they had subjugated and were now attempting to govern. Their own religious views were too rudimentary to contribute, in Chinese eyes, to their legitimacy.

Buddhism offered a splendid vehicle for the Wei's needs, but it encountered challenges before becoming the dominant religion. North China had been exposed to Buddhism over several centuries, and the first Wei emperor, recognizing Buddhism's potential, had recruited a monk to supervise the monasteries and to act as a political adviser. The patronage of the first two Wei emperors resulted in numerous conversions among the Tuoba. Yet Buddhism also elicited hostility among Daoist monks and Confucian scholars, who tried to sway court sentiment against the Buddhists. Several prominent Confucians – who were concerned about Buddhism's espousal of tax exemptions and celibacy for monks, its denigration of a hierarchical system where each acted according to his or her own social status, and its advocacy of a modified retreat from society – initiated a campaign to persuade Emperor Wu (424–452) to restrain the Buddhists. Their efforts bore fruit, as Wu issued an edict that led to repression in 446. With the explicit support of the court, monasteries were razed and scriptures were burned and an unknown number of monks were killed.

Emperor Wu's death and the accession of Emperor Wencheng altered court attitudes toward Buddhism. The Wencheng emperor issued an edict reversing the discriminatory policies and the repression sanctioned by his predecessor. He and, after his death, his widow provided funds for the construction of temples and stupas (i.e. reliquaries). In addition, the Northern Wei ruler began to supply both manual laborers and farm hands to perform chores in the monasteries and to work their lands. He and subsequent rulers turned over so-called Buddhist Households to the monasteries to labor on the Buddhist estates. This patronage fostered the growth of the monasteries; Chinese sources record that there were about two million monks and nuns by the end of the dynasty.

The two most lavish examples of government patronage were the construction of the Yungang and Longmen caves. The Yungang caves, built just a few miles from the Northern Wei capital in modern Datong, consisted of sculptures carved out of the rock. Some were colossal depictions of the figures in the Buddhist pantheon while others were smaller and more detailed and included representations from the Buddha's life. Although the court initially donated most of the funds for these sculptures, wealthy patrons eventually offered vast sums to pay for inscriptions and carved images in order to gain merit or Karma. Many of the sculptures exhibited Indian and central Asian influences, and indeed the whole idea of cave sculptures derived from south and central Asian sources, principally from the state of Bamiyan in modern

Figure 4.1 Ancient stone carvings of bodhisattvas at the Longmen Grottoes in Luoyang, China. © Michael Gray / iStockphoto

Afghanistan. As impressive as Yungang is, the cave complex at Longmen, near the city of Luoyang, to which the Wei shifted its capital in 494, is an equally extraordinary site. Situated adjacent to the nearby Luo River, the highly revered cave temples of Longmen contain sculptures and inscriptions produced primarily in the Wei and later dynasties. The region's gray limestone provided the material for the creation of images of greater delicacy than in the past and laid the foundations for a unique Chinese style that differed from the Indian and central Asian depictions.

The inscriptions reveal the political and social significance of the construction of cave temples. A few praised the emperor or an aristocrat; others offered prayers for the continued glory of the dynasty. The inscriptions funded by monks and lay people emphasized religious merit and assistance in securing a better life on Earth. Apparent in most of the inscriptions is the strong link between the state and Buddhism; many offered lavish praise and support for the emperor and the dynasty. Such expressions ensured Wei patronage and the apparent selection of Buddhism as the court religion. The inscriptions also show Chinese influence in the repeated references to the welfare of the family and the ancestors – vital conceptions to the Chinese and another indication of the flexibility of Buddhism and its ability to accommodate to native beliefs. This adaptability of the Buddhists in doctrine and practice served and attracted the Wei elite, but it also helped to gain adherents among the Chinese population. The attraction of the Wei to a more sophisticated religion, which also converted many Chinese, marked a transition toward greater sinicization.

Another indication of the Wei's efforts to accommodate to Chinese practices was its attempt to devise a mechanism of land distribution that ensured a reliable source of tax revenues. This creation of a land and tax structure is all the more remarkable when one considers that the Tuoba had scant experience with such regular administrative processes. Late in the fifth century, the Wei mandated an "equal-field" system – an imaginative method to retain peasants on the tax rolls instead of having them work as tenants on the often tax-free estates of the large landowners or aristocrats. To preserve its revenue sources, the Wei recognized that it needed to prevent the shifting of peasants into the private economy. It therefore "nationalized" all the land not directly owned by the estates and distributed it equally among working adults. Each would receive the same amount of land, of which only a relatively paltry portion, allotted for the growth of mulberry trees essential for silk production, could become private property. Control of the land reverted to the state when the peasant died or became too old to farm, and the government then redistributed it to young peasants who had reached adulthood and could assume the responsibilities of farming. In return for the state's generous grant, the recipient was required to provide taxes of grain and silk or other textiles produced on "his" land and to perform corvée labor for the central government or the local authorities. Later the court also imposed militia obligations on the peasants and sent some to the frontiers to form military colonies (*tuntian*). In addition, the government inaugurated a system of local organization, under the direction of a leader, to provide for self-defense, collection of taxes, and proper harmonious relations within the group. Because the "equal-field" system temporarily met the Wei's revenue requirements, it became a model for the two dynasties (Sui and Tang) that subsequently reunified China. Each modified and expanded upon the Wei system of land ownership and taxation. Even more impressive for a so-called barbarian (i.e. non-Chinese) dynasty, the military and local organizational systems the Wei introduced were imitated by other Chinese dynasties and ironically became perceived to be characteristically "Chinese."

Chinese civilization itself gradually influenced the Wei, with its transfer of the capital to Luoyang offering the most significant proof of its growing sinicization. In 494, the Wei rulers signaled a dramatic shift by moving their base from Pingcheng along the frontiers between the steppes and the sedentary agricultural territories to the heartland of China in Luoyang, the city that had been the capital during the Later Han dynasty. The Wei doubtless recognized the symbolism in choosing Luoyang, for the city had numerous associations with a more glorious past for China. By moving to the center of China, the Wei elite revealed its growing identification with Chinese civilization. Within a few years, the court issued regulations that confirmed this change. It enjoined its own officials to master the Chinese language, to refrain from using their own native tongues, and to avoid the donning of Xianbei attire. The government integrated both Chinese and Tuoba officials and did not discriminate against either in appointments and selection. Tuoba leaders who still dominated the military and had remained on the frontiers resented the privileges granted to their subjugated enemies, and the unity that had previously characterized the relationship between the frontier Tuoba and the Tuoba in Luoyang began to unravel. The more sinicized Tuoba residing in China were wary of devoting too many resources to the military – an attitude characteristic of Chinese officialdom and not of peoples who derived from the steppes, for whom military readiness was all important.

The consequent reduction of status for the military led to predictable results. Within two years of the move to Luoyang, the frontier Tuoba initiated a short and abortive uprising against their more sinicized brothers in the capital. Such outbreaks occurred with alarming regularity over the next few decades, weakening both the central government and the frontier military. By reducing the funds allotted to the military, the Wei limited the border army to a defensive posture. Instead of initiating forays into the steppes to deflect potentially hostile peoples, the army simply protected lands that lay within China's borders – a daunting task that made it vulnerable to incursions and attacks. Such intrusions reached their climax in 528 when a steppe army occupied Luoyang and killed much of the court elite. The Wei did not recover and indeed fragmented into two distinct, weak, and ultimately nonviable dynasties. In short, the fate of the Wei illustrates the perils of division between increasingly sinicized steppe leaders and their confreres who sought to retain their traditional lifestyles and values. This split ultimately prevented them from cooperating and led first to weakness and then to collapse. This same kind of internecine conflict would plague nearly all the steppe peoples who sought to govern China.

SPIRITUAL DEVELOPMENTS, POST-HAN

The collapse of the Han and the subsequent chaos undermined Confucianism – a philosophy that promised harmony and order. Confucianism, the state cult during the Han, had been unable to avert the instability that brought the dynasty to an end. It was thus in some disrepute. A new philosophy or religion was required to lay the foundations for a unified China.

This hobbling of Confucianism offered Daoism an opportunity to make inroads on the popular mind. In the late Han, messianic Daoist movements such as the Five Pecks of Rice and the Yellow Turbans had arisen to challenge the court. Daoism served as a popular manifesto during that time. However, when the Han dynasty fell, many men of letters, who were disillusioned with public life, also turned to Daoism, although they did not simply renounce Confucianism. Wang Bi (226–249), perhaps the most original of these thinkers, sought to reconcile Confucianism with Daoism. Heavily influenced by the works of Laozi and Zhuangzi, Wang was determined to preserve Confucianism as well. Thus, he had a vision of a blend of active participation in government and quietism in private. However, he argued that such participation ought to be based on the Daoist concept of the original force of the universe – "nothingness" – from which the "embodiment of existence" derived. An individual needed to be involved in this world, but his behavior ought to be predicated on a detachment and disinterestedness that led to proper Confucian conduct – that is, Wang Bi linked Confucian action to Daoist motivations. The ideal of a disinterested but moral official dovetailed with Confucian precepts as well. Simultaneously, Wang offered an outlet for Daoists by equally emphasizing individual cultivation of the path that led to the Daoist ideals.

Some Daoists followed this path without concessions to Confucianism. They sought solace or self-fulfillment in this turbulent era and refrained from an actively Confucian role in society. A few joined likeminded friends and associates in their efforts to attain the Daoist ideal. The Seven Sages of the Bamboo Grove was the most renowned and doubtless the most notorious such group. Claiming adherence to Zhuangzi's espousal of "naturalness" (*ziran*), the seven went beyond the acceptable limits of their society. Several of them shocked their contemporaries with their unconventional behavior by carousing, drinking, and appearing in the nude. Such hedonism eventually embroiled them in conflicts with the political authorities. Two of the Seven Sages were executed for what was perceived to be provocative and perhaps subversive behavior. Xi Kang (223–262), one of the two, had written the first essay on the Chinese lute and had also experimented with methods to prolong life. Others among the Seven Sages were less sybaritic and attempted to reaffirm Zhuangzi's thoughts in the context of society. Guo Xiang (d. 312), who produced the first edition of Zhuangzi's work, asserted that Zhuangzi's "naturalness" and "nonaction" did not imply abandonment of society. Indeed disinterestedness, the Daoist value par excellence, was an invaluable trait for a government official. True "nonaction" therefore lay neither in total separation from society nor in a hermit-like existence.

As the more learned form of Daoism developed, so too did a more populist formal organization. The philosophies of Laozi and Zhuangzi began to assume the characteristics of a religion or a formal Church. Feasts and celebrations fostered the rise of a Daoist community that took part in rituals, ceremonies, and even magic. Some of the more learned Daoists were distressed at what they perceived to be the vulgarization of the Daoist message. However, with the growing popularity of Daoism, they could do little to stem this trend, which also entailed searches for medical cures and for an elixir of immortality. Popular Daoism could not be rooted out; it had a hold on the populace. Moreover, the real threat to Daoism turned out to derive from the Indian religion of Buddhism, whose early practitioners originally sought to ingratiate themselves with the Daoists.

BUDDHISM ENTERS CHINA

Buddhism is linked with the Indian prince Siddhartha Gautama (ca. 563–483 BCE) of the Shakya tribe, who eventually became known as Shakyamuni ("sage of the Shakya"). Because descriptions of his life evolved centuries after his death, they offer an embroidered version designed to idealize the founder of the religion. Such writings are not reliable accounts, as they seek to use his biography as a means of inculcating the basic message of Buddhism. Actual events are so interlaced with myths and legends that it is impossible to separate them, and knowledge of the life of Siddhartha Gautama is blurred at best. Yet consideration of the mythical accounts conveys a sense of Buddhist teachings.

According to these narratives, Siddhartha Gautama was born to a princely family that ruled in northeast India, bordering on modern Nepal. His birth resulted in remarkable omens:

> In the ten thousand world-systems an immeasurable light appeared. The blind received their sight ... The deaf heard the noise. The dumb spoke with one another. The crooked became straight. The lame walked. All prisoners were freed from their bonds and chains. In each hell the fire was extinguished ... hunger and thirst were allayed. All men began to speak kindly ... All the heavens became clear ... The sea became sea water.[1]

Fabulous stories, which uncannily presage Siddhartha Gautama's later significance to the world, abound about his childhood, but the principal attested events were his marriage at the age of sixteen and the subsequent birth of a son. Despite the obvious advantages accruing to him because of his status and wealth, he remained an unfulfilled and dissatisfied man. His life of privilege did not blind him to the miseries afflicting others or to his own inevitable demise. A series of set pieces exposed him to such afflictions. He came across an old man, a sick man, and a dead man. Distressed by the sufferings they had endured, he continued to brood about the miserable fate of men who could not escape misery even after death. One day he encountered a recluse who had shaved his head and wore an old yellow robe. Impressed by the recluse's abandonment of possessions and his goal of acting meritoriously, Siddhartha Gautama left his palace and family and gave up his own possessions. Cutting off his hair and donning a yellow robe, he started on his mission to discover the causes of suffering. He visited one sage after another, but found their teachings unpersuasive. He led an ascetic, reclusive life for six years, but such a disciplined existence did not ease his mind.

Some years elapsed before he achieved enlightenment. At the age of thirty, frustrated with his lack of progress, he sat in the lotus position at the foot of what became known as the Bodhi tree and started to meditate. He wished to avoid, on the one hand, the hedonism of a life given over to pleasures and, on the other hand, the asceticism of a life of deprivation and austerity.

He ultimately recognized that illness, pain, separation from loved ones, and ultimately death were the common fate of mankind. Death was no panacea because all creatures are afflicted with repeated reincarnations in different forms and faced with the same ailments and suffering. Hope for those who suffered was based on good deeds and on leading a moral life, which is explained by the concept of Karma, which assumes a cause–effect relationship between events and actions. Good behavior would translate into a good effect, or would generate good Karma, leading to a more favorable position in the next life. On the other hand, nefarious behavior would result in a less advantageous status in the following cycle of rebirth. However, the principal objective of the good Buddhist would be to avert reincarnation and instead to achieve Nirvana, a blissful state of selflessness in which cravings had been extinguished.

Enlightenment came in the form of the Four Noble Truths, the first of which stated that life entailed suffering. According to the second truth, human suffering derived from craving for objects or pleasures, which ultimately caused frustration. The third truth embodied the individual's response to the pain he would be compelled to endure in this life, for it prescribed lack of passion and desire as an antidote. If the individual really understood the second truth and moved toward a cessation of desires, he would take the first step toward the alleviation of his own suffering. The fourth truth guided the individual to the moral life and to the meditation that would facilitate enlightenment. It defined the Eightfold Path of right views, right intent, right speech, right conduct, right means of livelihood, right endeavor, right mindfulness, and right meditation that would create good Karma and pave the way to Nirvana. Nirvana, in this earliest form of Buddhism, meant "extinguished," which signifies renunciation of passions and desires and avoidance of reincarnation.

Having become the Enlightened One (or Buddha), Siddhartha Gautama then set about promoting his teachings. He developed the Buddhist teachings (*dharma*) and emphasized the Buddhist monastic community (*sangha*). Having set forth the fundamentals of the faith and having personally spread the message for much of his life, the Buddha himself died or reached a higher consciousness after reminding his disciples of the impermanence of everything and urging them to work diligently to enlighten themselves. This simple sketch of the Buddha's life and ideas hardly does justice to the many episodes described in the traditional accounts and to the elaborateness of his views.

Nonetheless, even the Buddha's basic articulation of the essentials of his beliefs reveals reasons for their attractiveness to the people of his and later times. He emphasized that individual effort, in the form of good conduct, provided steps on the path to Nirvana. Leading an ethical life in each successive reincarnation could have tangible results. Yet the Buddha focused on concerns that transcended this life and may be said, critics have insisted, to have diverted attention from social injustice and instability. According to this line of thinking, the poor who followed these teachings would direct their efforts at achieving Nirvana and thus avoid confronting the social evils that plagued them. On the other hand, it could be argued that Buddhism offered solace in chaotic times by providing a means of responding to human suffering, by showing the evanescence of current afflictions, and by redirecting attention to eternal concerns. Whatever the reasons, Buddhism gained adherents rapidly in northern India and then gradually in central Asia.

Other Buddhist thinkers added to the initial doctrines. Eventually the basic tenets were grouped into three categories. The first were written by or at least deemed to represent the words of the Buddha (*sutras*); the second consisted of essays composed by Buddhist masters (*shastras*); and the third comprised monastic rules (*vinayas*). The resulting number of sources was sizable. Unlike Judaism, Islam, and Christianity, Buddhism had no specific holy book. Its message was scattered in numerous texts, and the doctrines differed in subtle and sometimes not-so-subtle ways. The large number of volumes and the incredible richness of ideas permitted the development of a wide variety of interpretations and sects. In turn, the rise of different sects and the lack of orthodoxy contributed to Buddhism's appeal; it did not appear to be monolithic and had elements that could attract various kinds of adherents. Without a pope or a highly structured ecclesiastical organization, it did not need to defend a specific orthodoxy. Buddhists could be flexible in attempting to spread the Buddha's teachings to other regions and could and did accommodate to native beliefs.

Despite such accommodations, Buddhism would probably not have been transmitted so readily without additional adjustments in doctrine and practice. The original form of the religion, which later came to be known as Theravada, was exceptionally severe and centered on individual salvation – through strenuous efforts, one could become an *arhat* (an enlightened one). The emphasis on rules meant that the individual virtually needed to become a monk or a nun to achieve enlightenment. Although Theravada gained adherents and still prevails in Thailand, Myanmar, and Sri Lanka, its vision did not attract a wide audience in the more populous lands in Asia such as China and Japan. Buddhism needed a more universal doctrine and the espousal of a less austere and forbidding lifestyle if it were to broaden its potential audience.

Mahayana Buddhism provided the vehicle for the wider dissemination of the religion. Adherents used the term "Mahayana," which is defined as "Greater Vehicle," to convey their desire for a more universal message, and they designated Theravada as "Hinayana" (or "Lesser Vehicle"). A major difference is that the Theravada texts were written in Pali, an ancient literary language, while the Mahayana scriptures were in Sanskrit.

To be sure, Mahayana differs in its doctrine from Theravada, but the more significant distinctions entailed the means of achieving enlightenment. The main doctrinal innovation was the Mahayana belief that duality characterized everything in the world, each concept consisting of both a negative and a positive aspect. Nirvana, like reality and the world we inhabit, appeared to the human mind as a void. Nirvana was equated with the wheel of life (*samsara*), a more appealing goal than the absolutely negative nothingness of the Theravada view. Nirvana, in essence, lay within daily activities and, more particularly, within the human mind.

An even more appealing element of Mahayana was the lack of strenuous activities demanded of the faithful. Theravada not only enjoined rigorous discipline, including meditation, fasting, and other physical deprivations, but also scorned sensual pleasures. In contrast, Mahayana, with its view that Nirvana and enlightenment could be found within the individual, offered Nirvana to all rather than to the few who could adopt a virtually monastic lifestyle. It emphasized that individuals ought to look inward, within their own minds, to grasp enlightenment rather than attempting to achieve it through such external means as denial of delights and desires, as recommended by the Theravada. Neither self-mortification nor more demanding analysis of and speculation on doctrine were essential. Understanding of doctrine was not as critical as simple faith and devotion.

Mahayana advocated faith in a remarkably different conception of the Buddha. Theravada sects portrayed the Buddha as a human being who had achieved an understanding of the universe and then transmitted this message to the world before moving into the higher consciousness of Nirvana. To the Mahayana orders, the Buddha was an eternal figure, and Siddhartha Gautama was one emanation of a being who transcended the ordinary boundaries of birth and death. This timeless Buddha had assumed the form of Siddhartha Gautama to bring his vital message to mankind. He had appeared in other forms on Earth and would continue to do so until the arrival of the Maitreya, or Buddha of the Future.

In later periods of Chinese history, new Mahayana sects would develop, having as their focus other emanations of the eternal Buddha such as Amitabha, the Buddha of Infinite Light or the Buddha of the Western Paradise, and Vairocana, the Cosmic Buddha. The different emanations of the Buddha began to be worshipped as divinities, with Siddhartha Gautama himself becoming transformed into a deity. In this conception, the Buddha was less forbidding and more accessible to the ordinary believer. He appeared to be more compassionate in this guise than in the manner he was depicted in Theravada texts.

Contributing to the more human face of Mahayana was the introduction of bodhisattvas, who resemble saints in the Christian tradition. Bodhisattvas had achieved enlightenment but had elected to remain within this world of suffering instead of migrating to Nirvana in order to help less fortunate others. Because of their love of their fellow man, they delayed their own entrance into Nirvana and even transmitted to others some of the merit they had accumulated as a result of the good deeds they had performed on Earth. Each bodhisattva represented a different virtue associated with the eternal Buddha; Manjushri reflected wisdom, for example. The most renowned and popular bodhisattva was Avalokitesvara (Guanyin in Chinese), who embodied compassion and mercy. As befitted a figure symbolizing these virtues, he was often depicted, in sculpture and painting, with numerous arms and eyes, which signified his eagerness to embrace mankind and to offer assistance to all who suffer. With the spread of Buddhism in China, Avalokitesvara began to be represented as a female and became increasingly associated with women. Indeed, the bodhisattvas, though originally conceived of as humans, were gradually deified and worshipped, perhaps filling a need for venerable figures to whom prayers could be directed. Their love of mankind and their compassion proved particularly attractive in times of social upheaval. The traits they symbolized differed considerably from the Theravada ideal of the *arhat*. Their concern for the whole population contrasted sharply with the *arhat*'s self-absorbed striving for Nirvana. No doubt the bodhisattvas conveyed a more universal and appealing image to the ordinary person. The lay believer was not alone. He or she could rely on the noble bodhisattvas as guides on the path to Nirvana.

Buddhism spread gradually from its original center in northeast India, with the Mahayana sects eventually emerging as the most popular forms. Two centuries after Siddhartha Gautama's appearance, Buddhist missionaries reached central Asia and began to convert inhabitants in the oases along what came to be known as the Silk Roads. Merchants carried the message to the western frontiers of China, and several central Asian oases became centers for the dissemination of Buddhism.

By the Later Han dynasty, Buddhist communities had been established in various parts of China. One probably spurious account attributes the introduction of Buddhism to a dream of Emperor Ming (r. 58–75) in which he saw a golden figure flying around the capital. The next morning the emperor's ministers identified the figure as the Buddha, who offered the possibility of salvation to mankind. Suitably impressed, the emperor sent emissaries to central Asia to learn more about the Enlightened One's doctrine, which led eventually to greater knowledge of and conversions to Buddhism. This account is ahistorical. How could a minister in Luoyang, in the eastern part of the country, so far from India and central Asia, have been so well informed about this religion? It appears that Buddhists of later times, seeking greater legitimacy, concocted this story to associate the arrival of their religion with the Chinese emperor. The more likely scenario is that Buddhists first penetrated China in the northwest and from there spread along natural internal routes of transport. By the second century CE Buddhism could be found in several sites in China, and in around 148 An Shigao (?–168), a Parthian most often known by his Chinese name, had settled in Luoyang to translate Buddhist writings into Chinese. Other foreigners joined him shortly thereafter and helped in his efforts to make the sutras and other Buddhist texts available to the Chinese.

However, considerable time elapsed before these and later translators overcame the difficulties entailed in producing Chinese versions of the Buddhist texts. Differences between Chinese and the Indian languages posed almost insurmountable obstacles for the many translators, who had no access to dictionaries. Literary Chinese – an inflected language with rudimentary grammar and a concise, almost telegraphic, style – contrasted sharply with the Indian languages, which were highly inflected with extremely involved and systematic grammars and a flowing, wordier style. The divergent traditions and institutions of the two cultures exacerbated the problems encountered by translators. Chinese philosophy had thus far centered on the attributes and virtues that led to a harmonious, stable, and ethical society while Indian thought focused rather on abstruse speculation and on concerns that went beyond this life. Such cultural distinctions ensnarled efforts to transmit the basic principles of Buddhism.

However, the success of the religion in China was based, in part, upon the Chinese terms used to convey its most important doctrines. Eager to make the teachings appealing and less foreign to Chinese, Buddhist translators decided to express specific Buddhist concepts in terms familiar to the Sinitic world. They chose Daoist terms to impart Buddhist ideas. The Daoists' *wuwei* (nonaction) was used to translate Nirvana and *jenren* (immortal) became *arhat*, while the *dao* itself was often designated as *dharma*. This tactic altered, in subtle ways, the message of Buddhism in order to attract Chinese adherents. By the deliberate use of so-called matching concepts (*geyi*), translators sought to make unfamiliar ideas more palatable to the Chinese. Groups of Buddhist concepts were linked with Confucian or Daoist classifications, sometimes slightly and sometimes not so slightly altering the message. By muting the differences between Buddhism and the native beliefs, proselytizers facilitated its wider acceptance.

Yet the potential for tensions remained. Certain Buddhist practices and doctrines clashed with long-standing Chinese beliefs and values. The celibacy of Buddhist monks conflicted with the value accorded to continuance of the family line by the Chinese. Similarly, Buddhist universalities and emphasis on Nirvana's applicability to all without reference to a specific group was at odds with the group and family orientation of Confucianism and the ethical code that linked behavior to status and role within the family, clan, or community. Theravada's injunctions about desires and anger, its implied condemnation of sensual pleasures, and its apparent advocacy of physical deprivation through fasting and a highly disciplined life ran counter to the Chinese acceptance of the physical and squeamishness about voluntary harming of the body. Later, when Buddhism gained imperial favor and Buddhist monks received a tax-exempt and draft-exempt status, Confucian Chinese hostility toward the religion increased. Chinese critics would also eventually capitalize on Buddhism's Indian heritage to characterize it as alien to Chinese traditions.

However, Chinese resentment and anger initially did not appear, and the Han dynasty's fall spurred efforts to develop an ideology that would simultaneously restore unity and provide solace to the individual in troubled times. Thus the translation of Buddhist texts, popular essays explaining the religion's main doctrines, and writings that led to the development of new sects continued unabated.

Together with such scholarly and missionary activities, a few Buddhists played public roles, sometimes either serving or advising the government. Among these prominent Buddhists were Zhi Dun (314–366), who attempted to reconcile Buddhist and Daoist doctrines; the fourth-century nun Zhi Miaoyin, who influenced government affairs during the Eastern Jin dynasty; Fotudeng, a central Asian monk who reputedly had magical powers, which he placed at the service of the Later Zhao rulers; and Kumarajiva (344–414), of mixed central Asian and Indian blood, who learned Chinese, settled in the ancient capital of Changan, and gathered together a large group of monks to produce precise translations of Buddhist texts in order to differentiate between Buddhist and Daoist teachings, which had become increasingly blurred. Kumarajiva's last goal sheds light on the beginnings of the complicated and increasingly hostile relationship between the Buddhists and the Daoists. Buddhism entered China with some Daoist trappings, or at least with Daoist terminology. Thus, the initial Daoist reaction was positive; however, as Daoist leaders began to realize that Buddhism diverged from their views and beliefs and that the Buddhists placed Buddha on a pedestal way above that of Laozi, they began to resent the foreign religion. Eventually, the ecclesiastical authorities of the two religions would clash, sometimes violently. Yet, by and large, Buddhism successfully adapted its message to Chinese sensibilities and sensitivities, and its success in China owed much to its ability to accommodate to Chinese civilization.

LITERATURE, SCIENCE, AND THE ARTS IN A PERIOD OF DIVISION

The chaotic conditions that gave rise to Daoism and Buddhism also spurred literary developments. The Seven Sages of the Bamboo Grove, of Daoist renown, sought to express their views through imaginative writings. As befit their appellation, the Seven Sages concentrated on nature as one of their principal subjects. They wrote about the beauty of the mountains and the wild, uncultivated lands but also about the serene mood these vistas induced in them. In addition, they celebrated wine, which they consumed in vast quantities in order to seek comfort and escape from their troubled, unstable times. As noted earlier, Xi Kang, one Sage, wrote a lengthy prose poem about the Chinese lute, praising it for the quality it shared with nature: offering the listener a calm interlude in an otherwise unstable era. Tao Yuanming (365–427) was the poet par excellence of those who espoused the beauties of nature and solitude and the physical labor of farming as well as the dissipation of despair offered by the drinking of wine. He also rejected the frustrating and perilous striving for wealth, status, and fame through official service. A worldly career could not compare with the pleasures of digging in the soil or calmly contemplating the trees, the birds, and the landscape, or overcoming inhibitions through a binge of wine drinking.

Artists too sought security and stability in reaction to the turmoil of the times. The principles of painting adduced by the sixth-century art critic Xie He conform to the Daoist ideals expressed in poetry. Xie He's Six Principles became the standard for evaluating painting for many years to come. They were: (1) animation through spirit consonance, (2) structural method in the use of the brush, (3) fidelity to the object in portraying forms, (4) conformity to kind in applying colors, and (5) proper planning and placement of elements (6) so that, by copying, the ancient models would be perpetuated. These principles, particularly the *chi* (the spirit that infused nature and mankind) dovetailed with the themes expressed in contemporaneous poetry. The painters' attempts to reflect the *chi*, the force that drives all human beings, as well as all natural objects, were similar to the Daoist poets' efforts to depict the beauty of nature.

An even greater indication of this conjunction was the development of landscape painting. Hardly any of these early paintings have survived, but several attributed to or in the style of Gu Kaizhi (344–406) have been transmitted. Gu Kaizhi's depictions of mountains, trees, and rivers reveal the same concerns with serenity found in the Daoist poetry. Records about other landscape painters whose paintings have not lasted into modern times indicate that they shared a similar interest in landscapes.

Calligraphy as an art form developed during this era, though precious few examples have survived. The works of the great calligrapher Wang Xizhi (303–361) reveal a relaxation from the more formal style of *lishu* (clerical

Figure 4.2 Leaves seven and eight from Wang Xizhi Book One, "Calligraphy of Ancient Masters of Various Periods," Section V of the "Calligraphy Compendium of the Chunhua Era," 1616, ink rubbing and yellow ink on paper, Chinese School, Ming dynasty (1368–1644). © FuZhai Archive / The Bridgeman Art Library

script) to *caoshu* (grass script), which permitted greater experimentation, creativity, and individuality – all traits that conformed to the Daoist precepts that dominated the art world.

The greatest concentration of surviving artworks are of Buddhist origin. They were found particularly in the Yungang, Longmen, and Dunhuang caves but also in other Buddhist sites in Binglingsi (about fifty miles along the Yellow River from Lanzhou) and in Maijishan (in the modern province of Gansu). The early sculptures in these caves were massive, heavy, and austere and reflected Indian and central Asian influences, but the later sculptures were refined and lighter, with flowing robes and with more human faces. The Dunhuang paintings (in their 492 caves), which survived owing to the dry climate in the desert regions surrounding the Dunhuang oasis, often provide vignettes of the Buddha's life; depict different emanations of the Buddha, bodhisattvas, and *apsaras* (flying figures, often of musicians); and illustrate tales concerning the Buddha's earlier incarnations in the form of animals. These charming frescoes, which originally consisted principally of Indian subjects and motifs, became increasingly Chinese in themes and styles.

Loosening of strict aesthetic standards and greater opportunities for individuality and creativity characterized the culture of this politically unstable period. Daoist poets deviated from established patterns in order to express their individual reactions to nature and their desire for a mystical union with all phenomena. Painters produced images that displayed their own feelings toward the landscape rather than stereotyped societal attitudes, and even painters of Buddhist themes and motifs sought to deviate from central Asian and Indian models and to create their own individual styles. Like the painters of Buddhist subjects, the sculptors who created images derived originally from the Indian religions began to introduce innovations on the acceptable mode of depiction. Non-Buddhist sculpture, particularly figures of humans and animals adjacent or leading to the tombs of emperors or prominent nobles along a so-called spirit road leading to the main burial site, also revealed a less stereotyped and more individual portrayal of secular figures.

All sorts of discoveries and innovations in techniques and practices developed, partly as a result of the experiments and activities related to Buddhism and Daoism and partly from the exposure to the outside world afforded by Buddhism. The burning of incense for ceremonial and religious purposes and the chanting of mantras that evolved into music became popular practices that had Buddhist origins. The translations of Buddhist writings into Chinese led to the development of dictionaries and grammars. Daoist attempts to prolong life resulted in experiments with alchemy and chemistry, which often brought with them valuable discoveries. Knowledge of a variety of specific herbs, metals, other elements, and chemical reactions increased. These discoveries contributed not only to medicine but also to technology and perhaps to science, or at least to an inquisitive attitude and a desire for additional knowledge of the physical world.

With their concern with helping the afflicted and ailing, Buddhists also contributed to medical discoveries and insights. Indian medicinal recipes reached China; a Buddhist text that offered descriptions of hundreds of ailments was translated into Chinese. Another Buddhist text described diseases of the eyes, ears, and feet. Several monks reputedly performed miracle cures, which permitted a paralytic to regain use of his limbs and stemmed an unspecified epidemic. These remarkable occurrences did not, in themselves, produce medical breakthroughs; nonetheless, they indicated interest in and support for efforts to cater to the ills of mankind. Amelioration of the ailments of the body became part of the Buddhist mission, no doubt spurring experimentation and advances in medicine.

Despite the evident breakdown of the old society, scholarship and cultural developments proceeded apace, in part abetted by the arrival of influences and individuals from abroad. Indian and central Asian Buddhists introduced not only the tenets of the religion and the attendant art and architecture but also innovations in other cultural areas – music, for example. Complementing the music meant to accompany Buddhist rituals and ceremonies was the secular music of the nomadic and oasis peoples of central Asia and Mongolia, to which north China was exposed with the establishment of non-Chinese dynasties there. The scriptures and paintings in the Buddhist caves depict orchestras with both Chinese and foreign instruments. The *sheng* (a blown reed instrument) and the *pipa* (or lute) had been known in China before this time, but the *suona* (a kind of oboe) and the harp had been imported, probably via central Asia, from Persia.

The southern Kingdom of Wu, one of the successor states to the Han, contributed to Chinese scholarship through its foreign contacts. Because of its position in the south, Wu and its rulers became increasingly involved with areas in Southeast Asia. They exchanged envoys with the Kingdom of Funan (roughly modern Cambodia), and Wu ambassadors returned from these journeys with invaluable information, increasing China's familiarity with the geography, customs, and accomplishments of some of the Southeast Asian peoples. Among the more important observations of one account concerns the scope of seaborne commerce conducted at this time, the sailors' knowledge of optimal trade routes, and the information about the spread of Indian religions. The size of some of the vessels that plied these trade routes is surprising. One perhaps exaggerated account indicates that junks could transport as many as five or six hundred men.

The greater contact between China and its neighbors in the south and north compelled an interest in geography and, in particular, cartography. A government official named Pei Xiu (224–271) produced a now lost map of China that delineated the various provinces and located the mountains, seas, and towns. This map, based on a grid system, spurred interest in cartography and served as one of the models for future mapmaking. A side effect of this interest was the compilation of local histories or gazetteers, the first of which provided information on the products, customs, flora and fauna, and meritorious men from the region of modern southern Shaanxi and northern Sichuan. Many provinces, districts, counties, and other local regions adopted the practice of collecting information and writing about their Buddhist and Daoist temples and monasteries, flood-control projects, prominent buildings and monuments, taxes, academies and schools, and trade, as well as compiling biographical sketches of leading individuals. Local governments often commissioned these collections but sometimes local scholars, as a leisurely diversion, contributed and produced these works, which often served as handbooks for officials unfamiliar with the local areas to which they were assigned. Thousands of these gazetteers have survived into modern times and offer a mine of information about Chinese history.

These advances in knowledge exemplify the remarkable innovations of this seemingly chaotic period in Chinese political history. Paradoxically, this era of turbulence witnessed the introduction of invaluable cultural contributions to China. Yet this period was not unique, for previously chaotic ages (e.g. the Warring States era of the Zhou dynasty) saw remarkable achievements in Chinese philosophy. Unstable political and economic conditions appear, on occasion, to have stimulated experiments and attempts to find underlying shared views that might facilitate unity and defuse the unsettled and violent environment. A centralized government was not essential for cultural developments and innovations. Vital changes could and did take place in times of unrest.

Thus, despite the turbulence, individual Chinese invented important devices and discovered new techniques or objects. The wheelbarrow, invented at this time, facilitated the peasants' work by permitting the transport of humans and animals more readily and with less labor and effort. The watermill also lightened the peasants' burdens by offering a simpler method of irrigating the land and grinding grain. Sedan chairs, which may have been used initially to carry the elderly and ailing, first came into prominence during this period. Within a short time, they became status symbols, as the elite appropriated them as a means of transport. The bleakness of the era may have spurred interest in games as distractions. Backgammon and elephant chess diverted many Chinese, and books on chess began to appear in the sixth century. Chinese flew kites as recreation and for practical effects as well. On one extraordinary occasion, an emperor, whose capital was besieged by the enemy, sought assistance by sending a kite aloft to inform allies of the perils he faced.

Perhaps less frivolous and of more consequence were the introduction of new plants and the discovery of uses for minerals. The new agricultural goods, several of which originated abroad, included onions, sesame, pomegranates, safflower, and broad beans, all of which enriched the Chinese diet and cuisine. However, the most influential discovery was tea, a beverage that would have profound effects on Chinese art and literature and on its economy. The first records of tea derive from the third century, though it may have been consumed earlier. Its use stems from the migration to south China, which had the proper soil for its growth. Tea was later associated with Buddhist ceremonies and became an integral part of such rituals. Throughout history, Chinese attributed wondrous benefits to tea drinking, including cures that cannot be proven. However, tea was valuable because it offered the benefits of boiled water, as opposed to impure and sometimes polluted water.

The use of coal to smelt iron and for fuel dates from this era as well, although a few references appear to point to an earlier origin. This discovery preceded by about a thousand years the application of coal for the same purpose in the West and averted the denuding of China's forests. Much of the remainder of China's timberland was nonetheless ravaged, but the damage would surely have been more widespread without the hot ember. The relative paucity of trees in parts of north China necessitated the tapping of another resource for fuel.

In sum, this period of disunion and the attendant often chaotic conditions did not preclude cultural, scientific, and economic developments. Many Chinese profited from the technological advances and foreign imports during this era. As in the Warring States period, political chaos and dynastic changes did not necessarily relate to social and cultural developments. Political stability was not essential for agricultural and economic growth. Neither was it vital for an efflorescent cultural and social life. Political chaos resulted from the lack of a central government capable of unifying the country. Local aristocrats contested efforts at centralization, and the various dynasties in both north and south China did not have the power or the policies needed to overcome such resistance. Also, ordinary Chinese who remembered the instability, corruption, and mismanagement of the Later Han dynasty may have been wary of supporting a powerful central government. Only when the lack of a central government fostered extraordinary unrest did common people recognize the desirability of a government to regulate society and to restore stability.

NOTES

1   Clarence Hamilton, *Buddhism: A Religion of Infinite Compassion* (New York: Bobbs-Merrill, 1952), pp. 3–4.

FURTHER READING

Albert Dien, *Six Dynasties Civilization* (New Haven: Yale University Press, 2007).

Jacques Gernet, *Buddhism in Chinese Society: An Economic History from the 5th to the 10th Centuries,* trans. by Francois Verellen (New York: Columbia University Press, 1995).

Liu Xinru, *Ancient India and Ancient China: Trade and Religious Exchanges, AD 1–600* (Delhi: Oxford University Press, 1988).

James Watt et al., *China: Dawn of a Golden Age, 200–750 AD* (New York: Metropolitan Museum of Art, 2004).

Arthur Wright, *Buddhism in Chinese History* (Stanford: Stanford University Press, 1959).

PART II

China among Equals

[5]   RESTORATION OF EMPIRE UNDER SUI AND TANG, 581–907

CHINA's unification in the late sixth and early seventh centuries led to one of the greatest periods in Chinese and indeed world history. The Tang dynasty (618–907) – which emerged after almost four centuries of misrule, warfare, lack of a centralized government, and diminution of trade and tribute with the outside world – proved to be a quintessentially prosperous, powerful, and culturally productive era. The dynasty devised the administrative structure the Chinese would employ, with some variations, until the collapse of the imperial

A History of China, First Edition. Morris Rossabi.
© 2014 Morris Rossabi. Published 2014 by Blackwell Publishing Ltd.

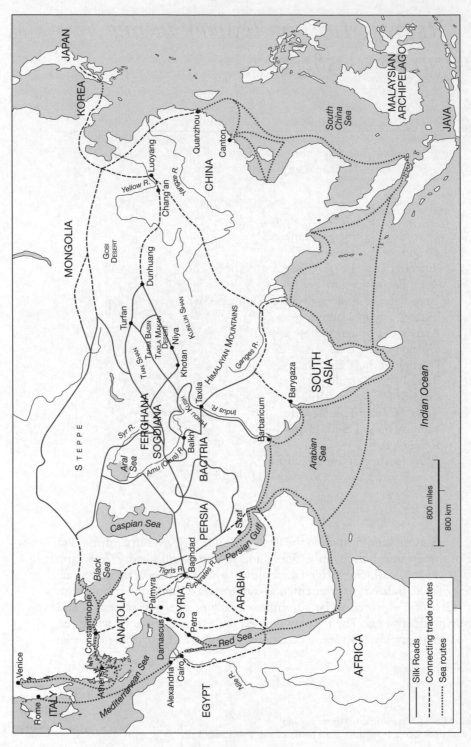

Map 5.1 Silk and sea routes in traditional times

system in 1911. It began to recruit officials through competitive civil-service examinations, a characteristic feature of Chinese civilization. Its cosmopolitanism attracted, via the Silk Routes and maritime trade, numerous merchants, entertainers, soldiers, missionaries, and envoys who exposed China to foreign religions, music and dance, products, medicines, animals, and technologies, contributing to the dynasty's resplendent culture. Simultaneously, China began to transmit paper, silk, tea, and other goods to numerous regions in Asia.

China's own creativity, as well as borrowings from foreign areas, contributed to this efflorescent culture. Poetry, tricolored ceramics, sculpture, architecture, and the other arts and literature reached extraordinary heights. The development of political and economic institutions set the stage for this dazzling culture. Military and political unification was the first step in devising the structure under which the arts, literature, and technologies flourished. This era began with a short-lived but important dynasty, the Sui.

SUI: FIRST STEP IN RESTORATION

Yang Jian (541–604), the founder of the Sui dynasty, was descended from an aristocratic family of officials who had served the non-Chinese dynasties during the period of disunion. In hindsight, his upbringing proved to be ideal for a unifier of China, whose people had become exhausted after three centuries of disorder and lack of unity. A Buddhist nun took charge of his early education until he was twelve. He then attended the Imperial Academy, where he was exposed to Confucian learning but also had time to devote to military training. His military prowess led, shortly thereafter, to an appointment in the army. At the age of twenty-four, he married the daughter of one of the heads of a leading non-Chinese family, the Dugu. The young man now had links with the most powerful forces in China: the traditional aristocracy, the Buddhist monasteries, the Confucian scholarly elite, the military, and the non-Chinese peoples. Later his accession to power was facilitated by his daughter's marriage to the heir apparent of the Northern Zhou dynasty, which offered a vital association with an imperial family. When the heir apparent died in 580, Yang Jian declared himself regent, then systematically murdered the princes of the Northern Zhou. In the following year, he proclaimed the founding of the Sui dynasty, with himself as Emperor Wen. Using his various associations, he suppressed opposition and within the decade had occupied and unified much of China. The culmination of his efforts was his conquest of the state of Chen in 581.

The question he now faced was how to rule a China that had been fragmented for over three hundred years. Recruitment of a loyal and effective group of advisers was essential. Emperor Wen first relied on his wife, one of the most influential empresses in Chinese history. Castigated in the sources as jealous and tyrannical, she played a vital role, nonetheless, in the government's patronage of Buddhism, which turned out to be crucial in harnessing support for a unified empire under Yang Jian. The new emperor also recruited three competent men as counselors and administrators. Gao Jiong (d. 607), a Buddhist, devised a financial system that ensured revenues for the military and for construction projects; Yang Su

(d. 606), a military commander, served as the dynasty's enforcer, ruthlessly crushing opposition and thus giving the government the opportunity to establish order; and Su Wei (542–623), a civilian adviser, focused on civil administration, rituals, and a philosophic rationale for the new dynasty.

Although the dynasty's initial successes were based upon its military force, its ability to govern depended upon its philosophical justification for rule and its creation of an effective government. The Sui was the first dynasty to use an eclectic ideology to legitimize its authority and to unify the various peoples within China. Its eclecticism revolved around its apparent support of and appeal to Confucianism, Daoism, and Buddhism. Confucianism, which had provided the ideological foundations of the Han, was deemed to be an insufficient stabilizing force after the collapse of the dynasty. Yet it was so closely identified with China that a prospective unifier needed to offer support. Emperor Wen, though a devout Buddhist, made overtures to Confucianism, first by restoring the Confucian court rituals (including music and dance) and by emphasizing such Confucian moral principles as filial piety and the Mandate of Heaven. Subsequently, he needed and selected Confucians as bureaucrats, since they tended to be the most educated members of the population. Yet he did not intend to rely exclusively on a corps of erudite Confucian scholars to serve as the main building block of his government. Instead he repeatedly expressed his desire to recruit pragmatic men who exemplified Confucian morality rather than academics without a practical bent. Yang Jian clearly sought Confucians who could offer tangible assistance in organizing a government, not a scholar who mouthed pious moral strictures.

Similarly, he patronized those elements of Buddhism and Daoism that could buttress his position and strengthen his government. For example, he tried to cloak himself in the mantle of a devout leader. He recognized that, if adopted by a large segment of the population, Buddhism could contribute to political unity. Since support from the major sects and monasteries would also help him consolidate his position, he provided funds for the construction of temples. These policies attracted many Buddhists to his cause. Daoism in its popular or, some would say, vulgar form had captured the imaginations of many Chinese, and Emperor Wen, though disdainful of excessive Daoist claims, still spoke favorably of the *dao* and its contribution to unity. On the other hand, he did not provide the same patronage to Daoist temples and monasteries that he had to Buddhist ones. In short, he attempted to bolster his claims to legitimacy by gaining the support of all three major systems of thought or religion in China.

Similarly, the governmental system that Emperor Wen and his advisers devised had elements of earlier institutions but was laced with some innovations. Like their use of the traditional philosophy of Confucianism as well as the newly introduced religion of Buddhism, the Sui rulers organized offices familiar to the Chinese population, along with new structures needed for the changed world in which they found themselves. They retained the old Han offices known as the Three Dukes but allowed them little real authority. Power was concentrated in the hands of the three central ministries: the Department of State Affairs, the Chancellery, and the Secretariat. The Department of State Affairs, consisting of six functional ministries – Personnel, Rites, War, Revenue,

Justice, and Public Works – was the most important body. A principal deviation from the Han pattern was the elimination of the position of chancellor (one of the Three Dukes in Han times), possibly the central figure of earlier bureaucracies. Without a chancellor, power flowed into the hands of the emperor. Apart from the later addition of a chancellor, this structure, with some alterations, prevailed throughout much of Chinese history until 1911.

The officials the Sui selected to staff the major offices turned out to be, in some ways, unrepresentative of the new, unified China. Almost all were northerners; south China, which had experienced a population explosion after the fall of the Han and had been brought into the Chinese orbit, lacked much representation in the government. Like Emperor Wen, most officials derived from the Northern Zhou, and many were related to Emperor Wen and the son who succeeded him as emperor. Yet, in the lower ranks of the bureaucracy, Wen established merit as the principal criterion for selection. He sought to subvert the authority of powerful aristocratic families whose sons had had the inside track on positions in central and local government. Civil-service examinations were initiated and provided men to staff the eighth and ninth (lower ranks) of the bureaucracy, limiting still further the opportunities for the aristocracy to dominate.

The Sui thus sought to establish centralized rule over its lands, a policy that no dynasty in at least three centuries had been able to achieve. It granted the Ministry of Personnel the power to appoint local officials, preventing the irregular arrangements that had permitted aristocratic families to dominate local government. The court was determined to abolish the system of recommendations that had allowed the local aristocracy to control appointments and to vitiate the possibility of selection on the basis of merit. The court also mandated that the officials chosen by the Ministry of Personnel could not be sent to their birthplace, an additional check on the power of local oligarchies. Their tenure in any one position was limited to three (later four) years, which reduced the possibility that they would fall prey to the blandishments of the local elite.

The Sui also needed to assure itself of revenues to finance government projects and the military. It adopted the equal-field system developed by the Northern Wei as a means of land distribution and as a way of ensuring sufficient tax income. The underlying assumption of this system was that the emperor owned the land of China personally and that he distributed this land to adults who could cultivate it. When they were too old or sick to farm, the land would revert to the state and would be redistributed to young men who were capable of farming the land. In return for this grant, each farmer had to provide a grain tax and a donation of cloth, as well as about three weeks of corvée labor a year. Such land and tax policies required proper implementation. Yet local officials had no vested interest in promoting this more equitable system. Nor was the local aristocracy eager to abide by the system and thus relinquish the lands to which they laid claim. The result was massive disregard for the government's land and tax directives. Many local officials, in collusion with aristocratic families, falsified land and tax records, removing considerable acreage from the system. Inadequate censuses and land registers naturally subverted the Sui court's intention to establish a stable and equitable mechanism for land distribution that would also guarantee its revenue needs. In addition to the abuses engineered by local officials and aristocrats, the Buddhist and Daoist monasteries had received sizable tax-exempt estates, which further eroded the tax base. The equal-field system worked best on the land confiscated by the two Sui emperors from opponents and enemies. No aristocratic family could claim this land, and the government thus encountered fewer hurdles in distributing it according to the regulations.

Having devised the institutions needed to govern and having the requisite resources to set up these institutions, the Sui could now turn its attention to the actual mechanics of ruling. Emperor Wen had a new legal code enacted, which curbed the severity of punishments. He then sought to propagate this code within the officialdom, but yet again he was dependent in carrying out the laws on the officials themselves – bureaucrats who were, on occasion, corrupt and who lacked interest in proper implementation of the laws. Government also required a center for its operations. Recognizing the need for such a capital, which could bolster his legitimacy, Wen selected a site near Changan that had rich historical associations with the Chinese. His architects designed a walled city that met the requirements of imperial residences and bureaucrats' offices and that blended with Confucian symbols and rituals.

The next step in the Sui's consolidation of power entailed control over its frontiers and possible expansion to provide itself with a buffer zone. Repair of the walls (or so-called Great Wall) on the northern border was the first self-defense measure. The court then sent an expeditionary force that briefly occupied the kingdom of Champa (in modern Vietnam). At about the same time, a Sui army overwhelmed the Tuyuhun peoples who inhabited the lands to the west of the dynasty's frontiers. Their principal adversary, however, was the Tujue, a group composed principally of Turkic peoples who controlled much of inner Asia, stretching from Mongolia to the borders of Persia. Having achieved unity under a khaghan (the title of the supreme ruler of the Mongols, often also termed a khan of khans) in the early sixth century, the Tujue had fragmented by the middle of the century into the Eastern Khaghanate, based along the Orkhon River in Mongolia, and the Western Khaghanate, which dominated much of western Turkestan. Emperor Wen attempted to control them through the Han dynasty tactic of divide and rule. By trying to exacerbate the tensions between them, he hoped to defuse the threat they posed to China's lands. He pursued this policy throughout his reign and ensured Sui primacy or at least relative control over much of its northern frontiers.

Emperor Wen's achievement in unifying China after almost four centuries of intermittent warfare and other disruptions was remarkable, which makes the brevity of the dynasty he founded seem puzzling. The Sui survived for only two reigns and lasted for about three decades. In this sense, it resembled the Qin dynasty, which also had only two emperors and lasted for about fifty years by one count and for fifteen years by another count. Yet both preceded two of the longest and most illustrious of China's dynasties, the Han and the Tang. The successor dynasties benefited enormously from the accomplishments of their short-lived predecessors and borrowed and refined practices and institutions developed by the immediately preceding dynasty. Without the completion of projects initiated by the Qin and the Sui, the Han and Tang would have encountered more serious obstacles in establishing stable and financially secure governments. Yet both the Qin and the Sui tried to do too much in too short a time. The projects they undertook were costly and often required the use of large numbers of forced laborers. Such vast expenditures of funds and labor gave rise to opposition that ultimately resulted in the downfall of each dynasty.

The Sui's troubles emerged in the reign of Yang Guang (569–618), the second emperor, who was Yang Jian's second son and whose mother was of Xiongnu ancestry. Before his accession, his father gave him responsibility over some of the newly incorporated lands of south China; Yang Guang patronized Buddhism, waived taxes in areas heavily damaged during the earlier warfare, and recruited advisers representing Confucians, the military, and Buddhists, among others. In short, he succeeded in bringing peace to the south by ingratiating himself with its leading constituencies. His brilliance as a manipulative politician is attested by his creation of an image as a pious Buddhist and an honorable leader, which led to his designation as heir apparent. In 604, his father's death propelled him to the throne as Emperor Yang. Because he was the last Sui emperor, the historical accounts portray him in a negative light and depict his policies as destructive. It is thus difficult to avoid the unflattering stereotypes in describing his reign.

Though later Confucian scholars and historians castigate him for his personnel policies, Emperor Yang's first few years in power were apparently stable. He was certainly guilty of executing several capable officials who had served him and had been candid in their advice. Such outspokenness was not tolerated in his court, and Emperor Yang relied instead on more conniving and secretive counselors who accompanied him on his frequent travels; restlessness served as a dominant motif throughout his reign. Yet he promoted Confucianism by starting schools for its study, built libraries, and sought to ensure that examinations and thus presumably merit were the route to high government office. At the same time, he temporarily waived taxes on the families of those who had died trying to help him assume the throne, and he restored Confucian court rituals and constructed granaries as insurance in case of poor harvests and food shortages.

His major construction projects, though bitterly criticized by Confucian historians, proved to be boons for the Tang and later dynasties. The building of new canals and the expansion of others, some of which formed the network known as the Grand Canal, were vital. They provided access to some of the rich agricultural lands of the south for the northern capitals of the dynasty. The canals were also extended directly north, linking the fertile south to that less prosperous region. The economic value of these canals is indisputable, as they permitted the flow of tribute grain to the capital and to the grain-deficient regions of north China. Yet they were also significant for the military because they allowed the rapid deployment of troops from the south to the more vulnerable northern and northeastern frontiers – the areas inhabited by non-Chinese peoples. Confucian historians criticized the Sui construction of a second capital at Luoyang as excessive and profligate. Yet Luoyang had been the capital during the Eastern Zhou and Later Han dynasties, was revered by the Chinese, and was closer to the southeastern regions, which were becoming increasingly important. The symbolism of its reconstruction, as a boost to the dynasty's legitimacy and to its associations with the glorious past, was probably as significant as the emperor's geographic and economic motivations.

These projects, together with less grandiose but still costly ventures such as repair of the walls along China's northern borderlands and building and maintaining roads throughout the empire, were invaluable, if not essential, for China's prosperity and defenses. Yet the money and manpower requirements posed an intolerable burden on the populace. The court drafted hundreds of thousands of laborers to extend and enlarge the canals and extracted considerable tax revenue, principally from those least able to afford such payments. No doubt a few officials, landlords, and merchants profited, either legally or illegally, from these projects, and some aristocrats and landlords, with ties to the bureaucracy, evaded court requisitions. The burdens of tax and corvée labor thus fell disproportionately on the least prosperous and least politically powerful constituencies, leading to social unrest in the second half of Emperor Yang's reign.

DISASTROUS FOREIGN CAMPAIGNS

Foreign adventurism brought the dynasty down. The court might have been able to survive the disruptions precipitated by its domestic policies, but ill-considered foreign military campaigns exacerbated its financial problems and contributed to the disaffection of large segments of the population. Not all of the Sui's foreign relations during Emperor Yang's reign were unproductive. In 606, the court received its first embassy ever from Japan, which initiated a relationship that profoundly influenced Japanese history. Emperor Yang also continued his father's policies of marital alliances, trade and tribute, and divide and rule in dealing with the western and eastern Turks, which led to peace along the northern and northwestern frontiers.

Punitive campaigns against the state of Koguryo, one of the contenders for power in Korea, proved to be the undoing of the Sui. Koguryo controlled the region of modern Manchuria east of the Liao River and North Korea, while the state of Silla dominated southeast Korea and the state of Paekche ruled the southwest. Koguryo had resisted the Sui, refusing to send tribute and sending troops across the Liao River, which Emperor Yang regarded as an encroachment on his lands. The Sui emperor was also concerned that Koguryo might ally itself with the Turks to the west or other groups in Manchuria in opposition to the Sui. Such fears, together with a desire to expand the territory under his control for his own and China's greater glory, prompted him to mount several expeditions against Koguryo. He set forth on his first campaign in 612 with alacrity, expecting to capture Koguryo's capital, around the modern city of P'yongyang.

His plans went awry, as the cities en route resisted and stalled his forces until late summer, when heavy rains compelled the Sui troops to withdraw. The Koreans' knowledge of the land, as well as the unfavorable climate, to which the Chinese troops had not adjusted, gave the Koreans a decided advantage over the Sui forces, who also had to contend with a one-thousand-mile supply line from their capital. In addition, Koguryo's strong defenses surprised the Chinese.

Undeterred, Emperor Yang raised a sizable force for another attack the very next year. This second expedition again faced opposition, but its failure was due to the outbreak of rebellions in China and the need to dispatch soldiers to quell such disturbances. Yang retreated to China, but, still obsessed with his goal of overwhelming Koguryo, he organized a third campaign that actually compelled the Korean king to submit. Yet he had to abandon the expedition to deal with rebellions that now wracked the entire empire. Returning to China, however, he refused to listen to advisers who sought to explain the gravity of the pressures facing his dynasty. Increasingly out of touch with events in his domains, he soon found many of his own relatives turning against him. In 618, he was murdered by one of his own underlings. The heavy obligations he and his dynasty had imposed on the population finally led to the Sui's destruction.

ORIGINS OF THE TANG

In a dramatic departure from the previous four centuries of Chinese history, the fall of the Sui dynasty did not lead to fragmentation. After the overthrow of the Han in 220, every collapse of a governing group that had sought to unify the country had resulted in disintegration. If nothing else, the Sui finally ended that pattern. Sui rule had fostered unity and recognition of the need for stability and order. Like the relationship between the Qin and Han dynasties, the Sui set the stage for the great Tang dynasty. Unlike the Qin, however, the Sui did not seek to impose a hideously despotic system. In any event, reversion to pre-Sui disunity and sporadic warfare seemed out of the question. A unified country offered economic advantages (state-supported transport and irrigation projects, for example) to the powerful elites, and an orderly, more organized political structure could lessen fears of social disruption that would challenge those elites' authority and power. A strong dynasty could facilitate and accelerate the integration of south China, which had gradually become more populous and wealthier in the post-Han period. It could also protect China's interests against political rivals along the northern and western frontiers and might even slowly and steadily expand into and incorporate some of these alien territories. In other words, the Sui had, from the standpoint of the elite, moved in the right direction, but its second ruler and his government and ministers had undertaken too many projects at enormous cost of labor and other resources and had squandered vast sums on luxuries and on hasty and far-flung military campaigns. Like the somewhat comparable Qin dynasty eight centuries earlier, it had alienated and lost the support of much of the Chinese populace. A successor dynasty could very well adopt many of the Sui's policies, avoid its excesses, and still gain the allegiance of the elite and of ordinary Chinese.

The founder and the first rulers of the Tang dynasty succeeded partly because they pursued this strategy. Naturally, they also had specific and distinct advantages. Descended from a family that appears to have had Xianbei and Turkic forebears, they were related to the ruling families and had served as officials in the Northern Zhou and Sui dynasties. They were most assuredly part of the aristocracy and did not represent the beleaguered and alienated peasantry of the Sui era. They were not advocates of dramatic social upheavals, and indeed Li Yuan (566–625), the Tang founder, had had a distinguished career as a Sui official and military commander. Because he himself had led campaigns to crush opposition to the reigning dynasty, he seemed an unlikely usurper. Yet, like other aristocrats of the time, he witnessed growing antagonism toward the weakening Sui and saw an opportunity to seek the throne for himself. However, he and his supporters were not revolutionaries and hardly desired a change in the social system.

In 617, he seized his chance to upend the Sui. Having secured a base in the form of his military command in Taiyuan in north China, he planned an attack on the capital. However, he first shored up his northern and western flanks by making peace with the eastern Turks, who sent him soldiers and weapons in return for pledges of booty from his campaign. Thus, late in 617 he occupied the Sui capital around Xian, and the following year he captured the eastern capital of Luoyang. Shortly thereafter, he proclaimed himself emperor of a new dynasty named after his fief, the Tang. Through a judicious blend of rewards and ruthless suppression, he and Li Shimin (599–649), his ablest son, gradually overwhelmed all rebel opposition by 624.

Li Yuan (known to history as Tang Gaozu) set about restoring unity and establishing a government. However, in conventional sources, his son Li Shimin received most of the credit for laying the foundations for Tang rule. Because Li Yuan reigned for only two years beyond the pacification of the rebel groups, he scarcely had time to leave an indelible imprint on the dynasty. Yet he pressed forward with the Sui efforts at centralization, initiating new domestic and foreign policies and some new institutions. His accomplishments in his brief reign permitted his successors to create a stable, long-lasting government. He bribed the eastern Turks with presents to prevent them from capitalizing on China's evident disorderliness and attacking along its northern frontiers. While this tactic did not lead to an enduring peace and, in fact, raids by the eastern Turks plagued the last year of his reign, it allowed him a short respite during which to take hold of the government and to install himself as the ruler. He formed military organizations in many local areas in order to gain control over them; he restored the Sui equal-field system and the associated taxes on grain and cloth to meet the dynasty's financial needs; he continued the previous dynasty's laudable irrigation and transport policies; he ordered the formulation of legal and administrative codes, which actually came into force in 624; and he gathered together a capable group of advisers, mostly from his own background.

His main failing was his inability to control the imperial succession, which set an unfortunate model for his descendants. Much of the first century or so of Tang rule would be afflicted by irregular successions, considerably weakening the dynasty. The Gaozu Emperor could not prevent his own sons from plotting against each other and thwarting the enthronement of his designated successor. As the commander at some of the most important victories against rebel forces and with one of the largest armies in the country, Li Shimin was angered that his father had passed him over as the legitimate successor. Thus, after making damning but false accusations about his brother, the designated successor to his father, he ambushed and personally killed his unfortunate sibling. Within two months, he had so consolidated his power that he could demand that his father abdicate. In 626, he assumed the throne as the second Tang ruler, eventually coming to be known as Emperor Taizong.

TAIZONG: THE GREATEST TANG EMPEROR

Barely twenty-six years old when he took power, Taizong overshadowed his father to become one of the most renowned monarchs in Chinese history. To many Chinese, Taizong would be revered as the quintessential emperor. They minimized his excesses and credited him with promoting a golden age in Chinese civilization. This view perhaps magnifies his role and fails to note that some of his policies and attitudes later generated serious problems.

Taizong achieved his greatest early successes as a military man, a career that shaped the first part of his reign. Thriftiness bred into him by military training caused him to condemn the lavishness of Sui projects and to seek to alleviate the burdens of taxes and corvée labor that the construction of elaborate palaces and other structures imposed upon the populace. Although he eventually succumbed to the desire for a luxurious court style, he still retained the image of a frugal and ascetic ruler. Asserting that his military background had offered him scant experience as an administrator, he professed interest in recruiting able officials to guide him. Like the ideal of the Confucian sage-ruler, he initially pledged to offer great leeway to his advisers. His brother-in-law Zhangsun Wuji (ca. 600–659) took the emperor at his word and thus played an active and, on occasion, decisive role in policy discussions. Wei Zheng (581–643) represented still another type of honest and competent counselor: the stern Confucian moralist who was blunt in his assessment of the emperor's performance. Although Wei at times reprimanded the emperor, he was neither harassed nor requested to tone down his criticism. Accepting and tolerating such critiques from a strict moralist actually served the emperor's interest because such behavior conformed to the Confucian model of proper relations between minister and ruler. Nonetheless, despite Taizong's perception of the significance of Confucian civilian advisers, transition from military conquest and rule to a civilian government proved to be difficult. Indeed, such problematic transitions plagued many of the Chinese and specifically foreign dynasties that sought to rule China.

The principal concern of this prominent galaxy of ministers and of Taizong himself was to establish stable central and local administrations. They quickly restored the Sui system of three central offices in which the Secretariat wrote up edicts, the Chancellery analyzed them, and the six ministries of the Department of State Affairs carried them out. In both the central and local governments, Taizong and his ministers sought to control corruption, to limit the power of the aristocratic families who still attempted to dominate government, and to include more geographic areas in recruiting officials. They wished to rein in the aristocrats who controlled local government, as the resurgence of localism or at least of a decentralized authority concerned them. Under pressure to offer hereditary appointments to imperial princes and trustworthy ministers, Taizong occasionally consented to such commissions, which could lead to a concentration of power in local elite families, but his closest advisers, opposed to such devolution of authority, persuaded him to limit such grants in order to avert the restoration of localism. His emphasis on the revival of the civil-service examinations, with the successful candidates constituting a pool of competent men, was designed to provide him with officials to help gain control over local affairs from the aristocratic elite. Taizong himself interviewed and questioned the most advanced candidates as part of the examination process. Although he also instructed the Directorate of Education to set up schools to prepare promising individuals for the exams, the number of successful graduates was still insufficient for the government's needs. Several decades would elapse before the exams became the principal supplier of officials. The civil-service examinations turned out to be one of the longest-lasting and most significant institutions in Chinese history. Abandoned only in 1905, they generated the bureaucracy that governed China. Because the examinations emphasized knowledge of Confucianism and the Confucian classics, they created an official class that often had Confucian cultural values.

Within a short time, the Tang also adopted a law code as part of restructuring the system. The Tang code, with some borrowings from earlier ones, was the earliest to be transmitted in toto to the present. In the early 620s, the first Tang emperor commissioned experts to devise the code, but three decades of assiduous efforts and critiques elapsed before it was proclaimed in 653. It would remain a standard for many future dynasties. Comprising twelve sections and over five hundred articles, it described offenses against the state, identifying transgressions of ordinary citizens and officials and specifying punishments for such offenses. The newly enacted code emphasized the individual's responsibility to society, not his or her rights. Protection of civil liberties was not a principal concern. The major objective was to ascertain the truth at any cost, including the use of torture to elicit confessions. Once the alleged facts had been uncovered, a defendant had to prove his or her innocence. A presumption of innocence until proven guilty was not integral to the code. Magistrates conducted investigations and presided over trials, acting as both prosecutor and judge, while the defendant argued his or her own case without legal assistance.

The code devoted considerable space to offenses against the imperial family and the state, including entire sections on laws concerning trespassing in forbidden places (palaces, city gates, and frontier walls) and transgressions by officials. The code's framers focused on state concerns such as taxes, land obligations, marriages of peasants, proper raising of troops, maintenance of stud farms and storehouses, and prevention of forgeries and counterfeiting. They also stressed order, emphasizing punishments for brawls and for offenses against individuals and property. Punishments depended on social status. Members of the elite received lesser punishments than ordinary Chinese for the same offenses. Joint responsibility could be invoked for what were perceived to be the most heinous offenses. Thus, family members who had no involvement could be punished if one of their kin were found guilty of treason or other high crimes. Punishments included flagellation with bamboo sticks, prison with hard labor, strangulation, decapitation, and death by slicing.

Meanwhile, the energetic Taizong proceeded to play an active role in strengthening his government. He pursued the Sui policy of organizing many of the empire's adult males into militias (*fubing*) to guard local areas and the capital; these troops furnished their own supplies but were granted exemptions from taxes and corvée labor in return. He still needed more professional soldiers for his foreign expeditions, but the availability of a militia relieved his regular army to take part in external campaigns. The use of the militia also reduced expenditures and thus minimized the court's burden of raising and collecting revenue. Most of its income derived from the equal-field system, but many in the elite were able to escape registration of their land and avoid taxation. The court also supplied grants of tax-exempt land to imperial princes, prominent civilian and military officials, and Buddhist and Daoist monasteries and Confucian temples and schools. Thus, the self-funded militia and the court's own financial restraints averted a fiscal crisis, but the relative ineffectiveness of the equal-field system and Taizong's inability to ensure its proper operation bequeathed a grave problem to later Tang rulers. One of his more successful ventures was reduction of the harshness of the legal code – for example, limiting the number of crimes for which capital punishment was mandated and demanding that officials send three separate reports about a case before actually executing anyone.

Having formulated policies for the militia, finances, and law, Taizong could turn his attention to cultural policy, which also had political implications. Because the Tang ruling family claimed descent from Laozi, Taizong was a generous patron of Daoism. Still, he had to adopt an even-handed policy toward the principal organized religions within the realm in order to ingratiate himself with every segment of the Chinese population. Thus, despite his misgivings about the Buddhist clergy and the minor restrictions he imposed upon the religion, he feared incurring the wrath of the increasingly affluent and powerful monks. His solution was to provide limited patronage to the Buddhists while endowing Daoist monks with benefactions unavailable to the Buddhists. His relations with Confucians were more direct and more positive. Needing skilled and educated counselors, he recognized the value of cultivating erudite Confucians. Having reinstituted the civil-service examinations, he also recruited scholars to write histories of the post-Han dynasties and devised the structure of an office of historiography. His support for Confucian scholars was also evident in his sponsorship of groups seeking to prepare standard editions of the classics and literary works. In essence, Taizong generally adopted the Sui policy of offering patronage to all three principal Chinese religions and philosophies, although he was less enthusiastic about Buddhism.

TANG EXPANSIONISM

Taizong also continued the Sui initiatives in foreign relations, which entailed an expansionist policy. Such an aggressive posture can, in part, be explained by the disruptions and chaos of the three centuries prior to Sui rule, during which foreigners capitalized on China's weakness to make incursions and even to establish dynasties on Chinese soil. An offensive policy could both deter such attacks and provide the Tang with buffer zones against any future foreign assaults. Scholars of the predominantly pastoral peoples living north of China offer still another explanation. They assert that the territories along the shared border of the Chinese and their neighbors consisted of land suitable for either cultivation or pasturage. Strong Chinese dynasties would seek to lay claim to this potentially arable land. Expansionism was also linked to control and protection of trade routes. Although the Tang, like other dynasties before and after, repeatedly asserted that China was economically self-sufficient, many Chinese benefited enormously from commerce. Trade and increased revenue for the court thus promoted attempts to safeguard routes and to control land beyond the Tang borders. Moreover, because Taizong himself aspired to be remembered as one of the most extraordinary rulers in the Chinese tradition, the enlargement of Chinese territory and the submission of foreigners would bolster his claims. Although the Chinese courts often disparaged and emphasized the emperor's moral leadership, historians would frequently designate those emperors whose achievements resulted in a more powerful empire as "great."

Thus, Taizong pursued an opportunistic and occasionally bellicose foreign policy, which was often successful, partly because of disarray among his neighbors. The eastern and western Turks were the first to experience turbulence, leading to civil wars and disastrous fragmentation (the fate of the primarily pastoral peoples north and west of China throughout much of recorded history). Capitalizing on a struggle between the khaghan and his nephew, Tang forces defeated the divided eastern Turks, occupying modern Inner Mongolia and the Ordos region and capturing the khaghan in 630. Similar divisions bedeviled the western Turks, who controlled the Tarim River oases along the Silk Roads to central and west Asia. Taking advantage of such tensions, Taizong ordered his forces to move expeditiously to dominate these vital halting places on the trade routes. This was no easy task, for a Tang army had to cross a vast stretch of inhospitable desert terrain in order to invade and lay claim to these fragile but significant sites.

In addition, Taizong was determined to control both the southern and northern Silk Roads, and this exacerbated the difficulties for his invading force. Yet, by the end of his reign, Chinese troops had consolidated their authority over the oases all the way to Kashgar. Quite a few non-Chinese merchants in the oases welcomed a Chinese presence because they wished to restore and doubtless surpass the trade of the glorious days of the Han dynasty. Thus Hami (the gateway to the northern routes) voluntarily acceded to Chinese rule in 630, and Khotan (an oasis on the southern routes that had vast quantities of white, black, and green jade) and Kashgar (the western juncture of the two routes) submitted in 632. However, Tang troops had to fight their way along the northern routes, reaching Kharashahr by 644 and Kucha by 648. This resounding success profoundly influenced not only the Tang's economy but also its culture. Its control of the oases resulted in increased contact with other Asian civilizations and in a more cosmopolitan court. Safe passage permitted merchants, clerics, and entertainers to flock to China during the seventh and eighth centuries, bringing with them new goods, ideas, and technologies. China would be in touch with developments in Persia, India, and central Asia.

Taizong was somewhat less successful in relations with Tibet and Korea, but suffered no major disasters. Tibet achieved political unity at this very time. King Srong-btsan-sgam-po (605?–649) unified the previously autonomous peoples and, perceiving himself to be the equal of the Tang ruler, requested a marital alliance, which would bolster his legitimacy. Denied such a concession, the king raided Chinese border settlements until Taizong relented, and in 641 dispatched Princess Wencheng (d. 680), his niece, as a marriage partner for the Tibetan monarch. The Princess brought Buddhist texts and artifacts from China in an attempt to win over the king to a Chinese Buddhist sect. At the same time, a princess from the Indian subcontinent was sent in marriage to the Tibetan king to lure him to join an Indian Buddhist sect. The Jokkang, the oldest Buddhist temple in Tibet, was reputedly built to house the treasures brought by the two princesses. In the event, Taizong's concession ushered in a period of peace, although tensions would erupt shortly after the Tang emperor's death. Like his Sui predecessors, Taizong was obsessed with Korea. He sought to establish suzerainty over Korea or at least to install Silla, the Korean kingdom he supported, in power. These aims prompted him to lead two separate expeditions against the kingdom of Koguryo, his principal antagonist in Korea. Both campaigns ended in failure, and their squandering of resources provoked some unrest in China.

IRREGULAR SUCCESSIONS AND THE EMPRESS WU

Taizong's mostly positive legacy did not extend to the succession to the throne. Machinations by unscrupulous court officials, as well as by several of his own ambitious sons, resulted in the crowning of one of his least able sons. Taizong himself contributed to this chaotic state of affairs. Appalled by his designated heir's infatuation with Turkish dress and lifestyle and by his homosexual liaison, he had his son's partner executed. The son tried to avenge himself, planning to assassinate one of his brothers, but the plot was discovered and Taizong stripped his son of the succession and exiled him. Later he was compelled to exile still another son and possible heir for involvement in yet another plot. His ministers eventually pressured him to appoint his son Li Zhi as his successor. His unease about this appointment proved prophetic.

Li Zhi, under the reign title Gaozong (628–683), seemed to preside over a prosperous China, but appearances were deceptive. An indecisive and weak person, he actually ruled for only a brief part of his reign, as strong officials and one of his empresses wielded power in his name. The Chinese economy of his time seemed to be booming, with relative peace enabling peasants to focus on the land and to increase agricultural production and with foreign merchants beginning to arrive in larger numbers to trade for Chinese products and to make available to the Tang elite an astonishing variety of goods. In addition, domestic regional trade resulted in the establishment of new towns and cities dependent upon commerce. Yet the government's fiscal underpinning was shaky because the equal-field system, the mainstay of court revenue, was not operating properly. It required registration of all who either worked or owned land. Yet administrative incompetence, corruption, and resistance meant that barely half of China's households had been registered by Gaozong's time, and the rest simply evaded taxes, imperiling the government's ability to meet its fiscal obligations for court, military, public-works, and bureaucratic expenditures. However, despite these problems looming on the horizon, China experienced no major catastrophes during Gaozong's reign.

His era is inextricably linked with the ascendancy of Empress Wu (624–705), the only woman to rule China in her own right. Because Empress Wu represented the antithesis of the most cherished values of the Confucian elite, her reputation in the traditional Chinese accounts is unenviable. These works depict her as ruthless, vindictive, and cruel and accuse her of pitiless and vengeful crimes ranging from purging and exiling her opponents to almost unimaginable brutality, including the suffocation of her infant daughter. Such characterizations should probably be somewhat discounted, for they reflect Confucian scholar-elite antipathy toward women in public life and toward what they perceived to be political machinations that violated Confucian morality. Naturally, this assertive and no doubt unsavory woman was cast in the most negative light.

A concubine at the court of Taizong, Wu adroitly maneuvered to gain power. She appears to have attracted the young Gaozong's attention and was thus able to avert the typical fate of concubines upon an emperor's death: consignment to a Buddhist nunnery. Shortly after his accession, Gaozong brought her back to court as one of his concubines. From her base at the court, she sought to attract allies in her effort to undermine Gaozong's empress and to have herself elevated to that position. According to the not unbiased Chinese histories, she killed her own daughter, making it appear that the empress was the murderess. Probably more important, she gave birth to a son, providing the emperor with an heir and giving her greater leverage in her rivalry with the empress. As a result, Gaozong raised her to the status of empress, enabling her finally to eliminate her rival. The histories revile her for supposedly having the former empress executed in a grisly manner. The executioner reputedly cut off the former empress' arms and legs, allowing her to bleed to death painfully. A few influential court officials who had supported the former empress were either exiled or killed. Such purges were not bloodier than court struggles in earlier dynasties. Thus, the historians' severe condemnation of Empress Wu seems overstated and hypocritical. Her rise to power was also facilitated by the emperor's weak personality and by his recurrent illnesses, including a severe stroke.

From around the mid 660s, the Empress Wu ruled in her husband's name, yet she still encountered opposition. Thus, she courted support from the Buddhist establishment and from those who opposed the old aristocracy. Deeply religious, if not superstitious, the empress favored the already powerful and affluent Buddhist monasteries, providing funds for the construction of religious buildings and for the fashioning of statues at the Buddhist cave complexes. She attracted scholars by subsidizing projects designed to produce definitive lay as well as Buddhist texts. With such support, she was able to have the first heir apparent who appeared to challenge her position exiled for reputedly plotting a coup d'état. Her own fourteen-year-old son, who seemed as weak as his father, was then designated the heir apparent, which strengthened her position, particularly after the death of Gaozong in 683.

Yet Empress Wu continued to face challenges to her authority until she finally assumed power in her own name in 690. Paradoxically, her first threat arose from the son she had selected as the new emperor. She had not counted on his wife, the Empress Wei, and her relatives, who had persuaded the young emperor to appoint members of her own clan to important positions at court, unnerving many of Empress Wu's allies in the bureaucracy. Within a couple of months, Wu reacted to this challenge by forcing her son to abdicate and enthroning his brother, Emperor Ruizong (662–716). This *putsch* did not end the turbulence, for a coup erupted shortly after the accession that the empress had imposed. Wu not only suppressed this ill-organized and ill-planned coup and killed or imprisoned the hapless plotters but also initiated a ruthless purge of both actual and potential dissidents. Quite a few prominent officials either lost their lives or were exiled during this period of excessive retribution. The only defense for Wu's actions stems from her fear that Confucian antipathy toward female rulers would jeopardize her position and her conclusion that officials who held such views needed to be rooted out. Indeed, when she was apprised of unjust accusations against loyal officials, she rescinded proceedings against them. Nonetheless, many were illegitimately condemned, particularly when Wu had an affair with a so-called Buddhist monk named Huaiyi (d. 694) and paid less attention to court affairs. She eventually tired of Huaiyi's highhandedness and had him murdered.

Having been the dominant figure at court for about three decades, it seemed only a matter of time before Wu would assert her own claim to the throne. She had already shifted most court activities from Changan to Luoyang, upon which enormous resources had been lavished. She commissioned a supposedly ancient stone tablet that proclaimed that a "sage" female would rule the world. At the same time, the suspicious discovery of a Buddhist sutra stating that the Maitreya, or Future Buddha, would be incarnated as a woman and that her arrival would usher in a period of great prosperity gave Wu the opportunity to act. In 690, after three ritual refusals, she accepted the throne as "emperor" of a new Zhou dynasty, the name chosen because of its evocation of a golden age in Chinese civilization. One of her first actions was to establish her capital in Luoyang, which was not only easier to defend and supply than Changan but also permitted her freedom from the aristocratic clans who dominated the capital in the west. Her main administrative innovation was increased reliance on the civil-service examinations, rather than dependence on aristocratic privilege, for appointments to office. Yet, despite strong support for a merit system, she herself often circumvented the bureaucracy, relying instead on the "Scholars of the Northern Gate," a group of her cronies, to help devise and implement court policy. Her patronage of Buddhism also contributed to irregularities in administration, as she offered Buddhist monks privileges and positions at court. In effect, Buddhism became the court religion during her reign.

Although the underlying problems of inadequate revenues from land taxes and their evasion by the elite persisted, Empress Wu made only half-hearted efforts to cope with the shortfall; as she aged, her energies were diverted elsewhere. Indeed, as her reign and her life drew to a close, she became ever more distant and allowed her favorites to run roughshod over government, as corruption, sale of offices, political abuses, and excessive opulence characterized the court. Reputable officials repeatedly attempted to rid the court of her parasitic and corruptible favorites, but she just as often either saved her cronies or simply did not cooperate in the effort to remove them. Finally, early in 705, a cabal of officials took advantage of her frailty to organize a coup that placed her son Zhongzong (656–710) on the throne as emperor. The Zhou dynasty came to an end, having had, like Wang Mang's Xin dynasty, only one ruler.

Unsettled conditions did not end with the enthronement of Emperor Zhongzong or his successor. Most of the next decade presented a chaotic tableau at court, as the emperor's relatives and the government's ministers competed for power. Bizarre intrigues, plots and counterplots, and corruption marred the history of this period of restoration. Shifting the capital back to Changan, Empress Wei, Emperor Zhongzong's wife, dominated the early stage, expropriated land for herself and her retainers, dealt harshly with any dissent, and may have poisoned her husband when he challenged her. Shortly thereafter, a coup led by Princess Taiping (d. 713), Wu's daughter, resulted in the assassination of Empress Wei and the brief restoration of Emperor Ruizong to the throne.

When Emperor Ruizong proved to be less than totally compliant, Princess Taiping forced him into retirement, and in 712 his son Li Longji (685–762) became emperor. The new emperor came to be known by his posthumous title of Xuanzong and proved to be a much more forceful ruler. Sensing that her power was threatened and that her position could be challenged, Taiping organized a coup to depose Xuanzong, but one of her coconspirators betrayed her. Xuanzong acted first, killing the principal plotters and forcing Taiping herself to commit suicide. The death of Taiping brought to an end the dominant roles of women and female rulers in Tang politics. Many Chinese historians have been vituperative in their denunciations of all these princesses and empresses. Such blanket condemnations do not square with the evidence, certainly not in describing Empress Wu. Despite her excesses and occasional capriciousness, Wu's reign witnessed impressive accomplishments. The prestige of the civil-service examinations was bolstered, as successful candidates staffed an increasing percentage of the bureaucracy. Wu's patronage of Buddhism, although it enraged Confucian officials, contributed not only to the development of the religion but also to art and architecture, to trade with Buddhist lands, and to knowledge of the outside world. Yet her drive for power and her circumvention of regular bureaucratic channels in decision making undercut the proper operation of government and laid the foundations for irregularities during the almost decade-long period from the end of her reign until the accession of Xuanzong.

TANG COSMOPOLITANISM

However, Wu's expansiveness and her lack of hostility toward trade, which also characterized Taizong's reign, fostered Tang cosmopolitanism. As a result, foreign merchants, who were less likely to be restricted than during most Chinese dynasties, flocked to China both along the caravan trails through central Asia and via the sea routes to China's southeast ports, areas that had become increasingly prominent after the fall of the Han dynasty. With them came official envoys from other lands; a few – such as the emissary from the Sassanid ruler of Persia, whose domains were threatened by the Islamic armies from Arabia – sought assistance from China, while others merely attempted to curry favor in order to secure the imprimatur of the greatest power in east Asia. Finally, a profusion of clerics – Buddhist, Nestorian, Manichean, and Zoroastrian, among others – arrived to establish a beachhead in China. These foreigners began to create their own communities within China. Quanzhou and Guangzhou (or Canton), for example, had virtually self-governing foreign settlements of Muslims and scattered groups of Indians and Southeast Asians. Changan, which received foreigners mostly from the land routes, had communities of Turks, Uyghurs, and Persians. Naturally, their clothing, music and dance, food, and native products stimulated Chinese interest and yearning for foreign customs and foreign goods.

Indeed, an amazing variety of foreign products and discoveries now entered China. Grapes, though introduced as early as the Han, became more popular, and the Persians and the Turks transmitted knowledge of how to produce grape wine. Pistachios, kohlrabi, spinach, pepper, sugar, nutmeg, saffron, and jasmine were among the foods, aromatics, medicines, and spices brought to China. Foreign dwarfs, musicians, acrobats, and dancers not only entertained at the Tang court but also introduced new fashions in hair and dress. Simultaneously, the Tang introduced tea, a beverage recorded as early as the Qin dynasty, to Korea and Japan and the Chinese introduced paper to central Asia.

Although part of this increased contact with foreign lands came about through trade, cultural interchange, and religion, part was also due to Tang expansionism in the latter half of the seventh century. During the reigns of Gaozong and Empress Wu, China reached the greatest territorial extent in its history. For example, internal disturbances within the state of Koguryo enabled the two Tang rulers to succeed where the Sui emperors had failed. Before challenging Koguryo in 660, Tang forces, with the help of the state of Silla, their principal ally in Korea, had vanquished the southern state of Paekche, which they could then use as a base for forays against Koguryo. In 668, Tang troops overran the weakened kingdom of Koguryo and stationed a force of about twenty thousand men in P'yongyang, its principal city. Within a decade, the Tang withdrew these troops, but they no longer faced a hostile power in the peninsula and even perceived of the Silla kings as vassals. Trade and tribute from Korea increased considerably with the fall of Koguryo. To the west, the Tang continued to capitalize on internal struggles among the western Turks and briefly occupied the very borders of Persia. The court also served as a haven for the son of the last king of Sassanid Persia, whose dynasty the Arabs had vanquished. Such control over the central Asian towns and oases facilitated long-distance trade across Asia.

This long-distance trade across central Asia required oases and garrisons. The oases or towns, such as Hami and Samarkand, needed to be multiethnic and multilinguistic – characteristics that would promote and facilitate relations with travelers. Foreign merchants could often find inhabitants who spoke the same language, making commercial transactions smoother. Each town required access to water, either from rivers or from the melting snow of neighboring mountains. The carefully preserved water and the elaborate irrigation works designed to make optimal use of this precious resource permitted the oases to be agriculturally self-sufficient. Needless to say, all were strategically located on one or more trade routes. These towns, which provided vital halting places for merchants journeying across Eurasia, were essential, but defense against bandits and marauders was critical for the survival of commerce. Like the Han, the Tang stationed garrisons beyond the traditional boundaries of China to protect travelers. It erected watchtowers, generally guarded by conscript soldiers, along the major trade routes. These forces used flag or smoke signals to warn travelers of perils and also provided them with hostelries and supplies.

Even with these institutions, merchants encountered innumerable difficulties on the trade routes. The first was the roads themselves, although "roads" is a misnomer and "trails" might be a more appropriate term. These trails were difficult to traverse and by no means easy to follow. Winter snows and summer floods occasionally obscured them or made them impassable. The inhospitable climate and terrain posed other obstacles. Desert travel was extremely hazardous, as travelers sometimes needed to walk across sand dunes as high as sixty or seventy feet. Vivid and frightening descriptions of sandstorms appear in the accounts of numerous travelers. The intense heat of the desert and the frigid temperatures in the mountains, leading to the perils of icy conditions, frostbite, and mountain sickness, were still other concerns for merchants. Finally, yet another difficulty was the enormous capital required for such long-distance trade. Many caravans failed to reach their destinations. Yet sufficient numbers of merchants were willing to risk sizable losses for a regular flow of caravans to persist throughout the height of the Tang. They took such risks because of the anticipated profits. The elites in the civilizations in central Asia, west Asia, and the West paid vast sums for Chinese goods, so the trade was extremely lucrative.

Tang pacification of the western Turks and other groups in central Asia resulted in a seemingly uninterrupted flow of caravans through the region. However, almost directly south the Chinese faced a real challenge, that intruded on their generally stable relations with their neighbors. In the early 660s, Tibet was at war with the Tuyuhun, a confederation of tribes around the Kokonor region. Within a few years, Tibetan forces used these newly subjugated lands as a base to expand into the oases of the Tarim basin, thus threatening China's Silk Roads trade to the west. The Tang responded to this challenge with several unsuccessful military expeditions, but in 692, capitalizing on internal disturbances within Tibet, a well-organized force recaptured the vital oases of Kucha, Khotan, and Kashgar. This potential impediment to commerce along the Silk Roads was thus removed.

ARRIVAL OF FOREIGN RELIGIONS

Extended relations with the outside world enriched Chinese culture. Nowhere was this impact more evident than in the profusion of foreign religions that reached China during this era. Since the court adopted a policy of toleration or at least of benign neglect to religions that did not create political or social disruption, foreign clerics faced no insuperable obstacles in building houses of worship, monuments, and monasteries in which to expound their religious views.

Chinese Buddhism benefited enormously from the opportunity for closer contact with other centers of Buddhism. Indians and central Asians arrived in China to introduce new sects, to explicate texts, and to teach acolytes. At the same time, a few Chinese monks traveled to the sites of the religion's origins to study with Buddhist masters, to collect texts, and to gather Buddhist artifacts. Xuanzang (596 or 602–664), the most renowned of these Buddhist pilgrims, followed in the footsteps of Faxian (337–ca. 422) by leaving China without specific imperial sanction and spending sixteen years journeying through the oases of Turfan, Khotan, and Dunhuang and through the Indian subcontinent, trekking overland in both directions. He learned about a variety of Buddhist texts and accumulated, through gifts or purchases, vast quantities of Buddhist objects. Having survived blizzards, bandits, and overzealous rulers who wanted to persuade this learned monk to settle in their lands, he returned to the Tang capital at Changan, bringing with him Buddhist writings and artifacts. Emperor Taizong was delighted with the intrepid Buddhist monk and the treasures he brought back to China. He granted Xuanzang a lengthy audience during which he questioned the cleric not only about religious matters but also about the customs, goods, and peoples he had encountered on his travels. Taizong and his successor, Gaozong, provided support and patronage for Xuanzang's efforts, over the next two decades, to translate the texts he had transported to China. While persisting in his translation projects, Xuanzang also wrote the *Da Tang Xiyuji* (*Record of the Western Regions in the Great Tang*), an account of his travels that broadened China's knowledge of another part of the world. Like Faxian, who wrote *A Record of Buddhistic Kingdoms* (*Gaoseng Faxian Zhuanyi juan*), he mentioned the products of the various regions he had visited; these were reports that would interest Chinese merchants and officials. The Buddhists thus contributed to China's store of information and perceptions of other lands.

The monk Yi Jing (635–713) was the most renowned of the Buddhist pilgrims to travel by ship to the Buddhist centers. In 671, he departed from Guangzhou via the sea route to India, where he remained for more than a decade to read and study the Buddhist texts. From there, he traveled to the Indianized states of Srivijaya (in southeast Sumatra) and began to translate the Sanskrit writings into Chinese. After more than two decades, he finally returned to China, where the Empress Wu greeted him as a hero and lavished numerous rewards and gifts upon him.

Such interest and knowledge led to the introduction and development of new Buddhist sects, several of which had little success in attracting adherents. The doctrines of the Sect of the Three Stages (*Sanjie*) met with hostility from the court, which eventually proscribed it. Its proponents contended that history would consist of a first stage of a true implementation of the Buddha's teachings, another stage of an adulterated version of the teachings, and the last stage of the degeneration of these messages. They insisted that their own times were part of the third stage, when no sages would appear, chaotic conditions would prevail, and people would not be able to understand true morality and would be unable to distinguish between good and evil. They contended that the proper response to these unsettled times was austere conduct and almsgiving. In effect, by maintaining that society was in a state of decay, the Three Stages sect challenged the Tang's claim that the dynasty had fostered prosperity and cultural efflorescence. By emphasizing the degeneracy of the times, the sect also appeared to be indirectly criticizing the Tang, which reacted, predictably enough, by seeking to prohibit its practice. Unlike the Three Sects, the Disciplinary school (*Luzong*) did not attract the hostility of the court, partly because it had limited popular appeal and partly because it did not impart a potentially threatening or subversive message. The monk Daoxuan (596–667), its originator, directed the school toward the monastic community, devising a comprehensive set of rules for monks and nuns. Because his rules would not have wide popular appeal and indeed the school's doctrines were limited primarily to clerics, his sect did not attract the court's attention.

The Characteristics of the Dharma (*Faxiang*) school and the Tantric or Esoteric school were two other sects of great doctrinal interest whose appeal to ordinary people was nevertheless limited. The *Faxiang* sect asserted that the only reality consisted of ideas or consciousness and that the world of appearances or external phenomena was illusory and simply a corrupt form of consciousness. They argued that realization of this basic truth led to an understanding of perfect wisdom. This emphasis on consciousness and on denial of external reality was overly abstract and thus attracted few adherents, though these doctrines captivated the pilgrim Xuanzang. Because the sect also offered no tangible formulas for achieving enlightenment, it restricted its potential audience. The Tantric school, borrowing from Hinduism, conceived of a large number of deities who could be influenced by magic, sorcery, and a variety of symbols. Mantras, the chanting of set formulas that are scarcely intelligible, offered one means to ward off evil and to resist the spells initiated by opponents. The most renowned such mantra, "Om mani padme hum," was deemed to be effective in the attainment of enlightenment or paradise. Mudras, or the positioning of hands or fingers of the deities in a manner designed to be imitated by believers, reputedly offered another means of enlightenment. The mandala, a representation of the Buddhas and bodhisattvas in their respective positions in the cosmos, offered still another technique for understanding the illusory nature of external reality. Indian masters of the Tantric school arrived in China during the early and middle Tang to propagate its views, but the sect gained prominence almost exclusively in Changan; with the cessation of visits from these Indian Buddhists, the sect withered away.

The Huayan school was one of the more successful Buddhist sects in China. Fazang (643–712), a learned scholar and erudite translator, and Guifeng Zongmi (780–841), a charismatic and persuasive lecturer, were among the most renowned proponents of this abstruse teaching, which required concrete illustrations to explain its major principles to baffled students and even to disciples. Its main teaching consisted of a belief in a world of emptiness characterized by the duality of principle (*li*) and phenomenon (*shi*), which were totally interlocked. Similarly, all phenomena were not distinct or separate, as all phenomena are, in turn, expressions of *li*. In seeking to illustrate this principle, Fazang wrote an essay titled *The Golden Lion*, pointing out that in the nose, ears, and other organs of the lion are found the entire golden lion and, in turn, the entire lion is found even in the tiniest element of its body. Every phenomenon is intertwined with all phenomena, with the Buddha at the core. Again, Fazang sought to illustrate this principle with a concrete example. He placed eight mirrors in line with the eight main points of the compass and added two others, one on top and one below, each facing the other. He then moved a Buddha figure, lit by a torch, into the center, and it turned out that the figure was reflected in the mirrors and that the figure in each mirror appeared in all the other mirrors. Thus he explained the identity of all phenomena with each phenomenon and indicated that the Buddha lay at the center of all phenomena and principles. Despite its somewhat enigmatic teachings, the Huayan sect did attract adherents and survived past the Tang era.

The Tiantai school, a sect with a similarly difficult message, also gained support during the Tang and lasted beyond the dynasty. Zhiyi (538–597), its most prominent adherent, actually lived before the Tang, but the sect achieved its widest following during the Tang. The sect's name derives from the location where Zhiyi decided to settle: Mount Tiantai, in the modern province of Zhejiang. Zhiyi himself sought to create an eclectic sect that would incorporate and reconcile the teachings of diverse other schools. Recognizing that believers were confused by the differing conceptions of the Buddha and Buddhism represented in the sutras and by the differing emphases of the various sects, he tried to offer an explanation for the seeming inconsistencies in the texts and schools. One rationale he put forth was that the teachings reflected different periods in the Buddha's life and that they were designed for different audiences. Because some of the early sutras, written after the Buddha's initial enlightenment, were simply too difficult for all but the most sophisticated believers, the Buddha proposed concepts that could be more widely understood. As more people became aware of these basic principles, he started to offer a third and more sophisticated version of his teachings. In addition, however, the Buddha, recognizing that his lectures reached individuals of differing abilities, simultaneously presented different messages to meet the levels of his diverse audience. The Buddha thus spoke in a variety of voices to reach his different listeners. Zhiyi did not deride any of the messages in the sutras, as they all represented the Buddha's message modulated to fit the needs of those with a lesser or a greater understanding of Buddhism.

The Threefold Truth embodied the ultimate Tiantai doctrine. The first truth was that things were empty. Yet they were not simply meaningless because they had a transitory existence in the world that we currently perceive, the second truth. The reality or the mean encompassed both emptiness and transitoriness – the third truth, which combined the other two and was superior to both. All of these phenomena were integrated in the absolute mind, which incorporated both the tiniest things, even a strand of hair (often used by the Tiantai school to represent the most miniscule element in the universe), and the most colossal. Although the concept of the absolute mind emphasized the nonmaterial world, the Tiantai did not reject the world of phenomena and instead perceived it as a useful place within the purview of the universe. It thus accorded the ordinary activities of human beings a role in the mostly spiritual component of Buddhist teachings.

Chan was still another sect that flourished during the Tang. This teaching slighted the use of the intellect to achieve enlightenment. Instead it proposed meditation as a means of attaining enlightenment, which was identified as the Buddha-nature that each individual possessed within himself or herself. Human logic would not lead to enlightenment, a state that culminated in a perception of the unity of all phenomena. This state could not be described in words. It could be perceived only in feelings, and an outside observer could not gauge whether an individual had achieved the spiritual awakening of enlightenment. Study of the Buddhist writings and proper conduct according to Buddhist precepts were irrelevant and could detract from the intuitive response essential for enlightenment. One school within Chan believed that such intuition and the ensuing breakdown of reason necessitated jarring and occasionally devastating "attacks" to undermine the logical defenses that impeded the effort to arrive at a Buddhist nature of spontaneous, intuitive responses. A Chan master might yell at or beat an acolyte, or insist that he stay awake for long periods – all deliberate attempts to undermine the rational faculties. The master might also pose problems (*gongan*) to assist the disciple in moving beyond human logic. These problems were often paradoxical and were designed to elicit intuitive, nonrational answers. Such questions as "can you hear one hand clapping?" defied reason and required an intuitive leap. A verbal response to these queries was not necessarily a good choice because Chan mistrusted words. A smile, a frown, or other facial or body signals were more effective means of communication.

Chan, with its individualism and spontaneity, appears to clash with Buddhist views and to have more in common with Daoism. Its disdain for Buddhist texts, worship, and rituals meant it diverged considerably from other sects, but its defenders declared that their objective – achieving enlightenment – was precisely what Buddhists valued. Moreover, they did not distance themselves from Daoism because they did not repudiate attitudes of naturalness and spontaneity, scorn for verbal communication, or the possibility of Buddhahood and *dao* within the individual; they shared all these beliefs with Daoist masters.

Numerous stories and myths have developed about the Chan leaders who introduced the sect in China. Bodhidharma, in particular, a patriarch of the sect in the fifth or sixth century, was the central figure in a number of accounts concerning the development of Chan in China. He arrived from central Asia and began to teach that enlightenment lay within the individual and that nonverbal means were the ideal vehicles for transmission and understanding of Buddhism. He and his fellow Chan proponents, however, by the nature of their teachings – which relied on a one-on-one master–disciple relationship – did not attract a wide following.

The Pure Land school became the most popular sect of Buddhism. It did not require a disciplined or ascetic life, deprived of sensual pleasures, nor did it demand extensive study or meditation. It emphasized salvation, not rigorous activities leading to enlightenment or self-knowledge. In other words, it was easy to practice, and its objective was appealing. The two versions of the *Pure Land Sutra* embodied its principal teachings; one version simply focused on sincere faith as the road to salvation while the other stressed that, in addition to faith, good works were essential. The version of the *Sutra* that attracted the largest number of adherents was the one that stressed faith alone. According to the text, the final objective was rebirth in the Pure Land, a Western Paradise presided over by Amitabha. This idyllic land, described as a virtually perfect environment with beautiful flowers and trees next to rivers redolent of sweet fragrance, was accessible if the worshipper believed in Amitabha with a sincere heart. It was taught that Buddha had facilitated the individual's rebirth into the Pure Land because of the merit he had accumulated, which he had then transmitted to the rest of mankind. The only criterion for entrance into this paradise was belief in Amitabha, as reflected in chants of devotion directed at the creator and guardian of the Western Paradise.

Guanyin assisted Amitabha in easing entry into the Pure Land. As a bodhisattva – that is, a person who had achieved Nirvana but returned to help others do so – Guanyin was a compassionate figure who protected humans from evils and threats and to whom childless women would pray to give birth to a son. Originally depicted in sculpture and painting in a male form, in later times, particularly after the Song dynasty, Guanyin appeared as a female. She was also often portrayed with numerous arms, indicating her desire and ability to embrace the world.

Pure Land's simplicity made it appealing, and some of its proponents further simplified it. Daozhou (562–645) advocated repetition of the Buddha's name as a means of assuring entry into the Pure Land, a proposal that reputedly led one of his disciples to utter the Buddha's name one million times in a week. Shantao (613–681), one of his other disciples, urged chanting of the sutras and worshipping of images of the Buddha, along with repetition of the Buddha's name, as useful recipes for entrance into the Western Paradise. As a result of its simplicity, Pure Land grew astonishingly during this era, as evidenced by the increasing number of representations of Amitabha and Guanyin in Chinese Buddhist art. They tended to supersede the depictions of the historical Buddha and of Maitreya, the Future Buddha. Also of great popular appeal were paintings of the horrors of Hell and the delights of the Western Paradise. No wonder that Pure Land was found attractive by many Chinese who did not wish to undergo the strict discipline or exercises in meditation or the reading and analysis of complicated writings required in other Buddhist sects.

While these sects gained adherents, the monasteries and nunneries flourished, and many became involved in secular activities. Under the equal-field system monks and nuns received land, and the Tang rulers also granted sizable holdings to the monasteries. By combining their allotments, some of the monasteries had substantial estates. In addition, the failures of the equal-field system led to the imposition of additional taxes on peasants, who were occasionally compelled to abandon their land or to sell it to large landlords or to monasteries. Wealthy patrons also contributed to the monasteries with donations of land, and monasteries could call upon a large number of peasants, many of whom were criminals, orphans, or farmers dispossessed of their lands, to farm their estates. Because their holdings were tax exempt, the monasteries garnered sizable profits that enabled them either to buy additional lands or invest in other enterprises. The monasteries had a variety of potentially profitable ventures, including loans with interest to merchants. They also established pawnshops, oil presses, inns, and even banks.

These secular activities generated funds for the monasteries. No wonder then that they could afford to construct beautifully landscaped temples of ample scale. Within the temples were splendid images of gold, silver, or bronze, as well as bronze bells, incense burners, and ritual vessels. The monks, in addition, did not deprive themselves, wearing elaborate silk robes and enjoying well-prepared and far-from-measly repasts. Some accumulated their own lands, animals, carts, and valuable religious articles. Quite a few did not lead a life of austerity and discipline. No wonder then that unscrupulous, ill-educated, and profit-minded individuals sought ordination as monks, compelling the Tang government to assist in expelling unfit slackers and profiteers from the monasteries. The government also devised examinations to test a prospective monk's knowledge of Buddhism before he was accepted into the monastic fold. However, being frequently in need of income, it also occasionally sold certificates that provided immediate ordination for monks. In addition, the emperors could furnish certificates enabling laymen to be accepted into the monastic orders. The monks had their own organization and hierarchy, but the government also appointed officials to scrutinize the monasteries' activities. As the dynasty waned, these officials were principally eunuchs who were often accused of expropriating some of the monasteries' property for themselves.

Aside from maintenance of the monasteries and perhaps ill-advised luxuries and corruption, the income generated from the Buddhists' property served a variety of purposes. It supported the various festivals organized by the monasteries in commemoration of state and religious rituals; the translation of Buddhist writings; schools for training acolytes; and the propagation of Buddhist teachings to the population through colorful and marvelous stories from the Buddhist sutras.

A variety of foreign religions from west Asia reached the Tang, but none had the same success as Buddhism. Persian merchants and travelers exposed China to Zoroastrianism and Manicheism, but these religions did not attract a wide following. Manicheism had a greater impact on the non-Chinese along China's northern frontiers. Jewish merchants traded along the Silk Roads, but no Jewish community settled in China until the twelfth century, and even then the community consisted of just a few thousand residents. West Asian traders and emissaries also introduced Nestorianism, a heretical form of Christianity that was banned from Europe in the fourth and fifth centuries, to China. Nestorianism had scant influence on the Chinese; its only surviving contribution is a stele that describes the religion's main tenets. It too found a more receptive audience among the peoples living north of China, especially the Mongols. All these west Asian religions espoused sole-truth beliefs that did not suit China's eclectic views. A Chinese who could simultaneously be Confucian, Daoist, and Buddhist in respective parts of his life would not wish to abandon his previous beliefs and practices for a sole-truth religion.

The only other west Asian religion was Islam. Muslim merchants reached China both by the Silk Roads and by sea. Arabs and Persians navigated across the Persian Gulf to the Indian Ocean and eventually arrived in Guangzhou, Quanzhou, and other ports of southeast China. Relations between them and the Tang were generally harmonious, partly because they did not seek to proselytize the Chinese population. Other than a battle near the Talas River in central Asia in 751 between an Arab force and a Tang army, the Muslims lived peacefully in virtually self-governing communities in southeast and northwest China. The Tang offered them considerable leverage because they performed valuable services for China. The court recruited them for positions as translators and interpreters and, perhaps as important, often employed them in the empire's horse administration. It recognized that the Arabs and Persians were more adept than the Chinese in breeding and tending horses. Muslim traders imported a variety of goods, and Chinese merchants and even officials profited from this commerce.

GLORIOUS TANG ARTS

The prosperity of the Buddhist monasteries had a positive influence on the arts. Other than the funerary figures at the tombs of emperors and nobles, most of Tang sculpture reflected Buddhist interests and patronage. The emperors and the monks themselves commissioned colossal statues – both life-size figures and miniature sculptures of Buddhas and bodhisattvas. Many of the sculptures revealed a combination of indigenous and foreign elements, with Indian sensuality combined with Chinese sensitivity to line, for example. This same mélange of the native and the foreign was integral to Buddhist painting of this era, much of which was destroyed during a devastating repression of Buddhism in the ninth century. Contemporaneous sources reveal that foreign painters worked in and were much admired by Chinese artists. A number focused on Buddhist subjects, and their techniques and themes influenced native painters. The Dunhuang caves, found along the Silk Roads, yield a treasure trove of wall paintings of events in the life of the Buddha and the bodhisattvas, with landscapes and portraits dominating.

Secular painting flourished as well, though few examples have survived. None of the portraits produced by Wu Daozi (680–740), one of the most renowned of these painters, are still extant. The excavation and opening of several tombs in the 1970s enriched knowledge of Tang painting because delicate portraits of court ladies, as well as poses of dynamic lions and other animals, adorn the walls. The tomb of Empress Wu, which is perched on a hill overlooking the tombs in the valley below, has not been excavated, but the presence there of a considerable cache of paintings,

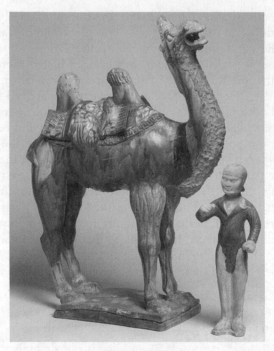

Figure 5.1 Tomb figure of a Bactrian camel, Tang dynasty. Philadelphia Museum of Art, Pennsylvania, PA, USA / Gift of Mrs. John Wintersteen / The Bridgeman Art Library

perhaps exhibiting both Buddhist and secular themes, is uncontested. Painters also depicted court scenes and landscapes, with Yan Liben (ca. 600–673) and the scholar and poet Wang Wei (699–759) leading the way respectively in the two styles.

As in painting and sculpture, Tang crafts reveal considerable foreign influence. Persian motifs and shapes had a significant impact on Chinese gold and silver vessels. Sassanid Persia had achieved a high level of craftsmanship in its metalwork, and borrowings and adoptions by Chinese craftsmen manifested their recognition of the striking Persian sophistication in the production of gold and silver vessels. Tang ceramicists also made great strides and adapted the shapes and designs of Persian metalwork in their plates, ewers, and bowls. The presence in China of Persians, who probably fled from the Islamic armies, facilitated the transmission of Persian styles, and the resulting forms and décor, including the foliate pattern on bowls and dishes, the pilgrim bottle, and grapevine, all evince Persian and central Asian influence. The figures represented in the decorations were often central Asian or west Asian entertainers, merchants, or soldiers. The ceramics frequently borrowed designs from textiles and other materials. The glazes, made of cobalt, iron, or copper, were more varied than in earlier dynasties, with colors stretching from blue and green to yellow and brown, culminating in the creation of the tricolored ceramics for which the Tang is justifiably renowned. Kilns in the north used a slip (clay made semifluid with water and used for coating pottery) and produced a white, high-fired ware that resembled though was not as hard as porcelain, while kilns in the south produced green ware, occasionally with lotus and flower designs. Central Asian designs and shapes had a greater influence in the north, which also had the more elaborate burials and which thus required ceramic figurines as tomb artifacts. These figurines varied in size from big camels and horses to much smaller musicians, soldiers, and servants.

DECLINE OF THE TANG

This cultural efflorescence in Buddhism and in the arts was offset by the turbulence of the imperial succession and the political disruptions of the late seventh and early eighth centuries. Only with the accession of Emperor Xuanzong in 712 did the political and economic problems of the dynasty temporarily recede. The new emperor was an able, intelligent monarch who tried to cope with the dynasty's financial difficulties. The ultimate failure of this remarkable ruler offered stark evidence of the Tang's decline. Having come to power via a coup, he was able to bring into office his own supporters, most of them graduates of the civil-service examinations and free of the corruption that had tainted Tang government since Empress Wu's reign.

Xuanzong's early policies aimed to establish more stability and less capriciousness in decision making at the court. With the advice of able Confucian counselors and ministers, he tried to restrict the political influence of the families and allies of his own consorts and of the eunuchs, to limit the building of Buddhist and Daoist monasteries, to prevent monks from meddling in government, and to reduce the inordinately heavy tax burden on the peasantry. In the first years of his reign, Xuanzong implemented some of these reforms. He introduced regular and orderly, rather than arbitrary, processes in government; he periodically moved his entourage to Luoyang, which was closer to the food-producing regions; he sought to reduce court expenses, which had spiraled upward since the relatively austere reign of Taizong; he appointed civil-service graduates to both central and provincial-level positions; he weeded out wealthy individuals who had been ordained as monks in order to evade taxation; and he attempted to restrict the amount of tax-free land and to register households, particularly wealthy ones, that had evaded taxation.

Like many other reform efforts throughout Chinese history, Xuanzong's attempts at change faced considerable obstacles. Wang Mang of the Han and, later, Wang Anshi of the Song, as well as other reformers, confronted many of the same difficulties. They all sought change via entrenched government officials and bureaucrats who either were profiting from the existing system or were allied with landlords and others who also benefited from the status quo. To be sure, the reformers recruited likeminded officials and appointed supporters to government positions, but they still needed the assistance of the regular bureaucracy if they were to be effective. Their dependence on the bureaucracy weakened attempts at reform. The prevailing ideology also contributed to their dilemmas, for Confucianism emphasized proper selection of competent and morally superior men, rather than changes in institutions or adoption of new policies, as the means to a good government and society. Reformers would be subject to criticism for according precedence to institutions over men, and such criticism would help to justify those entrenched interests in the government who opposed the reforms. Because reformers could not conceive of (and the institutional structure did not lend itself to) cultivating support from groups beyond the bureaucracy, the reformers faced an uphill battle in seeking implementation of their new policies. Even a fair trial of their innovations on a small scale was precluded, both because such experiments would necessitate a differing and nonstandard application of edicts and because of the undiminished opposition of and possible subversion by the bureaucracy in the site selected for these trials. The nexus of bureaucrats, landlords, and other allies often subverted reforms.

For Xuanzong, other problems also intervened. Imperial relatives appear to have concocted at least one plot against him, which he deflected, subsequently either exiling or executing the plotters. Xuanzong faced an even greater quandary in coping with the empire's finances. The farming of unregistered land by peasants and the creation by officials and landlords of ever-larger estates, which routinely secured tax exemptions, constricted the court. To cope with this quandary, Yuwen Rong (d. 730–731), one of Xuanzong's ministers, developed a program that offered six tax-free years if peasants registered their lands. Quite a few peasants took advantage of this generous offer, but Yuwen Rong himself alienated other officials and members of the imperial family and finally fell victim to a cabal, which persuaded the emperor to exile him. Other reformers – who sought fairness for nonelite candidates in the civil-service examinations; more-inclusive registration of households on the tax rolls; a better, speedier, and less expensive system of grain transport to the capital; and more direct control over local areas – followed him. Again and again, however, conflicts at court between the bureaucracy and the old aristocracy arose, often undercutting these efforts.

After this bureaucratic infighting, Li Linfu (d. 753) emerged as the most influential minister from 736 to 752 and thus as the architect of the last significant measure meant to bolster Xuanzong's rule. Yet Li's simultaneous attempt to strengthen his own position at court ultimately undermined his effectiveness. As part of the old aristocracy, Li was determined to deal realistically with the consequences of the failures of the equal-field system. First, acknowledging that the militia system (*fubing*), based upon three years of military service for adult males who received land grants, was not working well, he turned instead to the creation of a professional army. The ideal of a low-cost militia had not operated satisfactorily; Li's professional force initially turned out to be more effective, as it decisively defeated the Tibetans (for example). Yet it gave considerable authority to the military governors stationed along the frontiers and was extremely expensive. Second, Li sought to raise additional income by persisting with Yuwen Rong's efforts at the registration of land, but evasion of taxes remained a serious problem and exacerbated the Tang's revenue shortfalls. Third, Li introduced administrative changes, but his own jockeying for power and his purging of potential and legitimate rivals lent a striking irregularity and instability to the court. In effect, his attempts to bolster the Tang's military and revenue base actually weakened the dynasty.

However, there were no significant retreats or defeats in the dynasty's foreign relations. There were also no resounding successes, but China generally maintained an equilibrium with its neighbors. Moreover, China still had the respect of other civilizations in east Asia – respect demonstrated by their emulation of Tang institutions. In its efforts at centralization in the seventh century, Japan had borrowed, with significant modifications, many Tang administrative and fiscal practices and had even adopted the Chinese characters for the Japanese written language. Embassies from Japan continued to arrive during Xuanzong's reign, bolstering China's prestige. In Korea, during the reign of King Kyongdok (r. 742–764), government offices were modeled on those of the Tang. Buddhist monks studied in China and returned to Korea with new ideas, texts, and artifacts, which clearly influenced the culture of the Silla kingdom. The Buddhist grottoes at Sokkuram on the outskirts of the capital at Kyongju, highlighted by the pure, simple, and beautiful white stone statue of the Shakyamuni Buddha, were no doubt inspired by the Yungang and Longmen caves.

Chinese relations with Tibet were less satisfactory, as the two sides remained adversaries. In 715, Tang forces had defeated a Tibetan army in Ferghana, but within a year Tibetan troops were conducting forays reaching to the Tarim River basin oases, which were vital for China's continued commerce in central Asia. In 722, Tibetan forces moved into Little Balur, which lay along the principal routes from Kashgar to the Indus valley. The Tang responded in the same year, dispatching an army from Kashgar that wrested control of the region from the Tibetans and thus safeguarded China's route to the west. Some Tang officials feared, in particular, the possibility of an alliance between the Tibetans and the Arabs, who had been spreading eastward after their conversion to Islam and were fast becoming a major force in central Asia (between the Tibetans and the western Turk peoples – another potentially dangerous threat to China's frontiers). Despite pleas from one of his commanders to seek a compromise so as to reduce expenditures on defense, Xuanzong maintained a hostile stance toward Tibet until 730, when the Tibetans, faced with military campaigns in the west, consented to an agreement that delineated their common borders and permitted trade along the frontiers. Yet, within five years, hostilities erupted once again, and both sides reneged on their agreement, as the Tibetans and the western Turks joined together to resist the Tang. A decade of standoffs ended with the arrival of Gao Xianzhi (d. 756), a Tang commander of Korean descent, who decisively defeated the Tibetans in the late 740s. By 755, when the Tibetan king was murdered by a cabal of ministers, leading to disruptions and turbulence, it appeared that the Tang had finally gained the upper hand in its disputes with the Tibetans over territory and trade.

The Tang registered the same ambiguous results in relations with central Asia and Mongolia. Early in Xuanzong's reign, the western Turks dominated much of central Asia, particularly after their Khan Sulu halted the Arab armies seeking to conquer ever eastward. On several occasions, he supported oases along the Silk Roads in achieving independence from China. Like many other nomadic rulers, however, he could not forge unity among his retainers, and eventually one assassinated him, leading to warfare and the weakening of the Turks and facilitating the Tang's efforts to maintain influence and perhaps control the oases and trade routes to the west. Similarly, the eastern Turks were overwhelmed by disunity, with the defections and assassinations of important leaders characterizing their history in the eighth century. The Tang faced no threats from them. Finally, the Uyghurs, one of the groups in the eastern Turkish confederation, broke away and established their own identity. A more sedentary group with a capital city in Karabalghasun, they engaged in a lively trade with the Tang via the tribute system – again a peaceful resolution of a potentially troublesome border conflict.

The Tang established peace along its northeastern frontiers. The Khitans, a group from Manchuria that would later play a significant role in east Asian history, were intermittently hostile, but they did not make any dramatic incursions into China. Parhae (in Chinese, Bohai), another state in eastern Manchuria, ruled by a commander of the extinguished state of Koguryo, arose in the last decade of the seventh century and, on occasion, challenged Tang forces along the frontiers. However, by the mid eighth century, Parhae had become increasingly sinicized, adopting Chinese political institutions and even the Chinese language. Although Parhae remained an autonomous state, it fit in nicely with the Chinese world order, abiding by the tributary system in order to secure trade.

Xuanzong and his minister Li Linfu appeared thus to have stabilized China's frontiers without abandoning the territory acquired by earlier Tang emperors. The underlying domestic problems of the dynasty, which included revenue shortfalls and fractious infighting at the court as well as the resulting purges and instability, had been somewhat concealed during Li's tenure as the dominant figure at the capital. However, the eighth-century attempts at reform had not noticeably improved the dire financial and administrative straits that the Tang faced. Li's death in 753, after years of control at the court, exacerbated China's problems of leadership, but even before then the reign of Xuanzong had been veering toward turbulent times.

Traditional Chinese scholars have sometimes attributed this decline to changes in the emperor himself. Since the early 740s, he had become increasingly diverted from court affairs by fascination with Daoism and Esoteric Buddhism. He not only became an ardent patron of the two religions but was also attracted by their emphasis on meditation and transcendence of earthly concerns – certainly not auspicious qualities for a secular ruler. Traditional sources also accuse him of neglecting official duties because of his passion for his consort, Yang Yuhuan (719–756; better known by her title Yang Guifei or "precious consort Yang"), who exerted considerable authority at court and insinuated her own relatives into government. To be sure, the deflection of Xuanzong's interests from affairs of state contributed to the mid-eighth-century crisis, but no single ruler, however much attention he paid to governance, could have stemmed the tide without substantial institutional and political changes.

Such trends in Tang administration and finances did not, in any case, depend on any specific emperor. They often superseded any individual ruler and cannot be identified with one. The rulers frequently did not devise policies and simply supported their officials' plans. Although it is sometimes convenient to describe these developments in the context of specific reigns, these trends were ongoing throughout the years of several emperors. Blaming or praising a specific emperor for events is not historically accurate. Reforms in the registration of land, the collection of taxes, and the recruitment of a military force were vital, yet the Tang, not Xuanzong alone, could not cope with these problems amid a series of foreign-policy disasters in the early 750s, which resulted in the most severe challenge to the dynasty's very survival.

TANG FACES REBELLIONS

Unconnected military defeats in the early 750s revealed the weakness of the Tang armies and the growing power of the peoples and states along China's borderlands. In 751, Gao Xianzhi, who had earlier defeated the Tibetans and the western Turks and affirmed the Chinese presence along the Silk Roads oases, suffered a crushing blow near the Talas River in central Asia at the hands of an invading Arab army. The same year another Tang force was overwhelmed by the troops of the southwestern kingdom of Nanzhao (located in the modern province of Yunnan) and the Khitans vanquished a sizable Chinese army led by An Lushan. At this juncture, Li Linfu's health was deteriorating, and he died shortly thereafter, permitting Yang Guifei's cousin, Yang Guozhong (d. 756), to ascend to the leading position at court. During his brief tenure, Yang alienated many officials, including the military governors along the frontiers.

An Lushan (703–757), of Sogdian and Turkic heritage, represented the professional military and the military governors whom the court had started to rely on when its institutions began to falter. The decay of the equal-field system, the resulting drop in tax revenues, and the failures of the militia it had counted on compelled the Tang to turn over greater authority to the provincial military governors. Reining in these increasingly powerful military governors, many of whom were of foreign descent, became an almost impossible task. Yang Guozhong repeatedly tried to control An Lushan, accusing the foreign military governor of plotting a coup. Yang's prophecy was self fulfilling because his consequent hostility ultimately offered An a pretext to challenge the Tang court.

Late in 755, An rebelled, with the expressed intention of removing Yang from power. Shortly thereafter, however, it was clear that he intended to overthrow the emperor as well and to establish his own Yan dynasty. He struck quickly and decisively, moving from his base in Fanyang (in the modern province of Shanxi) south and capturing the secondary Tang capital of Luoyang by the end of the year. Although he encountered stiff resistance, he continued to advance toward Changan. The court responded by summoning its crack troops from the northwest to defend the capital, leaving that region vulnerable to attack by the Tibetans and Turkic groups. Even with this influx of forces, the turmoil, the devastating infighting at court, and the purging and execution of commanders who lost battles harmed the Tang cause. The panicked emperor was persuaded to flee the capital, but the soldiers accompanying him blamed the Yangs for the court's parlous condition. They trapped and murdered Yang Guozhong and compelled the emperor to execute his previously beloved concubine, Yang Guifei. Within a short time, the emperor's son, with the acquiescence of the hapless emperor, acceded to the throne.

The rebels under An Lushan appeared to have a good chance of winning in the initial stages, but they themselves lacked unity. An was assassinated by his own son, An Qingxu, who was in turn killed by another rebel leader, Shi Siming (703–761), who had been his father's close friend. Shi met the same fate at the hands of one of his underlings. Such internal struggles weakened the rebels and prevented them from striking a final blow at the Tang. The rebels' basic defect was that they had no social program; they had no plans to cope with China's revenue and land problems. They did not reflect the interests of those groups or classes who had not fared well under the Tang. Instead, they were primarily military men led by commanders of generally humble backgrounds who did not share the values of the court bureaucracy and its growing number of scholar-officials. Concerned by the turbulence at court after Li Linfu's death and wishing to profit from this obvious disarray, they challenged the central authorities. Their rebellion thus did not represent a breakdown or an attempt to deal with the Tang's socioeconomic dilemmas. Instead these commanders appeared to be principally interested in their own self-aggrandizement, power, and wealth and had scant concern for reforms that would lead to stability.

UYGHUR EMPIRE AND TANG

Yet this inchoate group of leaders posed a threat to the Tang dynasty's survival. Having little confidence in its own demoralized and inadequate militia, the court had no choice but to seek outside assistance. It first turned to loyal frontier military garrisons and then summoned the Uyghur Turks from Mongolia to crush the rebellion. By 763, this formidable force had overwhelmed the disunited rebels. Yet the Tang's victory inevitably came with some costs and with diminution of its authority. Civilian officials no longer controlled the military and certainly did not dominate the newly affirmed and bolstered military governors. Without such control, the court was hard pressed to enforce its regulations concerning landholding and taxes. Large estates developed and were increasingly able to evade the payment of taxes. Without sufficient revenues, the court was powerless to prevent greater assertions of provincial autonomy. Its relations with bordering foreign states or tribes did not offer a rosier picture. Having provided substantial support during the Tang's times of trouble, the Uyghurs now sought privileges commensurate with the assistance they had furnished in crushing the rebel forces. Like many of China's neighbors to the north, they wanted Chinese goods, and their leader, the khaghan, often requested Chinese princesses as brides. With a well-established capital in Karabalghasun, on the Orkhon River, they also differed from their nomadic predecessors in terms of the region they controlled, which stretched from the Altai Mountains in the west to the Kerülen River in the east and included sections of the Gobi desert. As more Uyghurs began to settle down, they attracted Chinese who moved across the borders to join them and offered skills in administration and craftsmanship, among other desirable qualities. Also, as they became increasingly sedentary, some of them turned to farming and others became merchants. Towns grew, and the range of opportunities and occupations broadened considerably. Their government became more elaborate and sophisticated in order to encompass the developing urban culture and the growing number of farmers.

The conversion of many Uyghurs to the Persian religion of Manicheism provided still another indication of the changes occurring in their society. A hierarchical religion based on warring forces of light and dark (which were mirrored in spirits and matter), Manicheism perceived of the world as consisting of the elect (the clergy, who exemplified the spiritual life of celibacy and abstention from meat) and auditors (ordinary people, who could marry and eat without restrictions but were to lead modest lives). The ultimate objective was to break away from the material world and to be transported to the land of eternal light. Abstemiousness and a pure life would guarantee admission into this region. Imbedded within Manicheism was a powerful zeal for proselytizing, which received the blessings of the khaghan and his court. The religion's emphasis on discipline and on a hierarchy appealed to the khaghans, and its relative insignificance in China also attracted them because they wanted to chart an independent course from the sedentary empire to the south. They may, in addition, have been influenced in their choice of religion by the fact that Manicheism put them in touch with west and central Asia via the numerous Manichean merchants.

Although the Uyghur Empire bore witness to a transition from a nomadic society to a mixed economy of agriculture, pastoralism, and trade, it encountered many of the same problems of previous steppe societies. Dynastic instability, not unlike the rifts that plagued the Xiongnu in the first century BCE, undermined the empire. Five of the thirteen khaghans were assassinated, as challengers repeatedly sprang up to depose the rulers and contributed a considerable measure of disorder. Similar rifts bedeviled relations between the pastoral nomads and the growing sedentary population, as their economic and social interests diverged. Leaders of the pastoral contingent, distressed at policies that veered away from customary practices, openly defied the khaghans, enfeebling the court and generating widespread conflicts and wars. The khaghans' army, which was clearly affected by these divisions, became less effective, making it and the whole Uyghur Empire vulnerable to enemies. In 840, it finally fell to the Kyrgyz, another group from the steppes, and those Uyghurs who escaped the destruction managed to flee southwest toward the northwestern region of modern China.

Despite the turbulence that afflicted the Uyghurs, they still had leverage in their relations with the Tang. They demanded trade with the Chinese, seeking in particular large quantities of silk in return for horses. The Tang, which needed horses for its cavalry, gained valuable steeds, but the dispatch of substantial amounts of silk to the Uyghurs burdened the Chinese economy. The Tang also found it difficult that the Uyghurs appeared to dictate the terms of their relationship rather than abiding by the Chinese world order, which was a blow to the pretensions of the court. Simultaneously, the khaghans frequently requested Chinese princesses in marriage, requests that often could not be refused. By the late eighth and early ninth centuries, Tang China – which had been an expansionist power and had dominated its relations with most of its neighbors – found itself offering tribute and acquiescing to the Uyghurs' other demands.

TANG'S CONTINUING DECLINE

The Tang court repeatedly sought to implement reforms in the late eighth and early ninth centuries to revive its flagging fortunes, although it was realistic in not seeking to implement these policies in clearly autonomous frontier areas. In 780, it initiated a two-tax system designed to rationalize taxes, which had grown into a confused, jumbled, and often-evaded multi-tax structure. This reform did indeed create a more equitable and less cumbersome means of raising revenues, but demanded an ability to collect these taxes. Undermining the Tang's efforts to do so was its reliance on the powerful regional governors to carry out these policies. These local rulers did not buckle to central-government authority and devised their own taxes. On several occasions, the court attempted to impose its will on certain provinces, but its tests of will with provincial governors bore little fruit, and the mobilization of military forces placed even greater stress on its finances.

Throughout the ninth century, the court's authority continued to erode. Its efforts to exert influence on provincial governors and administrations faltered, enabling the local landlord elites to amass great wealth and power. Landlords, capitalizing on the inequitable tax burden imposed upon the peasantry, on their own ability to evade taxes, and on the support of corrupt officials, had garnered more and more land. Peasants responded to these unsettled conditions with banditry, brigandage, and smuggling. The northeast, where An Lushan's rebellion had originated, witnessed among the highest incidences of such lawlessness, but violent disruptions spread to the south during the course of the ninth century. Both the central and provincial armies had been starved of funds by avaricious or cost-cutting governors and by the limited tax revenues available to the court, which itself was plagued by internal rivalries, by aggrandizement of power by eunuchs, and by demoralized and occasionally corrupt officials. In some areas, rebellions were joined or instigated by soldiers who were appalled by official corruption, by the deteriorating living standards of the peasantry, or by grievances concerning their own impressments into military service, or simply inspired by a desire for booty. In 878, the court was compelled to seek the help of the Shato Turks, who had already assisted the Tang in its efforts to crush the An Lushan outbreak. Based in the province of Shanxi, the Shato were to play an increasingly significant role in the late ninth and tenth centuries.

The court had changed considerably after the An Lushan rebellion, with an inner court gradually surpassing the power of the bureaucracy. Eunuchs assumed prominent positions in government, often frustrating the reform efforts of competent officials. A coup in 805, seemingly directed in part against the eunuchs, was abortive. One emperor, who reigned from 805 to 820, attempted to stem the erosion of the central government's authority and to arrest the illegal abuses and excesses of provincial governors. He also tried to curb the eunuchs, but his efforts did little to prevent them from amassing additional power. Later plots and attempts by such officials as Li Deyu (787–850) to subvert the eunuchs' authority were also doomed to fail.

The court's domestic dilemmas were mirrored by retreats in its foreign relations. It continued to withdraw from the Tarim River basin oases occupied by Tang armies in the seventh century. Tibetan forces had started to dislodge Chinese forces from these towns and oases almost immediately after the An Lushan debacle. By 763, the Tang had been forced to abandon most of its positions in central Asia, and from that year on "what little news of the West that reached China had to pass through the hostile territory of the Tibetans."[1] In 766, Tibetan armies moved into the important oases of Ganzhou and Suzhou, and in 781 they occupied Hami, one of the critical gateways to central Asia. Although the Tang dynastic history reveals that the population of Hami amounted to about ten thousand, the town's significance belies this puny figure. Hami was strategically located along the major trade routes to the west. Thus, the loss of Hami and neighboring oases and towns undermined the court's attempts to dictate commercial and tributary arrangements with the regions and states to the west and resulted in a disruption of the Silk Roads trade.

Tibet's expansion at the expense of China continued throughout much of the dynasty. The two powers signed treaties in 783 and 787, but disputes, which often erupted into battles, persisted. Adding to the turmoil was the involvement of the Uyghurs, who sought to capitalize on the confusion and on the Tang's evident weakness. Uyghur forces extracted sizable payments from caravans traversing their lands, as well as repeatedly demanding benefits and concessions from the Tang. Nonetheless, the prominent official Li Mi (722–789) persuaded the court to satisfy some of the Uyghur demands in order to have a credible ally against the Tibetans. He even conceived of an audacious plan to forge alliances against the Tibetans with the 'Abbasid Caliphate, which had its capital in Baghdad; the Nanzhao kingdom, which had its capital in Dali (in the modern Chinese province of Yunnan); and India. The extent of this plan is an indication of the truly breathtaking international relations of this era. After some initial hesitation, Emperor Dezong (742–805) followed Li's advice, sending one of his daughters in marriage to the Uyghur khaghan and establishing markets where the Uyghurs could trade their horses for Chinese silk. The idea of an alliance with India was extremely far fetched, but otherwise Li Mi's grand plan appeared to have been, in part, implemented. In 794, disaffected by Tibetan tax and military demands, the Nanzhao kingdom permanently defected from its previous vassal-like status to the Tibetans to cooperate instead with the Tang. The Uyghur Khaghanate cooperated with the Tang until 840, when the Kyrgyz defeated it, compelling the Uyghurs to migrate westward. Finally, in the early ninth century, Tibetans and Arabs became bitterly embroiled in struggles over control of western central Asia. Tibet was isolated, yet the ninth-century Tang court could not recover most of the oases that lay along the foothills of the Tianshan mountains. Instead the Tang and Tibetan rulers, who recognized that they needed to defuse tensions with at least one of their manifold hostile neighbors, finally came to an accommodation after decades of intermittent warfare. In 822 or 823, they signed a peace treaty that prohibited incursions by either side on the other's territory. The Tang thus achieved peace for about twenty years while the Tibetans could focus on their determined and implacable enemies, the Uyghurs, with whom they contested control over the central Asian oases and the resulting caravan trade to the west.

However, shortly thereafter, all three of these intersecting and interacting neighbors – the Uyghurs, the Tibetans, and the Tang – faced internal divisions and weaknesses, which contributed to their loss of influence and authority in central Asia. The Uyghurs were the first to be dislodged from central Asia, as they were bedeviled by conflicts among their rulers and their elite. In 840, the Kyrgyz nomadic confederation ousted the Uyghurs from Mongolia. At about the same time, turmoil wracked Tibet, as the king was assassinated and the succession was disrupted. The unsettled conditions undermined Tibet's foreign endeavors, and around 850 it began to lose its grip on one after another of its central Asian oases. The principal towns and oases that the Tibetans had so assiduously overwhelmed and occupied in the previous century now broke away and restored their independence, although most nominally accepted Tang sovereignty. However, the Tang's own pressing financial and political problems diverted it from efforts to reimpose its rule on these central Asian sites.

SUPPRESSION OF BUDDHISM

Additional evidence of the Tang's decline may be observed in the mid-ninth-century suppression of Buddhism, regarded as one of the few major religious persecutions in Chinese history. The Tang imperial family had, from the outset, been linked with Daoism, and the Dezong and Xianzong (778–820) emperors were ardent Daoists and less sympathetic to Buddhism. Paradoxically, the astonishing success of Buddhism during the Tang aroused suspicion and hostility, which the financially drained dynasty appears to have manipulated for its own purposes. An 819 memorial by the renowned Confucian Han Yu (768–824) expressed the resentment of intellectuals about Buddhism. In urging less court support for Buddhism, Han Yu emphasized its non-Chinese nature and its supposed clash with Chinese values and practices. Buddhism had been imported from abroad, and the Buddha himself was of "barbarian origin." The Buddha's message was expressed in "barbarian" language, which had prevented him from understanding the significance to the Chinese of the family and the emperor. Han Yu added several scurrilous remarks about an esteemed sacred relic, a bone of the Buddha. Other critics also dwelt on Buddhism as a foreign religion and its supposed deviation from Chinese customs and beliefs. Still other Chinese found the celibacy of Buddhist monks and the calls for deprivation of sensual pleasures repugnant.

Emperor Wuzong (814–846), who also favored Daoism, had more mundane motivations for unleashing an assault on Buddhism. The Buddhist monasteries, through lavish benefactions from fervent believers, through gifts and exemptions from the court, and through their own exertions, had amassed considerable wealth, making them vulnerable to a declining and fiscally strapped dynasty. Some had substantial estates, and careful cultivation of their lands had generated sizable profits, most of which was tax free. Similarly, monks and nuns were not liable for taxes or military service, a fact that enraged many ordinary Chinese. Such prosperity had enabled the monasteries to construct elaborate building complexes and to fashion gold and silver objects. This wealth attracted attention and made the Buddhists a prime target in the hostilities that erupted in unstable times. In 843, the fourth year of his reign, Wuzong and his minister Li Deyu signaled their intention to act against the Buddhist clergy. The court mandated that monks who had married, served as physicians, or in any other way breached monastic regulations be defrocked. Shortly thereafter, it expanded the order to include the Manichean clergy, the religious group with whom the Uyghurs were identified. Several thousand nuns and monks were expelled, and the court confiscated much of the property owned by the Manicheans.

From the initial mandate until Wuzong's death in 846, the court issued edicts and pronouncements that amounted to a full-scale campaign against the Buddhist religious establishment. Ennin (793 or 794–864), a Japanese Buddhist pilgrim, chanced to be in China at this very time, and his account of his observations offers a graphic description of the repressive policies directed against the Buddhists. According to his narrative, the court chipped away at one Buddhist custom or privilege after another. Initially it banned Buddhist fasting periods; then it prevented Buddhists from worshipping certain sacred relics and defaced or destroyed a number of Buddhist images and texts. Early in 845, it launched its most devastating assaults on Buddhism, first confiscating the estates of many monasteries and subsequently ordering local officials throughout the empire to provide a list of the monks, nuns, and monasteries within their jurisdictions. It used these lists when it unleashed its systematic attack later in the year. Within a short time, the court ordered the razing of about forty thousand small, predominantly rural temples and shrines and sanctioned the destruction of more than four thousand monasteries, permitting only one temple for each important prefecture and four each in Changan and Luoyang, the two capitals. About a quarter of a million monks and nuns were defrocked, and approximately 150,000 laborers who had toiled in the estates and workshops of the monasteries were "freed" (although they were now liable for taxation). Buddhist scriptures and venerated relics were damaged or irreparably destroyed, and court officials confiscated and then melted down gold and silver statues, the residue going into the government's coffers. Emperor Wuzong's death in 846 brought a halt to this devastating persecution of Buddhists. However, Buddhism never recovered the political and economic power it had attained during the Tang.

In light of this devastation, it might seem strange to argue that the suppression of Buddhism was probably not based on religious discrimination. Instead, economic considerations motivated the court's subjugation of Buddhism. There were, by and large, no major doctrinal disputes that precipitated the attack. Fervent believers continued to worship without hindrance. The more intellectually inclined were still attracted by the Buddhist worldview. Buddhism did not disappear from China, nor did the court proscribe its message or censor or ban its writings. The secular activities of the Buddhist hierarchy and its resulting economic prosperity, not its ideology, provoked the repression.

FINAL COLLAPSE

The court's newly obtained wealth from the Buddhist monasteries did not, however, stem its continued decline. Though Chinese and foreign contemporary observers wrote that the country was remarkably prosperous and appeared to be well organized, tax evasion and government corruption remained rampant. The number of landless and thus homeless peasants who had been unable to pay taxes or had been compelled to sell or commend their land to tax-exempt landlords or simply give up their lands increased. Government policies accelerated, rather than arrested, rural distress. Eunuchs continued to meddle in and control court decision making and to decide upon the imperial succession, and, in at least two cases, they murdered an emperor. The emperors were less competent, and instability and irregularities at court almost predictably led to banditry, rebellion, and outbreaks by the court's own demoralized troops. The initial insurrections in the 850s and 860s originated either along the frontiers or in regions far from the capitals, but the incidence of rebellions within the central core of China increased. To deflect such outbreaks, the court on occasion pledged to provide relief to the peasants and others who were suffering as a result of the turbulence afflicting China, but its efforts were feeble and were often subverted by its own officials.

Such minimal responses to the social and economic crises in the countryside naturally stimulated further outbreaks. It would be misleading to label these disturbances peasant rebellions since they involved such a mélange of criminals, peasants, disaffected military men, vagabonds, petty thieves, failed civil-service examination candidates, and locally powerful individuals who lacked formal education and were thus blocked from entrance into officialdom. In fact, peasants often suffered from the depredations of these groups. Commanders of the rebel bands were not of peasant origin. Huang Chao (d. 884), the eventual principal leader of a so-called peasant rebellion, had initially studied for but failed the civil-service examinations. Without other prospects, he then joined with a certain Wang Xianzhi (d. 878) in the selling and, allegedly, smuggling of salt.

Huang Chao's biography in the Tang dynastic history attributes the rebellion he and Wang Xianzhi organized to brigandage, but does not deny the famine that struck the peasantry in some regions. The difference in the rebellion led by Wang and Huang and other earlier outbreaks was location. Wang and Huang attacked and occupied areas in the heartland, not the periphery, of China, whereas the earlier violence had been confined to the frontiers. Starting in 874, Wang's forces moved into various sites around the eastern section of the country directly north of the Yangzi River, and by 876 they had captured towns close to Luoyang. Rifts between Wang and Huang surfaced at that point, temporarily weakening the rebels and leading to a Tang victory over and execution of Wang in 878. Huang became the unrivalled commander of the rebel forces and headed toward south China, the most prosperous region in the country. In 879, his troops entered and sacked Guangzhou, the formerly thriving port for trade with Southeast Asia, India, and west Asia. An Arab account written by Abu Zaid of Siraf within a couple of decades of Huang's rebellion estimated that Huang's forces massacred 120,000 Muslims, Jews, and other foreigners. Arab historian al-Mas'udi, in a text written in the mid tenth century, put the figure at 200,000. Both numbers are inflated, but they nonetheless indicate that the rebels attributed some of China's problems to the exploitation of foreigners, particularly merchants.

Despite his initial victories, Huang Chao had a fatal flaw: he was unable to gain the support of the skilled administrators who could have helped him govern the regions he had occupied. Perceiving him as a rebel, they steered clear of him, making him appear more like a plunderer than a ruler. Although he moved into regions of south China, he did not establish an administration. In 880 he occupied Luoyang and in 881 his troops entered Changan, but the results were no different. He failed to set up a government, and within a few months Tang troops challenged his control over Changan. The Chinese sources attribute his ineffectiveness in attracting educated administrators to his bloodthirstiness and his cavalier condoning of massacres. During the struggle for Changan, he reputedly slaughtered eighty thousand innocents when he recaptured the city. Such evidence naturally reflects the official viewpoint of the Chinese winners in this conflict and, as such, is suspect. To be sure, many noncombatants were brutally murdered, but there is no reason to believe that Huang's forces were any more vindictive or malevolent than the Tang troops. It was simply that the excesses of Huang's forces were recorded and, without doubt, exaggerated, while the violent misdeeds of the imperial armies were ignored. The view that Huang was responsible for the absolute devastation of Changan is also overstated. After about two thousand years of serving as one of China's capitals, Changan never became the capital of a united country. Huang's own actions appear, however, to challenge the notion that he deliberately ransacked the city. In 880, he founded the Greater Qi dynasty in Changan. There would seem to be little reason to destroy the city he hoped to establish as his capital. The four years of battles and sieges that followed his accession probably did as much damage to the city as the pillaging by his own forces. Here again the Chinese sources portray a loser – a "rebel" – in the most negative light.

By 882, the court had recognized that its army could not, by itself, overwhelm the rebels. A stalemate had developed around Changan. Like their ancestors in the mid eighth century who had summoned foreign troops to help in crushing the An Lushan rebellion, court officials made the fateful decision to call upon foreigners to subdue Huang Chao and to prop up the existing dynasty. In 883, the court sought the assistance of Li Keyong (856–908), a Shato Turk then residing in the modern province of Shanxi, to suppress the rebels. Within a year, Li Keyong had reasserted imperial authority in Changan and had so soundly trounced the rebels that Huang, unwilling to surrender or to fall into enemy hands, committed suicide. The Tang had been restored, and the court returned to the capital, but at a significant cost.

The Tang did not have a lengthy respite after the failure of Huang's rebellion. Its financial system was chaotic; it could not count upon a steady supply of revenue through taxes; many civilian and military governors had become ever freer of court control; foreigners such as Li Keyong dominated north-central and northeast China; and eunuchs persisted in exerting power in the capital. Court policy was almost suicidal. It antagonized Li Keyong, the very leader who had saved the dynasty, and by 890 a war had erupted with the Shato ruler. The court continued to decline, which permitted Zhu Wen (852–912), a former ally of Huang Chao, to occupy the capital, execute many eunuchs, and murder one of the emperors. In 907, he took the final step of overthrowing the last Tang emperor and establishing the Liang dynasty, with himself as Emperor Taizu. He controlled part of north China but was unable to assert his authority over much of the rest. Li Keyong ruled modern Shanxi and northern Hebei, and his Shato Turks contested the Liang's power for the remainder of its troubled tenure (less than two decades). South China fragmented into what became known as the Ten Kingdoms, none of which could forge unity. In effect, in its lack of a centralized government, post-Tang China came to resemble the post-Han era and the Warring States period.

EFFLORESCENCE OF TANG CULTURE

Before its almost anticlimactic demise, the Tang had witnessed a splendid cultural efflorescence. The economic prosperity, the political stability, and the spirited élan of the initial phases of Tang rule provided a favorable environment for literature and the visual arts, the latter of which was described earlier. Like the patronage offered to the arts, the imperial and elite support for literature nurtured the careers of remarkable writers. The support of Buddhism, Daoism, and Confucianism in the early Tang offered a philosophical and religious underpinning and thus fostered literature and art as well. Similarly, Tang cosmopolitanism offered exposure to foreigners and foreign ideas and products, which influenced the themes and styles addressed by the writers.

Poetry, in particular, flourished, as skill in versification became an asset for the true "gentlemen" in the elite. As a result, about fifty thousand poems by more than two thousand Tang poets are still extant. The most prominent of these poets aspired to literati status, which was certified by passing the civil-service examinations. In addition, the examinations tested skills in the writing of poetry, which, in turn, bolstered the prestige of poets.

Wang Wei, Li Bo (701–762), and Du Fu (712–770), three of the great Tang poets, were almost exact contemporaries, but their poems reflect different themes and styles. Wang Wei was conventionally the most successful because he passed the highest-level civil-service examination and served in various bureaucratic posts. Although later literary critics have not esteemed him as highly as his two fellow poets, he perhaps surpassed them in the range of his accomplishments, which also encompassed painting, calligraphy, and music. He continued to assume government positions, but his best-known and most revered poems reflect a desire to escape from the pressures and obsessions of ordinary life. He expresses this sentiment most clearly in his poem "Given to My Younger Paternal Cousin, Military Supply Official Qiu":

In younger years I knew little of worldly affairs:
I forced myself to learn to seek fame and power.
But vainly I heard of the years of frisking horses
And suffered for lack of wisdom surpassing others.
As for managing things, have I indulged in mere talk?
In post after post it's not that I haven't been tested.
Since there are few joys that satisfy my nature,
I fear being blamed for going against the times.
In clear winter I see the distant mountains,
The gathered snow, the frozen azure green.
Brightness emerges from the eastern woods.
And brings out my thoughts of escaping from the world.[2]

Wang Wei returned more than once to the theme of seclusion in beautiful natural surroundings. His growing attraction to Buddhism reinforced this emphasis on the natural. Yet his desire for detachment conflicted with his involvement in political affairs – a theme he addressed in "A Poem to Leave Behind at Parting from My Elder Brother Monk Wen-ku in the Mountains":

Taking off the hermit's robes, I will ascend to the emperor's morning court;
Going away from my master, I will meet prominent men of the time...
My younger brother is an official of high rank;
My older brother has this monk's shaved head...
At your brushwood gate, only sprinkle water and sweep;
When I have leisure, I will pass by and join you.[3]

Li Bo, the second of the triumvirate, did not achieve the same worldly success as Wang Wei. Yet, ironically, he was the one who praised secular and sensual values. Anecdotes about his alcoholic binges and his dissipated later life have occasionally blurred the essential seriousness of his work. The story that he drowned during one of his drunken nocturnal escapades when he fell from a boat while trying to clasp the moon that was reflected in the water has been discounted, as have other fanciful accounts of his adventures. However, his career was dogged by disappointments, failures, and exile. Like other prominent poets, he sought association with the scholar-official elite as well as imperial patronage, both of which he obtained sporadically and then lost through his alcoholic excesses or through such poor choices as appearing to support an abortive rebellion against the Tang. He surely did not have a typical civil-service career, which may be related to his mercantile origins and to his possible Turkic background. Born in central Asia, he seems to have been influenced by exposure to Turkic culture. His fondness for wine and his repeated references to black and white mountains and to the moon reverberate in Turkish culture. A few of his poems may originally have been intended to be accompanied by central Asian music, further evidence of Tang cosmopolitanism. The hedonism and the unconventional attitudes that character-ized his poetry may have been a reaction to his perception that many Chinese in his own times viewed him as an outsider, if not an alien. His paeans to liquor hardly jibe with the stereotypical Confucian values. The views expressed in his "Wine Will Be Served" surely alienated many traditional moralists:

> To be elated in life, one should enjoy oneself to the full
> And never let the golden goblet stand empty toward the moon...
> Roast the sheep, slaughter the ox! Let's take our pleasure,
> And with one long drink, empty three hundred cups!
> Young scholar Tan-ch'iu, Master Ts'en
> Wine will be served;
> Don't stop drinking! ...
> The five-colored horse,
> The thousand-gold fur –
> Let's call the boy to take them out and pawn them for good wine,
> That drinking together we may dispel the sorrows of myriad years.[4]

Li Bo's hedonistic poems tended to overshadow the more melancholy and more restrained sentiments he expressed in his other poetry. Love of nature, awe at the majesty of the mountains, and joy at the peace and stillness of the towering peaks were also common themes in his works. He repeatedly referred to the appeal of the quietude of a contemplative and hermit-like existence in the mountains – a far cry from the views with which he is commonly associated.

While Li Bo revealed, in part, the foreign influence on Chinese culture during the Tang and his somewhat romantic but individual reactions to society, Du Fu expressed a Confucian moral judgment of developments in turbulent mid-eighth-century China. Although Du Fu did not pass the highest-level civil-service examinations, he remained a staunch Confucian (a system of values that emerges repeatedly in his poems). His Confucian values resulted not only in poems championing family responsibilities and pleasures but also poems critical of social conditions. He lived during what was reputed to be the apogee of Tang power, but recognized that the disparity between the elite and the poor, along with the exploitation of the peasantry, were creating social fissures that could lead to the downfall of the dynasty. He was critical of the oppression that compelled, for example, peasants conscripted into the army to hire substitutes because they could not leave the land for long periods of time. He shows his dismay at the exactions imposed upon ordinary people in his "My Trip from the Capital to Feng-hsien":

> The silk that was bestowed at the vermillion court
> Came originally from some poor shivering women;
> Their husbands were whipped and flogged
> So that it could be levied as a tribute to the imperial city.[5]

Du Fu's descriptions of the An Lushan rebellion and its devastating aftermath are particularly heartrending in their evocations of the miseries and sufferings inflicted upon the masses. His poems graphically depict the sale of children by parents in order to pay for taxes or merely to eke out survival; bloodshed and rotting corpses; and discombobulated scholars and peasants. His concern for the common people and his rectitude as a good Confucian moralist, as well as his remarkable use of language and images, ensured that he would be esteemed in later generations, prompting his most important English-language biographer to subtitle his book "China's Greatest Poet." Du Fu was unable to have much effect on social conditions, and, in fact, spent most of his last years living in exile in a thatched cottage in Chengdu.

A number of other prominent poets lived during the Tang. Like Du Fu, Bo Juyi (772–846) was appalled at the inequities in the Tang system and the exploitation of common people, and some of his poetry reflected his concern and distress at the heavy taxation on the poor, the forced recruitment of peasants into the military and their dispatch to dangerous and unhealthy environments, and the elite's spending of vast amounts on luxuries while the bulk of the population barely eked out a living. Additional evidence of Bo Juyi's identification with ordinary people was his attempt to make his poetry accessible by limiting arcane allusions and using clear, simple language. In contrast, some esteemed Tang poets hardly dealt with the dynasty's social and political crises. Li He (790–816) wrote difficult poetry that often expressed personal, morbid, and gloomy views in somewhat abstruse language. Hanshan, a poet whose identity is unclear, wrote poems informed by the tenets of Chan Buddhism, by critiques of the secularization of the Buddhist monasteries, and by descriptions of the beautiful mountain retreat he sought as a recluse in Cold Cliff in the Tiantai Mountains. Li Shangyin (812–858) wrote poems replete with symbolism and mystical significance and allusions.

Although overshadowed by the remarkable achievements in poetry, prose also made strides during this era. Histories of the dynasties of the period of disunion were compiled (a traditional kind of enterprise) but at least one historical work was unique. Liu Zhiji (661–721) produced *Shitong* (*Generalities of History*), a work that analyzed the writing of history and was the first true critical investigation of earlier historical studies and their defects and virtues. The compilation of encyclopedias, which contained excerpts from other books on subjects such as medicine, foreign lands, and military and tax affairs, came into vogue. In 801, Du You (735–812) completed his *Tongdian* (*Comprehensive Institutions*), just such a compilation, which also included sections from an account, now lost, of the 'Abbasid capital of Baghdad by his relative Du Huan, who had been captured by an Arab army and may have resided for a time in the Arab capital. Local gazetteers, which consisted of compilations of facts ranging from geography to taxes to history to biographies of locally prominent figures, began to appear in large numbers.

Han Yu was the premier prose stylist of the time. Staunchly opposed to Buddhism, Han Yu tried to reassert the primacy of Confucianism. He emphasized the writings of Mencius and of the *Daxue* (Great Learning) section of the *Liji*, the early ritual text. To him, the object of philosophical and literary discourse was the explication of Confucian beliefs and morality and their dissemination. Literature had an obligation to foster the spread of Confucian doctrines. His staunch support of Confucianism in the face of a powerful Buddhist establishment earned him the plaudits of the founders of Neo-Confucianism in the Song dynasty, contributing further to his renown as a champion of the traditional morality. In his own time, however, his bitter critique of Buddhism and of corrupt court officials led to his banishment to an isolated region in south China. Beyond his specific policy objectives, he also supported the use of the old prose style (*guwen*) employed in the Confucian classics. He proposed restoration of the simple, unadorned language and lack of embellishments characteristic of the classical works. Objecting to the more elaborate and attention-attracting writing styles of the recent past, he opted for traditional prose untainted by artifice and by needlessly complex verbiage. His own essays satirized avaricious and exploitative officials and so-called great men of his times. Like other scholars of his era, he also dabbled in poetry. Although he never achieved the renown of his predecessors Li Bo and Du Fu, he used his poems to accentuate his support for Confucian doctrines, his nostalgia for the classical era, and his yearning for a restoration of the traditional prose style.

The art of fiction flourished during the Tang. The earliest and somewhat rudimentary stories had appeared during the Six Dynasties period, but the Tang witnessed significant developments. Many stories diverged from the earlier tales, which had emphasized the supernatural; instead they were more realistic, though some had fantastic elements. Love stories abounded, and a common theme was the sad fate of courtesans and concubines who were betrayed by their former patrons or lovers. Accounts of great swordsmen and swordswomen made up still another popular genre, with these courageous figures performing amazing feats of derring-do. It would have been unusual if Buddhism, with its striking influence during this time, had not inspired stories. Thus, the cache of texts in the Buddhist caves at Dunhuang contains simple stories illustrating basic Buddhist principles.

The development of a similarly simple theater was presaged by singing, dancing, and acrobatics productions. Performances by central Asian dancers, musicians, mimes, acrobats, and magicians were popular, and culminated in the creation of playlets. These dancers may also have initiated the practice of foot-binding, which will be discussed later. The Tang court recruited attractive and talented young people and trained them on the palace grounds in singing, dancing, and acting. However, a full-fledged theater, with a repertoire of carefully crafted plays, did not develop for several centuries.

Although not as significant in terms of science and technology as the subsequent Song dynasty, the Tang witnessed some development. Daoist adepts, who dabbled in alchemy, stumbled upon discoveries in chemistry. Elaborate engineering and irrigation works resulted in new understandings of mechanical engineering. However, the most significant development was the invention of printing. Some texts may have been reproduced earlier, but great strides in technology and in the production and dissemination of printed texts occurred during the Tang. A substantial market for books had been generated by this time. Fervent Buddhists were eager to own copies of the sacred texts, and candidates for the civil-service examinations required reproductions of the classics for their studies. As China had had access to paper and ink for some time and had developed the technique of fashioning seals out of metal, the development of block printing did not require much of a technological breakthrough. Because the Chinese delighted in making rubbings of images and writings on stone and bronze, they were primed for the evolution of a technique for reproducing texts. Early examples of Chinese block printing deriving from the sixth century have been found in Korea; small charms dated 764 were printed in Japan; and the *Diamond Sutra*, a major Buddhist text that used to be considered the earliest printed text found in China, dated 868, was found in the Dunhuang caves. The development of printing in the Tang laid the foundations for large-scale printing of multivolume texts that were disseminated on a wide scale during the Song dynasty.

The decorative arts also flourished in the Tang. Tricolored ceramics, some of which portrayed foreign merchants, entertainers, and guardian figures, were especially prized. Depictions of horses and camels were similarly popular. Because many of these ceramics were buried in the tombs of the imperial family or prominent officials, some have survived intact. The 1998 discovery of a ninth-century shipwrecked Arab dhow near Indonesia's island of Belitung, part of the maritime "Silk Roads," attested to the existence of other kinds of ceramics and ceramic centers. Wares from Changsha and the province of Zhejiang confirm the remarkable efflorescence of ceramic production in a variety of regions in China. Depictions of a lotus (a Buddhist symbol) as well as Arabic inscriptions and central Asian motifs offer additional evidence of Tang cosmopolitanism. Ceramics constituted the majority of the sixty thousand objects found in the cargo, but gold and silver ornaments and ritual objects were also plentiful. The motifs on the largest Tang gold cup ever discovered portrayed central Asian or Persian musicians and a dancer – additional affirmation of the popularity of foreign music and dance in the Tang. The exquisite quality of these gold and silver artifacts makes art historians, in particular, sad about the loss and destruction of gold and silver ritual objects during the 840s persecution of the Buddhists. Also disappointing is the relative paucity of textiles to have survived, especially in light of the renown of the Silk Roads. Climate and the fragility of silk took their toll. A few Tang silks, including a child's coat, have been preserved, and several reveal central Asian motifs, another indication of Tang cosmopolitanism.

NOTES

1 Christopher Beckwith, *The Tibetan Empire in Central Asia* (Princeton: Princeton University Press, 1987), pp. 146–147.
2 Pauline Yu, *The Poetry of Wang Wei* (Bloomington: Indiana University Press, 1980), p. 100.
3 Marsha Wagner, *Wang Wei* (Boston: Twayne Publishers, 1981), p. 127.
4 Liu Wu-chi, *An Introduction to Chinese Literature* (Bloomington: Indiana University Press, 1966), pp. 74–5.
5 Liu, p. 82.

FURTHER READING

Timothy Barrett, *The Woman Who Discovered Printing* (New Haven: Yale University Press, 2008).
Charles Benn, *China's Golden Age: Everyday Life in the Tang Dynasty* (Oxford: Oxford University Press, 2004).

Liu Xinru, *Silk and Religion: An Exploration of Material Life and the Thought of People, AD 600–1200* (Delhi: Oxford University Press, 1996).

Edward Schafer, *The Golden Peaches of Samarkand* (Berkeley: University of California Press, 1963).

Frances Wood, *The Silk Road* (Berkeley: University of California Press, 2004).

Sally Wriggins, *The Silk Road Journey with Xuanzang* (Boulder: Westview Press, rev. ed., 2003).

[6] POST-TANG SOCIETY AND THE GLORIOUS SONG, 907–1279

FIVE DYNASTIES AND TEN KINGDOMS

The fall of the Tang resulted in the same kind of fragmentation that characterized the collapse of two earlier dynasties, the Zhou and the Han. No government could gain control over the entire country; instead, local rulers or dynasties prevailed. The two earlier periods of division lasted for centuries, but the fragmentation after the Tang endured for only about fifty years. Perhaps China had become simply too large to be decentralized for so long. Chaos and turbulence could not be tolerated over the vast expanse of territory that had now become

A History of China, First Edition. Morris Rossabi.
© 2014 Morris Rossabi. Published 2014 by Blackwell Publishing Ltd.

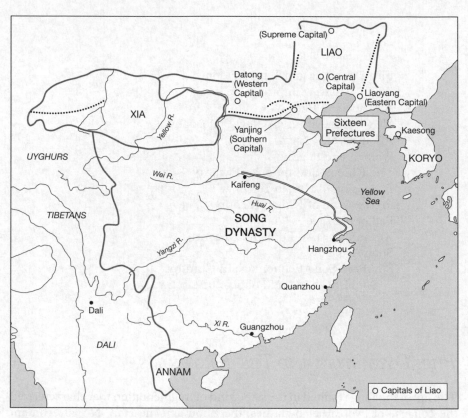

Map 6.1 Song dynasty and its neighbors, ca. 1005

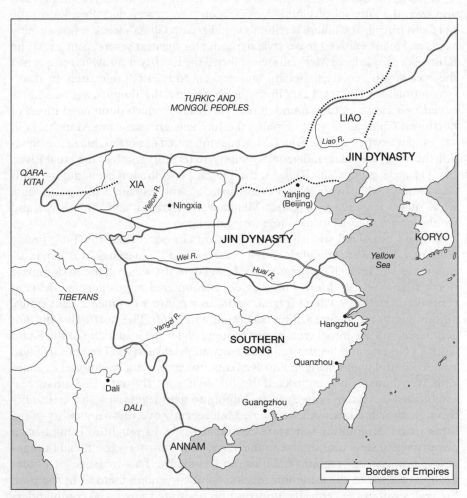

Map 6.2 Song dynasty and its neighbors, ca. 1127

part of the Middle Kingdom. The country and the growing population needed the stability that only centralized rule could provide. Or it could be that the Tang had built up such a sophisticated nexus of transport, communications, and commerce that centralization was facilitated. The indigenous Song dynasty eventually took power in much of China in 960, but was forced out of north China in 1126. The period from 960 to 1126 is known as the Northern Song, and the period from 1126 to 1279 is known as the Southern Song.

However, at the time of the initial collapse of the Tang dynasty, centralization and even the survival of Chinese civilization were threatened. Peoples on the northern fringes of Chinese territory capitalized on China's weakness to occupy lands and to establish Chinese-style dynasties for the next several centuries. The Khitans, a people from Mongolia, established the Liao dynasty, which controlled the area around modern Beijing and sixteen additional prefectures in north China from 907 to 1115. Later in the tenth century, the Tanguts, a group influenced by Tibetan culture, founded the Xia dynasty, which dominated much of northwest China until 1227. Finally, the Jurchens erupted from Manchuria in 1115 and overwhelmed the Khitans, occupying much of north China and expelling the Song, the ruling indigenous dynasty, to territory south of the Huai River. Each of these groups, the Khitans, the Tanguts, and the Jurchens, did not suddenly vanish when their dynasties collapsed. Some remained in north China while others scattered throughout Manchuria, Mongolia, and central Asia and would remain in touch with China for centuries.

China's heartland was similarly turbulent. In 907, when the Tang finally collapsed, Zhu Wen, one of the rebel Huang Chao's underlings, was in a position to declare himself emperor of the Liang dynasty, which came to dominate north China. Yet he almost immediately encountered opposition in efforts at centralization. South China fragmented into a number of independent states, amounting to ten before China was reunited in 960. The north also did not acquiesce, and the initial recalcitrant groups, under the leadership of the Shato Turk Li Keyong and his son Li Cunxu, actually defeated the Liang in 923 and gained control over Changan and Kaifeng, two important traditional capitals. Zhu Wen himself was murdered by his own son. By 926, Li Cunxu had established the Later Tang dynasty, hoping to gain legitimacy and credibility through association with the renowned but recently overthrown dynasty of the same name. Attempting to restore centralized rule, Li sought to bring back a governmental structure similar to the Tang, with ministers, an official bureaucracy, powerful aristocratic families, and eunuchs. This mélange of potent groups resulted in the same internecine conflicts among them as in the past. Struggles within the central administration permitted provincial commanders to assert themselves and to challenge the court.

Simultaneously, however, conflicts among the commanders and between the commanders and the court weakened all sides. Warfare devastated the provinces, undermining the power of the commanders. The various dynasties themselves were also devastated because the constant tumult caused the collapse of one after another. Yet each successive dynasty recognized the need for a powerful imperial army to restrain the provincial commanders, who themselves began to weaken because of the constant warfare. It seemed only a matter of time before one dynasty, with a sufficiently potent military force, would emerge to enforce its will on the country.

Meanwhile, the south fragmented into the Ten Kingdoms, which actually endured longer than most of the northern dynasties. However, the territory each kingdom controlled was relatively finite, and none expanded beyond its original domain. Yet no single state, either in the north or south, could attract sufficient support to establish a centralized government and unified rule. However, political disunity did not prevent increasing economic relations. Interstate trade flourished because, by this time, the various regions of China had become more and more economically interdependent. Specialization of production and commerce had forged a unity that was virtually irresistible.

SONG: A LESSER EMPIRE

The Song, under the leadership of the military commander Zhao Kuangyin (927–976), would ultimately unite the disparate states and regions into one centralized dynasty. Zhao benefited from the efforts of a few of the more competent rulers of the Han and Zhou dynasties in north China, who had enlarged the lands under their control and had begun to encroach upon the power of the military commanders. Thus, when the Song arose, conditions were propitious for an assertion of centralized authority. Zhao capitalized upon these developments to establish the Song in 960, and the dynasty moved quickly to dominate north China. Best known as Taizu (Grand Progenitor) of the Song, Zhao rapidly expanded his control into south China. By the time of his death in 976, he had incorporated the traditional centers of China, save for the states of Wuyue and Northern Han, which his successor and younger brother overwhelmed three years later. This second emperor, renowned as Taizong ("Grand Ancestor"; 939–997), ruled for another two decades and pursued many of the same policies, adding continuity to the dynasty. The relatively long reigns of the first two emperors, as compared to the brevity of rule that was characteristic of the Five Dynasties and Ten Kingdoms era, contributed to the dynasty's stability.

The accession of Zhao Kuangyin began to restore confidence in the proper operation of the Confucian system in China. He moved the capital to the city of Kaifeng, partly because Changan, the Tang capital, had been devastated toward the end of that dynasty. The Song diverged from Tang policies in order to avert the fate of its predecessor. Its officials were convinced that the Tang had fallen, in part, because of its expansionist policies and its inability to control its military forces. They thus opted to become a "lesser empire" by imposing civilian control over the military. By ruling less territory than the Tang, the court faced challenges from other Chinese states and, more important, from the foreigners who had seized lands within China. Its less expansionist and bellicose policies resulted in part from a realistic assessment of changes since the Tang. It now confronted a multistate system in northeast Asia, and it could not defeat these states, which often enjoyed military parity with the Song. It did not share the Tang luxury of being the only dominant power in the region. That is, the Song was necessarily woefully weak; its seminomadic neighbors who had established empires were powerful, and many Song policy makers took this new balance of power into account.

The Song thus tried to preserve its lands without a sizable military presence or a belligerent foreign policy and yet confronted a powerful and primarily pastoral nomadic people from Mongolia known as the Khitans, who had established the Liao dynasty. The Khitans had their own emperor, who challenged the supremacy of the Song in China proper, and their powerful military force could prove troublesome along China's northern frontiers. Recognizing that it did not have the military capability to expel the Khitans from Chinese territory, the Song opted for a peaceful resolution of its commercial and diplomatic relationship with the Khitans. The Treaty of Shanyuan, which resulted from letters sent by the two sides in 1005, entailed humiliating concessions for the Song. The court not only promised to make annual payments of 100,000 taels of silver and 200,000 bolts of silk but also agreed that the Song emperor would address the Khitan ruler as "emperor," not as a vassal. The treaty also demarcated the boundary between the two states and pledged both sides to peaceful relations. By signing a treaty that acknowledged the equality of a foreign state, the Song revealed its weakness. To state it perhaps too baldly, the Song bribed the Khitans in order to obtain peace. It made extraordinary concessions to deter its northern neighbor from incursions on Chinese soil.

Although a few officials criticized the court for surrendering to the so-called barbarians, most supported its realism and pragmatism. They concurred with the view that an aggressive foreign policy was deleterious to stability. They also contended that the expenditures on the annual payments to the Khitans would be considerably lower than expenses on repeated military engagements or maintenance of a large army all along the frontiers. Even when the Song signed a second treaty with the Khitans, which increased the annual subsidy to 200,000 taels of silver and 300,000 bolts of silk, the court could generally manage the payments. Silver was somewhat problematic because the Song's annual production amounted to 300,000–400,000 taels, but the court received sufficient foreign silver in payment for Chinese commodities to sustain the expense. The Khitans, in fact, used most of their gifts of silver to buy Chinese goods. The payments in silk did not burden the court because it received substantial amounts of silk on taxes and bought vast quantities (as many as two million bolts annually) for its army. Sending 200,000 or 300,000 bolts a year to the Khitans did not make a dent on the court's supply.

This policy of accommodation through the presentation of gifts of silk and silver was so effective that the Song used the same tactic to defuse tensions with the Tanguts, who occupied the lands to the west and northwest. Like the Khitans, the Tanguts established a Chinese-style dynasty, the Xia, and institutions resembling those of China. A year after the signing of the Treaty of Shanyuan, the Song began to provide annual gifts of forty thousand bolts of silk to the Xia. However, border disputes and controversies over proper names of address between the Xia ruler and the Song emperor erupted into wars in the mid eleventh century; these culminated in several Tangut victories and the negotiation of an agreement similar to the Treaty of Shanyuan. This agreement increased opportunities for trade for Tangut envoys to the court and pledged the Song to offer annual gifts of tea, silver, and 153,000 bolts of silk. Once again, the financial burdens on the court were relatively light compared to the military expenditures it would have incurred with continual warfare. Later in the eleventh century, officials who advocated a more aggressive approach toward the Tanguts gained power, and several wars erupted in which large Song armies with sophisticated logistics were mobilized. Because neither side emerged with overwhelming clear-cut victories, both reverted to the less belligerent policy in which gifts of silk, silver, and tea fostered peace along the border.

The Song rulers also had determined that they needed to curb the powers of the military commanders who had been instrumental in the Tang's collapse. A centralized and effective government would be undermined without restraints on these military officials. Thus, the court gradually had to restore civilian control over these incipient warlords. Taizu himself initiated such efforts by limiting his own commanders once he had consolidated his authority over much of China. He relegated some of the most successful to relatively minor posts to avert challenges from them. He encouraged or coerced others to retire, providing them with generous gifts for their previous military service. As these military commanders were transferred, retired, or died, he chose civilian replacements. The few obstreperous commanders were summarily dismissed, but Taizu preferred to attain his objectives through compromise and conciliation. Seeking to impose civilian control over the military, he gained the cooperation of military commanders by generosity toward those who acquiesced, as well as toward those who initially resisted but later accepted his overlordship. He frequently deferred to his ministers, he lauded the civil bureaucracy, and he embodied the traits of a sage Confucian ruler. His military force and his policy (tempered by moderation and judicious rewards) of promoting civilians over the military enabled him to achieve stability.

A NEW SONG ELITE

A shift in the composition of the elite facilitated Taizu's efforts at governance. The major aristocratic families, which had dominated from Han times on, had begun to be challenged during the Tang, as a regular bureaucracy had started to develop. The Song relied on a more merited-based system associated with the civil-service examinations, rather than on appointments based on social rank. Some scholars have assumed that this change presaged the transition from an aristocratic to a more autocratic society. They argue that the pre-Song-era aristocrats had the wealth, status, and influence to challenge the emperors whereas the new merit-based bureaucrats did not have the independence or wherewithal to contest or debate policies with the rulers. Lacking the opposition of a powerful group with equivalent status, the emperors could more readily impose their own will on the government. The aristocracy, which earlier restrained or at least counterbalanced the emperors' authority, was not as dominant a force. Without such countervailing forces, the emperors from this time on bent government to their own needs and were less tolerant of and less threatened by dissent among officials.

There is some merit to this view, but it perhaps overstates the significance of this political transition. Some pre-Song emperors had been autocratic; others, who either showed scant interest in government or were not overpowering, had been more willing to accept counsel from their ministers or other officials. Examples abound, on the one hand, of dominant emperors who brooked no criticism, and, on the other hand, of tolerant rulers who fostered active deliberations of court policies. Similarly, some Song and post-Song emperors ran roughshod over the bureaucracy, while others turned over most government affairs to officials. In theory, the post-Song emperors could more readily override opposition from the bureaucracy, but in practice officials were often granted leeway to disagree with the rulers.

The governmental structure reflected the growing emphasis on control, order, and regularity. Assisting the emperors in devising policies was a series of agencies designed to enhance the authority of the central government. The Council of State drafted reports to clarify policies, all of which ultimately required the emperor's imprimatur. Originally composed of less than ten men who had served in various capacities as academicians or drafters of documents, they consulted with the emperor on policy and then drafted, with the help of the Bureau of Academicians, decisions and proposals. Several agencies, most notably the Censorate, informed the court about local conditions, scrutinized the activities of the bureaucracy, reported on malfeasance and corruption to the emperor, assessed the performance of officials, and even criticized the emperor himself.

Although the Council of State on occasion administered government programs, other agencies generally implemented policies. A Finance Commission, eventually composed of the offices of Salt and Iron, Census, and Funds, took charge of the revenues and expenditures of the empire. It collected taxes, devised budgets, and managed commerce and the country's resources. The Bureau of Military Affairs, often supervised by civilians, planned for the defense of China and attempted to avert the rise of powerful military commanders as in the Tang. Finally, the Secretariat and Chancellery oversaw all civilian matters other than finances. Thus, it supervised the bureaucracy and the judicial system. Civilians predominated in this new governmental structure, and the highest government posts went to successful candidates of the civil-service examinations.

Similar emphases on civilian and central-government control prevailed in the Song local administration. The court relied on so-called circuit intendants to act as its representatives in the supervision, though not actual governance, of the prefectures and subprefectures, the principal divisions on the local level. The circuits were roughly equivalent to the contemporary Chinese designation of provinces. Intendants specialized in finances, justice, the military, and, for lack of a better word, commerce. The intendants for commerce actually oversaw all transactions involving exchanges, as well as the minting of coins and the transport of grain to the more populous centers in the empire. Prefectural and subprefectural officials really carried out the principal tasks of local government. About 1300 subprefectures, each composed of 2500 to 3000 households, were designated as the main government organs with which ordinary people dealt. Leaders of the subprefectures, assisted by sheriffs and registrars, collected taxes, ensured peace and safety, managed education, served as moral exemplars, and guided the moral development of their charges.

Prefectural leaders normally supervised ten to twelve prefectures, although a few who governed large cities or industrial centers might oversee only one or two such prefectures. Centered in a town or city, they inspected the work of subprefectural officials, focusing on the judicial system and on the government monopolies. In short, they added still another link between the central government and the local populace and officials. The court thus sought to maintain control over local areas to avert the fragmentation of the late Tang.

It also relied upon the civil-service examinations for recruitment or selection of its officials. Although a few officials received the imperial grace of protection (*yin*), enabling them to bring one of their relatives into government without taking an examination, the vast majority of the bureaucracy consisted of successful graduates of the examinations. The highest positions were reserved for those who passed the demanding third level of examinations, which granted one the title of *jinshi* and which, from 1067, were given only once every three years. The examinations, which were administered in law, letters, history, rituals, and classics, generally emphasized rote memorization of texts, which led eventually to criticism of their format and style. Critics pointed out that they did not evaluate ability or ethical character – a prominent failing in a Confucian-based system that emphasized moral worth. Seeking to ensure fairness and avert favoritism, the court devised a system of evaluation that guaranteed the anonymity of the candidates. Examiners did not know the candidates and thus could not judge their character.

Simultaneously, the court, seeking to impose civilian control over the military, kept increasing the number of successful candidates to enlarge the pool of eligible officials. By the mid eleventh century, the holders of degrees began to outstrip the number of official positions in the bureaucracy. Too many candidates were passing the exams, challenging the families who sought to bring their sons into the bureaucracy through the so-called *yin*, or grace of protection. Yet some in the elite found ways, through the *yin* privilege , to place a son in government without an examination and thus retained their prominence in the Song. These entrenched families, in a disguised attempt to restore patronage or nepotism, initiated more strenuous efforts to ensure successful admission into officialdom for their sons.

One way of reducing the number was to prevent the sons of men in specific occupations from taking the exams. Thus the court, at various times, prohibited the sons of monks, artisans, and merchants from participating in the exams. It also investigated the moral qualifications – particularly, adherence to filial piety and other Confucian virtues – of potential candidates, ruling out some in that way.

NEO-CONFUCIANISM: A NEW PHILOSOPHY

The elite identified and sought legitimacy through a new form of Confucianism. This so-called Neo-Confucianism developed beyond Confucianism's original concerns. Neo-Confucian thinkers became engaged with metaphysical questions such as the origins, nature, and composition of the universe, issues that Confucius and his school had avoided. They explored ideas that had been the province of the Buddhists, and these efforts could be said to be responses to Buddhist metaphysics. Neo-Confucianism may have developed without reference to Buddhism, but Neo-Confucians were critical of Buddhism as well as Daoism.

A slew of such thinkers contributed in their formulations to the reappraisal, revival, and resurgence of the traditional philosophy. Zhu Xi (1130–1200), also respected as a great calligrapher, summarized their views in his *Reflections on Things at Hand* (*Jinsilu*). Incorporating the ideas of Zhou Dunyi (1017–1073), Zhang Zai (1020–1077), Cheng Hao (1032–1085), and Cheng Yi (1033–1107), Zhu Xi's text delineated the philosophy's principles. Following the style of much philosophical discourse in China, it consisted, in part, of commentaries on Confucius's *Analects*, Mencius's text, and the *Great Learning* (*Daxue*) and *Doctrine of the Mean* (*Zhongyong*) sections of the *Liji* (*Book of Rites*), which became known as the Four Books and became the standard for the civil-service examinations. Although the discussions and analyses of these sources may have appeared to be mere scholarly speculation, the texts actually prescribed some of the same applicable tenets as traditional Confucianism. Thus, these thinkers still dwelt upon personal morality, proper relationships within the family, and the individual's relationship to the state.

However, they now supplemented the original Confucian precepts with analyses of the composition of the universe. Like the polarities between thought and action and *yin* and *yang*, the fundamental underlying forms of the universe were perceived of as a duality, the *qi* and the *li*. *Qi* consisted of matter or energy: the material components of the universe, or what is perceived by the senses. Traditional Confucianism had focused on that aspect of the universe. The Neo-Confucian thinkers added *li*, or the underlying principle or form. Material objects were infused with *li*, but so were values, relationships, and beliefs. Nothing could exist or be conceived of without *li*. Unlike *qi*, *li* could not be perceived by the senses. It constituted the metaphysical element in the new form of Confucianism and had not been integral to the original formulation of Confucianism.

The ideal was coequal forces of *li* and *qi*, but individual Neo-Confucians privileged one or the other. A few conceived only of the existence of *qi*, a conception that barely distinguished it from traditional Confucianism. Others cast *li* as superior because it was the most significant underlying force of the universe. In this formulation, it came to be identified with the Great Ultimate, the progenitor of the universe.

The Neo-Confucians' ultimate objective remained morality or creation of a better man. Human beings started out as pure, but their *qi* could deviate from goodness and proper behavior. If they adhered to *li*, they could move closer to the ideal of a good Confucian man. Adherence required knowledge of *li*. Zhu Xi asserted that "investigation of things" led to such knowledge. He stated that delving into the classics and implementing the moral conduct prescribed in them was the proper path. Scholarly study and use of the rational faculty were his prescriptions for obtaining knowledge of *li*. He tended to deemphasize the intuitive grasp of reality and Buddhist meditation techniques in the quest for *li*. His emphasis on study originally contributed to creativity and learning, but in much later periods Neo-Confucianism became static and increasingly stultified. In this era, it meshed with the openness to new ideas and discoveries. Yet it became identified with the scholar-official class and the new elite based on merit and examinations.

ATTEMPTS AT REFORM

The emphasis on privilege (*yin*), as well as on the content of the examinations, elicited criticism and proposals for reform. In 1043, Fan Zhongyan (989–1052) and Ouyang Xiu (1007–1072), two leading officials who were concerned about the threat of instability and war along the northwestern frontier, the growing economic tensions with the Khitans, and the resultant domestic disturbances, wrote a comprehensive memorial to the emperor in which they advocated a variety of reforms. The main changes involving the bureaucracy were calls for reduction of the *yin* privilege, which favored the elite; a greater emphasis on the candidate's moral character; and changes in the examination system – specifically, a focus on questions of policy and analysis rather than on poetry and the classics and on pure memorization. However, these changes were not implemented. Because the leading reformers, including Fan and Ouyang, were politically naïve, they did not foster alliances with the sympathetic bureaucrats in opposition to traditionalists. Their more politically astute enemies, therefore, outmaneuvered them and, within a year, had most of them reassigned to posts outside the capital. Any future attempts at reform would require savvier leadership.

Later in the century, Wang Anshi (1021–1086), more of a pragmatist than the initial reformers, sought and secured a prominent position in government to promote his reforms. Like those of Fan and Ouyang, his proposals were wide ranging, embracing economic, political, and educational changes. Wang's reforms of the exams entailed elimination of the poetry section and a strong emphasis on using the classics to consider questions of policy – that is, a more pragmatic bent. He wanted the exams to be more than stylistic exercises. He advocated the establishment of schools in the various prefectures to prepare promising young boys for the exams. He subsequently ingratiated himself with Emperor Shenzong (r. 1068–1085) and had himself appointed as the Second Privy Councillor. During the emperor's reign, Wang sought to implement his reforms despite considerable opposition, and his enemies included some of the leading figures of the Song. Such opposition and the death of the emperor, Wang's most important supporter, resulted in the subversion of Wang's reforms. Poetry and memorization of the classics remained the main subjects and the main skills to be evaluated in the exams. A similar reform during Emperor

Huizong's reign (1101–1126) also foundered. By then, the Song faced serious challenges to its survival from its northern neighbors, and the failures of the reforms would eventually harm China, making it vulnerable to foreign attacks.

The Song not only experienced a commercial upsurge but also witnessed the rise of the south to a more prominent position. The south was, in any event, the economic center, both due to seaborne trade and to the rise of commercial agriculture. Such new crops as tea and fruits as well as new, more productive strains of rice permitted substantial population and financial growth and the development of cities in the south. Simultaneously, coal mining, iron and porcelain production, and printing enterprises developed rapidly, and the government met the needs of these new concerns by issuing the first paper money in global history. A large number of wine shops, kilns, and silk, oil–pressing, and papermaking workshops were founded. The economic prominence of the south began to translate into greater power in government as a larger and larger percentage of official positions went to southerners. Yet the power of the government itself was eroding. The population increased dramatically, but there was no concomitant increase in government. It stands to reason that fewer officials would translate into less government control. Thus, the Northern Song's weakness paved the way for the fall of the dynasty in the early twelfth dynasty.

The so-called New Reforms of Wang Anshi constituted one of the last major efforts to stem the decline. Wang had developed a comprehensive program designed to alleviate the sufferings of the peasantry and to strengthen China. He first detailed his plans in his "Ten Thousand Word Memorial" to the throne in 1058. He suggested changes in education and in the civil-service exam, which have been described, but they were only part of a program that was designed to strengthen and enrich the country. It appears too that Wang may have represented the interests of the developing south against the entrenched power of the wealthy northern landlords. He and his close associates derived from middle-level landlords who had but recently entered the bureaucracy. He was thus not sympathetic to northern large landowners who evaded taxes. Identifying with the southern merchants who traded with foreigners landing in the southern ports, he did not oppose merchants or a money economy. In addition, he favored merit rather than the *yin* privilege in selection of officials. In short, he seems to have reflected the concerns and aspirations of a new group that sought to challenge the status quo, including the corruption and tax evasion of the northern landed elite. Because he and his supporters wanted to change, not repair, institutions, their program clashed with the views of officials who wanted merely to tinker with institutions or emphasized the selection of moral Confucian officials. Perhaps incomprehensibly to some Westerners, the two sides bolstered their differing viewpoints by citing ancient texts in their arguments.

Yet Wang also believed that government ought to pursue policies based upon current conditions and that such programs ought to be evaluated on pragmatic grounds. Unlike many Confucians of his time, he did not denigrate law and institutional change, although he did emphasize the employment of good officials in the bureaucracy. Again as distinct from the Confucians of his time, Wang considered excellence in an official to consist of competence and skill at the specific position, not simply the official's embodiment of the Confucian moral virtues.

This new kind of official, Wang said, ought to be concerned about the current financial shortfalls faced by the court and to remedy this deficiency both by preventing tax evasion and by helping to increase productivity. Such efforts would entail informing peasants about the latest advances in agronomy and helping them to preserve their lands from the control of rapacious landlords and moneylenders.

Aside from the aim of attracting additional competent officials, Wang's specific program was rooted in economic reforms. He proposed the creation of a Finance Planning Commission to consolidate the operations of the various government agencies that dealt with finances. He also suggested the conduct of a new land survey that would provide data for a fairer tax system and thus fewer opportunities for tax evasion by large landowners. Complementing the hard-line policy toward the landlords were programs designed to assist the peasantry. The government would provide low-cost loans at the time of planting, which peasants would repay at harvesting time. Peasants would thus no longer have to obtain high-interest loans from landlords and usurers. Under the "hired-services" system, peasants who had earlier been liable for corvée labor, sometimes at busy times in the agricultural cycle, could now pay an additional tax that could be used to employ a substitute. Another group that would benefit from Wang's reforms would be merchants. The government would mint more coins to promote commercial activity and would purchase goods directly from small merchants to prevent domination by the wealthy. Finally, local authorities would profit from Wang's additional innovations. He would organize a *baojia* system, in which each ten families would band together in a unit to maintain order on the local level. The *baojia* would save funds for the government by assuming some of the tax-collection, militia, and justice functions and would also offer more autonomy to local regions.

Sima Guang (1019–1086) – a renowned historian, essayist, and official – and other bureaucrats from the north criticized Wang's program because they opposed government activism and defended tradition and the existing bureaucracy. Perhaps unfairly accused of representing the interests of the large landowners and of de-emphasizing Wang's goals of increasing wealth and power, they tended to be concerned with recruiting capable officials rather than changing institutions to cope with China's problems. If the leading officials were competent, they could develop a system of rewards and punishments to ensure that lower-level bureaucrats performed their duties properly. Such an emphasis on individuals and on the hierarchy of authority would be the only means of coping with and overcoming China's fiscal, military, and social difficulties. Unity and order, based upon such a hierarchy, ought to be the objective of government, and reforms ought to be directed at making the bureaucracy perform better rather than at institutional changes.

Sima opposed an activist government. Rectifying the bureaucracy and ensuring that it performed its duties properly were his solutions to the problems the government faced. Thus, he was critical of Wang's New Reforms. Sima contended, for example, that Wang's Finance Planning Commission would be managed by inexperienced individuals who would supervise traditional bureaucrats. Such a disruption in the hierarchical structure would be doomed to fail. Similarly, government attempts to promote an increase in production – an integral motivation for Wang's New Reforms – would be counterproductive. Instead, the government ought to curb its own expenditures and recruit officials who were more knowledgeable about financial matters to manage the state's resources. The farming loans program marked further government intrusion in the economy, an intrusion that according to Sima actually subverted the order of society. It undercut the wealthy, who often provided the loans, while not substantially improving the peasants' lot. Local officials could, for example, compel peasants to request loans so that the government could profit from interest payments. Were the New Reforms designed to benefit the peasants or the court?

Sima was also critical of the hired-services program. He portrayed it as still another tax on the peasants. He argued that, in addition, payments in cash contributed to the commercialization of the economy. Peasants would become increasingly dependent on the commercial economy to obtain the cash necessary to pay the government for the program, and the rural economy would be subverted, with merchants making the greatest gains and peasants suffering the greatest losses from this system. Peasants would also be burdened by the *baojia* system, which would compel them to assume police and military responsibilities, which would distract them from their primary concerns of farming.

In short, Sima represented orthodoxy and the current elite while Wang reflected the interests of the reformers and the less favored. Wang sought an activist government while Sima opposed government intrusion into what he perceived to be the proper order and hierarchy in society. Sima went further, insisting that "it was in the interest of the state to leave wealth in private hands in order to maintain social stability."[1] Even in foreign relations, Wang sought a more assertive government that challenged rather than appeased foreigners, particularly the Tanguts, who shared a common border with China. Such a policy would entail a substantial increase in the army and in military expeditions. Sima disapproved of any such increases and instead proposed a policy of conciliation, though not submissiveness. He pointed out that stability in relations and peace with the Tanguts and other foreigners were preferable to instability and disruption.

The controversy between the reformers and the conservatives, as reflected by Wang Anshi and Sima Guang respectively, persisted throughout Wang's tenure in office, but a general bias against institutional reform and a less-than-supportive bureaucracy truly undermined Wang's efforts. Conservatives looked askance at the proposed institutional changes because such innovations were an implicit critique of the dynastic founders who had established the structures. Thus, any change encountered obstacles, and Wang's comprehensive reforms were even more subject to such criticism. However, the bureaucracy remained the most recalcitrant stumbling block to Wang's efforts to promote change. Although most bureaucrats were well-educated and respectable, low salaries inspired many to capitalize on their positions to extort funds and to extract bribes. Because they recognized that Wang's reforms might undercut such corruption, they were disenchanted with his New Reforms and attempted to avoid implementing them. Wang, himself a paragon of virtue in financial matters, raised the salaries of officials to prevent temptation and to curb corruption. However, clever manipulators who could fabricate or distort evidence to discredit Wang and his allies abounded among the officials.

Facing such opposition, Wang responded by recruiting and promoting his own supporters, which in turn opened him up to criticism for seeking to create his own clique within government. His enemies "charged that Wang recommended only unscrupulous bureaucrats who knew how to make profits, either for the government, which was contrary to conventional Confucian ideas, or for themselves, which was even worse."[2]

Wang's efforts to tame the bureaucracy failed, which incalculably jeopardized the New Reforms. Even more troublesome was the lowest level of the bureaucracy (the clerks), who received even worse pay and were thus even more tempted to accept bribes. Wang used rewards and punishments to deal with them, offering them higher salaries while imposing stiff penalties on corruption. Because even the higher salaries could not match the sums the clerks could garner through illegal means, they were not deterred from misappropriating funds and persisted in practices that sabotaged the New Reforms. For example, the land survey that Wang envisioned as the basis for a fairer tax system relied upon measuring and proper reporting by the lower levels of the bureaucracy. Thus, when unscrupulous clerks collaborated with large landowners to shield land from registration, they effectively sabotaged Wang's efforts. Similarly, when they compelled peasants to request interest-bearing loans whether or not they needed such funds, they subverted the spirit of the reforms.

Wang was fighting a losing battle. Without the wholesale replacement of such corrupt officials and clerks by bureaucrats intent on implementing the reforms, he could not hope to carry out his New Reforms. In turn, even assuming that he had sufficient qualified men as replacements, a program of this kind would provoke the hostility of many Confucian scholars as well as the powerful landlords. Wang could not, even if he had wanted to or had conceived the notion of mobilizing the less privileged (the peasants and small merchants), have provided the sustenance needed to challenge the entrenched bureaucracy and landlords. Lacking strong allies among the groups he championed, he relied instead on attracting the support of Emperor Shenzong, which was a risky gambit. Because the emperors could be capricious, their favorites at one time could easily be abandoned at another time. The current favorites' competitors, seeking the emperor's attention, would repeatedly look for opportunities, either directly or indirectly, to criticize Wang. This was precisely the scenario that confronted Wang and the emperor, as orthodox Confucians, eunuchs, and bureaucrats whose activities, positions, or wealth were adversely affected by the New Reforms questioned Wang's ideas and the effectiveness of his reforms, at first privately and later publicly and vociferously. These critics achieved their desired result because the emperor began to deny some of Wang's demands, jeopardizing efforts to introduce and properly implement important parts of his package of reforms. His dependence on the emperor meant that he was subject to the ruler's changes of heart, if not capriciousness. Yet, during the emperor's reign, Wang remained in power, and his reforms were, at least officially, put in place.

The death of the emperor in 1085 marked the end of Wang's power and ushered in a period when his rivals held sway. With the support of the empress dowager, who now became the dominant force at court, they dismantled many of the reforms and replaced the advocates of reform with their own antireform supporters. Bureaucratic stagnation and corruption quickly reappeared. Clerks in local government, their numbers continuously swollen by their success, retrieved their authority and reverted to the extortion and bribery that had characterized the pre-Wang era. The failures of the bureaucratic reforms mirrored the failures of efforts to impose a more equitable tax system and to facilitate and improve the lives of the peasantry. Thus, neither the government's revenue shortfalls nor the livelihood of the vast majority of the population improved. Evidence of the Song's internal weakness and instability emboldened the foreigners living along China's northern and western borders to make substantial economic demands on the court and, if denied these special requests, to initiate forays into Chinese territory. The treaties the court had negotiated with the Khitans and the Tanguts started to be ignored. Conditions along the frontiers became increasingly unsettled.

Factionalism continued to handicap the government. Although the conservatives gained the upper hand in 1085 and dismissed many of Wang's supporters, they still had to contend with covert opposition from the reformers. Their restoration of ineffective and corrupt bureaucrats offered Wang's old allies an opportunity to act and to succeed in creating a postreform era, starting in 1093. Wang's brother-in-law and, in particular, the latter's brother Cai Jing (1047–1126) took charge, and, like their predecessors and opponents, purged the conservatives and reinstated their own allies. Although some modest reforms were implemented, Cai, who was also renowned for his excellent calligraphy, tolerated favoritism and corruption among his own adherents, and proposed the dispatch of gifts and tribute to the emperor, the Son of Heaven, in an attempt to win him over. Government deteriorated, and the dichotomy between reformers and conservatives was not bridged. Cai remained in power until 1126, when he was denounced for corruption and exiled (though he died en route to his place of exile); his departure no doubt contributed to the collapse of the Northern Song dynasty in the same year. Later historians portrayed him in such a negative light that he appears as a villain in *Shuihuzhuan* (*Water Margin*), one of the most famous Chinese novels. His policies actually assisted the Jurchens, the foreigners who eventually defeated and compelled the Song to flee to the south. There the Song set up a new capital in Hangzhou and reestablished its dynasty (later known as the Southern Song dynasty), which enjoyed a great, though precarious, prosperity based upon bountiful agriculture and far-flung commercial networks.

WOMEN AND THE SONG

Just as there have been many Chinas, there have been considerable variations in the statuses and roles of women in different regions and during different dynasties and eras. Confucian orthodoxy would, in theory, dictate a patriarchal society in which the stereotypical woman had limited authority in the family, clan, or polity. To be sure, women could not take part in ancestor worship and were generally not eligible for formal education, but they often had considerable leverage within the family, especially if they gave birth to a male heir or brought a sizable dowry. The stereotype of women who were totally dominated within the family and scarcely played any role in the public area requires some modification.

The Song witnessed an apparent decline in the status of women, although some of their economic rights were affirmed. Families arranged marriages based on status and wealth and did not consult the couple. Men, in theory had leverage in relations with women. Traditionally, they could divorce their spouses for barrenness, licentiousness, failure to serve parents-in-law, loquacity, theft, jealousy, or serious disease, while women did not have the right of divorce. However, divorce was relatively rare, partly due to the paucity of women caused, in part, by female infanticide. Moreover, women who had observed a three-year mourning period for their parents-in-law or had no relatives to whom they could return or whose husbands had suddenly become wealthy could not be divorced.

Women could hold on to their dowries and could inherit property in early Song but their positions had eroded by the late Song. If a husband died young, his widow had jurisdiction over and protected the household's property until her sons gained maturity – a vital responsibility for the family's survival. The revival of Confucianism, which accorded women a lower position in society, may have undermined their position. Greater physical separation between men and women, in line with the separatism dictated by the association of women with *yin* and men with *yang*, limited the role of women in rituals.

Foot-binding, which began on a limited scale in the late Tang and perhaps originated with Turkic dancers at the court, became more common – still another impediment for women. Excavations of late Song tombs prove that elite girls had their feet wrapped in cloth to prevent them from growing and had specially made small shoes. The practice, which was first adopted by courtesans, originated among the elite, who did not need much mobility, and then gradually spread to the lower classes. Eventually, prospective bridegrooms' parents sought to arrange marriages with women whose feet had been bound because the practice came to represent modesty and a moral reputation. Poor parents bound their daughters' feet in order to improve their chances of social mobility. Families who wished to have their daughters marry well were under considerable pressure to have their feet bound. The older women were responsible for binding a child's feet when she was five to eight years old. The precise day for binding the feet with cloth was carefully chosen, and rituals were performed and offerings made to the Tiny-Footed Maiden Goddess and especially to Guanyin, the bodhisattva to whom women, in particular, prayed. Girls were taught to make their own shoes, some decorated elaborately with symbols of good luck and other things. This turned out to be an important skill because the shoes, often made of silk or cotton, frequently needed repair or replacement. In addition, a prospective bride showed her mettle by making shoes for her future in-laws.

Whatever the ritual and marital significance, the physical impediment of bound feet restricted not only women's movement but also their participation in social and political life. In later times, many Westerners who reached China would find the practice to be evidence of sexual depravity and of bizarre and cruel infliction of pain and deformity on young children. In any event, these limitations accorded with the Confucian perception of women as playing roles primarily in the household – as supervisors, major caretakers for children, respectful providers for the needs of their in-laws, and confidantes and assistants for their husbands.

Recent studies imply that women were less submissive than this image may convey. Although only one major woman writer, the poet Li Qingzhao (ca. 1081–1141), published her works, literacy among elite women was not uncommon. Women could, on occasion, make choices about remarriage, their children, and their own dowries. They had significant economic leverage because they could contribute to their households through their work as weavers. The Song witnessed an extraordinary rise in demand for silk, offering women a more important position in the family's finances.

The increase in the number of concubines in wealthy families may, paradoxically, have bolstered the position of women. Concubines, who generally derived from lower-class backgrounds and lived with the family, rose in status and thus ensured somewhat closer relations between elite and ordinary families. Moreover, wives would presumably have been more secure because their husbands could satisfy their sexual urges within the household rather than expending untold sums in visiting and maintaining courtesans outside the household.

To be sure, women faced numerous constraints. Young couples had no choice in marriages. Girls were married at a young age, in many cases just as they became teenagers, and in their new families their relations with their mother-in-law were vital. Images of conflict between daughters-in-law and mothers-in-law were pervasive in popular literature. Other potential hazards were high incidences of maternal mortality as well as the psychological damage of female infanticide. Poor families with scant resources might allow an infant daughter to die, as she would have to be maintained and reared and would be married before she made a financial contribution to the household. Still, overall, one of the main limitations imposed upon women was exclusion from the public sphere.

THE KHITANS AND THE LIAO DYNASTY

The Liao dynasty (907–1125) of China and the Western Liao (1124–1211), its successor, were founded by the Khitans, a proto-Mongol people who were originally nomadic pastoralists residing in modern Inner Mongolia, Mongolia, Manchuria, and perhaps as far north as Lake Baikal. Mentioned in the Chinese sources as early as the fourth century CE, the Khitans, like other pastoral nomads, depended largely on their animals for survival, although a few groups supplemented their incomes by fishing and farming. Their reliance on animals in regions plagued by high winds and considerable snow and ice made them vulnerable to their capricious environment. A devastating winter could lead to the deaths of many of their animals. In those circumstances, China often provided a safety net by permitting the pastoral nomads to trade for such necessities as grain and craft articles and such luxuries as silk and tea. On the other hand, when China was disunited, its northern pastoral neighbors would, on occasion, capitalize on its weakness to annex Chinese territories.

Indeed, the Khitans sought to take advantage of the turbulence following the collapse of the Tang dynasty. Having been influenced by the Uyghurs, the first of the pastoral peoples of Mongolia to build a capital city and to devise an administrative system, they had begun to shift from a small pastoral organization to a larger confederation. They became intent on ruling rather than plundering the territories they occupied in China. By 938, when China was still disunited, the Khitans had wrested control over sixteen prefectures, including the area of modern Beijing.

Even earlier, they had manifested their desire to govern the Chinese regions they had seized and to establish a true dynasty. In 907 their ruler, Abaoji, proclaimed himself khaghan of a Khitan confederation, and within a decade he adopted a Chinese title for his reign. Khitan precedent dictated elections every three years for a new ruler, but Abaoji (872–926), known to the Chinese as Taizu, rejected that custom and instead sought to impose a hereditary rather than an elective system of succession that had been characteristic of the pastoral nomadic societies. He overwhelmed opposition to his plan and retained power for almost two decades, setting a precedent for a Chinese-like system, which, however, continued to be contested. To bolster his legitimacy and to indicate his intent to rule both sedentary agricultural and mobile pastoral societies, he began to construct a capital city in 918. Although the capital, known by the Chinese name Huangdu (later changed to Shangjing), was based in modern Inner Mongolia, not at that time part of China, it signaled a change in Abaoji's conception of governance. He now attempted to rule the sedentary population in his domains from a stationary site, with a regular administration. Inhabitants could count on relatively fixed and stable taxes rather than irregular and perhaps capricious demands. They could also rest assured that the government would not expropriate their farmland and convert it to pasture.

Development of written scripts marked still another change for Khitan society. As the Khitans sought to rule rather than plunder the domains they had subjugated, they recognized the need for a written language for their proto-Mongol spoken language (which also incorporated Tungusic words). They developed both a large script and a small script, each of which had similarities to Chinese characters. Because neither has been fully deciphered, knowledge of their society is somewhat limited. Yet their creation of these scripts reveals recognition of new responsibilities incurred with annexation of new lands and the need to govern them.

Having adopted a Chinese name for their dynasty and Chinese reign titles and temple names for their emperors, having built a Chinese-style capital city, and having devised a Chinese-influenced administrative system and written scripts, the Khitans governed in their traditional domains and in the territories they occupied in China for about two centuries. By the middle of the tenth century, the Khitans, with a population of about 750,000, directly ruled about two and a half million Chinese, with whom they traded and had diplomatic relations; they also stayed in touch with a China whose population numbered in the tens of millions. How did they retain their identity and remain under their own dynasty and leadership with so much exposure to and adoption of many features of Chinese civilization? How did they resist assimilation?

EXPANSION OF KHITAN TERRITORY

The Khitans' relations with China, although initially hostile, eventually bolstered their self-image and contributed to the preservation of their identity. By 926, Abaoji had crushed and occupied the Bohai kingdom (in Manchuria), which China had perceived as a vassal state. Twelve years later, his immediate successor gained control over the sixteen prefectures in China, including the area around modern Beijing. In 947, his troops ventured as far south as the Yellow River, briefly occupying the city of Kaifeng. However, the Khitans had overstretched their supply lines and could not maintain their hold over a region so distant from their base. They abandoned the city, but not before the emperor adopted the Chinese name of Liao for his dynasty. Emperor Shenzong (982–1031) turned his attention to Korea, and in 994, after several Khitan military expeditions, the kingdom of Koryo accepted a status as a vassal of the Liao. Meanwhile the Song dynasty reunified China in 960, fifty years after the collapse of the Tang dynasty.

After an initial fracas, the Song achieved a rapprochement with the Liao court, thus offering prestige to the Khitan emperors. The second Song emperor led an abortive attempt to recover the sixteen prefectures. After this failure, the Song began to reevaluate its policies toward its northern neighbors. Analyzing the reasons for the collapse of the Tang dynasty, Song officials concluded that its predecessor had expanded beyond the Chinese cultural frontiers, in part precipitating its fall. Thus, as mentioned above, the Song determined to be a "lesser empire" in order to avert the fate of the Tang. It deemphasized the use of the military and valued a peaceful relationship with its northern neighbors, including the Liao. To achieve this objective, it negotiated the Treaty of Shanyuan, described earlier.

Coexistence with the Liao proved beneficial and contributed to what some scholars have labeled a Song technological and economic revolution. The Song witnessed the development of a substantial iron industry, a profusion of inventions in agriculture and navigation, an increase in population and an ensuing accelerated pace of urbanization, and a cultural efflorescence in painting, porcelain production, literature, and philosophy. Peace along its northern frontiers allowed greater Song investment in the economy and was one factor in these remarkable economic and cultural developments.

PRESERVATION OF KHITAN IDENTITY

The Liao also benefited from the new relationship with the Song. Treatment as equals by the most powerful dynasty in east Asia bolstered the Khitan image. They could borrow Chinese institutions and practices without blurring their own identity. Recognizing that they needed such institutions to govern their Chinese domains, they selectively adopted Tang-dynasty institutions without totally abandoning their own system of governance. They maintained a balance between the Chinese institutions and their own more rudimentary administrative structure, choosing what they perceived to be the most useful or appealing Chinese practices.

Establishment of a dual administration was thus a second means of preserving their identity. Two governments ruled from the supreme capital. The northern government, manned by Khitan officials, dealt principally with the mostly pastoral peoples of the steppes, while the southern administration, staffed mainly by Chinese officials, governed the mostly sedentary agricultural society with agencies and institutions familiar to the mostly Chinese inhabitants. The Khitans eventually constructed five capitals, with four of them administering local regions within the Liao domains. Although the Khitans were the first seminomadic people to build cities in the Mongol steppelands, the dual administration permitted the Khitans in the north to maintain their traditional lifestyles as stockbreeders.

The means of selection of the ruling families furthered the Khitan efforts to retain their identity. The Yelü clan supplied the emperors but was limited to consorts from the Xiao clan. The ruling emperors could not marry women from the Chinese, Tungusic, Uyghur, or other foreign communities that the Khitans had subjugated. The purity of the imperial family was thus assured.

Although the imperial family enjoyed opulent lifestyles in the palaces built in the various capitals, they persisted, both symbolically and in practice, in maintaining their links to their pastoral nomadic heritage. The Chinese chronicles indicate that the Liao emperors periodically moved from one capital to another and one site to another, continuing the Khitan legacy of mobility. Even after the construction of elaborate palaces, the emperors and their retinues, on occasion, slept in tents. It may be that this supposed link was a gesture and perhaps artificial. Nonetheless, the courts appeared to have felt duty bound to share the traditional lifestyles of their people. A likelier and probably more heartfelt link to their heritage was the emperors' repeated organization of hunts and other outings – a standard activity in Khitan society designed both to obtain food and to sustain proper rituals.

Several of the Liao's policies also diverged from traditional Chinese practices and beliefs and thus charted a unique identity. First, unlike the Confucian scholar-official class, the Khitan supported merchants and commerce. Traditional Confucians considered trade to be a parasitic pursuit, but the Khitans, whose nomadic pastoral economy required the exchange of goods, had a much more favorable attitude toward merchants. They developed extensive commercial networks, trading with the Song, the Tungusic peoples, Koryo, the Tangut of northwest China, and other peoples as far away as central Asia. They provided horses, sheep, furs, carpets, lumber, and slaves to the Song and received silver, silk, tea, and gold and silver ornaments in return. Their other trading partners offered ginseng, jade, and cotton cloth among other goods.

Second, the Liao elites adopted Chinese religions, particularly Buddhism, but they did not abandon their traditional beliefs. The Liao emperors provided funds for the construction of monasteries and temples and for the printing of texts. To be sure, Buddhism influenced their views and their funerary practices. However, they also maintained practices associated with divination and shamanism, some of which the state sponsored. Even as they adopted Chinese-style ancestral rituals, they made offerings of deer meat rather than the traditional Chinese fruits and grains. Third, although Buddhism inspired some of their artworks (which were often produced by Chinese craftsmen), the Khitans also valued objects that reflected and glorified their nomadic pastoral heritage. They commissioned artisans to produce elaborately designed and often gold-encrusted saddles, stirrups, boots, funerary urns in the form of tents, and amulets, all of which evoked their love of horses and other animals. Fourth, their development of two written scripts reflected still another means of differentiating themselves from the traditional Chinese dynasties.

Their political culture differed somewhat from the Chinese model. At least three Liao empresses had tremendous power and often decided on court policies – a distinct deviation from Chinese practices, where historians reviled strong women, such as Empress Wu of the Tang dynasty, who sought to play political roles. The authority and status of ordinary Khitan women are not known, but some elite women had more power than their Chinese peers.

FALL OF THE LIAO

More critical was the Liao's inability to settle on a regular system of succession to the imperial throne. In the predynastic state, the Khitan leaders would convene and elect the next leader. The Chinese favored a hereditary system. As a result, clashes repeatedly arose between different elite factions about the principles of succession. At the same time, conflicts reared up between the nomadic pastoral Khitans and the more sinicized Liao court elites. The traditional lifestyle was pitted against the increasingly Chinese values that began to characterize the Khitans in the south. These internal struggles weakened the Liao.

The dynasty's neighbors and subordinates capitalized on such disharmony and the ensuing disarray at the Liao court. The Bohai of Manchuria rebelled and sought assistance from the Jurchens, a Tungusic people who had previously accepted the supremacy of the Liao. Aguda, a capable Jurchen military leader, challenged Liao control, and in 1115 proclaimed himself Emperor Taizu of the Jin dynasty. The Song, renouncing the Treaty of Shanyuan, also attacked the Liao, but without much success. Nonetheless, these hostilities made the Liao vulnerable and facilitated the Jurchens' final defeat of the dynasty in 1125.

The Khitans did not immediately disappear. Yelü Dashi (1087–1143), a descendant of the imperial family, led remnants of the Khitan military and their families westward to modern Xinjiang and neighboring regions in central Asia to found the Khara Khitai (in Chinese, Xi Liao) dynasty, which survived until the Mongol conquest of 1211. Some capable Khitan officials who remained in China served later dynasties. Yelü Chucai (1190–1244), the most prominent such official, helped Chinggis Khan (r. 1206–1227) and Chinggis' son and successor, Ögödei (r. 1229–1241), to devise institutions suitable for ruling China.

The Liao was the first foreign dynasty that sought to combine its traditional system of governance with the Chinese administrative structure. It succeeded for about two hundred years and served as a model for other foreigners, including the Mongols, who attempted to rule China.

XIA AND JIN: TWO FOREIGN DYNASTIES

Also during the Song period, a group called the Tanguts occupied northwest China, which encompassed the Gansu corridor and the Ordos region and stretched farther west to Dunhuang and Yumen (Jade Gate), the traditional end point of the so-called Great Wall. Including elements of Tibetan, Chinese, and Turkic–Mongol culture, the Tanguts had a mixed economy of agriculture, herding, and commerce. Although their population and the size of their domain paled in comparison to those of the Liao and the Song, they had a sizable military force and controlled a strategic location on the routes to central Asia and west Asia. They accepted a tributary status to the Liao and Song, although they were clearly autonomous, and established the Xia (ca. 982–1227), a Chinese-style dynasty with a Chinese name, and built a capital city. Notwithstanding the Tanguts' "tributary" status, hostilities with the Song prevailed until the two dynasties came to an agreement in 1044. Like the Song's Treaty of Shanyuan with the Khitans, the new arrangement was advantageous for the Tanguts, as the Song pledged to provide gifts of silk, tea, and silver in return for a Xia guarantee of peace along the frontiers. Although the agreement was maintained, the Song also dispatched troops on several occasions in the late eleventh century to suppress the Tanguts.

The Xia dynasty, which the Tanguts founded, was culturally sophisticated and engaged in considerable commerce. Construction of a capital city distinguished it from nearly all of China's mostly nomadic neighbors. Even more unusual was its development of a written script, which has, in fact, been deciphered. Printing with moveable type was another of its remarkable achievements, as was its enactment of an elaborate law code. However, its most noteworthy characteristic was state adoption and patronage of Buddhism. Devotion to Buddhism as the state religion provided for the allocation of resources for the construction of temples, for the translation and printing of sutras, and for the fashioning of ritual objects. Emperors, officials, and monks believed that they accumulated merit by subsidizing the creation of beautiful Buddhist manuscripts, drawings, paintings, and textiles. Russian archeologists who excavated the Xia capital discovered a treasure trove of such works that is now found in the State Hermitage Museum in St. Petersburg. Trade generated some of the revenues required for the sponsorship of Buddhism. The Xia sent salt, rhubarb, horses, sheep, camels, and carpets to China and received tea, silver, silk, porcelain, lacquerware, and silver and gold ornaments.

The Xia's political history did not match its efflorescent religion and growing economy. Although the dynasty was influenced by Confucianism, which prided itself on stability and order, the Xia was plagued by periodic unrest. Struggles over the throne after a ruler's death, as well as the power of such extralegal authorities as empress dowagers (who dominated at least one reign), led to some turbulence. The dynasty was, on occasion, plagued by banditry and uprisings and frequently acted as a tributary of the Song and Liao emperors and eventually the Jin dynasty, which drove the Song out of north China in 1126. Vulnerable to such powerful adversaries as the Mongols, in 1207 it sought assistance from the Jin against a projected attack by Chinggis Khan. The Jin refused its request, permitting the Mongols a free hand in the Xia territories. In 1209 Chinggis launched an invasion, but his troops, having no experience of laying siege to a city, had to flee from a bungled attempt to capture the Xia capital in order to avoid inundation by a river they had attempted to divert. Chinggis had to be content with the Xia ruler's perfunctory submission, symbolized by the dispatch of the emperor's daughter to his harem. Later the Xia emperor showed his independence by rejecting the Mongols' demand that he supply troops for their campaign in central Asia from 1219 to 1225, which proved to be his fatal misstep. In 1227, seeking revenge for such insubordination, Chinggis and his forces, now having mastered the techniques of siege warfare, defeated the Tanguts, occupied and sacked the capital, and killed the Xia emperor. Many Tanguts survived and played roles in later history but they never reestablished an independent state.

The Jurchens, who would later play a vital role in Chinese history, were a Tungusic-speaking people with a mixed economy who were based in what was formerly called Manchuria. Those in the northern domains of the Jurchen territories hunted and fished for survival (an economy similar to their neighbors in Siberia). Those in the west were herders, and those in the south were farmers but also hunted and migrated with their animals. The Jurchens in the south had greater contact than their confreres with the various groups that arose in the post-Tang-dynasty world in east Asia.

The more organized Khitan Liao dynasty imposed a tributary status on the Jurchens, compelling them to provide annual payments of falcons, furs, and pearls. On the other hand, in 1042, the Jurchens signed an agreement with the Song by which the Chinese dynasty pledged to offer annual "gifts" of tea, silver, and silk. The Song also permitted a controlled system of trade under which the Jurchens received tea, grains, and rice and supplied pearls, ginseng, and horses in return. Despite these Song economic concessions, conflicts between the Song and the Jurchens flared up throughout the eleventh century and weakened both.

The Jurchens' relationship with the Liao was even more volatile. Chafing under the Liao demands for tribute, the Jurchens often battled with their Khitan overlords. Such struggles with the Liao and Song required the Jurchens to develop a larger and more sophisticated military organization, which, in turn, necessitated a more complex administration to match those of their neighbors. The Jurchens learned from both, and by the end of the eleventh century could muster a huge military force to challenge the two dynasties. In 1115, they adopted the Chinese dynastic name of Jin, and in the same year defeated the Liao dynasty. The panicked Song leaders quickly agreed to a treaty that provided annual payments of silk and silver to the Jin. Yet the treaty did not lead to peace. By 1127, Jin troops had routed the Song, compelling the native Chinese dynasty to abandon China north of the Yangzi River and create the Southern Song dynasty, setting up its capital in Hangzhou.

For the next century, the Jin ruled north China, using Chinese institutions with slight variations. Jin rulers used the traditional Chinese civil-service examinations to select officials but also saved some top positions for the Jurchens. They devised a law code, conducted censuses, and developed their own written scripts. Increasingly influenced by Chinese institutions, they set up land and commercial taxes and imposed monopolies on vital goods, which they could then sell at a profit. Yet, like the Chinese dynasties, the Jin had officials who enriched themselves; the dynasty was plagued by considerable corruption, leading to revenue shortfalls. The government was thus unable to maintain the country's infrastructure, and disasters, including catastrophic Yellow River floods in the 1190s, struck its lands. Peasants made homeless by the floods began to rebel against the Jin. Adding to such disruptions were the increasing conflicts with the Song. From 1206 to 1208, the native Chinese dynasty tried to regain control over northern China. Although the Southern Song failed, this period of unrest made the Jin vulnerable to other attacks.

Chinggis Khan arose at this point, and in 1211 initiated campaigns against the Jin. The Mongol ruler recognized a golden opportunity to capitalize on the splits between the Jurchens and the Southern Song, and on the Jin dynasty's attendant weakness. Having already renounced his status as a Jin vassal, he began to challenge the established commercial relationship with the Jin. Conflict erupted in 1211 and, after considerable loss of life and devastation, in 1215 Mongol troops moved into the Jin stronghold in the area around modern Beijing. The Jin emperor fled to Kaifeng, but the dynasty fell to Chinggis's son Ögödei in 1234.

Although many in the Jurchen elite had been attracted by Chinese civilization, the bulk of the population was not sinicized. Yet the Jin emperors restored Confucian rituals at court, supported productions of plays (including so-called *zaju* or skits), and sought legitimacy in China. Recent excavations of Jin tombs indicate that culture flourished during the dynasty. The brick carvings in the elaborately decorated tombs depict theatrical productions as well as local festivals. They portray dancers performing lion dances and musicians playing drums, flutes, clappers, and other instruments. The carvers created models of stages for these performances, but they also chose subjects such as paradigms of filial piety (a Confucian concern), scenes of daily life (including cooking and horseback riding), and even religious figures such as the immortals (who were virtually deified in Daoism). As more research on the Jin is conducted, it seems likely that additional evidence of Jin support of culture, literature, and the arts will emerge. Nonetheless, those Jurchens who remained in their homelands northeast of China and even quite a few within China retained their own identities. After the Mongol conquest, many Jurchens went back to their native lands, from which they would play important roles in Chinese history four centuries later.

SONG ARTS

Buddhism, with its pantheon and emanations of the Buddhas and bodhisattvas and its granting of merit for visual representations of its teachings, had inspired artists ever since its arrival in China and continued to do so. Daoism, with its message of mysticism and its evocation of nature, also provided artists with themes that could be illustrated. Similarly, Song Neo-Confucianism, with its emphasis on investigation and study as a means of attaining knowledge, influenced and spurred artists to produce realistic depictions of nature.

A large number of extraordinary painters appeared in the Northern Song. Several of them wrote essays that embodied their views of landscape painting. Guo Xi (ca. 1020–ca. 1090), one of a slew of impressive artists, wrote that the painter must study nature in order to depict it precisely. The true artist must convey the images of mountains, water, and trees as they appear at specific times during the day or in specific seasons. Yet, according to Jing Hao (855–915), a late-Tang painter and critic whose views were influential, surface realism is insufficient. The painter "must capture both exterior verisimilitude and inner substance."[3] The integration of the external appearance and the innate spirit constitute reality at any given time. Although the artist recognizes that these images are transitory and can never be considered "complete," he still provides an opportunity for the viewer to examine, explore, and enjoy the mountains,

Figure 6.1 Fan Kuan (ca. 990–1030), *Travelling among Streams and Mountains*. Hanging scroll, ink and color on silk. China, Northern Song, eleventh century. 206.3 × 103.3cm. This painting is amongst the most famous of all Chinese paintings, and is one of the best examples of the Northern Song "monumental" landscape style. Photo: akg-images / Erich Lessing

hills, rivers, and bridges. The viewer should be transported out of his or her daily routine into a new vision of landscape and nature.

The culmination and embodiment of this unique conception of realism is the renowned painting *Travelling among Streams and Mountains* by Fan Kuan (fl. 990–1020). Fan had studied the works of such earlier Song landscape painters as Li Cheng (919–967), but eventually recognized the need to chart his own course. He retreated to the mountains of his native Shaanxi province, and after lengthy observations and study of the terrain emerged with his great painting. In this dramatic and arresting work, the viewer confronts a steep and majestic mountain, spectacular waterfalls, and massive rocks and trees. Dwarfed by this powerful landscape is a pilgrim accompanied by pack animals. This depiction of mankind fits well with the injunction to represent nature and humans in a realistic perspective. The dynamism and movement of nature, in the form of massive jutting mountains and waterfalls, propel the viewer into the active, ever-changing character of phenomena. The realism is so intense that "the very mountains seem to be alive."[4]

The Qingming scroll, which has been dated to around the late eleventh century, yields perhaps the purest example of realism. Measuring approximately 5.25 meters in length, it depicts the countryside and suburbs of a great city and finally the bustling city itself. Although the city has traditionally been identified as the Northern Song capital of Kaifeng, its pristine quality, the omission of beggars or the ailing, the relative paucity of women, and the lack of police or other security officers have caused some scholars to believe that the artist intended to portray an idealized city, where everyone dressed and behaved according to social status. Nonetheless, even these detractors admit that the artist painted in a realistic manner. The stores, restaurants, warehouses, river, and bridge represented in the scroll convey the image of an authentic Song city, even if not the capital of Kaifeng.

Other styles of painting also developed and flourished. Flower painting, which had appeared in the Tang, now showed birds adjacent to or perched on bushes or flowers, creating a new style. Xu Xi, one of the pioneers as well as one of the most accomplished of the painters of this genre, was renowned for the grandeur of his works, which resembled in their monumental scale Fan Kuan's "Travelling among Streams and Mountains." His rapid and spontaneous style of brush painting contrasted sharply with the precise, realistic, and artfully colored works of Huang Quan (903–965), the other great master of bird and flower painting. The influential connoisseur and calligrapher Mi Fu (1052–1107) championed a style of landscape painting that differed from the genre reflected in the overpowering scenes in the paintings of Fan Kuan and other northern Chinese. He admired southern Chinese painters such as Dong Yuan (ca. 934–ca. 962) for their serene and clear representations of nature, which consisted principally of the gentler landscapes – meandering rivers, graceful clouds, and beautiful lakes. Although the painters of north and south differed in their conceptions of the natural surroundings, they shared the goal of realistic portraits of landscapes.

Li Gonglin (1049–1106), a high-born official, preserved and added to the genre of figure painting while also helping to create a respect for beautiful objects of the past. An acquaintance of Wang Anshi and other luminaries of his age, he gained renown as a collector of ancient bronzes and jades and was extraordinarily knowledgeable as a connoisseur of the great Chinese artworks of earlier dynasties. In line with this reverence for antiquity, he devoted considerable time to copying the works of painters whom he admired. Such copying made him vulnerable to accusations of derivativeness in his own painting. His detractors, particularly Mi Fu, criticized his lack of creativity. Yet, ironically, he shared the concern for realism of the landscape painters lauded by his critics. His paintings of horses, for example, were based on such exhaustive observation and study of the imperial stables that "he was warned of the danger in becoming so imbued with their images that he would transmigrate into a horse."[5] He also painted human figures, particularly as he began to focus on Buddhist subjects, but his interests did not encompass landscapes.

In other ways, however, Li reflected many of the themes and aims of Northern Song painting. His realism and attention to detail mirrored the similar concerns of landscape painters, though his subjects were different. His practice of copying paintings he admired was mimicked and persisted as a means of training young painters. His reverence for ancient Chinese objects was part of a rising concern for connoisseurship among Song artists. These objects served as models for aspiring painters, and the copies they produced with such remarkable care could not, on occasion, be distinguished from the originals, leading to an increased incidence of fakes and frauds. Unscrupulous individuals, be they artists or owners, would emboss the seal of a prominent earlier painter on works and pass them off as originals. Even the most knowledgeable curators, collectors, and art historians in modern times have sometimes been unable to detect these fakes.

Finally, Li continued in the great tradition of Buddhist painting. Here, too, he reflected a Northern Song genre; his subject matter and themes related to Buddhism, which persisted in inspiring the arts but not as profusely or innovatively as in earlier dynasties. Chan Buddhism, with its emphasis on meditation and sudden enlightenment, had begun to supersede some of the more popular sects of the past and gave rise to a focus on spontaneity and quietism in painting.

These developments in painting would no doubt have been remarkable even without government support, but imperial patronage created a favorable environment for artists. Such support had originated in the early Northern Song court but reached its height during the reign of the last emperor, Huizong (r. 1101–1125). An ardent patron of court painters, Huizong also demanded adherence to his aesthetic principles. Painters who sought the court's favor needed to abide by the dictates he proclaimed. His rigidity helped to ensure that court painters selected only certain themes and produced works according to his specifications. Some merely copied the paintings of the emperor himself or sought his endorsement of works similar to his. Most of the paintings associated with him are precise and simple descriptions of birds on branches. The popularity of bird and flower paintings may, in part, have derived from their link with Huizong and the painters he supported at court.

Poetry was, on occasion, an integral part of paintings. For example, Mi Fu incorporated poetry and splendid calligraphy in his paintings. Although the

Tang was the glorious period in Chinese poetry, the Song produced excellent poets who often dealt with the highly personal themes of love, sorrow, and frustration. Su Shi or Su Dongpo (1037–1101), the most renowned of these poets, was a multitalented calligrapher and painter but achieved fame in poetry. His poems often reflect events in his own life, including criticism of Wang Anshi's New Policies. Exiled due to his opposition to these reforms, he wrote some poems about loneliness and longing. He also used his poems to reflect his personal relationships and career.

Li Qingzhao, a poet from an elite family who married a member of the elite, is one of the most renowned poets in Chinese history. Her early poems show the deep and loving relationship she had with her husband, which was in part centered on their shared love of intellectual and aesthetic pursuits. However, her later poems reveal the shocking changes in her life. In 1127, she and her family fled from north China when the Jurchens of Manchuria attacked the Song. Leaving her beloved artifacts and her former life behind, she headed south with her husband. Two years later he died, an event that transformed her poetry. Her writings became epistles of her sorrows and distress after these misfortunes.

Developments in Song ceramics and porcelain matched those in painting. The elegance and simplicity of the pottery resembled the same characteristics in painting, and these similar attributes may have been caused by the fact that the target audience – the scholar-officials, the intellectuals, and the landed elite – was the same for both arts. The wares, which many Chinese believe to be the most elegant and beautiful of their porcelains, were occasionally named for the locations where they were produced. Ding ware, in its original form a white porcelain, derived from the area around Dingzhou in the modern province of Hebei, and Jun ware, with its deliberate purple splotch brought about by copper oxidized in the glaze, was produced initially in Junzhou. Celadons were also prized throughout Asia, and Korean potters, in particular, borrowed the Chinese technique and began to develop exquisite celadons of their own. The veneration of antiquity resonated with the ceramics because potters used many of the same forms and shapes found on the Shang and Zhou bronzes. Similarly, some of the decorative motifs on the porcelains resembled the plant and flower motifs in Song paintings – still another example of the borrowing of shapes and motifs from one medium to another that has characterized Chinese art.

Knowledge of the extraordinary quality of Song porcelains spread throughout Asia and created a demand for them. Porcelain became an important commodity in trade. Although the Silk Roads to west Asia had become more precarious, partly because China had withdrawn from the oases and towns in modern Xinjiang in the late Tang dynasty, commerce still persisted. The mostly Turkic peoples residing along the northwestern borders of China transmitted goods to and from the Song. The quantity declined, but trade, including traffic in porcelain, was conducted. A contemporaneous Song account also reveals that porcelain was an important item in seaborne trade with Korea, Southeast Asia, Persia, and Arabia, reaching all the way to Fustat, adjacent to modern Cairo.

SOUTHERN SONG ECONOMIC AND CULTURAL SOPHISTICATION AND POLITICAL INSTABILITY

The Southern Song witnessed an even greater commercial prosperity. Expelled from north China by the Jurchen peoples of Manchuria who founded the Jin dynasty, the Song court shifted its capital to Linan (or Hangzhou), which became one of the world's most resplendent cities. The bountiful agriculture and the seaborne trade fostered prosperity for the elite and the merchants. Improvements in navigation and mapmaking and developments in naval technology promoted shipping in south China. The use of a mariner's compass facilitated Chinese shipping. Proximity to good harbors in the south offered greater opportunities for travel and commerce. The ports of Hangzhou, Quanzhou, and Fuzhou prospered and attracted merchants from west, south, and Southeast Asia. These cities eventually had resident communities of Hindus and Muslims who formed virtually self-governing units and maintained their own cultural identities. They built temples and mosques and even had their own cemeteries. The hospitable welcome they received in south China, as well as in the north, encouraged ever-larger numbers of foreign merchants to bring their goods. In north China, a small group of Jewish artisans and merchants settled in and built a synagogue in the city of Kaifeng.

Increasing commercialization in south China affected domestic markets as well. Merchants were no longer limited to the capitals of specific counties and thus traded in small towns and villages as well. Although government officials continued to supervise markets, merchants faced fewer restrictions in trade. Enclosed markets became rarer, allowing merchants to trade in neighborhoods that had earlier had restricted commercial areas. The growth in commerce led to an increase in the use of money, which in turn encouraged the government to collect taxes in cash. The quantity of paper money increased – another step in facilitating commerce.

The flourishing agricultural economy provided the foundation for this commercialization. Fertile soil in south China had attracted migrants from the north since the third century and had also generated surpluses, which were then transported to markets. The resulting prosperous economy created a wealthy elite who desired domestic and foreign luxury goods. As noted earlier, foreign trade grew, and some scholars assert that the Chinese had a favorable balance of trade in seaborne commerce. Yet not all groups benefited from what appeared to be a dazzling economy. Many peasants did not profit from the seeming prosperity, and the government itself often faced financial shortfalls. Thus, lying below the glittering surface of Southern Song court life in Hangzhou, the city that enchanted Marco Polo more than any other in China or perhaps in the world, were serious fiscal realities and great deprivation for much of the population. The remarkable achievements of the elite in broadening and contributing to Neo-Confucian thought and in creating beautiful paintings coexisted with the exploitation of much of the populace as well as the deterioration in the government's performance of its duties. An economy of abundance, of paper money, of an expanding population (which reached at least sixty million by the early thirteenth century), of prosperous tea plantations and silk workshops, and of extensive foreign (mostly seaborne) trade nourished a small elite but left many at or below subsistence. Although "in the spheres of social life, art, amusements, institutions, and technology, China was unquestionably the most advanced country of the time,"[6] only a small segment of the population profited from these advances.

Hangzhou, the greatest capital city in the world, reveals much about the lifestyles and values of the elite. Situated between the Yangzi River and the port cities of Ningbo, Fuzhou, Quanzhou, and others dotting the southeast coast, Hangzhou was extremely attractive, bordered on one side by the man-made West Lake and on the other by the Zhe River. Yet its location on a nexus of rivers, lakes, and canals was clearly more valuable than its natural beauty. It could readily export goods while also being easily supplied. These fortuitous circumstances created a large population, probably more than one million (some estimates run as high as two million). Lavish multistorey houses; markets offering perfumes, spices, and bronze and iron vessels; and restaurants, taverns, theaters, and singing girls attracted many. Wealthy officials and merchants no doubt concurred in Marco Polo's assessment that Hangzhou was "the most noble city and the best that is in the world."[7]

Commercialization created a prosperous merchant class but did not result in the new socioeconomic system associated with postmedieval Europe. Despite their wealth, merchants did not have commensurate political power. A strong state that valued agriculture above all other economic pursuits did not permit much leverage to merchants and suppressed any assertions of merchant independence. The state itself participated in trade and officials clambered on to foreign ships before the entry of individual merchants and garnered some of the most precious goods. Then and only then would merchants be permitted to trade for the rest of the foreign merchandise. In addition, wealthy merchants would, on occasion, buy land as a possible first step toward their families' eventual acceptance as part of the gentry. They also would aspire to have sons who passed the civil-service examinations.

Despite the civil-service examinations, the bureaucracy remained rife with abuses. Nepotism (which favored the sons of the leading families and officials) and sale of offices were rampant, particularly in the thirteenth century. Maintenance of a sizable military force to resist the encroachment of the non-Chinese dynasties north of the Yangzi River created fiscal problems, as did the elaborate and costly court and the elite's craving for expensive foreign products. The government responded to these problems by inflating the currency. Its lower-paid officials generally received no additional funding, despite the inflation, and became increasingly corrupt. Deterioration in government efficiency and infighting among cliques at court contributed to the growing disarray. In the last few reigns, empress dowagers and their relatives sought to dominate the young and occasionally infant emperors who ascended the throne, and this fostered an even more negative image of the court.

The grand lifestyles at court and among the elite resulted in an unfavorable balance of trade, which necessitated the export of precious metals and money to foreign lands. The elite's penchant for foreign luxuries generated ongoing fiscal problems.

To be sure, some peasants did well because they had land that was more fertile or were more enterprising or hard working or grew marketable products or had good connections with local officials. Most, however, either owned small plots or were tenants compelled to pay high rents. The government demanded stiff taxes, including nuisance or sales taxes on important commodities such as salt, and wealthy merchants also imposed higher prices for essential goods. Many peasants fell into debt to landlords or usurers and would often remain so for the rest of their lives because of the high rates of interest. A bountiful harvest was insufficient to rescue them from debt.

More and more peasants became unable to compete with the large and more commercial estates, and they increasingly abandoned their lands and migrated to cities. They served as laborers or servants to the wealthy. The servants, though economically dependent on their prosperous employers, were generally better off than the laborers, who often undertook backbreaking work under insecure conditions. The growth of urban centers, together with the flight of poor girls and women to these towns and cities, inevitably gave rise to increases in prostitution. A few prostitutes achieved fame and wealth as courtesans or due to talents as musicians or dancers who performed for the elite, and these women lived comfortable and secure lives. However, the vast majority were ill-educated, had scant talent, and were herded into singing-girl houses or tea-houses or restaurants where proprietors served as their protectors but also pocketed much of the income for entertaining the establishment's guests.

The new elite, which had for the most part dispersed the old Tang aristocracy, had achieved its success through the civil-service examinations rather than family or position. It naturally had a vested interest in the content and philosophy of the exams, which were intertwined with Confucianism. At the same time, the late Tang attacks on Buddhism diminished the Buddhist establishment's ability to play the political role that it had earlier in the dynasty. Such developments offered Confucianism an opportunity to supplant Buddhism as the most significant force at court. Buddhism was not eclipsed as a religion and, in fact, continued to prosper. However, monks did not have the political power and economic leverage that they wielded in the times of the Empress Wu or other Tang rulers.

Recent research has shed light on Southern Song popular religions that accompanied what is said to have been an increase in localism in the country. After the fall of the Northern Song and in the context of the governmental problems confronting the Southern Song, local elites allegedly devoted their efforts to security and economic development in their own localities instead of focusing on positions in the central government, which due to corruption, weakness, and ineptitude was less effective. Popular religions mirrored that transformation, as the devout worshipped and appealed to local deities rather than to the more distant gods, who did not have the same personal relationship with the ordinary person and have been said to be as remote as the hierarchical bureaucracy that ruled the country. These local deities were, on occasion, recently dead figures and not the anthropomorphic deities or the heroes of the past. Popular Daoism and its deities and immortals, in particular, became part of and bolstered this new localism. There were exceptions to this emphasis on local deities. The growing number of merchants who traveled to distant areas prayed to regional deities.

The earlier deities were not abandoned. Guan Yu, one of the most popular of these gods, had been a real military hero during the chaotic times that led to the fall of the Han dynasty in 220 CE. Defeated in battle and then decapitated, he was honored even by his enemies for his military prowess and his devotion to his leaders. By the sixth century, he had become deified as the God of War, and numerous shrines, with his image represented as a figure with a red face and long beard, were dedicated to him. His reputation developed so quickly that he became an important figure not only in popular religions but also in Daoism (as a guardian and destroyer of demons) and in Buddhism (as a bodhisattva). This depiction fit in with the syncretism of Chinese religions.

Paradoxically, the dynasty was open to new technologies and scientific investigations. Its seaborne contacts with Southeast Asia, India, and west Asia; the Neo-Confucian emphasis on investigation; and the government's focus on civilian rather than military matters contributed to remarkable advances in the sciences. As the leading historian of Chinese science has written, "Whenever one follows up any specific piece of scientific or technological history in Chinese literature, it is always at the Sung [i.e. Song] dynasty that one finds the major focal point."[8] Medicine and medical therapies attracted great interest. Acupuncture became widely used, and medical specialists produced an imperial medical text known as the *Recipes of the Department of Favoring the People and Harmonizing Preparation of the Taiping Era (Taiping huiming heji jufang)*. A pharmaceutical text that emphasized the use of plants as medicines appeared, and a variety of studies on bamboo, birds, fishes, lichees, and flowering trees added to knowledge of botany and biology. New developments in bridge building (such as the transverse shear-wall and the caisson) and in hydraulics (such as lock gates) complemented striking advances in agriculture, including better seeds. Similarly, larger junks, the sternpost rudder, and the magnetic compass facilitated greater seaborne commerce. Less positive was the use of gunpowder for explosives, specifically for grenades and bombs ejected from catapults and cannons.

Shen Gua (1031–1095) was the most renowned writer on science in the Song and was one among its many remarkable figures. An unusually large number of extraordinarily capable officials, artists, and thinkers lived during the Song, and, like many of them, Shen was multitalented. Having passed the civil-service examinations and having supported Wang Anshi's New Policies, he served in a variety of official positions, each of which required a move from one location to another. During his peripatetic life, he kept notes on the technological and scientific marvels he witnessed or learned about. He compiled his observations in a work entitled *Mengxi bitan (Dream Pool Essays)*, which included sections on astronomy, mathematics, physics, chemistry, engineering, music, and other areas of study. It provided a summary of Song knowledge of these mostly scientific fields.

In sum, the Song witnessed remarkable achievements in science, technology, the arts, philosophy, overseas commerce, and the examination system, but political instability and an inadequate revenue base for government weakened the dynasty. Had the political excesses, including corruption, succession problems, and exploitation of the populace, been controlled, the Song would not have been as vulnerable to foreign attack. The Southern Song, in particular, with its sophisticated urban culture in the capital of Hangzhou, reached a level achieved by few civilizations. Marco Polo was entranced by its natural beauty, its lovely West Lake, the wealth of its inhabitants, its hospitals, its bathhouses, and its restaurants. He pronounced Hangzhou to be a place "where so many pleasures may be found that one fancies himself to be in Paradise."[9]

This cosmopolitan culture would face the most powerful steppe military adversary China had ever encountered. What is truly amazing is that the Southern Song managed to hold off this seemingly irresistible foreign force for more than four decades. Its wealth, its patriotic fervor, its military, and its cultural heritage sustained it and averted an immediate collapse.

NOTES

1 Peter Bol, "Government, Society, and State: On the Political Visions of Ssu-ma Kuang and Wang An-shih" in Robert Hymes and Conrad Shirokauer, eds., *Ordering the World: Approaches to State and Society in Sung China* (Berkeley: University of California Press, 1993), p. 180.

2 James T. C. Liu, *Reform in Sung China* (Cambridge, MA: Harvard University Press, 1959), p. 66.

3 Richard Barnhart, "Ching Hao" in Herbert Franke, ed., *Sung Biographies: Painters* (Wiesbaden: Franz Steiner Verlag, 1976), p. 25.

4 Michael Sullivan, *The Arts of China* (Berkeley: University of California Press, 3rd ed., 1984), p. 159.

5 Hsio-yen Shih, "Li Kung-lin" in Herbert Franke, ed. *Sung Biographies: Painters* (Wiesbaden: Franz Steiner Verlag, 1976), p. 81.

6 Jacques Gernet, *Daily Life in China on the Eve of the Mongol Invasion, 1250–1276*, trans. by H. M. Wright (Stanford: Stanford University Press, 1962), p. 18.

7 A. C. Moule and Paul Pelliot, trans., *Marco Polo: The Description of the World* (London: George Routledge & Sons, Ltd., 1938), p. 326.

8 Joseph Needham, *Science and Civilisation in China* I (Cambridge: Cambridge University Press, 1961), p. 134.

9 Moule and Pelliot, p. 326.

FURTHER READING

John Chaffee, *The Thorny Gates of Learning in Sung China* (Cambridge: Cambridge University Press, 1986).

Patricia Ebrey, *Inner Quarters: Marriage and the Lives of Chinese Women in Sung China* (Berkeley: University of California Press, 1993).

Jacques Gernet, *Daily Life on the Eve of the Mongol Invasion, 1250–1276*, trans. by H. M. Wright (Stanford: Stanford University Press, 1962).

Valerie Hansen, *Negotiating Daily Life in Traditional China: How Ordinary People Used Contracts, 600–1400* (New Haven: Yale University Press, 1995).

Robert Hymes, *Statesmen and Gentlemen* (Cambridge: Cambridge University Press, 1986).

Dorothy Ko, *Every Step a Lotus: Shoes for Bound Feet* (Berkeley: University of California Press, 2001).

James Liu, *Reform in Sung China: Wang An-shih and His New Policies* (Cambridge, MA: Harvard University Press, 1968).

Alfreda Murck, *Poetry and Painting in Song China: The Subtle Art of Dissent* (Cambridge, MA: Harvard University Press, 2000).

Morris Rossabi, ed., *China among Equals* (Berkeley: University of California Press, 1988).

PART III

China and the Mongol World

[7] Mongol Rule in China, 1234–1368

> Rise of Chinggis Khan
> Legacy of Chinggis Khan
> Expansion and Early Rule of Empire
> Sorghaghtani Beki, Möngke, and Khubilai
> Unification of China
> Khubilai's Policies
> Multiethnic and Multireligious China
> Khubilai and Chinese Culture
> Decline of the Yuan
> Legacy of the Mongols

After the Khitans, Tanguts, and Jurchens came the Mongols, who differed from these other non-Chinese groups who dealt with the Song dynasty because they eventually conquered all of China. Paradoxically, the Mongols' lifestyle and culture differed most markedly from those of the Chinese. Yet perhaps they had the greatest influence on China. To be sure, China had an impact on the Mongols, as its civilization attracted many of them. However, most Mongols did not become sinicized and retained their own identities.

Their identities, like those of the Xiongnu and other groups based in Mongolia, centered, in part, on their environment and traditional economy. A landlocked domain, a harsh continental climate, and severe winters confronted the Mongols in their native territories. Below-freezing temperatures in winter and spring and limited precipitation in summer, occasionally leading to droughts, impeded agriculture in nearly all locations and compelled the

A History of China, First Edition. Morris Rossabi.
© 2014 Morris Rossabi. Published 2014 by Blackwell Publishing Ltd.

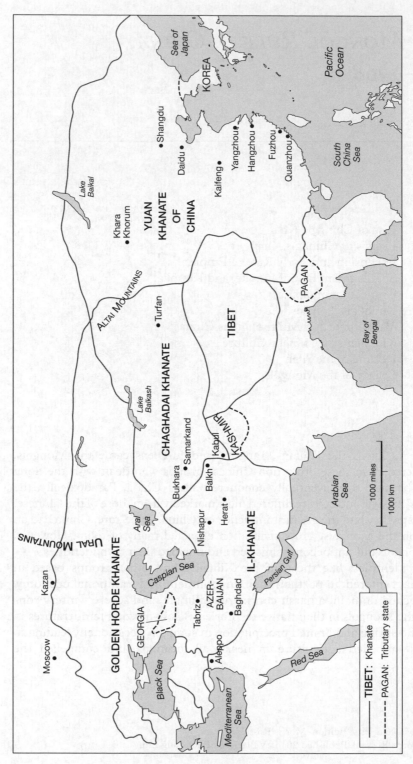

Map 7.1 Mongol Empire, 1279

Mongols to rely on pastoralism. Even nomadic pastoralism was precarious because of dreaded winters with extraordinary amounts of snow and ice that prevented the animals from reaching the life-saving plants and grasses in the grazing lands. Hundreds of thousands or perhaps millions of animals perished under those conditions.

The Mongols migrated from one location to another to find water and grass for their animals. Two such movements per year were characteristic, but herders living in or near the Gobi desert might be compelled to move more frequently. Mobility was critical, especially during a bad winter, when the animals' survival was at stake. Sheep, goats, and oxen provided food, fuel, clothing, shelter, and means of transport. Camels carried the Mongols' belongings during their travels, and horses supplied the mobility required to round up the animals and to maintain a powerful cavalry – an extraordinary asset in warfare. Some Mongols supplemented their pastoral economy by hunting, and a few of them cultivated wheat, millet, and other grains, despite the short growing season.

Like pastoral nomads of the past, the Mongols needed to trade with China because of their precarious economy. They sought Chinese goods for their very survival, and their elites eventually desired silk and other luxuries in stable times. In turn, they supplied animals and animal products to the Chinese. When denied such commerce, they raided Chinese settlements to obtain the products they craved. Such engagements required larger and larger groups of Mongols and more sophisticated military organizations. The scale of warfare with China and among the Mongols themselves and various Turkic groups in Mongolia widened, devastating the grasslands and undermining the herders' strategies for survival. The Mongols needed unity.

RISE OF CHINGGIS KHAN

Temüjin (ca. 1162–1227) proved to be the charismatic and powerful leader who would unify the steppe peoples. The murder of his father when he was eight or nine years old was pivotal in his career. The *Secret History of the Mongols*, the only contemporary indigenous source on the thirteenth-century Mongols, writes that, with his mother and siblings, he was then forced to eke out an existence by gathering nuts and berries in the steppes. At that point, Temüjin recognized that he needed friends and allies to survive in this demanding environment; this was perhaps his most important insight. He forged one alliance after another, especially after he reputedly managed a hair-raising escape from a rival group that had imprisoned him. On occasion, he broke with his allies, defeated them, and incorporated some of his former enemies into his army, ensuring that they were personally loyal to him.

Other Mongol leaders had attempted to unify their people, but Temüjin developed more successful policies and practices. He chose his commanders based on merit, not on their aristocratic backgrounds. Those who were capable administrators or were courageous in battle were elevated into progressively higher positions. This policy of rewarding merit ingratiated him with his forces. His equitable division of spoils and rewards earned him additional support.

After some notable victories, he assumed the title of "khan," and once he had defeated all other Mongol leaders and had unified the Mongols, he was awarded the title of Chinggis Khan.

Chinggis capitalized on the Mongols' military prowess to organize a powerful army. The Mongols required boys and many girls to participate in athletic contests, including horse racing, archery, and wrestling, which served as part of their military training. Chinggis also mandated that they take part in hunts as an additional aspect of their preparation for warfare. They learned how to shoot the Mongols' composite bow, which had double the range of any other known in the world, while riding at full speed on their horses. Proficiency in the use of helmets, axes, and armor also contributed to their martial successes. In addition, Mongol tactics were highly developed. They placed felt puppets on horses to give a misleading impression of their numbers; they employed psychological terror by devastating a few towns and massacring the inhabitants in order to induce others to submit voluntarily; they feigned retreats to lure their pursuing enemies into a trap where their largest detachments were stationed; and they took great pains to set up supply lines and develop logistics. Chinggis demanded tight discipline. Commanders and ordinary soldiers who defied his orders or instructions were severely punished. Perhaps most important, the Mongols never set forth on a campaign without considerable intelligence information provided by merchants, defectors, and spies.

Another vital component of Chinggis' successes as he ventured beyond Mongolia was his willingness to recruit foreigners. The Uyghur Turks, who voluntarily submitted in 1211, proved to be important subjects, as they had skills in commerce, administration, and finance. Even before their submission, Chinggis had commissioned one of his Turkic advisers to develop a Mongolian written language based on the Uyghur script. Chinggis also incorporated Turks into his army, and Turkic forces constituted a large segment of the forces for his son's conquest of Russia.

Numerous explanations have been offered for the Mongols' eruption from Mongolia to create the largest contiguous empire in world history. One is simply the attraction of spoils. Once Chinggis had developed a sizable army, there was an almost inexorable drive to secure booty through additional conquests. China's possible denial of trade may also have prompted Mongol raids. A series of bad winters in the late twelfth and early thirteenth centuries doubtless compelled movement out of Mongolia and attacks on the dynasties in China. A reputed injunction by Tenggeri, the Mongols' Sky God, to Chinggis to conquer the world does not jibe with Chinggis' actions. Other than his campaign in central Asia, Chinggis did not seek to occupy the states he had defeated, which challenges the view that he attempted to fulfill a divine mandate to conquer the world.

Chinggis' initial campaigns led to the eventual destruction of the two non-Chinese dynasties in China and then the first Mongol occupation of a different land. In 1209, after an indecisive campaign, the Tangut Xia dynasty of northwest China sued for peace, and in 1227, a few months after Chinggis' death, his commanders demolished the Xia. In 1215, Chinggis' troops entered and sacked Zhongdu, near the modern city of Beijing, compelling the Jurchen Jin emperor to flee to the south, and in 1234 Chinggis' son overwhelmed the

Jin and occupied all of north China. In a campaign that lasted from 1219 to 1225, Chinggis swept through central Asia and occupied Samarkand, Bukhara, Herat, and other major commercial emporia. The Mongol conqueror died in 1227, probably of natural causes, although some sources attribute his death to injuries sustained in a hunt or to an unspecified illness.

LEGACY OF CHINGGIS KHAN

Chinggis bequeathed a considerable legacy, both positive and negative, to his descendants. A positive contribution was his unification of the Mongols. On the other hand, he established a large army and introduced a level of violence that the world had never seen. Yet, once the destruction and massacres had been accomplished, his other policies paved the way for his descendants. He devised and articulated rules collected in a set of instructions known as the *Jasagh*, which provided a semilegal precedent for his successors. His recruitment of foreign advisers and administrators influenced his sons and grandsons to trust and employ foreigners whose states they had subjugated. His support for commerce prompted his descendants to impose a *Pax Mongolica* in the territories they conquered, a peace that facilitated a spectacular growth in international trade in the thirteenth and fourteenth centuries. His toleration of foreign religions as a means of ingratiating himself with foreign clerics also became a standard policy for his successors, although, on occasion, they initiated campaigns against Daoism, Islam, or other religions.

Chinggis chose one of his sons as his successor but did not mandate a system of succession, a disastrous flaw that would weaken the Mongols. Once they had become unified, the Mongol leaders abandoned two traditional means of selecting leaders. Older brother to younger brother and ultimogeniture, or the youngest son as successor, were discarded. Instead, the Mongol nobility would meet in a so-called *khuriltai* (assembly) to choose the khaghan, or khan of khans, from among Chinggis' descendants. Naturally, different noblemen would support different Chinggisids, leading to disputes and often to civil wars. The first transfer of power worked out well, as Chinggis' wishes were respected. His son Ögödei became the khaghan while Ögödei's three brothers received territories in central Asia, Mongolia, and the Western Regions (which eventually encompassed Russia) respectively and were granted the title of "khan."

EXPANSION AND EARLY RULE OF EMPIRE

Ögödei (r. 1229–1241) expanded the empire and was the first khan to conceive of actually ruling the vast domains that the Mongols had conquered. His troops added Korea, north China, and lands up to the Iranian border, and, most dramatically, conquered much of Russia and initiated successful forays into Hungary and Poland. Perhaps as important, he began to set up an administrative structure to govern the lands under his control. His first step was to build a capital city in Khara Khorum, a site in the Mongol steppes. Khara Khorum became a magnet for an international coterie of clerics, merchants, and artisans. Recent excavations at the site have attested to the existence of a mosque and a Buddhist temple, as well as numerous Buddhist artifacts. Stalls for craft shops have been found, and Chinese ceramics, gold objects, and other luxury products indicate the development of a sophisticated society. A pathway or road leading to the city served as a link both to China and to the Silk Roads. Although the Franciscan friar William of Rubruck compared Khara Khorum unfavorably to the Parisian "suburb" of St. Denis, it was still remarkable for a city with a multiethnic population in the steppes. However, its location was so remote that it could not readily maintain the large number of people needed in what was a world capital. William of Rubruck mentioned that four hundred wagons reached the town daily to supply its inhabitants. Such a logistical effort could not be sustained. Within three decades, the Mongols had moved their capital to a more central location in China.

Stationed in Khara Khorum, Ögödei was determined to rule the northern Chinese territories he had subjugated in 1234. Lacking expertise in governance among his own people, Ögödei recruited Chinese and central Asians to assist in developing the proper institutions to rule the venerable civilization of China. He employed a sinicized Khitanese named Yelü Chucai, whom his father had also consulted. Yelü, whose ancestry stretched back to the Liao dynasty, sought to restore the traditional order in north China and advised Ögödei to reestablish institutions and practices resembling those of the previous Chinese governments. The sources credit him with preventing the Mongols from converting the agricultural land into grasslands and turning north China into a herder economy, although Chinese accounts also mention others, Chinese and Mongols alike, persuading the Mongol leadership to avoid such a radical step. Yelü also proposed the reintroduction of the civil-service examination as the main means of selecting officials. His efforts were frustrated, as Ögödei did not wish to be limited simply to Chinese officials and sought a multiethnic group of administrators. Yelü's other principal suggestion was the development of a regular tax structure rather than the capricious system the Mongols employed. The Mongol leaders traditionally levied taxes when a need, such as a military campaign, arose, but the Chinese were accustomed to a specific annual tax burden. Yelü persuaded Ögödei to accept a yearly tax levy, but central Asian Muslims interceded and undermined his policy. They proposed a tax-farming system in order to reduce state expenditures. Muslim agents, rather than paid officials, would collect taxes, saving on the expense of paying state tax collectors. The state would assign quotas to the Muslim merchants who acted as tax farmers, and the merchants would retain any funds above the quotas, a policy that led to serious abuses. The tax collectors benefited from squeezing as much revenue as possible from the Chinese, who responded by developing a negative image of both the Muslims and the Mongols. Yelü had tried to avert such exploitation of the Chinese, but Ögödei had not followed his advice.

Ögödei's death in 1241 ended the Mongols' campaigns but also witnessed the onset of a decade's long struggle for power among Chinggis' descendants.

Ögödei's family became embroiled in a conflict with his brother Tolui's sons. Partly due to this struggle, more than five years elapsed before Ögödei's son Güyüg ascended the throne as the khan of khans. His death two years later precipitated still another conflict that was, on this occasion, bloody.

SORGHAGHTANI BEKI, MÖNGKE, AND KHUBILAI

Sorghaghtani Beki, Tolui's widow and Khubilai Khan's mother, was the principal protagonist during this struggle. Portrayed as one of the most remarkable figures of her age by contemporaries in both East and West, she played a vital role in her sons' accession to power. Chinggis Khan had defeated her people in his drive toward unification of the Mongols and had given her in marriage to his son Tolui. Extraordinarily intelligent, she was ambitious for her sons and prepared them to be the rulers of the entire empire. As a Nestorian Christian, she recognized that toleration of a variety of religions would facilitate rule over a multiethnic and multireligious populace. Granted her own lands in north China after her husband's early death, she provided funds for Islamic, Buddhist, and Nestorian religious institutions. Instead of exploiting the Chinese peasants in her domain or compelling them to convert their property to Mongol-style grasslands, she encouraged them, through advice from agricultural specialists and through fewer corvée burdens, to grow more grain. She reasoned that the greater the increase in production, the greater the tax revenues that would accrue to the Mongols. Although she was illiterate, she ensured that her sons became literate, and her son Khubilai, who would have considerable influence on China, even learned spoken Chinese. Sorghaghtani Beki's political skills were unmatched. She had ingratiated herself with influential Mongol leaders by offering gifts and valuable intelligence information to them. Strong support from the nobility thus enabled her to overcome the opposition of Ögödei's descendants. Her son Möngke became the khan of khans in 1251, but she did not live long enough to enjoy the fruits of her labor. She died within a year.

Like his immediate predecessors, Möngke was determined to annex additional territories for the growing Mongol Empire. Because he needed revenue and troops to pursue such campaigns, he quickly proclaimed that only the court could levy taxes, impose corvée labor, and raise military forces for attacks and invasions. Once he had enforced these regulations, he turned to his plans for expansion. He directed his younger brother Hülegü to head toward west Asia to encroach upon the Islamic lands. After meticulous preparations, Hülegü led his forces, in 1256, in an attack on the Ismaili mountain stronghold of Alamut. The Ismailis, a small order within Islam, used suicide missions to assassinate their enemies, the Muslim leaders of the Baghdad-based 'Abbasid Caliphate (750–1258), which governed the Sunni or majority order of Islam. They assumed that such violence would create instability and would lead to the downfall of the caliphate, which was the most important contemporary Islamic state. Hülegü's troops scaled the mountain and crushed the defenders. Shortly thereafter, in February of 1258, Hülegü overwhelmed the 'Abbasid Caliphate and initiated a bloody massacre at its capital in Baghdad. Within a few years, Hülegü founded the so-called Il-Khanate, an indication that he planned to remain in west Asia. However, the Mongol rulers in Russia, who eventually became known as the Golden Horde, believed that Chinggis Khan had granted the Western Regions, which included west Asia, to his alleged son and their ancestor, Jochi. Their resentment against Hülegü and the Il-Khanate resulted in tensions and then in actual battles. These internal disputes and wars would harm the Mongol Empire and would eventually contribute to its collapse.

Möngke also set his sights on the Southern Song dynasty, which still ruled the Chinese territories south of the Yangzi River. Concerned that the Song rulers would lead a revanchist effort to oust the Mongols from north China, he wanted to destroy this opposition force. In 1259, he and his commanders devised a plan for a three-pronged assault on the Song. His own troops would embark from northwest China to the southwest and then march eastward to attack from the west. His younger brother Khubilai would meet the Song forces head on by crossing the Yangzi River and moving toward the Song's eastern lands. A naval force would then raid and seek to occupy the flourishing ports along the east coast. The campaign was successful until Möngke's death in August of 1259. The succession struggles that had plagued the Mongols for several generations now led to a cessation of the planned conquest of the Song. Khubilai and his brother Arigh Böke, each advocating different philosophies of governance, fought for the throne. Khubilai suggested that the Mongols needed to adopt some Chinese institutions and practices to rule China. Fearful that the Mongols would become increasingly sinicized, Arigh Böke objected to policies that might detract from the Mongol way of life and would erode Mongol values. Naturally, a drive for power also contributed to this civil war. China's abundant resources coupled with the traditionally powerful Mongol military, especially its cavalry, enabled Khubilai to overcome Arigh Böke. By 1264, the conflict had ended, permitting Khubilai to focus on ruling China.

UNIFICATION OF CHINA

However, the Mongols needed to overwhelm the Southern Song dynasty and unify China to gain credibility and legitimacy with the Chinese population, which was eager for a restoration of a China ruled by one dynasty. The Song, through increases in agricultural productivity, infant industries, and trade, had built a flourishing economy and a resplendent social and cultural life. But its government was chaotic and corrupt, with weak emperors often influenced by empress dowagers. As soon as Khubilai gained power, he ordered an attack on the Song. Toward the end of a five-year siege of the important town of Xiangyang, two Islamic engineers brought and employed powerful catapults and mangonels that led to victory. Success in overcoming this resistance meant that the Mongols could cross the Yangzi River. They gradually moved toward the Song capital at Hangzhou. Their reputation had reached the Song court, prompting the empress dowager to submit. Patriotic ministers swept up the child emperor and fled south. The sickly child died during the constant moves needed to keep one step ahead of the pursuing Mongol forces. The ministers who accompanied the court officials simply enthroned another child emperor. In 1279, the Mongols caught up with the Chinese, and the chief minister, with the young emperor in tow, dove into the sea and drowned. The Song dynasty had come to an end, and the Mongols had reunified China, a goal the Chinese had sought for four centuries and had been unable to accomplish.

KHUBILAI'S POLICIES

Khubilai (1215–1294) generally chose governmental institutions similar to the traditional Chinese ones. The six ministries founded during the Tang dynasty remained in place, and the system of local government scarcely differed from the structure in the Song dynasty. However, there were a few fundamental differences. Khubilai abolished the civil-service examinations as the only avenue to officialdom because he did not want to rely exclusively on the Chinese to staff his government. Examinations in Chinese based on knowledge of Confucianism would limit the pool of candidates for bureaucratic posts. Recommendations, perceived merit, and inherited positions were the principal roads to social mobility. Even when the Mongol court restored the examinations in 1315, they were not the sole means for entrance into the bureaucracy. This policy resulted in the development of an international coterie of officials, with Mongols dominating the military and the hierarchy, supported by Chinese, central Asian Muslims, Turks, Tibetans, and others. Most officials were Chinese, but the Mongols placed checks on them by appointing censors who traveled around the country incognito to survey the performance of officials and to report directly to the emperor about malfeasance and bribe-taking. Although the censors apparently conducted their work professionally and efficiently, corruption persisted among both Chinese officials and Mongol nobles.

Khubilai principally deviated from Chinese patterns in his social policies. Like the traditional Chinese emperors, he supported the peasantry through waiving taxes in times of distress and by setting up local organizations to provide information on optimal agricultural practices and to supply legal and police functions. However, he differed from the Chinese in his treatment of other social groups. For example, although the Chinese prized the beautiful bronzes, jades, porcelains, and textiles produced by artisans, they traditionally accorded craftsmen a relatively low social status because they worked with their hands, not their minds. The Mongols in the steppes had few artisans because of their frequent migrations and their ensuing inability to transport the often heavy tools and equipment required for such work. This paucity of craftsmen led the Mongols to value Chinese craftsmen and to provide them with tax and corvée exemptions, as well as special privileges. Such favorable treatment resulted in a Chinese craft renaissance during the Mongol era. The Mongols and Khubilai in particular also prized occupations that offered practical benefits. He especially valued doctors because the Mongols' rugged life and ensuing culinary and alcoholic excesses often led to severe illnesses and, on occasion, to early death. He also prized scientists such as astronomers, who could provide information on weather conditions and could offer, in their guise as astrologers, predictions that appeared plausible to the Mongols.

Merchants were probably the group that benefited the most from Mongol rule in China. Confucian officials had relegated merchants to a low social position, portraying them as exchangers, not producers, of goods. Bureaucrats considered merchants of lesser importance than the scholar-official class that dominated the government and even of lesser importance than the peasantry, who produced the most significant commodities. Mongol attitudes differed from those of the Chinese because they so desperately needed and craved foreign goods. Thus, Khubilai and his successors reduced tax burdens on merchants and eliminated sumptuary regulations aimed at traders. They also made positive contributions to commerce. The government built roads and canals to facilitate travel, made greater use of paper money, allowed merchants to stay at state postal stations while on their travels, and offered low-cost loans to merchant organizations undertaking long-distance trade along the Silk Roads. A trade revolution ensued, resembling the craft revolution that the Mongols had, in part, prompted. Merchants from Asia and then Europe reached China. The Mongols' domination of much of Asia also facilitated merchants' journeys.

MULTIETHNIC AND MULTIRELIGIOUS CHINA

Foreign missionaries, scientists, entertainers, military men, craftsmen, women, sailors, and physicians accompanied the arrival of merchants, creating a much more multiethnic and multireligious China in a global environment. Central Asian and Iranian Muslims were the most numerous and influential of these foreigners. Their positions in the social hierarchy as second only to the Mongols, with north Chinese third and south Chinese fourth, attested to their importance. The khans recruited many Muslims from central Asia and Persia. For example, Jamal al-Din, who arrived from west Asia, assisted in the construction of astronomical instruments and an observatory and in the development of a new calendar. Iranian physicians helped in the translation of Iranian medical texts into Chinese and the building of Iranian-style hospitals in the Mongol capital in China. A few Muslims from west Asia served in the Mongol military and offered skills in using catapults in besieging towns and cities. Khubilai selected the Muslim Saiyid Ajall Shams al-Din (1211–1279) to be the first governor of the newly conquered region of Yunnan in southwest China. Saiyid Ajall followed the Mongol lead in tolerating a variety of religions, not merely Islam, in his domain and, in fact, fostering Confucianism and Chinese civilization in an area inhabited by non-Chinese peoples. Khubilai also chose Muslims to manage the dynasty's financial administration. Muslim officials devised budgets and acted as tax collectors because of their perceived expertise in finances. Khubilai then employed several Muslims as superintendents of maritime trade in the southeastern port cities, giving them responsibilities for collecting tariffs and taxes, banning contraband, and regulating commerce. Muslim communities spread throughout the country as a result of the esteem in which the Muslims were held. Relations with the Islamic world outside China benefited enormously from favorable policies toward the Muslims within the country. Commerce in Chinese silks and porcelains and west Asian spices and medicines, among other products, grew exponentially during the Mongol era.

Similarly, Mongol support for Buddhism promoted relations with south Asia. The Mongols were not attracted by the more intellectual sects, which required sophisticated reading and understanding of the sutras. They sought instead Buddhist orders that entailed relatively easy practices and had practical benefits. Tibetan Buddhism, with its emphasis on the esoteric and magic and its toleration of monks playing an active role in secular and political life, was particularly appealing. Khubilai recruited a young Tibetan monk named the 'Phags-pa Lama (1235–1280) to teach his family the precepts of Tibetan Buddhism. 'Phags-pa turned out to be successful in initiating Khubilai's wife Chabi (1227–1281) into the mysteries of Tibetan Buddhism, and Khubilai rewarded him with the title of State Preceptor and eventually appointed him the ruler of Tibet. 'Phags-pa, in turn, assisted his benefactor by proclaiming that Khubilai was a reincarnation of Manjushri, the bodhisattva of wisdom, and a "Chakravartin" or "Universal King," which bolstered Khubilai's credentials as ruler of China.

Khubilai continued to rely on 'Phags-pa for a variety of tasks. When Khubilai sought to develop a written script that could be used for many languages in the Mongol domains, he entrusted 'Phags-pa with the responsibility of creating that script. 'Phags-pa's Square Script was based on the Tibetan and Sanskrit languages and was phonologically sound. It received the court's blessing, but it proved impossible to persuade the population to use a script mandated from the top. The government employed the script on such official documents as passports, seals, and paper money, and potters decorated a tiny group of porcelains with it. In any event, 'Phag-pa's manifold contributions prompted the court to provide tax exemptions for Buddhist monasteries, to construct temples, to incorporate Buddhism into court rituals, and to fund the production of ritual objects and sculptures.

Despite these appeals to foreign religions and peoples, Khubilai and his successors recognized that China was the center of their newly subjugated domains. They had to win over the Chinese. Khubilai responded by making concessions to Chinese culture. He first restored Confucian rituals at the court. Because Confucianism and China could not be separated, his use of these ceremonies impressed the Chinese. His construction of temples for his ancestors also fit in with traditional Chinese practices. Even more convincing was his shift of the capital from Khara Khorum in Mongolia to north China. In 1267, he ordered the construction of Daidu, in the vicinity of modern Beijing. Perhaps as significant, he had the capital built to Chinese specifications. Although Khubilai employed quite a few non-Chinese to design and construct the city, Daidu did not differ substantially from earlier Chinese capitals, except in its massive scale. Once Khubilai had chosen a capital in China, he adopted a Chinese name for his dynasty. "Yuan" derived from the *Yijing*, one of the most notable texts in the Chinese canon.

KHUBILAI AND CHINESE CULTURE

Khubilai and the Mongols supported specific features but not all of Chinese culture and art. They did not value cultural manifestations that required sophisticated knowledge of the Chinese language. Poetry, which was traditionally an attribute of a good Confucian, did not interest the Mongols and would not secure their support. Similarly, philosophical essays scarcely had an impact on them, although Khubilai and his successors recruited many Neo-Confucian thinkers for their governments. Calligraphy was not an art that they encouraged. They patronized the forms of Chinese culture that they could readily appreciate and comprehend.

Theater witnessed a golden age during the Mongol era, and Khubilai even set up stages in the Imperial Palace complex. Dramas, which were characterized by singing, dancing, pantomime, and acrobatics, appealed to them. The Yuan plays had their antecedents in less formal Song-dynasty expressions. Storytellers held audiences (consisting principally of nonelite individuals) spellbound with tales of great heroes, of love affairs, and of corrupt officials. In such cities as Kaifeng and Hangzhou, actual performances developed from storytelling. Audiences were captivated by both puppet shows and live actors. In Yuan times, historical events were popular in theater. Colorful and well-known figures were often the principal characters. Yang Guifei, the consort of a Tang-dynasty emperor who had had great influence over the emperor until her execution, and the Buddhist pilgrim Xuanzang, who had traveled to central Asia and India, were popular in such dramas. Judge Bao, based upon a real Song-dynasty personage of the eleventh century, was a heroic figure in a series of plays. He was depicted investigating instances of official corruption and malfeasance that harmed ordinary people and then punishing the criminals. Love stories that showed romance triumphing over arranged marriages or over obstacles imposed by the different class backgrounds of couples were a staple in these dramas. Such stereotypes as villainous officials and lovely heroines, including courtesans, abounded and appealed both to Chinese and foreign audiences. The use of the colloquial language rather than the somewhat arcane classical Chinese also found favor with the common people. Songs with dynamic music, played on the lute and the zither, enlivened performances and added to their popularity. The elite and later critics were entranced by the poetic lyricism in the songs, while general audiences enjoyed the stories and the spectacle.

The visual arts, which naturally did not necessitate knowledge of the Chinese language, received the greatest Mongol patronage. Although some artists refused to work for or cooperate with the Mongols, several major painters were willing to serve the foreigners who had, in fact, unified China after several centuries of disunity. The painters opposed to the new Mongol leadership either retired or rejected Mongol offers of bureaucratic positions. In contrast, Zhao Mengfu (1254–1322), who turned out to be the most renowned Yuan-dynasty painter-calligrapher and was a descendant of the Song imperial family, accepted official posts in the Ministry of War and as president of the Hanlin Academy, the most prestigious organization for the country's scholars, and still had the leisure time to paint. Li Kan (1245–1320), a famous

Figure 7.1 Liu Guandao, *Khubilai Khan*, ink and color on silk. National Palace Museum, Taipei, Taiwan / The Bridgeman Art Library

Figure 7.2 Zhao Mengfu (1254–1322), *Sheep and Goat*. Washington DC, Smithsonian Institution, Freer Gallery of Art. © 2013. Photo Scala, Florence

painter of bamboo, became the minister of personnel. Patronage of these and other painters fostered the efflorescence of Yuan-dynasty painting. A few of the artists could be described as court painters. Liu Guandao, who in 1281 painted a portrait of Khubilai Khan on a hunt, could be classified as part of this group. Emperor Renzong (r. 1311–1320) was the ruler most active in support of painting and initiated the practice of commissioning imperial portraits. Mongol patronage naturally influenced the painters' subjects. It is no accident that paintings of horses were extremely popular and that Zhao Mengfu's "Sheep and Goat" was one of his most famous works. Bearing in mind the greater freedom enjoyed by elite women in Mongol society, it should be no surprise that this period saw a Chinese female painter – Guan Daosheng (1262–1319), Zhao Mengfu's wife – rise to prominence for the first time.

Naturally, most Chinese paintings were not produced to Mongol specifications and were not based on Mongol patronage. Some scholar-officials who did not serve the Mongols produced such traditional painting genres as landscapes, portraits, and bamboo depictions. Even those who assumed government positions under the Mongols continued to paint within the Chinese traditions. Zhao Mengfu, for example, emphasized a return to the ancients in painting, especially the Tang-dynasty models rather than the more recent Song-dynasty paintings. His depictions of horses fit into the models provided by the Tang. At the same time, he perceived his calligraphy to be as important as his painting, an attitude that the Mongols would not necessarily have appreciated. Yuan painters persisted in executing other traditional genres. Daoist painting flourished; it was neither derived from nor influenced by the Mongols. Buddhist painting owed some influences and motifs to the Mongol patronage of Tibetan monks. Mahakala, a deity often portrayed in Tibetan art, achieved greater prominence in Yuan art, and influences from India and the Himalayan regions may be seen in Chinese art during the Mongol era. An even greater deviation from the Mongol-employed painters was found in the work of artists who reflected despair at the current conditions and indirectly criticized the Mongol rulers. Images of emaciated horses representing Chinese Confucians who had been displaced by the Mongols and were powerless in this new society were one example of such denunciations of the Yuan-dynasty court.

The Mongols in China continued their ancestors' patronage of craftsmen, first influencing ceramics. Although art historians traditionally discounted the role of the Mongols in the production of Yuan-dynasty ceramics, recent research has modified that view. The Mongols were not the potters who fashioned celadons or blue-and-white porcelains, but they had an impact in fostering the production of ceramics. The Yuan's close relations with the Il-Khanate of west Asia led to the importation of cobalt blue into China. West Asian potters had, for some centuries, employed cobalt for pottery and, via the Mongols, the Chinese learned of the practice. As a Mongol commissioner supervised the kilns at Jingdezhen, the center of blue-and-white production, a Mongol role is indisputable. The Mongols also alerted Chinese potters to west Asian tastes, providing them with information about the shapes and decorative motifs that would appeal in the Islamic world. Their enforcement of migrations of craftsmen from one region of their empire to another facilitated the transmission of shapes and motifs.

The Yuan porcelain exported to west Asia catered to the clientele of that region. Jingdezhen and other sites produced massive plates, jars, dishes, and vases designed for this market. The Mongols knew that west Asian peoples characteristically placed their food on large plates for all the diners to consume. Mongol supervisors at the kiln sites recognized the west Asian preference for decoration and encouraged Chinese potters to depict plants, flowers, trees, dragons, phoenixes, and cloud collars, all derived from Chinese symbols. West Asian artists would themselves adopt some of these Chinese motifs in tile, pottery, textiles, and illustrations. To be sure, the Mongols were primarily interested in profit from the trade in Chinese porcelains, but their information and instructions had a significant aesthetic influence.

Figure 7.3 Yamantaka-Vajrabhairava with imperial portraits, ca. 1330–1332, silk and metallic thread tapestry (*kesi*), 96⅞″ (245.5) × 82¼″ (209 cm). New York, Metropolitan Museum of Art, Purchase, Lila Acheson Wallace Gift, 1992. Acc. no.: 1992.54 © 2013. Image copyright The Metropolitan Museum of Art / Art Resource / Scala, Florence

The Mongols also played a role in textile production. Textiles, which were light and thus easily transportable, blended well with the Mongols' migratory lifestyle. Because Chinese and central Asian weavers knew of the Mongols' fondness for gold, they used gold thread for the clothing, Buddhist mandalas, and decorations they produced. The Mongols themselves took steps to foster the development of luxury textiles. They moved central Asian and Persian weavers to China to collaborate with Chinese weavers in producing the *nasij*, or cloth of gold, that they prized. More than half of the agencies they established in the Yuan Ministry of Works supervised the fashioning of textiles. Like nearly all craftsmen, weavers received tax reductions from the Mongols.

In sum, the Mongols in China contributed to the efflorescence of Yuan art. Because they were frequently the consumers of goods produced by craftsmen, artists and artisans had to cater to their tastes. Their enforced movements of artisans from one land to another resulted in considerable diffusion of motifs and technology. Aware of west Asian tastes, they offered guidance to craftsmen who wished to trade with the mostly Islamic populations in that region. The Yuan government offered tax exemptions for artists and craftsmen, allowing these artists to focus on their arts and crafts. The government also made substantial efforts to preserve the beautiful objects that were produced – in part through the Imperial Palace collections.

The Mongols appeared to be the supporters and protectors of many features of Chinese culture. They reinstated traditional rituals and ceremonies at court and restored most Chinese government offices (including the Hanlin Academy) as a center for the worthiest Confucian scholars; they recruited Chinese for their administration; and they built Chinese-style ancestral temples. They adopted the traditional Chinese policy of toleration or at the least benign neglect toward foreign religions as a means of ingratiating themselves with foreign clerics. They were ardent patrons of drama and the visual arts, which contributed to striking renaissances in these fields. In short, the Mongols showed great concern for the Chinese people and their culture.

DECLINE OF THE YUAN

These positive developments characterized the first half of Khubilai's reign, but dramatic events led to reverses in the last decade or so of his life. His principal wife died in 1281, and his son and designated successor predeceased him. These personal losses coincided with almost catastrophic problems of state. The construction of a capital city at Daidu and of roads and canals, the campaigns against Southern Song China, and expeditions against foreign states required tremendous expenditures. Khubilai chose a Muslim named Ahmad to raise the needed revenue, and the new minister fulfilled the government's needs by enrolling more households on the tax lists, imposing higher prices on essential products on which the government had monopolies, and levying additional taxes on merchants. These policies, which were harshly implemented, alienated many in the Mongol and Chinese elites, and they responded by assassinating him and justifying themselves by accusing Ahmad of corruption and embezzlement of state funds. Ahmad's successors were similarly dispatched, with some killed and some merely dismissed. Revenue problems plagued the remainder of Khubilai's reign and persisted throughout the Yuan dynasty.

Foreign expeditions exacerbated these revenue shortfalls. Khubilai sent two expeditions against Japan, which had refused his orders of submission and had actually harmed his envoys. Bent on revenge, he did not consider the different environment he faced in sanctioning such a campaign. His troops had to be transported across rough and dangerous seas to Japan, and their remarkable advantage of a powerful cavalry would at least be partially neutralized. Koreans and Chinese were recruited to man the ships that took Mongol soldiers toward Japan. The first expedition was curtailed en route because of dangerous weather, but the Japanese were prepared for the second expedition in 1281, having constructed a lengthy wall all along the beaches where the Mongols would have to land. The Chinese sources report that the expedition, which consisted of 140,000 troops, set forth in two waves, one from south China and the other from the north Chinese– Korean border. The size of the force was no doubt exaggerated, but it nonetheless might have posed a threat to Japan had it landed. However, on August 15, a typhoon struck and sank quite a number of ships. Sailors and troops drowned, and those who had reached the shore found themselves without additional supplies and reinforcements and were no match for the Japanese samurai.

Although campaigns in mainland Southeast Asia were not as catastrophic, they were similarly costly and did not result in substantial gains. Expeditions in Champa and Annam (both in modern Vietnam) ended ambiguously, with offers by their rulers to present tribute to the Yuan court. The Mongols did not secure clear-cut victories. Their troops were not accustomed to the tropical and semitropical heat; they were vulnerable to new types of infectious and parasitic diseases; their horses were stymied in the forest regions; and guerilla warfare by the native inhabitants plagued them. Even more disastrous was the undertaking, with only limited naval expertise, of an expedition in Java (in modern Indonesia) in 1292, which faced the same difficulties as in mainland Southeast Asia. After a year of conflict, the Mongols withdrew.

In addition, continued fissures in the Mongol world were devastating for Khubilai. In 1287, a Mongol commander rebelled in Manchuria. This Nestorian leader, who was the Great Khan Ögödei's grandson, posed such a threat that Khubilai, afflicted with gout and rheumatism, personally went onto the battlefield, leading a sizable force. Khubilai's troops routed the enemy and killed its commander in the traditional Mongol way. Marco Polo described the execution:

> He [the commander] was wrapped very tightly and bound in a carpet and there was dragged so much hither and thither and tossed up and down so rigorously that he died; & then they left him inside it; so that Naian ended his life in this way. And for this reason he made him die in such a way, for the Tartar said that he did not wish the blood of the lineage of the emperor be spilt on the ground.[1]

At the same time, the Yuan's border with central Asia was unsettled. Ögödei's grandson Khaidu, still angered that his line had been replaced for the Great

Khanate, challenged Khubilai throughout the 1280s and almost reached Khara Khorum, the former capital of the Mongol Empire. Khubilai's forces pushed Khaidu away from Khara Khorum, but he persisted in his relentless raids and attacks from central Asia. Khubilai was more successful in crushing a revolt in Tibet. In 1290, his grandson virtually wiped out the Buddhist sect that had initiated the rebellion. Despite this victory, these outbreaks revealed disarray in Khubilai's domains.

Two years after the Java expedition, Khubilai Khan died. A caravan carried his body to an undisclosed location, perhaps in modern Mongolia, for burial in what may have been an elaborate tomb. His alcoholic and culinary excesses following the deaths of his wife and son had contributed to illnesses and then to his death. The problems of revenue shortfalls and poorly planned and executed military expeditions attest to the inadequate policy formulations in the last years of his reign.

The Yuan court experienced repeated failures after Khubilai's death. His grandson Temür legitimately succeeded Khubilai in 1294, but future successions were frequently contested. Struggles between the candidates often reflected the decades-long disputes between those Mongols who believed that they needed to accommodate to Chinese practices and institutions in order to rule and their brethren who emphasized an assertion of the traditional Mongol way of life and values. Such disunity weakened the Mongol elite, leading to repeated purges and assassinations of emperors. The most important crisis happened in 1328–1329, when two brothers fought for the throne. The early deaths of other emperors from natural causes added to the Yuan court's instability. Bribery, a bloated bureaucracy, and substantial government grants to Mongol princes and Chinese officials contributed to chaotic conditions, which alienated the Chinese population. Reformers tried to limit these excessive grants to the Mongol and Chinese elites, but the bureaucracy and several emperors stymied them. The woeful shortages of revenue and the scandalously outsized payments to elites prevented the Yuan from preserving its military readiness and maintaining its infrastructure.

Inattention to dams and irrigation works, predictably enough, led to floods and the spread of waterborne diseases. Unusually cold winters in the fourteenth century exacerbated the pressure on the Mongol rulers. Floods and changes in the course of the Yellow River in the 1340s were the final blows. Some Chinese died, and many had to abandon their lands. The changes in the course of the Yellow River interrupted the flow of grain from south to north China, a real threat for the dynasty. A Mongol reformer ordered the building of a new channel for the river to the area of Shandong province, a seemingly effective means of taming the waters. The government mobilized a large labor force and expended substantial resources for this construction project. The channel was built, but the expense in funding and in imposition of corvée labor turned out to be burdensome and generated greater Chinese hostility toward the Mongol rulers. The court defrayed some of its expenses by printing more paper money, leading to devastating inflation and a devaluation of paper currency.

The Chinese approved of one specific policy during this period. In 1313, the Yuan court decided to restore the civil-service examinations, and two years later it administered them. However, it suspended them on at least one occasion and did not mandate that fine performance on the examinations would be the only route to an official position. It also devised different and simpler examinations for Mongols and other non-Chinese and offered them a disproportionate number of posts in the bureaucracy. This policy reinforced the four-class system of Mongols, Muslims and other foreigners, northern Chinese, and southern Chinese, with the latter two often relegated to lower-level positions. Perhaps even more galling to the Chinese was the Yuan policy of favoring the military over the civilian authorities. Civilian scholar-officials had dominated in China for centuries. Thus the overturning of this long-held tradition offended many Chinese.

Banditry increased, and many Chinese found millenarian sects appealing. The White Lotus Society arose; this was a millenarian group that believed that the era's chaotic conditions presaged the arrival of the Maitreya, or Future Buddha, with an ensuing last judgment in which the foreigners, the corrupt, and the exploiters would be punished. Such views prompted the society's members to act in a major outbreak against the dynasty. In 1352, the so-called Red Turbans (founded by members of the White Lotus), identified as such due to the color of their headgear, initiated a rebellion that was surprisingly successful. Three years elapsed before the Yuan suppressed this millenarian movement. The inadequate Yuan response finally led to attacks on large local estates and government offices, leading eventually to the dynasty's collapse in 1368.

LEGACY OF THE MONGOLS

Despite its inglorious end, the Yuan performed the invaluable service of linking China up with many areas of Eurasia. China and Europe had their first direct contacts with each other. European merchants, envoys, missionaries, adventurers, and craftsmen arrived in China, while at least one person born in China, a Nestorian Christian named Rabban Sauma, traveled to Constantinople, Naples, Rome, Paris, and Bordeaux. In 1245, the pope dispatched the Franciscan John of Plano Carpini to urge the Mongols to cease and desist from further incursions in Europe and to convert to Christianity. In 1253, the Franciscan William of Rubruck reached the Mongol encampments with a similar message. Although the Mongols rejected both pleas, the two Franciscan emissaries returned to Europe with valuable reports on their travels and observations, which, in turn, helped to prompt Genoese and Venetian merchants to travel to the central Asian, Indian, and Chinese sites the emissaries described. A sufficient number of traders journeyed to China for a fourteenth-century author, Francesco Balducci Pegolotti, to be able to provide a detailed itinerary, with an indication of distances from one town to another and with suggestions about the number of horses, camels, and men required for such trips.

Marco Polo was the most famous European of mercantile background to reach China. His father and uncle had visited China and had meetings with Khubilai Khan, who invited them to return with one hundred learned Christians to proselytize for Christianity. The two brothers did not lure

Figure 7.4 Khubilai gives the Polo brothers a golden passport. Image from *Le livre du Grand Caan*, France, after 1333, Royal 19 D. I, f.59v. © British Library Board / Robana

Christian companions but brought their twenty-one-year-old son or nephew Marco from Venice with them. Marco remained in China, at the court or on travels throughout the country, for sixteen years. He departed from China in 1291 to escort a princess sent by Khubilai to marry the Mongol ruler of west Asia. In 1298, the Genoese captured Marco during a war with Venice. Fortunately for history, Marco was in a prison with a storyteller named Rusticello, who collaborated with him on a volume describing Marco's journeys and observations. The account provided a vivid description of China and in particular of Khubilai. Marco was deeply impressed with both Daidu (or modern Beijing) and Hangzhou, the capital of the former Southern Song dynasty and the world's most populous city. He did not mention bound feet, tea and teahouses, or the Chinese writing system, which has caused a few to question whether he actually reached China. However, the details he provides about events at court, Shangdu (or Xanadu), Daidu, the circulation of paper money, and the use of coal for heating tally well with Chinese sources. Although Europeans initially doubted Marco's account, they eventually accepted it as an accurate description, which prompted them to seek a sea route to Asia.

The travels of the Nestorian Rabban Sauma attest to the attempted political links between Europe and Asia. Rabban Sauma had departed from Daidu to undertake a pilgrimage to the Holy Lands. Arriving in the Il-Khanate, in present-day Iraq, he found that Muslims controlled the Holy Lands, which would prevent him from achieving his religious objective. He remained in west Asia until the Mongol ruler chose him for a delicate diplomatic mission. The Mongols proposed an alliance with the Europeans to attack the Mamluks, the major Islamic dynasty in the region and the occupiers of the Holy Lands. Rabban Sauma met with the pope and the kings of France and England, but his visit did not lead to collaboration. Nonetheless, the very idea of such cooperation reveals the scope of intersocietal contacts and the development of a true Eurasian history.

During the Yuan, China was influenced by Eurasia. It generally benefited from the technological, religious, scientific, and commercial relations with west Asia and Europe. The western countries began to acquire knowledge about China, and the Chinese came to be better informed about west Asia. Maps from this period attest to China's great knowledge about the lands to its west. The Mongols of the Yuan maintained a strong relationship with the Mongols of west Asia and thus exposed China to developments in that part of the world. Although the Ming, the Chinese dynasty that replaced the Mongol Yuan, sought a more isolationist policy, it could not divorce itself from the world. From the Yuan period on, China was inextricably bound up with its neighbors, as well as faraway places in the west.

NOTES

1   A. C. Moule and Paul Pelliot, trans., *Marco Polo: The Description of the World* (London: George Routledge & Sons, Ltd., 1938), p. 199.

FURTHER READING

James Cahill, *Hills Beyond a River: Chinese Painting of the Yüan Dynasty, 1279–1368* (New York: Weatherhill, 1976).

William Fitzhugh, William Honeychurch, and Morris Rossabi, eds., *Genghis Khan and the Mongol Empire* (Seattle: University of Washington Press, 2009).

John Langlois, ed., *China under Mongol Rule* (Princeton: Princeton University Press, 1981).

Morris Rossabi, *Khubilai Khan: His Life and Times* (Berkeley: University of California Press, 1988).

Morris Rossabi, ed., *The Travels of Marco Polo: The Illustrated Edition* (New York: Sterling Publishers, 2012).

Naomi Standen, *Unbounded Loyalty: Frontier Crossing in Liao China* (Honolulu: University of Hawaii Press, 2007).

[8] MING: ISOLATIONISM AND INVOLVEMENT IN THE WORLD, 1368–1644

THE parlous economic conditions of late Yuan exacerbated the earlier dormant ethnic antagonisms and resulted in banditry and full-scale rebellions. Economic upheavals opened the floodgates to a wide variety of rebel groups, all of whom tried to galvanize the support of the dispossessed and pauper populations. Yet the rebel leaders represented diverse constituencies and had different objectives. Each attempted to identify with the oppressed populace and assumed a strong antiforeign stance. Nativism had its appeal in a country controlled by foreigners for almost a century, not to mention the four centuries of alien rule endured by north China.

The White Lotus Society, one of the most powerful rebel groups, grew out of a secret religious organization. It was ecumenical and incorporated elements of Buddhist, Manichean, and Daoist beliefs; it gathered together many of the

A History of China, First Edition. Morris Rossabi.
© 2014 Morris Rossabi. Published 2014 by Blackwell Publishing Ltd.

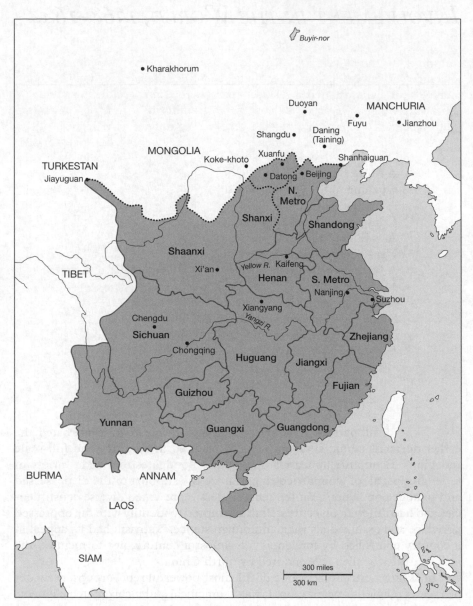

Map 8.1 Ming China

discontented; and it promised the destruction of the Yuan dynasty with the arrival of the Maitreya, the Buddha of the Future. This millenarian movement depicted the Maitreya as representing the liberating force that would overcome the decay of the Law, which had resulted in the evil and corruption dominating the world (the decay that was associated with the Mongols). First organized as a cohesive sect by a Buddhist monk, it spread quickly beyond the monasteries and attracted lay leaders who could marry, thus assuring greater continuity for the movement. Its growth also may have been stimulated by its tolerance for lay leadership. Traditional Buddhist sects were dominated by monks, and laymen played a relatively passive role in these organizations. In contrast, laymen were accorded considerable authority in this new organization. Acceptance of women into the sect was another unique feature of the White Lotus movement. Members initially met for religious assemblages, usually focusing on the means of achieving salvation, but soon the White Lotus assumed secular functions, serving as a mutual assistance group.

Its ideology, which provided a splendid vehicle for insurgencies against established authority, and its secular activities, which created a strong sense of community, had generated repeated government attempts at suppression. The government had already quashed the White Cloud Society, another dissident Buddhist sect; it had been easily dispersed in part because it had not truly branched out into the secular world and attracted laymen. The Yuan banned the White Lotus Society; yet it survived and in fact flourished, partly because it was ecumenical and incorporated elements from Daoism, Manicheism, and folk religion. Moreover, as the Yuan floundered and declined, leaders of the White Lotus Society took up the cause of resistance against the discredited and increasingly despised Mongol rulers. After some unorganized and ineffective outbreaks, they finally but briefly coalesced around a child named Han Liner, who was purported to be a direct descendant of the Song imperial family and was proclaimed as the first emperor of a newly restored Song dynasty in 1355. Some of the White Lotus leaders started another rebel movement, known as the Red Turbans because of the red headbands they wore. Although they recruited a sizable force in the Huai River areas north of the Yangzi River, lack of unity plagued them. Without centralized leadership, they could not mount a devastating challenge to the Yuan.

Most other rebel groups were also flawed. Two smugglers, Zhang Shicheng (1321–1367) and Fang Guozhen (1319–1374), initially threatened the Yuan in the 1350s and early 1360s, but poor administrative skills hampered them. Fang, a pirate involved in illegal salt trading, was successful in attacking at sea but could never establish governance on land. Zhang had a grand opportunity to topple the dynasty, as his troops occupied an area that provided one-third of the agricultural tax revenues and had one-fifth of the total population in the country. However, according to later, hostile, and possibly unreliable Chinese sources, he and his subordinates abandoned themselves to the pursuit of sensual pleasures and failed to pay attention to government. Neither Fang nor Zhang succeeded in setting up a government and left themselves vulnerable to other rebels who could mobilize support from those Chinese with administrative skills.

Chen Youliang (1320–1363) was still another potential adversary for the Yuan, and (even more to the point) for the rebel leaders who were vying to determine which one of them could unify the Chinese and deal the final blow to the Yuan (which for many Chinese had lost the Mandate of Heaven). A violent opportunist, Chen joined other rebel organizations but betrayed one leader after another until he assumed the title of "emperor" of a revived Han dynasty in 1360. He created a powerful military force, well-balanced between an army and a navy. Yet his lack of foresight, his unthinking belligerence, and his almost exclusive reliance on the military culminated in his downfall. In 1363, in a major battle on Poyang Lake, in the province of Jiangxi, with his principal opponent, Zhu Yuanzhang (1328–1398), he had the superior naval force but was outmaneuvered, outplanned, and outthought. He was killed when a stray arrow pierced his eye, and his leaderless forces panicked and either died while attempting to escape or surrendered.

The fates of the Red Turbans and the rebel leaders of late Yuan resemble the course of other unsuccessful dissidents in Chinese history – or, at least, the Chinese sources portray them in that way. They seemed to show greater interest in plundering than ruling. Unable to develop a plan or a vision for China, they moved from place to place, providing their supporters with tangible opportunities for profit but without establishing stable institutions or an orderly government. They did not permanently occupy specific regions with the intention of governing. Without such intentions, they could not attract the essential assistance of skilled administrators or experts in devising a stable, long-lasting system. Naturally, the Chinese Confucians who later wrote the histories of these rebel groups depicted them simply as marauders (perhaps a distorted image). Yet we are dependent on the victors' version of events. The groups who lost did not offer a competing scenario.

In any case, the rebel groups continued to proliferate, partly due to the Yuan's ineffectiveness. It did not develop a cohesive plan for coping with the economic distress of the peasants and other inhabitants whose lives had been shattered by the floods along the Yellow River and Huai River areas. Even its military responses to the rebellions were surprisingly weak. Chancellor Toghto (fl. 1340–1355), the most successful Mongol commander, had defeated several rebel units and appeared on the verge of crushing the dynasty's principal antagonists. However, his victories led to resentments and a fear that he, a sinicized Mongol, would depose the emperor and place himself on the throne. He had tried to recruit more Chinese into the bureaucracy, had tried to deal with the Yellow River floods, and was simply too powerful an official, and in 1355 his opponents persuaded the emperor to strip him of his position. Within a year he had been murdered, which eliminated the most capable commander under the court's supervision. With such actions and policies, the court, in effect, defeated itself.

A MORE POWERFUL STATE

Zhu Yuanzhang was the ultimate beneficiary of the Yuan's decline. Although his childhood and early life were on the surface not a propitious background for a future emperor, his early days actually positioned him for his later career. Born into a poor peasant family and then orphaned at the age of sixteen, he went to work at a Buddhist temple as a domestic. He could thus identify with and eventually gain popularity among the rural pauper population. His stay in the temple also offered him opportunities to learn to read and write, to gain exposure to Buddhist teachings, and to use Buddhism as the mantle for his own secular objectives. However, fearful of a sudden Yuan attack on his temple because of its association with rebels, he joined the Red Turbans and thus gained experience in forging links with the military. After several years with the disunited and conflict-laden Red Turbans, he began to build his own forces. In attempting to develop a military, he had the advantage of knowing about Buddhism and thus attracting Buddhist support and expertise in warfare and in command as a result of his years with the Red Turbans.

Capitalizing on these advantages, he mobilized a force that captured Nanjing in 1356. Most important, as he occupied new territories, he cultivated scholars and officials who helped him to administer these lands. Such attention to government differentiated him from other rebels. He actually meant to rule his newly conquered domains. Thus, his success was almost inexorable. He defeated Chen Youliang at the battle of Poyang Lake in 1363 and over-whelmed Zhang Shicheng in 1367. In the following year, he compelled the last remnants of the Mongol armies to flee northward to Mongolia. Having quelled his rebel opponents as well as the tottering Yuan dynasty, he now proclaimed himself as the emperor of a new Ming (Bright) dynasty in 1368, with a capital in his original base in Nanjing in south China. Since most of the rebels and Zhu himself had been centered in the southern part of China, his choice of location for the Ming capital was not surprising. The locus of political power appeared to be shifting to the south.

Having endured at least a century of foreign rule, Ming China sought to avert still other attacks and invasions from peoples beyond its northern and western borders. Zhu Yuanzhang and the court were determined to limit Chinese contacts with foreigners and to dominate foreign relations. Restrictions on dealings with foreigners would presumably reduce the potential of foreign conquests because foreign agents would be unable to gather intelligence that would facilitate military expeditions against China. Simultaneously, because the Ming required powerful armed forces to avert further foreign assaults, the court initially accorded military commanders a high status. In addition, it needed the military to overwhelm the dissidents and rebels within China, an enterprise that consumed several decades.

An emphasis on internal stability accompanied the pressure to limit relations with foreigners. The court concluded that a strong emperor was needed to maintain domestic peace and thus a potent country able to stave off the so-called barbarians. The resulting government was more despotic than in earlier dynasties, with fewer restraints on the emperors' power. Chinese scholars often ascribed this growing despotism to Mongol influence, with the Mongol khans portrayed as autocratic rulers. A likelier explanation is that the Ming emperors legitimized their greater authority by referring to the reputed oppressiveness of the Yuan period and the need to avoid such a fate.

Legitimacy and stability were, without doubt, the principal concerns of the first emperor. His elaborate accession to the throne and his restoration of the sacrifices to Heaven and Earth and other Confucian and Buddhist rituals were his initial attempts to secure recognition as a legitimate ruler. Establishment of an imperial capital in Nanjing and choice of his eldest son, Zhu Biao (1355–1392), as his heir were additional efforts to bolster his and his dynasty's authority. He entrusted his nine sons with lands throughout the country to ensure his own power and thus to centralize control. In 1370, he reinstated the civil-service examinations to recruit additional competent civil administrators, an important symbolic step as well because it offered a sharp contrast with the Yuan, which had not used the examinations as the exclusive means of selecting officials. In effect, the emperor sought to reestablish indigenous and stable institutions with a more dominant ruler and carefully circumscribed and regulated relations with foreigners. Consolidation and control were basic concerns.

Yet he continued to face impediments throughout his reign. Campaigns against the Mongols persisted until his last years, as the threat they posed did not readily dissipate. One such Chinese assault resulted in the virtually total destruction of the first Mongol capital at Khara Khorum – a blow to the prestige of the previously powerful rulers of the greatest empire in world history. Yet no final crushing blow had been administered to the Mongols. Similarly, the emperor's harsh domestic policies did not impose the total control he craved. Execution of corrupt or ineffective officials in the mid 1370s did not lead to the stability and consolidation he sought. Thus, he initiated a relentless and all-encompassing purge directed mainly at a previously favored official in the Secretariat named Hu Weiyong (?–1380). Hu had made a sharp ascent in the bureaucracy. had ensconced associates and allies in important official positions, and appeared to be a rising star in government. The emperor, somewhat paranoid and fearful of any challenges to his authority, noticed Hu's growing prominence and became concerned about a potentially influential clique in the bureaucracy that was loyal principally to Hu. In 1380, he moved to avert such a possibility, accusing Hu of contemplating a coup d'état and executing him and several thousand of his reputed supporters. He then abolished the venerable agency known as the Secretariat, placing its own authority and responsibility in his own hands and in those of the later emperors of the dynasty. The abolition of the Secretariat, which had, on occasion, served as a bureaucratic check on the absolute power of the emperors, contributed to the growing despotism, as the first emperor (renowned as Hongwu) became his own "prime minister."

The purges persisted even after the elimination of the so-called Hu Weiyong clique and were particularly directed against any questioning or challenge to the emperor's wishes or policies. Critics of Emperor Hongwu's favorable tilt toward Buddhism were severely punished. Others who alluded to the arbitrariness of the judicial system were similarly harassed or harmed. During the last decade of his reign, few men, even the most renowned figures in the empire, were spared from the emperor's purges. In the period from 1393 to 1395, he ordered the executions of three of the most eminent generals in the country as well as some of the most competent nobles. He even demanded that one of his sons-in-law commit suicide. Simultaneously and ironically, the emperor issued injunctions that emphasized concern for the proper administration of justice. A law code known as the *Da Ming lü*, a set of regulations referred to as the Grand Pronouncements, and instructions to his descendants he labeled the Ancestral Injunctions were produced at his behest, and each enjoined against injustice, treason, and corruption. Despite such pronouncements, the emperor sought total control, using purges and the full authority of the imperial throne.

Yet the emperor could not dominate all events. In 1392, his carefully selected and groomed heir apparent died, disrupting plans for the succession. The emperor named the deceased heir apparent's son, Zhu Yunwen (1377–1402?), as his designated successor, but age was taking its toll, and he could not as readily impose his youthful candidate on his own older sons. Zhu Di (1360–1424), one of his sons, who had a sizable army based along the northern frontiers of China, resented his father's passing him over as a potential successor. Having a powerful force under his command, he bided his time to challenge his young nephew, who resided in the dynastic capital in Nanjing.

The death of Emperor Hongwu in 1398 permitted Zhu Di to reveal his imperial ambitions openly. The resulting civil war and Zhu Di's victory meant that the official histories offer his version of events, and many of the documents and records representing his nephew's viewpoint were either lost or destroyed. Despite the one-sided depiction in the accounts transmitted to the present, the records still indicate that the nephew's short reign witnessed an amelioration of the first emperor's severe policies. He restored power to the leading ministers, revised some of his grandfather's harsh laws, and eliminated some of the privileges that the first emperor had granted to Buddhists and Daoists. Recognizing the threat posed by Zhu Di, he conceived of abolishing the title of "prince," which had been bestowed on the first emperor's son, among others. Zhu Di, who was referred to as the Prince of Yan and charged with the defense of Beijing and the surrounding regions, considered this new policy as provocative and used it as a pretext for a coup d'état.

Zhu Di, asserting that opportunistic and corrupt court officials had misled the youthful emperor, initiated a rebellion against his nephew. With a powerful army and an excellent command structure, he made significant inroads against his nephew, whose forces were not as well organized or as ably led. After several years of intermittent warfare, Zhu Di's troops reached the capital at Nanjing. During the ensuing battle the young emperor's palace was set afire, and the emperor supposedly burned to death. Yet, shortly thereafter, rumors circulated that he had donned a monk's garb and managed to escape from the conflagration that consumed the palace. Whether he died or survived by assuming a disguise, the young emperor would never reappear.

Yet the uncertainty surrounding the ousted emperor's disappearance shadowed and somewhat unnerved Zhu Di for the rest of his reign, to which he had given the title Yongle ("Eternal Joy"). Fear that the deposed ruler might suddenly emerge and challenge his authority plagued Emperor Yongle, as an aura of illegitimacy persisted. His policies, on occasion, reflected efforts to affirm his legitimacy. His court historians, for example, falsified court records to denigrate his nephew's status and to bolster his claim to be the true designated successor to the throne.

OPENING TO THE OUTSIDE WORLD

Emperor Yongle's deviation from his father's foreign policy may also have stemmed from an attempt to justify his ascendance to the throne. He reversed his father's efforts to reduce contact with the outside world, partly to support his own claims to legitimacy. A good Confucian emperor would, in theory, induce foreign rulers to come and transform themselves (*laihua*) – that is, to become sinicized. The more virtuous the emperor, the more foreign potentates would arrive. Conversely, the greater the number of foreign rulers and envoys arriving in China, the more legitimate the ruler. Thus, it was in Emperor Yongle's best interests to stimulate the arrival of foreign embassies at court. On the other hand, the court, having experienced a century of Mongolian rule, may not have had the same traditional self-confidence about its cultural superiority. The old system may have been maintained as a ritual, and it is possible that the court no longer believed in the underlying principles of this paradigm. Indeed, as China weakened in the late fifteenth and early sixteenth centuries, it allowed deviation from the formulas of the traditional system.

No doubt Emperor Yongle's most grandiose attempt to promote the arrival of foreign officials was the dispatch of the embassies of the Muslim eunuch Zheng He (1371–1433). Leading an enormous flotilla of ships and transporting substantial gifts for foreign rulers, Zheng undertook seven journeys, traveling to Southeast Asia, India, Persia, and west Asia and becoming the first attested Chinese to reach the east coast of Africa. He commanded as many as sixty large vessels with thirty thousand men on several of the expeditions. His mission fulfilled the goal of eliciting foreign delegations to travel to the Chinese court. Leaders from as near as Champa (in modern Vietnam) and as far away as modern Mogadishu (in Somalia) sent embassies to Yongle. Other motives – the goal of affirming China's power, the desire to obtain foreign products, and the objective of increasing China's knowledge of the outside world – may also have spurred the dispatch of the missions, which turned out to be the most impressive expeditions in world history until the journeys of Christopher Columbus, Vasco da Gama, and other European explorers of the late fifteenth and early sixteenth centuries. Another objective may have been to ferret out information about the emperor's missing and presumed dead nephew, but this goal, if intended, was not fulfilled.

The missions, nonetheless, resulted in exchanges of goods, which stimulated trade. Zheng He presented gifts of silk, porcelains, and other commodities to the rulers of the various regions he visited, and generated a market for these products. Foreign potentates, in turn, sent the emperor, via Zheng, exotic animals, including lions, leopards, and giraffes. Even more important, they provided so-called tribute of spices and medicines, which appealed to many Chinese. Southeast Asian merchants continued to bring spices to China even after the cessation of the expeditions.

After Emperor Yongle's death, the court sanctioned only one more mission for Zheng. The climate of opinion about such foreign expeditions altered upon the demise of the leading patron, Emperor Yongle. Court officials complained of the tremendous expense entailed in outfitting and manning such missions.

Yongle's successors also reverted to the foreign policies of the Ming's founder, policies that did not jibe with the expansiveness and perhaps expansionism of the Zheng He explorations. Later courts focused on domestic policies and sought to limit foreign relations.

Emperor Yongle dispatched still other emissaries to elicit tribute embassies from other states. He sent Chen Cheng (d. 1457) to the central Asian centers at Herat and Samarkand, which had previously been hostile. Temür (or Tamerlane, 1336–1405), the conqueror and ruler of central Asia, was, in fact, mounting an invasion of China when he died in February of 1405. His son and successor, Shahrukh (1377–1447), was less bellicose and sent an embassy to establish relations with the Ming court. Elated by what he dubbed a tribute mission, Emperor Yongle dispatched Chen Cheng on at least three occasions to generate even closer contacts. Chen returned to China with a valuable record of the customs, products, and conditions in the states and regions through which he traveled. Shahrukh, in turn, dispatched an embassy, one of whose officials, Ghiyath al-Din Naqqash, wrote a revealing account of Ming China, principally about the court. This account yields a unique glimpse of an emperor at work and at leisure. The Chinese court, in attempting to convey an image of emperors as divine beings, rarely in its histories permitted views of the emperors as flesh-and-blood creatures. Shahrukh's envoys, however, accompanied Emperor Yongle on a hunt, dined with him, and observed his listening to appeals for those condemned to death. Ghiyath al-Din Naqqash's report thus depicts Emperor Yongle as a real human being rather than as a shadowy, omnipotent, and semidivine decision maker and dispenser of justice. These exchanges of missions ensured continued tributary and trade relations between the Ming and central Asia and buttressed the emperor's claim to legitimacy.

Yongle was similarly successful with other embassies. The mission of the eunuch Isiha (fl. 1409–1451) led to the arrival at court of the leaders of the Jurchen peoples of Manchuria. Yongle's embassies to Tibet resulted in reciprocal missions of Buddhist monks. Although Tsong-kha-pa (1357–1419), the renowned founder of the dGelugs-pa (or Yellow Sect) of Tibetan Buddhism, parried the Chinese emperor's invitation to come personally to court, he sent a leading religious dignitary to pay his respects. The Tibetan missions presented lavish tribute goods, and the court rewarded the envoys with elaborate gifts of silk robes, banners, and wearing apparel. By the end of Yongle's reign, a number of Tibetan Buddhist sects had exchanged missions with the court. Similarly, Yongle's embassy to the Korean king led almost directly to the arrival of a mission from the Choson dynasty's ruler and to regular exchanges of envoys and goods. Finally, the Japanese shogun began to send tribute missions to the Chinese court.

But Emperor Yongle could not secure the acquiescence of other foreigners. Here he deviated from his father's policies in initiating military expeditions to impose the Chinese world order on neighboring states and rulers. His father had cautioned his successors not to seek territories beyond the Chinese cultural sphere, noting that rule over restive non-Chinese peoples would require enormous military expenditures for a standing army in newly acquired territories. He also had asserted that such an occupation force would face continuous resistance.

However, his son Yongle personally led five campaigns into the Mongol steppe lands to coerce the Mongols into halting their raids along the frontiers. The campaigns were unsuccessful because they did not take into account the Mongols' underlying motivations. The Mongols needed and coveted Chinese products, and, if the court did not grant them sufficient opportunities for trade and tribute, raids were their only recourse. Chinese restrictions on tribute or trade along the frontiers often provoked conflicts, and the Mongols had a tactical military advantage. After a raid or a skirmish, they could simply flee farther and farther away and thus elude Chinese armies, which did not have effective supply lines to enable pursuit of the Mongol cavalrymen for long periods of time. Thus Yongle's campaigns, which are often portrayed in the Ming dynastic history as great successes, did not quell disturbances along the Ming frontiers. The emperor's bellicose policy offered no relief for the border. Divide and rule, another tactic he employed, also failed. Providing benefits, gifts, and titles or offering additional opportunities for trade to one group of Mongols in hopes that such favoritism would cause rifts among them and deflect attacks on China scarcely ensured peace along the frontiers.

Yongle's policy in Annam was even less successful. Learning of the overthrow of the Tran dynasty by a usurper, he sent a force not only to crush the rebels but also to institute Ming rule, a disastrous error because this effort antagonized patriotic Annamese. A war flared up, and Chinese troops would be bogged down in fighting for the next two decades. In 1427, China finally withdrew, admitting its mistake in seeking to annex Annam. However, considerable damage had been done to the Ming army and economy.

Despite such resounding achievements as the Zheng He missions, Yongle's foreign policy was extremely expensive. Although the arrival of tribute embassies from a diverse array of foreign lands bolstered Yongle's claim to legitimacy, the expansionism evinced in the Mongolia and Annam campaigns was a costly failure. Ignoring the conventional wisdom, as well as his father's injunctions, Yongle sought to subjugate and incorporate lands beyond China, a policy that most traditional Chinese officials would have considered to be misguided. The expeditions imposed financial burdens on his successors, which contributed to the dynasty's fiscal problems.

Other grandiose policies of Emperor Yongle would also create difficulties, both dynastic and financial. His fabrication of texts to denigrate his nephew and bolster his own claims to the throne set a poor precedent for later historical record keeping. His abandonment of his father's capital in Nanjing and his construction of a new capital in Beijing, though eminently reasonable from his perspective, turned out to generate additional burdens on China. Because the area around Beijing was his center, he would naturally want to set up his seat of government there. Moreover, he recognized the need for a capital city that lay close to and thus could more readily defend the northern frontiers. This reasoning was sound, but his other motivation – building a majestic and awe-inspiring capital city to bolster his legitimacy – was more

Figure 8.1 Tian Tan, the Temple of Heaven, one of the grandiose structures built by Yongle in Beijing. © eye35.pix / Alamy

problematic. The capital was planned on a grand scale and wound up consuming vast resources of manpower and funds. Hundreds of thousands of laborers toiled on its construction, which was intended to be much more impressive than even the capital of Khubilai Khan. The large scale of Beijing presumed a large population, which could not be maintained from local sources. The court needed to devise a costly system of transporting grain and other provisions from its economic heartland in south China along the Grand Canal to Beijing. It had to increase the tax burdens on the peasantry in order to supply the burgeoning population in the capital.

In sum, although Yongle expanded China's contacts with the outside world and constructed an imposing capital city, his legacy was ambiguous. China began to trade with a wide variety of regions, states, and peoples, and the Ming had an impressive administrative center. Yet these successes were accompanied by insidious problems that would repeatedly plague the Ming. Later courts would have to contend with the sizable debts and the heavy taxes required to provide revenues for Yongle's embassies to foreign lands and his construction projects. In addition, his choice of eunuchs to head some of the foreign missions accorded them great authority and was the first step toward the overwhelming power eunuchs eventually garnered during the Ming.

It is no accident that a decade after Yongle's death a eunuch named Wang Zhen (d. 1449) began a rise to power that would propel him to one of the most important positions in government. Gaining the support of a child emperor enthroned in 1435, he overcame the resistance of court officials through clever maneuvering. This extralegal seizure of power exacerbated other government abuses. Excessive corvée labor and tax demands, together with devastating floods and droughts in various regions of the country, contributed to disarray and popular discontent, but the court managed to crush the minor uprisings that erupted during this time.

A COSTLY FAILURE

The court and Wang Zhen were less successful in dealing with the Mongols. A Mongol ruler named Esen had, in the 1440s, expanded his area of control to include Hami and other towns and oases along the traditional Silk Roads. Even more irritating to the court was the ever-increasing frequency of his tribute missions and the larger number of men in each, which increased the Ming's costs in transporting, feeding, and offering gifts to the emissaries. Such rising expenditures caused Chinese officials to limit the number of Esen's embassies and to reduce the presents and products granted them in trade. Esen's reaction was predictable. Accusing the Chinese of unfair commercial practices and of exploitation and mistreatment of his envoys, Esen prepared for a confrontation with the Ming court. These tensions over tribute and trade finally erupted into warfare. In July of 1449, Esen initiated an assault on China. Wang Zhen persuaded the emperor to personally command the Ming army to resist the incursions. Chinese accounts castigate Wang for encouraging the emperor to join the expedition and convey the impression that such imperial-led campaigns were unusual. Yet, only three decades earlier Emperor Yongle had commanded five expeditions against the Mongols. Wang simply followed the precedent established by an earlier Ming emperor.

Wang had underestimated the power of the Mongol leader, and the expedition proved to be disastrous. With scant intelligence concerning the enemy, Ming troops crossed into the lands of the steppe pastoralists. Vulnerable from the very outset due to poor planning and logistics, they were surrounded. Wang was killed and the emperor was captured in a battle near Tumu, the site of a postal station. However, Esen did not capitalize on his victory. He waited for a month before marching on Beijing, affording the Chinese time to construct additional fortifications and to enthrone the emperor's younger brother as the new ruler. By the time Esen's troops reached the capital, Beijing could readily withstand a lengthy siege. Faced with such resistance, Esen abandoned his siege and returned to the steppe lands. A year later, he repatriated the emperor, and in 1454 he was murdered in one of the many struggles for leadership in Mongol history. The threat posed by the Mongols receded, but the debacle at Tumu had revealed weaknesses and poor judgment at court.

CONSPICUOUS CONSUMPTION

Nonetheless, the rapid acceleration in the commercialization of agriculture and the development of urban centers encouraged some landlords to move to the cities. Such absentee landlords settled in towns both to have greater access to luxury products and as protection from peasant dissatisfaction and uprisings. Their profits as well as those of wealthy merchants were not always used for capital accumulation that would be invested in advances in technology or other means of increasing production. Instead they expended vast sums on luxurious lifestyles. Wealthy merchants also sought luxury goods and evaded sumptuary laws that the government could not enforce. The state could not control the lively market economy and limit extravagance. Merchant handbooks, which publicized specific luxury goods from various areas of China as well as exotic products from abroad, began to be published, although the status of merchants themselves was not elevated. What art historian Craig Clunas has labeled "superfluous things" assumed greater significance for the elite's social status and aesthetic appeal. The choices the official class and merchants made – for example, about clothing, furniture, gifts, food, types of tea, and interior decoration – played a vital role in defining them. This pattern of consumption was especially prominent among the nouveau riche in the lower Yangzi valley of south China.

Such conspicuous consumption did lead to cultural efflorescence. Art collection became important as a means of "taste," which, in turn, related to social stratification. Connoisseurship about bronzes, rocks, jades, inkstones, calligraphy, lacquer, ceramics, seals, and furniture helped to confirm elite status, and these decorative arts, as judged by prices in the market economy, were, perhaps for the first time in Chinese history, valued as highly as painting, formerly the province of the elite. Painters also produced for the market and not merely for the use of the traditional official class and for their edification and pleasure. Painting became just as much a luxury product as the decorative arts, and owners became more concerned about a painting's authenticity and possible forgery and fraud, as well as proper care and preservation of paintings, including limitations on exhibiting these fragile artworks.

The emphasis on material culture altered perceptions of the decorative arts. Craftsmen gained in stature, and potential owners strove to discover the names and the geographical origins of artisans before purchasing an object. At the same time, officials and merchants became interested in collecting jades, bronzes, and calligraphy of the past. They also sought foreign luxury products, and merchants were in a position to obtain these goods even if it required them to engage in smuggling.

Although the economy became increasingly monetized, and China was gradually becoming part of the world economy, the segment of the population affected by these trends was relatively small. Most peasants produced for themselves and for local markets. The larger estates that produced specialty crops designed for export were the main institutions and groups influenced by regional or global developments and were, on occasion, consumers for the Chinese and world material culture.

Growing urbanization, the greater economic opportunities afforded by regional and global developments, and the somewhat freer environment allowed a few women to break away from the traditional stereotypes, although countryside women did not benefit. Women with more independent status became merchants, entertainers, midwives, artists, or shamans. The growth of the textile industry, mostly a female enterprise, provided additional opportunities. However, women's property rights had eroded since the Song dynasty. Households without sons now had to find nephew successors to land and property. At the same time, widows could no longer inherit land and also faced considerable pressure, due in large part to Neo-Confucianism, to remain chaste after a husband's death.

ARTS IN THE MING

Ming cultural developments reflected the urbanization and interest in material culture and yet the aversion to foreign influence that characterized court policy. Like its prospective officials – who, in the so-called "eight-legged essay" to pass the civil-service examinations, needed to master the rigid form, with a specified number of sentences, considerable parallelism, and numerous allusions to classical texts – many thinkers, artists, craftsmen, and writers often, but not always, worked within traditional modes. Yet important innovations were introduced in philosophy, literature, and the arts. Creative individuals produced works within existing forms but also experimented and developed new types of expression.

Although Ming porcelains reflected many of the shapes and designs of the past, an attempt to cater to foreign markets also influenced the decorations and types of ceramics produced. Jingdezhen, the major porcelain center in the province of Jiangxi, and Dehua, another center in Fujian province, had produced ceramics during the Song and Yuan periods. In Ming times, Jingdezhen became renowned for its blue-and-white porcelains and Dehua for its white wares. The fine clay nearby as well as a reservoir of skilled potters enabled Jingdezhen to produce flasks, bowls, jars, brush rests, and lamps, which were often decorated with flowers, grapes, waves, and other motifs, some of which had been used earlier in paintings and textiles. The cobalt blue used in decorations came from central Asia, an indication of the impact of the world beyond China. In addition, some of the wares had Persian or Arabic (or, less frequently, Tibetan) inscriptions, an indication that they were produced either for Muslims and other foreigners in China or, more likely, for foreign trade. The sizable collections of blue-and-whites and indeed other porcelains at the Topkapi Museum

Figure 8.2 Jar, porcelain painted in underglaze blue, H. 19″ (48.3 cm), Diam. 19″ (48.3 cm). New York, Metropolitan Museum of Art, gift of Robert E. Tod, 1937. Inv. 37.191.1. © 2013. Image copyright The Metropolitan Museum of Art / Art Resource / Scala, Florence

in Istanbul, the Ardebil Shrine in Iran, and various Southeast Asian states attest to the scale and range of the market for Chinese porcelains. By the late sixteenth century, market demand had fostered mass production and a resultant decline in quality. As relations with central Asia became more turbulent, Ming potters could not readily obtain what the Chinese referred to as "Muslim blue" or fine cobalt, which further undermined quality. Yet both the domestic and foreign demand for Chinese porcelains continued to grow. The foreign market increased with the arrival of Europeans in China and, within a short time, Ming potters began to produce wares suited to European tastes. These wares would influence Turkish, Iranian, Southeast Asian, and Japanese ceramics, as potters would borrow designs, shapes, and colors from Chinese craftsmen.

As in earlier dynasties, textiles continued to be of great consequence in the economy for the roles they played in foreign relations, social and political status, and domestic and foreign trade. Mass production of silk in large workshops and small factories in Suzhou and other nearby centers near the Yangzi River began to characterize the silk industry, as did porcelain production in the late sixteenth century. Tremendous foreign and domestic demand led to the rapid growth of the industry. The increased amount of silk meant that it could be used ever more frequently and in even larger quantities in foreign relations. Like the dynasties from the Han on, the court offered bolts of silk, as well as silk robes, to nearly all the tribute missions that reached China. The court granted even the valuable dragon robes to foreign emissaries. These long robes were generally reserved for officials and for the emperors and princes, but envoys or rulers from foreign lands with strong bonds to China occasionally received them. The robes were embroidered with up to twelve symbols (solely for the emperors), the most prominent being the dragon. Robes with the five-clawed dragon were reserved for the emperors and princes while officials and foreign envoys were accorded the four-clawed dragon. So-called mandarin squares also served to differentiate social status. Those badges worn on the front and back of costumes used animal or bird symbols to distinguish among various levels of civilian and military officials.

Ming craftsmen also introduced new designs and shapes in lacquer, cloisonné, and jade. As with porcelain, they borrowed some of these motifs and forms from other media and adapted them to the needs of their own materials. They adopted and altered motifs and forms from as early as the Shang dynasty, fitting in with Ming conservatism, but they also introduced elaborate designs and unusual shapes.

Like the Ming decorative arts, painting consisted of a combination of close associations with tradition and of deviations from orthodox patterns. Painters centered at the court in Beijing tended to follow the traditional works, depicting birds and flowers designed to embellish the walls and ceilings of the palace buildings. Landscape painters modeled their works on those of the Southern Song masters Ma Yuan (1160 or 1165–1225) and Xia Gui (fl. 1195–1224). Technical perfection and decoration rather than individual creativity or expression were the painters' principal concern. Supervised by eunuchs in the Bureau of Painting, court painters were reluctant to deviate from tradition for fear of incurring the wrath of their eunuch overlords. Yet when Tai Chin (1388–1462; one of the landscape painters who alienated the court and was compelled to return to his birthplace in Hangzhou) was freed from court restrictions, he founded the Zhu school of painting, which produced more flexible and more individual versions of the types of landscape represented by Ma Yuan and Xia Gui. Tai Chin's followers and associates were more independent and thus less bound by tradition.

Nonetheless, the court painters in general blended with the conservatism and stagnation of much of the elite centered around the capital. Perhaps intimidated by the eunuchs, by officials, and by court standards, these painters produced conventional and, on occasion, trite works. Because deviation from the accepted models might result in reprisals or dismissal, most court painters remained within accepted norms.

The painters of south China, particularly in the provinces of Jiangsu and Zhejiang, broke away from the accepted models, carving out new directions in painting. The garden culture they developed in such cities as Suzhou and Wuxi symbolized their elite lifestyle; it incorporated splendid pavilions and flowers adroitly situated near rocks and ponds to foster serenity and contemplation. Yet recent studies challenge this idyllic image and the idealized conception of the elite. According to their interpretations, the gardens provided the elite with a means of preserving wealth and avoiding taxation. Gardens offered a method of storing capital that the government could not touch. Production of useful and income-generating commodities rather than decoration or aestheticism was integral to the garden culture. However, increasing commercialization in the late sixteenth century led the elite to shift from a financial to a more aesthetic perception of the garden, partly to distinguish themselves from crass

Figure 8.3 Humble Administrators Garden, Suzhou, Jiangsu province, China. © Henry Westheim Photography / Alamy

merchants. Unusual plants, rocks, and other deliberately unproductive landscapes began to supplement and substitute fruit trees and other economically viable pursuits in these gardens, where aesthetics overwhelmed agronomy. In this new vision, the owner was conceived of as a detached, reclusive gentleman who contemplated and enjoyed nature through his garden and scorned the commercial world and urban scenes and dabbled in the arts, including painting. A few went beyond mere dabbling and created great works of enduring value.

The most renowned among them formed the Wu school of painters. Shen Zhou (1427–1509), a wealthy gentleman who did not serve as an official, lived in semiretirement and began to paint landscapes in the style of the Yuan reclusive painters. He imitated the Yuan painters in rejecting government service, although they had the additional motivation of unwillingness to work for foreign conquerors. His scrolls and album leaves reveal the same simplicity as some of the Yuan landscape painters. However, unlike them, he occasionally populated his landscapes with small figures, lending them a greater sense of humanity. Several decades later, Wen Zhengming (1470–1559) painted landscapes in his own style; however, as important were his poems and prose works, many of which deal with gardens. His paintings and writings, which in part reflected his eremitism, contributed to the garden culture and to the conception of nature as a source of solace for the elite who failed to become officials or were rejected for government service. He offered a vision of a withdrawal from the hurly-burly of official or commercial life and a concern for personal cultivation and lofty pursuits.

Figure 8.4 Dong Qichang (1555–1636), *Reminiscence of Jian River*, ca. 1621, hanging scroll, ink and color on paper, without mounting: 49 ⁵/₁₆ × 18 ⁹/₁₆ ″ (125.3 × 47.1 cm); with mounting: 102 × 24 ⁹/₁₆ ″ (259.1 × 62.4 cm). New Haven (CT), Yale University Art Gallery. Leonard C. Hanna, Jr., B.A. 1913, Mrs. Paul Moore, and Anonymous Oriental Purchase Funds. Acc. no.: 1982.19.2. © 2013. Yale University Art Gallery / Art Resource, NY / Scala, Florence

It was left to Dong Qichang (1555–1636) both to embody and to provide an intellectual rationale for the literati in painting. A painter and calligrapher, he made a clear-cut distinction between the court painters and the literati artists, the latter of whom were freer from most restraints. They could, for example, paint landscapes more creatively and spontaneously than could the more rule-bound artists. Free both from the court and from the pecuniary concerns of the market and entrepreneurs, they could afford to explore the meaning of nature through art and to invest their explorations and insights with Confucian values. Dong classified those painters as part of the Southern school and the court painters as part of the Northern school, making a definite demarcation between the two. He perceived the independent and more scholarly painters of the Southern school to be superior to those attached to the court and those of the Northern school. The corruption and decline of the Ming court no doubt bolstered Dong's negative views of those associated with the dynasty.

NEO-CONFUCIANISM: SCHOOL OF THE MIND

Developments in Ming thought mirrored the paradox of Ming political stagnation and commercial dynamism. Neo-Confucianism embraced both conservatives and innovators and both orthodox thinkers and creative individualists. Toward the end of the Ming, some thinkers even challenged Neo-Confucianism, offering scathing criticism of the status quo.

Ming Neo-Confucianism has traditionally been associated with Wang Yangming (1472–1529), who surely delineated the parameters of thought in the dynasty. Wang's views are embodied in the life he led. In his works, he emphasized the strong links between moral cultivation and practical action. Thus, his active career as an official represented the fusion of meditative and social involvement. He believed that the meditative search for truth should not be equated with study of orthodox texts, even the Confucian writings. Although these works ought not to be discounted, they did not have a monopoly on the truth. Influenced by Chan Buddhism, Wang emphasized the "mind and heart" (xin) as the fount of knowledge, which could be achieved through looking within oneself, not through intensive study of authoritative Confucian classics. He challenged Zhu Xi's School of Neo-Confucianism, which had focused on investigation of the external world as a means of obtaining knowledge.

The mind, which Wang equated with li (principle), was the final arbiter of truth, partly because the operation of the world mirrored that of the mind. True knowledge of the pure mind ought to be the major objective of those seeking enlightenment. Wang himself attempted to achieve sagehood and to instruct others in how to do so. Like the stereotypes of other Confucians, Wang had an optimistic view of mankind. He believed in the essential goodness of human beings and asserted that the mind could lead to this innate goodness of the individual. Thus, each individual could aspire to sagehood. Indeed, the mind contained the knowledge of goodness, but the path to such purity required considerable effort to overcome hurdles en route. Once such impediments as selfishness and acquisitiveness had been cast aside, the individual could reach the ideal of sagehood. No doubt Chan Buddhism influenced Wang in his disdain for external sources of wisdom, for constant study of Confucian texts, and for careful analysis of logic or experimental knowledge. His emphasis on looking within one's own mind in attaining sagehood resembled the Chan Buddhist concern with intuitive attempts to achieve sudden enlightenment.

What distinguished Wang from Chan Buddhism was his belief in the fusion of knowledge and action. Unlike Chan, which focused specifically on meditation as the road to knowledge and enlightenment, Wang accorded action as crucial a position as knowledge. Knowledge could not be said to be understood unless it informed the individual's action. The two were part of the same continuum. Knowledge needed to be translated into action to be considered true insight. Separation of knowledge and action revealed a lack of understanding. If knowledge and action diverged, the individual did not really "know." For Wang, knowledge could not be separated from action, and his active official career testifies to his view of the fusion of the two.

Wang's involvement in the politics of his time provided a model for officials. Scholars whose objective was the pursuit of knowledge had a rationale for undertaking positions as bureaucrats. They did not need to shy away from official careers because knowledge was intertwined with action. Because sagehood was predicated on such involvement, scholar-officials received justification for their roles in government. Such an approach jibed with the scholar-officials' need for a rationale for public involvement yet offered tranquility through its emphasis on the clear and peaceful mind as the source of knowledge.

Although Wang was the dominant philosopher of his era, several who were influenced by his views charted new courses in thought. They also diverged from orthodox Neo-Confucianism or at least introduced Buddhist and Daoist beliefs into their conceptions. Each of these thinkers questioned the authority of the Confucian classics and suggested few limits on self-expression. Wang Gen (1483–1541), one of these thinkers, took Wang Yangming's exaltation of the mind seriously and was, in particular, attracted by the great philosopher's view that the mind superseded conventional morality concerning good and evil. The younger disciple, deriving from a nonelite family of salt producers, expanded upon Wang Yangming's ideas to offer a greater threat to conservatism. Identifying with ordinary people, he concurred with Wang Yangming's conception of the potential sagehood of all men. However, Wang Gen went one step further in advocating liberation of the common man so that he could achieve his potential – a clear challenge to the Confucian emphasis on the individual's duty to society and on his obligations to the network of relationships in which he was embedded. However, he did not translate his seemingly egalitarian ideas into policies that might influence the court. Instead he lectured to and taught a wide array of disciples, not limiting himself to students preparing for the civil-service exams. He and Wang Ji (1498–1583) were considered to have founded the Taizhou school of Wang Yangming's brand of Neo-Confucianism. Unlike Wang Gen, Wang Ji passed the civil-service exams and obtained the *jinshi* degree. Meetings and dialogues with Wang Yangming had a more pervasive influence. Although he served in government early in his career, he eventually retired when his ideas aroused corrupt or conservative officials to criticize him. He spent the last years of his life refining and supplementing Wang Yangming's ideas. He, too, emphasized sagehood but asserted that it lay in faith in the mind. This devoutness would be construed as tantamount to religion, and Wang stressed, in particular, inner enlightenment and proper breathing techniques, deliberately relating his views to Daoist and Buddhist beliefs and practice. This digression from orthodox Neo-Confucianism left him vulnerable to criticism from Confucians, but gained him the respect and adherence of many Daoists and Buddhists.

The dramatic economic and social changes of the late Ming influenced the intellectual currents of the time and gave rise to unconventional thinkers who diverged from the prevailing Neo-Confucianism. Rural markets had developed amid a growing commercialization of the economy. Greater specialization in crops spurred the economy, as did the large quantities of silver imported into China. Prosperity, in turn, provided more leisure time and greater opportunities for an increase in literacy. Advances in printing offered access to a growing corpus of written materials, and publishers catered to the newly literate audience by issuing practical handbooks, short stories, and abbreviated and less difficult versions of the Confucian classics. Woodblock printing had developed earlier and a printed version of a Buddhist sutra dated 868 has been found, but the Song through the Ming dynasties witnessed an expansion in the number of printed works.

A FEW UNORTHODOX THINKERS

Several thinkers responded to these changes, deviating from the concerns of traditional Confucian orthodoxy. Liu Kun (1536–1618) emphasized practical knowledge in contrast to the often arcane theorizing of some of the Confucian philosophers. His works concerned proper local organization, the education of all (not merely elite) children, and the value of commerce and merchants – decidedly un-Confucian sentiments. Writing in the colloquial style, he reached a wide audience, including women and ordinary individuals from nonelite backgrounds. He Xinyin (1517–1579), another unorthodox thinker, challenged the most basic Confucian institution, the family. Echoing the theories of universal love espoused by Confucius's opponent Mo Zi, he criticized the family unit as parochial and limiting. He also defended free and unimpeded discussion, which contested all orthodoxies. His outspokenness and his ideas resulted in his detention in a prison, where he was killed.

Li Zhi (1527–1602) was the most unorthodox of these late Ming thinkers. Born into a merchant family, he took and passed the second level of the civil-service exams and had a two–decades-long minor career as an official. He then retired from government and started to study, write, and lecture on his novel ideas. An unrelenting critic of the orthodoxy of his time, Li enraged many traditional Confucian thinkers, and his heretical views aroused the hostility of officials, leading to his arrest for "immoral" and "subversive" ideas and behavior and to the suppression and destruction of his publications. While in prison, Li committed suicide.

Li Zhi's criticisms of Confucianism stemmed, in part, from what he perceived to be its conservatism. He insisted that schools of thought needed to change with the times. Ideas and institutions had to adapt to ever-changing circumstances, but Confucianism had not been modified to conform to such changes. Li himself was fascinated with the novel, the latest literary genre, and wrote annotations for two such works of fiction. He actively sought to promote social change, championing the rights of women and the lower classes (groups who suffered as a result of the turmoil of the late Ming). His own outsider status, deriving from a commercial Muslim background, may have contributed to his empathy for other Chinese who were not part of the elite.

MING LITERATURE

Developments in Ming literature, including the essay form, reveal the same dissatisfaction with orthodoxy and the social system. Growing commercialism and a larger printing industry (which catered to the growing number of literate individuals) provided fertile ground for popular writings. Printing establishments sprouted in the cities of Suzhou, the Southern Song capital of Hangzhou, and Nanjing, supplementing the earlier printing center of Fujian. The audience for works that offered practical advice was sizable. Morality books, which prescribed proper behavior and etiquette, were popular, particularly among the newly wealthy merchants. Copies of the notes of students who prepared for the civil-service exams, as well as model exam papers, had a substantial audience. Story books, encyclopedias, and simple commentaries and explications of the Chinese classics also sold well. Woodblock prints began to appear and found an appreciative clientele. Hu Jingyan (1582–1672) achieved the greatest successes in the production of these color prints, depicting flowers, fruits, and rocks. His remarkable collection of prints inspired other, more worldly artists to dabble in erotica. Albums filled with erotic prints began to appear on the market in late Ming times. The prints (illustrated in black, blue, red, green, and yellow, with each color used for a specifically designated part of the body or dress) offered depictions of nudes, suggestive erotic scenes, and explicit bedroom venues with half-dressed lovers. Such depictions, which occasionally illustrated Daoist conceptions of the conservation of male sexual energy and the masculine absorption of the female *yin* element during sex, had a considerable vogue, challenging Confucian orthodoxy.

The novel, which developed during this time, decried social conditions and challenged the status quo. Because it defied convention and originated in storytelling, the elite originally relegated it to a relatively low status. It did not have the same prestige as poetry or philosophical works. The mostly anonymous authors combined stories and organized them into novels, which as a result were lengthy and appeared to be patched together. The popularity of the novels attested to the increasing rate of literacy and indicated that the new audience relished accounts of elite corruption and injustice. The most popular among them often dealt with historical events and eventually would be mounted as plays or operas and even later reproduced on television or in video games.

The major ones can largely be characterized as social-protest novels. *The Romance of the Three Kingdoms* (*Sanguozhi yanyi*), which is attributed to a certain Luo Guanzhong of the fourteenth century (although the earliest surviving edition derives from around 1522), dealt with the era after the collapse of the Han dynasty and cataloged the court's failings –dissipation, intrigues, official malfeasance, and exploitation by the eunuchs. Neither the scholar-official bureaucrats nor the military commanders appeared in a favorable light. The thrust of the narrative cast several of the military contenders for power as tyrannical and evil, while others such as Guan Yu and Zhuge Liang were portrayed as brilliant strategists and moral rulers or commanders and as possessors of magical or supernatural powers. The novel judged these stereotyped figures on the basis of their humaneness and incorruptibility. Perhaps because they were stereotypes, the leading characters became popular and romantic heroes.

Water Margin (*Shuihuzhuan*, also translated as *All Men Are Brothers* or *Outlaws of the Marsh*), which Luo Guanzhong allegedly edited, offers an even clearer example of a novel that exposed social injustices. It described the adventures of a group of 108 bandit-heroes toward the end of the Northern Song dynasty who rebelled against an exploitative and oppressive government. These heroic figures defended the poor and powerless against cruel, avaricious, and tyrannical officials. Their leader, Song Jiang, a Robin Hood-like character, still believed in loyalty to the emperor, despite his hatred of many at the court. In one version of the novel, he ultimately joined the imperial forces to stave off a rebel whom he considered to be an even greater threat to China. The exploits of these heroes, which included feats of almost superhuman strength, appealed to a wide audience. Mao Zedong was entranced by the work and proclaimed it his favorite novel. The adventure stories aside, the novel's portrayal of a group advocating social justice reputedly appealed to him. Its use of the colloquial also attracted and increased the number of its readers.

Although *Journey to the West* (*Xiyouji*, also translated as *Monkey*), a sixteenth-century work, was not a novel that exposed social or political injustice, it gently satirized the Buddhist establishment and Chinese officialdom. Based on the travels of the Buddhist monk Xuanzang in the seventh century, the novel invented three characters who accompanied the renowned traveler. Monkey, the most significant of these escorts, protected Xuanzang from an array of ogres and ghosts. His magical powers, together with the assistance of Buddhists and deities, permitted the Buddhist monk to reach his destination safely. After harrowing adventures, including debates and struggles with Daoist monks and battles with monsters, both Xuanzang and Monkey achieved salvation. In the course of this fantastic and often comic journey, the travelers encountered avaricious and ignorant Buddhist monks, as well as official bureaucrats. Although Buddhist and Daoist themes, adventurous tales, larger-than-life characters, and humorous and sometimes earthy incidents constituted the main thrust of the novel, the revelations about the religious establishment and the bureaucracy could not be discounted as themes. Wu Cheng'en (ca. 1500–1582), an official, is credited with paramount but not exclusive authorship.

The Golden Lotus (*Jinpingmei*), also a sixteenth-century work, was renowned not only for its candid and unflinching depiction of erotica but also for its exposure of a decadent and corrupt society. Its vivid pornographic description of sex acts shocked and captivated its audience, but its account of the lecherous nouveau-riche Ximen Qing also revealed a decaying and amoral culture. The rich and corrupt owner of a pharmacy, Ximen Qing was an inveterate womanizer who sought sexual gratification not only with his wives and concubines but also in numerous adulterous relationships. Abetted in his sexual adventures by the so-called Golden Lotus, another reprehensible character who poisoned her husband, Ximen Qing reflected some of the worst excesses of late Ming profligacy. Along with hedonism, bribery and corruption were rampant, and the newly wealthy, according to the novel, would resort to any action, including murder, to satisfy their desires. The author showed that behind the elaborate entertainments, banquets, and parties lay a decadent and corrupt society. He concluded the novel with the two most pernicious characters receiving their just desserts. The Golden Lotus's brother-in-law exacted his revenge for his brother's murder by killing his sister-in-law whereas Ximen Qing died while imbibing an aphrodisiac that was, in fact, poisonous. After his death, nearly all his family members had disastrous lives. Only his principal wife, a faithful and virtuous woman, and one son, who joined a Buddhist monastic order, survived the fall of his family.

Short stories also witnessed the same development of realistic descriptions of the new commercial and urban elites and a sympathetic portrayal of those who were oppressed and discriminated against. Feng Menglong (1574–1646), who gathered and issued a valuable collection, and Ling Mengchu (1580–1644), who compiled a similar collection mostly of his own works, selected stories representing various genres, from tales of the supernatural and Buddhist and Daoist immortals to accounts of historical figures to realistic portraits based on contemporary events. Hypocritical and avaricious monks and nuns, rapacious merchants and pawnbrokers, and harsh and cruel judges populated the stories and revealed Feng's and Ling's views of the decline of the Confucian virtues of love, filial piety, and righteousness in their new money-oriented society. Feng and Ling countered this decline with the Buddhist teaching of retribution. The unjust, the evildoers, and the criminals, often associated with the merchants and monks, would eventually be punished in this world or in the afterlife, while the virtuous would reap their just rewards.

Ming dramatists were not as concerned about social problems or about appealing to a wider audience. A new form of dramatic opera deriving from south China, dubbed the *chuanqi*, was extraordinarily long, and its arias were sung in the Wu dialect. Although the playwrights did not deliberately inject social themes in their dramas, the plays often reflected the tensions arising between the values of the newly ascendant middle class and those of the scholar-official elite. Gao Ming's (ca. 1305–ca. 1370) *Lute Song* (*Papa Ji*) offered one example of this tension. The leading character was tempted from the proper Confucian path by his yearning for wealth and renown, but he eventually returned to the "right" road of abiding by filial piety and by respecting his admirable first wife, who lived by the traditional Confucian virtues. His first wife brought him to his senses by pursuing him and playing plaintive songs on her lute. Because members of the elite wrote many of these plays, they tended to reflect the conventional orthodoxy. However, in reaffirming Confucian principles, they disclosed that traditional values were being challenged.

Tang Xianzu (1550–1616), the most famous of the Ming playwrights, was associated with dissidents, including Li Zhi, but his plays did not generally represent his social or political views. Instead they concerned themes of seemingly eternal verities. The transience of life and the fear of death loomed large in his works; in his early plays, he offered love as a means of coping with the impermanence of human existence. In *The Peony Pavilion* (*Mudanting*), one of his most revered plays, the young heroine had a dream in which she and a handsome youth met and fell in love. Unable to find love in this life, she died but left her portrait behind. The young man fortuitously visited her home and found her portrait. That very night he had a dream during which the heroine appeared and instructed him to dig up her body. When he did so, she returned to the world of the living, and the couple was reunited. Love appeared to overcome the transience of human life. In another of his plays, dreams again propelled the action and addressed his major themes. The protagonist repeatedly had dreams at critical points in his career. One dream led to a propitious marriage, which in turn led to a distinguished career and a reward for his meritorious service (the imperial gift of a sizable estate and twenty-four female quasi-entertainers and quasi-bed partners). The playwright implied that fame and sex compensated for the brevity of life. Yet Tang's later plays were less optimistic. Did this more sober view reflect his growing disenchantment with the corrupt and incompetent leadership at court? The available sources do not yield an answer. However, he now seemed to regard fame, wealth, and love as ephemeral. His heroes abandoned the weak and sought refuge in Daoist detachment or Buddhist enlightenment. The inexorable march of time, the approach of death, or disillusionment with his society probably contributed to his growing emphasis on religious salvation.

The plays and life of Li Yu (1610–1680?), the most eccentric of the Ming playwrights, revealed the individualism of the dynasty's later years. Failure in the civil-service exams deflected Li from a bureaucratic career, a depressing outcome for most Chinese, but Li took it in stride. Faced with the prospect of supporting a slew of concubines, he worked, at various times, as a publisher, bookseller, commercial gardener, essayist, critic, and playwright. His plays differed from those of other dramatists in that he did not have a message to convey. He simply sought to create entertaining plays that expanded a range of plots and used well-crafted dialogue suited to each character. Yet he was serious in his efforts to portray ordinary people, not the elite, in his dramas. In addition, the intelligence and individuality of his female characters conformed with his support for education for women, which included exposure to the classics, literature, and painting and the other arts.

Theater, particularly the southern drama known as *kunqu*, persisted for several more centuries, owing its success in part to the continued growth of southern Chinese urban centers that nurtured it. A larger potential audience was available for the theatrical productions. Yet the *kunqu* was less appealing because of its almost exclusive association with south China, and its plays were increasingly divorced from the lives of the populace. Beijing opera arose later in the eighteenth century and introduced more popular and entertaining elements in drama. It innovated in music, dance, and costume, and makeup was more colorful than in the *kunqu* theater. Brilliant acting, singing, and dancing, which mesmerized the audience, took precedence over themes, dialogue, and poetry. Because the spectacle often superseded the ideas, Beijing opera did not have the same literary quality as earlier traditional theater. Yet the remarkable acting attracted attention while it overshadowed the playwriting.

Chen Zilong (1608–1647), a poet most often renowned for his loyalty to the Ming court, also reflected the growing individualism of the era. A loyalist who resisted the Manchu conquest of 1644 and ultimately committed suicide after the enemy captured him, Chen was highly praised for his devotion to the Ming. It may seem strange to extol a man who remained steadfast in his support of a corrupt, increasingly mismanaged, bankrupt, and demoralized dynasty, but many Chinese clearly valued such figures. Even more significant, Chen's songs and poems to his beloved Liu Shi, a poet in her own right, were remarkably candid. His open acknowledgment of romantic love reflected individualism and a great concern for individual feelings. The relatively independent life and career of Liu Shi, who also openly expressed her love for Chen, indicated the greater opportunities for women.

BUDDHISM: NEW DEVELOPMENTS

Neo-Confucianism overwhelmed Buddhism, as few original thinkers arose to infuse new ideas into the religion. Yet the Neo-Confucian School of the Mind owed much to Buddhist conceptions. In addition, the number of ordinations of monks increased at a rapid pace. Buddhism had profited because the first Ming emperor had spent part of his youth in a monastery. Yet, despite these successes, Buddhism tended to be eclipsed by the other Chinese religions and cults and needed to adapt in order to retain its influence. One such adaptation entailed borrowing from Daoism the concept of merits and demerits as a means of determining the individual's status or the path to Nirvana. Buddhist monks explained that noble deeds earned a specific number of points (e.g. helping a person to recover from a serious illness resulted in the award of ten merits), while transgressions led to demerits (e.g. one hundred demerits for killing another person). A grand total of ten thousand merit points would almost surely lead to Nirvana. This formulaic concept contributed to public-spiritedness and philanthropy, but hardly to Buddhist ideology.

Monks worked out the schedule of merits and demerits in part to stem the decline of Buddhism. Believing that only the Chan and the Pure Land sects were still vibrant, they sought to reconcile these sects to strengthen the cause. Many Buddhists were scornful of Pure Land because of its seemingly easy path to Buddhahood, but these monks countered that chanting and calling on the name of Amida in an effort to enter the Western Paradise were not facile exercises with scant intellect and appeal. The believer had to focus his mind on Amida, an intense experience that resembled the Chan meditative process. An emphasis on the mind characterized both of these sects and indeed the other remaining sects. The monks' eclecticism extended to Confucianism as well. In their effort to bridge the gap between their religion and Confucianism, they noted that the two complemented each other. As one monk stated, Confucius was a this-worldly sage and Buddha an another-worldly sage. Other monks also maintained that Buddhist monks needed to purify themselves if the *sangha* (or community of monks) were to be sustained. Thus they imposed strict discipline in the Yunqi temple, which they constructed in Hangzhou, in order to reverse the negative image that lazy, incompetent, or avaricious monks had conveyed. They hoped in this way to bolster the image of Buddhism.

Almost two centuries earlier, Tsong-kha-pa (1357–1419) had reformed the dGelugs-pa, the Yellow Sect of Tibetan Buddhism, the other form of that religion that attracted some Chinese. The Chinese rulers did not forge the same links that the Mongols of the Yuan had created with the Tibetan religion. Yet the Ming emperors provided elaborate gifts for Tibetan Buddhist envoys and expressed interest in their religion. Information about Tsong-kha-pa's reputation reached the court, promoting a growing interest in his sect. He had transformed the dGelugs-pa by insisting on celibacy for monks, rooting out magic, demanding a disciplined lifestyle from the monks, and establishing a curriculum for them. News of his rejuvenation of the sect spread to China, and Emperor Yongle repeatedly invited him to court. The ensuing high regard for the sect prompted greater interest and more Chinese conversions to Buddhism.

SOCIAL DEVELOPMENT AND MATERIAL CULTURE

The changes in material culture belied the Ming's reputation as staunch supporters of isolationism and resisters of innovation. Eyeglasses were introduced from Southeast Asia. Maize reached the Ming, probably circuitously from the New World, via some of the Muslims of Spain, north Africa, and west Asia. Sweet potatoes and peanuts arrived via the Europeans who came by sea to China starting in the early sixteenth century. These crops proved to be boons because they could be grown in inhospitable areas. Food production increased as sweet potatoes and peanuts were planted in soil unsuited to millet, wheat, and other traditional crops. Such an increase contributed to a growth in population in the late sixteenth century and offers a partial explanation for the dramatic jump between the mid seventeenth and mid nineteenth centuries. Tobacco, also from the New World, began to be planted, originally in south China but later in the north as well. It probably reached China through Southeast Asian intermediaries and turned out to be a useful cash crop. Although some in the elite initially resisted its introduction, it continued to be grown. Planters even defied government efforts to ban tobacco, and by the middle of the seventeenth century it had become accepted throughout society.

The numerous investigations in geography, pharmacology, and botany, among other areas, challenged the perception of the Ming as lacking interest in the outside world and as conservative in its views of the natural universe. Not only were specific individuals seeking to expand their own knowledge of the world but the government too, by supporting specific projects, disclosed its desire for such information. The court sponsored two imperial geographies, the *DaMing yitongzhi* (*Records of the Unity of the Great Ming*) and the *Huanyu tongzhi* (*Comprehensive Records of the Universe*), which offered descriptions of numerous lands. The two works described the customs, the products, and often the topographical features of the foreign territories with which China had relations. Most of this information was based upon the reports presented by the envoys dispatched abroad early in the dynasty. The court was thus well informed about neighboring and distant lands in Asia. In addition, works on foreign relations revealed that the court trained specialists in foreign affairs. Ma Wensheng (1426–1510), the minister of war in the late fifteenth century, wrote detailed texts about China's relations with the peoples along its northwestern and northeastern borders. Xu Jin (1437–1510), another long-term official in the northwest, produced a sophisticated narrative and analysis of political and social conditions in central Asia. The *Huayi yiyu* (*Sino–Barbarian Dictionary*), which contained Sino–foreign glossaries or rudimentary dictionaries of Mongol, Jurchen, Sanskrit, and other languages, revealed a similar interest in foreigners and a growing scholarly expertise. The Siyiguan (College of Translators) and the Huitongguan (College of Interpreters), two government agencies that trained translators and interpreters, provided the court with personnel proficient in Burmese, Jurchen, Mongol, Persian, Thai, Tibetan, Uyghur, and other languages. To be sure, the level of expertise was often mediocre, a product partly of the court's own policies. It allocated scant resources to the two agencies and accorded the interpreters and translators relatively low status and pay, limiting their ability to recruit the most capable and motivated young men. Nonetheless, as interpreters and translators, these men dealt with and learned about foreigners, thus increasing China's knowledge.

Geographic knowledge of China itself also attracted attention. Remarkable explorers were, in large part, responsible for advances in such knowledge. They compiled diaries of their expeditions, which incorporated information on the topography and the spectacular sites they saw. One such explorer undertook a dramatic and dangerous trip in the remote areas of southwest China. Enduring bitterly cold weather, bandit raids, and loss of supplies, he persisted and discovered the source of the Yangzi River and traversed the Mekong and Salween rivers.

The Ming also witnessed innovations in and greater knowledge of technology. The *Wubeizhi* (*Treatise on Armaments Technology*), compiled by Mao Yuanyi (1594–ca. 1641) in 1628, offered descriptions of armor and weaponry and disquisitions on strategy. More military texts were written during the Ming than in the entire history of China until that time. The *Tiangong kaiwu* (*Exploitation of the Works of Nature*), edited by Song Yingxing (1587–1666), was a valuable compendium on Chinese methods of production. Song wrote about agronomy (including the growing of grain); clothing materials; dyes; salt; sugar; ceramics; the casting of pots; statues and mirrors; vegetable oils; paper; the forging of weapons; the mining and use of silver, copper, tin, zinc, and lead; vermilion; and ink. Illustrations peppered the work, facilitating efforts to identify the tools and techniques of production. Even more comprehensive was the remarkable *Bencao gangmu* (*Compendium of Materia Medica*) of

Li Shizhen (1518–1593), the descendant of a long line of physicians and dispensers of drugs. A description of beliefs about medicinal use of plants, animals, and inanimate substances, this monumental text preserved many of China's contributions to materia medica. It surveyed approximately 1900 species and offered more than 8100 prescriptions for both ailments and chronic diseases. A sampling of these recipes yields the use of the fresh river snails for conjunctivitis, jaundice, and difficulties in urination; of dried and powdered cattle louse to ward off smallpox; and of ground-up "dragons' teeth" for arthritis and for diseases of the liver. Also included in the work were descriptions and treatment for syphilis and smallpox and an analysis of the curative properties of wild rhubarb, which grew primarily in Gansu. According to Li, the root of the plant, which the Chinese referred to as "Great Yellow," served to cure gastrointestinal disturbances and congestion of the pelvic organs as well as to cope with malarial fevers, among numerous other applications. Europeans, who started to trade for Chinese rhubarb in the late sixteenth century, made even greater claims for it. An English herbal published in 1597 prescribed rhubarb for diseases of the liver, kidney, and spleen, for swellings of the heart, spitting of blood, shortness of breath, ringworm, inflammation of the lungs, madness, and frenzy. M. Pomet, chief druggist to King Louis XIV of France, added that it could be used to eliminate worms in children. Europeans valued it so highly that an extensive commerce in rhubarb developed between the seventeenth and nineteenth centuries. It is unclear whether the other recipes were as effective.

VIOLENCE IN THE SIXTEENTH CENTURY

After the disastrous capture of the emperor in 1449, the court recovered and managed several decades of peaceful rule despite repeated purges and executions of officials and the growing power of eunuchs. Aside from a few minor insurrections, the dynasty encountered few crises for the remainder of the fifteenth century. However, disquieting trends appeared beneath the surface. Eunuchs were becoming increasingly prominent in all facets of government, reaching even to the judiciary and beginning to supersede the authority of judges. The skills of the Ming military were dissipating, and the court provided scant funding for its troops, in accordance with the dynasty's professed opposition to expansionism and the attendant lack of prestige for the military.

These developments started to translate into serious problems and abuses at the outset of the sixteenth century. Unstable and oppressive eunuchs, insufficient revenues (as a result of widespread evasion of taxes by the elite), and elaborate and expensive struggles for power among court bureaucrats led to several revolts, and to brutal punishments being inflicted on officials critical of the eunuchs or the emperors. The court initiated enormous construction and public-works projects and insisted on larger and more elaborate palaces, imposing substantial burdens on ordinary people. Yet it scarcely sought to register on the tax rolls the lands of those members of the elite who had evaded taxes. Similarly, it could not control and mandate the collection of commercial taxes, placing still additional burdens on the population at large.

The early-to-mid-sixteenth-century court did not make sufficient efforts to promote reforms, which would have generated revenues for legitimate undertakings. It thus encountered considerable domestic and foreign turbulence. Internal uprisings as well as piracy and brigandage, which it could not entirely control, undermined stability. Capitalizing on such disturbances, Altan Khan of the Mongols attacked China and reached the gates of Beijing in 1570. His invasion was prompted by a desire for additional trade and for an expansion of the horse markets along the Sino–Mongol borders. When the court rebuffed his demands, he ordered an assault. Like other Mongol rulers after the height of the Mongol Empire, however, he could not forge the unity required to pose a true threat of conquest. Although his forces briefly occupied the area near Beijing, they eventually withdrew, but they coerced the court to create horse fairs where ordinary Mongols could trade for badly needed grains. When the court reneged on its pledges shortly thereafter, Altan Khan's forces renewed their raids on Chinese territory.

The court sorely needed reforms to achieve stability and to forge peace along its borders. Seeking to prevent additional incursions from the north, the Ming initiated an era of wall building, which resulted in much of the modern so-called Great Wall. This new construction did not necessarily end attacks, but it deterred or curtailed some. At this time, an official named Zhang Juzheng (1525–1582) assumed the challenge of reinvigorating and preserving the Ming. Faced with revenue shortfalls, he first limited expenditures at court and in the army. Confronting a maze of taxes, he mandated tax quotas for local officials, placing the onus on them. To facilitate their efforts, he converted the existing system in which individuals contributed a variety of service-in-kind and monetary obligations into one payment of silver bullion, a process that came to be known as the "single-whip system." He relied on riding roughshod over the bureaucracy to secure his objectives. Unable to initiate a new set of laws or to sack or circumvent government bureaucrats, he was compelled simply to enforce existing regulations and to root out corruption. He could scarcely broach institutional innovations and thus relied on tight control over and intimidation of the bureaucracy to achieve his objectives. While seeking to tame the bureaucracy, Zhang suffered the misfortune of his father's death, which, under Confucian rituals, required him to retire from government service to observe a period of mourning. When Zhang maneuvered to obtain a waiver from the emperor from such an enforced retirement, he alienated orthodox Confucian scholars and officials who criticized him and further barred his efforts to promote changes. Although the initial pressure on local officials resulted in substantial gains for the dynasty, continued opposition from the bureaucrats whom Zhang called upon to implement his policies ultimately subverted his reforms. Like other reforms in Chinese history – those sponsored by Wang Mang and Wang Anshi, for example – they faced considerable resistance because they sought to undermine the privileges and power enjoyed by the bureaucracy (the group reformers counted on to foster change). In addition, Zhang and other reformers were often stymied by their aversion to institutional transformation. Recommendations for changes in institutions could be construed as indirect criticism of a dynasty's founders, which consequently placed reformers in a defensive position. Reformers such as Zhang thus faced serious obstacles.

After the failure of Zhang's reforms, the dynasty's problems mounted. Foreign opponents and domestic adversaries capitalized on these difficulties. For example, the court faced rebellions among minority peoples in the provinces of Sichuan and Guizhou for almost a decade until 1600. In 1592, it suppressed, not without difficulty, an outbreak of mostly Mongol troops stationed in and protecting the province of Ningxia. However, its major campaign of the last decade of the sixteenth century was support for Korea against a Japanese invasion. Toyotomi Hideyoshi, who with his predecessor Oda Nobunaga had restored centralized government in Japan after a century or so of disunity and turbulence, initiated two invasions of Korea in order to secure a foothold on the Asian mainland. The Ming court assisted Korea on both occasions – in 1592 and again in 1597 – and dispatched at least seventy-five thousand troops during these campaigns. The combined efforts of Korean and Chinese naval forces led to victory on the sea, isolating the Japanese samurai on Korean soil and blocking the arrival of supplies. Yet the Japanese continued to fight until they learned of Hideyoshi's death in 1598. At that point, to the relief of the exhausted and battered forces on both sides, a peace agreement was negotiated, enabling the samurai to withdraw. The Ming court had realized its objective of resisting Japanese encroachments on the Asian mainland, but its expenditures on these campaigns and on the internal rebellions were staggering, adding to its fiscal woes.

FALL OF THE MING DYNASTY

Dissidents who were distressed at the disarray at court and in the country at large began to join together to (at the very least) express their dismay and dissatisfaction. The Donglin Academy was the most renowned such association; it used Confucian precepts to question the venality of court officials. Adherents of the Donglin maintained that reaffirmation of Confucian ethics and their implementation at court were more important than institutional changes or reforms. Having founded its academy in 1604, the Donglin partisans convened meetings and sessions designed to preserve Confucianism and to discuss and assess the role and moral cultivation of officials. Such meetings often resulted in sharp criticism of certain officials; this alienated those officials from the Donglin cause but did not substantially halt the steady decline of the court, which faced revenue shortfalls while ironically the elite (both at court and among officials, large landowners, and newly prosperous merchants) spent considerable sums to purchase luxuries. The Donglin's moral suasion scarcely affected the course of government, and indeed the court, in its last year, initiated proceedings against its leaders. Excluded from authority and power, the Donglin, as well as other talented men of the late sixteenth and early seventeenth centuries, were unable to contribute to attempts to form a less corrupt and more stable reformist government. Lacking such capable officials, the court continued to decline.

The fiscal and personnel problems of the court aside, factors beyond its control contributed to the dynasty's crises in its last two decades. An extraordinary cold spell afflicted China for much of the 1630s, no doubt reducing the food supply. Floods and droughts further worsened economic conditions during that decade. Silver, which had flooded into the empire's coffers from trade with Europe and Japan, diminished: such commerce witnessed ups and downs and, on occasion, silver exports from the New World decreased during the early seventeenth century.

The machinations of the notorious eunuch Wei Zhongxian (1568–1627) exacerbated these problems. His rise to power during this time came at the expense of the Donglin adherents. When officials either allied with or a member of the Donglin group wrote memorials to the emperor criticizing Wei for his extravagance and his usurpation of authority, he simply outmaneuvered and defeated them in bureaucratic infighting, executing several of them, imprisoning others, and murdering still others. With these opponents silenced, Wei could appoint his relatives and allies to positions at court and could acquire even more wealth and property. Internal discussions about unrest, disturbances, and threats posed by the newly risen and vibrant Manchu confederation northeast of China became increasingly chaotic, resulting in greater turbulence. Rebellions erupted in southwest and northwest China, enabling the Manchus to capitalize on this internal disarray to encroach on Chinese lands. Wei's abuses created numerous enemies who bided their time to challenge the seemingly all-powerful eunuch. The accession of the next emperor in 1627 offered them their opportunity because the young ruler from the outset signaled his opposition to Wei. Within a few months of the new reign, Wei had learned that the emperor planned to have him executed. The eunuch averted this ignominious fate by committing suicide.

Wei's death did not alleviate the dynasty's precarious state. Chaotic economic conditions and a distressed population in various sections of the country precipitated unrest and violent outbreaks. Starting in the western provinces of Shaanxi and Shanxi, rebellions spread eastward and toward the south in the 1630s. Li Zicheng (1606–1645?), the principal rebel in the northwest, had been a postal-station attendant with strong links with the local Muslim community. Organizing a band of army deserters, postal-station attendants, outlaws, and peasants, he challenged the Ming court and, after some initial mistakes and defeats, headed toward the capital with one victory after another. Much of the Ming army, bereft of supplies and corrupt and demoralized, either defected or was defeated. By April of 1644, Li's forces reached the gates of Beijing. A few hours before the rebel troops entered the city, the last Ming emperor hanged himself. Finding scant treasure in the imperial coffers, Li's forces extorted booty from officials and the populace. They contributed to the turbulence rather than attempting to restore stability through the reestablishment of institutions. Li lost considerable support because of the looting and massacres he appeared to sanction. When he proclaimed himself emperor of a new dynasty a couple of months later, he faced powerful opposition. The Confucian scholar-official class feared that Li might engineer a social revolution that would deprive them of power and transfer authority to an underclass composed of peasants and others on the fringes of society. Having no choice and having no independent military force to defeat Li, they turned to outsiders, the Manchus, to oust him. The Manchus had, by this time, received considerable assistance from those Chinese who wished to preserve an imperial system but with a Manchu emperor. Believing that they would fare better under a Manchu imperial structure than under a rebel, the Chinese elite ordered its commanders to permit Manchu forces entry into China. A few days later, a force of Manchu troops, supported by several Chinese detachments, ousted Li from the city, and a new longer-lived dynasty, the Qing, was established.

The Manchus did not suddenly appear out of nowhere. Most derived from the Jurchen peoples who had overwhelmed the Northern Song dynasty in 1126 and established the Jin dynasty that ruled north China for a century. The Mongols had crushed the Jin in 1234, leading many to return to their Jurchen homelands in Manchuria. They remained under Mongol sovereignty but regained their autonomy during the Ming, though they accepted a so-called tributary status in order to obtain trade with China. In the north the Jurchens were hunters and fishermen; in the west they survived as nomadic pastoralists; and in the south they farmed. The farmers lived a sedentary existence and could more readily develop an administrative structure. Foresight and unity were required to forge the Jurchens into an important force in east Asia.

Nurhaci (1559–1626) proved to have the skills needed to unify the Jurchens and neighboring peoples. His father had helped the Ming in a 1582 campaign against an obstreperous Jurchen leader, but a Ming commander had inadvertently killed him. Nurhaci demanded compensation for his father's death, which he received. One reward was appointment as leader of one of the most significant Jurchen groups. Increasingly, however, he and the Ming came into conflict over trade and land, and he then conceived of creating a political organization to challenge the dynasty.

Styling himself on the sedentary agricultural contingent among the Jurchens and neighboring peoples and employing the advances they had made in developing iron and other industries, Nurhaci initiated his efforts at unification. Recognizing that he required revenues, he monopolized the Manchurian trade in ginseng and reaped huge profits from selling that "life-giving root" to the Chinese. He reopened gold and silver mines and gained control over the commerce in furs and pearls within Manchuria. Having considerable financial resources and a few industries, he could subsidize the production of weapons for his army and did not need to rely on foreigners for warfare. However, he quickly recognized that he needed foreign assistance in conducting censuses, devising a tax system, and the myriad other governmental tasks. Because his own people had had scant experience in administering an empire, he turned to the Chinese living across the border for such expertise. Many Chinese who had become disillusioned with the Ming's corruption and misadministration defected to Nurhaci and served him by devising institutions similar to those found in China. Their assistance as well as his own military prowess led to his conquests of Jurchens and others in Manchuria. Additions of non-Jurchens to their cause eventually prompted Jurchen leaders to adopt the name "Manchu" for the entire new grouping.

Administrative reorganization was required as the Jurchens, or now Manchus, incorporated more units into their confederation. They broke up the original groups and dispersed them among the so-called Eight Banners, which consisted of Plain White, Bordered White, Plain Blue, Bordered Blue, Plain Red, Bordered Red, Plain Yellow, and Bordered Yellow. The Banners served as both the administrative units and the military organization for Manchu families. Consisting of companies of about three hundred, the Banners were originally made up of families of the same lineage, but soon many families were separated into different units. Dependence on their new associates eroded old alliances and led to loyalty to the new Banner leaders. As Mongol and Chinese defected, they sometimes joined the Manchu Banners or, when they began to outnumber the Manchus, formed their own Mongol or Chinese Banners. A few Chinese adopted Manchu names and identified with the Manchus, but most remained attached to Chinese culture. The Manchus gradually became more standardized as the troops received salaries instead of relying on booty. With such a strong financial and military base, the Manchus increasingly opposed the Ming forces. Battles frequently unsettled border inhabitants. In 1616, the Manchus raised the stakes by proclaiming the Later Jin dynasty, a direct reference to the earlier Jurchen Jin that had conquered China about five centuries in the past. In 1636, Hong Taiji (1592–1643), Nurhaci's son, signaled that the confederation now consisted of groups other than the Jurchens by changing the name of the dynasty to Qing.

By the mid 1640s, the Ming dynasty no longer ruled the country, but remnants of the imperial family, along with Chinese patriots in south China, resisted the Qing until 1660. The patriots who undertook to preserve the Ming represented different interests and were often in conflict with each other, which undermined their efforts. Nonetheless, relying on naval forces and control over ports in the south, a so-called Southern Ming cohort withstood the Manchu Qing dynasty for almost two decades. In 1661, Zheng Chenggong (1624–1662), known in the West as Coxinga, the last remaining Ming loyalist, fled from the province of Fujian to Taiwan.

Zheng's defeat of the Dutch East India Company in Taiwan attests to the military parity between China and the European colonial empires at this stage. Zheng capitalized on the Ming's advances in military technology. The Ming's development of cannon technology and artillery, its use of guns, and its skill with the tried and true bows and arrows contributed enormously to Zheng's success. Dutch forces had needed to be powerful to conquer and occupy the East Indies (or modern Indonesia), but they could not resist Zheng, who commanded a hundred thousand troops and three thousand vessels in Taiwan. As seafarers, the Dutch had a stronger navy, but Zheng's army was larger, better equipped, and more united than the Dutch troops. The Dutch forces lacked unity, their leaders were inadequate, and their supply lines were precarious. They had made peace with the aborigines in Taiwan and had succeeded in building forts on the island, but they were no match for Zheng's troops. The Dutch withdrew, and Zheng even contemplated an attack on the Philippines. His death in 1662 prevented the dispatch of such an expedition. His son succeeded him, but in 1683 an expeditionary force from the mainland overwhelmed Zheng's descendants and gradually integrated Taiwan under the government of Fujian province.

FURTHER READING

Timothy Brook, *The Confusions of Pleasure: Commerce and Culture in Ming China* (Berkeley: University of California Press, 1999).

James Cahill, *Painting at the Shore: Chinese Painting of the Early and Middle Ming Dynasty, 1368–1580* (New York: Weatherhill, 1978).

Victoria Cass, *Dangerous Women: Warriors, Grannies and Geishas of the Ming* (Lanham, MD: Rowman & Littlefield, 1999).

Craig Clunas, *Superfluous Things: Material Culture and Social Status in Early Modern China* (Honolulu: University of Hawaii Press, 2004).

Craig Clunas, *Empire of Great Brightness, Visual and Material Cultures of Ming China, 1368–1644* (Honolulu: University of Hawaii Press, 2007).

John Dardess, *Ming China, 1368–1644* (Lanham, MD: Rowman & Littlefield, 2012).

Edward Dreyer, *Zheng He and the Oceans in the Early Ming Dynasty, 1405–1433* (New York: Pearson Longman, 2006).

Ray Huang, *1587, A Year of No Significance: The Ming Dynasty in Decline* (New Haven: Yale University Press, 1981).

Andrew Plaks, *Four Masterworks of the Chinese Novel* (Princeton: Princeton University Press, 1987).

Moss Roberts, trans., *The Romance of the Three Kingdoms: A Historical Novel* (Berkeley: University of California Press, 1991).

David Roy, trans., *Plum in the Golden Vase or Chin P'ing Mei* (Princeton: Princeton University Press, 5 vols., 1993).

Sarah Schneewind, *Tale of Two Melons: Emperor and Subject in Ming China* (Indianapolis: Hackett, 2006).

Henry Tsai, *The Eunuchs in the Ming Dynasty* (New York: State University of New York Press, 1996).

Henry Tsai, *Perpetual Happiness: The Ming Emperor Yongle* (Seattle: University of Washington Press, 2011).

Arthur Waldron, *The Great Wall of China: From History to Myth* (Cambridge: Cambridge University Press, 1992).

Anthony Yu, trans., *The Journey to the West* (Chicago: University of Chicago Press, rev. ed., 2012).

PART IV

China in Global History

[9]   EARLY QING: A MANCHU DYNASTY, 1644–1860

> Preserving Manchu Identity
> Kangxi and the Height of the Qing
> Western Arrival
> Jesuits in China
> Expansion of China
> Qing Cultural Developments
> Qing Faces Economic Problems
> Stirrings of Discontent
> The Western Challenge
> Opium Wars
> Explanations for the Decline of the Qing

HISTORIANS of China have generally portrayed the Qing as a typical Chinese dynasty and the Manchu rulers as gradually adopting the style and trappings of traditional Chinese emperors. The Manchu origins of the Qing are thus slighted and possible deviations from the norms of Chinese dynasties have hardly been explored. Although the Qing restored and used many Ming institutions, its rulers and officials, on occasion, initiated new policies that diverged from Chinese practices and views. However, traditional Chinese historians have asserted that the various ethnic groups, including the Manchu conquerors, in the Qing accommodated to Chinese civilization and eventually became sinicized. They applied the same paradigm to the foreigners who temporarily annexed or actually conquered part or all of China. A number of specialists, who espoused the so-called New Qing History, challenged this view, arguing that the Qing developed a multiethnic empire. They

A History of China, First Edition. Morris Rossabi.

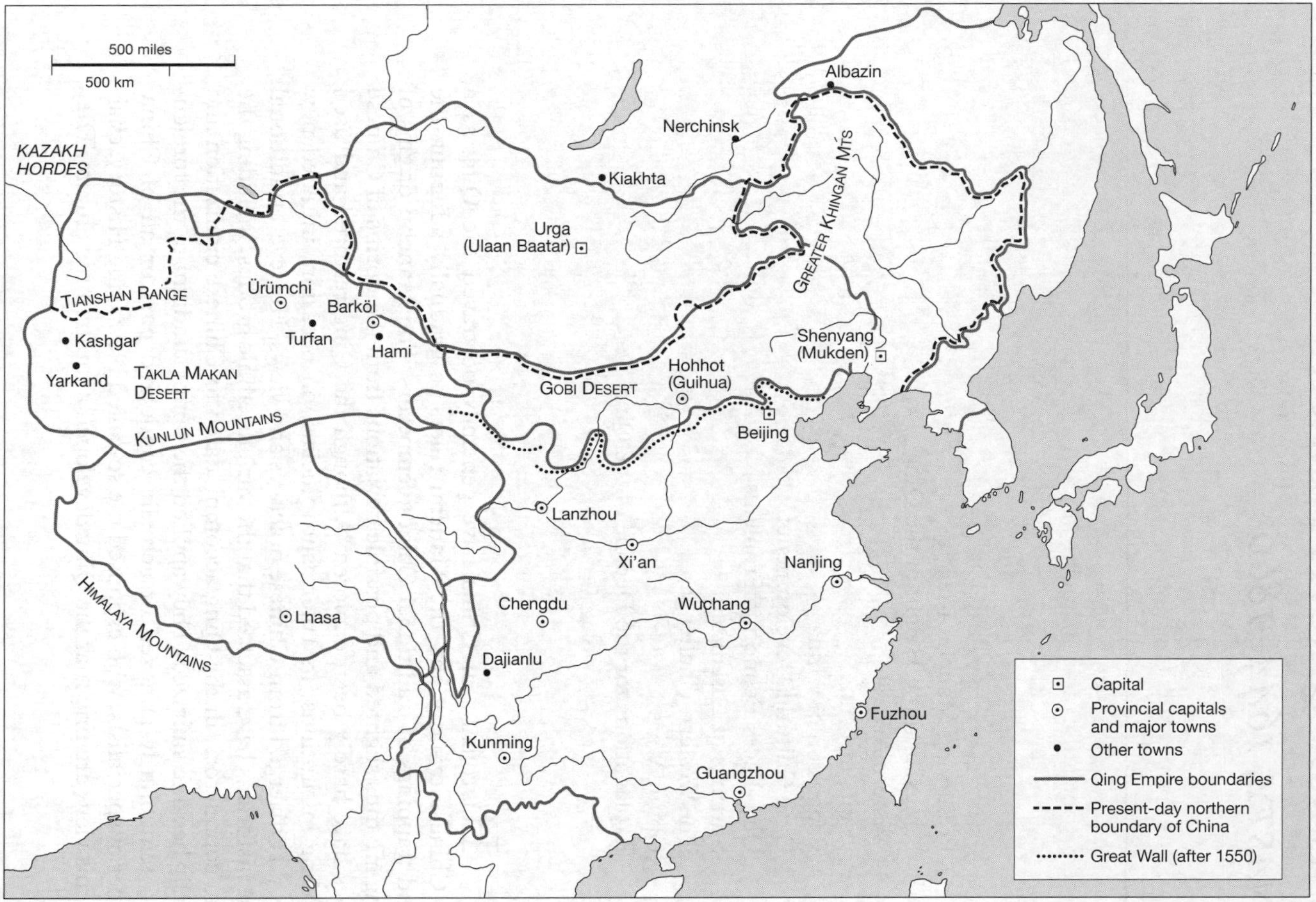
500 miles
500 km
KAZAKH HORDES
TIANSHAN RANGE
Kashgar
Yarkand
TAKLA MAKAN DESERT
KUNLUN MOUNTAINS
HIMALAYA MOUNTAINS
Ürümchi
Turfan
Barköl
Hami
Lhasa
Kiakhta
Nerchinsk
Albazin
Urga (Ulaan Baatar)
GOBI DESERT
GREATER KHINGAN MTS
Shenyang (Mukden)
Hohhot (Guihua)
Beijing
Lanzhou
Xi'an
Chengdu
Dajianlu
Kunming
Nanjing
Wuchang
Guangzhou
Fuzhou
Capital
Provincial capitals and major towns
Other towns
Qing Empire boundaries
Present-day northern boundary of China
Great Wall (after 1550)

Map 9.1 Qing dynasty, ca. 1760

note that the early Qing emperors perceived themselves to be Manchus and different from the Chinese, that they favored and patronized Tibetan Buddhism, and that they initially incorporated aspects of Mongolian culture, including the use of the Mongolian script for the Manchu written language. In addition, they embarked upon territorial annexation and created the significantly larger China of modern times, a policy of expansionism that ran counter to the dictates issued by most emperors and officials in the Chinese tradition. Both viewpoints are useful in understanding different aspects of the Qing dynasty.

Before the conquest of China, the Banners had become the principal means of organization and included not only Manchus but also Chinese, Mongols, and Koreans. Indeed, the Manchus' successes may have been due, in part, to their ability to recruit foreigners who offered skills that they lacked. By incorporating skilled foreigners into their administration, they not only strengthened their ability to rule but also helped to turn the dynasty into an empire.

Hong Taiji, ambitious and politically astute, succeeded his father Nurhaci and laid the foundations for the establishment of the new dynasty. After he consolidated his position, he turned against one of the more vulnerable foreign groups adjacent to the Ming border, the Chahar Mongols of modern Inner Mongolia. Despite his direct connection to the Chinggisid line, the Chahar ruler, Lighdan Khan, though a supporter of Buddhism and a patron of a number of literary compilations, had alienated many Mongols, who betrayed him and joined Hong Taiji. By 1634, Lighdan Khan's lands in Inner Mongolia had fallen to the Manchus. Shortly thereafter, Hong Taiji constructed a capital city in Mukden and began to establish a bureaucracy composed originally of Chinese officials. With the assistance of these foreigners, he organized a government and, as noted earlier, in 1636 he proclaimed himself the emperor of the newly minted Qing dynasty.

Hong Taiji died in 1643, leaving behind a five-year-old son who would assume the title of emperor. Hong Taiji's brother Dorgon became regent for his nephew. For the next seven years, until his premature death, Dorgon determined policies for the dynasty. He actually crossed into China and devised the strategy for the defeat of Li Zicheng, the rebel who had captured Beijing and overthrown the Ming. He set the stage for Sino–Manchu rule over China by recruiting Chinese advisers to establish a government. He imposed some control over the Manchu princes and leaders of Banners and placed himself in charge of two Banners. His extraordinary power as regent to the young emperor generated considerable hostility among influential princes, and his sudden death permitted his enemies to imprison or execute his allies and to vilify him. They accused him of seeking to usurp power, of humiliating effective officials, and of living in a grand style in newly constructed palaces. These kinds of splits among the Manchus subsided in the late seventeenth and eighteenth centuries, when the Qing was at its height, but revived again in the nineteenth century and contributed to the erosion of the dynasty's power.

Almost four decades elapsed before the Qing finally overcame resistance from Ming-dynasty loyalists. Once Qing forces had defeated Li Zicheng, they moved quickly to occupy most of north China. Parts of south China remained havens for Ming loyalists. A descendant of the Ming proclaimed himself to be emperor in Nanjing, but Qing armies overwhelmed him. Another descendant, based in Fuzhou, challenged the Qing, but in 1646 Manchu troops crushed his forces and executed him. Zheng Chenggong and his descendants maintained their control over Taiwan until 1683, when the Qing pacified the island. Wu Sangui (1612–1678), a commander who had earlier cooperated with the Manchus, challenged Qing authority in Yunnan and Guizhou, again in south China. A prolonged conflict, known as the War of the Three Feudatories, lasted from 1673 to 1681, when Qing armies overcame Wu's forces.

The Qing had defeated these opponents by the early 1680s, at which point it emerged as one of the world's great empires. The Moghul Empire in India and the Ottoman Empire in the Middle East were at their height, but no other country in Asia was as populous or had as powerful an army as the Qing. Its agricultural economy produced sufficient food for a growing population as well as such cash crops as tea, tobacco, and sugar. Domestic commerce increased, leading to the development of new vibrant cities, especially on the southeast coast. The cities also housed factories and workshops producing silk, clothing, porcelain, and printed books. Western merchants reached China seeking silk, tea, and porcelain and were willing to pay in silver for these goods. Jesuit missionaries, originally dispatched to convert the Chinese to Christianity, were so dazzled by China's glorious civilization that they did not abide by papal instructions to condemn Confucian rituals and to depict Confucius as a heretic.

When the Manchus took power, they faced the same governance dilemmas the Mongols had confronted four centuries earlier. How could they, as a tiny group, rule the vast Chinese population? Moreover, as an expansionist dynasty, which eventually conquered and occupied large domains in Mongolia, Tibet, and what came to be known as Xinjiang, how could the Qing dynasty govern a variety of non-Chinese peoples? As important, how could the Manchus retain their identities in a basically Chinese domain in which they were colossally outnumbered? The closing of Manchuria to Chinese colonization, support for the Manchu language and shamanism, and maintenance of cultural distinctions such as avoiding the adoption of the Chinese practice of bound feet for women all helped.

Yet the Manchu bannermen were in a precarious position. They received land grants and stipends from the state, but officers frequently commandeered the land and the stipends became increasingly insufficient. Many had to borrow funds to survive. Most were illiterate because the court had not provided them with an education in Manchuria. Without this skill, they could not serve in the bureaucracy. Several Qing emperors, especially Kangxi (r. 1662–1722), sought to foster literacy but found that many bannermen had turned to spoken but not written Chinese and had scant knowledge of the Manchu language. The court thus had to rely on Chinese to staff much of the bureaucracy. The civil-service examinations used the Chinese language, favoring the Chinese.

PRESERVING MANCHU IDENTITY

Dorgon and Emperor Kangxi, who eventually acceded to the throne in 1662, had devised policies to set up and preserve Manchu rule, especially among the military. The basic quandary they faced was to preserve their identity in an almost totally Chinese environment, in which they were outnumbered by about a hundred to one. Their strategy first entailed continued use of the Manchu language. Government documents were to be written in Manchu as well as in Chinese, and the Manchu elite continued to be taught the language. A second part of the strategy was affirmation of traditional Manchu customs and rejection of certain Chinese customs. The Manchu men distinguished themselves by compelling Chinese men to wear the queue hairstyle. A third element of their strategy was to maintain Manchuria as their homeland and to prevent Chinese colonization in their traditional domain. Manchu culture and civilization would presumably flourish and avert tainting by Chinese customs. The Manchus in Manchuria would remain unpolluted by Chinese practices and beliefs and the region would provide an escape hatch should the Chinese overthrow and expel the Qing rulers.

Yet, ironically, the Manchus needed Chinese collaborators. Without them, they could neither have defeated the Ming nor have established their new dynasty. With Chinese support, they adopted the traditional Chinese system of six ministries, the Censorate, and a local administration based upon division of the country into provinces. Loyal Chinese staffed many of these offices under the watchful eyes of Manchus. Similarly, the Qing restored the civil-service examinations as the principal means of selecting officials. With such Chinese assistance, the Manchus achieved stability in north China within the reign of the first Qing emperor.

KANGXI AND THE HEIGHT OF THE QING

Kangxi was disappointed over the paucity of Manchu bannermen who could become scholar-officials, but otherwise he presided over a generally prosperous and expansionist China. His father succumbed to smallpox, compelling him to take the throne at the age of nine, in 1662. Five years later, chafing under the restrictions on his power imposed by Regent Oboi, he asserted his authority, had Oboi arrested, and executed several of the regent's allies. His own writings, which have been translated in the form of a diary, show him to be a man of great intellect and sublime sensitivity who understood the value of learning, as well as of military training.

Unlike many emperors in Chinese history, Kangxi paid considerable attention to governance. He sought to stabilize Manchu rule in China, in part by ingratiating himself with the Chinese literati. Like a typical Chinese emperor, he supported Neo-Confucian philosophy and such scholarly enterprises as work on dictionaries of the Chinese language (for example, the *Kangxi zidian*), the Ming dynastic history, and a major encyclopedia. He recruited Chinese so-called bondservants to perform a variety of tasks, including acting like the Ming-dynasty censors in surreptitiously reporting about the performance of provincial and local officials. These censors also handled the imperial court's personal affairs. Probably most important was Kangxi's own diligence and involvement in government. He devised a system of secret memorials by which officials could contact him. He was serious about undertaking tours of inspection throughout the empire to gauge for himself conditions in his far-flung domains. He cultivated the Chinese literati and was an avid student of both Chinese and foreign (especially Western) knowledge, and he reduced the monetary and labor demands on his Chinese subjects. At the same time, he was determined to affirm his Manchu identity by maintaining Manchu customs at court and by participating in martial activities such as hunting. In sum, he and the other early Qing-dynasty rulers attempted to achieve a proper balance in their roles as emperors of China and leaders of the Manchus.

WESTERN ARRIVAL

Having proven his mettle in domestic affairs, Kangxi also confronted foreign-policy issues that earlier emperors of China had not faced. Instead of dealing with the primarily pastoral peoples north and west of China, whom the Chinese often considered to be barbaric and less sophisticated, and the agricultural but less populous states south of China, Kangxi had to devise policies for dealing with the representatives of the Western civilizations. To be sure, earlier Chinese dynasties had had relations with Indian, Iranian, and Arabic empires, not to mention the various rulers of central Asia, and had been influenced by their religions, cultures, and technological accomplishments. However, such relations had often been on China's terms, and these civilizations were far enough away and had not made sufficiently great leaps forward in weaponry that they could challenge and perhaps threaten China. The newer arrivals from the West, who reached China overland and by sea, proved to be more troublesome.

Within a few decades of Vasco da Gama's discovery of the sea route around the Cape of Good Hope from Europe to China, Portuguese merchants began to land on China's eastern coast. Having learned about the spices from the East and seeking to extract profits from this lucrative trade, Portuguese sailors and pirates were determined to establish bases or colonies in Asia from which to dominate the commerce. Because their men-o'-war were superior to the Asian ships and navies, in 1510 they occupied Goa (an island adjacent to the Indian coast) and Malacca (in present-day Malaysia), which was directly across the island of Sumatra and commanded the straits that led to southeast China. Their powerful naval forces permitted them to play a vital role in Asian trade and to be labeled the Pepper Empire. By the early sixteenth century, they were serving as intermediaries in the commerce among the east Asian countries while also transporting spices and earning considerable profits. Initially they did not make a good impression because they avoided court regulations on commerce and also traded for Chinese children, whom they sold as slaves. After numerous unpleasant incidents, including the imprisonment of an official Portuguese ambassador, the two countries came to an agreement in 1557, with the Portuguese securing a base in Macao, an island off the southeast coast of China, which the Chinese continued to govern. However, in 1887, when China was at its nadir, Portugal established its own rule over Macao that lasted until 1997, the year China reasserted its claim to the island.

Western merchants other than the Portuguese began to arrive in the late sixteenth century. The Spanish and the Dutch, who eventually created another seaborne empire, sought trade with the late Ming dynasty, but, as the Dutch became involved in the East Indies (modern Indonesia), they played a gradually lesser role in China. For a time, the Spanish superseded other Westerners due to their domination over the Philippines and South America. The seemingly inexhaustible supply of silver from America provided Spanish merchants with a commodity that lured the Chinese into trading their silk. The Spanish use of silver set the pattern for Western commercial exchanges with China, which appeared interested in only one European product: precious metals. The Qing, like the traditional Chinese dynasties, continued to profess self-sufficiency and did not seek to exchange its silks, tea, or porcelains for European commodities. Thus, China was awash in silver up to the late Ming dynasty and then again from the seventeenth to the early nineteenth centuries. Despite repeated efforts, Europeans could not find products other than precious metals to trade with China. The Qing court began to depend upon a steady supply of silver for its own expenditures, as well as for state projects.

When the Manchus took power, Kangxi did not turn away these European merchants but did impose the same restrictions as in earlier Chinese–European relations. He described Westerners as tribute bearers and had government officials supervise their activities. Once the Westerners had concluded their affairs, they departed for their homelands. Although Kangxi's government did not encourage this commerce, it was no doubt profitable and initially posed no threat. Prompted by an insatiable curiosity, Kangxi learned a great deal from these European merchants.

However, he learned much more from the missionaries representing the Society of Jesus. Founded in part as a response to the Protestant Reformation, the Society's members (known as Jesuits) differed from what they perceived as the corrupt and ignorant clergymen who had found places in the Protestant Church. The Jesuits needed to be well versed in Church doctrines; to lead disciplined, incorruptible, and even abstemious lives; and to be sincere in their devotion to Church beliefs. They served as exemplars for the regular clergy in reaffirming Catholic principles as Protestants challenged them. Part of their regimen was an emphasis on careful study, knowledge of Church teachings, and intellectual rigor. They respected scholarship and attempted to convey an image as learned religious leaders. In addition, they kept up with the latest developments in the secular world and in the sciences – skills and knowledge that Kangxi valued. Their knowledge, sophistication, and persuasiveness prompted the papacy to dispatch them as missionaries to the parts of the world that Europeans had reached in the sixteenth century.

When Franciscans and Jesuits initially arrived in Japan and China, they were cordially received. Some of the Japanese elite were captivated by their message, especially since the Jesuits respected Japanese culture and sought to conform to Japanese sensitivities and customs. By learning the Japanese language, the Jesuits could explain Christian theology, hoping to couch it in terms that the Japanese could fit into their own culture. Having experienced a century of disunity and violence, the early unifiers of Japan – Oda Nobunaga (1534–1582) and Toyotomi Hideyoshi (1536 or 1537–1598) – at first welcomed the Jesuits. However, Hideyoshi and his successor and founder of the new Shogunate, Tokugawa Ieyasu (1543–1616), began to suspect the Jesuits of trying to subvert their government and to fear that Christianity, the new ideology, was disturbing the rigid social class system they had created. The Jesuits' apparent involvement in the Shimabara Rebellion of 1637 to 1641 against the government prompted the shoguns to ban Christianity and foreign missionaries and to institute a policy of "closing the country" (*sakoku*) to Westerners. Only Dutch traders who had not attempted to proselytize for Christianity were permitted to enter Japan and even they were limited to Deshima, an island off the coast of Nagasaki.

JESUITS IN CHINA

After initial misunderstandings, the Jesuits in China also received a warm reception, partially because they strenuously tried to accommodate to Chinese culture and to learn the Chinese language, which impressed the Chinese elite. Arriving during the last decades of the Ming dynasty, Matteo Ricci (1552–1610) became the most renowned Jesuit of the era; his journals were published and became a vital source of knowledge about China for Europeans. His book, which was published posthumously in Rome in 1615, revealed the extraordinary respect with which he viewed Chinese civilization. It lavished praise on the Chinese, Confucian values, and the educated elite and described geography, products, and customs. His residence resulted in great achievements and in his eventual appointment as Superior General of the Jesuit order in China. After having learned spoken and classical Chinese in Macao, he spent five years in Guangzhou province before a local governor expelled him in 1589. Returning to Macao, he compiled, with an associate, a Portuguese–Chinese dictionary and a map of the world in Chinese. Later, with the help of a Chinese Christian named Xu Guangqi (1562–1633), he translated the Chinese classics into Latin and translated Western works on science and mathematics into Chinese. At the same time, he received a visitor from the Jews in Kaifeng and was the first Westerner to report on this community of so-called Chinese Jews. In 1601, Emperor Wanli (1563–1620) permitted Ricci and other Jesuits to reenter China as a reward for sending a chiming clock to him. Over the next decade, Ricci and his brethren converted a few members of the scholar-official class, but they did so without condemning Confucianism and the associated ancestral rituals. In fact, Ricci, in describing Christianity, linked it with Confucian precepts, thus making Christian doctrines less foreign to the Chinese. He also began to wear Chinese garb in order to ingratiate himself with the men in the Confucian elite whom he had befriended. The Ming court respected him so highly that the emperor, responding to Jesuit entreaties, allowed Ricci to be buried in Beijing on his death in 1610.

Many of the Jesuits who arrived in Ricci's wake gained the approval of the Qing emperors, especially if they could make practical contributions. Ferdinand Verbiest (1623–1688), a Flemish Jesuit well versed in mathematics and astronomy, transmitted the latest European discoveries in those fields. He engaged in a contest with a leading Chinese astronomer who had already bested the German Jesuit Adam Schall von Bell (1592–1666). Having proved that European astronomy was more accurate, Verbiest received an appointment as Director of the Main Observatory while his opponent was executed. Kangxi substituted Jesuits for Chinese and Muslims in the Bureau of Astronomy. Verbiest, through his position as Director of the Main Observatory, met with Kangxi to teach him geometry, music, and philology. Kangxi became even more impressed when Verbiest introduced the Chinese to new methods of casting more powerful cannons. Kangxi's good impression of Verbiest led him to recruit Jean-François Gerbillon (1654–1707), a French Jesuit, and Tomás Pereira (1645–1708), a Portuguese Jesuit, as interpreters and translators in negotiations with Russia, which led to the Treaty of Nerchinsk, the first modern treaty that China signed. Later, Guiseppe Castiglione (1688–1766), an Italian Jesuit, was so attracted by Chinese culture that he modeled his works on those of Chinese painters and even assumed the Chinese name Lang Shining. In turn, Qianlong, Kangxi's grandson, was so entranced by Castiglione's work and knowledge that he had the Jesuit artist draw up plans for a Western-style palace in the Old Summer Palace.

Kangxi, in particular, patronized and then recruited Jesuits for government positions. His support of the Jesuits stemmed from the Europeans' practical contributions. The Jesuits' scientific and technological expertise tantalized the Qing monarchs. The Jesuits delighted Kangxi with their gifts of clocks while also producing such vital products as cannons for him. Their instruction in music, mathematics, optics, and medicine appealed to him. As long as the Jesuits offered practical and tangible benefits, Kangxi appreciated their efforts and assigned them to specific tasks. He also recognized that they tried to accommodate to Chinese culture by wearing Chinese dress, learning the Chinese language, and emphasizing the common features of Christianity and Confucianism. He himself expressed little interest in their religious teachings and did not perceive of them as threats merely because they had converted a tiny segment of the Chinese population. Still he valued, in particular, their secular contributions and their assistance in science and technology.

Relations between the Jesuits and the emperors would readily have been maintained had internal disputes within the Church not created instability and undermined the ecclesiastical mission. Others in the Vatican and other orders disputed the Jesuits' approach toward China. They disapproved of the Jesuits' accommodation to Chinese culture and insisted that Confucius had to be condemned as a heretic and that Confucianism and its rituals, including ancestor worship, could not be tolerated. Approval of such practices and rites would translate into acceptance of major errors in Christian principles, and such errors would divert Chinese Christians from the true path. The Jesuits countered these arguments, noting that they could not denigrate Confucianism and still hope to convert the Chinese. Instead, they would portray Confucius as a great teacher and the practices and ceremonies associated with him as secular. In short, they would treat Confucianism as a moral philosophy and the rituals simply as an expression of cultural pride. The Vatican responded that the deviations proposed by the Jesuits led to significant alterations of the Christian message and would vulgarize and distort Christianity simply to appeal to the heretical Chinese.

This fundamental disagreement subverted the Jesuit enterprise in China. The popes, siding with the religious orders in Rome, ordered the Jesuits to censure the Chinese rituals. In the early eighteenth century, the Jesuits continued to act in their own way, but the popes responded by dispatching only those missionaries who subscribed to Vatican policies. The adamant and nonconciliatory messages of the missionaries alienated the emperors and the courts. In 1724, the emperor who succeeded Kangxi banned Christianity. Individual Christians were allowed to remain in China, but anti-Christian members of the elite ordered many churches closed or razed. By the middle of the eighteenth century, there was only a minimal Christian presence in China.

By 1760, China appeared to be in control of its relations with Westerners. Most foreign Christian missionaries had either been expelled or had departed of their own volition. Foreign merchants generally abided by Qing-dynasty regulations and accepted a status as tribute bearers. These traders, especially those employed by the British East India Company, which was fast becoming the leading trading company in China, enjoyed such substantial profits that they were willing to accept what they perceived to be unusual, government-imposed restrictions on commerce. Transport of Chinese tea, silks, and porcelains to the European market was so lucrative that the representatives of the British East India Company chose not to challenge Qing rules. The monopoly granted to the East India Company by the British government ensured that it did not face competition, permitting it to charge high prices for the Chinese products it shipped to Britain.

EXPANSION OF CHINA

The Qing's success accompanied similar outstanding achievements along its frontiers. Unlike earlier dynasties, which steered clear of expansionism, the Qing set forth to annex the steppelands and, in the process, also expanded into the regions northwest of China. The expansion was motivated by attempts to pacify the Zunghar or Western Mongols, who were based in western Mongolia and in the regions in modern Xinjiang, north of the Tianshan mountains. The Qing had harmonious relations with many Mongols and had adopted some features of Mongolian culture, but their relations with the Zunghars were often hostile, with both sharing the blame. The Zunghars had undergone a transformation in the seventeenth century, which permitted them to supersede the Eastern or Khalkha Mongols in the international struggles of the late 1600s. They had made strides toward the creation of a more sedentary society. Their leaders encouraged crafts and industries, promoted agriculture, embraced Tibetan Buddhism, and developed a new and more precise written script for Mongolian.

The rise of the Zunghars is connected to the accession of their leader Kharakhula. He initiated the internal consolidation of confederations to create a powerful union. He and his son Erdene Baatar built a palace, an indication that the Zunghars sought to settle down and deviate from the seasonal migrations of the nomadic Mongols. Erdene Baatar promoted agriculture and industry, economic activities that required a more sedentary society. He sought to suppress shamanism and to foster the spread of Buddhism, considering shamanism a more rudimentary form of religious expression and organization that was ill suited to the social structure that he was attempting to create. Buddhism was more organized and more in tune with unification.

By the time of Erdene Baatar's death in 1653, therefore, the Zunghars were well on their way to becoming a powerful confederation. They could indeed be troublesome to the Qing if they were able to unify all the Mongols. Yet unification would prove to be difficult. The Khalkha themselves were divided into four separate khanates. The ruler of one of these khanates tried to use Buddhism as a unifying force by selecting a Mongol boy as the Bogdo Gegen, a reincarnate who would become a symbol around whom all Mongols would rally. The so-called Bogdo Gegen's value as a unifying figure would supersede his role as a religious leader. However, this "Living Buddha" did not fulfill the khan's expectations. His devoted followers did not unite, as his religious prestige did not translate into political authority. Capitalizing on the lack of Khalkha unity, the Qing established a typical tributary system with them, with the Mongols providing horses and animal products to the court while it reciprocated with grain, tea, pots and other manufactured articles, as well as luxury products such as silk.

Disruptions among the Zunghars undermined this seemingly stable system. After Erdene Baatar's death, his son Sengge had succeeded him, but in 1671 two elder half-brothers assassinated him. His brother Galdan (1644–1697), who had been studying in Tibet to become a Buddhist monk, decided to avenge his sibling's death. Before departing from Tibet, he sought and received the Dalai Lama's blessing. Within a few months, Galdan overwhelmed the usurpers and established himself as khan of the Zunghars. At that point, Galdan was not satisfied with his position as leader of his own group of Mongols; he wished to restore the old Mongol Empire with himself as the Great Khan. The divisions among the Khalkha offered him the opportunity to gain control, but such an attempt to annex their lands would inevitably lead to conflict with China, and possibly with a new force in east Asia: the Russian Empire.

After the collapse of Mongol and Turkic domination around 1505, the new Russian government sought to create a buffer zone against any future attacks from the east. It therefore encouraged colonization of what came to be known as Siberia. Russian colonists crossed the Ural Mountains into Asia in the late sixteenth century, and by following the flow of the Siberian rivers had reached the Pacific by 1648. Adventurers, fur trappers and hunters, fur-trapping merchant families, prospectors, soldiers, and farmers, learning of the minerals, furs, and other rich resources in the region, led the way into the new territories, where they came into conflict with the Qing in the Amur River basin. The Russians built forts and tried to extract tribute from the native inhabitants, and the Qing was concerned about this belligerent group right across its northeastern border. The tsar sent several ambassadors to establish a more peaceful relationship with China, but the envoys returned empty handed. The resulting battles between the Qing and the Russians appeared to presage a full-scale war between the two great empires.

Galdan appeared well positioned to take advantage of this conflict. While China was occupied with the perceived Russian threat, Galdan first moved against the oases and towns along the old Silk Roads. By 1679, he had attacked and occupied Hami and Turfan, and shortly thereafter his troops moved into Kashgar and Yarkand. His next step was to dispatch several thousand men, instead of the prescribed two hundred, on tribute (actually covert trade) missions. The Qing court was unwilling to sustain the enormous costs entailed in supplying embassies. Galdan became ever more hostile when the Qing thus denied him an increase in trade. His most important challenge was his dispatch in 1688 of troops into the Khalkha lands and his occupation of much of eastern Mongolia. Recognizing that he could not, by himself, defeat the Qing, he entertained the notion of an alliance with the Russians.

He was too late because, by the late 1680s, the Russians and the Qing had realized that they had complementary objectives. They recognized that they could gain more from each other than they could from Galdan. Russia wanted trade to obtain China's silks, tea, porcelains, and rhubarb while China sought a favorable demarcation of its borders with the tsarist empire. Russia already had a vast domain in Siberia and could afford to be generous in delineating the border. With the assistance of two Jesuit missionaries based in China, the two sides signed the Treaty of Nerchinsk in 1689. By treating Russia as an equal and signing the treaty, the Qing accepted an alteration in the tribute system, which denied the equality of other states. Faced with the possibility of a Zunghar–Russian alliance, the Qing was realistic enough to modify its traditional conduct of foreign relations. Under the agreement, the Russians withdrew from the Amur River valley, burned down their forts and towns in the region, and pledged to return deserters to the Qing; the Manchu dynasty agreed to allow a specified number of Russian caravans to reach Beijing for trade. As a result of later treaties, the Qing founded a school to teach Chinese and Manchu to a small number of Russian students and permitted the establishment of a Russian Orthodox mission to cater to the students' spiritual needs.

Galdan was now vulnerable. He could not attract the support of the Bogdo Gegen, nor could he unify with the Khalkha Mongols. Indeed, by 1691 the Khalkha had accepted Qing overlordship, and the Manchu court quickly appointed officials to govern the Khalkha domains. Even Galdan's own nephew, Tsewang Rabtan (d. 1727), betrayed him by attacking his uncle's troops along the old Silk Roads. Lacking allies, Galdan tried to elude the Qing forces, but in 1696 they caught up with and defeated him. The following year he either died of natural causes or committed suicide. The last effort to restore a Great Khanate in inner Asia suffered an inglorious end.

However, the Qing still had to contend with the Zunghars who had fled from Mongolia. Tsewang Rabtan and his troops roamed throughout inner Asia for a time but finally, in 1717, occupied Lhasa, thereby instilling fear at the Qing court that he would install a new Dalai Lama and use him to unite the Tibetans and the Mongols. The Qing had to act, and in 1720 they rooted out the Zunghars, who had alienated the Tibetans by their oppressive rule. Tibet and the nearby territory of Qinghai became tributaries of the Qing, and a Manchu official known as an *amban* governed the region. Yet some Zunghars escaped and established a base in Xinjiang, from which they harassed the Qing or, from the Zunghar perspective, sought to dislodge the Manchus from their ancestral homeland in Mongolia. Battles persisted for more than three decades, until the Qing devised the supply lines and logistics to dispatch an army to travel through some of the world's most daunting terrains to reach the area that eventually came to be known as Xinjiang. In 1757, its forces, aided by disunity and a smallpox epidemic among their enemies, decisively defeated the Zunghars. In fact, the Zunghars disappeared from the historical record. Not all were massacred; many escaped westward and joined or intermarried with other Mongol groups. The Qing now had substantially increased the territory under its control while incorporating non-Chinese peoples along its borders, a fact that required new policies. By 1760, the Qing had annexed Inner Mongolia, Mongolia, Tibet, and the area across the northwestern frontiers now known as Xinjiang. The Lifanyuan, a newly founded government agency, supervised many of these new domains.

Internal peace, as well as expansion along China's frontiers, gave birth to an optimism that pervaded Emperor Qianlong reign. Qianlong (1711–1799) proclaimed universalist ambitions while affirming Manchu identity. He laid claim to Mongolia, Tibet, and Xinjiang, part of which was based upon his conquest of the Zunghars and of their link to Chinggis Khan, which he himself appropriated. He began to connect with the Mongols and their aspirations for a world empire, and Tibetan Buddhism, which he patronized, offered ideological justification and legitimacy for his claim. To be sure, his support for Tibetan Buddhism also stemmed from a sincere desire for personal enlightenment through the religion. His and his grandfather Kangxi's construction of a summer retreat in Chengde, a site north of the Great Wall, with temples modeled on several in the Tibetan capital of Lhasa, and his and his predecessors' building of numerous Tibetan temples in Beijing, including the Yonghegong, reveal a devotion to the religion. In addition, he learned Sanskrit and Tibetan and was initiated into a Buddhist sect. One should not discount his devotion to Tibetan Buddhism, but perhaps part of his dedication to the religion may have been due to his attempt to maintain control over a multiethnic empire. The Qing did so not only by adopting some of the ethnic groups' practices and beliefs but also by themselves influencing the social, economic, political, and cultural patterns of the peoples whom they subjugated.

On the other hand, the Qing, especially Qianlong, wanted to affirm its identity. Qianlong repeatedly enjoined his Manchu subjects to maintain Manchu language, dress, social status, shamanism, and customs and emphasized retention of military skills. He also sought to remind Manchus of their lineage, stretching to the Jurchen Jin and other conquest dynasties of China and culminating in his attempts to identify himself with Chinggis Khan. It is no accident that he commissioned the writing of Manchu histories and genealogies and descriptions of rituals that emphasized the Manchus' relationships with the other great conquest dynasties. His predecessors' and his own deviations from the Chinese model of foreign policy offered additional evidence of affirming a separate Manchu identity. Chinese rulers had inveighed against seeking to expand beyond the Chinese cultural boundaries. However, the Manchus annexed a tremendous amount of territory and then ruled numerous ethnic groups who did not subscribe to Chinese customs and practices.

QING CULTURAL DEVELOPMENTS

Despite underlying economic and political problems, the Kangxi and Qianlong reigns witnessed considerable cultural developments. The economy seemed prosperous, cities grew, and the number of potential patrons and consumers increased. China was at its height in the seventeenth and eighteenth centuries and ranked among the world's great powers, annexing new territories and

Figure 9.1 Plate, eighteenth century (ca. 1715–1720), hard-paste porcelain, Gr. H. 1⅜" (3.5 cm), Diam. 9⅛" (23.2 cm). New York, Metropolitan Museum of Art, the Lucile and Robert H. Gries Charity Fund, 1970. Acc. no.: 1970.220.1. © 2013. Image copyright The Metropolitan Museum of Art / Art Resource / Scala, Florence

contributing to an efflorescent society. Although much of the population continued to lead a hand-to-mouth existence, the governing elite and the wealthy could afford luxury goods and great works of art. At the same time, Westerners craved beautiful objects from China.

Porcelain remained attractive to both Chinese and foreign consumers. Some connoisseurs preferred the Song, Yuan, and Ming ceramics, which often had limited decorative motifs. Song ceramics, for example, were often plain. By contrast, the Qing blue-and-white vessels, some of which were designed for export, were often elaborately decorated, and quite a few wound up in stately homes in the West. The fashion for Chinese porcelains spread throughout the Western world, with the English gentry being avid consumers. Chinese producers must have believed that Westerners preferred pictorial representation to plain and unadorned works. Thus, they depicted scenes with humans, animals, and plants. In addition, Westerners commissioned specific motifs such as coats of arms and Western figures or scenes. Westerners became so enamored of porcelains that they also clamored for highly decorated lacquerware, textiles, and cloisonné.

Nonetheless, Qing potters added to the innovations of their Ming predecessors. They developed new colors in their monochromes, including yellow and turquoise blue. From copper they produced pieces (mostly vases) in so-called oxblood, a reddish color that consumers found attractive. Enamels of vases and bowls of a rose color (*famille rose*) and of a green color (*famille verte*), with depictions of birds and plum blossoms, also secured a receptive audience. Striking and bright colors in general became popular.

Yet other developments that were not as aesthetically pleasing began to appear. Jingdezhen, the important site for Ming porcelains, especially blue-and-white wares, became a center for mass production, with dozens of individuals contributing to the production of one piece. Although the objects were often technically perfect, creativity and refinement were frequently lost. As more porcelains were produced on demand for Europeans, quality declined. Potters fulfilled European requests for specific motifs on porcelains that were gaudy and lacked taste. Some nouveau-riche members of the Qing also served as consumers for such wares. The Song elite, which favored understatement, would have perceived these plates, bowls, and dishes as garish. The fussiness and the elaborateness of the decorations would perhaps have disturbed Song consumers. By contrast, the Qing elite and foreigners were captivated by these ornate objects because they attested to the owner's wealth and status.

Painting also served the elites because it linked them to the traditional scholar-officials. However, some of the most prominent Qing painters did not serve in government. Like some Yuan-dynasty painters who had rejected employment in the Mongol government, several of the more important Qing painters sought havens outside public service. Because the seventeenth-century artists, in particular, witnessed the destruction wrought by the Manchus, they distrusted the invaders and would not have wanted to assist them in ruling or perhaps exploiting the Chinese.

These artists turned away from public life to focus instead on their own private pursuits. Zhu Da (ca. 1626–1705), who signed his work as Bada

Shanren, was perhaps the most individualist of these painters and joined a Buddhist monastery. Preferring to have limited contact with others, he no longer talked and issued only a few guffaws or other strange noises. Reflecting the influence of Chinese Buddhism, his technique aimed at quick strokes that would elicit the essence of an object or scene. His sketches of birds and rocks are strange but expertly depicted. Shi Tao (1642–1707), one of the so-called Two Stones (because the "Shi" in their names means "stone"), was also isolated. He originally joined a Buddhist monastery but eventually converted to Daoism and returned to secular life. In a major text on art, he emphasized the union between artist and nature and sought to implement this insight in his paintings. Other seventeenth-century painters also found the Manchu conquerors repugnant and would not hold office in the Qing.

Yet several prominent painters followed the trajectory of traditional art and a few of them actually served the Manchus. Four men known as the Four Wangs, only two of whom were related, fit into that context. Wang Yuanqi (1642–1715), the most prominent of the Wangs, became a government official in the Qing and continued the landscape tradition. The so-called Eight Eccentrics of Yangzhou represented the era's individualism, yet, like many painters of earlier generations, they engaged with antiquity. They sometimes veered away from the past and poked fun at earlier tradition but at least they were well aware of it.

One important work of fiction proved to be dazzling. *The Story of the Stone* (*Hongloumeng*, sometimes also translated as *Dream of the Red Chamber*), a great novel published in mid-Qing times, reflected both the height and the growing troubles of the dynasty. Cao Xueqin (1715 or 1724 to 1763 or 1764), the author, was descended from an illustrious family. His grandfather Cao Yin had been one of the most influential Chinese bannermen of the seventeenth century, and his grandmother had been a wet nurse for Kangxi. The family's favored position offered power, prestige, and wealth. Throughout Kangxi's reign, it secured special privileges that began to descend into corruption. Kangxi's son and successor, Emperor Yongzheng (1678–1735), perhaps concerned about the family's authority, accused its members of corruption, undercut it, and confiscated its wealth. The family fell into poverty, and Cao Xueqin did not have the distinguished career of his immediate forebears.

The Story of the Stone, which is semiautobiographical, documents the fall of a powerful and prosperous household, but it goes beyond the specific events described. The conception of reality and illusion are significant themes, and there is a psychological acuity about the dozens of characters the novel portrays. The leading figures are not stereotypes but are depicted in a nuanced manner. Cao himself died young, without finishing the novel. He had written about two-thirds of the work, and two authors completed it some years later.

Composed in written vernacular rather than in classical Chinese, the novel offers a panoramic view of the eighteenth century. It offers insights into family structure; filial piety; status; religion; the roles of music, opera, and the arts; and medicine and food. It documents, in particular, the power accruing to rich families on the local level and their control of the justice system, which allowed them to dominate local government and to engage in illegal behavior without fear of sanctions. It also shows fathers playing a dominant role in the household and, in this case, ensuring that the son marries the woman he has chosen for him. The son's own beloved dies shortly after this, and he reacts by leaving his wife and becoming a pilgrim. The novel attests that the power of the patriarch and the filial piety owed to him had not diminished by that time. Another pattern that prevails is the performance of elaborate and costly Confucian, Buddhist, and Daoist rituals. These ceremonies confirm the family's wealth and status, which is also revealed in elegant clothing, tea ceremonies, and musical and theatrical extravaganzas.

QING FACES ECONOMIC PROBLEMS

Only a few years elapsed after Qianlong's death before the problems that underlay the foreign expansionism and the domestic prosperity surfaced. A few of these problems derived from the dynasty's successes. Some of the territories it had occupied and the foreign peoples it had subjugated proved to be troublesome. Violent outbreaks erupted in Xinjiang as early as 1781 (still during Qianlong's reign). The early nineteenth century witnessed repeated rebellions in the region. Mongolia and Tibet were not as unstable, but soon disruptions and foreign threats in those lands began to subvert Qing control. The military expenditures required to control and to station garrisons in these territories increased dramatically, imposing severe financial burdens on the government. In some cases, corruption consumed the funds allocated to these garrisons, rendering them undersupplied and increasingly ineffective.

Qianlong added to the financial problems through a series of costly military campaigns. In 1747–1749 and 1771–1776, he dispatched troops to suppress a rebellious hill people in Sichuan province. These so-called Jinchuan wars, which were designed to crush an ethnic group of about thirty thousand people who were related to the Tibetans, entailed enormous expenditures and loss of life. From 1765 to 1769, Qianlong initiated four abortive invasions, and a similar campaign was undertaken against Vietnam in 1788–1789. His only major success was a defeat in 1788–1793 of the Gurkhas, who had attacked Nepal. The Qing bore extraordinary expenses in these generally fruitless campaigns, exacerbating the dynasty's financial difficulties.

Moreover, the early Qing's domestic successes, including a bountiful agriculture, could, strangely enough, prove counterproductive. More extensive use of fertilizers, better seeds and strains of grains, and more sophisticated irrigation systems had translated into striking increases in agricultural production. Introduction of such New World imports as peanuts and sweet potatoes, which could be grown in marginal lands, and corn (and tobacco) also contributed to this increase. The initial surpluses facilitated the development of cash-crop farming. Land could be devoted to tea, cotton, silk, sugar, and other goods designed not for local consumption but for trade. As this commercial agriculture began to play a greater role, transportation facilities and market towns developed for the convenience of merchants. Such centers sprang up particularly in south China, the site of much of this production. However, the north, which was less productive, benefited from such growth in trade, leading to larger and larger towns along the Grand Canal, which provided many of the north's supplies. Merchant networks grew to service the trade, and soon increasingly sophisticated banks were organized to meet the merchants' needs. Ever-larger workshops and factories supplanted household enterprises in the processing and production of textiles and ceramics.

However, the bountiful economy resulted in an extraordinary increase in population. At the outset of the Qing, the population was about 150 million, but two centuries later it had more than doubled to over 400 million. Part of the explanation was the previously mentioned agricultural production and economic growth. Another factor that may have contributed was the textile factories. Because these factories employed mostly female labor and provided the girls and women with wages (however meager), females, even from poor families, could be said to have economic value. Poor families who might have been tempted to allow a baby daughter to die or actually snuff out her life might now perceive her as a potential contributor to the household. Female infanticide may have declined, and, with more girls surviving, population naturally increased. It is difficult to ascertain how much this factor may have contributed to population increase, but it is a plausible hypothesis. Equally as important, the growth in population led to an excess of labor and thus a disincentive to develop new technology. The government found itself in a trap. The surplus of labor undercut efforts to improve technology, a major distinction between China and eighteenth-century western Europe.

By the early nineteenth century, population growth had nearly outstripped food supply, and peasants were turning to marginal land to attempt to feed the populace. Poverty increased and raised the potential of famine if a bad harvest or a natural disaster were to afflict part or much of the country. The potential for social disorder also increased. Nuisance and sales taxes and payments for simple government services imposed additional burdens on the lower social classes. A general increase in grain prices, prompted by the food required by the growing population in the cities and market towns and by the sizable horde of silver from Europeans, permitted peasants to pay these sharply increased taxes for a while. However, by the early nineteenth century, the payments had become onerous and generated considerable discontent. Aware of the growing rural animosity with the system and the government, a few local officials, on occasion, falsely claimed that peasants in their region had suffered from natural disasters and appealed to the central government to waive taxes. Yet, even with some tax holidays, many peasants, faced with continuous government demands, became increasingly restive.

Corruption and so-called gifts to superiors exacerbated these tensions. Local landowners, who lived luxuriously and also had to offer customary payments as gifts to high-level bureaucrats, demanded an ever-increasing amount of tax from peasants, often for their own benefit. Officials also often received gifts from litigants in court cases, adding to the stigma of an unfair judicial system that favored the rich. Heshen (1746–1799) was the quintessential symbol of the corruption that plagued the official system. A bannerman, Heshen attracted Emperor Qianlong's attention and favor and was repeatedly promoted and granted greater and greater authority. Soon he occupied numerous offices and began to appoint his own followers to influential government positions. In 1790, he arranged the marriage of one of his sons to one of Qianlong's daughters, which offered him greater leverage. Corruption and nepotism advanced hand in hand, particularly as Qianlong aged, lost control, and became mesmerized by Heshen. Eventually Heshen accumulated vast quantities of gold, silver, sheep, cattle, and other commodities through Qianlong's bequests and others' "gifts," as well as through extortion, bribery, and, most ominously, higher taxes. He also owned vast tracts of land, employed hundreds of servants, and had a sizable harem. This state of affairs had a debilitating effect on the dynasty. Heshen's recklessness and his illegally secured wealth showed the dynasty's weakness and decline. Shortly after Qianlong's death, Heshen's enemies placed him in jail and compelled him to commit suicide. However, the damage had been done. Gross corruption had eroded trust in the dynasty and could not be readily controlled.

In addition to corruption, the bureaucracy was riddled with other problems. The number of officials did not increase in proportion to the growth in population. The larger number of civil-service examination candidates led to a higher failure rate, creating still another discontented group – and an educated one, to boot. Moreover, the relatively understaffed government offices could not respond to the population's needs. Frustrated by the lack of opportunities, some turned to extralegal or indeed illegal activities. Even if they did not initially succumb to illegal behavior, they still were a volatile and potentially troublesome force. The Qing did not find outlets for this educated citizenry.

Evidence of the late eighteenth and early nineteenth centuries' decline may be gleaned from the grain-shipping system, which was vital for north China. South China was generally self-sufficient in its food supply, but the north could not sustain itself and repeatedly faced acute shortages. Thus, the proper operation of the transport system via the Grand Canal was essential. The waterways and canals needed to be maintained, and avaricious local officials had to be prevented from imposing illegal levies on boats trading along the waterways. Contemporaneous accounts indicate that inadequate supervision and maintenance led to silting and flooding, and that corruption compelled shippers to pay excessive fees for use of the Grand Canal. Illegality in the grain-transport system and the ensuing exploitation bred frustration and anger. Honest officials proposed substitution of sea transport for the canal, and grain and other commodities were, on occasion, delivered along the coast. However, these deliveries were insufficient.

STIRRINGS OF DISCONTENT

Corruption and nepotism in the bureaucracy, educated men stalled in their careers due to a low number of official positions, and the turbulence precipitated by expansion into Xinjiang all contributed to unsettled and volatile conditions by the early nineteenth century. The economic disparities between the gentry/official class and the peasantry and between the rich merchants and ordinary urban dwellers, together with the exploitation of much of the population, almost inevitably led to disturbances and violence. Early-nineteenth-century China, which on the surface still appeared to be a great power and was at that time still regarded as such by the Western countries, actually faced corrosive social divisions. Development of secret societies was one reaction to these dislocations. Initially found in south China, they assisted rural migrants who had come to the cities for work, mostly as manual laborers, and had scant support in the harsh and alienating urban environments. Known familiarly as the Triads, one of these societies at first provided hospitality and aid to newcomers but soon became linked to piracy, smuggling, gambling, and eventually drugs. These antisocial activities gradually became antidynastic. Demonizing the Qing as a foreign, Manchu dynasty that exploited China, some members of these secret societies sought a return to Chinese rule, as reflected in an attempt to restore the Ming dynasty. Thus, they became a revolutionary force that the government needed to suppress and, by the mid nineteenth century, had actually suppressed.

Like earlier dynasties, the Qing also faced religious millenarian opposition. The White Lotus Society, which had undermined the Yuan dynasty, reemerged as a force in the late eighteenth century. Its beliefs centered on the arrival of the Maitreya, or Future Buddha, which would lead to the destruction of demons and other evildoers and would bring about prosperity and universal peace. As its leadership turned more and more against the dynasty, it attracted adherents who did not necessarily share its spiritual and (particularly) ascetic vision. Still later, bandits, oppressed peasants, and disloyal merchants and smugglers joined the sect. Thus, it may be misleading to refer to the White Lotus disturbances and their rebellion as religious movements. In any event, the Qing army could not suppress the White Lotus Society and had to rely extensively upon the elites in local areas and their militias and mercenaries to crush the dissidents. Even then, about a decade elapsed before the White Lotus Society was finally defeated around 1805.

At the dawn of the nineteenth century, the Qing was vulnerable. Corruption, misadministration, banditry, squandering of sometimes inadequate tax revenues, rebellion, and gentry and merchant aggrandizement hobbled the government. The dynasty's own exploitation of peasants added to its disarray, as the disgruntled joined with diverse other groups in violent acts against the Qing. The much-weakened dynasty now began to face Western pressure to alter its commercial and diplomatic relationships – structures that the Qing had mandated and enforced.

THE WESTERN CHALLENGE

Concerned about the increasing number of Western merchants arriving in China and fearing that the court could not control them, Qianlong had imposed restrictions on this trade. Around 1760, he demanded that Western traders land their ships only in Canton (modern-day Guangzhou). Setting aside a special quarter or island within the city for the merchants, he required them to trade only with the Cohong, thirteen merchant firms specifically licensed to deal with foreigners. In turn, a government official whom the Westerners referred to as the Hoppo extracted fees from the Cohong members and ensured that foreigners kept within the boundaries imposed upon them. Because some of this revenue went to the court, the Hoppos were under pressure to provide ever more funds to the imperial coffers. They also sought to pocket any additional income they could extract from the Cohong. This was still additional evidence of the corruption that was plaguing the dynasty by the late eighteenth century.

The British East India Company, the dominant trader by that time, accepted the court's restrictions because it profited from the trade. Its leaders were not upset that the Qing had separated this so-called Canton system it had established from any intergovernmental connections; the system was merely a commercial connection. They also did not mind that they had no access to the court in Beijing, nor did they object to the Qing demand that they not bring wives to China. One concern was their position in Britain. However, in the late eighteenth century, Adam Smith's *The Wealth of Nations* (published in 1776) and other classical economists' writings challenged the mercantilist system that had supported monopolies. The ascendancy of liberal economics then reached the political arena. In 1813, the British Parliament abolished the East India Company's monopoly on the China trade but gave the firm twenty years to divest itself of its control of this market.

The subsequent opening of the China market to a variety of British firms created demands for a change in commercial and diplomatic relations. Their greatest concern was the unfavorable balance of trade with the Cohong. They could find few goods the Chinese coveted and often had to pay for goods in silver, an increasingly expensive arrangement that led to a diminution of the British supply of the metal. In addition, the proliferation of British firms in the China trade meant that they faced stiff competition when they returned to Europe with Chinese products. Thus, confronting reductions in their profit margins and animated by their liberal economic belief in free trade, they chafed under Qing government restrictions and sought greater price competition in China, which would mean either abolition of the Cohong's monopoly or permission to trade with any merchants they chose. They began to lobby the British government to press China for such changes. As they became more involved in commerce, they wanted, in addition, more ports open for trade and a steady and regular, rather than capricious, system of customs levies. Although they did not emphasize changes in diplomacy, they surely would benefit if China and Britain could establish regular relations.

By this time, the British and other foreigners had other concerns as well. In 1784, a gunner on the British ship *Lady Hughes* had issued a gun salute for distinguished Chinese guests who had dined aboard and had accidentally caused the deaths of two Chinese citizens. The Qing, asserting legal jurisdiction over events in China, had demanded that he be turned over for trial. After considerable hesitation, the captain handed the unfortunate sailor over to the Qing authorities, who accused him of murder and had him summarily executed without allowing appeals and without allowing Westerners to attend the proceedings. Appalled by what they perceived to be cruel and barbarous actions, the foreigners wanted to gain control over legal cases concerning their own citizens, which would undermine China's legal sovereignty. When they had the opportunity, they would infringe upon China's sovereignty in order to protect their own citizens.

The British government had tried at least twice to develop proper and equitable relations with China. Unlike the British East India Company, it could not accept an inferior position to the Qing court. Capitalizing on the celebration of Qianlong's eightieth birthday, the British sent George Macartney (1737–1806) to lead an official embassy to seek changes in the Sino–British relationship. In 1793, Macartney arrived in China, having received instructions to demand diplomatic parity with China and thus the establishment of permanent embassies in both countries; to expect proper treatment as an envoy of the British king; to resist any demeaning demands; and to request improvements for Sino–British commerce. The most telling consequence of these instructions was that Macartney would be obliged to object to performing the kowtow (three kneelings and nine prostrations) as humiliating and intolerable in relations between two sovereign states. The Qing would then inevitably perceive such a response as a barbaric challenge to two thousand years of foreign relations in which China treated foreign states as tributaries rather than as equals. Macartney's instructions were thus guaranteed to undermine his mission.

Indeed, the mission did not achieve any of its objectives. First, Macartney informed court officials that he would not abide by their regulations regarding the kowtow, which caused considerable consternation. The court demanded a show of obeisance as part of the traditional rituals. After complicated negotiations, Macartney compromised by bending on one knee, the European custom in audiences with monarchs. This contretemps did not augur well for the remainder of the mission. Claiming that it did not require more goods, the court rejected demands for additional ports to be opened. It could not conceive of diplomatic parity between the Middle Kingdom (the Chinese name for China) and any other state. It also saw no need for an official British representative or ambassador in Beijing. Rebuffed at every turn, Macartney returned to Britain with as much information about China and as many Chinese works as he could. Despite the mission's failure, he received a substantial pension.

The British did not follow up on Macartney's embassy, although the country's concerns about China grew. The Napoleonic Wars diverted British attention from Asia for the next two decades. Yet the groups propelling efforts to alter the Sino–British commercial and diplomatic relationships gained force. Liberalism, with its emphasis on free trade, lack of government interference in the economy, and the dismantling of monopolies, dominated Britain's political and economic life. Within a year of Napoleon's defeat, therefore, the British government dispatched William Pitt, Lord Amherst (1773–1857), to China, providing him with a similar set of instructions to Macartney's. Yet again, ritual disputes between Lord Amherst and the Qing authorities beset the mission, which concluded with no concessions from either side. In fact, the British envoy was not permitted to go to Beijing because he refused to perform the kowtow.

The stage was set for a clash between two world orders, two economic philosophies and structures, and two legal systems. The British Empire could not accept a status as a Qing tributary nor could its king be portrayed as a vassal of the Qing emperor. British merchants and companies, with their laissez-faire philosophy, continuously challenged the Qing state's intrusiveness in the economy, the monopolies with which they were compelled to deal, and the constant drain on their silver supply caused by the unfavorable balance of trade. British law could not accept the Qing legal system's perceived indifference to individual rights and to proper treatment of the accused. As relations deteriorated, one or the other would have to alter its views and policies. The British had the greater incentive to compel such changes because of their less advantageous position in commerce. Having failed to secure changes through diplomacy, they had the option of adopting a more belligerent policy.

On the other hand, almost no dynasties in China had faced a country with such highly developed and almost completely different conceptions of international relations, commerce, and law. China had managed to maintain its tribute system of foreign relations for about two thousand years. It had modified the system when necessary, especially at times of weakness. However, it had never fundamentally abandoned the principles that China was a superior civilization and that the emperor, as the Son of Heaven, was the central ruler of the world. Even when foreign dynasties conquered China, they generally adopted this worldview. The British and the Westerners in general had their own conceptions of international relations between sovereign states, a system that collided with the empire–tributary structure of traditional China. One of these systems would have to best the other.

Commerce would precipitate change. The volume of tea, silk, and porcelain imported by Britain and the Western nations was much higher than the volume of goods imported by the Chinese. The Westerners could find few commodities, other than cotton from India, that had a market in China. They had to provide silver to cover the costs of the Chinese products they wished to buy. This draining of the West's silver supply was not sustainable. The British, in particular, needed to find a commodity that the Chinese wanted.

OPIUM WARS

Opium, which the Qing court had banned in the early eighteenth century, proved to be that product. The British knew that land in northern India was ideally suited for cultivation of opium. Having occupied much of India, they could develop a triangular trade with China, providing the Middle Kingdom with Indian opium and cotton in return for Chinese tea, silk, and porcelain. The new commerce overturned China's previously favorable balance of trade. The Chinese now had to pay silver for opium, diminishing their supply of precious metals at a rapid clip. From about 1800 to 1832, there was a five-fold increase in the British delivery of opium into China. Alarmed by the evidence of growing addiction, the court first banned importation of opium and later prohibited opium smoking. It proved unable to enforce these edicts, as avaricious British and Chinese merchants, in collusion with corrupt local officials, avoided the restrictions.

The 1830s witnessed a rapid increase in the illegal opium trade. As the East India Company's monopoly on the China trade ended, more firms sent ships to China for commerce, and many offered opium for sale to Chinese adventurers and merchants. The government was unable to squash this illegal trade, leading to court discussions about future policies. One faction advocated the growing of opium in China, so as to eliminate the power of criminals over the trade. Another faction supported simple legalization of opium, without necessarily giving an impetus to domestic growth of the drug. This option too would drive criminals out of the trade. A final group opted for banning opium and a more concerted effort to crush this illegal trade. After a heated debate, the court decided on the most difficult policy: total eradication of opium and the opium trade.

In 1839, the court dispatched an experienced official named Lin Zexu (1785–1850) to enforce this demanding directive. Arriving in Canton, he used persuasion and pressure on Chinese officials and merchants to combat the opium trade. He jailed some smugglers, tried to educate young Chinese about the dangers of opium addiction, and confiscated supplies of the drug. He demanded that the British turn over their cache of opium. When Charles Elliot (1801–1875), the British superintendent of trade with Chinese merchants, refused, Lin compelled the Chinese support staff in the British enclave to withdraw. This mini-blockade forced the British to relent. Having collected approximately twenty-one thousand chests of opium from British merchants, Elliot gave them to Lin, who destroyed the entire quantity. Lin wrote a letter to Queen Victoria, pressing her to prevent her merchants and navy from illegally importing the noxious substance into China. He noted that the products the British received from China, tea and rhubarb, were vital to their health and vitality while opium, the illegal substance the British smuggled into China, was deleterious to the Chinese people's health and wealth by addicting them and by draining away their silver supplies. This part of his letter concluded with a threat: if the queen did not restrain her subjects, China would prevent them from obtaining tea and rhubarb and, without those salubrious products, how could Britain prosper?

The British response, not long in coming, was predictably negative. British firms, outraged by the blockade, demanded that the government adopt a harsher policy in China to protect their economic interests. The British court itself was upset by what it perceived to be mistreatment of Elliot. On an even grander scale, it resented the Qing court's portrait of the British monarch as a vassal and the British government as a tributary. Lin's seizure of opium from Elliot offered a pretext for challenging the whole Qing system. In June of 1839, Elliot would not turn over several British sailors who, in a drunken state, had killed a Chinese, and this heightened Sino–British tensions.

After minor incidents, the Qing ended trade with the British in December of 1839, prompting a British declaration of war the very next month. The Chinese ships were outmatched. The British navy, the world's most powerful such force, either blockaded or attacked Canton and Tianjin and other sites along the coast. The Qing court, trying to relinquish as little as possible, appointed Qishan (1786–1854), a Manchu governor-general who was regarded as an able diplomat, to negotiate peace with the British. In January of 1841, after delays and considerable stalling, Qishan and Elliot concluded an agreement by which the British received Hong Kong, a monetary indemnity, and diplomatic equality and attained a guarantee that Canton would be reopened for trade. Neither government approved of the agreement, and both dismissed the two negotiators. Frustrated by the slow pace of the negotiations after a war they thought they had won, the British resumed attacks along the coast. Starting from Canton, they captured Xiamen and Fuzhou and then headed north to Shanghai, which they seized. Having failed to secure the Qing's surrender, the British moved, via the Yangzi River, into the interior; the conflict culminated in the occupation in 1842 of Nanjing, a populous center and a capital city for the first Ming emperor. Shocked by the fall of Nanjing, the Qing acquiesced and agreed to the Treaty of Nanjing.

The British had now achieved most of their objectives. They received the island of Hong Kong; four additional ports for trade as well as permission to have consuls and to bring their families to the ports; compensation for the opium Lin Zexu had destroyed; and payment for the losses they had incurred during the so-called Opium Wars. They compelled the Qing to abolish the Cohong and to permit them to trade with any and all merchants in China. Tariffs, they emphasized, ought to be standard and not capriciously imposed. They added that the Qing court would need to address Britain as an equal in any correspondence, a major deviation from traditional Chinese foreign policy. A provision in the supplementary 1843 Treaty of the Bogue proved to have far-reaching consequences. It extracted a most-favored-nation clause from China, which guaranteed that any privileges granted to any other power would automatically accrue to Britain. This clause was aimed at deflecting a traditional Chinese tactic of "using barbarians to regulate barbarians" – that is, favoring one group with commercial and diplomatic privileges and denying them to others, creating a rift among them. The treaty scarcely mentioned the reputed cause of the conflict. In fact, "Opium Wars" is a misnomer. The basic struggle revolved around two conceptions of trade and foreign relations. Opium was important but was much more of a symptom of the underlying issues.

Shortly thereafter, the other Western powers negotiated similar treaties but with additional privileges. In 1844, the USA, which had started to trade with China in the 1780s and now had considerable commercial interests in the so-called Middle Kingdom, pressed for and received permission in its treaty to set up hospitals and churches for its Protestant missionaries, who began to arrive in China in steadily increasing numbers. The treaty with the USA and a subsequent treaty with France enshrined the concept of extraterritoriality – that is, foreigners accused of crimes in China would be tried in their own countries' courts. China was, in this way, compelled to relinquish sovereignty over its own territory.

The opium trade, the misidentified cause of the conflict, persisted. British smugglers accelerated the pace of trafficking. Unable to cope with the opium blight, the Qing legalized the drug in treaties signed with France and Britain after conflicts in 1856 and 1860. Only at the beginning of the twentieth century did the Qing reinstate the prohibition on the drug and initiate serious attempts to stamp out the trade. By then, most production had shifted to China, facilitating efforts of consumers to purchase it. Judging from the reports of both Chinese and foreign observers, opium was readily available in the first half of the twentieth century. Emily Hahn (1905–1997), the intrepid journalist who traveled throughout Asia and Africa from the 1920s on, wrote a harrowing account for *The New Yorker* magazine of her initial experience with and then addiction to opium in the 1930s and of the German physician who helped her to overcome her addiction. Most addicted Chinese either resisted or did not have such assistance. Repeated depictions of opium dens in movies and trashy novels offer clues about the scope of the problem in the 1930s and 1940s. In the 1950s, the People's Republic of China mounted a campaign to eradicate opium production and to "cure" addicts through punitive measures. The government claimed victory, but China remains a conduit for and consumer of drugs produced in Southeast Asia and Afghanistan.

Westerners did not anticipate the Opium Wars' consequences. They perceived that free trade and the elimination of monopolies would open up a market of more than four hundred million Chinese consumers. This dream was really a delusion because the vast majority of Chinese could not afford to pay for Western goods. Moreover, the Opium Wars had generated animosity toward the British and indeed all foreigners. Recognizing this hostility and being themselves ambivalent about the implementation of the humiliating provisions of the Treaty of Nanjing, Qing officials stalled in implementing some of their treaty obligations. Canton, a particularly antiforeign center, remained closed to the British, and the four other ports did not generate the volume of trade that the British assumed they would. The British began to believe that they needed an ambassador in Beijing to reflect their views and to adjudicate disputes with local officials. Such support in dealing with the highest levels of government would be of assistance in preventing officials in Canton and the other ports to act as what the British merchants perceived to be stumbling blocks. Once the barriers were removed, the British would reputedly be able to tap into the huge Chinese consumer base.

However, despite the number of treaties in the post-Opium Wars period, Western merchants and governments were disappointed with the relative paucity of economic activity. Merchants wanted their governments to elicit concessions from the Qing and to compel it to abide by its treaty obligations. Tensions were high throughout the 1840s and early 1850s. In 1856, Qing authorities gave British hard-liners the pretext they sought in order to undertake a harsher policy. Officials in Canton boarded the *Arrow*, a ship allegedly flying the British flag, and arrested several Chinese whom they accused of piracy. The men were eventually released, but local officials neither apologized for the false arrests nor offered assurances that they would refrain from boarding other British ships. War erupted, but the Sepoy Mutiny of 1857 in India diverted the British for a time. In 1858, the French, one of whose missionaries had been killed, collaborated with the British; the combined forces attacked and occupied Canton and then their ships attacked north China, compelling Chinese officials to sign the Treaty of Tianjin. However, the Qing court repudiated its officials' actions and rejected the treaty. In 1860, the war resumed, and the Franco–British army marched into Beijing, razing the emperor's Summer Palace (Yuanmingyuan) en route. This show of force prompted the court to relent and accept the Treaty of Tianjin as well as conventions newly negotiated in Beijing. The most significant provisions were the opening of eleven additional ports, authority for missionaries to buy buildings throughout China, permission to enter the interior, Qing payment of an indemnity, granting of Kowloon to the British, and the stationing of ambassadors in Beijing. At the same time, in 1858, Russia forced the Qing to sign the Treaty of Aigun, giving the tsarist court the left bank of the Amur River. Two years later Russia was also granted land east of the Ussuri River.

China's reactions to these losses and to the infringement on its sovereignty were not uniform. Different groups of Chinese people responded differently to this extraordinary challenge posed to their system of values and government. Other invaders had reached an accommodation with China, leading to a merging of Chinese and foreign practices and institutions in governance, the military, an underlying philosophy, and the economy. Engagement with the Western countries, as well as with Russia and Japan, would not turn out to be so easy. Some Chinese institutions would be overturned or transformed. However, even without a contretemps with the West, China might still have, as some historians have argued, undergone changes through the rising tide of commercialism and industrialization. The Western challenge probably accelerated the pace of transformation, but it is important to keep in mind that nineteenth- and twentieth-century China's policies were not merely a response to the British, the French, the Americans, the Russians, and the Japanese. Such domestic developments as the rapid increase in population, the growing corruption and ineffectiveness of government, and the heightened antagonism between the Manchus and the Chinese and between the state and its Muslim population frequently shaped Qing policies.

In addition, many Westerners exploited China, but, perhaps as important, they disparaged its culture, its values, its government, and its institutions. Past invaders had been impressed with Chinese civilization. Although they may have set up a harsh and repressive rule, they did not depict the Chinese as backward and did not attempt to alter Chinese customs and values. However, Westerners denigrated the practice of bound feet, Chinese traditional medicine, Chinese standards of sanitation and health, and Chinese philosophies and religions. They criticized the educational system, which enshrined the seemingly rote civil-service examinations, because it did not prepare the Chinese with the tools (science, engineering, etc.) to progress. These analyses and critiques dealt a severe blow to Chinese cultural pride. A civilization with at least a four-thousand-year history of glorious accomplishments was now being ridiculed and its institutions and morality described as incompatible with the modern world. Yet these criticisms would develop gradually throughout the nineteenth century.

Meanwhile, China had to cope with defeats in the Opium Wars and the wars of 1856 and 1860. Many educated Chinese did not initially understand the dimension of the new Western threat. Several simply assumed that adoption of Western weapons, without other changes in the economy, organization, methods of work, and mores, would be sufficient to protect China and to compel the foreigners to relinquish their favored position in China. As China faced loss after loss in the mid to late nineteenth century, more sophisticated analyses and solutions would be proffered. However, before Qing officials devised more serious proposals for dealing with the foreigners, they faced major domestic disturbances and insurrections.

EXPLANATIONS FOR THE DECLINE OF THE QING

By the mid nineteenth century, China was no longer among the great powers. Defeated by Britain in the Opium Wars of 1839–1842, it also faced serious internal disturbances. At least four major rebellions had afflicted the dynasty by the early 1860s. The population had increased dramatically to over four hundred million people, creating great strains on agriculture and the available food supply. A bad harvest or a natural disaster could be catastrophic, leading to starvation and possibly famine. China's relatively rudimentary workshops and factories could not compete with many of the Western countries and their industrial revolutions. For example, the Qing did not have the arsenals and dockyards to produce advanced weaponry and ships. Without such sophisticated armaments, the dynasty was vulnerable in foreign conflicts. The decline of the Qing Banner forces, once one of the world's most powerful armies, exacerbated the court's difficulties. Corruption, inadequate weapons and supplies, demoralized soldiers, and lack of modern strategy and tactics had eroded the Banner forces' skills and competencies. It was no accident therefore that Russia encroached on China's northern territories and that Britain had a base in Hong Kong and had detached the Himalayan kingdoms from China. France had substantial interests in mainland Southeast Asia and southwest China. Later, Japan and Germany would make additional inroads on Chinese soil. Social relations had been disrupted. Overpopulation and poverty afflicted China, leading to migrations to towns or cities and even to foreign emigration. Overseas communities developed in Southeast Asia, as Chinese saw and seized possibilities for economic opportunities in neighboring lands. A few Chinese ventured to South America, especially to Peru to work in the mines.

Some Chinese migrated to the USA because of employment opportunities. They originally arrived during the California gold rush in the late 1840s and early 1850s. Later they labored on the Transcontinental Railroad. American workers began to resent Chinese competition, and anti-Chinese sentiments increased rapidly. The Chinese deflected some of this criticism by shifting employment to starting laundries and restaurants. Yet they still attracted hostility, especially after the declining economy that followed the US Civil War. After considerable lobbying by their opponents, the US Congress passed the

Chinese Exclusion Act of 1882, the first of several anti-immigrant laws directed at east Asians. The Act stipulated, among other clauses, that neither skilled nor unskilled Chinese workers would be admitted into the USA for the next ten years.

How did China reach such an impasse? Specialists on Chinese history have offered numerous, sometimes conflicting, answers to this question, although a few interpretations can be reconciled. One view is that the imperial system and the Confucian scholar-officials imposed restrictions on the activities and power of the merchant and entrepreneurial classes, blocking the development of industrialism and capitalism. Another is that the large population undercut the need for machinery, as there was sufficient labor to undertake farming. Moreover, China had to use land for food crops instead of nonfood crops that required machinery for processing. Technological development was limited by the imperative of feeding the ever-increasing population. Still another, and the most recent, explanation is based on the fact that the industrializing European nations, especially Britain, possessed coal and other natural resources for industrialization and garnered substantial profits from their colonies in the New World to supplement the capital available for investment. Thus, they underwent an industrial revolution earlier than China and could capitalize on their advanced military and industrial technology to impose a colonial system on the Chinese. A combination of all these factors perhaps helps to explain China's descent into chaos by the mid to late nineteenth century.

FURTHER READING

Pamela Crossley, *The Manchus* (Oxford: Wiley Blackwell, 2002).

David Hawkes, trans., *Story of the Stone: A Chinese Novel in Five Volumes* (Hammondsworth: Penguin, 1973–1986).

Philip Kuhn, *Soulstealers: The Chinese Sorcery Scare of 1768* (Cambridge, MA: Harvard University Press, 1990).

Ichisada Miyazaki, *China's Examination Hell: The Civil Service Examinations of Imperial China* (New Haven: Yale University Press, 1981).

Jonathan Spence, *Emperor of China: Self-Portrait of K'ang-hsi* (New York: Vintage, 1988).

[10] *Late Qing, 1860–1911*

T HE mid-nineteenth-century convulsions in many regions of China reflected the Qing government's decline and its inability to cope with economic, military, ethnic, and political problems. Faced with an ineffective government, local officials assumed some of its responsibilities, particularly through defense and military forces. These organizations were eager to maintain the peace but not to deal with some of the underlying problems, such as the exploitation and distress of the peasantry. The peasants' position did not improve, providing recruits for greater disturbances. Peasants who were dependent on proper maintenance of the Yellow River and the Grand Canal were particularly concerned

A History of China, First Edition. Morris Rossabi.
© 2014 Morris Rossabi. Published 2014 by Blackwell Publishing Ltd.

because the government's mishandling of these infrastructure projects harmed both agriculture and transport of farm produce to markets and consumers. A corrupt and ineffective bureaucracy, powerful local landlords and gentry, and a growing class of impoverished peasants created a volatile stage. As evidenced by the development of secret societies and the early-nineteenth-century White Lotus uprisings, poor peasants and many on the fringes of existence in the countryside needed only a spark to join an antidynastic movement.

NIAN AND OTHER MINOR REBELLIONS

The Nian, a curious group composed of poor peasants, gangs, and secret-society members, was among the first to seek the overthrow of the Qing. Unlike some of the other rebels, the Nian (the term for a specific dialect) did not adhere to any religion but was an antidynastic movement. Its major deficiency was its lack of centralized leadership. In 1851, a Nian rebellion erupted after floods on the Yellow River drowned masses of people, and a second flood in 1855 exacerbated the population's misery. The rebels would, on occasion, gather around a specific individual, but these alliances did not last long. Zhang Lexing (1810–1863) initiated the uprisings but, even after government troops killed him, the rebellion persisted. The Nian campaigns in Anhui, Henan, Jiangsu, and Shandong provinces, areas afflicted by the Yellow River floods, created considerable damage, and the Qing could not, at first, contain the rebels. Nian troops, boasting an excellent cavalry division and firearms, occupied a number of cities. Taking advantage of the Qing's preoccupation with the more important Taiping Rebellion, they gained control of locations in Jiangsu, a formerly prosperous province, and denied the government the area's rich tax revenues. However, the Nian forces harmed themselves by not establishing an administration to govern the regions they conquered, undermining regular relations with the local people, and instead alienating them by foraging for food on their lands. They appeared to be exploiters or criminal gangs engaged in marauding, raping, and destroying rather than offering relief from an oppressive government and elite.

Despite much Chinese antipathy toward them, the Nian were not easily suppressed. After Zeng Guofan (1811–1872) had crushed the Taiping, the Qing court ordered him to lead punitive expeditions against the Nian. He proved unable to defeat the Nian. Li Hongzhang (1823–1901) and Zuo Zongtang (1812–1885), two of Zeng's chief lieutenants, eventually organized the so-called Huai army and, using recently bought European weapons, finally crushed the Nian in 1868. The Nian's failures may be linked to its lack of an ideology and its inability or unwillingness to collaborate with the Taiping, which would have created a formidable force. This campaign was also the first of many crucial nineteenth-century events in which Li and Zuo would play vital roles. They were later among the dominant figures in late-nineteenth-century efforts at economic modernization and in relations with foreigners.

China's borderlands were similarly restive, but ethnic problems complicated the difficulties. The southwestern province of Yunnan was home to a variety of ethnic groups, some of whom the Qing had mistreated. Hui or Chinese Muslims were particular targets, and several Chinese campaigns from the 1830s to the 1850s had resulted in the killing of numerous Muslims. Early-nineteenth-century migrations of Chinese into Yunnan had also exacerbated tensions. Perceived exploitation and oppression erupted into the so-called Panthay Rebellion, which lasted from 1856 to 1873. Although animosities between the Chinese and the Hui played a role in the accelerating violence, minority ethnic groups who were not Muslims also joined in the rebellion. "Panthay," which derives from the Burmese term for Muslims, gives a misleading impression of the rebellion because it emphasizes only Muslim participation. In fact, Du Wenxiu (1823–1872), who became the leader of the rebellion and founded a so-called sultanate in the city of Dali, sought to attract the various non-Muslim peoples to his side. Recognizing that trade with Southeast Asia was vital for revenue, he cultivated the Tai, Yi, and other minorities who had links with the peoples in modern Thailand and Burma. Unity proved elusive, and he even had Muslim opponents – an indication that the rebellion was not simply a Muslim struggle against the Chinese and the Qing. On the other hand, some Chinese joined his cause, again challenging the view that the Panthay was exclusively a Muslim revolt. Defections by previous allies and a concerted Qing military effort turned the tide against Du and led to the collapse of his Dali sultanate.

The most significant of these revolts sprang from a new direction, a religion that had played only a minor role in Chinese history. Christianity, or at least a version of it, was the inspiration for the most devastating attack on the Qing. The rebels' knowledge of Christianity was actually limited, partly due to the lack of reliable information as well as a somewhat inaccurate translation of the Bible. The Christianity espoused by those opposed to the dynasty adapted parts of the religion that suited their political and social purposes. Recognizing that the rebels were not well aware of and not implementing what the Western missionaries perceived to be Christian principles, those missionaries eventually turned against the rebels. Similarly, Western officials and merchants concluded that the rebels simply used Christianity without being devout. The various rebel groups made decisions that were often counterproductive and translated into loss of support from foreigners and from potentially sympathetic Confucian officials.

TAIPING REBELLION

Hong Xiuquan (1814–1864) led the movement that offered the greatest challenge to the Qing. Born to a poor family of the Hakka, or guest peoples, who were classified as such because they had moved from north to south China, he aspired to an official career but failed the civil-service examinations three times. Bitterly frustrated, he looked for a scapegoat to explain his failures. At this very time, he was exposed to Christianity in his native province of Guangdong and especially in Guangzhou or Canton. Missionaries had arrived there as early as the 1830s, and Hong gained some knowledge of Christianity through simple pamphlets they had written to describe the rudiments of the religion. Christianity offered him a means of expressing dissent

303

and of identifying scapegoats. He had a dream or seizure that fused his two concerns. In his vision, he encountered a bearded old man, whom he identified as God, and Jesus, who told him to destroy the evil spirits who threatened Christianity. Hong referred to Jesus as his elder brother, implying that he too was a son of God and had now been entrusted with a mission to eradicate the demons, whom he identified as the Manchus. A fourth failure in the examinations and nothing to look forward to except a career as a teacher in countryside schools prompted him to take decisive steps to undertake his mission. His limited knowledge of Christianity notwithstanding, he started to explain its doctrines and to convert Chinese and Hakka and other minorities in the poverty-stricken province of Guangxi. He had fertile ground on which to propound his ideas, with a poor and largely uneducated populace who had grievances against both the local elites and the government. By the late 1840s, he had honed his message to identify the Manchu rulers as devils and the Confucian elite as abetting the Manchus and purveying a heretical philosophy. After a brief period of study with Issachar Roberts (1802–1871), an American missionary in Canton, he began to organize his Christian converts into a movement, the Society of God Worshippers, and to attack Confucian structures, be they ancestral shrines or temples.

The organization he and several charismatic followers devised was a curious blend of fundamentalism and utopianism. Yang Xiuqing (d. 1856) and Shi Dakai (1831–1863), important recruits, probably had as much influence as Hong in setting up a proper structure. They organized themselves in multiples of five into companies, squads, and battalions. Leaders of these units trained their forces, produced weapons, and attempted to inculcate an esprit de corps. Under this scheme, they were to ensure that all profits and wealth accrued to a Heavenly Storehouse and to divide land equitably. The amount of land allotted to families reputedly depended on their size. Once families were able to provide for themselves, the surplus produce would revert to the central organization. In theory, the surplus would be used in times of bad harvests or for others less fortunate. Similarly, the organization's policies toward women challenged traditional values. For example, unlike in many periods of Chinese history, women could own property, work in the fields, and serve in government. Hakka women were quite independent and did not approve of arranged marriages, adultery, concubinage, or prostitution and did not enforce the practice of bound feet; these factors influenced the rebels' policies. The rebel leaders lambasted Confucians and the Manchus for the restrictions they imposed on women. The leaders' emphasis on equality attracted many women, prompting the more enthusiastic to take part in combat. However, these ideas and values were not always implemented.

The rebels' fundamentalism also attracted adherents who despised what they believed to be the immorality of the times. The more educated converts also appreciated the rebels' critiques of the superstitions associated with Confucianism, including ancestor worship. Instead of Confucian examinations, the rebels initiated their own civil-service examinations that emphasized knowledge of the Bible and of Hong Xiuquan's writings. Yet the message of equality, which resonated with the majority of rebels, centered on destruction of an oppressive and evil government. The poor and powerless formed a natural constituency for the purported radical reorganization of society.

However, the leadership of this so-called Christian movement eventually turned out to be less supportive of change. Instead it set up a hierarchical structure that resembled the imperial system. As early as 1851, egalitarianism eroded. Hong proclaimed himself to be the Heavenly King of the Taiping Tianguo or "Heavenly Kingdom of Great Peace," which became abbreviated to Taiping. He also appointed other kings, including his early supporters, Yang Xiuqing and Shi Dakai. To many, he appeared to be reverting to a dynastic system. An indication of his dynastic ambitions was his granting of the title of "king" to his son Hong Tianguifu (1848–1864), whom the official sources portray as spoiled and indulged. Hong Xiuquan seems to have conceived of creating his own dynasty. However, his son was quite young when extraordinary responsibilities were thrust upon him. Spoiled and indulged or not, he could not assume his position at such a young age. Qing troops captured and executed him when he was only sixteen years old. The more equitable structure that Hong Xiuquan pledged to implement was also not fulfilled. His other social and economic policies were scarcely carried out. To be sure, wars against the Qing and Chinese forces and the ensuing chaotic conditions interfered with plans to adopt some of the more radical programs that he and other leaders proposed. However, there is considerable evidence that the policies they pursued did not jibe with or reflect the Taiping message – perhaps the principal reason for their failure to oust the Qing dynasty.

Hong Rengan (1822–1864), one of Hong Xiuquan's cousins, sought to stem the Taipings' decline. A Christian who had been exposed to Westerners, including employment as assistant to James Legge, a translator of the Chinese classical texts, he attempted to foster Western-style reforms and to promote a better image of Westerners among the Taipings. He supported the building of railroads, the establishment of banks, and the development of a more efficient and reliable central administration. Leaders who profited from the status quo opposed his reforms and prevented their implementation. Nonetheless, he persisted in advocating change until Qing forces captured and executed him during the last days of the Taipings.

The rebel Taipings devastated China for about fourteen years before they were finally suppressed by the Qing. They succeeded at first in the rural regions, and from 1850 on moved gradually north from Guangxi through Hunan. By 1852, they had actually raided and occupied towns and cities, culminating in the capture of Nanjing in 1853. South China, in particular, was devastated. With the pomp and circumstance that he professed to despise and that undercut his egalitarian ideology, Hong moved into the palace in which the first Ming emperor had resided. Nanjing became his capital and the northernmost city he and his forces occupied. They initiated forays farther north but were unable to hold substantial territories north of the Yangzi River. Even within the lands they subjugated, traditionally minded Chinese were chagrined by their practices, their seeming fanaticism, and their incessant demands for supplies and taxes. The Taiping egalitarianism simply vanished, undermining political support among the oppressed.

The Taipings' attacks on Confucianism deprived them of skilled officials who could have assisted them. Destruction of temples and shrines and repeated critiques of Confucianism alienated officials who might have sided with the rebels. Some of them had lost confidence in the Qing government because of its ineffectiveness and corruption. However, they would not join or serve a rebel group that challenged their most cherished values and social beliefs. They also suspected that the Taipings would not support a hierarchical social system, with the gentry in charge. Without such literate and skilled men, the Taipings did not have a sufficient number of able administrators who could help to establish a government with a regular tax and judicial system.

The Taipings also harmed themselves by their own fractiousness. Several of the kings considered themselves to be more competent than Hong, and Yang Xiuqing, in particular, opposed Hong's attacks on Confucianism. Yang believed that Confucianism could be a positive force. The struggle between them ended only when Hong's allies killed Yang in 1856. Repeated conflicts arose among the kings, leading to assassinations, pitched battles, and desertions. In addition, their inability to win over Western missionaries, diplomats, and merchants to their cause created considerable vulnerabilities. The missionaries concluded that the Taipings knew little about Christianity and represented a violent, power-seeking movement that used Christianity to justify pillaging and plundering. Western governments were determined to prop up the Qing government lest China fragment into chaos, which would harm their political and economic interests. Thus, individual Western military leaders actually assisted in the suppression of the Taipings. An American named Frederick Townsend Ward (1831–1862), who died fighting against the Taipings, and several American officers led a contingent of Chinese troops in battle against the rebels. Charles Gordon (1833–1885), a British officer who took part in the destruction of the Summer Palace in 1860 and was later killed in the Sudan, eventually commanded these soldiers, who came to be known as the "Ever Victorious Army" and helped to defeat the Taipings.

Yet fourteen years elapsed before the Qing suppressed the Taipings; only in 1864 did the government finally have sufficient manpower and resources to trounce the rebels. Since the middle of the nineteenth century, the Qing Banners had ceased to be an effective fighting force. That is, the central government's troops had been demoralized, afflicted by corruption, and lacking an esprit de corps. The court was thus compelled to rely on local Chinese officials who, faced with inadequate, if any, support from the Manchu Banner armies, had organized their own self-defense forces. These independent militias had a vested interest in protecting their lands from what they perceived to be Taiping "bandits." Thus, they had a stronger will to fight than the regular Manchu Banners. Zeng Guofan, an ardent and incorruptible Confucian from Hunan, organized the most renowned such personal army and was probably the most successful military commander in the anti-Taiping campaigns. Later Chinese leaders, including Chiang Kai-shek (1887–1975), admired and tried (some successfully and some not nearly so) to emulate Zeng. Zeng ensured that his troops knew what was at stake in the struggle against the Taipings, which generated a real esprit de corps. By 1864, these armies and militias had crushed the Taipings, but the Qing's difficulties had not ended.

Untold numbers of people had been killed during the battles between the Taipings and the Qing as well in the massacres that on occasion followed the fighting. Contemporary descriptions of the damage portray extraordinary devastation. Important historic sites were destroyed, leaving modern Chinese with few remainders of the past in the regions around Nanjing and the other battle sites. Both sides damaged property and land, contributing to the pauperization of the rural populations in their paths. Destruction of land led to famines, and the pollution of water and earth during the campaigns resulted in the spread of infectious and parasitic diseases. The beleaguered Qing government could do little to stem the environmental damage and the disease, and often local Chinese officials and governors, including Zeng Guofan, Li Hongzhang, and Zuo Zongtang, had to cope with the distress. Despite their efforts, appalling conditions in many parts of the country resulted in migration both within China and to foreign countries. Many people moved to Southeast Asia, and some traveled as far away as the USA and Latin America.

The way the Taipings had been defeated reinforced, rather than erased, suspicions about the Qing's competence and strength. The Qing, by itself, could not have crushed the rebels. Instead local militias, led by Chinese commanders, had been victorious and thus had considerable leverage in dealings with the government. These militias did not disband after defeating the Taipings and, in fact, assumed greater responsibilities in maintaining the peace in the countryside. The government was compelled to permit them to retain a tax on goods passing through their domains (known as a *likin*), which gave them funds to outfit their military forces. Their troops would need such equipment because rebel groups other than the Taipings challenged the Qing.

OTHER REBELLIONS

The northwest frontier proved to be even more unsettled, though the Qing court adopted a moderate policy. It attempted to foster the region's economic recovery after the devastation caused by the eighteenth-century conquest and instructed its officials to avoid interference with the local people's customs and religion. It also sought to collaborate with the *begs*, or native chiefs, in governing. However, the court was dependent on officials to implement these policies and found that it could not attract the most competent and honest personnel. Instead, many officials who traveled all the way to the relatively barren northwest, where they governed a mostly non-Chinese and Islamic population, attempted to enrich themselves. They demanded excessive taxation, allowed Chinese merchants to take advantage of the local people, and interfered with the practice of Islam.

Exploitation and anti-Muslim policies provoked disturbances and then rebellions along the northwestern border. Islamic religious leaders who maintained relations with coreligionists in central Asia and as far away as Yemen articulated a so-called New Teaching, based on a Sufi order of Islam, to galvanize the Muslim population against Qing overlordship. They advocated a loud chanting of God's name and a return to a form of Islam untainted by foreign influences. Rebellions under their leadership erupted in 1781, 1815, 1820, and 1847, and several years elapsed before the Qing pacified each of them. The central Asian Khanate of Kokand abetted the rebels because its merchants, who profited from an illegal northwestern border trade for Chinese tea and rhubarb, resented Qing restrictions on commerce.

The most destructive rebellion erupted in 1862 in the province of Shaanxi and then spread throughout the northwest. A commercial dispute between a Muslim and a Chinese merchant, flared up, leading to disturbances and massacres in both communities. Gansu, a province west of Shaanxi, witnessed the first organized revolts. By 1864, Ya'qub Beg (1820–1877), a military commander from Kokand, had arrived and became the rebel leader. Bellicose and authoritarian, he became, through manipulation and the use of draconian punishments, the dominant figure in northwest China, particularly in the modern region of Xinjiang. Adopting the title of "Athalik Ghazi" or "Champion Father," he set up a secret police force to ferret out dissenters to his harsh policies. He used fear of this force to induce merchants to pay for "police" protection and imposed stiff taxes on peasants. Naturally these policies alienated the populace and eventually undermined his rule. As a result, Ya'qub could not recruit many soldiers from Xinjiang and was compelled to rely on his Kokandian army, which then appeared to be an occupation force. Peasants, merchants, and other inhabitants, mostly Muslims but with some Chinese as well, suffered during Ya'qub's rule, and this should have facilitated Qing efforts to oust him from the region.

However, the Qing faced its own problems. Only after the government crushed the Taipings in 1864 could it turn its attention to the northwest. Even then, officials were divided about policy priorities. Li Hongzhang, who ultimately defeated the Nian rebels, believed that the government had to focus on preserving and defending the central core of Chinese territory, mostly along the eastern coast. He added that Xinjiang, which had been brought under Qing control only a century earlier, was a barren and unpopulated land, and had scarcely any economic value. China, he argued, ought to use its financial resources to develop a modern navy, which would be able to avert incursions on China's southeastern coastal areas. Zuo Zongtang, who had led troops against the Taipings, challenged Li, noting that China had never been invaded from the south or east and that nearly all raids and invasions had originated from across China's northern frontiers. He agreed that Xinjiang was not a promising domain but argued for his own domino theory: that is, if China abandoned Xinjiang, the rebels would be emboldened to initiate incursions in the nearby core territories in China's north and, if successful, would venture into the northeast as well. To avert this precipitous loss of territory, Zuo proposed a greater emphasis on army modernization and on recovery of Xinjiang. The court eventually supported Zuo, deciding that immediate preservation of land was more important than maritime defense.

Tsarist Russia's expansion into central Asia complicated Zuo's planned campaign in the northwest. In the eighteenth century, khanates in central Asia had prevented Russia from annexing the traditional heartland of the old Silk Roads, and their merchants, particularly those from Bukhara, had controlled commerce and often excluded Russian traders. The Russian government, under pressure to act on behalf of its commercial interests, gradually turned its attention to the region starting in the 1830s. By that time, both the predominantly nomadic Kazakh peoples and the various more sedentary khanates lacked unity and had not developed modern military forces or a modern economic system. Facing a fractured opposition, Russia targeted one group after another. Despite involvement in conflicts (such as the Crimean War) in other areas, Russian forces gradually defeated the Little Horde, Middle Horde, and Great Horde of Kazakhs by the late 1850s. They then moved quickly against the khan of Kokand, overwhelming Tashkent in 1865 and naming it the capital of Turkestan, the new region that supplanted the Khanate of Kokand. In 1868, they crushed the Khanate of Bukhara and occupied its major towns of Bukhara and Samarkand, and in 1873 they compelled the Khanate of Khiva to become a Russian protectorate. Russian merchants now had access, on an equal footing, to central Asian trade. The original economic objectives of expansion had been increases in commerce and incorporation of additional territory, but a new motive developed because of the civil war in the USA. Russia had been receiving most of its cotton from the US south, but the north's blockade of the south had temporarily cut off supplies. The lesson Russia learned from this crisis was that it needed to produce its own cotton. Its newly acquired lands in central Asia seemed ideal for growing cotton, but the decision to invade those lands proved catastrophic for the vast domain.

As Russia became increasingly drawn into central Asia, it developed a greater interest in the adjacent region of Xinjiang. China's weakness, as demonstrated in the Opium Wars, prompted Russia to capitalize on the Ya'qub Beg-led rebellion. Even before the rebellion, it had demanded opportunities for trade in Xinjiang, and the Qing, hoping to use Russia as a counterweight to Britain and France, had granted such commercial privileges, counting on the tsarist government to act as an advocate against the Western powers. This policy of "using barbarians to regulate barbarians," which China had developed as early as the Han dynasty, was ineffective as long as the Qing continued to deteriorate. China simply did not have the authority to demand that Russia resist British and French encroachments. The Qing permitted Russia to trade and to station consuls in the town of Kashgar yet denied those privileges to any other foreign power. Russian traders arrived in Xinjiang, but so did geographers, adventurers, explorers, and natural scientists, some of whom may also have worked for the intelligence services. Russia accumulated a vast storehouse of information, including precise maps and descriptions of critical locations in Xinjiang.

Increasing involvement in Xinjiang prompted Russia to react to the instability resulting from Ya'qub Beg's rebellion. Asserting that the chaos affected its central Asian lands, in 1871 the tsarist government sent troops to occupy Ili, in northern Xinjiang, but pledged that it would withdraw once the Qing restored order. The government in Beijing could not avert this brazen occupation, but Britain could voice its concerns. The British were the foreigners most distressed by the turn of events because they were engaged in a struggle with Russia known as the Great Game. Seeking to protect India, the crown jewel of the British Empire, they feared Russian expansion into central Asia. The Russian foray into Xinjiang also troubled the British because it offered the Russians a base for additional incursions into China. Yet at this point they could not argue with Russia's premise that chaos in Xinjiang threatened Russia's newly subjugated territories in central Asia. Lacking any counterbalance to the Russians, the Qing had no choice but to tolerate their presence in Ili. It needed to focus on suppressing Ya'qub Beg.

Zuo Zongtang, the commander in charge, recognized that victory required winning over the population (some of whom were ethnic Chinese) on his route to the northwest. Poverty and damage incurred during the various rebellions bedeviled the northwestern provinces of Shaanxi and Gansu. Some peasants had abandoned the land and others barely eked out an existence. Recognizing the parlous conditions in these provinces, Zuo was determined to foster the local economies before setting forth for the military campaign. His troops initiated irrigation projects, dug wells, planted trees, built roads and bridges, and fostered silk and cotton production. He encouraged the local population to start modern, mostly military enterprises, such as foundries and arsenals. In the late 1860s, after such economic reconstruction had begun to revive the northwestern economies, he led his troops forward. Despite the demanding desert terrain, he overcame resistance in Shaanxi by 1869 and in Gansu by 1871. Ya'qub Beg now began to show concern over his position. Having alienated the Muslim majority and the Chinese minority in Xinjiang through excessive taxation, autocratic rule, and intrusive and pervasive secret police forces, he unsuccessfully sought assistance from Britain and Turkey against Zuo. Without such foreign aid he was vulnerable, but he did not receive the foreign support. Meanwhile, Zuo used the same strategy in seeking to pacify Xinjiang as he had in Shaanxi and Gansu. After lengthy preparations, in 1876 he marched on Xinjiang and quickly captured the town of Urumchi, which had become the most important center in the region. By the following year, he had restored Qing control over nearly all of Xinjiang, and Ya'qub Beg had either committed suicide or been murdered.

The Qing court now confronted Russia. Building on its success in defeating Ya'qub Beg, it requested that the Russians withdraw from Ili and turn it back to Qing jurisdiction. Russian diplomats in Beijing demurred and sought to secure significant economic concessions in return. After considerable negotiations and misunderstandings, the two parties arrived at an impasse. Zuo, supported by belligerent officials at court, proposed a war to oust Russia from Ili. Less bellicose officials prevailed and succeeded in appointing Zeng Guofan's son Zeng Jize (1839–1890) to negotiate with the tsarist court. The Russians, for their part, were in a difficult position. They had devoted considerable resources to a victorious war with Turkey in 1877–1878, but British pressure had prevented them from gaining the warm-water port that they had sought on the Black Sea. Aside from their parlous financial condition, they faced domestic disturbances and challenges to autocracy and economic inequality, which led to the assassination of Tsar Alexander II in 1881. Naturally, Britain did not want Russia to annex Ili. Under such pressures, Russian diplomats met with Zeng Jize, a sophisticated diplomat who had represented China in France,

Britain, and Russia and knew English, and accepted a compromise in the Treaty of St. Petersburg in 1881. They agreed to withdraw from nearly all of Ili and from passes that threatened towns in southern Xinjiang in return for the establishment of consulates in Turfan (in Xinjiang) and other locations and for permission for Russian merchants to trade, without the imposition of taxes, permanently in Mongolia and for a limited time in Xinjiang. A disastrous war had been averted, but Qing China faced additional pressures on its border-lands.

FOREIGN THREATS

The breakdown of the Chinese world order, as exemplified by the tribute system of foreign relations and Chinese assertions of cultural superiority, and the ravages of the internal rebellions against the Qing court provoked a crisis. Foreigners, whom the traditional dynasties had considered to be "barbaric," had defeated China and appeared to be trampling upon the heritage of Chinese civilization, one of the longest-lived and most glorious of the world's cultures. Simultaneously, both Chinese and non-Chinese ethnic groups had challenged the Qing and sought to topple it. In some cases, a decade or more elapsed before the dynasty crushed rebel groups. The foreign wars and the internal convulsions shattered Chinese cultural assumptions and undermined the Qing's invincibility. Past dynasties had proclaimed that the Chinese civilization would last for ten thousand years. The heavy blows the Qing suffered in the mid nineteenth century seemed likely to contradict that confident prediction.

Making matters worse were the challenges to the Qing in its own homeland of Manchuria. At the outset of the dynasty, Manchu officials had planned to use Manchuria as an escape valve should they be forced to retreat from China. Therefore, they had forbidden Chinese immigration into the region in order to keep Manchuria untainted by Chinese civilization. This ban was relatively well enforced for the first half of the dynasty, but by the early nineteenth century Chinese merchants were evading the regulations, traveling to Manchuria, and trading silk, cotton, and grain for furs, ginseng, soybeans, and leather. At the same time, Chinese peasants, suffering from excessive taxation and natural disasters in the north, were crossing into Manchuria and buying land from the Banner forces.

The Russians quickly capitalized on the disruptions in the Qing system in Manchuria. Nikolai Muraviev, appointed governor-general of eastern Siberia after the Opium Wars, initiated an aggressive policy to take advantage of the Qing's weakened position in Manchuria. In 1854 and 1855, he deliberately transgressed upon the 1689 Treaty of Nerchinsk, which had delineated the boundary between Russia and China, by sailing down the Amur River and bringing settlers with him to set up colonies along its banks. The Qing authorities had no choice but to capitulate and sign the Treaty of Aigun in 1858, which turned over 158,000 square miles to Russia. Two years later, the Qing agreed to a Sino–Russian Treaty that added 100,000 square miles to the area granted to the Russians in the earlier treaty. In addition, Russia received trade concessions in Manchuria.

The tsarist court also challenged Qing domination of Mongolia. By the early nineteenth century, the Qing policy of preventing Chinese merchant trading companies from setting up permanent presences in Mongolia had failed. Chinese merchants readily crossed into Mongolia, took advantage of credulous herders and offered them loans at usurious rates of interest, and generally pauperized the country. Even the Mongolian elites fell into debt in order to buy Chinese luxury goods. Stiff taxes imposed upon herders by the Qing court and their own nobility added to the misery of many Mongolians. A few moved into towns but had limited economic opportunities, forcing many men into servile positions and some women into prostitution and concubinage. Buddhist monasteries, which the Qing supported because they preached nonviolence, were powerful and controlled much of the area's wealth. Although the monasteries helped to preserve Mongolia's art and literature and offered the most important formal educational structure and the only medical system, the elite monks dominated ordinary lamas and exploited workers and servants assigned to them by Qing officials. With the notable exception of Zanabazar (1635–1723), the first Bogdo Gegen (leader of the Buddhist establishment), most of the monks were oppressive and obscurantist. Zanabazar was an excellent sculptor and painter and a learned Buddhist scholar. Most of the remaining seven who held the title "Bogdo Gegen" through 1924 were undistinguished and not necessarily pious.

Noticing the instability in Mongolia and recognizing the possibilities for gaining a foothold in this vast neighboring domain, the nineteenth-century tsarist court encouraged Russian merchants to compete with Chinese merchants and set about to discover more about the country. Russian geographers, explorers, naturalists, and ordinary travelers began to arrive in Mongolia to map the country, to identify its flora and fauna, and to study its pastoral nomadic society. Nikolai Przhewalski (1839–1888) was perhaps the most renowned of these explorers, partly because he discovered one of the few remaining species of wild horses, which was then named after him. Other Russians wrote about the Buddhist monasteries, and still others offered vivid descriptions of countryside life. Russian merchants were not as successful as their scientist, traveler, and explorer compatriots. They were at a decided disadvantage. Fewer than three thousand of them ventured into Mongolia, while twenty thousand Chinese either lived or traveled through the country. The Russians settled in the capital whereas the Chinese merchants were willing to head to the steppe lands and the countryside, where they could obtain goods much more cheaply. Finally, Russian merchants came on their own and thus had less capital and fewer products than the Chinese, who often represented large firms or banks. Nonetheless, the Russian presence reflected a challenge to Qing domination of Mongolia.

Naturally, the court, officialdom, and civilian and military leaders reacted to these reversals at the hands of foreigners, as well as to the domestic insurgencies. Their responses differed considerably, and their prescriptions for changes or lack thereof would compete for the rest of the dynasty. The remaining decades of the nineteenth century and the first decade of the twentieth, until the Qing's collapse in 1911, witnessed one faction after another trying to dominate policy. This inconsistency weakened the court and simultaneously frustrated Westerners.

DIFFERING COURT RESPONSES TO CHALLENGES

One faction at court favored the adoption of Western technology in order to preserve Chinese culture. However, before China could do this, it needed to devise a suitable means of dealing with foreigners. China had never established a foreign office to deal exclusively with foreign states, kingdoms, or khanates. The Ministries of Rites and War and the Lifanyuan, which had been established in the Qing to deal with Mongolia and Russia, had been the principal agencies responsible for foreign relations, but they had other tasks that the court often perceived as more significant. In 1861, about two decades after the first Opium War and a year after the second, the Qing, under pressure from the Franco–British force that had occupied Beijing and had burned down the Summer Palace, was forced to sign the Convention of Peking. Prince Gong (1833–1898), the emperor's uncle, was compelled to stipulate the founding of a new foreign office known as the Zongli Yamen, which would eventually have access to international law in the form of the American W. A. P. Martin's translation of Henry Wheaton's *Elements of International Law*. The Qing did not necessarily abide by the book's precepts, but officials became aware of the Western system of international relations and recognized that they might ultimately have to subscribe to Western-style ways, which emphasized diplomatic parity. Foreigners also promoted the establishment of the Tongwenguan, a school for interpreters in Beijing. Students initially studied foreign languages, but by the late 1860s, under the leadership of W. A. P. Martin (1827–1916), who served as the school's president from 1869 to 1895, students were also studying science, "Western learning," and international law. Within a short time, such schools were also founded, with the acquiescence of Prince Gong and the court, in Shanghai, Fuzhou, and Guangzhou.

At the same time, the court sent young men abroad to study Western science and culture. Yung Wing (1828–1912), who received a BA from Yale and was the first Chinese to receive a degree from a foreign university, served as a model for the dispatch of students to Yale and other universities. In 1863, Zeng Guofan sent him to the USA to buy equipment for an arsenal. This shipyard, which became known as the Jiangnan Arsenal, built the first modern Chinese steamship in 1868 and also served as a center – led by an American named John Fryer (1839–1928), who eventually became a professor of Chinese at the University of California – for the translation of Western books on science. After considerable lobbying by Yung, in 1872 the government sent 120 students as part of the so-called Chinese Education Mission to study engineering and science in institutions in New England. However, by the end of the nineteenth century, most students who studied abroad were going to Japan because of its geographic propinquity and more familiar written language.

The dispatch of ambassadors to and from China as well as the creation of a Maritime Custom Service facilitated China's adoption of Western technology and ways. Foreign ambassadors streamed into China right after the second Opium War, and the Qing court sent an envoy to found its first embassy in Britain. At the same time, the Maritime Custom Service developed and collected fixed and regular tariffs, in part to pay the indemnities they owed after the wars with foreigners. Robert Hart (1835–1911), born in Northern Ireland and one of the early directors of the Service, proved to be exceptionally able and was sympathetic to China. He ensured that Chinese officials played a vital role in administration of the Service and did not relegate them to the position of clerks. To his credit, he placed the monies secured from the Service at the disposal of the Qing government to pay its debts to foreigners.

During the reign of Emperor Tongzi (r. 1862–1874), the first steps toward change took place. The leaders of military modernization set up arsenals and shipyards, mostly along the east coast. Fuzhou, Guangzhou, Shanghai, and Tianjin were among the sites selected for these new construction projects, which would bolster the country's defense capabilities. The schools linked to these arsenals and shipyards would train a few of the prominent figures of the late nineteenth century. Li Hongzhang, one of the leaders in suppressing the mid-century rebellions, founded a military arsenal at Tianjin to foster a so-called Self-Strengthening Movement, a term coined by Feng Guifen (1809–1874), a Chinese scholar-official. At the same time, Zuo Zongtang, another of the military leaders, established the Fuzhou dockyards to modernize the navy. Yan Fu (1854–1921), who eventually studied in Britain, translated English works on political thought, and became president of Beijing University, was, in part, educated in the Fuzhou school. It should be noted that he eventually joined the conservatives and supported a royalist government; many other reformers did not.

By the early 1870s, Li Hongzhang and other reformers recognized that military modernization was insufficient for the reforms required in China. The Self-Strengthening Movement, which originally focused on military modernization and the construction of shipyards and arsenals, spread almost inexorably into a drive for greater industrial development. Li himself began to recognize that guns, cannons, and ships were insufficient for China's defense. Beyond weapons, military uniforms were another necessity. An industrial infrastructure was also needed to ensure China's security. Trains, telegraphs, and merchant ships were essential in modern warfare.

Although the reformers understood the necessity of development, they formulated a hypothesis known as *tiyong* to justify their efforts. They identified *yong*, translated as "practical use," with the economic and military changes they sponsored and *ti*, translated as "essence," with the enduring Chinese culture. They sought to legitimize *yong* by emphasizing and actually stating that their ultimate goal was to preserve *ti*. They tried to assure the Chinese that the economic development they fostered would not undermine the fundamental nature of Chinese civilization. Yet they apparently did not realize that industrialization would result in social changes. More people would move into and live in cities; there they would work in factories or workshops, where lateness on an assembly line could not be tolerated; they would need to become literate to read instructions about equipment and myriad other responsibilities in their new workplaces; and they would require the development of new attitudes and values to cope with alienation from their native lands and families. At the very least, their perceptions of Chinese culture and civilization would be somewhat transformed.

Li Hongzhang's career embodied the reformers' ideals. Although he devoted much of his life to foreign policy, he also fostered military and economic modernization. Adopting a policy of so-called government supervision and merchant operation, he supported continuous industrial development. Naturally, he initially lobbied for industries that would make China more powerful, including armaments and coal mining. Yet he also supported the textile industry and a shipping company. He helped elicit subsidies for these firms, engineered monopolies and reduced tariffs for the most favored firms, and even played an active role in supervising some of them. In 1872, the state helped to found the China Merchants' Steam Navigation Company, which within a few years fostered the establishment of the Kaiping coal mines, the Shanghai cotton mills, and the Imperial Telegraph Administration. Nepotism, corruption, a dearth of technical skills and capital, conservative opposition, a hostile bureaucracy, and tax evasion hobbled these enterprises, yet they made some progress. By the 1880s, some private enterprises had developed without government supervision. Yet the pace of such change was nowhere near as fast as it had been in Britain, France, and other industrialized countries.

These undertakings were made, in the words of a biography of Yan Fu, "in search of wealth and power."[1] A more powerful China would be able to stave off the West and protect its indigenous culture. Some Western-educated leaders, influenced by a conception of the social Darwinism to which they were exposed in their studies abroad, believed that only the strongest civilizations could survive. Thus, they advocated military and industrial modernization, especially a strong navy, but not necessarily Western economic or political institutions. Nonetheless, the external influences, via education, journals, and books, created a climate in which the Self-Strengthening Movement had some successes.

Even this reform movement, which could not be labeled revolutionary, faced opposition, particularly at court. A contingent at court was adamant in its unwillingness to adopt any Western ways. Historians have often, fairly or unfairly, chosen the empress dowager Ci Xi (1835–1908) as the personification of such opposition. Ci Xi was principally interested in securing and retaining power and aligned herself with conservative forces by default. A concubine of Emperor Xianfeng (1831–1861), she gave birth to a son, which elevated her status at court. Through adroit manipulation, she ensured that her young son became the emperor in 1862. He was a sickly and weak boy, and was dominated by his mother, who became the true power behind the throne. A complex but decisive woman (unlike the stereotype of a typical female in traditional China), she has generally received a bad press in China. Chinese sources often portray her as unscrupulous and vindictive in her rise to power and accuse her of serious crimes, perhaps even murder. They also revile her policies and depict her as a major stumbling block to the reforms needed for modernization.

The most damning critique of Ci Xi involved her diversion of funds meant for naval modernization to rebuild the Summer Palace, which the Franco–British troops had destroyed in the second Opium War against China in 1860. As an ironic and oft-cited response to her critics, she built an immovable marble boat on the Summer Palace lake (which has endured as a major tourist attraction).

Figure 10.1 Empress dowager Ci Xi. © Mary Evans Picture Library / Alamy

Some historians believe, rightly or wrongly, that the lack of a fully modern navy later left China vulnerable in the Sino–Japanese War of 1894–1895. Literate and shrewd, Ci Xi's adeptness at court politics and her ruthlessness in dealing with opponents also generated severe criticism. For example, after her son's death in 1874, she maneuvered to have her young nephew placed on the throne, which offered her additional opportunities to dominate the court. She occasionally cooperated or allied herself with reformers and Chinese officials, including Li Hongzhang, and was not averse to reform, but her main preoccupations were siding with favorites and obtaining bribes from transactions to which she consented. One deficiency was lack of knowledge of Western technology and tradition, which caused her to be suspicious of the West. In turn, this attitude contributed to an image of her as a conservative opposed to reform. In any event, Ci Xi alone could not derail modernization.

Indeed, many at court and in the population at large looked askance at both the Westerners who arrived in China as well as the changes wrought by the Western presence. Traditionalists at court opposed the industrialization and modernization that gradually crept in to China, concerned that such developments would undermine their Confucian-based society. At the same time, ordinary Chinese were appalled by the intrusion of the Westerners, with their unusual dress, values, and interests, and by the appearance of new types of frightening weapons and technology. Eventually, they also objected to the evidence of industrialization in the country. They bided their time to act.

Simultaneously, the native economy was facing challenges. Continued population growth placed a burden on the arable land, and the poor and unfortunate were compelled to farm marginal land. Periodic droughts and natural catastrophes resulted in hunger and starvation, leading to social unrest, which, on occasion, bubbled up into attacks on foreigners and foreign technological innovations. Economic distress sometimes prompted leaders of dissidents to blame foreigners for parlous conditions. It is true that foreigners and foreign goods had, to a certain extent, affected the Chinese agrarian economy. As China was drawn into the global economy, it faced stiff competition in areas where it had been supreme. British textiles and Ceylonese and American tobacco cut into China's share in the world market for these commodities and even began to supersede local production. However, international competition and colonial relations with foreigners did not, by themselves, generate the increasing pauperization of the population. Social and economic inequality contributed at least as much, if not more, to peasant poverty. Many peasants fell into increasingly greater debt, despite (for example) attempts by women to use their skills at weaving to earn a wage in order to shore up their household's survival. Poor peasants and poor urban dwellers, who were frustrated by their economic instability, blamed foreigners for their problems.

ANTIFOREIGN ACTS AND FOREIGN REACTIONS

Several notorious incidents created considerable tension between the Chinese and Westerners. In 1870, a French consul in Tianjin, enraged by Chinese officials' support for anti-Catholic stories about nuns kidnapping and either harming or murdering Chinese orphans, stormed into a magistrate's office, fired his revolver, and inadvertently killed an innocent observer of the scene. In turn, a crowd of Chinese killed the consul and the nuns and then destroyed the nunnery. The French government demanded that the court punish those responsible for the so-called Tianjin Massacre, and the Qing authorities complied by executing over a dozen men, some of whom may have been innocent. Later a British consul named Augustus Margary (1846–1875) was killed in southwest China. Although the Qing court had absolutely no connection to the murder, the British demanded and received, via the Chefoo Convention, compensation in the forms of a substantial payment, the opening of four additional ports to trade, and an embassy dispatched to apologize to Queen Victoria.

There were other less reported incidents until the Boxer rebellion in 1900 (discussed below), which involved Western missionaries. Both Catholic and Protestant clerics, representing a variety of Christian sects and orders from many Western countries, had arrived in China even before the first Opium War, but the British victory resulted in an onrush of missionaries. Most arrived with a sincere desire to convert the Chinese to what they perceived to be a truer religion and to introduce other elements of Western culture to China. Some, however, adopted condescending attitudes toward Chinese culture while also enjoying appurtenances (such as amahs, servants, and a luxurious lifestyle) that they could have not dreamed about in their native lands. Such denigration of Chinese culture elicited harsh reactions from the Confucian elite, who were genuinely distressed by the perceived attack on their traditional culture. They were also concerned about the missionaries' challenge to the elite's status in Chinese society. Thus, some in the elite gave credence to outlandish rumors such as that mentioned above concerning the supposed kidnapping and brutal treatment of Chinese children in nunneries and churches.

Although the missionaries' ultimate goal was to convert the Chinese to Christianity, they contributed significantly to Chinese society in other ways. They started the first modern periodicals, founded schools with a Western curriculum, established schools and colleges for girls, introduced modern medicine (via clinics and hospitals), and translated classical Chinese texts into Western languages. In short, they exposed the Chinese to Western ideas, technology, and culture, not simply Christianity. Their schools taught secular subjects as well as the Bible and various Chinese texts. Together with secular organizations, they encouraged and sponsored capable students to study in the West. They also produced dictionaries and language texts to facilitate study of the Chinese language. A small minority traveled into the hinterlands and offered the first Western-language descriptions of rural conditions among non-Chinese ethnic groups. Marshall Broomhall and Isaac Mason, for example, provided valuable reports about the Islamic peoples in China, a subject barely known in the West.

All of these were worthy contributions, but Chinese conservatives often associated missionaries with the exploitation of China and with promoting the advent of Western-style industrialization in China – a heinous crime in their eyes. The missionaries' most resented activity was their attempt to provide special benefits for Chinese converts to Christianity. They secured both legal and extralegal privileges for Chinese Christians, and many Chinese came to resent both the Chinese Christians and the missionaries.

The missionaries themselves had a very different experience from that of the seventeenth-century Jesuit missionaries who came to China. Because the Jesuits had dealt with the elite, they had had a favorable impression of Chinese culture and society; at the time, the Qing had been at its height, and had therefore impressed the foreign clerics. The Jesuits and the Confucian scholar-officials had shared a love of learning and a support for proper behavior. Even the Qing emperors were comfortable with the Jesuits, and vice versa.

Conversely, the nineteenth-century missionaries, mostly Protestants, met with ordinary people and only a small group within the elite. They encountered less sophisticated and sometimes illiterate Chinese. Perhaps as important, they failed to recognize the stresses and hardships the Chinese faced as a result of the turbulence in the country. Several thousand years of Chinese civilization had been challenged. Confucian values and Chinese attitudes toward foreigners and foreign states were all brought into question. Some Chinese feared that China could not survive in the new, more threatening world. Protestant sects and missionaries traveled into China's interior and sought influence over ordinary people and were perceived as a great threat. Christianity appeared to represent turbulence both in the cities and in the countryside. The Chinese abhorred chaos, and they associated Christianity with the Taiping rebels and the Western encroachment on China. Thus, they distanced themselves from the missionaries, who made relatively few converts and wound up dealing with Chinese whom they perceived to be uneducated and unsavory. The missionaries' characterizations of the Chinese were inaccurate, but they shaped the condescending attitudes of some missionaries toward the Chinese.

By the mid 1870s, China was under considerable pressure. Although it had suppressed the major domestic insurrections and turmoil, it confronted a growing population, peasants suffering from landlord exploitation, stiff taxes, and repeated natural disasters exacerbated by poor maintenance of environmental safeguards. Some peasants, despondent due to their inability to sustain themselves, turned to banditry; others became heavily indebted to landlords or usurers; and still others migrated to cities or towns, where they either found jobs in the newly developing enterprises or barely eked out an existence. Westerners intensified the pressure on China as they encroached upon its territory, with each country seeking influence on specific provinces or regions. The British, French, and Russians had already staked their claims. Britain detached Bhutan, Sikkim, and Nepal from alleged Chinese jurisdiction and sought influence or domination in China proper; France successfully challenged Chinese claims to modern Vietnam, Laos, and Cambodia, as well as southwestern China; and Russia annexed lands all across China's northern frontiers. Other powers would soon join in the attempt to capitalize upon China's weakness.

LOSSES IN SOUTHWEST CHINA

Conflict erupted with France, which sought control especially over Vietnam. Ironically, the Chinese had attempted to dominate Vietnam since the Han dynasty. They had attacked in the Tang and had actually annexed the country from 1406 to 1427, during the Ming dynasty. After the withdrawal of Ming forces, the Later Li dynasty (1428–1789) was founded, and then during the late Qing the Nguyen dynasty (1802–1945) governed the country. Yet Vietnam followed a Chinese model. Like the Chinese, the Vietnamese had set up a civil-service examination, the successful candidates of which staffed the bureaucracy. Buddhism, which had also spread to Vietnam from China, had been a vital spiritual force, which affected secular life as well. Yet centralized control proved elusive because of poor transport and communications, divisions between a more sophisticated north and a less well developed and poorer south, a tremendous disparity in income between the wealthy elite and much of the peasantry, and a variety of different ethnic groups who did not necessarily identify with the state, the dynasty, or each other. Such disunity plagued the Nguyen dynasty and facilitated the efforts of rapacious foreign states to dominate the country.

Napoleonic-era France had expansionist impulses not only in Western Europe and Russia but also in Southeast Asia. French merchants, advisers, and missionaries began to arrive in Vietnam in the early nineteenth century. The missionaries had greater success in Vietnam than in China, and Catholicism spread rapidly among the elite and commoners. Fearful about the growing number of conversions to Catholicism, the Nguyen dynasty cracked down on missionaries and Vietnamese converts. However, the government was ineffective against French incursions. By the mid 1870s, France had signed treaties that allowed it to dominate in South Vietnam and in modern Cambodia. Nationalists in North Vietnam pivoted against France, which responded by occupying both Hanoi and Haiphong in 1882. The Nguyen court appealed to the Qing for assistance. Li Hongzhang, the chief foreign-affairs statesman for the Qing, wanted to negotiate for a peace settlement, but the court opted for conflict with France. The Qing navy was no match for the French ships, which approached Fuzhou on China's southeast coast and sank about a dozen Chinese vessels without losing a single one of their own. The Qing forces were able to defeat the French on land in southwest China. However, news of their victories did not reach the Qing court in Beijing until after a peace agreement had been concluded. Under this arrangement, the Qing relinquished its claim to Vietnam, which became part of the colony of French Indochina. Within a decade, the French added Cambodia and Laos to their growing domain in Southeast Asia. Meanwhile, in 1885, the British established a protectorate over Burma. Siam proved to be the only Southeast Asian country to preserve its independence.

JAPAN EMERGES

Japan was, from the Chinese perspective, the most surprising of the foreign countries to take advantage of the Qing's decline. After Japan was opened up to foreign contact by US commodore Matthew Perry in 1854, different factions in the country debated its future course. In 1868, reformers took power and ousted the Tokugawa Shogun. The emperor moved from the ancient capital of Kyoto to Tokyo and ushered in the Meiji Restoration, named for the title of his reign. Claiming that they were merely restoring the emperor as head of state rather than initiating a revolution, the reformers skillfully and swiftly guided Japan toward modernization. They developed a modern army and navy to replace the samurai class; allegedly dispensed with the Confucian four-class structure of samurai, peasants, artisans, and merchants; and emphasized a new form of nationalistic Shinto to legitimize their reforms. At the same time, they sent a mission, under the leadership of Iwakura Tomomi (1825–1883), to study and then select the best Western institutions upon which to model their own modernized structures. They examined the West's militaries, social and economic organizations, technologies, legal codes, and educational systems and chose the optimal forms for Japan. About sixty students accompanied the mission, and some remained behind to study at Western educational institutions.

Within a short time, the centralized leadership of reformers had propelled Japan into an increasingly industrial economy. Its navy, in particular, had been enormously strengthened. China, which had barely begun to build modern ships and to train naval commanders in modern warfare, was at a decided disadvantage. When a crisis erupted in 1874–1875, this lack of a powerful navy forced China to accede to Japanese wishes. Japan claimed the Ryukyu Islands, which had sent tribute to China and was considered a Qing vassal state. The resulting dispute between China and Japan was resolved peacefully: with the threat of violence hanging over them, Qing diplomats agreed that Japan had special interests in the islands. This was Japan's first victory, but the Japanese would later make even more demands on the Qing, leading ultimately to war.

SINO–JAPANESE CONFLICT

The most devastating blow to the Qing came from Japan's expansionist efforts. From the 1870s, the Meiji reformers had been eager for a base on the Asian mainland. Japan needed a reliable source of mineral and natural resources for an industrial economy and it lacked such supplies within the country itself. The Asian mainland, especially China, provided a huge potential market for Japanese finished goods, or so the Meiji reformers believed. Concerned also that Japanese population growth would soon outstrip the resources and land available in the four main Japanese islands, they sought nearby lands in which to settle the excess population. Manchuria satisfied all these requirements: it had valuable resources, it could form a base from which to approach and access the Chinese market, and it was a relatively underpopulated region as a result of Qing efforts to preserve the Manchus by closing the area to Chinese settlers from the seventeenth century on.

Korea was an intermediary step toward Manchuria. Yet nineteenth-century Korea had energetically attempted to exclude foreigners and had earned the epithet "Hermit Nation." The long-lived Yi dynasty (1392–1910) had successfully kept most Westerners out of the country, but it failed to cope with domestic inequalities and the ensuing disturbances. Throughout the nineteenth century, considerable turbulence had been created by stiff taxes on peasants, the limited size of peasant holdings in comparison with huge landlord estates, and the fact that a large percentage of peasants did not own land but rather farmed the land of landowners. A reform movement in the 1860s sputtered to a halt; it neither altered the domestic issues nor opened the country to foreigners.

Japan was determined to change Korea's attitude toward the world. Following its success in challenging China's claim to the Ryukyu Islands, Japan almost immediately set about asserting itself in Korea. In 1876, it opened Korea's doors by signing a treaty that initiated regular relations with the Hermit Nation and secured access to three ports for commerce. However, China still laid claim to Korea, despite Korea's independent signing of a treaty. Meanwhile, Japan persisted in its missions to detach Korea from

Chinese suzerainty and to make it a dependency. Violence and revolts in Korea facilitated Japanese efforts. In 1884, the Korean king and the rebels called for military assistance from both China and Japan. Each sent troops, and a confrontation seemed imminent. Li Hongzhang prevented a war by signing an agreement with the Japanese that appeared to pave the way for a long-lasting peace. Each side pledged to withdraw its forces and to notify the other if, at the Korean king's request or by its own decision, it dispatched armies to Korea. This understanding seemed to create a mechanism for stability. The Qing then appointed a Chinese Resident to represent its interests in Korea and to confirm its fleeting special claims in the Korean court.

However, appearances were deceptive, partly because of domestic outbreaks in Korea. The Tonghak movement, based upon a murky blend of Buddhist and indigenous beliefs and practices, had developed by the middle of the nineteenth century and added adherents over the decades as it protested against domestic exploitation and corruption and the court's acquiescence to foreign countries. Its invocation of political discontent caused the Korean government to ban the movement and provoked a rebellion, which gained traction due to parlous economic conditions. The Korean king sought assistance from China to crush the rebellion, and the Qing dispatched a force and informed Japan of its intention to do so. Unwilling to be left out, Japan itself sent troops, who turned out to be more effective than the Chinese forces. They reached the king's palace and captured the king and queen, an action that demanded a response from the Qing. It could not stand idly by while its perhaps closest "vassal" was in such danger. Li Hongzhang ordered that additional troops be sent to Korea and mobilized China's relatively few modern ships.

The conflict seemed to be a colossal mismatch. A struggle between China (traditionally one of the world's great empires, with a sizable population and abundant resources) and a group of four islands (with a population a seventh or an eighth of that in the reputedly powerful state across the sea) appeared to be no contest. Most Chinese had perceived of the Japanese as students who modeled their culture and institutions on those of China. They considered Chinese civilization to be superior and Japanese civilization to be a pale imitation. However, a few Chinese recognized that Japan had made a tremendous surge forward with the onset of the Meiji Restoration. Turning to the Western model of industrialization, Japan had created a powerful military force with a strong esprit de corps while Qing armies had scarcely been bolstered and wallowed in corruption and poor morale.

The Sino–Japanese War and the resulting treaty did not turn out gloriously for China. Japanese troops readily overwhelmed the Chinese force in Seoul and then headed north into China. The Japanese navy virtually demolished the outmatched northern Chinese navy, compelling the Qing court to seek peace within a year of the onset of hostilities. The Treaty of Shimonoseki in 1895 turned out to be a cause of national humiliation for China. The Qing was forced to abandon any claims to control over Korea, which it subsequently recognized as an independent country. It had to pay an indemnity for Japanese losses during the short-lived war and to open additional ports for trade. Japan also gained control over Taiwan and the Pescadores. The treaty granted the Liaodong peninsula to Japan, but Russia (fearful that Japanese annexation might threaten its own interests in Manchuria) and Germany and France (concerned about Japan's increasing power in east Asia) compelled the Japanese to abandon that provision. Finally, Japan elicited a most-favored-nation clause in the treaty, placing it on a par with the Western countries. Japan's image in the world had been bolstered while China's place had deteriorated.

In the fifty or so years since China's defeat in the first Opium War, it had become a virtually powerless giant. China, which had been the dominant force in east Asia since the Han dynasty, had now been bypassed and seemed a spectator, not an active participant, in developments. Japan had inherited China's status and, in doing so, had revealed ever more clearly the Qing's weakness. Westerners now concluded that if Japan, a minor Asian land in their view, could decisively overwhelm China, then they would not face considerable opposition in staking greater claims to the East.

SCRAMBLE FOR CONCESSIONS AND US RESPONSE

Such logic drove the so-called scramble for concessions. One after another, foreign powers sought both special economic privileges and political influence in various regions in China. Germany, which had been virtually excluded from the colonial expansion in Asia and Africa, now attempted to compensate by asserting itself in Shandong province. Under the agreement it negotiated with the Qing, Germany leased land in the province and received mining and railroad rights. A tangible German influence was seen in the establishment of breweries; Tsingtao, the most popular beer in overseas Chinese restaurants in modern times, was originally produced in the German concession. Russia and France obtained leases on harbors. The tsarist court, with its fixation on warm-water ports, received Port Arthur on the Liaodong peninsula, and France opted for Guangzhou Bay in the south, where its interests lay. The powers went even further, demanding that China not relinquish specific regions to any other countries. The Japanese, for example, claimed privileges in Fujian province right across the sea from Taiwan, which it had detached from China. Britain received a similar guarantee for the Yangzi River region, as did Russia for Manchuria and France for Chinese regions adjacent to Indochina.

This apparent dismemberment of the country worried some foreigners because they feared that their companies and businessmen would be excluded from the various concessions. The USA, which had not participated in the scramble for concessions, sought to play a role in east Asia, but the other powers seem to have locked it out. The US Secretary of State John Hay responded by sending two letters to the powers, which articulated what came to be known as the Open Door Policy. The letters emphasized the concept of free trade in the concession areas for all powers, not simply the dominant country, and affirmed support for the Qing dynasty and its continued rule over China. Economic self-interest in the USA dictated the creation of the Open Door Policy, not idealism or an attempt to protect China, as is often portrayed in

US history textbooks. The USA wanted to maintain commerce, on favorable terms, with China, and the Open Door Policy, if implemented, would secure its position in this trade.

CHINA HUMILIATED AND THE REFORMERS

Defeat in the Sino–Japanese war and the ensuing scramble for concessions among the powers were devastating blows to Chinese prestige and self-image. Patriotic Chinese were shocked not only by the loss to Japan but also by the great powers' continual encroachment on Chinese territory. China had been laid low by a country it traditionally perceived as imitative of Chinese culture and by Western barbarians. Some nationalists blamed the Manchus while others were appalled by the corruption and the deterioration of Confucianism. They bristled and expressed displeasure with Western influence, in the form of banks and companies in the port cities and in the activities of compradors (Chinese who acted as agents for the Western firms). They believed that a reaffirmation of the past and a return to Confucian principles and values were the only means of staving off the decline and disappearance of Chinese culture.

Yet a few Chinese opted for change and reform. Some had been trained in classical Confucianism and passed the civil-service examinations but had begun to question the relevance of the traditional ways and patterns. Paradoxically, Kang Youwei (1858–1927), probably the most renowned of these reformers, actually used Confucianism to legitimize his philosophy. Using his comprehensive knowledge of Confucian texts, he argued that Confucius believed in change to meet changing circumstances. Confucius would not have sided with the conservatives who opposed change and claimed to be the upholders of Confucian beliefs. Kang had not adopted the fervent anti-Manchu attitudes of some reformers, and he apparently believed that the Qing rulers could be persuaded to move in a new direction. Thus, he did not advocate the dynasty's overthrow and would, in Western terms, be considered a constitutional monarchist. His own ideas smacked of utopianism – a wish for a more egalitarian society – but his advice to Emperor Guangxu (1871–1908) was pragmatic and reflected the moderate reforms championed by the *tiyong* group (which, as mentioned above, advocated protecting the essence of Chinese culture but making use of foreign innovations). His young student Liang Qichao (1873–1929) joined him in his appeal to the emperor. Like some of the other reformers, Liang was also concerned about the roles of women. He believed that women should be offered employment, and also asserted that women should become literate so that they could be better teachers for their children.

By the late Qing, women were becoming more active in demanding rights, although there were considerable setbacks. Demands for the abolition of arranged marriages complemented the campaign against foot binding. The number of girls' schools increased, and education provided a vehicle for greater activism. Qiu Jin (1875–1907) represented the era's feminism and activism. Married with two children, she went alone to study in Japan. On her return, she started a feminist magazine that promoted women's rights. In essays and poetry, she urged women to work so that they could have their own independent incomes. At the same time, she joined secret societies and groups intent on overthrowing the Qing dynasty. The authorities discovered a revolutionary plot with which she was associated and arrested and beheaded her. Despite the efforts of Qiu Jin and other feminists, women did not have the right of divorce and had few, if any, property rights. They also had scant recourse in cases of domestic violence and adultery. Families, husbands, and in-laws could, in theory, sell girls into prostitution or servanthood.

Meanwhile, on the basis of the crisis of the scramble for concessions and the threat of the dismemberment of China, and also on the advice of Kang Youwei and other reformers, the emperor issued a series of edicts from June to September of 1898 to change the Qing. These "Hundred Days of Reform" consisted of practical changes, with scant assertion of ideological or more overarching doctrines. First, the reforms altered the kinds of government officials the Qing would recruit by mandating a new civil-service examination. Instead of emphasizing evaluation of the candidates' knowledge of the Confucian classics, the examinations would consist, in large part, of questions concerning practical problems that officials might encounter. Similarly, schools and institutes that trained specialists for jobs in the industrial economy would be established, and the curriculum for a university in Beijing would principally be based on Western science, technology, and medicine. The emperor also founded, for the first time in Chinese history, government offices to foster industry and commerce and to produce exports. Instead of using pronouncements and maxims on morality or general policies, the emperor concentrated on very practical matters. He was similarly pragmatic in his approach toward developing a modern army and navy. New weaponry and warships would be manufactured, and at the same time a more sophisticated and disciplined training regimen would be initiated. These reform proposals were down to earth, without any of the grandiose sentiments expressed in Confucian texts.

Yet the emperor and the reformers were naïve. They scarcely sought political and military allies until the very last of the Hundred Days. In September, they contacted military commanders, belatedly hoping to attract the physical force they required to stave off the opposition, which appeared to be mobilizing against the reformers. However, these attempts to recruit military commanders offered the conservatives a pretext for action against the reformers. The empress dowager, with the support of the powerful military commander Yuan Shikai (1859–1916), quickly engineered a coup d'état against her nephew, the emperor, who remained under virtual house arrest for the next ten years. Her agents seized and executed six prominent reformers, though both Kang Youwei and Liang Qichao escaped and fled the country. They would continue to write and their views would continue to evolve, but they would not again play a political role. However, Liang, based mostly in Japan, would propagandize and influence the Chinese students in Japan, who constituted the largest number of overseas Chinese students and a few of whom would play important roles in twentieth-century Chinese history.

The crushing of the reformers who inspired the Hundred Days of Reform had profound implications. Conservatives, flush with victory, began to develop an exaggerated view of their power and of their attempts to reaffirm traditional values. They concluded that, if they acted in concert, they could even tame the foreigners. An antiforeign movement could conceivably overcome the so-called foreign devils. On the other side, some of the reformers concluded that the Qing dynasty would never agree to sharing power or to instituting changes in political life and the economy. Compromise with the dynasty was precluded because of its unreliability and its betrayals during the Hundred Days of Reform. The only alternative was overthrow of the imperial system, for it could not be trusted to embrace change.

BOXER MOVEMENT

An antiforeign movement, which started outside the court but was subsequently assisted by the Qing, erupted first. Along with bitterness toward foreigners, economic deprivation contributed to the movement and instigated part of the violence. The poor and, to a certain extent, the court elite blamed foreigners for their miserable conditions, which were exacerbated by floods and the resulting chaos, famine, and starvation in Shandong, the province the Germans wanted to claim in the scramble for concessions. Religious conflicts

Figure 10.2 *Too Many Shylocks*, 1901, color litho, Pughe, John S. (1870–1909). Private Collection / © Look and Learn / The Bridgeman Art Library

A Group of Chinese Boxers.

Figure 10.3 A group of Chinese Boxers. Artist: Ogden's Guinea Gold Cigarettes. London, The Print Collector. © 2013. Photo The Print Collector / Heritage-Images / Scala, Florence

added to the turmoil. Catholic missionaries laid claim to a temple in Shandong that native inhabitants said belonged to them. A local court sided with the Catholics, which embittered the local Chinese population.

The secret society known as the Boxers (*Yihequan*, or "Righteous and Harmonious Fists"), which opposed Western influence, was the most prominent group in this antiforeign movement. The Boxers, composed principally of poor peasants but including many on the fringes of the rural and urban areas, were disturbed by poverty and the rising force of Christianity, as well as the Western innovation of railroads, which pounded on the earth and generated tremendous noise, disturbing and allegedly damaging the ancestors' graves as well as ordinary housing. They were also enraged that the railway lines cut across traditional farming plots, that the land adjacent to the tracks was unusable for agriculture, and that people and livestock crossing the tracks were jeopardized and some actually killed. Characterized by specific rituals and symbols, training in the martial arts, and claims of supernatural powers, the Boxers were subverted by a belief that Western weapons could not harm their adherents, who were supposedly immune to bullets and swords. This assertion brings to mind Mao Zedong's later observation that the atomic bomb was a "paper tiger." Each reflects a concept of self and its power to deflect seemingly harmful objects. The Boxers were to pay heavily for this misconception. Many contemporary communist historians have praised the Boxers and have portrayed them as anti-imperialists who simply did not have the ideological sophistication and leadership to succeed. They have tended to downplay the Boxers' violence and fierce antiforeignism. Despite their conservatism, the Boxers recruited women to their cause and employed them to obtain intelligence information, among other responsibilities. The Red Lantern group consisted of young women, the Blue Lantern of middle-aged women, and the Black Lantern of elderly women.

The Boxers reacted violently to the Western presence in China, using their rigorous training in the martial arts. In 1900, their first step entailed opposition to the Catholics' expropriation of a temple in Shandong. They then damaged or destroyed railroad tracks and telegraph lines and any other items that smacked of the West. They also killed Chinese Christians, and murdered the envoy from the German Empire on June 20, 1900. The province of Shanxi, which was plagued by a drought and the ensuing disturbances, was the site of the so-called Taiyuan Massacre, in which thousands of Chinese Christians were murdered. The most renowned Boxer campaign was the siege of the foreign legations in Beijing from June 20 to August 14 of 1900. The Boxers' initial successes prompted the Qing and the empress dowager Ci Xi to support them and to appoint officials to command them, but they would not accept court leadership. They surrounded the foreign quarters but did not break through and did not elicit the legations' surrender. In short, they were disorganized, and no charismatic leader arose to unite the disparate Boxer groups. The inordinate length of the siege permitted the foreign states to organize a relief effort. Britain, Germany, the USA, Russia, France, Japan, Italy, and the Austro-Hungarian Empire raised an army of about fifty thousand to lift the siege. Starting with a victory in Tianjin, the army headed toward Beijing. On August 14, it entered the capital and defeated the Boxers, many of whom fought with rudimentary weapons, believing themselves to be invulnerable to Western bullets, only to learn that they had erred.

The foreign states held both the Boxers and the court responsible for the antiforeign attacks. By blaming the Qing, foreign powers could demand concessions. In September of 1901, they compelled the court to sign a Boxer Protocol, which forced the Qing to execute a number of officials, to suspend the civil-service examinations in a number of provinces, and (perhaps most important) to pay reparations for the losses foreigners had allegedly incurred. China had to make such payments until 1939. The USA used its portion of the reparations to provide scholarships for Chinese students. Discovering that few Chinese candidates knew English, the USA started an English Institute to instruct students in the language. The Institute eventually turned into Tsinghua University, a full-fledged educational organization. Despite this specific benefit, the humiliation of paying reparations was damaging for the Qing's pride and image. The indemnities were also sizable, exacerbating the chronic financial problems of the Qing court. Many Chinese now turned against the government, while foreigners began to distrust the court. Foreign states, which earlier might have supported the Qing for fear that its collapse would lead to chaos and endanger their economic interests, now were less willing to bolster the court.

Court Reforms

Responding to its failures and to renewed pressure, the Qing court rapidly made concessions. In 1902, it forbade the practice of foot binding – certainly a useful means of gaining the attention and support of Westerners in China. In the same year, it permitted the founding of *Nübao* (*Women's*), the first women's magazine. Within a the next year, it established ministries of commerce and foreign affairs to foster modern trade and modern international relations. Two years later, it abolished the civil-service examinations, the main source for recruiting officials for at least a thousand years, if not longer. This date (1905) and this decisive step could be said to be the beginning of modern China. The civil-service examinations had been central to the Confucian system. Abolition of this institution, as well as the ensuing impact on government, signified a dramatic change in Chinese civilization. Military commanders, business leaders, and doctors and other professionals could compete for power, and could challenging the traditional relationship between the scholar-officials (who passed the examinations and earned government positions) and the imperial court. The new groups, which were still heavily weighted toward the elite because they were more likely to offer a modern education to their children, sought a clear, written demarcation of powers in government. That is, they would not accept a monarch, with absolute and unrestricted authority, and were eager to share power. Studying both the West and Japan, they demanded a legislature and a constitution. The court reluctantly gave in and sent a mission, resembling the Japanese-dispatched embassy of the early 1870s, to Japan and the West to study their governments. The envoys returned and recommended reforms modeled on the Japanese transformation. In 1908, the Qing thus pledged to set up a constitutional government within nine years, but the court would still dominate the judiciary, the military, and foreign policy, offering little real authority to the new legislators.

Yet the dynasty had offered an opening to supporters of restrictions on its powers. By 1909, provincial assemblies, chosen with limited suffrage and reputedly with scant power, became one of the opposition forces. Although they tended to represent the new commercial, military, and political elites, they still championed greater civil liberties, women's rights, and a less authoritarian regime. As they grew disenchanted with the Qing, they evinced anti-Manchu sentiments and sought Chinese control of government. Such Chinese nationalism spread and animated patriots, who began to blame the Manchu dynasty for China's weaknesses. Figures as disparate as the political leader and revolutionary Sun Yat-sen (1866–1925) and the twentieth century's most renowned Chinese short-story writer and essayist Zhou Shuren (1881–1936), better known by his pseudonym Lu Xun, were influenced by these currents, and Sun, in particular, viewed the Manchus as enemies. Coincidentally or not, both men had connections with Japan. Sun devoted himself to studying the Japanese model, courting Japanese support, and, in 1905, founding the Tongmenghui, a party to unify all revolutionary groups, in Japan. Lu Xun studied medicine in Japan but turned away from that profession after witnessing the Japanese audience's raucous reaction to the execution of a Chinese by a Japanese soldier.

The Chinese found Japan to be an attractive model, especially after its resounding victory in the Russo–Japanese War of 1904–1905. Japan could now take its place among the Western powers. In less than four decades, Japan had leapt from a traditional system based upon an agricultural economy and dominated by a samurai class (which scarcely used modern weapons) to a major great power that could readily compete with the West. Many young Chinese found Japan's path worth emulating and believed that, since its written language was close to Chinese, learning Japanese was not as demanding as learning Western languages. The Japanese attracted the largest number of Chinese students, some of whom were exposed to new ideas and became radicalized by their foreign experiences. They received good training in medicine, engineering, and other practical subjects, and on their return to China played a vital role in efforts at industrialization.

The waning decade of the Qing witnessed a growth in industrial development. Because the government recognized that transport was a high priority, it entered into agreements for foreign loans and assistance in the construction of railroads. The pace of such construction accelerated between 1901, the year the Boxer Protocol was signed, and 1911. By the terms of a Mutual Defense Treaty in 1896, Count Sergei Witte (1849–1915), the former Director of the Railways and the then Russian Minister of Finance, had extracted, perhaps with a bribe, from an elderly Li Hongzhang the right to build and to enjoy a ninety-nine-year lease and joint ownership of the so-called Chinese Eastern Railway through northern Manchuria to the Siberian port city of Vladivostok. The treaty appeared to offer Russia a major advantage in Manchuria, but this gain placed it on course toward a collision with Japan, which also sought to expand into the Manchus' native territory. The Russo–Japanese War of 1904–1905 ended tsarist penetration into northeast China, but the Chinese Eastern Railway was built and survived Russia's loss in the war. In other areas, France built tracks from Kunming to Hanoi, Germany started to construct railway lines in its concession in Shandong, and Britain built tracks from Beijing to Wuhan, the collective name for the cities of Wuchang, Hanyang, and Hankou.

Such improvements in transport contributed to industrialization in parts of the country. The Wuhan area became one of the centers of such development, and other regions housed both native and foreign enterprises. Textile mills, copper and coal mines, and cigarette factories (among others) had been established and had elicited foreign partners or investment, although an indigenous capitalist class, known as compradors, became wealthier and more powerful. Thus, new groups gradually perceived that the dynasty was irrelevant to their interests and, in fact, impeded industrialization and modernization. Support for the Qing eroded among these increasingly prominent groups, whose discontent complemented the frustrations of many peasants, intellectuals, and reformers. A large number of manufacturers became opponents, proclaiming the Qing to be obstructing modernization.

FALL OF THE QING

The Qing, having lost the ardent support of much of the population, barely survived the first decade of the twentieth century. The empress dowager and the emperor died in 1908, within a day of each other. Manchu court officials enthroned a three-year-old (not a good choice during a crisis) because they believed that they could more readily wield power with a child emperor on the throne. However, they alienated Chinese who feared that they would retard or impede reforms. Moreover, nationalism, in the form of anti-Manchu attitudes, was rampant, creating greater animosity toward court officials who wished to maintain power over the mass of the population. More and more Chinese believed that they had no choice but to overthrow the dynasty, and revolutionary groups began to attract a large number of adherents.

An accident at one of the revolutionaries' secret bomb-making sites in Hankou, one of the cities in Wuhan, led almost inexorably to the dynasty's fall. On October 9, 1911, an explosion rocked the hideaway. The police quickly occupied the house and found a file that listed the revolutionary group's members. Faced with the prospect of being identified and then arrested and probably executed or imprisoned, the revolutionaries were compelled to act. Violence erupted on the following day, which is celebrated by Chinese around the world as "10/10." Within a short time, many Qing troops in Wuhan joined the revolutionary forces. The court tried to fight back and restore order, but by the end of October troops in many provinces had allied with the antidynastic movement. Provincial assemblies, which had been organized just a few years earlier, started to support the revolution. In desperation, the court appointed Yuan Shikai (the powerful military leader who had assisted in suppressing the Hundred Days of Reform movement in 1898) as premier, and approved of his organizing a cabinet that signaled that it would accept a constitutional monarchy. This concession was too little and too late, and the court's military position worsened. In December, the revolutionary forces occupied Nanjing after a major battle. On January 1, 1912, Sun Yat-sen, the leader most closely associated with revolution, who had just returned from a trip to the USA and Europe that aimed to gain support from the West and from the overseas Chinese, accepted the title of provisional president from the provincial assemblies.

However, Sun, whose life, ideas, and skill will be discussed in the next chapter, was in a weak position and would be unable to seize power after the dynasty's fall. He had no military force, and the Tongmenghui, the revolutionary organization he had established in 1905, was not a cohesive political party. He was not an especially good administrator. Without a strong base, Sun had little choice but to make a deal with Yuan Shikai. He did so almost immediately, yielding the presidency of the new republic to Yuan, who negotiated with the court about the conditions for an end to the dynasty. Yuan guaranteed the safety of the boy emperor and his entourage, and ensured that the court would receive an annual stipend and would retain its property. On February 12, 1912, the young emperor – Puyi (1906–1967) – abdicated, and the more than two–thousand-year history of the imperial institution ended. Free of Qing regulations, Chinese men now cut off the despised queues that the Manchus had forced them to wear.

NOTES

1   Benjamin Schwartz, *In Search of Wealth and Power: Yen Fu and the West* (Cambridge: Harvard University Press, 1964).

FURTHER READING

Joseph Esherick, *The Origins of the Boxer Uprising* (Berkeley: University of California Press, 1987).

Kenneth Pomeranz, *The Great Divergence: China, Europe, and the Making of the Modern World* (Princeton: Princeton University Press, 2001).

William Rowe, *China's Last Empire: The Great Qing* (Cambridge, MA: Harvard University Press, 2009).

Jonathan Spence, *God's Chinese Son: The Taiping Heavenly Kingdom of Hong Xiuquan* (New York: W. W. Norton, 1996).

[11] THE REPUBLICAN PERIOD, 1911–1949

The 1911 Revolution and Its Aftermath
Warlords in Power
The May Fourth Movement and Intellectuals
    in the Post-First World War Period
Communist Party
Rise of Chiang Kai-shek
Guomindang Dominance
Communist Party Revival
Long March and Aftermath
The Sino–Japanese War
The Pacific War, the Communists,
    and the Guomindang
Civil War in China

THE end of the dynastic system left a vacuum in China. Earlier in its history, the Middle Kingdom had experienced periods of uncertainty and chaos. It lacked true central governments during the last centuries of the Zhou dynasty, again following the Han dynasty's collapse, and also after the Tang dynasty's downfall. Although these eras witnessed remarkable cultural innovations, such as the development of Confucianism and Daoism and the introduction and spread of Buddhism, disunity had led to considerable political and military turbulence. As China became more populous and incorporated additional territory, it could not endure such periods of decentralization. After the Yuan dynasty reunified the country in 1279, central governments ruled China, without interruption, until 1911. Specific emperors and administrators

A History of China, First Edition. Morris Rossabi.
© 2014 Morris Rossabi. Published 2014 by Blackwell Publishing Ltd.

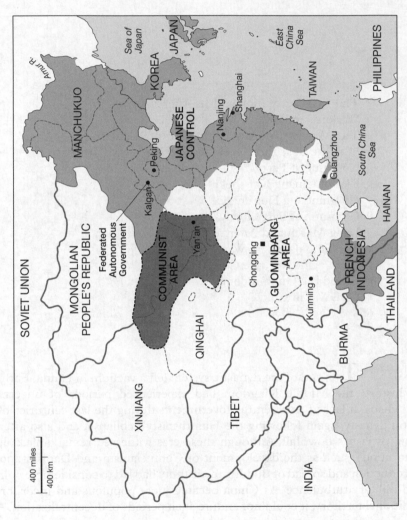

Map 11.1 China after Japanese attack, 1938

may not have been effective, but (at least in theory) centralization prevailed, and successive dynasties continued to rule from the capital, generally in Beijing. The Qing emperor's abdication in 1912 could and did lead to disruptions. Six centuries or so of unity had prevented the country's dismemberment. However, the lack of an emperor, a symbol of unity, cast China into uncharted waters, creating unstable conditions. Although a central government was established in Beijing from 1912 to 1916 and in Nanjing and Chongjing from 1928 to 1949, neither controlled the entire country. Japanese encroachment starting in 1915 and culminating in the Japanese attack of 1937 contributed to disunity and chaos.

THE 1911 REVOLUTION AND ITS AFTERMATH

Sun Yat-sen is the leader most often associated with the 1911 revolution, although, in fact, he scarcely played a role in the events leading directly to the downfall of the Qing. His encomium as "Father of the Chinese Republic" may be somewhat misleading. He became a national figure and even a national hero, but he hardly ever wielded much authority over China during his own lifetime. He never became the country's chief executive and played an entirely different role.

Sun had disadvantages as a political leader in China. Although he was born in Guangdong province, he spent most of his life outside China. He was educated in Hawaii and attended medical school in Hong Kong. Perhaps

Figure 11.1 Sun Yat-sen in 1912. Photo: akg-images / Interfoto

even more significant, Sun had been converted to Christianity. Thus, he differed considerably from most Chinese because of his religious views and his residence abroad. When he turned to politics, he remained abroad and devoted most of his time and efforts to obtaining financial support from overseas Chinese communities. Sun seemed to be separated from the vast majority of the Chinese population. On the other hand, this could also have been an asset. Chinese who were entranced by Western civilization may have appreciated Sun's apparent identification with the West. He wore Western clothes, at least in most of his photos. He identified and sought assistance from the Japanese, who had modernized their economy and educational and banking systems expeditiously, although their political structure differed from that of the West. His ability to connect with ordinary Chinese would appear to have been limited, but his appeal to advocates of modernization and possibly Westernization helped him to gain support among the general population.

Sun's ideas and program also derived from the West but were vague and difficult to identify. His so-called Three People's Principles of nationalism, democracy, and people's livelihood were ill defined because his views consisted of a mélange of his unsystematic reading in Western sources. People's livelihood could refer to either socialism or a kind of people's capitalism. Nationalism could be anti-Manchu beliefs or a modern form of nationalism for the Chinese. The unclear definitions may actually have worked in his favor because a variety of different peoples or groups, who represented different policies, could join his movement. A lack of a more focused ideology proved to be a boon because he had no rigid criteria for membership in his Tongmenghui (or Revolutionary Alliance), the movement he founded in Japan in 1905. Travel outside China impeded efforts to organize a tightly knit political party or a military force that could offer him the leverage he needed to deal with commanders and warlords throughout China. Indeed, he did not turn out to be a skilled administrator or an adept military leader, which prevented him from assuming power over any sizable domain in China.

When he returned to China (by early 1912), Sun had no choice other than to negotiate with Yuan Shikai, the dominant military figure in north China. Sun agreed to resign as provisional president and to support Yuan as president if he abided by the provisional constitution, permitted political parties, and sanctioned an election for the Chinese parliament. By the time of the election in January of 1913, the Tongmenghui had become the loosely organized Guomindang (or Nationalist Party), a political party. Despite its newness, the Guomindang won the largest number of seats in the parliament, and Sun's young protégé Song Jiaoren (1882–1913), the leader of the party, was poised to become the premier and to limit the president's power. However, Yuan could not tolerate the threat of the erosion of his presidential power. This prompted several of his underlings to assassinate Song, although Yuan himself escaped official guilt for involvement in the plot. Without Song in opposition, Yuan compelled the parliament to name him president for five years. When the parliament proved to be a nuisance late in 1913, the Yuan abolished it. Sun, fearing for his life, fled to Japan.

Yuan set about shredding his commitment to Sun, gradually assuming an imperial role and ultimately weakening himself and China, thereby making the country vulnerable to foreign incursions and demands. He had grand visions of restoring China's dynastic structure, with himself as the new emperor, and, after alleged calls (instigated by his underlings and allies) to take the throne, he agreed to become emperor as of January 1, 1916. However, there was little support for reestablishment of the imperial system, leading many commanders in various provinces to detach themselves from the central government. Provincial warlords had gained power before 1916, but the pace of such challenges to the Beijing government accelerated after Yuan's attempt at imperial restoration.

At the same time, Yuan faced another quandary. In 1915, capitalizing on the great powers' involvement in the First World War and the attendant focus on Europe, Japan sent the so-called Twenty-One Demands to the Chinese government. The most controversial of these demands was Chinese recognition of Japan's dominance over Shandong province, a dominance it achieved by expelling Germany, which had maintained a concession there since the 1890s. Germany was using nearly all its resources for the First World War and could not afford to defend its preeminent position in Shandong. Japan also sought and received greater economic concessions in Fujian, Inner Mongolia, and Manchuria and leverage over important iron and steel companies, thus assuring itself of access to these resources. With no countervailing force from any other foreign power, Yuan had to acquiesce to nearly all the demands, which further alienated the population. His death in 1916 ended his aspirations but also ushered in a chaotic period, with a decline in central governmental authority and an increase in warlord power. It turned out that, the greater the distance from Beijing, the greater the opportunity for warlords to establish autonomous regions.

WARLORDS IN POWER

The northwest province of Xinjiang illustrates the potential for dismemberment of the country. Conquered by the Qing in the middle of the eighteenth century and riveted by rebellion throughout the nineteenth century, Xinjiang had, in any case, loose connections with China. The Qing had ruled a mostly non-Chinese population composed of pastoralists and oasis-dwellers who engaged in subsistence farming. Although the vast majority of the people were Turkic and Muslim, a Chinese warlord named Yang Zengxin (1867–1928) took power in the aftermath of the 1911 revolution. A tough-minded, oppressive, and shrewd leader, he had the advantage of a well-organized military force. He combined ruthless suppression of the local, non-Chinese inhabitants with some relief measures and protection from exploitative Chinese merchants. His forces dealt harshly with both Chinese dissidents (including secret societies who sought greater autonomy) and Turkic governors who demanded independence. He devised agreements with some non-Chinese governors, but in some cases duped and murdered recalcitrant chieftains. One of his successful tactics was to generate conflicts among them and thus prevent them from allying with each other. Within a few years, he had enforced a certain stability in Xinjiang, although tensions remained beneath the surface and would, on occasion, flare up into violence. In dealing with these domestic problems, Yang paid lip service to Yuan Shikai's leadership and to the later rule of a hobbled central government after Yuan's death, but, in fact, he was virtually independent and devised his own policies.

Tensions along the Russian border also plagued Yang. Tsarist Russia's control over central Asia, the region bordering Xinjiang, had weakened considerably with its entrance into the First World War. Its own general deterioration led to poor performance in the early stages of the war. Deaths, demoralization, and desertions devastated the Russian forces, compelling the government to draft its central Asian, mostly Muslim subjects, into the armed forces in 1915 – a policy that it had tried to avert because it knew that it would antagonize these less-than-loyal groups. Many central Asians perceived the war as a European problem and saw no great benefit in them becoming involved. Moreover, their economic conditions had become ever more parlous. In the nineteenth century, the tsarist court had forced them to substitute cotton for grain cultivation, making them dependent on other parts of Russia for some of their food. The onset of the war created food shortages for central Asia, as the country's western regions retained, and did not export, their grain. Thus, turbulence erupted in central Asia because of limited food supplies and resistance to recruitment into the tsarist army. The Russian Revolution of 1917 exacerbated the instability and violence, forcing Yang to pay attention to his western and northern borders with Russia.

Yang feared that the violence in Russia and central Asia would spill over into Xinjiang. The struggle between the Bolshevik communists and the White Russian forces (the anticommunists, who were the main anti-Bolshevik group) often took place in Siberia and central Asia, where the anticommunist groups found a hospitable environment. This civil war was waged relentlessly from at least 1918 to 1921, with the Whites often using central Asia as a base. As the Bolsheviks defeated one after another of the White groups, some soldiers sought sanctuary in Xinjiang. Yang faced a dilemma. Should he assist the Whites or should he seek to establish good relations with the Bolsheviks? He eventually chose to deal with the Bolsheviks, and in 1920 signed an agreement calling for the repatriation of the White Russians, for proper commercial relations, and for an exchange of diplomats. Yang did not ally with the Muslim central Asian opponents of the USSR (the Union of Soviet Socialist Republics, which came into being in 1922 as a consequence of the Russian Revolution). Instead, in 1924, he signed a treaty permitting the USSR to establish five consulates in Xinjiang and allowing for his own government to open the same number in central Asia. As a result, trade between Xinjiang and the USSR increased at a faster rate than the Chinese central government's commerce with Xinjiang. The most revealing aspect of these developments is that Yang had the right to negotiate with foreign states without seeking the central government's approval. His power typified that of many provincial warlords.

Yan Xishan (1883–1960) represented still another warlord of this era. A native of Shanxi who commanded a large military force, Yan took power in the province right after the 1911 revolution. Yuan Shikai's government had scarcely any influence over Shanxi, and after Yuan's death Yan supported one or another of the succeeding military men who controlled the government in Beijing – but without relinquishing authority over his own province. He survived, and in fact flourished, during the almost constant changes in the central government from 1916 to 1927. In 1928, when Chiang Kai-shek's military campaign united at least China's east coast, Yan at first collaborated with the new leader, who happened to be Sun Yat-sen's brother-in-law. However, Chiang and Yan soon came into conflict, and only eventually established a fragile peace because of the Japanese and communist threats in the 1930s. The so-called alliance with Chiang granted Yan autonomy over Shanxi; he used this free hand to ingratiate himself with the population via a policy of economic modernization. He promoted industry (especially mining), built roads and a railway line, fostered agronomy, and instituted social reforms, including establishment of public schools and greater emphasis on women's rights. After the Second World War, his efforts were insufficient to halt the Chinese communists' inexorable rise to power. In late 1949, recognizing the defeat of Chiang Kai-shek's armies, he fled to Taiwan.

There were many other such examples. Warlords, some of whom had been Yuan Shikai's underlings or commanders, gained control over numerous areas in China. Criminals or bandits who had significant forces took power in some regions and generated fear and instability. Some of these figures, such as Yan Xishan and, to a lesser extent, Yang Zengxin, advocated and implemented policies emphasizing social reforms and economic modernization. But many were simply rapacious and contributed to poverty and oppression, as well as to a weakened Chinese state. Foreign governments took advantage of this disunity to back one or another of the warlords, creating even greater havoc. Japan, increasingly concerned with Shandong, Manchuria, and Inner Mongolia, supported its own candidates among the warlords or simply precipitated disruptions upon which the warlords could capitalize. The USSR meddled in Xinjiang, and by the late 1920s had virtually supplanted China as the main external force. It also helped to detach Mongolia from China's control and facilitated its efforts to become an independent country. Britain, the USA, and, to a lesser extent, France, in part due to investments and stakes in trade with China, also became involved in the country's tempestuous politics in the first and second decades of the twentieth century. In these chaotic circumstances, foreign involvement and alliances were destabilizing. Different foreign states had differing economic and political interests and exerted their authority over a weak and decentralized China for their own benefit, contributing to continued misery but also to stirrings of nationalism.

Decentralization offered greater power to local officials and landlords. Some in the old gentry class profited from the lack of an effective central government. Virtually without restrictions, these landlords had flexibility to enforce their own will in local areas. Alliance with local officials, who either derived from the elite class or were readily corruptible, permitted landlords to evade taxation and to dominate their regions' peasants and workers. Chinese who believed themselves to be exploited had no agency to which they could appeal. They became increasingly frustrated with government, which did not appear to be protecting the weak and the powerless.

THE MAY FOURTH MOVEMENT AND INTELLECTUALS IN THE POST-FIRST WORLD WAR PERIOD

At the same time, nationalism, which, on occasion, developed into antiforeign demonstrations or boycotts, spread. Some Chinese blamed foreigners, together with social divisions and inequality in the country, for China's predicament. They became increasingly alienated and suspicious of foreign intentions. The USA was somewhat excepted because it had not demanded a specific Chinese territory as a concession. It sought free trade rather than a monopoly of the territories' economic activity. Chinese intellectuals were captivated by President Woodrow Wilson, who had, after all, been an academic. Via his Fourteen Points (proclaimed at the outset of the USA's entrance into the First World War), Wilson championed the principle of national self-determination, which meant that colonies could opt to regain their independence. Some Chinese intellectuals assumed that Wilson would therefore support their nationalist aspirations and would assist in persuading foreign states to abandon their virtual occupation of Chinese territories.

They were to be disappointed when the Western powers that met at Versailles at the conclusion of the First World War acquiesced to Japan's claim to Germany's concession in Shandong province and to Japanese occupation of the region. Many Chinese intellectuals believed that the West had undermined its commitment to China. The pledge of national self-determination had not been honored. Instead, Chinese territory had been turned over to a country that had traditionally borrowed much from China, including Confucianism, Buddhism, and even much of its written language – a land that the Chinese considered a younger brother who learned from China.

On May 4, 1919, several thousand students organized a demonstration to protest the Japanese occupation of Shandong. Followed and restricted by the police, the students originally marched around Tiananmen (The Gate of Heavenly Peace) in Beijing, but scuffles soon broke out. Students damaged the house of a prominent Chinese official, violence erupted, and one student was killed during the fighting that ensued. Much of the Chinese population was appalled at the violence and the loss of life. For a country that had been governed by scholar-officials and where education was so highly valued, the death of a student was shocking. Many lost faith in the Western democracies and began to search for political and social alternatives.

The May 4 incident took on great symbolic significance. Reformers clustered around the concept of a May Fourth movement, which appeared to encompass the changes they sought. All agreed that Yuan Shikai and the other leaders who assumed power after his death had failed to rectify China's international image and to implement domestic reforms, but each of the figures proposed different solutions. Nonetheless, they agreed about specific issues, including the use of *baihua* (colloquial language) in written Chinese, women's rights, human rights, and elimination of the stifling aspects of Confucianism. The political institutions they advocated differed, but they concurred about these basic social reforms. Each would side with different political factions in the struggles that plagued China from 1919 to 1949.

Who were these nationalist intellectuals? Several of the most important had been educated abroad – in Japan, but also as far away as Germany, France, and the USA. Some of the most renowned either taught or were associated with Beijing University, which had been founded in 1898 and had rapidly become the country's most famous intellectual center. It was a hotbed for discussion of China's future, with individual writers, teachers, and speakers reflecting a wide variety of philosophical, literary, and political views. Intellectuals had not formed a consensus. Representatives of many stripes, from anarchism to social Darwinism to Wilsonian idealism, expressed their viewpoints. Some were concerned about literature and writing, others focused on women's rights, and still others sought democracy and alleviation of social and economic inequalities. Chinese intellectuals capitalized on the disorder in China to present widely diverging ideas.

One of the most important figures in promoting and protecting the intellectual ferment at Beijing University was Cai Yuanpei (1868–1940). Cai had received a classical Confucian education and had passed the civil-service examinations so brilliantly that the Hanlin Academy, the most prestigious organization for scholars in traditional China, had selected him for admission. The disastrous Sino–Japanese War of 1894–1895 had shocked him into questioning whether a classically trained official could provide China with the skills and strength to protect itself and to foster economic development. He sought to learn about Western education and obtained funding to attend Leipzig University from 1908 to 1911, then eventually extended his university training in France. Even before his sojourn in France, he had served briefly as minister of education in Yuan Shikai's cabinet. However, he quickly grew disillusioned with Yuan, resigned, and went back to Europe.

Only after Yuan's death in 1916 did Cai return to China to assume the post of Chancellor of Beijing University. During his off-and-on service at Beijing University until 1926, he contributed enormously to its development. He did so not necessarily through his own ideas but by fighting for freedom of expression and by tolerating and permitting an extraordinary range of ideas to be presented and discussed. By rallying popular support, he prevented local warlords and the Beijing government from intruding and suppressing such outpourings of intellectual discourse. When the government tried to intervene, he would threaten to resign, and his great popularity and the esteem he enjoyed among the general public would often compel officials to back down. His position as chancellor led to an intellectual flowering, as well as considerable student and faculty interest in and involvement in politics. Both students and faculty were free to present dissenting opinions and to participate in demonstrations and political activities because of the safe haven he provided. In 1928, after his position at Beijing University had ended, he founded the Academia Sinica, the most important organization for high-level and cutting-edge research in China, and became its first president. By then, he had already had a significant impact on the burgeoning intellectual atmosphere in Beijing.

Hu Shi (1891–1962) was one of the intellectuals who took advantage of the freedom at Beijing University to have a major impact on Chinese society.

A brilliant boy from a family in straitened circumstances, he managed, at the age of thirteen, to move from his native village to Shanghai, where he studied so-called Western learning in several schools, which prepared him to pass a test for a Boxer Indemnity Scholarship to study in the USA. He initially attended the College of Agriculture at Cornell University, seeking pragmatic skills that China could use. However, his intellectual interests outweighed his practical concerns, prompting him to major in philosophy at Cornell and then to earn a PhD at Columbia University under the tutelage of John Dewey, the apostle of pragmatism and of the use of the scientific method as a source of knowledge. Returning to China, he became a professor of philosophy at Beijing University. Like Cai Yuanpei, he was a moderate and did not take an active role in politics, emphasizing only his hatred of violence and revolution. His reform efforts centered on use of *baihua* rather than the classical language in written texts, be they newspapers, literature, or government documents. He argued that such a change would, in itself, be revolutionary because the written language would be simpler, leading to a higher rate of literacy. This populism accorded with his emphasis on reason and science and his dedication to the political and social values of Western civilization. He championed women's rights, good government, and democracy, among other features of Western civilization. Although Hu later served as ambassador to the USA and presidents of both Beijing University and the Academia Sinica, he may have made his most important contributions in his early years at Beijing University with his support for *baihua*.

Chen Duxiu (1879–1942) of Beijing University turned out to have the greatest political influence of these three representative figures. Although he started out with a classical Confucian education, in his late teens he studied at a modern Westernized school. He learned French and English in China, and also studied abroad in Japan and France and became conversant with and impressed by Western civilization. He started a magazine in Japan, and on his return to China *New Youth*, his newly renamed magazine, became extremely popular with intellectuals. His espousal of Western liberal values, as personified in his concepts of Mr. Democracy and Mr. Science and his publication of young but increasingly distinguished authors in *New Youth*, bolstered his reputation, prompting Cai Yuanpei to offer him the position of Dean of the College of Letters at Beijing University in 1917. He served in that position for two years, during which time he associated with Hu Shi, the chief university librarian Li Dazhao (1889–1927), and other future luminaries. The intellectual ferment of the time was heightened by the lack of respectable central government and by the influence and manipulation of Western powers and Japan. Chen himself was captivated by Woodrow Wilson's vision and pledge of national self-determination. Chen looked askance at what he perceived to be the Western betrayal of China in the Treaty of Versailles that came at the end of the First World War; he thus supported students who called for an activist response on May 4, 1919.

The most renowned of these figures was Lu Xun (1881–1936), a pseudonym for Zhou Shuren. Like many of his sophisticated and intellectual peers, when he went abroad to study in Japan, he chose medicine, a practical subject.

However, he revealed in later writings that he abandoned medicine after viewing a Japanese documentary that recorded the decapitation of a Chinese, accused of spying for Russia, at which fellow Chinese simply looked on without protesting or registering emotion. He decided at that point that China's priority ought to be spiritual uplift, not merely physical health. Returning to China, he had a twenty-year career as a writer of short stories and essays. His stories, such as "Diary of a Mad Man" (*Kuangren Riji*), offer devastating critiques of the unpleasant underside of the traditional Confucian values, portraying them as oppressive and metaphorically cannibalistic. His most popular short story, "The True Story of Ah Q" (*A Q Zhengzhuan*), yields another metaphorical image of the depths and false self-images that China had fallen to in the face of the foreign powers. It also satirizes the retardant effects of the Confucian values. All these critiques were produced with a satiric light touch, and Lu Xun did not adhere to a specific political or social ideology. In 1936, he joined a so-called League of Left-Wing Writers, but never belonged to a political faction. Communist critics pilloried him for his seeming cynicism and his lack of a leftist solution to China's problems, but he had a large readership throughout the 1920s and 1930s until his death in 1936.

COMMUNIST PARTY

Chen Duxiu, in particular, was disillusioned by the lack of Western support for preventing Japan from occupying Shandong. Turning away from his earlier faith in the Western emphasis on national self-determination, he began a search for an ideology that would help China. His espousal of Mr. Democracy and Mr. Science appeared to be ineffective. Prompted by his colleague Li Dazhao, he joined a group studying Marxism. Li had studied in Japan, and on his return to China in 1916 became an editor of a newspaper that advocated reforms. Shortly thereafter (as mentioned above), Cai Yuanpei appointed him head of the library at Beijing University, where he became acquainted with Chen Duxiu. He threw himself into the life of the university and helped and became popular with students. Perhaps his most fateful assistance for students was offering Mao Zedong a job in the library. Disappointed by the West's lack of support for China at Versailles, he sought another source of aid for China. Influenced by the Russian Revolution of 1917, he turned to Marxism and persuaded his friend and colleague Chen Duxiu to join him in a study group. The following year, an agent from the Communist International (or Comintern) arrived in Beijing to advise and influence the group. Marxism's emphasis on class struggle, its espousal of industrialization, its support for the proletariat, and its opposition to imperialism appealed to Chen and his compatriots. They also found the dynamics of so-called dialectical materialism of great intellectual interest. However, the Marxist-Leninist resistance to colonialism was especially attractive.

Developments in Russia (later the USSR) would help shape events in China in the 1920s. When V. I. Lenin took power in Russia, he assumed that the success of the Bolshevik Revolution would prompt so-called proletarian revolutions in the advanced capitalist countries such as Britain, France, and Germany. The failure of his prediction that proletarian revolutions would topple the bourgeois governments necessitated an explanation. He attributed this failure to imperialism. He argued that Britain, France, and the other capitalist countries had gained so much revenue from their colonies that they could provide a pittance of social welfare (pensions, unemployment insurance, etc.), which was a sop to their people but nevertheless undermined attempts to overthrow the bourgeois governments. They could also allocate substantial funds to bolster their military and police forces to suppress recalcitrant members of the proletariat and their communist vanguard. Lenin asserted that only the smashing of imperialism would lead to economic crises and then revolution in the capitalist countries. The Comintern focus would thus shift somewhat to Africa and Asia, the principal colonial regions.

Lenin recognized that the colonial areas scarcely had industrial economies and had not reached the capitalist stage of development. He argued that the proletariat in these countries was tiny, that it could not by itself overcome the existing social system, and that it could not immediately set up a communist government. The proletariat thus needed to cooperate with the similarly tiny native bourgeoisie in opposition to the imperialists. Such cooperation, which the Comintern would label a "united front," would entail a temporary restraint on calls for social revolution and would instead emphasize nationalism. The enemy would be the foreign imperialists and their so-called lackeys, natives who worked for or collaborated with the foreigners rather than with the indigenous bourgeoisie. Comintern agents would be dispatched to help identify the representatives of the bourgeoisie and to assist in forging alliances with them.

The Comintern's representative, Grigori Voitinsky (1893–1956), identified the Guomindang, Sun Yat-sen's political party, as the natural partner for a Chinese Communist Party because it represented the progressive elements of the bourgeoisie. The Chinese Communist Party itself was in its infancy. Fearing arrest and possibly worse, Li Dazhao and Chen Duxiu had not attended the initial meeting that founded the party on July 1, 1921 on a boat coasting in the waters off Shanghai. Nonetheless, Chen was elected as secretary of the party. The small contingent of about fifty men who met on the boat lacked unity because of ideological differences, and a few would eventually leave the party and would later provide valuable accounts of its founding and initial operations. Comintern instructions to form a united front with the Guomindang added to the disputes within the party. Many members were displeased with these instructions. Yet they could not challenge the dictates of the leader of the only successful communist revolution, the USSR, which included the Ukraine, central Asia, the Caucasus, and regions in Siberia and was the preeminent center of the communist movement. Chinese communist leaders chafed at the USSR's instruction to cooperate with the Guomindang, but they abided by it. This disagreement was to be the first of many such ideological, territorial, and economic differences that culminated in a split between the Chinese communists and the USSR in the late 1950s. The Chinese Communist Party would eventually conclude that the USSR's principal objectives relating to China were based on Soviet, not Chinese, national interests.

In 1921, however, the fledgling Chinese Communist Party acquiesced to Soviet demands and sought to collaborate with Sun Yat-sen's party. Earlier, however, it had started to organize its less than one thousand members into a cohesive force. Facing considerable pressure to ally with the Guomindang, the party nonetheless continued on its own path in attempting to serve as the vanguard of the proletariat. Some of its members traveled to factories and mines to meet with workers and to proselytize for the movement. They were offered fertile ground, for the post-First World War period witnessed an increase in industrial production. The construction of railroads facilitated transport of goods and lured substantial foreign investment. Foreign companies aided by compradors developed new industries such as tobacco production, metals, coal, cotton and silk textiles, and soybeans. Workers were exploited in most of the plants, with low wages, long hours, few benefits, and scant health and safety precautions. The various governments throughout China dealt harshly with those who dissented or tried to organize workers or to initiate protests and strikes. The communists faced obstacles, as the number of workers was paltry. Factory and mine owners were not bound by restrictive laws or regulations and often had the support of the local government, police, and army. Dissenters were suppressed, workers were intimidated, and some of their leaders were executed. These circumstances confirmed Lenin's observations about China's limited industrialization and weak proletariat.

While the Chinese Communist Party continued its efforts to rouse the proletariat, the Soviets and Sun Yat-sen sought to come to an agreement. The relatively miniscule number of members in the party precluded much influence. The USSR dispatched Adolph Joffe (1883–1927) to work out an agreement with Sun. In a pronouncement in January 1923, Joffe concurred that communism was not suited to China and that the USSR would help the Guomindang to unify the country and expel the imperialists. Within a few months, the Comintern sent a political operative named Mikhail Borodin (1884–1951) to strengthen the Guomindang, using the USSR's Communist Party as a model. Other Soviets assisted in the development of a military elite by founding the Whampoa Military Academy near Canton, with Sun's future brother-in-law Chiang Kai-shek as its military commander and Zhou Enlai (1898–1976), a communist who had studied in France, as its political commissar. Although the USSR would be the Guomindang's most important partner, their agreement ensured that the Chinese communists would be subordinate to Sun's party. Lenin had concluded that the Chinese communists were too weak to take power and had also decided that the most significant priority was national revolution, or expulsion of the imperialist powers. Only after the success of the national revolution would Lenin sanction a social revolution, which would lead to a communist struggle against the bourgeois Guomindang. Until then, the Chinese communists would, in Lenin's formulation, play a subsidiary role.

Although many Chinese communists disapproved of Lenin's policy, they acquiesced to Soviet demands and suffered the consequences. At first, the communists' so-called united front with the Guomindang proved to be effective. Tensions remained beneath the surface. However, Lenin's death in 1924 and Sun's death in 1925 subverted the alliance at a time when unrest and instability were accelerating. In the aftermath of a strike in a Japanese-owned cotton mill in Shanghai, a worker was shot and students were arrested. The workers and students responded by initiating a boycott and then, on May 30, 1925, organizing a demonstration near the police station where the students were held. In panic, Sikh, British, and Chinese guards shot at the assembled group and killed anywhere from thirty to two hundred demonstrators. This incident on May 30 reverberated throughout the country and aroused nationalist sentiments. Chinese protested by demonstrating in the streets, which led to more violence and deaths, and by boycotting foreign products. The Shanghai Municipal Council imposed martial law in the city, exacerbating the tensions, although the violence had finally ceased by the end of the year. These signs of unrest offered the Guomindang–Chinese communist united front an opportunity, but they first had to find new leaders for their respective parties.

Meanwhile, leadership in the USSR ultimately centered on a struggle between Leon Trotsky (1879–1940) and Joseph Stalin (1878–1953). Trotsky veered away from Lenin's views. Distrusting the bourgeoisie, he advocated a much more radical policy. He opted for world revolution or an immediate proletarian accession to power and an avoidance of united fronts and coalitions. His views, if accepted, would spur the Chinese communists to sever relations with the Guomindang and to move expeditiously toward proletarian rule. His Jewish background was a potential disadvantage because of the covert anti-Semitism of many of the communist leaders. Stalin, his adversary, appeared to be more conservative. He instructed the Chinese communists to maintain their alliance with the Guomindang. However, he faced a dilemma that eventually proved damaging to the Chinese communists. By adopting Lenin's formulation, he would have to support the united front in China, at least until he could overwhelm Trotsky. Whatever the circumstances or however costly, he demanded that the Chinese communists back the Guomindang.

RISE OF CHIANG KAI-SHEK

Meanwhile, Sun Yat-sen's death eventually led to the unraveling of the united front. The landlords and industrialists, an important constituency in the Guomindang, were concerned about their communist "allies," while some leftists feared the right wing of the party. After Sun's death, suspicions between them exploded into violence. In August of 1925, the same year as Sun's death, Liao Zhongkai (1877–1925), a prominent leader in the Guomindang who had studied in Japan and who supported closer relations with the USSR, was assassinated, and many Chinese blamed the rightists within the Guomindang umbrella for the murder. Liao had been a potential rival for Chiang Kai-shek and via his murder the moderates' and leftists' preferred candidate to succeed Sun was removed. By March of 1926, the right-leaning Hu Hanmin (1879–1936) and the left-leaning Wang Jingwei (1883–1944), both of whom had also studied in Japan and were potential challengers to Chiang's supremacy, had been accused of conspiring to kidnap Chiang and ousted from the top leadership,

Figure II.2 Chiang Kai-shek. © Bettmann / CORBIS

which provided Chiang with undisputed domination over the Guomindang. His marriage in December of 1927 to Soong Meiling (1898–2003) – younger sister of Sun Yat-sen's widow Soong Qingling (1893–1981) and daughter of the successful Christian businessman Charlie Soong (1863–1918), who had originally been close to Sun Yat-sen – provided additional confirmation of his increasing stature. Charlie Soong had broken with Sun when his daughter Soong Qingling had, over his wishes, married Sun (who, embarrassingly, had not yet divorced his first wife). In this case, the Soong family apparently overcame its embarrassment and tolerated Chiang's marital status. A few years later, he regained their allegiance by converting to Christianity. Chiang himself profited from his association with the Soongs because he secured not only a powerful, American-educated wife but also his wife's brother, T. V. Soong (1891–1971), a Harvard- and Columbia-educated businessman who would eventually become minister of finance and proved to be adept at raising revenue, and H. H. Kung (1881–1967), his wife's brother-in-law, the richest man in China and also a minister of finance.

Facing no competition for the leadership of the Guomindang, Chiang now was determined to expand the territory under his control. Based primarily in Canton, he conceived of what was known as the Northern Expedition up the east coast of China to establish jurisdiction over the traditional centers of Chinese civilization. He wanted, in particular, to overthrow the warlords based in Beijing lest they attract foreign support and become entrenched. Mikhail Borodin, the Comintern agent in China, the remaining power broker, and the main conduit for USSR aid, did not entirely approve of such an expedition and did not trust Chiang. However, his objections did not impress Chiang, nor did Stalin support the Comintern agent. Still engaged in his struggle with Trotsky, Stalin could not afford to alienate and thus subvert his relationship with Chiang. He had differentiated himself from Trotsky by avidly embracing the united front and collaborating with the bourgeoisie. Having placed himself squarely in the united-front camp, he had no choice but to support Chiang in his military campaigns.

Labor-union leaders, communists, and leftists in general served as the advance detachments during the expedition, without realizing that Chiang was increasingly allying himself with rightists. Chiang had been meeting with landlords and industrialists and had sought to curry favor with them. Simultaneously, he began to cooperate with the Green Gang, a secret society in Shanghai that was involved in such criminal activities as gambling, narcotics, protection rackets, and prostitution. Du Yuesheng (1888–1951), the sybaritic leader of the Green Gang, who had dozens of concubines and four official wives, provided Chiang with funds and equipment. With such support, Chiang planned to suppress the leftists who would unwittingly assist his expedition. The leftists provoked demonstrations and work stoppages in cities and towns, facilitating the often peaceful entrance of Chiang's forces. Once his troops had occupied a site, they quickly unleashed an assault on the leftists who had helped them win. Borodin reported on these so-called betrayals to Stalin and appealed to the USSR leader to issue a call to sever the alliance with the Guomindang. However, Stalin had to hew to the united-front policy. He rejected Borodin's advice, leaving the Chinese communists vulnerable to Chiang's armies and their civilian supporters, as well as to troops controlled by warlords. For example, in April of 1927, Zhang Zuolin (1875–1928), a warlord from Manchuria who occupied Beijing, raided the Soviet embassy in the capital, helped himself to secret documents, and captured and then executed Li Dazhao, one of the principal leaders of the Communist Party.

The culmination of what the Chinese communists perceived to be betrayals and massacres took place on April 12, 1927. After strikes and demonstrations led by leftists, Chiang's troops and allies had moved into Shanghai in late March and early April. On April 12, his military and civilian forces and the Green Gang initiated a murderous rampage against labor unions and Communist Party members, imprisoning and killing many of them and putting an end to strikes and demonstrations. News about the killings spread throughout China, preventing Stalin from dismissing the betrayals and from seeking to maintain an already frayed, if not disastrous, alliance.

Stalin tried to deflect criticism away from himself in three ways. First, he criticized the Chinese communists for not attracting sufficient support from the proletariat. Second, he asserted that Chiang Kai-shek had finally revealed himself to be a rightist who represented landlords, industrialists, militarists, and criminal gang leaders. Third, he interpreted April 12, 1927 in this new light as reflecting a rise in the revolutionary wave. The Chinese communists could now, according to Stalin, adopt increasingly radical policies because of the duplicity of the bourgeoisie, which had revealed itself to be an unstable ally. He called upon the Chinese communists to cooperate with the Guomindang leftists against Chiang and immediately to take up arms. However, his earlier insistence upon maintaining the alliance with Chiang had left the Chinese communists vulnerable. Chiang's troops, the Green Gang, and other forces had murdered or imprisoned the top leftists and communists. Despite this, the Chinese communists would attempt to fulfill Stalin's intentions.

The communists would work on three fronts. As Stalin suggested, they sought to collaborate with a Left Guomindang government based in the industrial heartland in Wuhan. Wang Jingwei, who had been one of Chiang Kaishek's competitors as successor to Sun Yat-sen, had moved to Wuhan to lead the Left Guomindang. Sun Yat-sen's widow and Sun Fo (1895–1973), Sun's son from an earlier marriage, joined him, bolstering his position. However, the Left Guomindang did not have a powerful military force at its command. Moreover, its leaders were wary of the Chinese communists and instead began to negotiate with Chiang. Further, because the bulk of the population lived in the countryside and distress in the rural areas was pervasive, the communists foresaw that revolution could originate from there. Mao Zedong had just started to emerge, and, based on his investigations of peasant life in his native province of Hunan, he had concluded that a communist victory would require peasant support. However, the communists had scarcely made any efforts to propagandize and organize among the peasants. Yet they abided by Stalin's instructions and called for immediate rural outbreaks and disturbances. The ensuing Autumn Harvest Uprising in August of 1927 involved small groups who were not well organized or well supplied. The Guomindang, aided by local forces, quickly suppressed them. Similarly, an urban insurrection, known as the Canton Commune, barely lasted for four days, from December 11 to 15. Poor organization and inadequate supplies and preparation doomed the rebels.

By the end of 1927, Chiang and the Guomindang appeared to have achieved most of their territorial ambitions. Their troops occupied the east coast from Guangzhou to Shanghai and had eliminated the threat posed by the leftists and the communists. In 1928, Chiang defeated Zhang Zuolin and forced him out of Beijing. Fortunately for Chiang, Japanese expansionists in the military perceived of Zhang as a stumbling block, while other Japanese were appalled that he had lost Beijing. When Chiang's allies headed for Beijing, the Japanese urged Zhang to withdraw in return for a guarantee that the Guomindang would not be permitted entry into Manchuria. As Zhang headed back to Manchuria by train, Japanese militarists planted a bomb that detonated and killed him. Although Chiang now controlled Beijing, he decided to select a capital in Nanjing in southern China, where he had a strong base.

GUOMINDANG DOMINANCE

The Guomindang had optimal circumstances to establish its rule after the volatile conditions since 1900. Its Chinese communist opposition was on the run, and important warlords, along with the notorious Green Gang, pledged to support Chiang. Peasants sought relief from landlord exploitation and from punitive taxation. An agrarian reform program, which provided them with their own land, would surely be popular. Industrialists and traders, whom the communists had labeled as part of the national bourgeoisie, hoped the new government would protect their economic interests against foreign-owned enterprises and even foster industrialization through loans. Professionals, including attorneys, physicians, professors, students, and other intellectuals, hoped that the government would create stable conditions and would endorse and promote civil liberties. Workers in factories and mines, who were grossly underpaid and had hardly any safety and health guarantees, looked to the Guomindang for assistance and assumed that this nationalist party would protect their interests. Feminists lobbied for laws that would protect women's rights. All these groups appeared to have confidence in Chiang, but the Guomindang would lose the support of one after another.

Over the next few years, the Guomindang would disappoint them. Naturally, Japanese pressure and the actual occupation of Chinese territories until the 1937 outbreak of war between the two countries impeded efforts to deal with domestic issues. Japanese expansionism elicited criticism from much of the rest of the world but did not result in significant military aid to China. The Guomindang was on its own in coping with its aggressive neighbor. Yet its policies during the late 1920s and early 1930s did not inspire confidence in its desire for reform, its fairness, or its efficiency.

Landlords and often corrupt local officials still dominated in the countryside. They paid little or no attention to peasant distress and, in fact, continued to demand taxes even as farmers reeled from the effects of the Depression in the early 1930s. The foreign demand for tea, silk, cotton, and other Chinese products declined precipitously, driving many peasants to bankruptcy and a few ultimately to bare survival, if not starvation. Most peasants who worked in the large holdings of landowners received a pittance for their efforts and could barely eke out an existence. Those peasants who farmed on their own had small plots, which were, on occasion, scattered over long distances; this precluded mechanization, even in the remote possibility that peasants had funds to buy labor-saving devices. They generally used their own labor rather than machines. Local officials exacerbated the difficulties confronting peasants by not properly maintaining irrigation complexes, canals, dams, and other infrastructure projects. Floods and droughts plagued rural areas, leading to great rural distress and famines in the 1930s and the deaths of millions.

Social conditions in the rural areas were also not altered or reformed. The government scarcely fostered public-health programs, which contributed to significant incidences of infectious and parasitic diseases, especially after floods or other natural disasters. Rates of infant, child, and maternal mortality were similarly high. Countryside children frequently did not go to school, leading to low levels of literacy. From 1928, the time of the Guomindang's accession to power, until the onset of war with Japan in 1937, there were scant discernible changes in the lives of most peasants, which translated into considerable loss of support for the government.

A few urban residents profited from Guomindang rule, yet even they registered complaints about its policies. The government, lacking regular income taxes until the mid 1930s, imposed heavy financial burdens on industrialists and merchants. Nonetheless, the urban elites benefited from government, private, and foreign expenditures. As a result, universities and colleges sprang up, and a few students were granted the opportunity to study abroad. The USA used the Boxer indemnity funds to provide student scholarships. The Chinese government and foreign groups constructed hospitals and established medical schools, including the Rockefeller Foundation-funded Peking Union Medical College, which became a major research center and a transmitter of Western-style medicine. At the same time, Western cultural developments attracted the Chinese elite. Movies, radios, and translated novels and plays gained audiences in the larger cities, especially in Shanghai, the most dramatically Western-influenced urban area. European-style buildings dominated the skyline in the Bund, the Shanghai port area. Jazz bands in the Bund's Peace Hotel catered to foreigners and Chinese. The city's so-called foreign concessions reflected French, British, and other foreign styles, which the Chinese elite emulated in their clothing, music, and mannerisms. Shanghai became the most sophisticated of all of China's urban areas, with the problems (prostitution, gambling, and opium) as well as the advantages of cosmopolitanism. Yet, despite this fad for Western culture, some of the industrial and mercantile elites resented the Guomindang's punitive taxation, occasionally capricious economic policies, and demands for bribes and gifts. Corruption impinged upon some in the bourgeoisie, who were also disturbed by the Green Gang's criminal pursuits and the Guomindang's inability to restrain opium and human trafficking, among other illegal activities.

The professional and intellectual classes became increasingly disenchanted with Chiang and the Guomindang, which limited civil liberties and became repressive. The government censored newspapers, books, and movies, restricted freedom of speech and assembly, and, on occasion, arrested or executed dissenters, especially those at universities. Students and faculty, who had expected a new era of freedom after the removal of the warlords from Beijing, were dismayed by Guomindang policies. The Guomindang repeatedly accused dissenting or protesting students and instructors of communism and swept many of them to prison or had them killed. Government repression alienated not only many university students and students but also many professionals.

Advocates of women's rights were initially elated but were to be somewhat disappointed. The May Fourth movement had emphasized love as opposed to arranged marriages, as well as suffrage and better pay for women. Women in the urban areas, who were not as bound as their sisters in the countryside, were exposed to feminist journals and media and literary works, leading to calls for change. The law codes of the late 1920s and early 1930s abolished arranged marriages, prohibited the sale of women, and allowed widows to remarry. Women obtained the right of divorce in cases of desertion, rampant physical abuse, or attempted sale into prostitution. Men could not, as in traditional times, initiate divorce for barrenness, loquacity, theft, or jealousy. Women gained new legal rights, but implementation of these law codes lagged behind, especially in the countryside. Women in the rural areas confronted even more difficulties. Arranged marriages and domestic abuse were still common, and widows were still vulnerable in their deceased husband's family. They received low prices for their crops, especially during the Depression of the 1930s, and were subject to substantial taxes and onerous rents.

A few Chinese and Westerners have recently argued that the Guomindang era from around the mid 1920s had some positive features, partly due to a growing link with the global economy. They point out that China borrowed or appropriated numerous institutions, goods, and services from the West and profited as a result. The first modern shops and department stores displayed suits, neckties, cosmetics, perfumes, leather shoes, lamps, clocks and watches, razors, and cameras. New modes of transport, such as bicycles, taxis, and public buses, reached China. Homes were modernized with gas radiators, indoor plumbing, telephones, somewhat reliable electricity, tap water, and carpets. New schools, with adequate supplies of pens, erasers, books, and typewriters, were built. In Shanghai and a few other cities, hospitals and colleges were founded. A wide variety of restaurants and cafes were established. Chinese, especially those living in the urban areas, were exposed to international cuisine and to such foods as pasta, ice cream, and white sugar.

Yet this view that the Republican era witnessed economic progress has to be qualified. These new products and institutions were enjoyed by and catered to a small elite. The vast majority of the population had no access to these Western luxury goods, nor did many attend schools or colleges, have treatment in hospitals, or live in comfortable housing. These technological advances, useful and luxury goods, and modern institutions were available only in Shanghai and a few other cities. Trade with foreigners increased, foreign companies fostered some economic development, a stock exchange developed, and a panoply of foreign goods could be purchased in a few markets, shops, and department stores. Yet again, a small group profited from such changes and accessibility.

To an extent, China showed greater openness to the outside world. More foreigners arrived and provided valuable assistance. Ida Pruitt (1888–1985) was principal of a girls' school and head of the Department of Social Services at Peking Union Medical College, and subsequently wrote extraordinarily empathetic accounts of Chinese women. The art connoisseur John Ferguson (1890–1975) donated a fine collection of Chinese art to Nanjing University. Sidney Gamble (1890–1968) helped to conduct important social surveys of Beijing and north China. John Dewey (1859–1952), an influential American philosopher, lobbied so that the Boxer indemnity funds could be used for scholarships for Chinese to study in the USA. Many other foreigners devoted themselves to the welfare and modernization of China. Foreign advisers and Chinese promoted prison reform, human rights, and development of employment and professional organizations. They encouraged political debates at teahouses and parks, and meetings of chambers of commerce and other private organizations. However, these reforms and changes affected only a small part of the population. Parlous economic and social conditions prevailed for the vast majority of Chinese.

Novelists were among the first to publicize social ills and exploitation and to criticize the government. Li Feigan (1904–2005) showed his anarchist views by adopting the pseudonym Ba Jin, taking the first syllable of the name of Mikhail Bakunin (1814–1876) and the last syllable of the name of Pyotr

Kropotkin (1842–1921), both major anarchists. He wrote a novel describing the horrendous conditions facing coal miners. Having studied in France, he may have been influenced by Emil Zola's *Germinal*, another searing portrait of the exploitation of miners. His semiautobiographical and most popular novel, *Family (Jia)*, described the oppressiveness of the traditional patriarchal family structure. Ye Shengtao (1894–1988), an essayist and novelist, wrote about intellectuals who witnessed social evils but found themselves depressed and unable to act. Shen Yanbing (1896–1981), an editor, translator, essayist, and novelist who would eventually become minister of culture in the early communist period, depicted the travails of women both in marriage and as concubines. *Midnight (Ziye)*, his most renowned novel, shone a light on the bourgeoisie in Shanghai, their manners, their betrayals, and their doom. Believing that his frank and realistic novels and short stories jeopardized him, he adopted the pseudonym Mao Dun to protect himself.

Several of these writers, including Lu Xun, the twentieth century's most famous Chinese literary figure, joined the League of Left-Wing Writers in 1930 but were concerned about its formulaic communist line on literature. Lu Xun himself never became a Communist Party member. Ba Jin remained an anarchist until the communists took power in 1949. Mao Dun would, on occasion, criticize works produced only for ideological purposes, and Ye Shengtao did not play an active role in politics until the communists emerged victorious.

Such negative reactions to the first years of Chiang's and the Guomindang's rule provoked an attempt to offer attractive alternatives to these various constituencies. Because of the links and alliances between the Guomindang and groups who benefited from existing conditions, accommodating those who were discontented proved elusive. The government thus provided scant concessions or support for peasants, as it could not afford to alienate landlords. Links with the Green Gang and some powerful and wealthy entrepreneurs, in part through Chiang's brothers-in-law T. V. Soong and H. H. Kung, precluded much effort to ameliorate the conditions for workers in their workplaces.

In the mid 1930s, Chiang sought to appeal to intellectuals and students through the announcement of a so-called New Life movement. Harking back to the tenets of Confucianism and blending them with aspects of Western morality as filtered through his recent conversion to Christianity, Chiang emphasized the development of an ethical society as a means of restoring China to its rightful place among the world's powers. He asserted that proper behavior and adherence to traditional moral principles would strengthen his principal objective of strengthening the state. A puritanical approach to cleanliness, sex, and civic responsibility would create an environment for China's resurgence. Part of this campaign, including propaganda against spitting in the streets, derived from Sun Yat-sen's expressed views. Neither intellectuals nor students were impressed by the movement, which they found oppressive for the educated and women and subversive of human rights. They concluded that the movement was a cover for the corruption and continued exploitation of much of China.

One low-key individual and one militant organization arose to support Chiang. Liang Shuming (1893–1988), labeled the "last Confucian," had been on the Beijing University faculty and later became a school principal. He had been exposed to Westernizers and Marxists early in his career. Arguing that China had a unique culture, he asserted that it could not readily apply Western models. He believed that democracy was ill suited to China and that the Marxist formulas did not apply to Chinese society. Instead, he advocated education of the peasants, as well as the literati, to provide competent and moral examples for a revival of the traditional culture and state.

The Blue Shirts, which was composed of military officers from the Whampoa Military Academy, under Chiang's jurisdiction, had a different vision from Liang's relatively benign approach. They admired and attempted to model themselves on the European fascist movements. Disdainful of democracy, they sought other means to solve China's problems. Concerned about instability and lack of order, they supported a powerful executive. A strong leader such as Chiang and a resulting strong state were their aims. They could not tolerate dissenters who, in their view, weakened the state, and they certainly had no patience with free-living and hedonistic students. Echoing Chiang's views, they reviled the so-called sybaritic lifestyle of their opponents and were dedicated to a militaristic system and to destroying the Communist Party. Their mission was to eradicate what the Guomindang labeled "communist bandits." Dai Li (1897–1946), who had studied at the Whampoa Military Academy, was one of their leaders and was the head of Chiang's secret service. Reviled as the "Himmler of China," he employed secret agents to spy on leftist and communist groups and employed brutal means against alleged enemies.

COMMUNIST PARTY REVIVAL

In 1928, the communists appeared to be doomed. Li Dazhao, one of the earliest leaders, had been executed; Guomindang forces and allies had easily suppressed the Autumn Harvest Uprising of August 1927 and the Canton Commune of December 1927; and the Communist Party leadership was in disarray, with nearly all its members subscribing to Stalin's views but with some dissenters. In early 1928, the remaining communists had been forced to withdraw from the cities, where much of the proletariat, their alleged prime constituency, resided. The Western countries tended to support the Guomindang, while the USSR, the communists' alleged ally, could not or perhaps was unwilling to provide military or economic assistance to them. They had few resources and did not control any key economic centers. Their ray of hope was various groups' increasing disillusionment with Guomindang policies and governance.

Mao Zedong (1893–1976) appeared on the historical stage at this time. After the failure of the Autumn Harvest Uprising in 1927, he gathered the remnants of that disastrous outbreak and led them to the Jinggang Mountains in a remote region of his native province of Hunan. Shortly thereafter, continuous Guomindang attacks compelled Mao and his supporters to move eastward to a rural area in Jiangxi province. Here Mao organized the Jiangxi

Soviet (which lasted from 1931 to 1934) in imitation of the USSR, and here too he began to justify communist reliance on peasants, whom traditional Marxists had considered to have a petty bourgeois attachment to land ownership. Mao challenged the communist dependence on the proletariat by analyzing the peasants of China and by identifying some as potential allies or almost semi-proletarians. He asserted that rich peasants, who often had their own land and tools and a grain surplus, would not support a communist revolution. On the other hand, he suggested that the communists could trust the middle peasants, who barely eked out a living, and the poor peasants, who had insufficient food and would, on occasion, be on the verge of starvation. Those on the fringes of rural society – beggars, the unemployed, seasonally employed laborers – could also be potential supporters. The bulk of the rural population could supposedly be attracted to the communist message, and, since the vast majority of Chinese lived in the countryside, the communists, according to this theory, had a vast potential pool of support.

Mao thus not only questioned Marxist orthodoxy but now also tailored his policies to accommodate his theoretical formulations. Not wishing to alienate any segment of the peasant population, he did not encourage radical efforts. A few landlords were executed, and land owned by some landlords and rich peasants was confiscated. However, moderation prevailed in his Jiangxi Soviet. Mao was relatively weak and was more concerned about building up a military force. He depended upon Zhu De (1886–1976), who remained loyal to him throughout the ups and downs of Mao's career, to organize his guerilla army. Mao and Zhu became so closely identified that many in the outside world referred to them as Mao-Zhu and may have believed them to be one person. They had no choice but to rely upon guerilla warfare. They were vastly outnumbered by the Guomindang army, and also did not possess the massive weapons available to these adversaries. Their strategy of guerilla warfare centered upon avoidance of full-fledged battles, in which they could not match the Guomindang's advantages in manpower and armaments. Ambushes and skirmishes would be much more effective because they could determine the terrain and the numbers of combatants. Such a policy could be successful only if they had the local populace's support. They needed not only grain and other supplies but also information and intelligence from the peasants. The local inhabitants would act as their protectors.

Mao, Zhu, and their troops certainly needed such protection because Chiang Kai-shek was determined to crush them. Guomindang forces initiated "bandit extermination" campaigns. The first two campaigns led to standoffs, with neither side emerging as a clear-cut victor. Communist survival in the face of such overwhelming force prompted Chiang to seek outside assistance in suppressing them. He turned to German military advisers who suggested a serious blockade, the use of air power, and the construction of new roads to facilitate Chiang's army's movements. Based upon these recommendations, the fifth bandit extermination campaign finally surrounded the communists in Jiangxi. Recognizing that they were in mortal danger, the communist leaders decided that they would have to gamble by trying to break out of this stranglehold.

LONG MARCH AND AFTERMATH

In October of 1934, the communists set forth on the so-called Long March, a touchstone and almost mythical event in their history. It gave them a romantic aura, although the actual grinding drive across treacherous rivers, lofty mountains, and often barren terrain was perilous and led to great loss of life. Encounters with enemy troops, ambushes by local inhabitants, and wintry weather added to their woes. After a year of such extraordinary movement, the various communist contingents reached a safe sanctuary in the remote region of Yan'an in Shaanxi province. Many soldiers perished en route, and the Guomindang captured and executed a few leaders. Yet several commanders who were to play critical roles in twentieth-century China took part in the Long March, an approximately six-thousand-mile journey, and made it to safety. Mao himself managed to survive, although illness compelled soldiers to carry him for part of the way. Zhou Enlai, who had studied in France and was perhaps the most sophisticated of the communist leaders, was overall commander for a time, and Zhu De was the best-trained military commander of the older generation. Lin Biao (1907–1971) and Peng Dehuai (1898–1974), two young commanders who later would appear to have been tapped as Mao's successors, led two detachments.

Their success in this demanding expedition temporarily forged unity among the leaders. Such unity did not endure, as rival factions would repeatedly arise throughout Chinese communist history. All, however, hoped that their new base in northwest China – closer to the USSR, their principal ally – might translate into Soviet assistance. The USSR could not have helped when their base had been in Jiangxi and they had been surrounded by Guomindang troops. Migration to a less populated region, which was geographically isolated from the rest of China and relatively free of Chiang Kai-shek's forces, offered not only a respite but also the possibility of supplies from the USSR.

This rosy prospect did not coincide with USSR policy. By 1928, Joseph Stalin, having defeated Leon Trotsky and facing no serious opposition to his rule, had initiated radical collectivization in the rural areas and nationalization of enterprises in the cities. His foreign policies mirrored his hard-line domestic policies. He perceived the Western capitalist countries as enemies who sought the overthrow of the communist system in the USSR. At first, he did not distinguish between the Western democracies and Nazi Germany and Fascist Italy. From 1928 to 1935, he remained opposed to collaboration with Britain, France, and the USA, the leading Western democracies, to contain the Nazis and Fascists. Similarly, in east Asia, areas adjacent to the USSR's Siberian territories, he did not seek to create an alliance in opposition to imperial Japan's expansionist aims. In 1935, after two years of Adolph Hitler's rampage against leftists and communists in Germany, he began to differentiate between the threats posed by the Nazis and the competition with the Western States and sought a rapprochement with the European democracies. In east Asia, he perceived Japan to be a dangerous force and decided to emphasize a united-front policy against its territorial objectives in China and Southeast Asia. He called upon the Chinese communists to join with all Chinese, including Chiang Kai-shek's Guomindang, in a nationalist campaign against the Japanese.

The communist leaders' initial response to Stalin is not recorded, but they quickly adhered to a united-front policy. Having reached Yan'an after the Long March, Mao Zedong had praised what he believed to have been a miraculous achievement and condemned Chiang Kai-shek and his forces for their relentless attacks on the Red Army (the military forces organized by the communists, also called the People's Liberation Army) and for their exploitation of the Chinese people. It must have required a dramatic reversal of his views and values to accept Stalin's message. Nonetheless, he swallowed his pride, and by early 1936 he had begun to advocate for a united front. Some of his opponents agreed with his position. Zhang Xueliang (1901–2001), the son of Zhang Zuolin (the old warlord of Manchuria, who had been assassinated by the Japanese), had been Chiang's staunch ally in trying to suppress the Chinese communists. Naturally, he despised the Japanese, which made him receptive to a nationalistic effort to resist China's increasingly powerful neighbor. He even met secretly with Zhou Enlai to discuss an anti-Japanese coalition. Others among Chiang's followers and allies wanted to join in a patriotic movement to protect China from further Japanese incursions, but Chiang wished to focus on the communists. On December 9, 1935, students in Beijing organized a demonstration to protest Japanese aggression. The authorities dispersed the demonstrators, but other protests persisted. However, Chiang Kai-shek was determined to pursue his "bandit extermination" campaign against the communists rather than opposing Japanese incursions. Despite continued Japanese encroachment, even in north China and not simply in peripheral areas with large non-Chinese populations, Chiang remained focused on crushing the communist guerillas. Chiang's unwillingness to confront the Japanese infuriated more and more Chinese.

These tensions and hostilities erupted in December of 1936. Chiang convened a meeting of his top military commanders and allies in Xian to plan a campaign to "extirpate" the communists. Zhang Xueliang, one of the participants, had become so frustrated with Chiang that he decided to act. He kidnapped Chiang and demanded that his captive conclude his conflict with the communists and instead collaborate with them to save the country. Ironically, the communists were, in part, responsible for Chiang's release. Stalin had sent them a message asserting that Chiang, not Zhang, had the national reputation and support that could galvanize the bourgeoisie and other segments of the population in an anti-Japanese coalition. He urged them to line up behind Chiang. The communists responded by dispatching Zhou Enlai to Xian to facilitate a compromise between Zhang and Chiang. After oral assurances from Chiang, Zhang agreed to Zhou's plan to release Chiang. The Guomindang leader returned to his capital in Nanjing, and Zhang, to demonstrate his loyalty, accompanied Chiang. Zhang was detained and remained under house arrest for about five decades in China and then Taiwan, when the Guomindang was compelled to leave the mainland. During those years, he became an ardent Christian, built up a collection of Chinese art, and stayed clear of politics. Meanwhile, Chiang restated his opposition to a united front with the Chinese communists. Stalin had erred, not for the first time, in his perceptions of Chinese politics and society.

THE SINO–JAPANESE WAR

The lack of collaboration subverted China's response to Japan, which had grand ambitions in Asia. Seeking to take its place as a world power, Japan felt humiliated by what it perceived to be Western insults. After the Sino–Japanese War of 1894–1895, the Western countries had compelled Japan to abandon some of the territorial concessions it had obtained via the Treaty of Shimonoseki. At the conclusion of the Russo–Japanese War of 1904–1905, the Treaty of Portsmouth, brokered by US President Theodore Roosevelt, had limited the gains Japan thought it deserved. In the 1907 Gentlemen's Agreement negotiated with Roosevelt, it had acquiesced to limitations on Japanese immigration to the USA, although Japanese who were already residents would be granted US citizenship and Japanese students could obtain visas to study in the USA. In 1924, the US Congress enacted further restrictions on east Asian immigration, an even greater humiliation. During this time, Japan's only Western ally was Britain, with which it had signed an agreement as early as 1902. Yet at the Washington Naval Conference of 1921–1922, Britain joined the USA in applying a ratio of 5:5:3 to the tonnage of warships of each country, and Japan was accorded the lowest number. The Western powers reasoned that they had to station their vessels in the Atlantic and Mediterranean, among other places, and had to defend more territories than Japan did in the Pacific. The Japanese accepted this interpretation because it seemed to offer them a privileged position in the Pacific and, from their standpoint, a sphere of influence. They also compromised and refrained from demanding economic and territorial privileges in the old German concessions they had occupied during the First World War.

Yet all these incidents rankled Japan, which resented the way it had been forced to relinquish territorial and commercial gains and had not, in its view, been accorded proper respect. The rise of increasingly nationalist leaders in the late 1920s made the Japanese more assertive, and economic problems, exacerbated by the worldwide depression, added to their discontent. They started to make more forceful claims by creating the Greater East Asia Co-Prosperity Sphere, a vaguely described organization that was designed to bolster Japan's status in the region. Pointing to the US position in the Americas, Japan wanted to play the same role in east Asia. Yet the government did not want to act precipitously and thus to risk creating an incident in China. It sought to restrain the firebrands in the parts of the Japanese army based in Manchuria, but its officers provoked an incident in September of 1931, defeated Chinese troops, and occupied Manchuria. They quickly sought legitimacy by placing Puyi, the last Qing-dynasty emperor, at the head of and eventually as the emperor of the new country of Manchuria. They ignored the relatively feeble League of Nations response rejecting recognition of the new state, and Manchuria was effectively detached from Chinese control.

Figure 11.3 Invading Japanese forces moving into Nanjing, 1937. © Bettmann / CORBIS

Having not faced significant opposition in their occupation of Manchuria, the Japanese were emboldened to take additional steps to dismember China. In 1933, they moved into northern Hebei province, the area closest to Manchuria and, more ominously, the province nearest Beijing. Shortly thereafter, they supported the Mongol prince Demchugdongrob (1902–1966) in his effort to break away and to establish an independent country of Inner Mongolia. Some of their scholars helped the government by emphasizing the distinctions between the Chinese and the Mongolians and by promoting Mongolian ethnic identity. Prince De (as Demchugdongrob would be known to the Chinese) became the so-called ruler of much of Inner Mongolia but with Japanese advisers and commanders making the crucial decisions. Like Puyi, Prince De was virtually a Japanese puppet. Japan appeared to threaten many northern Chinese provinces. One incident after another followed until a confrontation between Chinese and Japanese soldiers in July of 1937 at the Marco Polo Bridge, ten miles west of Beijing, led to the outbreak of war. Within the next few months, Japanese troops, despite considerable loss of life, occupied much of China's east coast. When these soldiers entered the capital city of Nanjing, they were primed to exact revenge against the Chinese. They unleashed an assault on Chinese soldiers and civilians and men and women that the Chinese labeled the Nanjing Massacre. The number of dead, wounded, and raped Chinese is still in dispute, but that there was a seemingly uncontrolled rampage seems unquestionable.

Meanwhile, Chiang Kai-shek did not surrender and simply moved farther and farther inland. The Japanese had apparently hoped to break down resistance and to set up friendly puppet governments without having to use an enormous number of soldiers to pacify the Chinese interior. In any event, they did not have sufficient troops to occupy the whole country. It is not clear whether Chiang's retreat to the interior with him winding up in Chongqing was a deliberate strategy or merely a response to repeated Japanese threats and his own loss of men and territory. However, the net effect was to prevent a Japanese victory, leading to a protracted stalemate in the war. Yet Chiang's control over China had indeed receded. Japan dominated much of China's east coast, Manchuria, Inner Mongolia, and sections of north China; Xinjiang and other border areas were virtually independent; and the communists controlled an increasing part of the northwest. The Japanese recruited Wang Jingwei, one of Chiang's most ardent opponents in the late 1920s, to serve as the alleged governor of the central sections of China (including the Shanghai and Nanjing regions) – or, more accurately, to be the Japanese puppet in the region, detaching still more territory from Chiang's control.

Chiang's position was thus fragile. He did not fear a ground invasion by Japanese forces, but enemy planes pummeled Chongqing and other sites. The USSR initially provided some assistance, but by the end of the 1930s and early 1940s it had turned its attention to threats posed in the West. After the summer of 1939, it could focus almost entirely on the West because it had helped Mongolia to end incursions on its territory by defeating the Japanese at the battle of Nomonhan (or Khalkhin Gol, to the Mongolians). Marshal Gyorgy Zhukov (1896–1974), one of the great Russian heroes of the Second World War, earned his first successes in this battle. After this battle, because the USSR no longer feared the opening of a second front against Japan, it could marshal its troops in the West, which translated into reduced support for Chiang. The USA provided minimal economic assistance, and Chiang's main American supporters were the pilots recruited by Claire Lee Chennault (1893–1958). This volunteer group, which eventually came to be known as the Flying Tigers, challenged Japanese superiority in the air and offered some protection for Chongqing.

Chiang had not dealt with the serious problems that plagued his government in Nanjing. Corruption and nepotism appeared to be endemic, and the differences between rich and poor were still wide. Taxes on the peasantry were often high and capricious. Little was done to alleviate the peasants' poverty and suffering, which often translated into famines. Workers were exploited and lacked government support in the form of legislation to control the minimum wage and maximum hours. A few workers, especially those who labored in the arms industry, responded by developing a real class consciousness and solidarity. Although the war complicated efforts to introduce reforms or changes, the lack of progress on land reform, protection of industrial workers, and implementation of the Marriage Law (which had been enacted in 1931 and had abolished arranged marriages and offered more rights to women) undercut support for the Guomindang. In addition, a seeming reluctance to employ its best troops against the Japanese alienated patriotic Chinese.

THE PACIFIC WAR, THE COMMUNISTS, AND THE GUOMINDANG

After the Japanese attacked Pearl Harbor on December 7, 1941, the USA began to play a role in the Pacific. President Franklin D. Roosevelt appointed General Joseph Stilwell (1883–1946) as commander of the US forces in east and Southeast Asia to represent US interests in China and to collaborate with Chiang Kai-shek. As the war progressed, Stilwell became increasingly disenchanted with the Guomindang. He was appalled by the government's incompetence and corruption. Derisively referring to Chiang as "Peanut," he repeatedly but unsuccessfully pressed the Guomindang leader to use his best forces against the Japanese. Stilwell also faced opposition from Claire Chennault, who emphasized air power rather than ground forces. Limited resources meant that a decision was needed about these differing strategies. Both Chiang and the major US decision makers opted for air power and started to build airports and to seek planes from the USA, stymieing Stilwell, whom Roosevelt eventually recalled from China.

The Chinese communists did not achieve a true united front with the Guomindang and faced other difficulties as well. Not only did they not forge an alliance with the Guomindang but also the armies of the two Chinese parties, on occasion, clashed, with considerable loss of life and damage to the land. Each side blamed the other for these counterproductive hostilities, and the Guomindang went one step further by denying the communists in the northwest products they required. Nazi Germany's attack on the USSR in June of 1941 exacerbated the communists' problems because the Russians, intent on their own defense, could provide almost no assistance. The British, having surrendered Singapore to the Japanese, were also preoccupied, which prevented them from helping the Chinese.

Nonetheless, the communists did engage the Japanese. Their forces attacked Japanese positions in north China but did not make substantial progress. Instead, these battles provoked the Japanese into harsh reprisals on the Chinese population, sometimes leading to destruction of whole communities. With such a relatively weak position, the communists could not afford to alienate people they ruled by initiating radical policies. They needed to be pragmatic rather than ideological. Their leaders did not advocate confiscation of land owned by landlords or rich peasants, nor did they institute significant social reforms.

The Communist Party itself underwent dramatic change, as it identified its new leadership and clarified and supplemented its ideology. Party membership had increased spectacularly, but the communist hierarchy believed that many new recruits lacked knowledge of and dedication to communism. The party had grown from the ten thousand or so who survived the Long March to about 2.8 million in 1942, the year that Mao Zedong initiated efforts that would make him the virtually undisputed leader of the party. He started a so-called Rectification Campaign, which lasted from 1942 to 1944, to weed out those whom he considered to be ignorant of communist ideology, and this led to a decrease in party size. Many of the new recruits had been peasants from the communists' base in Yan'an and the surrounding regions. Party leaders started schools to train those who retained their party affiliation in proper behavior and ideology and welcomed urban youth, intellectuals, and professionals who had been entranced by the communists' message and had moved to Yan'an. The schools instructed party members to be egalitarian, to live simply, to maintain ties with the local population, and to adhere strictly to Marxist–Leninist–Maoist ideology. It was significant that Maoism now came to the fore. Mao perceived himself to be on a par with Marx and Lenin as a thinker, and he wanted to distinguish himself from the Soviet leaders, some of whom he began to distrust.

Perhaps the main thrust of the Rectification Campaign was "thought reform," a means of "purifying" party members. They met in discussion groups as part of the so-called brainwashing. Each participant was criticized and then wrote a self-criticism about his or her divergence from Marxist–Leninist–Maoist thought and deviation from party instructions. After considerable group discussion, the participant would write a self-confession in which he or she apologized for past mistakes. The campaign spilled over into an attack on supporters of Mao's previous rivals and on independent-minded intellectuals (a group Mao often considered to be insufficiently loyal to him) who were hesitant to acquiesce to the party's and his dicta. This was the first of a series of purges that would characterize Chinese communist history. Mao also brought communist cadres back to schools.

His lectures to the assembled groups were then published. In addition to the standard Marxist ideology, he charted new ground in his speeches. He again set forth his reasoning for communist reliance on support from the peasants for victory. In his work on art and literature, his instructions to writers and artists were that they represent the proletariat. Their works could not be neutral. Mao denigrated the concept of art for art's sake. He insisted that art and literature always reflected particular class interests. Artists and writers needed to support the working classes' interests. "Socialist realism" had to guide their works. They had to portray society realistically but also needed to point to the socialist future by describing the values and attitudes of a new socialist mankind. It was no accident that simplistic but colorful posters imprinted with party slogans became popular works of art. Literature and art that did not subscribe to the strictures of socialist realism would not be tolerated, and writers and artists who deviated from this model would have their works censored and could be imprisoned or, in extreme cases, hounded to death. Mao's formulations on these issues became party dogma and solidified his position as party leader.

As the Pacific War began to turn in favor of the Allies, principally the Americans, both the Guomindang and the Chinese communists were affected. From late 1942 on, US forces had gradually been defeating the Japanese and compelling them to abandon one Pacific island after another, moving ever

Figure 11.4 Mao Zedong (left) and Zhou Enlai (right) in Yan'an in northwest China, 1945. Photo: akg-images

closer to the Japanese islands. By 1944, US airplanes were bombarding Japan itself. General James Doolittle (1896–1993) had already pounded Tokyo and other cities as early as April 18, 1942, but by 1944 the raids were more frequent and deadlier. The most important contribution of both Chinese parties was to pin down Japanese forces in China, improving the USA's chances in the conflict with Japan. However, the actions of the Guomindang and the Chinese communists differed. The Guomindang continued to be accused of harsh treatment and exploitation of peasants and of forced conscription into the army. Income disparities and corruption persisted in the Guomindang-controlled regions, and morale in these areas was damaged. The Guomindang's campaigns against the Japanese were lackluster, with Japanese troops often inflicting heavy damage on Guomindang forces. Meanwhile, the communists appeared to have a disciplined, loyal, and efficient army. Having created greater stability toward the last few months of the Second World War, Mao Zedong could start to implement more dramatic changes, including a more sustained land reform that benefited the poor peasantry. The communists seemed so much more competent and dedicated that outside observers were sympathetic to them. Some Americans, including government officials, considered them to be more reliable partners than the Guomindang. Several presented favorable reports about the communists to President Roosevelt and portrayed them as "agrarian reformers." This was a crucial moment in US–Chinese relations because there was a possibility of an entente between the USA and the so-called agrarian reformers. However, Chiang Kai-shek ruled out collaboration with the communists, and Roosevelt abided by that decision.

Thus, the Allies permitted Chiang, not the communists, to attend the Yalta Conference in February of 1945, which would make plans for the postwar Pacific. Franklin Roosevelt, Joseph Stalin, and Winston Churchill, the British prime minister, were the principal actors and decision makers at the conference, while Chiang was a subordinate participant with scant leverage and had to accept the conference's consensus views. Roosevelt was eager to persuade Stalin to declare war on Japan in order to have Soviet troops participate in an invasion, a campaign that promised to generate numerous casualties because the Japanese would presumably fight to the death to protect their homeland. The US president, seeking to reduce America's casualties, was willing to make concessions to secure USSR involvement in the invasion. China was critical as a lure for Stalin. For example, Stalin demanded that Chiang endorse a plebiscite in Mongolia to determine whether its people wanted independence (which was, in theory, their current status) or to "remain under China's rule." China and the Guomindang had continued to claim that Mongolia was part of China, despite the fact that the Mongols now had their own communist government and institutions. In the ensuing election, the Mongols naturally opted for independence. Roosevelt also infringed upon China by agreeing to let Soviet troops liberate Manchuria and to grant the USSR special privileges there, particularly in ownership and access to railroads. In a weakened position, Chiang could not object to these concessions, which mostly concerned China.

Thus, the Japanese surrender in August of 1945 did not necessarily improve Chiang's position. The USSR had declared war on Japan a few days earlier and almost immediately sent troops to Manchuria, which seemed about to be detached from China. Tibet had been autonomous since at least 1911, if not earlier. In 1944, Turkic peoples had proclaimed an Eastern Turkistan Republic in Xinjiang, still another potentially independent entity. Warlords along China's periphery were de facto autonomous, a further blow to Chiang. The communists were expanding the territories under their jurisdiction. Chiang appeared unable to control events.

CIVIL WAR IN CHINA

The end of the Second World War initiated still another struggle for the control of China. The communists and the Guomindang, the two principal antagonists, had different strategies in this renewed civil war. The communists persisted in their policy of dominating the countryside, surrounding the cities, and then overwhelming the Guomindang. Reliance on the peasantry necessitated policies that appealed to the rural areas. Abandoning their earlier moderation, the communists now supported land reform. They targeted landlords, confiscating their land and permitting peasants to intimidate, harm, and sometimes kill them. This activist approach ingratiated the communists with the peasantry, though it resulted in capriciousness and violence. On the other hand, by not moving expeditiously to support land reform, the Guomindang did not identify itself with the peasants. Chiang was fixated on destroying the communist "bandits" before initiating significant changes that might attract the Chinese population. Much of Guomindang support also derived from the landlords and the bourgeoisie, groups that opposed such reforms. The communists definitely had the populist appeal, although they still had to contend with Guomindang troops trying to wrest control over territories that they had occupied. They could not compete with the Guomindang's weapons, but they were highly motivated, honest, and disciplined, attributes that Guomindang forces generally lacked.

Ironically, the communists had their first notable postwar victories on the country's fringes. In 1947, they occupied Inner Mongolia, ousting Mongols whom the Japanese had supported, and established the Inner Mongolian Autonomous Region, led by Mongols whom they considered to be reliable and loyal. Shortly thereafter, Ulanhu (1906–1988), a Mongol trained in the USSR and China, became the leader of the Inner Mongolian Autonomous Region. Manchuria, still another region on China's border, also proved to be a vital venue in the communists' ultimate success. The Yalta Conference had permitted the USSR to liberate Manchuria, and few, if any, restrictions were imposed on the Soviets in their occupation. Japan's surrender in August of 1945 allowed the Soviets a free hand in one of China's major industrial centers. Blessed with substantial natural and mineral resources, Manchuria had been the site of considerable investment by the Japanese in the 1930s. Factories and mines developed, and the population had increased. Good transport facilities linked the major cities, which had also benefited from Russian immigration from the early twentieth century on. Russian Jews, many with prized technical skills, had fled principally to the city of Harbin from pogroms in their homeland, and White Russians had sought sanctuary there after the Russian Revolution. Control of Manchuria thus offered significant advantages, and the Soviets capitalized on their liberation of the region. They dismantled machinery in factories and mines and shipped it to the USSR, where industries had been devastated by the Nazi invasion. They also confiscated tools, gold, and other items of value. Although they stripped a number of factories and mines, much of the industrial infrastructure remained an invaluable asset. The weapons abandoned by Japanese soldiers could also be useful. Russian troops recognized that, so they tried to ensure that the Chinese communists would obtain the abandoned arsenals. Similarly, they often turned over the lands they occupied to the communists. Chiang, unwilling to give up Manchuria without a fight, sent troops to prevent the communists from controlling this vital region, but his efforts failed. Despite massive superiority in manpower and military equipment, the Guomindang forces were riddled with corruption. Officials abused their positions for their own pecuniary gain. They managed enterprises, exploiting workers and carrying away and selling machinery from factories. The Guomindang was vulnerable, and Lin Biao, later to become the second most important figure among the communists and apparently Mao's successor, led the armies that forced Chiang's troops to withdraw from Manchuria.

Similar scenarios occurred throughout China. The Guomindang repeatedly harmed itself by its inefficiency, mismanagement, and toleration of corruption. Unemployment and inflation were rampant. Factory workers were exploited and paid poorly. In 1947, women workers in a cotton mill initiated a successful strike, adopting an aggressive response to employer elimination of New Year bonuses, child-care facilities, and maternity leave; other such incidents may have occurred. However, such victories were few and far between. In addition, morale among Guomindang troops was low. Many soldiers were either unwilling to fight or deserted. By contrast, the communist forces were disciplined and had high morale and a low rate of desertion. Foreigners residing in or visiting China noticed and wrote about the differences between the two sides. As early as the 1930s, the American journalist Edgar Snow and other visitors had praised and perhaps idealized the communists. Similarly, foreign observers provided withering criticisms of the Guomindang in its last days of control over China.

Under these circumstances, the communists were now ready to challenge the Guomindang in the cities. Although they still relied on the peasantry, the industrial workers began to provide support as well. In any event, their troops moved from the west and began to attack the eastern or central core of Chinese civilization. From Manchuria they headed south, and by late 1948 they had occupied much of north China, including the ancient capitals of Kaifeng and Luoyang. Communist forces had made a great leap forward: they could lay siege to sizable cities and actually seize them. After their campaigns in the north, they drove forward to the Yangzi-area cities, including Hangzhou and Shanghai. Probably as early as late 1947 or early 1948, Chiang and his associates must have known that they were losing the civil war. They began, at that time, to dispatch valuables, including precious artworks and manuscripts, to Taiwan. The three hundred thousand or so objects in the National Palace Museum in Taibei could not have been transported from China just in the last days of Guomindang domination of the mainland. Elaborate preparations must have been made much earlier, which confirms Chiang's recognition of the Guomindang's failure.

On October 1, 1949, Beijing provided the venue for Mao's proclamation of the People's Republic of China.

FURTHER READING

Ba Jin, *Family* (Prospect Heights, IL: Waveland Press, 1989).

Marie-Claire Bergère, *Sun Yat-sen* (Stanford: Stanford University Press, 1998).

Frank Dikkötter, *Things Modern: Material Culture and Everyday Life in China* (London: C. Hurst & Co., 2006).

Gail Hershatter, *Dangerous Pleasures: Prostitution and Modernity in Twentieth-Century China* (Berkeley: University of California Press, 1999).

Emily Honig, *Sisters and Strangers: Women in the Shanghai Cotton Mills, 1919–1949* (Stanford: Stanford University Press, 1992).

Peter Hopkirk, *Foreign Devils on the Silk Road* (London: John Murray, 2006).

C. T. Hsia, *History of Modern Chinese Fiction* (New Haven: Yale University Press, 1961).

Hsu Meng-hsiung, trans., *Midnight by Mao Dun* (Peking: Foreign Languages Press, 1957).

Leo Ou-fan Lee, *Shanghai Modern: The Flowering of a New Urban Culture in China, 1930–1945* (Cambridge, MA: Harvard University Press, 1999).

Stephen MacKinnon, *Wuhan, 1938: War, Refugees, and the Making of Modern China* (Berkeley: University of California Press, 2008).

Elizabeth Perry, *Shanghai on Strike: The Politics of Chinese Labor* (Stanford: Stanford University Press, 1997).

Ida Pruitt, *A Daughter of Han: The Autobiography of a Chinese Working Woman* (Eastford, CT: Marino, 2011).

Stuart Schram, ed., *Mao's Road to Power: Revolutionary Writings 1912–1949* (Armonk, NY: M. E. Sharpe, 7 vols., 1992).

Benjamin Schwartz, *Chinese Communism and the Rise of Mao* (New York: Harper & Row, 1951).

Jonathan Spence, *Gate of Heavenly Peace: The Chinese and Their Revolution* (New York: Viking Press, 1981).

Jay Taylor, *The Generalissimo: Chiang Kai-shek and the Struggle for Modern China* (Cambridge, MA: Harvard University Press, 2009).

Frederic Wakeman, *Policing Shanghai, 1927–1937* (Berkeley: University of California Press, 1996).

David Wang, *Fictional Realism in Twentieth-Century China: Mao Dun, Lao She, Shen Congwen* (New York: Columbia University Press, 1992).

Yang Hsien-yi and Gladys Yang, trans., *Complete Stories of Lu Xun* (Bloomington: Indiana University Press, 1981).

Yang Xianyi and Gladys Yang, trans., *Sun Shines Over the Sangkan River* (Beijing: Foreign Languages Press, 1984).

Madeleine Zelin, trans., *Rainbow by Mao Dun* (Berkeley: University of California Press, 1992).

[12] THE COMMUNIST ERA IN CHINA, 1949 ONWARDS

Early Pacification of Border Areas
Early Foreign Relations
Recovery from Wars
Cracks in the Communist World
Great Leap Forward
Return to Pragmatism
An Isolated China
Great Proletarian Cultural Revolution
China Reopens Its Doors
Dramatic Changes and Modernization
Tiananmen Disturbance of 1989
    and Its Aftermath
The Present Status of China

THE period since October of 1949 has witnessed remarkable fluctuations in Chinese government and Communist Party policies. Changes have, on occasion, been rapid and sometimes capricious. Often they have been predictable, but at other times the transformations have been sudden and so drastic that they have been difficult to understand. Motivations for these changes have ranged from perceived foreign threats to retention of ideological purity to personal struggles at the top of the hierarchy to decline in productivity to communist leaders' disenchantment with intellectuals or other segments of the population. Causes of these dramatic shifts have varied from realistic assessments of political and economic conditions to commitment to a rigid Marxist–Leninist-Maoist doctrine of development. The changes have caught

A History of China, First Edition. Morris Rossabi.
© 2014 Morris Rossabi. Published 2014 by Blackwell Publishing Ltd.

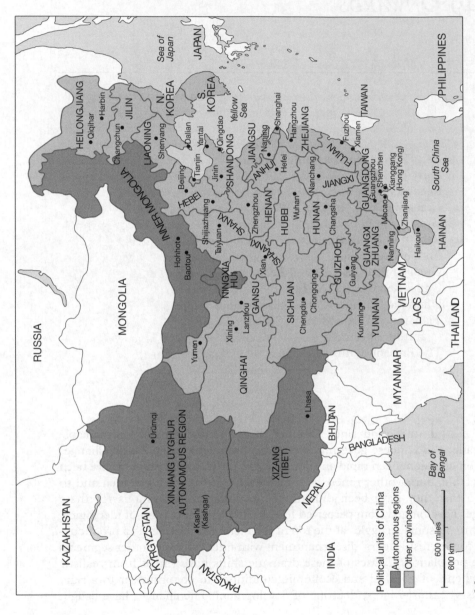

Map **12.1** China, 2013

many unawares and generated considerable instability and even chaos. Many Chinese have been confused by six decades of wavering and, at times, contradictory policies, which have occasionally prompted demonstrations and violence by police, army, and unruly crowds. Greater stability developed, in general, after Mao Zedong's death in 1976, but there were still periods of harsh and sudden fluctuations in government policies.

EARLY PACIFICATION OF BORDER AREAS

When the communists took power in late 1949, they had more substantial problems facing them than the capricious development of policies. They did not occupy specific regions, especially the borderlands. The regions that the Qing had added to China in the seventeenth and eighteenth centuries had capitalized on the dynasty's collapse to assert their autonomy or even independence.

Mongolia, the first of these regions to submit to the Qing, sought independence immediately after 1911. Plagued with disunity and an inability of the secular leadership and religious hierarchy to achieve peace for the country's benefit, Mongolia spent the period from 1911 to 1921 in limbo. Individual Mongol khans, Chinese warlords, and Japanese-backed White Russians, as well as a bizarre and murderous commander of Russian extraction named Baron Ungern von Sternberg (1885–1921), fought for control. Tsarist Russia, to which the Mongols appealed for support, feared antagonizing Japan and China and did not fully support the Mongols. In 1915, it brokered a vague arrangement by which Mongolia became autonomous but remained under Chinese suzerainty. Once the Bolsheviks took power, Lenin turned out to be more supportive and helped Mongolia to become an independent country and, in 1921, the second communist state in the world. The Mongolian People's Republic, as it came to be known after 1924, was heavily influenced by the USSR, but its legal status remained ambiguous. China claimed jurisdiction until 1945, when Stalin compelled Chiang Kai-shek to consent to a plebiscite in Mongolia. The Mongols opted for independence, but territorial disputes between Chiang and the Mongol government in Xinjiang prompted him to renounce the previous agreement. Mongolia was still not recognized by China, and Mao Zedong had also said that he looked forward to the country's incorporation into China. In 1950, under pressure from the USSR, Mao had to acknowledge Mongolia's sovereignty and exchanged ambassadors with the land to the north.

Mao was determined to maintain China's control over Inner Mongolia and Xinjiang. When his troops occupied Inner Mongolia in 1947, he ended the area's claims either to independence or as a region within the country of Mongolia (a policy that Japan had tried to implement during the Second World War). The communists would not permit such an outcome, yet they needed to appease the large Mongol population. They quickly appointed the sinicized Mongol leader Ulanhu to be the chief official in the so-called Inner Mongolian Autonomous Region. Their principal solution concerning minority areas was the development of the concept of an "autonomous region," which they have continued to use since that time. The term implied that the area's minority or minorities would have considerable decision-making power on the local level. Indeed, Mao and others in the communist leadership repeatedly stated that they would protect the minorities' cultural heritages, languages, and religious expressions. However, the policies they have pursued since 1949 have often clashed with their avowed intentions. They have, on occasion, undermined and attacked the minorities' unique cultural characteristics, which prompts speculation that they believed that the advent of communism would ultimately lead to increased assimilation and sinicization. Decades after the communists' assumption of power, minority "problems" remain intractable in China.

In the case of Inner Mongolia, the communists encouraged or coerced Chinese to move into the region. They sought to outnumber the Mongols, and, in fact, achieved their objective. Within a decade, the Mongols became a decided minority in their so-called autonomous region. The lure for the Chinese was extraordinary economic development. They could and did grow crops, cutting into the Mongols' pasture lands, and they found jobs in the burgeoning iron, steel, and chemical industries. The Chinese became the dominant force in the economy, but the communists adopted a flexible approach toward the Mongols by not interfering with their language, lifestyle, and culture. With this moderate approach and with a Mongol as the leader of the government, Inner Mongolia was relatively peaceful by the mid 1950s and had certainly fallen within the Chinese sphere.

Xinjiang experienced greater turbulence. After the collapse of the Qing, Yang Zengxin, a Chinese warlord, had taken command and initiated carrot-and-stick policies. Within a few years, he had crushed opposition from Chinese secret societies and, most important, from the local Muslim communities. Fewer corvée burdens and reductions in taxes had accompanied his repressive policies. The Bolshevik revolution posed problems for Yang, as central Asian Muslims and White Russians sought to use Xinjiang as a base for attacks on the USSR or at least as a sanctuary. Although he allowed a few of them to resettle in Xinjiang, his primary objective was peaceful relations with the USSR, which led to a treaty in 1924. This agreement permitted the USSR to set up five consulates in Xinjiang, and Yang was allowed a similar number in central Asia. Trade increased dramatically, surpassing Xinjiang's commerce with China. Yang seemed to be aligning himself with central Asia and the USSR rather than with China.

Even after Yang was assassinated in 1928, Sheng Shicai (1897–1970), one of Yang's most important successors, maintained relations with the USSR. Soviet advisers and technicians helped to develop the economy, and the USSR dispatched workers to build roads and railway lines. It also sent troops and supplies to assist Sheng to crush opponents. When the Soviet involvement in the Second World War prevented it from providing any further assistance, Sheng turned back to China and started an anticommunist campaign within his own ranks, executing Mao Zedong's brother during this time. Chiang Kai-shek did not trust Sheng and relieved him of his position in 1944. Without a Chinese strongman dominant in Xinjiang, the Turkic majority capitalized on the power vacuum to proclaim an independent Eastern Turkistan Republic in 1945.

For a time, it appeared that Xinjiang would become an independent country. Yet Chiang was able to impose a repressive Uyghur ally as the provincial leader. By 1949, the Uyghur ally had generated such hostility that he had been replaced by Burhan Shahidi (1894–1989), a communist ally. In the midst of these disputes, Mongolia's ruler Kh. Choibalsan (1895–1952) tried to lay claim to territories in Xinjiang. Because Kazakhs, one of the minorities in Xinjiang, constituted five percent of Mongolia's population, Choibalsan believed that he had a strong case for adding many Kazakh domains to his country. The USSR opposed his plan, and Mongolia would no longer be involved in Xinjiang.

The years after the Second World War offered the peoples of Xinjiang a golden opportunity to achieve autonomy or possibly independence, but disunity, the involvement of outsiders, and a terrible accident resulted in Chinese communist control. Some in the Turkic population sided with and sought assistance from the Guomindang; others allied with the communists; and still others hoped for USSR intervention. Fragmentation permitted the Chinese communists to become dominant. An accident – an airplane crash in which three of the most important Eastern Turkistan Republic leaders were killed – removed nationalists who might have challenged communist rule. The convenient elimination of these leaders aroused suspicion that either the Chinese communists or the USSR had deliberately sabotaged the plane.

Whether an accident or sabotage, the People's Liberation Army (the Chinese communists' military force) faced scant immediate resistance when it moved into Xinjiang in September and October of 1949. The USSR still planned to have influence in Xinjiang, but the People's Liberation Army asserted itself by defeating the dissident minority groups and occupying the areas it seized. By 1955, the Chinese communists were sufficiently secure to organize a Xinjiang Uyghur Autonomous Region, with autonomous districts and counties as well for the less numerous minorities such as the Kazakhs, Kyrgyz, and others. Critical to these efforts to control Xinjiang was Chinese migration, specifically into the eastern and northern sections of the autonomous region but with small pockets of settlements throughout. Some came as farmers and increased the amount of cultivated land, others were employed in the developing mining and industrial sectors, while still others followed the traditional model of herding in northern Xinjiang. The government organized them into a so-called Production and Construction Corps under the aegis of the military, entrusting them with militia duties along with their usual occupations. The Production and Construction Corps (or the Bingtuan, as it was commonly called in Chinese) became the wealthiest institution in the region. By the mid 1950s, the communists appeared to have stabilized Xinjiang through a relatively moderate policy that emphasized lack of confrontation with and meddling in the cultures, languages, and lifestyles of the minorities.

Tibet had been even freer of China's domination. From the early nineteenth century on, Qing-dynasty control had eroded. Tibet had become a source of contention between Britain and Russia, which were engaged in the Great Game, a struggle over their interests in central and south Asia. By the early twentieth century, however, Britain had become the principal foreign influence over Tibet, and in 1904 Colonel Francis Younghusband (1863–1942) and his troops entered Lhasa, compelling the Dalai Lama to flee, and imposed a treaty that basically turned Tibet into a British protectorate. After the Qing dynasty fell in 1911, Tibet was virtually detached from China, thanks to substantial influence from Britain. The events leading to and the onset of the Second World War diverted Britain, offering Tibet breathing space. Tibet tried to take advantage; the fourteenth Dalai Lama was selected in 1938, and throughout the war and in the immediate aftermath the Tibetan elite sought foreign support to retain its independence from China. Tibetan envoys attempted to elicit US recognition of Tibetan independence, but the US Department of State considered Tibet to be part of China.

The Chinese communist victory in China galvanized the USA to support Tibet and particularly to aid dissidents seeking Tibetan independence. In November of 1950, communist troops occupied Lhasa. The Dalai Lama fled, but he assigned a delegation to negotiate with the Chinese communists. In May of 1951, the negotiators devised a Seventeen-Point Agreement, which ratified communist rule over Tibet. Yet the Dalai Lama, who returned from exile later in the year, would still be Tibet's religious leader, and Tibet would be granted some flexibility, with the founding of a Tibet Autonomous Region. The communist regime would allegedly not interfere, at least temporarily, in the social class or theological systems. It would simply foster economic development through construction of roads and mining but would not move quickly to alter Tibetan society. Some Tibetans were certainly hostile to the Chinese, but, by the mid 1950s, the communists controlled Tibet.

EARLY FOREIGN RELATIONS

Once in power and while establishing their authority over the frontier terrain, the communists faced daunting problems in foreign relations. They first had to devise a proper relationship with the USSR. Their three-decades-long contacts with Stalin and other Soviet leaders had often been tense, although they had almost always abided by Soviet advice and instructions. Stalin was, in part, responsible for the almost disastrous policies the communists had pursued from 1925 to 1927. He had scarcely provided much economic or military assistance when Mao and his cohorts were based in Yan'an from 1935 through the Second World War and had not consulted with them about the structure of the postwar world. The Chinese communists were shut out of the Allied conferences at the end of the war and relied on Stalin's espousal of their interests. They eventually realized that Stalin was more concerned with his own and the USSR's special needs. Even harder for them to swallow was Stalin's support for an independent Mongolia, free of Chinese control. In December of 1949, Mao visited the USSR, his first and only journey outside China. Mao should have been prepared for Stalin's reactions at their meetings, which turned out unfavorably for the Chinese leader. Stalin pledged minimal assistance in the communists' efforts to overwhelm Chiang Kai-shek and then occupy Taiwan, but he promised to provide some economic aid. Once again, this agreement offered little to China. Even more exasperating was the considerable Soviet influence and economic involvement in the border areas of Xinjiang, Manchuria, and Inner Mongolia. Xinjiang had been linked to the USSR since the 1920s; Soviet troops had liberated Manchuria and still had considerable influence and possible allies there; and many Mongolians in the Soviet-influenced Mongolian People's Republic conceived of a Pan-Mongolian state that included Inner Mongolia. The potential for disagreements and conflicts was substantial.

Similar conflicts involving Taiwan were also on the horizon. Chiang Kai-shek had retreated to Taiwan after his defeat on the mainland in 1949, and the communists were poised for an attack on the island. Mao and his military commanders recognized that an invasion of Taiwan would be arduous and entail numerous casualties, but they appear to have been prepared for huge losses in such a campaign. Policy makers in the USA assumed that the communists would be successful and were reconciled to their takeover of Taiwan. The Korean War, which started in June of 1950, undermined this scenario. The onset of war between North Korea and South Korea prompted the United Nations Security Council to sanction the dispatch of United Nations troops, composed primarily of soldiers from the USA, to assist South Korea. The USA's massive firepower compelled North Korean troops to withdraw from Seoul, which they had occupied, and to retreat. The USA-led forces pursued the North Koreans and crossed into North Korea. At the same time, the USA dispatched naval forces to ply the waters between China and Taiwan to prevent a communist takeover of the island. Responding to what they perceived as US threats and fearing a strong US presence in the Pacific, the Chinese communists permitted so-called volunteers to come to the assistance of North Korea. Despite massive casualties, the communists pushed back the United Nations forces and temporarily reoccupied Seoul until the clear United Nations advantage in weaponry compelled them to withdraw from the city. From 1951 to 1953, neither side could gain a substantial advantage over the other, and each did not give up much ground. Finally, after a protracted and debilitating war, the two sides signed a truce agreement in July of 1953.

The Korean War was devastating for China. Deaths of soldiers, together with the diversion of financial resources to provide supplies for the military, were obvious results, but other consequences also harmed the country. China became isolated, as many countries, especially the USA, refused to grant diplomatic recognition to the new administration in Beijing. They maintained that the regime in Taiwan was the real government of China. The Chinese communists were unable to trade or have economic relations with many countries, forcing them to rely on the Soviet bloc for commerce and investment. Such lack of harmony with the West, particularly the USA, contributed to the prolongation of a cold war, which led to serious misconceptions on both sides. Chinese fears of a military attack resulted in the squandering of limited financial resources to build up a military force and sophisticated weaponry. The Chinese government also used the impasse to whip up hysteria about alleged US belligerency.

Simultaneously, anticommunist hysteria, partly due to a media and government campaign about the USA's "loss" of China to communism, struck the USA. Congressional committees investigated Chinese specialists in the Department of State as well as the so-called Old China Hands to lay blame for what was held to be failure in China. In the early 1950s, some of the leading government experts on China and east Asia, including John S. Service (1909–1999), O. Edmund Clubb (1901–1989), and John Paton Davies (1908–1999), had their security clearances revoked and left government employment. Congressional committees also targeted Owen Lattimore (1900–1989), John K. Fairbank (1907–1991), and other nongovernment employees who had criticized Chiang Kai-shek's government and had advocated a policy of moderation toward the Chinese communists. Supporters of Chiang in the academic community joined in the denunciations of these university faculty members as sympathetic to the Chinese communists. The bitterness of these struggles created a damaging rift in the field of Chinese studies. Owen Lattimore, arguably the greatest expert on China's borderlands, eventually left the USA and developed a program of study on east Asia at Leeds University in Britain, while John Fairbank, a pioneer in the study of modern China, remained at Harvard University, whose administrators generally supported him. In short, both communist China and the USA were hurt by these actions.

RECOVERY FROM WARS

In the early 1950s, the communists had to recover from the Japanese invasion, the civil war with the Guomindang, and the Korean War, and could not undertake radical policies. They first had to deal with the most pressing problems, some of which were not controversial. Foremost among these were infrastructure repairs, restoration of law and order (which entailed control over prostitution, secret societies, gangs, narcotics, gambling, and other criminal activities), establishment of such basic services as electricity and running water, and an increase in agricultural production to meet the population's needs. Public health was one of the critical difficulties that the government tackled. It initiated a Four Pests campaign, directed at rats, flies, mosquitoes, and sparrows. Killing of sparrows proved counterproductive because these birds served as predators for more harmful species of insects. Nonetheless, better sanitation, access to clean water, vaccinations, and training of medical personnel reduced the levels of infectious and parasitic diseases.

The status of women was still another difficulty that the communists immediately tried to alter. The Marriage Law of 1950 forbade female infanticide, arranged marriages, domestic abuse, and discrimination against women in the labor force. The effects of the law in the early 1950s were decidedly mixed. The government-controlled press acknowledged the persistence of arranged marriages and domestic abuse as late as the 1960s. Communist media also documented unequal wages for women in many enterprises, reluctance of many managers to hire women, and the paucity of crèches and child-care facilities, which were an impediment for women seeking employment. Simultaneously, the right of divorce led to dislocations. The communists, who still relied on the traditional household as the basic economic unit, were stunned by the dramatic increase in applications, mostly by women, for divorce. In 1954, the government quietly issued instructions to judges to seek to reconcile couples and to limit the granting of divorces to the most egregious instances of domestic abuse or to irreconcilable differences. Some progress was made in improving the position of women, but extraordinary changes, especially an increase in the number of women in the labor force and the strengthening of their economic rights, would be delayed. The government did not have the resources to provide nationwide care for children, nor did it seek an immediate challenge to traditional social practices, which might have generated considerable opposition. Advocates of moderate and incremental change dominated the government and were averse to disruptive and radical transformations.

On the other hand, the government initiated a series of campaigns directed at the populace. A Three-Anti campaign against waste, corruption, and bureaucratization was initiated; it was especially directed at Communist Party members who sought to use their honored status for their own profit. Many such cadres were perceived to be not entirely reliable. Shortly thereafter, the government initiated a Five-Anti campaign consisting of measures against tax evasion, fraud, bribery, purloining of state property, and theft of economic secrets. Most of the population avidly supported these efforts, which, in theory, offered a sharp contrast to Guomindang policies. Urban dwellers were particularly supportive of these movements, which served as models for future campaigns. The government used the media to announce the campaigns, which were then discussed in workplaces and educational institutions. "Spontaneous" mass rallies, which Communist Party cadres frequently organized, galvanized the people in a region and often resulted in abusive treatment of those labeled as anticommunists, who, at this time, were mostly members of the bourgeoisie or owners of large enterprises. The crowds and the cadres demanded confessions and criticized the alleged miscreants. To be sure, some were criminals or saboteurs or spies, but many were simply identified as bourgeois and had not committed any crimes. They merely derived from the wrong social class. These attacks spilled over into the remaining foreigners in China, especially foreign Christian missionaries, who were accused of spying and criminal activities. Most left the country, but a few were forced to confess and then imprisoned.

Regular efforts to establish a government accompanied these disruptive demonstrations and other activities. The Communist Party naturally dominated the top positions in government, and support from the People's Liberation Army, which had played an important role in the victory over the Guomindang, also was critical for anyone seeking power. The Central Committee of the party would devise policy, while the State Council, composed of such functional ministries as foreign affairs, justice, agriculture, finance, and education, implemented them. Economic planners were vital in these ministries, as the Communist Party pledged to increase production and to be more successful in economic development than the capitalist countries. Local government did not shift dramatically from the traditional Chinese system. China was divided into the basic traditional unit of provinces. However, Beijing and Shanghai had their own municipal governments and were not part of the provincial administration.

The major deviation from the past was the establishment of autonomous regions in the so-called minority nationality areas. The government eventually identified fifty-six such nationalities, with one – the Han, or ethnic Chinese – constituting about ninety-five percent of the population. The fifty-five others were a curious blend of religious, ethnic, or culturally distinct groups whose identification related to political agendas. For example, the Hui were ethnically Han people except that they were Muslims and were classified as such to distinguish them from ordinary Chinese. Most of the minorities resided in specific regions, but the Hui were scattered throughout the country. The government identified Turkic and Southeast Asian-related groups and further subdivided them, possibly to prevent unity between them. The minorities in southwest China were less troublesome to the government than those in the north. The northern groups – the Mongols, the Turkic and Iranian peoples of Xinjiang, and the Tibetans – had written languages, age-old cultural heritages, and strong senses of ethnic identity and had often clashed with Chinese dynasties over the centuries. The southwest had witnessed conflicts over Chinese expansionism but did not pose the same threats as the north's incursions or even conquests of China.

These ethnic groups and indeed the Han (or ethnic Chinese) had abiding faith in a variety of religions. Like other Marxist political parties, the Chinese communists perceived of religion as part of the social superstructure and designed to facilitate exploitation of the lower classes. According to this interpretation, the feudal and capitalist elites used temples, monasteries, churches, mosques, and religious experience in general to deflect the masses from focusing on economic bondage. Once such exploitation ended, religion would wither away. Yet the government needed to supervise religious organizations, and, within a few years of the founding of the People's Republic of China, it established a Chinese Buddhist Association and a Chinese Islamic Association and appointed reliable clerics and imams to coordinate and maintain control over these religions. The People's Republic of China actively promoted atheism in schools, the media, and propaganda. In its radical phases, the government initiated campaigns against religious organizations. It eventually targeted Tibetan Buddhism, Islam (especially in Xinjiang), and Christian house churches, the latter because they met secretly and were thus viewed as subversive. Believing that many clerics were traitors, young people at various times damaged monasteries and temples, destroyed ritual objects, and burned down mosques and churches. Nonetheless, Buddhism, Islam, and Christianity survived, challenging the view that religion was an ephemeral part of the superstructure.

Despite the disturbances caused by the mass campaigns and the accompanying purges of some leading governors, including a certain Gao Gang (1905–1954), the chief official in Manchuria, the government adopted relatively moderate policies until 1958. It followed the Soviet model of a reputedly rationally based Five-Year Plan. Planners did not make radical or absurd claims about increases in production. Again following the Soviet model, the planners focused on the growth of heavy industry and extraction of stiff taxes on agriculture to provide capital for the expansion. This may not have been the optimal strategy, but it was certainly not bizarrely irrational, as some later plans would be. Soviet experts and advisers arrived and promoted the efforts at industrialization. To be sure, the Five-Year Plan from 1953 to 1958 did not increase industrial production as much as the planners had predicted. Their policies in agriculture were similarly moderate, save for the rather demanding tax burdens. As early as 1952, they started to encourage formation of mutual-aid teams in which peasants would contribute their land and labor and would receive rewards based on the amount of land they owned. Starting in 1955, they pressed peasants to develop agricultural producers' cooperatives, which entailed even greater collaboration among peasants. In this new organization, peasants would be paid for their work, not on the basis of their land holdings. They would become, in Marxist terms, semiproletarians. In theory, the land still belonged to them, but they did not receive rewards based on the profits from their own land. To compensate for their losses, they received small private plots of land, the produce of which they could consume or sell. The government's rationales for encouraging or compelling peasants to join cooperatives were efficiency and potential for greater production. Larger and contiguous plots of land would facilitate the use of machinery and fertilizer, which would presumably lead to increased harvests. Politics was secondary to economics. The thrust of these organizational reforms was pragmatic, not ideological. Planners embraced the logic of increased production.

Part of the communist leadership's emphasis on rapid growth was due to isolation from the rest of the world. The USA, one of the world's major powers, not only had no relations with them but also granted diplomatic recognition to Chiang Kai-shek's regime in Taiwan as the legitimate government of China. Although China and the USSR were allegedly allies, the sources of tension between them stretched back to their first contacts in the 1920s. The USSR had acted as the big brother in the relationship but often considered its interests as paramount. Similarly, China's relationship with India was unstable because of territorial disputes. Japan appeared to be strongly linked to one of China's principal enemies, the USA. Facing such difficulties with the great powers, the Chinese sought to curry favor with the so-called Third World. Foreign Minister Zhou Enlai's attendance at the Bandung Conference in Indonesia in 1955 was a pivotal event. Zhou attempted to bond with the preeminent leaders of the world's nonaligned countries, stressing his view about the USA's imperial ambitions in Asia. Zhou and the Chinese communists would now align themselves with the underdeveloped countries in Asia, the Middle East, and African lands still under Western colonial administration. They often opted to side with the anti-imperialist and antiforeign groups in these countries, which in some cases meant supporting revolutionaries who wanted to overthrow the existing governments. This view eventually led to disputes with the USSR, which counseled direct diplomatic relations with governments and labeled China's willingness to support guerillas and revolutionaries "adventurist." Chinese communists appeared to be following the Trotskyite position of fostering world proletarian revolution rather than accommodation with the bourgeois states. From then on, the Western countries treated China as a pariah, which contributed to its isolation.

CRACKS IN THE COMMUNIST WORLD

Yet China would not be totally isolated, especially in the pivotal year of 1956. In February, the Soviet leader, Nikita Khrushchev (1894–1971), startled the communist world, particularly the Chinese, with a secret speech (which was eventually leaked to the world) condemning the crimes of the Stalin era. From the "liquidation" of the "kulaks" (or rich peasants) to the Moscow trials of the 1930s and ending with the post-Second World War purges, he enumerated Stalin's murderous and paranoid policies. These accusations reverberated first in Eastern Europe and contributed to disturbances and even revolutions in East Berlin, Poland, and Hungary. Shocked by the speech and what they perceived to be its repercussions, the Chinese communists and, in particular, Mao Zedong, were concerned about these rumblings in the Soviet bloc. In part, they blamed Khrushchev for precipitating the calls for change and the resulting violence in Eastern Europe. Nonetheless, they were also aware that overwhelming repression had generated the outbreaks in Eastern Europe. Even more important, they recognized that intellectuals and professionals frequently took the lead in challenging the communist governments.

Mao responded with a speech in 1956 (published in February of 1957) directed mostly at intellectuals, who could be disruptive but also had skills required for Chinese development. He urged them to make public their complaints and their critiques of the Communist Party and the government. Such dialogues and conversations would permit "one hundred flowers" to bloom. Here Mao referred to the Warring States period of the Zhou dynasty, when a hundred schools of thought and a hundred flowers had allegedly bloomed. Mao often used historical references to bolster his views, offering him a legitimacy associated with the Chinese tradition. However, the campaign did not develop as planned. Intellectuals criticized the limits imposed upon them, the ignorance of cadres, and the government's economic failures. They went way beyond what Mao had anticipated. Some of the most celebrated intellectuals participated in the Hundred Flowers campaign. Ding Ling (1904–1986), a pseudonym of Jiang Bingzhi, the most renowned Chinese woman novelist, who had received the Stalin Prize from the USSR in 1951 for her novels, including *The Sun Shines Over the Sangkan River* (*Taiyang zhaozai sanggan heshang*), was outspoken in her espousal of greater freedom for writers. Other writers and academics were similarly candid. A few trained in the West – especially the distinguished anthropologist Fei Xiaotong (1910–2005), who had trained at the London School of Economics, had written *Peasant Life in China*, and had been an advocate for rural industry – were particularly critical of restraints on basic freedoms, and especially concerned by the party's ban on the discipline of sociology. By June, the Communist Party, concerned about the intensity and scope of criticism, had initiated a propaganda effort, labeled the Anti-rightist Campaign, against the more vociferous critics, who were labeled "anticommunists" and "rightists." It compelled many intellectuals to engage in "self-criticism," renouncing their earlier views about the party, its cadres, and its policies. Ding Ling and her husband were exiled to labor in a bitterly cold region of what was formerly known as Manchuria and her works were banned. Fei was sent to the countryside and assigned to do manual labor. Many less renowned or prominent individuals were effectively silenced or imprisoned or assigned to hard labor in remote regions. This attack on intellectuals, technocrats, and professionals was counterproductive, for it deprived the educational system, public institutions, and the economy of skilled and intelligent men and women.

Some leading intellectuals survived, even though they had been critical of the party and government. Ba Jin, the formerly anarchist novelist who wrote the semiautobiographical *Family*, was criticized but did not, at this time, endure any hardships. Ma Yinchu (1882–1982), the president of Beijing University, who had been educated at Yale and Columbia universities as an economist, had been a thorn in the side of the orthodox Marxists but he managed to retain his position. Distressed by China's high population figures (as revealed in the 1953 census) and the continued rate of growth, Ma warned that overpopulation would undercut economic development, as profits would need to be plowed back into production for the immediate consumption of the increasing number of people. It would also impinge upon accumulation of capital for industrialization and would ultimately lower living standards. He noted that, without a birth-control policy, China could not expect dramatic economic growth. Orthodox Marxists accused him of echoing the retrograde economic views of Thomas Malthus (1766–1834), the nineteenth-century advocate of classical economics who feared population growth. Yet he retained his position during the disruptive aftermath of the Hundred Flowers movement and resigned only in April of 1960.

The turbulent reaction to the Hundred Flowers campaign had been terminated by the end of 1957, but the following year the government initiated policies that were even more radical. Part of the explanation for these extreme policies was Chinese estrangement from much of the rest of the world. The Chinese communists' campaign against dissenting intellectuals aroused even greater concerns and condemnations from foreign countries, which led to a relationship of foreign embargos, radical policies, and Chinese and foreign belligerence.

The year 1958 posed what the Chinese government perceived of as a threat. In October of the previous year, the USA had provided advanced missiles to Taiwan and repeatedly insisted that it would defend the island against attacks. Quemoy and Matsu, two islands that were very close to the mainland but were occupied by Guomindang troops, continued to be contested, and in the summer of 1958 troops on each side kept bombarding the other. The USA moved part of its fleet to the Taiwan Straits, and Vice President Richard M. Nixon (1913–1994) threatened the massive use of force to defend the islands. Hoping to counter this threat, Mao sought help from Khrushchev to develop nuclear weapons. China and the USSR had signed an agreement in October of 1957 to share nuclear information, but Khrushchev renounced it during the Quemoy and Matsu crisis. Mao now believed that China was on its own and realized that the USSR would not be a reliable partner. On the other hand, Khrushchev considered the Chinese government to be overly radical and "adventurist" and did not trust it to be a responsible nuclear power. The USSR leader had proposed a thaw in the Cold War with the West and was eager to establish traditional diplomatic relations with other states. China's "adventurism" threatened Khrushchev's policy. Mao, already critical of Khrushchev's secret speech exposing the crimes of the Stalin era, began to think that the USSR had adopted a rightist position in line with the capitalist West.

At the same time, Mao was disappointed both in China's economic performance and in his people's lack of ideological fervor. He recognized that China was way behind the world's great powers. Increases in agricultural production had not achieved the results he had anticipated, limiting the capital available for industrialization. Thus, mechanization had been similarly limited. Mao's solution was to focus on China's sizable population, allegedly its most important asset. He would develop policies that emphasized labor rather than machines as the engine for economic growth. The lack of ideological purity also concerned Mao. He found it disconcerting that cadres and ordinary people had lost some of the ideological fervor of the revolution. Some cadres, he noted, seemed more interested in climbing the bureaucratic ladder than in implementing policy. Many falsified economic statistics for their own and their areas' benefit. Mao also recognized that communist policies had favored workers and had alienated peasants and the rural areas. Nonetheless, blaming the cadres, he labeled them "corrupt" or "rightists."

GREAT LEAP FORWARD

Mao decided that China needed a sense of urgency to cope with these problems. He proposed a Great Leap Forward to raise production at least to the level of the lesser industrialized nations, promising to outstrip the United Kingdom within fifteen years. He was sufficiently realistic to acknowledge that China could not match the economies of the USA, the USSR, and the other great powers. Yet he was not pragmatic enough to recognize that some of his specific proposals would wind up badly. One of the most disastrous was encouraging the population to build furnaces "in their backyards" to produce steel. He assumed that the steel would not be of the highest quality but still would be usable for ordinary purposes such as pots and pans. It turned out that nearly all the steel in the approximately 500,000 backyard furnaces was useless. Even worse, considerable timber was cut to provide fuel for the furnaces. More successful was the recruitment of large groups of people for sizable infrastructure projects. Masses of people were galvanized to construct or repair (with scant employment of tools or machinery) dams, irrigation works, and public buildings. Many of the dams were badly built and collapsed. Nonetheless, a considerable number of such projects were finished in record time. Like the USSR, communist China praised Stakhanovite workers – that is, laborers who, through incredible hard work and will power, produced an abundance of goods. The media, as part of mass campaigns, virtually deified such model heroes and heroines. Their achievements and behavior heralded the development of a "New Man" or "New Woman" whose values

Figure 12.1 A dam built with little mechanical equipment in the Great Leap Forward era. Photo: Keystone-France / Gamma-Keystone via Getty Images

coincided with the Communist Party's message and who thought almost exclusively of the reputed "public good." Imaginative literature written and published during this time reinforced this image of the New Man and New Woman who devoted themselves to the cause of the Chinese people and communism above all else, including family relations.

State-sponsored culture emphasized the values of the New Man and New Woman. Painting broke away from traditional-style ink painting, characterized by landscapes or portraits that sometimes illustrated Confucian, Buddhist, or Daoist precepts but were also concerned with line, form, calligraphy, and color. The new socialist art emphasized content over form, barred abstractions, and often depicted the human figure in the form of the peasant, worker, or Mao or other celebrated leaders. Realism dominated, and poster art was especially popular, as it often accompanied such mass campaigns as the Anti-Three or Anti-Five movements, which have already been described. Bright colors rather than the often discreet black of ink painting were favored. Critical to the art were depictions of heroic figures who embodied the attitudes of the New Man or New Woman.

The Great Leap Forward in agriculture demonstrated the new values Mao wished to inculcate. Land was collectivized, and about twenty-six thousand so-called people's communes were organized throughout the country. Communes now owned nearly all the land, although peasants were granted small private plots in which they could grow food or supplies for their own consumption. Commune managers, most often party cadres rather than individual peasants, decided upon crops to be grown, assigned commune members to specific types of labor, provided taxes and production statistics to the government, and policed member activities. Members were enjoined to work for the common good rather than for their own or perhaps selfish desires. Many communes established mess halls where members ate their meals, and thus gained control over food. Communes organized crèches, nurseries, and primary schools to free women from child care so that they could join the labor force. The large-scale infrastructure projects and the decision to base economic growth on the large labor pools meant that female workers were essential, and the communes needed to provide facilities to permit women to work.

In the Great Leap Forward, Mao was counting on spectacular successes in grain production to promote industrialization. The greater the produce from agriculture, the more China could trade for heavy machinery from the USSR. Despite the innovation of the communes, China still relied on the Soviet model of economic development. Such a policy dictated extraction of as much revenue as possible from agriculture to fuel the development of industry. The organization of such larger and presumably more efficient entities as the communes appeared to be the optimal means of increasing agricultural production, but this assumption proved to be illusory.

Commune managers had to fulfill specific norms. Knowing that increases were the key both to retaining their positions and being considered for promotion, they had an incentive to match or exceed these quotas. Thus, when they sent reports to the central government, many falsified production figures. Some of the figures they cited were patently absurd but were accepted as legitimate by planners in the government. Based on these statistics, government tax collectors extracted more produce from the communes. Inexperienced cadres, many of whom were not experts in agronomy, had specific political agendas, which exacerbated these difficulties. As managers, they had the power to determine the crops to be grown and to countermand the views of experienced peasants, and often demanded deep plowing and close planting, exhausting the soil. Recognizing that their superiors in the government would appreciate an increase in cash crops to be traded with the USSR and the Soviet bloc, they could, on occasion, convert land designed to produce grain for local consumption to such specialty crops as tea and fruits meant for trade and export. They also adopted Mao's directives to plant rice stalks closer together and to crossbreed various animals, which both turned out to be disastrous.

The grain shortages that resulted from such falsifications and evasions were catastrophic. Power was often in the hands of the mess hall's kitchen personnel because they determined who would get the life-saving food. Many dissidents who opposed these policies were beaten, tortured, or killed. Events spun out of control, and, on occasion, local officials themselves were blamed for the disasters and severely punished. Famines struck many rural areas, leading to an untold number of deaths by starvation. There were reports of cannibalism in some areas in the countryside. Many children died, and parents sold, abandoned, or, in extreme cases, murdered their children. Cadres had some access to food and gorged themselves when they had meetings or seminars. Trafficking in women, who sought to survive through prostitution, increased. The Communist Party blamed some of the agricultural failures on a series of natural disasters, which also resulted in casualties. It scarcely mentioned deficiencies in policies or mistakes in implementation. Those who challenged the party's views and criticized specific government policies as contributing to famines were themselves criticized. For example, Peng Dehuai, the minister of defense and a great military hero, pointed to the failures of the Great Leap Forward. Although Mao, as one of the principal architects of the radical policies, was on the defensive, he was still able to stave off this critique at a major meeting in Lushan in August of 1959 and gained sufficient support to oust Peng from his position.

Conditions in the minority nationality border areas echoed the chaos in the central part of China. The radical policies of the Great Leap Forward increased the pressure on the minority nationalities to learn Chinese, to deemphasize their ethnic distinctiveness, and to detach themselves from their religions. Communization of animals and land and the propaganda against Islam prompted about sixty thousand Kazakhs in Xinjiang to flee to the USSR – an embarrassment in light of the Sino–Soviet dispute. Tibet proved to be even more of a challenge. In 1959, Tibetan Buddhist monks (assisted by foreigners) initiated a revolt. A Chinese army suppressed the revolt, but, accompanied by a contingent of Tibetans, the Dalai Lama departed and reached Dharamsala in north India, where he has remained since. India itself became involved in a territorial dispute. Within a few months in 1962, China emerged victorious, though tensions along the border remained.

RETURN TO PRAGMATISM

Despite this victory, Mao was in a weaker position because of the Great Leap Forward's failures, and this offered more moderate leaders greater opportunities to shape policy. Liu Shaoqi (1898–1969; the head of state from 1959 to 1966), Deng Xiaoping (1904–1997), and other of their associates, many of whom had been trained abroad, denounced the Great Leap Forward and sought a return to a careful and planned economy. By 1960, Mao was apparently somewhat in retreat from his dominant position and from the Great Leap Forward, which he had earlier championed. The chaotic Great Leap Forward policy, which had resulted in the deaths of millions of people and had exposed incompetent and corrupt cadres, had aroused considerable opposition, and the opponents wanted a steadier course for society. These opponents, including Liu Shaoqi, began to demand more accurate and less inflated economic statistics and sought to root out cadres involved in nefarious activities or those who capitalized on their positions to make substantial profits. The moderates took command of the economy and then ordered the closure of the backyard steel furnaces and other experiments designed to promote self-reliance. These enterprises had simply squandered local resources. The moderates were especially concerned about the food supply and adopted a pragmatic policy to raise production. They dismantled or reduced the size of some communes, allowed peasants to have larger private plots of land, and offered farmers greater incentives to produce more and to sell their goods for their own gain. The new policy turned out to be successful, as more food reached the government and the markets. Mao appeared to have accepted moderation in the economy and ideology. Yet this turned out to be a period of quiet before the storm. Whatever additional capital was available was invested in state-owned industrial enterprises.

Moderation was, in part, subverted by foreign relations. The US involvement in Vietnam, which shared a border with China, had been initiated with the dispatch of an advisory military force to South Vietnam in the early 1960s to ward off North Vietnam. In August of 1964, an alleged naval confrontation between the USA and Vietnam, which proved to be fraudulent but served the interests of American policy makers who sought to intervene to help South Vietnam, prompted a buildup of US forces, which culminated in the arrival of half a million men in the south by 1965. Some US government officials attributed the conflict in Vietnam to China, referring to a domino effect in which the Chinese communists, who reputedly dominated North Vietnam, would first seek to conquer South Vietnam and then all of Southeast Asia. This interpretation and the assumptions underlying it were ahistorical. China and Vietnam had traditionally been hostile. Several dynasties in China had attempted to conquer Vietnam and had been rebuffed. There was no love lost between the two, and communist China did not dictate policy or strategy to North Vietnam. Yet this fallacious interpretation caused the USA to send troops to block the communist empire from overwhelming Southeast Asia. The Chinese communists viewed this sizable contingent of US forces not far from its borders as a clear threat. The USA's support for Taiwan had already angered Mao. Now the USA, with massive firepower and with bombing of sites in North Vietnam, was intervening in a war virtually on China's doorstep. Mao perceived the US involvement as a deliberate provocation.

AN ISOLATED CHINA

The escalation of the Sino–Soviet dispute exacerbated China's concerns. Conflicts between the two heightened throughout the 1960s. Insults were hurled back and forth between the erstwhile allies. Soviet leaders repeatedly condemned the Chinese communists for their radicalism and their unwillingness to work within the boundaries of the established world order. The Chinese communists distrusted and disdained dialogue and possible collaboration with the capitalist countries. In turn, they portrayed Soviet policy makers as "capitalist roaders" and as betrayers of Marxism for seeking to cooperate with the West. Government-controlled media produced scathing analyses of the Soviets' acquiescence to the capitalist world.

This open breach with the USSR led to the final withdrawal of Russian technical experts and advisers and of Soviet economic assistance. Chinese leaders could no longer rely on trade for products it needed from the USSR. Assistance from or trade with the Soviet bloc in Eastern Europe also diminished and, in some cases, ended. Ideological disputes with the USSR translated into territorial conflicts. During the honeymoon period in Sino–Soviet relations, boundary disagreements had not surfaced, though there certainly

were numerous potential problems. The 1689 Nerchinsk Treaty had been relatively equitable in border delineation, but the mid-nineteenth-century tsarist
court and its officials in Siberia, capitalizing on China's military weakness, had
encroached upon Chinese territories and compelled Chinese officials to sign
treaties turning the lands along the border with Manchuria over to Russia.
After the Second World War, the USSR had assisted Mongolia in breaking
away from China and establishing a sovereign country. In 1950, China had
reluctantly abandoned claims to Mongolia, but it had not formally acquiesced
to the mid-nineteenth-century so-called unequal treaties that had been forced
upon the Qing dynasty and entailed loss of territory and sovereignty. As tensions in the Sino–Soviet dispute heightened, the potential for violence
increased, and claims to land became prominent. Both sides amassed substantial numbers of soldiers along their frontiers, and Mongolia, under pressure
from the USSR, permitted more than 100,000 Soviet troops to be stationed
along its borders with China.

The Chinese communist leaders now faced 500,000 US troops in South
Vietnam and at least as many Soviet forces along China's northern borders.
China had no allies among the major powers in the world. It distrusted Japan,
which was, in any event, allied with the West, and it had just fought a successful
war with India along its frontiers. In 1964, Indonesia had engaged in a purge
of so-called communists, many of them its Chinese citizens. China's ties with
many African states had become frayed, and much of the Middle East, ruled
by dictators or monarchs, feared the Marxist message.

Mao himself had become disenchanted with the moderate and incremental
policies of the early 1960s, which were implemented by bureaucrats, intellectuals, and experts. Cloistered in his compound in Beijing and perhaps embittered by the failure of the Great Leap Forward and the communization
movement and the ensuing loss of prestige, Mao planned new policies to challenge the status quo. He wanted to restore his tarnished image and, as a first
step, in 1962 he initiated a Socialist Education Campaign to eliminate "reac-
tionary" elements from politics, the economy, organizations, and ideology.
At the same time, he began to develop a Stalin-style cult of personality. First,
the government issued *Quotations from Chairman Mao Zedong* (*Mao zhuxi yulu*,
later known as "The Little Red Book"), which came to be the most important
book from that year on. In July of 1966, Mao took another step in the form of a
highly publicized swim in the Yangzi River to symbolize his continued presence
and desire to play a greater role in the country.

GREAT PROLETARIAN CULTURAL REVOLUTION

Two other prominent figures influenced Mao's thinking during this time, which
by 1966 had culminated in a bold, adventurist policy. Jiang Qing (1914–1991),
an actress who had become Mao's third wife in the late 1930s, was dismayed by
the "bourgeois" and "decadent" expressions of culture in the theater and in the
arts. Focusing on opera and theater, her areas of special interest, she claimed to
be offended by the ideas and values represented in these two art forms. Wu Han

Figure 12.2 Chinese Red Guards publicly parade their victims, wearing dunce caps and signs proclaiming their crimes, through the streets of Beijing. Mao's Cultural Revolution of the 1960s unleashed radicalized youth against so-called antirevolutionary groups. 1970. Courtesy Everett Collection / Rex Features

(1909–1969), a historian who had written a play about a sixteenth-century official that appeared to be critical of Mao, earned Jiang Qing's and Mao's wrath. Criticism of Wu's production and other artistic works were the first targets of the new movement, which came to be called the Great Proletarian Cultural Revolution. Within a short time, Jiang Qing would mandate that only six operas, which represented the correct political stance, be performed. Lin Biao, the other prominent supporter of Mao's radical policies, was the head of the People's Liberation Army, a highly influential group in the new society. Lin shared Mao's disdain for the moderate bureaucrats, offering Mao a valuable and powerful ally for his new policies. He joined in the attack against those labeled counterrevolutionaries.

Mao and his allies asserted that many in the bureaucracy harbored capitalist views and urged loyal communists to act against them and the "Four Olds": old customs, old culture, old habits, and old ideas. Students were in the vanguard in these demonstrations and constituted the so-called Red Guards. Mao unleashed these discontented students and young people to challenge the bureaucrats and all those who were allegedly counterrevolutionaries. The closing of schools and colleges permitted students to engage in the struggle against so-called enemies of the revolution, especially those with "old-fashioned ideas" and those with links to the West or Western culture. By late summer of 1966, workers and some intellectuals had joined in the Cultural Revolution campaign, which became increasingly violent. The Red Guards attacked whatever smacked of the old society – monasteries, museums, and elaborate houses and courtyards. They then moved from destruction of objects to harassment of people. Members of the old elite and even Communist Party leaders were compelled to wear dunce caps or to stand in physically painful positions and paraded around the streets. President Liu Shaoqi, who had been regarded as Mao's successor, was placed under house arrest, beaten, and at times denied his diabetes medication. This mistreatment led to his death in 1969. During the looting and devastation, thousands of people were killed or permanently injured. Intellectuals were perhaps the group that suffered the most, and students, often in collaboration with workers, accused local party leaders of antiparty activism and displaced them. Even more destabilizing were Red Guard and worker takeovers of universities, conservatories of music, and newspapers and magazines. They dismissed experts and sought to manage these institutions on their own, contributing to chaos in education and media outlets. They were prevented from moving into the Forbidden City, military installations, factories, and important artistic and religious sites. However, by early 1967, the top leadership faced difficulties in controlling the fury it had unleashed.

Life was unpleasant for the accused, even those who had been guilty of only minor infractions. They were often sentenced to hard labor, as well as seemingly constant self-criticism sessions and propaganda. Prominent writers were targeted. Ding Ling (as mentioned above, the most renowned Chinese woman writer of the time, who had already been exiled during the anti-rightist campaign of 1957) was sentenced to another five years in prison; the novelist Ba Jin was harassed and his wife allegedly died because she was denied medical attention; and as early as 1964 the writer Mao Dun was forced to resign as minister of culture. Microphones blaring the latest radical proclamations were everywhere from town centers to trains. Broadcasting of the message was relentless and undermined technical knowledge, which was vital for the economy and for society in general. Party propaganda emphasized that Redness, or loyalty to communist ideals, was more important than expertise – a serious challenge to the educated and to intellectuals. Red Guards and workers adhered to this message and took aim at the educated.

Eventually, Mao, along with Jiang Qing and three of her close associates (who became known as the Gang of Four), became concerned that the Cultural Revolution was getting out of control. They worried about the economic disruptions precipitated by the increasingly unruly demonstrations. Fearful of the growing disarray, Mao and his cohorts began to moderate their message and to criticize ultra-leftists for uncalled-for and illegal violence. They quickly recruited the People's Liberation Army to restore order. Lin Biao responded, with alacrity, and the People's Liberation Army quashed some of the demonstrations and helped to dismiss party cadres. Mao urged the Red Guards to go "up to the mountains and down to the villages." He wanted to curb the urban unrest by having the Red Guards join the rural labor force. The party then urged some of the students to return to school. Mao and Lin seemed to be collaborating in bringing the party under their control. As a result of playing such a vital role, Lin began to be portrayed as virtually on the same level as Mao. By 1969, he had been elevated to the position of Mao's successor. Yet soon thereafter Mao, fearful that the party had been devastated and concerned that the army appeared to be the dominant institution, became suspicious of Lin's increasing power, and in 1970 turned against his chosen successor. By 1971, their divisions were irreparable. According to official Chinese sources, in September, Lin allegedly plotted to assassinate Mao. The failure of his "plot" prompted him to flee on an airplane toward the USSR. Lacking fuel, the plane was reported to have crashed in Mongolia, leaving no survivors. Rumors spread that the plane had been shot down, but there was no way to verify these reports.

Lin Biao's disaffection and death symbolized the growing concerns about both domestic failures and China's isolation from the rest of the world. The Cultural Revolution, with its attack against established institutions and especially on intellectuals, had robbed China of expertise in various fields. Closing of schools and universities had disrupted the educational system and had subverted the careers of promising students. Appointment to leadership positions of "Reds" rather than experts had damaged the economy, education, and numerous institutions. Disdain and attacks on the West and on intellectuals who had any connections with Western knowledge and culture exacerbated China's difficulties and blackened China's image in the world. The economy had stalled, and the population needed ration coupons even to buy basic goods. China's relations with the outside world were chaotic. In 1969, pitched battles with the USSR along the Manchurian frontiers resulted in the stationing of even more Soviet troops all along the border. The potential for a Sino–Soviet war accelerated. Relations with many of the Western nations had come to an abrupt halt, and many in the West were shocked by the turbulence and violence of the Cultural Revolution. China had no official contacts with the USA, the major Western power. Taiwan represented China at the United Nations. During the height of the Cultural Revolution, the government had recalled many of its foreign ambassadors and had closed down embassies, even in the Third World. China maintained poor relations with the most populous Asian countries. It had engaged in battles with India along their joint borders in 1962 and had deplored attacks on overseas Chinese communities in Indonesia in 1964. China needed to reevaluate its policies.

CHINA REOPENS ITS DOORS

Changes in China's international relations were the first evidence of such reevaluation. In April of 1971, Chinese officials invited a US ping-pong team playing in Japan to visit China to take part in table-tennis exhibition matches. In the fall, after secret and delicate negotiations, the US and Chinese governments announced that President Richard M. Nixon would visit China in the

Figure 12.3 Nixon in China. President Nixon meets with China's Communist Party leader Mao Zedong. February 21, 1972. © Everett Collection Historical / Alamy

spring of 1972. Nixon, who had been one of the most prominent anticommunists in the 1950s, capitalized on the Sino–Soviet split to restore contacts with China. The meeting did not end with unanimity, especially on the issue of Taiwan. Yet it set the stage for renewed relations. Shortly thereafter, the two countries began, at a rapid pace, to exchange political, educational, scientific, and cultural delegations. Even before President Nixon's visit, the USA had dropped its objections and agreed to China's membership in the United Nations as a replacement for Taiwan. With these two stumbling blocks removed, China now began to reestablish formal diplomatic relations with Western and Third World countries. Its seeming moderation led to tangible results. On January 1, 1979, the USA and China restored diplomatic relations and, within a short time, Britain agreed to return Hong Kong to Chinese control in 1997 and Portugal agreed to return Macao to China. However, tensions with the USSR persisted, although both sides pulled back from the violence that had erupted in 1969. Chinese and Soviet officials and the media continued to criticize the other country's policies, but they kept within the bounds of discourse and no longer fought.

Domestic policies turned out to be more complicated. The Gang of Four, with Jiang Qing in the lead, accepted the changes in China's international relations but wanted to maintain radical internal policies, especially the commune structure in the countryside. They promoted "continuous revolution" and vigilance against bourgeois elements in the Communist Party. Using historic parallels, they started a "criticize Confucius policy" and praised Shi Huangdi, the first emperor of the Qin and indeed the First Emperor of China. They portrayed Mao as Shi Huangdi, the praiseworthy Qin ruler. Dependence on labor rather than use of expensive machinery was also at the height of their agenda. They repeatedly emphasized the peasants' ingenuity. Similarly, their agenda spilled over into industrial development. They relied on allegedly conscientious, idealistic, and exceptionally hardworking proletarians, as opposed to capital investment in technology. Asserting that leadership was crucial, they focused on proper political considerations in selecting managers in communes, factories, and mines. They tended to deride expertise and the capitalist model of economic growth and development. In short, they had barely altered their views as expressed in the Cultural Revolution, and had made only perfunctory concessions in light of the failure of their radical policies. They criticized Zhou Enlai, Deng Xiaoping, and other government and party officials whose views were not as driven by ideology and who sought to adopt foreign technology to propel the economy. Like Zhou, Deng had studied in France, had joined the communists during the Jiangxi Soviet, and had taken part in the Long March. He had been a target during the Cultural Revolution for his opposition to its radicalism. In 1974, he returned from exile, and the Gang of Four responded with severe criticism.

As of 1974, Jiang Qing's Gang of Four, seemingly with Mao's support, appeared to have the advantage. Yet within two years the political landscape changed drastically. First, Zhou Enlai died in February of 1976, stimulating extraordinary expressions of public grief. Demonstrations developed that were covertly, and on occasion overtly, critical of the radical policies and even of Mao himself. The demonstrators portrayed Zhou as a moderate and as closer to the true proletarian cause than most of the leadership. At this point, the Gang of Four launched its own broadsides against the less ideological opposition. The struggle continued through the summer, a season punctuated on July 28 with a catastrophic earthquake in Tangshan, an area within a hundred miles of Beijing, that led to the deaths of several hundred thousand people. Chinese who remembered the traditional dynastic view of the past knew that natural catastrophes were often harbingers of dynastic change or collapse. Within two months of the earthquake, Mao had died, an indication to believers that the earthquake signaled significant changes. The tensions between the two factions were exacerbated. Yet, without Mao's protection, the radical and despised Gang of Four faced perilous circumstances. Although Mao had tapped Hua Guofeng (1921–2008), a colorless bureaucrat who seemed to favor the radicals, as his successor, Hua found the Gang to be his competitors and overly radical as China reentered the world. Within a month, he arrested the Gang, including Mao's widow, and initiated a campaign to blacken their reputations.

Meanwhile, Deng Xiaoping, one of Mao's comrades-in-arms, who had had a tempestuous relationship with the deceased party leader, emerged as the leader of the moderates, who wanted a rational and carefully planned approach to the economy that was not based on ideological blinders. Deng and his allies were pragmatists who would, if necessary, contravene orthodox Marxist–Maoist thinking to foster economic growth. They opted for modernization, which, in practice, often meant adoption of foreign technology in key economic sectors. Such a policy necessitated the training of skilled personnel, which, in turn, required the restoration of universities. Higher education, which had suffered inordinately during the Cultural Revolution, had to be stabilized and organized. Within a short time, the government developed stiff entrance examinations for admission into major universities, which had been restaffed with outstanding academics and researchers. Simultaneously, the authorities negotiated with the Western powers and Japan to offer opportunities for Chinese students to train in their lands. These new policies overturned the Cultural Revolution dictum of the greater value of "Reds," or ideologically pure individuals, than experts. Deng and his supporters in the Communist Party and the military were convinced that economic planning and the use of experts, rather than the seemingly anarchic and disorderly Cultural Revolution policies, were the optimal means of fostering economic growth. They also believed that incentives were required for greater productivity.

However, before they could embark on their pragmatic policies, they had to deal with the most prominent radicals, as well as those who had been harmed by the Cultural Revolution. Their principal opponents could defend themselves by claiming that Mao had approved of their radical views, with the result that Deng and the pragmatists were left with no other choice and the difficult task of questioning Mao's policies without denying him a place in the pantheon of communist heroes. After considerable discussion and several pronouncements, they devised an evaluation of Mao that was mostly positive but also revealed his deficiencies. They portrayed him as a great leader who had his faults, with a percentage of good traits and a percentage of bad traits. His body was embalmed, and a special memorial hall, where the public could view it, was built in Tiananmen, the central square in Beijing. Under this cover, Deng and his collaborators could deal with the Gang of Four. Mao's wife Jiang Qing and another member of the Gang were tried and received sentences of capital punishment, although they were eventually resentenced to life imprisonment. The other two Gang members received lighter sentences. On the other hand, the government worked quickly to undo the excesses of the Cultural Revolution. The writers Ding Ling, Mao Dun, and Ba Jin were rehabilitated, allowed to return from the countryside to the capital, and permitted to travel abroad. Deng then outmaneuvered Hua Guofeng and became the undisputed leader of the country.

Having routed the radicals, Deng and the pragmatists could focus specifically on the economy, but they faced an immediate, almost insurmountable problem. As Ma Yinchu, the economist and former president of Beijing University in the 1950s, had predicted, the continued increase in population was threatening to undermine advances in the economy. The 1950s attacks on advocates of birth control for allegedly adopting the views of such classical economists as Thomas Malthus had harmed efforts to limit population growth. Even when the government began to pursue birth-control policies and provided contraception in the 1960s, it had relied on education and propaganda and had not imposed sanctions on multiple births and large families. Faced with a population of 1,200,000 people, in 1979 it decided to initiate more stringent policies to cap this growth. Without such a reduction, the government could not expect as rapid economic advances as it had hoped for. It formulated the so-called one-child-per-family policy, mandating disincentives for families that opted for multiple births. Couples who had one child would receive the state's health, educational, and welfare benefits for free. Those who chose to have more than one child would pay for these somewhat reduced benefits and would encounter more difficulties in employment and promotion at work.

Abuses and exceptions marked the policy's history. Local authorities often assigned elderly women to check on young women's menstrual cycles – an extraordinary invasion of privacy. Couples, on occasion, had to request permission to try to have a child. Government and party officials were accused of forcing pregnant women who already had a child to undergo an abortion. Another abuse was related to the traditional Chinese desire for a male heir. Limited to one child, couples would revert to subtle forms of infanticide inherited from earlier times – for example, abandoning a baby in inhospitable climates. Some spared a girl's life by giving her to an orphanage. The development of sonograms that could detect gender reduced the rate of infanticide. If the sonogram showed a girl, couples chose an abortion. The long-term implications of the one-child-per-family policy were also problematic. The resulting shortage of women as marital partners for young men in their twenties and thirties is a serious concern. A few women from North Korea and Mongolia have married Chinese men, but an increasing number of young men have not and will not find mates. However, there have been recent exceptions to the policy. Peasants with a daughter have been given the opportunity to have a second child, in hopes of producing a son who could work the land. In addition, non-Han Chinese ethnic minorities, which the government had classified into fifty-five groups constituting about five percent of the population, have never been bound by the one-child-per-family policy.

Having devised a policy, however flawed, on population, the new leadership could turn to other pressing issues. Deng and his allies adopted the slogan "Four Modernizations," referring to the engines for rapid growth. Modernization in agriculture, industry, science and technology, and defense would be the means by which China would progress and attain the level of the world's dominant powers. Here too expertise would replace ideological purity as the criterion for advancement. Individuals would be selected and promoted on the basis of their technical knowledge, not their political correctness. In 1980, Deng recruited supporters to help in implementing these policies: Zhao Ziyang (1919–2005) became premier and Hu Yaobang (1915–1989) became general secretary of the Communist Party. They described their new policies as "socialism with Chinese characteristics": a program centered on economic performance, not the ideology of the old mass campaigns. Deng also deviated from radical policies by emphasizing wealth as part of the Communist Party's program. He asserted that the initial enrichment of a few would be valuable because it would inexorably lead to prosperity for much of the rest of the population. Wealth rather than strict adherence to socialist ideology was his principal concern. The new policy was enshrined in the slogan "to get rich is glorious."

DRAMATIC CHANGES AND MODERNIZATION

The new authorities first took aim at agricultural reforms. The communes had offered the peasants few incentives because additional yields on the land they farmed did not translate into significantly greater income. Under the new so-called responsibility system, incentives were restored and the communes abolished. Households had to meet specific quotas for output but could sell any extra produce on the open market, which in the early 1980s provided substantial income. The communes were decollectivized, offering peasants greater autonomy. The ideological communist decision making that had characterized the Great Leap Forward and the Cultural Revolution was eliminated. However, these two campaigns had done considerable damage in rural areas. Planting of inappropriate crops, construction of faulty dams, leaks of chemicals into the ground and into the water supply, and the encroachment by a larger population on the land, as well as increased urbanization, had created difficult problems. Yet, free of earlier restraints, many peasants flourished, and produce became more readily available in rural and urban markets.

An adequate food supply enabled the government to turn its attention to industrial development. However, the increase in agricultural production led to lower prices, and the government now also required payments for the peasants' health and welfare benefits, which generated financial burdens in the rural areas. Variations in price levels, a growing population and the resulting intrusion on the land, and poverty in the countryside compelled some peasants to migrate to the towns and cities to seek work in factories or in ancillary urban organizations (established from the 1980s on). Simultaneously, cultural, social, and economic opportunities lured some ambitious peasants who wanted to live beyond the confines of the countryside. A substantial migrant population, amounting to tens of millions, developed, but they faced considerable difficulties. After they moved, they lacked the household registration (*hukou*) granted to all citizens and thus lost claims to housing, medical and welfare benefits, and education for their children. They were in a precarious position, yet they offered a labor force for industry and construction projects.

Modernization of industry also required investment and greater flexibility and freedom for managers and entrepreneurs. Zhao Ziyang, who had introduced successful economic reforms as party secretary in the province of Sichuan, now supported the privatization of state-owned enterprises and the decentralization of industry. He facilitated the use of enhanced revenues from agriculture to promote industrial development. The economic planners decided upon export-led growth and investment in light industries (such as textiles) rather than heavy industries (which required more investment) as strategies for economic development. As critical, the government actively sought foreign investment in so-called joint ventures. It offered favorable terms for foreign, often overseas Chinese, investors, including reduced taxes and the ability to fire lazy or inefficient workers. One remarkable innovation was the establishment of special economic zones in which private entrepreneurs dominated. The Shenzhen zone, near Hong Kong, was the first such special region where government regulations were minimal. The government adopted the so-called policy of "one country, two systems," maintaining communism in China and accepting capitalism in Shenzhen and later in Hong Kong and Macao. By the early 1990s, a large number of foreign firms, taking advantage of relatively cheap labor, few environmental regulations, and state inducements, had invested funds or built factories in China. Gross domestic product rose throughout the 1980s, markedly so from the mid 1990s on. China began to supply increasingly more sophisticated consumer goods to the West and indeed much of the world and started to enjoy a favorable balance of trade. It soon became the world's fastest-growing economy.

This dramatic growth necessitated a secure supply of natural resources. In the 1980s, China had sufficient supplies for domestic purposes, and the government ensured that prices for Chinese consumers remained low. For example, oil from Daqing, a highly touted site during the Cultural Revolution, met the country's needs during the early stages of industrialization. However, by maintaining low prices, the government prevented the oil companies from investing in and thus searching for new oil reserves. Eventually recognizing that under these circumstances supplies would remain low, the government finally liberalized prices in 1990 in order to obtain sufficient oil for its burgeoning industrial base. By the mid 1990s, the pace of industrialization had increased so rapidly that domestic supplies of oil were insufficient. The oil companies then were permitted to invest abroad and sought diverse sources to avert dependence on any one country. Iran, Kazakhstan, Russia, the Middle East, Africa, Indonesia, and Sudan and even India, Syria, and Myanmar attracted Chinese investment. Because some of these states were authoritarian and did not respect human rights, the Western democracies criticized China for supporting or at least not ostracizing such regimes. China generally ignored these objections and tried to ingratiate itself by providing economic aid and offering military training to the countries in which it was investing. Chinese oil companies had the advantage that the government did not expect them to make substantial profits. Thus, they were in a better position than other countries' oil companies, which required considerable profits.

The spectacular economic growth from the 1990s on resulted in a frenzied effort to secure a variety of mineral and natural resources. Chinese companies, often with low-interest loans from the government, traveled around the world – from East Asia to the Middle East to Africa and even to Latin America – to negotiate deals for these precious reserves. They either invested in foreign extractive industries or purchased commodities such as copper, coal, and gold. Their traders also traveled to buy such raw materials as wool and cashmere for the light industries they had developed.

Having a favorable balance of trade based on its industries, the government now fostered the third modernization, science and technology. Its first step entailed the dispatch of students to the more developed countries, including Japan and the West. Most studied engineering, science, or other practical subjects, often with subsidies provided by such international financial agencies as the World Bank or by the individual advanced states. However, China suffered somewhat from a "brain drain," as quite a number of students decided to settle in the lands where they had studied. Yet, once economic growth accelerated in China in the twenty-first century, more students appeared to return. The government's financial support for scientific research centers and universities has increasingly enticed well-trained researchers and engineers to go back to their native land.

Economic growth has also translated into development of China's defense capabilities, the fourth modernization. By the early 1980s, the Sino–Soviet struggle had receded, so China could begin to concentrate on other nonthreatening defense issues. At that point, the government moved its focus to expanding its military forces and updating its weaponry. The People's Liberation Army became an increasingly professional organization. Although the size of its army, navy, and air force has grown, the government has been relatively cautious and has not, until very recently, adopted an adventurist policy of encroaching on its neighbors, especially after the cessation of hostilities with the USSR and the end of a territorial war with Vietnam in 1979. It has brandished its weaponry during unstable times in its relations with Taiwan; to affirm its claims in the South China Sea in disputes with Southeast Asian countries and Japan; and to challenge US observation or spy planes that appeared to cross into Chinese airspace. Yet it has generally avoided bellicose acts and instead has often used economic pressure to resolve disputes. For example, in 2010, the Chinese suspended trade in rare minerals, vital for industry, to Japan during a conflict.

Political developments after Deng Xiaoping's rise to power around 1979 did not prove to be as smooth. Having ousted Hua Guofeng, Deng initially recruited pragmatists and more liberal officials to implement the economic reforms he supported. He did not, however, contemplate drastic political changes and did not advocate the kind of liberalization for the political system that he had championed for the economy. Because his position as chair of the Military Affairs Commission had been crucial in his victory over Hua, he did not foresee a decline of the military's power. Moreover, he acted decisively when dissidents placed posters on the so-called Democracy Wall in Beijing. Wei Jingsheng (1950–), perhaps the most renowned such activist, appeared to challenge not only specific policies but also the entire communist system, by emphasizing democracy as the fifth modernization. The government brought him to trial, and he was found guilty and sentenced to fifteen years in prison. Other dissenters met similar fates. At the same time, any perceived challenges in art, literature, and the cinema faced government censorship. The greater access and exposure to Western models in the arts, journalism, and television affected and stimulated some Chinese to seek greater individual freedom. University students, in particular, found lack of choice about their venues for employment galling. The government continued to determine where they would work – a specific enforcement of Communist Party policy. There was increased resentment against this and other policies that limited freedom of choice. Cynicism was also prevalent, especially as levels of corruption accelerated. Entrepreneurs with *guanxi* (connections with high officials in the local or central government) could secure lucrative contracts, dispossess peasants from their lands, and evade regulations or even the law to enrich themselves. More and more students and intellectuals were appalled by these conditions.

The government severely criticized dissenters and sometimes dealt with them harshly, prompting reactions from the growing body of dissatisfied people in the country. It dismissed a few prominent figures from their positions, expelled dissidents from the Communist Party, and detained those it perceived as obstructive or potentially subversive. It also adopted a harsher policy toward the writings and performances of dissenters. Yet student demonstrations persisted. In 1986, Deng began to blame the liberal officials he had brought to power during his accession to his leading position in the late 1970s. He would eventually target Hu Yaobang and Zhao Ziyang, two pragmatists who were identified with economic reform and greater openness to the West and had risen to be secretary generals of the Communist Party, for inspiring such demonstrations. Hu and Zhao had antagonized many officials by attempting to streamline the bureaucracy, fighting corruption, investigating the activities of children ("princes") of high-ranking party and government officials, demanding greater transparency, supporting free-market reforms, rehabilitating victims of the Cultural Revolution, promoting freedoms of speech and the press, expressing concern about the growing gap between rich and poor, calling for reduction of military expenditures, and advocating fewer controls on ethnic minorities. Deng specifically criticized Hu for encouraging bourgeois sentiments and "spiritual pollution" – that is, acceptance of Western values and ideas. In 1987, Hu was compelled to resign his position as secretary general of the Communist Party.

TIANANMEN DISTURBANCE OF 1989 AND ITS AFTERMATH

Despite the government crackdowns, students continued to demonstrate against policies limiting freedom and democracy, culminating in a confrontation in spring of 1989. Two unrelated events prompted the crisis. First, in April, Hu died of natural causes. Many students, to whom he had been a hero and who had been chagrined when he had been denounced and had lost his Communist Party position, decided to rally in Tiananmen Square, the true center of political power in Beijing. In addition to mourning his death, they started to demonstrate on behalf of the democratic and economic reforms Hu had championed. They started with rallies and were joined by ordinary citizens, and within a month the pace of protest had quickened, leading to a hunger strike in the square. To be sure, some opportunists had joined the crowds, but the massive number of people indicated considerable dissatisfaction with corruption, nepotism, and lack of freedom of expression. The government temporized and appeared to be paralyzed, prompting the demonstrators to make increasingly dramatic demands, including Deng's resignation. The second crucial event was the visit of Mikhail Gorbachev (1931–), the secretary general of the USSR's Communist Party. Many students recognized and revered him

Figure 12.4 June 4, 1989, Tiananmen Square riot. The June Fourth movement, or the 1989 Movement for Democracy, consisted of a series of demonstrations led by labor activists, students, and intellectuals between April 15 and June 4, 1989. © Durand-Langevin / Sygma / Corbis

as a kindred spirit because of his advocacy of *perestroika*, or "reconstruction of the economy," and *glasnost*, or "openness and greater freedom of expression." He represented the economic and political reforms sweeping the USSR, and inspired the students to greater activism and more demands. Zhao Ziyang was viewed as another kindred spirit because he visited the demonstrators.

The more radical the demonstrators grew, the more concerned and intractable the leadership became. A meeting between students and the political leadership did not go well. The government finally acted on the evening of June 3, by trying to clear students and others from Tiananmen. Troops moved in and beat and shot at the demonstrators. In turn, a few demonstrators turned to violence and killed some soldiers. By daylight of June 4, military forces had occupied the square and had dispersed demonstrators. Violence then erupted beyond the square, and ordinary citizens and protestors were killed. Estimates of the dead ranged up to three thousand. Similarly, the government dealt harshly with demonstrators in other cities; many were arrested, although a few, recognizing the perils, left the country.

Deng and his allies had to contend with world reactions to such violence. They could not conceal the military's use of excessive force because television cameras had witnessed events at Tiananmen. Leaders in many parts of the world condemned the severity of the government's response to dissent, and the media outside China offered biting critiques of the violence. Deng and other hard-liners appeared to be oblivious to or perhaps feigned ignorance about the reactions of foreigners. Deng himself portrayed the demonstrators as subversives who wanted to destroy the communist system and to impose the dreaded bourgeois control over society. He placed Zhao Ziyang under house arrest and initiated an anti-rightist campaign. He did not denigrate the post-1979 economic reforms, which had encouraged entrepreneurship and liberalization and rapid expansion, but simply excoriated the dissenters for attacking the Communist Party and its leadership and for promoting liberal capitalist policies.

Deng's formulation characterized Chinese policies from that time on, even after his own retirement in 1992 and his death in 1997. He himself did not opt for the "cult of personality" associated with Mao Zedong. His explicit instructions were to cremate his body and to scatter his ashes at sea. Unlike Mao, he did not have his writings disseminated throughout China, nor did he insist on statues in his honor.

Having dismissed Zhao Ziyang in 1989, Deng assisted Jiang Zemin (1926–), the mayor of Shanghai, to become general secretary of the party, the president of the country, and chairman of the Central Military Commission. After Deng's retirement in 1992, Jiang continued to support the market economy and dismantled some unproductive state-owned enterprises, leading to considerable unemployment. Zhu Rongyi (1928–), whom he brought with him from Shanghai, became premier and took charge of the economic reform program, which resulted in astounding growth. Zhu sought to modernize state-owned enterprises but also tried to guarantee a social safety net for the unemployed. At the same time, he eliminated taxes on the hard-pressed peasantry and attempted to deal with the growing disparity between the rural and urban areas. His partial success facilitated Chinese entrance into the World Trade Organization, with the attendant advantages, in 2001. However, his economic successes and the emphasis on rapid economic growth came at considerable cost. China was afflicted with urban air pollution, sandstorms, and lakes and rivers overflowing with poisonous residue from factories.

The Jiang/Zhu era also had mixed results in noneconomic areas. China became more engaged in the world and established better relations with many Western countries and, to a certain extent, with Taiwan. Hong Kong and Macao reverted to China, but the government generally did not adopt heavy-handed policies to alter their economic systems. It joined Russia and several central Asian countries to found the Shanghai Cooperation Organization in 2001. The organization focused initially on security and emphasized joint actions against terrorism, intelligence sharing, and military exercises, but it also served as a counter to the North Atlantic Treaty Organization and sought to limit US influence in central Asia, especially after the US invasion of Afghanistan and the establishment of US military bases in Uzbekistan and Kyrgyzstan to eliminate the Al-Qaeda terrorists who had attacked the USA on September 11, 2001. China also attempted to use the Shanghai Cooperation Organization to prevent central Asian countries from aiding and providing sanctuary to Uyghur nationalists, or what it labeled "terrorists," who sought greater autonomy or independence for Xinjiang, a region that had traditionally had a large Uyghur population.

Ordinary Chinese had somewhat greater freedom during the Jiang/Zhu ascendancy, but the government acted rapidly if it felt threatened. In 1999, government troops suppressed a demonstration by Falungong, a quasi-spiritual and moralistic order associated with the ancient Chinese practice of *qigong* (translated as "life energy cultivation"). The government labeled it an "evil cult" and described its founder, Li Hongzhi (1952–), as a ne'er-do-well. Adopting a strict moral code, spiritual cultivation, exercise, and meditation, the order appealed particularly to women and the elderly. The government tolerated it for a while but by 1999 had begun to perceive it as similar to such subversive secret societies as the Taipings, White Lotus, and Triad. It initiated a media campaign attacking the Falungong ideology and arrested, tortured, or killed quite a number of adherents. The self-immolation of several alleged practitioners of Falungong in 2001 at Tiananmen Square prompted even greater repression of the group. Similarly, the government banned Christian house churches, portraying them as subversive.

Another damaging legacy of the Jiang/Zhu era was its secrecy. Public health was compromised by a lack of transparency. For example, the government tried for some time to avoid acknowledging the extent of the HIV/AIDS epidemic, because admission of considerable drug use and prostitution would cause it embarrassment. A state-run blood-donor project that employed contaminated needles and spread the disease was an even more acute embarrassment for the government, which attempted to conceal the program.

The government of Hu Jintao (1942–), who ruled from 2003 to 2012, had a similarly mixed record. In his previous post as governor of Tibet, Hu had declared martial law in 1989 and had been accused of brutal suppression of Tibetan demonstrators. When he became president, general secretary of the party, and head of the Central Military Commission, he had a mandate of rapid economic development. Yet he faced pressure to protect the poor and those left behind by the sharp economic growth. His government reduced the poverty rate and provided support and a basic safety net for migrants who had moved to the cities and therefore lacked access to medical services and to educational opportunities for their children because they lacked household registration. It pledged to invest more capital in China's interior, which had not received the same attention as the coastal regions. It even committed itself to protecting the environment and to building better housing and facilities for the bulk of the population. The 2008 Beijing Olympics and the 2010 Shanghai Expo proved to be successful and bolstered China's image in the world. After some preliminary failures, the government acted expeditiously to deal with the infectious and deadly Severe Acute Respiratory Syndrome (SARS) epidemic.

Despite these successes, Hu and his government failed to fulfill many of their objectives. Income disparity accelerated; environmental disasters continued to be troublesome and resulted in numerous demonstrations against local authorities; cronyism, corruption, and illegal enrichment of officials persisted; and officials illegally colluded with factory and mine owners to expropriate lands from peasants, which also resulted in antigovernment demonstrations. In 2011, Liu Zhijun (1953–), the minister of railways, was accused of accepting $20 million in bribes and of laxness in safety considerations that led to a 2011 collision of a high-speed train and the deaths of forty people. The most sinister and notorious case of corruption involved Bo Xilai (1949–), the son of Bo Yibo (1908–2007), one of the communist movement's great heroes. Bo Xilai had pursued an initially well-regarded populist policy as leader of the city of Chongqing in Sichuan province, but in 2012 was arrested on charges of extraordinary corruption. His second wife, Gu Kailai (1958–), an attorney and businesswoman who was the daughter of a prominent communist elder, was then convicted of murdering Neil Heywood, an English associate with whom she had had a commercial dispute after years of collaboration in illegal activities.

The government also did not move expeditiously to implement the rule of law or to foster democracy. Despite some professed concerns for national minorities and pledges to support affirmative action, bilingualism in schools, ethnic unity, and religious freedom, the government in Xinjiang encountered considerable turbulence. In 2008, Uyghur activists attacked a police station and killed seventeen policemen. Relations between Uyghurs and Chinese remain tense. Throughout 2012, Tibetan activists immolated themselves to protest Chinese policies – a disastrous blow to the government's image. Another action that tarnished the government's image was the 2009 arrest on charges of subversion of the literary critic and human-rights advocate Liu Xiaobo (1955–), who received the Nobel Peace Prize in 2010. The rights of Chinese with a lesser profile than Liu have faced similar transgressions.

In sum, since the Tiananmen incident, the communist leadership has tried a mixture of a liberalized economy and a generally authoritarian political system. It has sought to stave off critiques by orthodox Marxists who blamed this policy for the Tiananmen incident and for the abandonment of communist principles. Yet it has also faced denunciations from liberals who resented restrictions on freedom of expression. Government policy has wavered from relaxation of authoritarian policies and freedom of expression in public to repressive policies and detention and imprisonment of critics, even if they had not committed a crime. In repressive times, the authorities have often directed their wrath at civil-liberties attorneys, journalists, and writers. Censorship has persisted in venues ranging from newspapers to the Internet. At times, the central government has refrained from squashing demonstrations against unscrupulous entrepreneurs, corrupt officials, and rapacious factory and mine owners and managers who polluted the environment. Nor has it silenced or detained individuals if they criticized specific conditions and not the system.

Divisions within the leadership have complicated the development of policies. The Tiananmen incident revealed such splits. During the crisis, prominent leaders who had supported the demonstrators lost their positions, and some were denounced. Since then, contradictory views within the top leadership have not readily erupted into the open. Foreigners have not been able to easily identify different factions. Yet the wavering of policies indicates contradictions within the governing elite. The jockeying for power among the top leaders has exacerbated the conflicts in policy. The rise in corruption and bribery has contributed to some of the difficulties. On occasion, corrupt high-level officials have been dismissed, imprisoned, and even executed. Yet considerable corruption has persisted, leading to numerous protests on the local level.

THE PRESENT STATUS OF CHINA

Economic growth has satisfied most of the population and has quelled potential disturbances. The country's east coast has benefited from foreign and private entrepreneurs' investment. Cheap labor has enticed many companies from highly developed countries to move their plants to China, leading to the world's greatest rate of economic growth. Less efficient, less productive, and occasionally corrupt state-owned enterprises remain a problem, as is theft of intellectual property and technology, which has enraged many in Japan and the West. With the rise of a private economy, income inequality has increased at a rapid pace, leading some urban dwellers to have a more comfortable life while others in the city and countryside barely eke out a living. Rationing, which has even included cotton, has ended, as stores, which had few consumer goods in the 1960s and 1970s, now have sufficient quantities of necessities and luxuries for those who can afford them. The public transportation system, including buses and roads, and sanitation facilities have improved in many areas, and the more prosperous families have televisions, washing machines, and the other appurtenances of modern life that were barely available earlier. Nonetheless, the government has focused on an export-driven policy, not on consumption by Chinese. Other than the very comfortable, most Chinese have saved their money. Moreover, foreign imports are expensive because of the high value of Chinese currency. However, as foreign demand shrinks, Chinese consumption needs to increase, especially if workers in manufacturing enterprises are to retain their jobs.

To be sure, economic development has not been uniform. Rural areas have not always had access to the machinery and the conveniences of modern technology. China's western regions have lagged behind, as investment and prosperity have grown disproportionately along the east coast and neighboring regions. In the late 1990s, however, the government, apprehensive about possible turbulence in these relatively remote areas, initiated efforts to foster the economy in the poorer regions of the west. The authorities have committed themselves to greater support and investment in the west, especially in the minority areas. It remains to be seen whether this policy will translate into significant economic gains and to reducing the tensions between Han, or ethnic Chinese, and the various minorities in the northwest and southwest.

After sixty years of communist rule, albeit with a measure of private entrepreneurship or capitalism over the past three decades, where does China stand as of the second decade of the twenty-first century? The Chinese government's lack of transparency makes it difficult to assess China's status and condition. The reports of fervent anticommunists about developments in China offer extraordinarily negative views. Evaluations of China's present, not to mention its future, are perilous. The assessment here is not designed to be a catalog of potential difficulties or disasters. Nor is it meant to be a list of the consequences of instability. The present system could survive, particularly if the government is adept at adapting to its problems. Here the goal is merely to describe the problems and opportunities.

The Communist Party still dominates the government and is the only legal political party. The government itself has turned out to be more pragmatic than in the days of Mao's leadership. Practical results rather than ideology crop up in policies and pronouncements. Transitions in leadership have been peaceful (a change from Mao's era). Mao ultimately turned against his chosen successors (Liu Shaoqi, who was arrested and died during the Cultural Revolution, and Lin Biao, whose plane crashed as he tried to flee after a reputedly abortive attempt to assassinate Mao). All these events contributed to instability in China. Since Mao's death, changes in leadership have not been as fraught, and transitions have not resembled the purges that earlier afflicted the party and government. Nonetheless, this authoritarian system scarcely makes any bows to democracy, and the political power of the military is another impediment to democracy. Dissent is limited, and, if construed as counter-revolutionary, is not tolerated. Democracy activists have emerged but have thus far had scant success. A few observers have asserted that China has never had a democratic government and yet has flourished. They argue that the lack of a democratic heritage may preclude such a development in China but that this will not necessarily harm its people. However, although traditional China had not been exposed to democracy, in the modern world, involvement with democratic countries cannot be avoided. Unlike the Chinese of the past, today its citizens are familiar with democratic principles.

A substantial movement that demands greater transparency in the government and the Communist Party and more citizen participation in decision making has not developed. Groups advocating human rights and more attention to civil liberties have sprung up both inside and outside China (among Chinese living abroad and among foreigners), but thus far they have had little resonance among the general population within the country. Officials have paid lip service to the rule of law and human rights, but sensitive trials are often secretly convened; accused citizens are, on occasion, detained but not charged with a crime and are not allowed visits from family and friends; and prisoners are frequently treated harshly or, in some cases, tortured. Political participation is limited, as voting is merely an endorsement of candidates already vetted and supported by the Communist Party. The lack of a multi-party political system limits choice and any potential for reducing the power of an authoritarian state.

There are also plentiful opportunities for abuses in local government. China's large population and territory allow great flexibility for local officials. The central government's control is hampered by distance and complexity, giving leverage to unscrupulous local officials. Some have collaborated with entrepreneurs, landlords, and factory owners to expropriate land, to evade environmental regulations and thus contribute to land and water pollution, and in general to exploit the local population. A few have concealed any problems that might reflect badly on them. For example, in the early to mid 1990s in Henan province, the poor sold their blood to unscrupulous companies that did not abide by proper precautions, and were infected with HIV/AIDS by contaminated needles. Yet officials tried to hide this public-health disaster. Similarly, officials in Yunnan and Xinjiang have, on occasion, sought to prevent public knowledge of drug addiction and the ensuing HIV/AIDS epidemic, which was spread by unclean needles. Authorities merely detained addicts and compelled them to follow a regimen of immediate withdrawal from their drugs.

Central- and local-government officials have frequently shown a flagrant disregard for ordinary citizens. Having decided upon a so-called Three Gorges Dam to generate hydroelectric power and to avert floods on the Yangzi River, the government simply moved more than a million people from their homes as they diverted the water onto their lands (in addition, the water has become infested with garbage and algae, and some experts have insisted that the dam has increased the possibility of landslides and earthquakes). Lack of official supervision has permitted contaminated food and liquor to be sold and to jeopardize the population's health. Food safety is a serious public-health issue, yet there is scant government regulation of the food industries. In 2009, Chinese leaders razed traditional Muslim buildings in Kashgar, a predominantly Muslim city, and, without consulting the local population, moved the residents to newly constructed housing. In May of 2009, the government reacted belatedly to a devastating earthquake in the province of Sichuan. Revelations about local officials permitting shoddy construction of schools, which trapped and led to the deaths of many children, embarrassed the government. Other examples of official malfeasance and lack of concern for citizens have become commonplace and, somewhat unusually, have also become public in the twenty-first century. China has the largest number of coal-mining fatalities in the world, a striking indication of a lack of implementation of its safety regulations.

Nepotism and corruption have also undermined the government's performance. As of 2012, China is 75th of 178 countries on Transparency International's corruption index – a poor record for a country among the more developed states and currently the world's second-largest economy. Partly due to the Confucian emphasis on devotion to family, nepotism has been characteristic throughout much of Chinese history. It is not surprising that connections and relationships (*guanxi*) persist as a means of educational, economic, and political advancement. The communist system has not subverted this tradition. Hopes that the corruption that plagued China's traditional dynasties would be more controllable in modern times have not come to fruition. Cases of bribery and corruption regularly appear in the newspapers. In addition, the media, which are controlled or influenced by the government, do not report quite a few instances.

The media and Internet continue to be regulated. The government dominates newspapers, television, and other outlets and limits information that criticizes or embarrasses officialdom. Foreign television and radio broadcasts in China are monitored and censored, and untrustworthy Internet sites are blocked. The media almost never challenge the government or the status quo. In effect, the media do not represent the individual citizen and merely reflect the official view, which barely takes note of the growing economic inequality.

The government has also censored or criticized some of its leading writers and artists. Gao Xingjian (1940–), who received the Nobel Prize for Literature in 2000, has lived in France since the 1980s, partly because his critiques of the government led to censorship. He spent years on a farm performing manual labor during the Cultural Revolution, and, even after his return from the countryside, the government continued to harass him. Ai Weiwei (1957–), the artist son of poet Ai Qing (1910–1996), has used his sculptures and installations to criticize the government's corruption and authoritarianism, especially in light of the shoddy construction of schools in Sichuan that led to increased fatalities in a 2009 earthquake (as mentioned above). His repeated criticism of the authorities may have prompted his arrest and imprisonment in 2011 on charges of tax evasion. Mo Yan (1955–), winner of the Nobel Prize for Literature in 2012, has not aroused the government's hostility, although he has written about corruption. Because his work employs the techniques of magical realism, he has not been perceived as a threat to the state and the official ideology. His general lack of support for dissidents has also contributed to a positive image with the government.

On another note, although economic growth has been remarkable over the past thirty years, distribution of income has not conformed to the Marxist model. Income inequality has continued to accelerate since the early 1980s. A few entrepreneurs and relatives of prominent leaders have profited in these years, and many have prospered because of special benefits or relations with officials who offered lucrative advantages. For example, bank loans have often been obtained by favored customers who had a unique relationship with bank employees. The loans have created a housing bubble, and banks have experienced losses but have averted disaster because of the population's high rate of savings. Having so many depositors, the banks have not needed to provide high rates of interest. However, the more prosperous and more sophisticated Chinese have begun to demand higher rates, placing greater pressure on the banks to make better and more productive loans. They could provide loans for additional low- and middle-income housing, which is desperately needed, but thus far an excess of luxurious and expensive housing has been built.

Until 2000, the newly rich had not flaunted their wealth, but in the early years of the twenty-first century they have begun to revel in pecuniary excesses, sending their children to expensive US universities, patronizing private clubs and entertainment centers, and purchasing helicopters and flying them without informing air controllers. The Gini coefficient, which measures levels of inequality, has continued to increase, signifying a considerable deviation from Communist Party professions of equality.

There are a substantial number of people living below the poverty line – the reverse of the nouveau riche. The government has done remarkably well in reducing the number, but even a conservative World Bank estimate has found more than 135 million counted as poor. The floating migrant population, consisting of tens of millions of people, has among the most precarious of existences. Members of this group – mostly peasants and those on the fringes of rural areas who cannot eke out a living in the countryside – travel to larger towns or cities to find employment. Most of the jobs they have secured have been seasonal, and they barely earn enough money to survive during slack times. Because they have not been registered as residents in their new workplaces, they have not been entitled to benefits, including housing, health care, pensions, and schools for their children. They have not, until recently, obtained the privileges available to ordinary citizens, which has set the stage for a descent into poverty. Over the past few years, the government has belatedly begun to provide them with a safety net. The lack of vibrant labor unions, most of which have been co-opted by the Communist Party and have little power, means that the poor have few advocates and scant leverage in an authoritarian state.

Access to state-provided health and educational facilities has declined, and the social safety net has been frayed. Rudimentary health care, which was available even for remote rural areas during the early years of communist rule, is not readily provided. There are fewer "barefoot doctors," or lay people trained by the government who cater to basic medical needs. Patients have to pay for their own medical insurance, care by physicians, clinic or hospital stays, and medicine, while the government has abandoned free and very-low-cost medical care. An additional problem is that medical facilities in the big cities are superior to those in the countryside. Similarly, schools and universities in the urban areas are generally better than the ones in the rural areas, and indeed the rate of literacy is lower in the countryside. Even in the cities, students in so-called key schools have superior teachers and better facilities and a much better chance of gaining admission into universities. Parents, on occasion, pay or provide gifts to administrators or teachers to ensure admission to these key schools. Entrance into universities is based on examinations, generally offering an advantage to educated or middle-class families, which is antithetical to the communists' professed egalitarianism. The social-welfare system, composed of pensions and child-care and housing allowances, among other benefits, has also been reduced. The government has begun to tackle these health and social-welfare problems, but much needs to be done.

Many of these changes have particularly affected women. The elderly, for whom women generally have greater responsibility, have fewer state guarantees and benefits than in the early days of communist rule, which imposes financial burdens on their families. At workplaces, employers often violate the equal-pay-for-equal-work principle, offering lower wages and salaries to women. Many firms have been reluctant to hire young women because female employees might become pregnant and would have to be granted maternity leave. Women are also poorly represented in the higher administrative positions in government, education, and the economy. No important government official is currently a woman. The one-child-per-family policy, which translates into numerous abortions of female fetuses, has resulted in an extraordinary shortage of women as marital partners, and this paucity gives women a major advantage. The fervent desire for continuance of the family line means that young and unattached women have some leverage because fewer women are available for the men who want to produce a son to continue the family line. As of 2013, however, the government faces greater demands to modify the one-child-per-family policy because the aging population creates more pressure on the working young to support the elderly.

Spectacular economic growth has had its impact on the environment. In the early 1980s, regulations about air, ground, and water pollution were limited and generally unenforced. Factories discharged chemicals into the land and water. North China, which has often been plagued by droughts, currently suffers from a shortage of water, and pollution of lakes and rivers compounds the region's difficulties in securing sufficient potable water for its inhabitants. The substantial dependence on coal for heating and other purposes has contributed to air pollution, especially in the big cities. Automobile emissions and traffic tie-ups have resulted in other environmental difficulties.

The environment for humans has also been criticized. Safety conditions at many factories and mines have been appalling. Scandals have repeatedly erupted over exploitation of factory workers, making conditions in the mills appear comparable to those in the early stages of the Industrial Revolution in the West. Workers have been compelled to work long hours, sometimes with dangerous materials, at low wages and in poorly lit buildings that lack proper ventilation. Protests about these conditions have increased, and suicides of workers have aroused concern both in China and abroad. Child labor in construction projects and mines, child trafficking, and prostitution persist. Human-rights activists have also condemned China for its liberal use of capital punishment. China continues to execute far more people than any other country. During so-called "Strike Hard" campaigns, sentences of capital punishment have often been excessive and capricious. More and more organizations have begun to lobby for prison sentences rather than execution for nonviolent crimes, and the government, perhaps in response, has reduced the number of people executed. Human-rights organizations have also objected to the harsh conditions faced by prisoners assigned to forced-labor camps. The Internet, despite considerable government censorship, has proven to be an effective galvanizing force in protests against abuses of the human environment. The government has been unable to totally control or close down this means of communication.

Concerning human rights in other areas, although China has plenty of coal and rare earth minerals (in fact, over 90 percent of the world's supply of such minerals as of 2013), it has had to import many other natural resources for its economic growth, leading to relations with oppressive dictatorial regimes. Much of its oil comes from Kazakhstan, Iran, and Africa. Its copper, gold, and other resources derive from all corners of the world, including its neighbors in East Asia but also Latin America and Africa. The government and private entrepreneurs have invested in numerous Third World countries (including recently concluded agreements to obtain oil and copper from Afghanistan) to ensure steady supplies of raw materials for its growing industries. By supplying finished consumer goods and by purchasing raw materials from many countries, it has generated considerable leverage for itself in a variety of states. However, it has dealt with what many in the outside world consider to be rogue regimes. The USA and its allies have frequently criticized China for its willingness to collaborate with these governments, but they are not as dependent as China is on such ostracized lands as Iran for supplies that would fuel economic growth.

Sino–American relations have had their vagaries. The USA, on occasion, has criticized China's human-rights violations, while China has accused the USA of adventurist and bellicose policies in Eastern Europe, Iraq, and Iran.

The Chinese authorities portray US involvement in human-rights issues as intrusions in China's internal affairs. For example, they portray US calls for religious freedom for Buddhists, Christians, and Muslims as support for subversives, anti-Communist Party dissidents, and so-called capitalist roaders. These tensions continue but have not led to the kinds of confrontations that characterized the Korean War and the early stages of relations. Tensions have at times erupted into brief contretemps, such as when the USA probably inadvertently bombed the Chinese embassy in Belgrade and when the Chinese brought down a US plane that violated China's airspace. However, no real armed confrontation has evolved since the Korean War. Indeed, the USA has tried to elicit Chinese assistance in dealings with Iran and North Korea – countries with which the USA has no formal diplomatic relations. However, economic relations continue to plague the Sino–American relationship. Faced with a decidedly unfavorable balance of trade with China, the USA has repeatedly asserted that Chinese currency has been deliberately undervalued and has urged the communist authorities to revalue the yuan, the basic unit of Chinese currency. On the other hand, consumers in the USA have benefited from the relatively cheap prices of Chinese goods. Businesses in the USA have complained that the Chinese have imposed barriers on the sale of American products in China. Businesspeople in the USA want a cheaper dollar so as to compete with Chinese products in the USA and around the world.

Simultaneously, as the second-largest economy in the world, China has begun to flex its muscles in its foreign relations. It expects to be respected and treated as a great power. Over the past few years, it has become embroiled in disputes with Vietnam, Japan, and the Philippines concerning oil, fishing and shipping rights, and ownership of islands between China and these other lands. The USA has decided to play a more significant role in the Pacific and has stationed more vessels and forces in the region, alarming and alienating the Chinese. In this connection, US officials have asserted that China has increased the size of its armed forces. Although China has devoted a somewhat higher percentage of funds to its military than previously, its budgetary increase does not compare with the amounts allocated by the USA. Yet China has been using its economic leverage in trade and investment to influence the policies of countries with which it has economic relations. After all, the Marxism that China espouses emphasizes the economic underpinnings and indeed significance of politics.

Taiwan represents one of the most crucial issues in Chinese foreign relations. The Chinese government has persisted in its claim that Taiwan is a Chinese province. Ironically, the government in Taiwan concurs but believes that Taiwan itself is the legitimate republic of China. Taiwan turned to a more democratic system after the death of Chiang Kai-shek in 1975 and the succession of his son Chiang Ching-kuo (1910–1988), who permitted greater freedom for the population and recruited more native Taiwanese into government. Its economy boomed from the late 1960s, creating a modernized and high-tech country. Conflicts between China and Taiwan have flared up into small-scale battles or bombings over the past sixty years, but they appear to have subsided. On occasion, one or the other side rattles its saber by testing weapons. Yet entrepreneurs from Taiwan have invested in China, and, at the time of publication, no substantial conflicts have taken place. Some observers have suggested the Hong Kong model for Taiwan. In 1997, Hong Kong reverted to nominal Chinese control after a century of British rule but was not compelled to abandon its economic system in favor of the communist system. However, because the fate of Taiwan is a more viscerally charged issue, it may be more difficult for both the Chinese and the Taiwanese to accept the Hong Kong formulation.

The problem of the so-called national minorities is similarly fraught. As of 1950, the communists had regained the territories that the Qing dynasty had conquered by the 1750s and had incorporated, according to their own count, fifty-five minorities. Many have acquiesced, and some have prospered under Han, or ethnic Chinese, rule. Southwest China, which has numerous minorities, some of whom are related to the Tai peoples, has generally been relatively peaceful, although the identities of many of the locals have begun to erode. Inner Mongolia, which has undergone considerable turbulence (especially during the Cultural Revolution), appears to have achieved a peaceful equilibrium. There are still Mongol nationalists who seek greater autonomy, but the Chinese in the so-called Inner Mongolian Autonomous Region now vastly outnumber the Mongols. Chinese peasants have encroached on pastoral lands, generating considerable erosion and dust storms. Despite this setback, which has resulted in the loss of grazing land, many Mongols have found other employment in the burgeoning industrial economy. Because Inner Mongolia produces more coal than any other region in China, mining has provided many, albeit hazardous and polluting, jobs. Mongol identity survives, as does the Uyghur script associated with early Mongol history and created by order of Chinggis Khan. Occasional incidents have given rise to demonstrations but have not translated into significant disruptions. Yet the potential for violence persists.

Xinjiang has been more problematic for the communist authorities. The continued migration of Chinese into the so-called Xinjiang Uyghur Autonomous Region has alienated the mostly Turkic but also Iranian and Mongol peoples in the area. There has been little intermarriage between the Chinese and the traditional local inhabitants, and Xinjiang is now approximately evenly divided between Han and non-Han residents. Many non-Han accuse the Han and the government of seeking to undermine their culture in every area, from Uyghur poetry to the Uyghur language to Muslim religious observances. The government has responded with ever-changing policies. In moderate times, it has emphasized affirmative action for the non-Han in employment and education and toleration toward Islam and non-Han customs and language. In repressive times, it has cracked down on the expression of the indigenous Islamic and Turkic cultures and on evidence of ethnic sentiments. Another source of irritation has been the general paucity of non-Han in leadership positions in local government, education, and the economy. Moreover, the non-Han population earns less than the Han because they have less training and less capital to invest, and face greater discrimination.

Violence has punctuated Xinjiang in the twenty-first century. The authorities have cracked down on the non-Han population and have made even more strenuous efforts to dissuade the neighboring central Asian Muslim countries from providing sanctuary for Uyghur "splittists," or nationalists who yearn for independence. The government has tried to portray these dissidents as Islamic fundamentalists in order to gain support against them. In short, six decades after the communists gained control over Xinjiang, animosity and turbulence between Han and non-Han persist.

Tibet has been similarly turbulent. After violence erupted in 1959, the Dalai Lama, the spiritual leader of Tibetan Buddhists, left his land and went into exile in Dharamsala, India. Despite occasional informal discussions between the government and the Dalai Lama's representatives, no compromise has been reached. As in Xinjiang, a substantial number of Chinese have moved to the capital city, Lhasa, where they play an important economic role. Many Tibetans resent the Chinese presence, and, like the Turkic peoples of Xinjiang, fear erosion of their identity and culture. The Tibetan response has been a spiritual revival and a persistent attachment and devotion to the Dalai Lama. The Tibetan leader has been an attractive figure for many influential people in the world, placing the Chinese government, which mistrusts him, in a defensive position. The worldwide "Free Tibet" movement, which has the support of well-meaning celebrities, has actually aroused the government's suspicions of the Dalai Lama's intentions and has perhaps hardened its position. As in Xinjiang, the government has used economic incentives to ingratiate itself with the Tibetan population. The authorities have invested considerable resources in Tibet, including the construction of an extraordinary railway line (one of the world's most expensive infrastructure projects) linking it to China. They have also provided funding for educational and medical facilities. However, many Tibetans fear that their culture will be overwhelmed. On the other hand, Tibetan music and arts are popular and have had an influence in China. To be sure, China would like to resolve the Tibetan problem, especially because of its resonance throughout the world and the ensuing negative image for the government. So far the parties have not been reconciled. Occasional violence, as well as suicides and self-immolations by Tibetans, have heightened tensions between China and, in particular, the community of Tibetan monks. However, the Chinese authorities can afford to wait for a settlement because the death of the current charismatic Dalai Lama may leave Tibet without a similarly popular and recognized leader.

It is appropriate to end this history with a reference to many Chinas. China and its history cannot truly be gauged without consideration of the non-Chinese within the country and on its borders. The relations between the two have vastly influenced Confucian China. Moreover, society over the past two thousand years has consisted not only of the Confucian elite but also of peasants, merchants, artisans, monks, doctors, and a variety of others. Because most of the primary sources derive from the elite, the principal literate group, knowledge of other groups and thus of Chinese civilization is limited. Archeology, careful study of indirect references in written sources, and the reports of foreigners, among others, supplement the elite's viewpoint, but the religions, lifestyles, and political and economic roles of the nonelite often lie beyond our grasp. The lives and contributions of women in traditional times have only come into partial view over the past few decades. In essence, a portrait of segments of the nonelite population who did not leave behind material remains can scarcely be recovered.

Similarly, modern China comprises many different Chinas. It is a diverse and sprawling country with the largest population in the world, eight percent of which is non-Chinese, meaning that there is no rigid uniformity. Different provinces and regions have had different experiences and have had different ways of implementing policies over the past sixty years. Cities and rural areas have been exposed to different influences, and Han and non-Han have reacted differently to government policies. Generalizations about all of China have to be carefully qualified.

At the same time, predictions about China's future have to be similarly guarded. The study of Chinese history is humbling. Unlike many of the stereotypes about traditional cultures, Chinese society has been ever changing.

FURTHER READING

Richard Baum, *Burying Mao: Chinese Politics in the Age of Deng Xiaoping* (Princeton: Princeton University Press, 1994).

Leslie Chang, *Factory Girls: From Village to City in a Changing China* (New York: Random House, 2008).

Elizabeth Economy, *The River Runs Black: The Environmental Challenge to China's Future* (Ithaca: Cornell University Press, 2004).

Gao Yuan, *Born Red: A Chronicle of the Cultural Revolution* (Stanford: Stanford University Press, 1987).

Dru Gladney, *Muslim Chinese: Ethnic Nationalism in the People's Republic* (Cambridge, MA: Harvard University Press, 1991).

Melvyn Goldstein, *The Snow Lion and the Dragon: China, Tibet, and the Dalai Lama* (Berkeley: University of California Press, 1997).

Kenneth Lieberthal, *Governing China: From Revolution through Reform* (New York: W. W. Norton, 2nd ed., 2004).

Ma Bo, *Blood Red Sunset: A Memoir of the Chinese Cultural Revolution*, trans. by Howard Goldblatt (New York: Penguin, 1996).

Roderick MacFarquhar and Michael Schoenhals, *Mao's Last Revolution* (Cambridge, MA: Harvard University Press, 2006).

Maurice Meisner, *Mao's China and After: A History of the People's Republic* (New York: The Free Press, 3rd. ed., 1999).

James Millward, *Eurasian Crossroads: A History of Xinjiang* (New York: Columbia University Press, 2007).

Michael Sullivan, *Art and Artists of Twentieth-Century China* (Berkeley: University of California Press, 1996).

Andrew Walder, *Fractured Rebellion: The Beijing Red Guard Movement* (Cambridge, MA: Harvard University Press, 2009).

INDEX

A History of China, First Edition. Morris Rossabi.
© 2014 Morris Rossabi. Published 2014 by Blackwell Publishing Ltd.

Roosevelt, Theodore
(1858–1919), 358
Rouran, 105
Ruizong, emperor of the Tang
dynasty (662–716),
141–142
rural distress (1930s), 350
Russia, 308
Central Asia and, 308–309
Jews and, 365
occupation of Xinjiang, 309
Port Arthur and, 323
revolution and Xinjiang,
338
Russo–Japanese War
(1904–1905), 330, 358
Rusticello (fl. late thirteenth
century), 230
Ryukyu islands, 321

Saiyid Ajall Shams al-Din
(1211–1279), 220
sakoku ("closing the
country"), 278
Samarkand, 143, 215, 241
Sanguozhi yanyi (The Romance
of the Three Kingdoms)
(novel), 98–99, 255
Schall von Bell, Adam
(1592–1666), 279
"scramble for concessions,"
323
Secret History of the Mongols,
213–214
Sect of the Three Stages
(Sanjie), 145
Self-Strengthening Movement,
314–316
Sengge (d. 1671), 281
Sepoy Mutiny (1857), 296
Service, John S. (1909–1999),
376
Seven Sages of the Bamboo
Grove, 109, 116
Seventeen-Point Agreement
(Tibet), 374
Severe Acute Respiratory
Syndrome (SARS), 401
Shahrukh (1377–1447), 241
Shakyamuni (ca. 563–483
BCE), 36

shamanism, 194
Shangdu (Xanadu), 230
Shang dynasty, 21–23
merchants (shangren),
22–23
social classes, 21–23
tax structure, 22
Shanghai and 1930s
prosperity, 351
Shanghai Cooperation
Organization, 400
Shantao (613–681), 149
shanyus (rulers of Xiongnu),
102
Shato Turks, 160, 165–166,
176
sheng (reed musical
instrument), 119
Sheng Shicai (1897–1970),
372
Shen Gua (1031–1095), 205
Shennong, 13
Shenzhen economic zone,
395–396
Shen Zhou (1427–1509), 249
Shenzong, emperor of the
Song dynasty
(r. 1068–1085), 183, 187
shi, 34, 59
Shi Dakai (1831–1863),
304–305
Shi Hu (295–349), 103–104
Shi Huangdi ("First
Emperor") (r. 246–210
BCE), 63, 67
Daoism and, 67
Mao and, 391–392
standardization of coins, 66
standardization of written
language, 66
tomb of, 65
Shiji (Records of the Grand
Historian), 61, 89–91
Shi Le (274–333), 103
Shimabara Rebellion, 278
Shi Siming (703–761), 158
Shi Tao (1642–1707), 286
Shitong (Generalities of
History), 169
Shu Han dynasty (221–263),
97–98

Shuihuzhuan (Water Margin)
(novel), 188
Shun, 13
Siberia, Russian colonization
of, 181–182
Sichuan earthquake, 405
Siddhartha Gautama see
Buddha
Silk Roads, 75, 78, 82, 94, 127
Buddhism and, 114
Ming and, 247
Mongols and, 216, 220
Tang and, 160–161
silver and trade, 277
Sima Guang (1019–1086),
185–186
Sima Qian (ca. 145–86 BCE),
61, 89–91
Sima Tan (ca. 165–110 BCE),
89–90
Sima Yan (236–290), 99–100
"single-whip" system, 262
Sino–British disputes, 293
Sino–Japanese War
(1894–1895), 316, 322,
358
Sino–Japanese War
(1937–1945), 359
Sino–Soviet relations,
374–375, 380
battles along border (1969),
390
conflict, 387–387
Siyiguan (College of
Translators), 260
Snow, Edgar (1905–1972),
366
Socialist Education
Campaign, 387
Society of God Worshippers,
304
Socrates and Confucius, 37
Sokkuram, 155
Song (state in Warring States
period), 32
Song dynasty (960–1279),
177
Censorate, 180
central government, 180
civil-service examinations,
181